Re

of

A Wayward
Altar Boy

An Archaeology of Memory

David M. Brewer

September 2014

Introduction

I personally do not like long introductions. Some explanations however, may be necessary for the reader to help understand the text: things like motive, style, spellings, and so forth. First of all, the motive for writing this memoir (and that's what it is, a collection of memories, most of which are anecdotes, some of which are mere vignettes, and some that are rather long stories) was to present odd and engaging incidents and events of my life to my sons and hopefully, their progeny as well; a sort of record of coming-of-age in the latter half of the twentieth century and then, crossing over into the new millennium. Maybe in this way I can make up for much of the time I was gone, either in the office or in the field, while they were growing up.

I do enjoy hearing stories from other people's lives… when they're interesting of course, as opposed to the usual alternative. So I've tried to keep that as a working basis throughout. I've read a number of memoirs in my life, and more than a few just before and after getting started on this work, right after Mom died in January, 2010, including among others *The Liars Club*, by Mary Karr, *The Tender Bar*, by J.R.Moehringer, and the monumental *A Heartbreaking Work of Staggering Genius*, by Dave Eggars (which, in my opinion, was both and neither, but great nonetheless). All of these were well-written, interesting, and somewhat touching emotionally, but they weren't very inspiring, adventuresome, or exciting, or even quirky and ironic (save Eggars), all of which made me think, "Hell, compared to these guys, my life is goddamn fascinating!" As to whether it's as well-written as theirs, well, I doubt it, but I'll let the reader judge for him or herself how accessible it is.

Other than the chapter titles, which are self-explanatory, the silly little story headings were created as more of a mnemonic device for me than anything else, and they would often pop up later, on re-reading and editing. I know a lot of them are goofy, but it's the only thing close to Joycean goofiness you'll find herein, and I realize that some are so punny and unfunny that I ought to be horse-whipped, and for that I apologize. The reader may notice different spellings for the word "archaeology" throughout, one with the central British "a" and one without. This follows the dictates of present-day professional usage, and you'll find that the only place it's used without the "a" is when referring to Federal "archeology" and its agencies, as per the mandate of the Paper Reduction Act of 1980, where omitting the "a" from all Federal publications was intended to save a good many of our national forests. (Who says Reagan didn't care about the environment?)

Some names have been changed, not necessarily to protect the innocent (although that may have been a factor in a few instances), but more than likely so that I wouldn't either get sued or ambushed (some of the bad guys in here were seriously dangerous, and some still are). The good guys however, mostly my friends and family, have remained intact. Although a few of them have either challenged or questioned my recollections, in almost every case I have proven to be the better witness to history. This is another reason I wanted to get this stuff down on paper, before my own dim bulb eventually flickers out.

I've tried to be honest, even to the point where I often inevitably come out looking like an idiot. That's because it's been the mistakes in my life that have allowed opportunities for learning, growth, and what little wisdom I've accumulated. Without the setbacks I could never have moved forward. Mom used to say that I was a very attentive child, and would listen carefully and with the deepest respect to the advice (and warnings) both her and Dad would share with me about the best way to meet life's challenges—and then I'd just go ahead and do what I pleased. It's been a lifelong problem.

The original title was *Genuine Reflections of a Wayward Altar Boy* because that part of my life was probably the most definitive. To be at a point where you truly believed, and then try to access the spiritual directly, especially in the ritual of the Mass, to strain your mind to discern the mysteries, and to be in the company of people who built and lived their lives around it, the priests, nuns, and the whole *catholic* culture (in the true sense of the word), was an amazing education for a young boy in the 60s, in a world that no longer exists. When I started serving Mass, we did it all in Latin. The priest faced the altar, his back to the congregation; we had your incense, your hymns… wine, bells… the works. It was a strange and wondrous "sacrifice" to an almighty, omnipresent, and *personally involved* deity, the idea handed down from antiquity by our Jewish brethren, and one that had been carried on in the Christian West intact for well over a thousand years. *Gone in less than a decade.* I was there for the changes, some of which the faithful still claim were for the better, and maybe so. A funny co-ink-a-dink, or maybe it's just a twist of time, but this all just happened to coincide with my reaching puberty, young adulthood, teenager-ism, and the Conscious Revolution ("Tune in; Turn on; Drop out"). Despite my working hard against the inevitable, it was time to grow up. That growing-up part though, was no easy ordeal and makes up the bulk of the narratives herein, with a few observations on the way. Heck, I never felt (or apparently acted) like a grown man til I was over forty, after my own Father had died. But then I became an archaeologist, a scientist, an agnostic, a Buddhist, …and a skeptic.

That's why there's two major parts—in the latter, once I was condemned to be an adult (wife, children, and career, or as Zorba put it, "the full catastrophe"), the world had changed, and not always necessarily for the better. The second section is therefore somewhat more serious, the risks being greater, the mistakes more consequential, and the tone a bit less humorous and off-handed. Still, there was plenty of good stuff a' happenin' and life got no less interesting; we are all products of our collective learning.

One last item… I realize that we all view the world, the events within it, and its many manifestations as unique individuals in a many-sided *Rashomon*-ish sort of way. Nonetheless, I have really taken very few liberties, other than stylistic, with the stories contained herein. Sure, many other things happened, but they are omitted for being either too personal or inconsequential. There will be more than a few individuals however, who didn't see things the same way I did, and will likely not agree with my comprehension of both the events and the intent. That's fine. I've tried to label any opinions as such where possible. If they don't like it, they can write their own version; I'd love to see it. Of course, any inaccuracies, mistakes, and/or unintended hurtful statements, just like the memories themselves, are solely the responsibility of the author. "Nuff said."

For Amy, Robin, Sam, and Dennis,
my inspiration and my legacy

Part I
Childhood

*... If Socrates leave his house today he will find the sage
seated on his doorstep. If Judas go forth tonight it is to
Judas his steps will tend.* Every life is many days, day after
day. We walk through ourselves, meeting robbers, ghosts,
giants, old men, young men, wives, widows, brothers-in-
love. But always meeting ourselves.

(Stephen Dedalus, citing Maeterlinck, while instructing the
elders at Dublin's National Library)

Ulysses, James Joyce

1.   Early Times (Family History to 1961)

BJ had fallen asleep in the bathtub. It was Sunday, June 8, 1952. Truman was still president, and it was the day my Dad graduated with a degree in Journalism from the Jesuit-run University of Detroit, the day I was born. He had stayed up all night at the hospital from the evening before, waiting for Mom to deliver, and I didn't arrive until 2 p.m. the following afternoon. He then had to get ready for his graduation ceremony and made his way back to their tiny apartment (with a Murphy bed), took a hot bath and fell asleep in the tub. His buddies came banging around 6 that evening, and woke him up to get him ready for the 8 p.m. mandatory attendance, no-excuses, U of D graduation ceremony. They barely made it on time. But later that evening, after a few celebratory drinks, and still in his black graduation gown with mortarboard, he was able to get back to the hospital, show Mom his degree, and meet his new-born son, amusingly dubbed The Crown Prince. I was supposed to have been a girl, according to the doctor, so they had already decided on the name Susan Carol, and now had to scramble for a male moniker. Dad decided D. Mark Brewer would make for a notable *nom de plume*, if it ever came to that. On looking at the newborn, Dad's friends suggested that considering how big and broad the Brewer nose was, and how long Mom's, it was a wonder that I didn't have to be delivered via Caesarean.

The Brewers

Dad was the oldest son of a seven-kid family of Irish descent, and though I've never been able to substantiate this story anywhere else, he once said that the name "Brewer" didn't come from beer-making, as everyone assumed, but was an Anglicization of being a "Boru-er" or descendant of those of the tribe loyal to Brian Boru, the semi-legendary First King of Ireland. The combined family tradition was that, being descended from the Brewers ("Boru-ers") on one side and the O'Briens (clan o' Brian Boru) on the other, we were thus descended on both lines from the kings of Ireland. The Brewer-side family saga starts with my Dad's grandfather, on his father's side, who was Irish right off the boat, and then scurrilously abandoned his family in Pittsburgh sometime in the late 1800s, never to be heard of again. This fellow's name was James, though I've also heard of him referred to as William as well. That's all that anyone knew about him, since he was not to be spoken about, and there was also some speculation that he might have been an outlaw of sorts, possibly worse (there was even a conversation I once overheard, which I shouldn't have, where the older women expressed their mutual feeling that, "he should have been hanged"). After this ne'er-do-well had run away, his oldest son, Bernard, my grandfather and my Dad's dad, whom I remember fondly when I was a young child, dropped out of school and went to work as a printer's apprentice, and supported the remaining family until he got married to my grandmother, then-Mary Elizabeth O'Brien. He became very adept at fixing the presses, and had some great stories he passed on to my Dad about life in 1920s Chicago and Detroit. Like the time the guy who worked the paper cutter, but drank profusely, jimmied the machine so that he didn't have to put both hands on the safety buttons, and then he could cut twice as much paper and get his work done in half the time (thus having more time for drinking). Until the day he drank too much *before* work and lopped off his eight primary digits (but not his thumbs). Appropriately, they kept the fingers in a jar of alcohol on top of the machines, as sort of an iconic warning trophy, and after he healed up, the guy went back to work, but drank a bit less, or at least a little slower, since it sometimes now took both hands to lift a glass. My grand-dad's developing mechanical skills however, led to moving his burgeoning family from Pittsburgh to Chicago, where my father was born, and then to Detroit, the new manufacturing center of the world, where they ended up around 1929 when the stock market crashed. I remember seeing my Grandpa often as an usher in the 60s in their local church on Sundays, and I once saw him decked out in the full

3

regalia of the Knights of Columbus (countervailing the godless Freemasons), with the feathery captain's hat, the cape and sash, and of course, the full sword-and-halter hanging from his side. Dad told me that this had not always been the case, and that Grandpa only came back to the Church later on in life, after at least six of his seven kids had grown and left home, and then he had single-handedly subdued his own wild ways. Those six kids were all grown up (one had died in childbirth), and then (surprise!) came the youngest, my Aunt Helen, ten years my senior (and sixteen years younger than my Father, despite his inexplicable embarrassment at having his Mother pregnant *again*). It was Helen who taught me how to dance, as well as to sing along to Mitch Miller albums when I was around five (my folks just loved it when they'd pick me up, hearing me bellowing "I'm a Ramblin' Wreck from Georgia Tech, and a hell of an engineer—A helluva, helluva, helluva, helluva, hell of an engineer. Like all good jolly fellows, I drink my whiskey clear. I'm a Ramblin' Wreck from Georgia Tech and a hell of an engineer."). Dad said that while he was growing up, what with the seven kids to keep in line, the neighbors always referred to Grandpa as "The Lion-Tamer."

My own father was also named Bernard Joseph Brewer, but he was never considered a Junior. He answered to Sonny by his family, BJ by his friends, and Barney by my mother, but always signed his name as Bernard J. Brewer, without the junior. He was renowned for his handwriting, humor, intellect, and both culinary and literary skills. In fact, after college, even though he had a degree in Journalism and was offered a job at the Detroit Free Press, he turned it down, considering the starting pay too low to raise a family on, so his first job was with Mack Trucks, editing tech manuals. But this was pretty dry and uninteresting stuff, and very soon he moved to Ford and helped write a lot of their promotional materials; you know, the glossy flashy advertising pamphlets, etc. Later he was made an offer to be an editor at Chrysler's Marine Division to do the same type thing, making more money every time he jumped, talented as he was. At some point, what with Chrysler being one of the Big Three back then, along with Ford and General Motors, which was also producing Chevrolet, and him now being somewhat of a public-relations guy, he was once invited to participate in a small private luncheon with Dinah Shore, who was at the time promoting "See the USA in your Chevrolet!" on her evening television program. We were all very impressed by that. And rightfully so.

Okinawa

Dad had been in the Army in World War II, volunteering at 17, right out of high school, and after basic training and getting shipped out halfway around the world, he was eventually blown apart by shrapnel on Okinawa after trudging along for six weeks, never getting enough time to stop and change his socks the entire trek. He only talked about it once, with my brother and myself, one night when we were all grown up and we'd decided to take him on a boys-night-out trip to a strip club (The Doll House), here in Orlando. He didn't like the club at all: too noisy, too crowded, and the girls were all too young. Oh yeah, and the beers were too expensive. He was right about the beers, so we headed down South Orange Blossom Trail (commonly referred to as OBT, or sometimes, S.O.B. Trail) to his own favorite hangout, Gary's Duck Inn. He knew everybody there, the bartenders, waitresses, owner, and especially, the cooks. The head cook would often spot him in the restaurant or bar and take him back into the kitchen to try some new dish he'd be working on and get Dad's opinion. Everyone always wanted Dad's opinion. Anyway, this one time my brother and I were sitting here at the bar with him at Gary's on a Saturday night, and Dad was drinking his usual, a Shark-tini, which was a triple dry martini, with lemon; I had a rum and tonic, and Paul had a gin and tonic.

After a round and a re-order, as we had previously conspired, my brother and I brought up the war, and asked him to tell us what had really happened. He took a long draw off the drink and said matter-of-factly, "Well, to be honest, I really don't remember very much. We had been pushing hard for over six weeks, it rained all the time, and it was always muddy. I was at the top of a cliff, and we had dug in along its edge. We knew that the Japs were at the bottom of this very high cliff we were on because we could hear them yelling to each other down below. So, we'd toss hand grenades over the edge, but we didn't know if they were having any effect. At some point they began lobbing mortar shells over the top toward us, but they didn't know exactly where we were positioned either, so it was hit and miss. After a few volleys, in the foxhole to our right, someone yelled at us, asking if we were okay. I had my rifle in my right hand, and I stood up and waved with my left hand, letting him know we were alright, and the next thing I knew I was just blown up. When I came to, I saw that my foxhole buddy was dead, and someone was calling for a medic. Well, there weren't any medics around, so some officer told another guy to help me get back away from the cliff edge to a first-aid station about a mile away. I got up, left my rifle, and noticed that my intestines were spilling out. I pushed them back in, and held them in with my shattered left arm, the bones just hanging out. The guy who was with me was more in shock from the sight of it than I was, so I knew it was bad. He asked me if I could make it, and I said yeah, but my leg had been hit too, so I had to limp along holding my guts in with my stumpy arm as he helped me to slowly make our way. When we got to the first aid station, they took one look at me, pumped me full of morphine, and I was out. The next thing I remembered I came to briefly and was lying on a table in a makeshift operating room, like they have on M.A.S.H. I looked over to my right and they were operating on some guy, and I watched as they were dropping large chunks of meat into a bucket below the table. Then I passed out again, and was out for four days."

Shit. He didn't have to tell us any more. We knew the story from then on. We'd heard the rest from various family members over the years. They stabilized him, cleaned out most of the dirt, patched him up as best they could, and put him on a troop ship to Hawaii, where they could finish the more intricate details. He remembered nothing of the trip to Hawaii, being kept doped up until he got there. They'd already sent a telegram to his family in Detroit telling them he was injured, and that *he'd lost his left arm*. But he hadn't. Once he got to Hawaii, the doctors looked him over and decided that with enough screws and hardware and some scraps of bone from his leg wound, and a flap of skin from his stomach, they could save the arm. He knew nothing about his, and said that he didn't really regain consciousness for a week or so, and when he did he was in a hospital bed, in a full-body cast, with his left arm and leg elevated. Then he was put on a plane to Seattle, to be put on another plane to Percy Jones Hospital in Battle Creek, Michigan, and there to recuperate as near home as possible. It's a bit of family lore that when he was being carried off the plane in Seattle, his older sister Kathleen ("Kitty"), who was a nurse lieutenant, happened to be the triage nurse on duty at the time to determine where each injured patient was supposed to go. They recognized each other as he was being off-loaded. She didn't even know that he'd been hit. It's also a little known piece of family legend that Dad and some of the other more badly wounded soldiers were flown down to San Francisco later that year to sit in the front row for the signing of the Charter for the newly-established United Nations in late June of 1945. Really more of a publicity stunt than anything. There ought to be pictures of them somewhere; I'm pretty sure I've seen one.

Once he got to Percy Jones, it was a year and a half of recuperation and rehabilitation. Dad said that at the beginning of his recovery the pain was so bad, and they were otherwise so bored, he and some of the other guys would save up their pain pills, taking several at once, and would sometimes sleep for days on end. When awake, the rehab concentrated on walking and getting back the use of their otherwise affected limbs. As part of his therapy, Dad took up making flies for fly-fishing, and became very good at it, even with the limited use of his left arm, still in the elevated and out-from-the-body cast. Apparently Bob Dole, later Senator Dole, was there at the same time undergoing similar rehabilitation; only it was his *right* arm that had been shattered. Dad didn't remember him specifically, but said they must have crossed paths repeatedly, since their injuries were similar and the rehabilitation routine was so regimented. Later, when they got to moving around more, Dad and his buddies would smuggle in cases of beer and keep them hidden and cold on ice in the toilet water tanks.

Eventually, once he got ambulatory, Dad got to go and visit his family in Detroit, and they were all very proud of him. When he went out, he had to wear a uniform draped over his body cast because he was still in the service. He told me once about going out to a bar with his father, who was kind of showing him off, and some of the guys were buying him drinks. After a while he decided to go outside and get a little fresh air, and a cigarette. While he was limping around under the streetlight, smoking, some neighborhood roughneck nearby started making fun of him, calling at him "Hey, Gimpy," what with his left arm in a cast sticking out, and him limping, if not being a bit tipsy. Dad was never one to hold his tongue, and he told the guy to go fuck himself. Well the guy came over and gave Dad a poke. Dad told me he was going to take a swing at the guy with his left arm, figuring the cast would lend a little extra weight, but before he could move, *his* father (who had followed him outside eventually) came flying over his shoulder and cold-cocked the jackass with a single blow, dropping him like a rag doll onto the pavement. Without a word they turned, nodded to each other, Dad flicked his butt into the street and they went back inside and finished their drinks with their friends.

A Driving Fear

Around this time, while Dad was still recuperating in the body cast, some of his buddies would pick him up, drive him down to Detroit and carry him around for a weekend, visiting friends and family and having a few drinks. It was on one of these trips, while they were taking him northward in Michigan, back to Kellogg's and Percy Jones, Dad was lying prone in the back seat, the most comfortable position for him, and a friend, who happened to be a young priest just out of the seminary, was driving, with another friend sitting up front. They had all been drinking, and Dad fell asleep. At some point a car crossed the center line, either theirs or the other car, and there was a horrifying crash. The two friends up front were killed, as were two people in the other car as well, but Dad, maybe *because* he was in a body cast, and was lying down in the back seat, had no injuries whatsoever. The suddenness and shock and horror of it apparently initiated a post-traumatic event from the war, and Dad never drove a car for over twenty years thereafter, until I learned to drive in the late 1960s. I think he finally forced himself to get behind the wheel when he couldn't stand the fact that his kid was driving and he wasn't.

When I asked him once about why he'd never tried driving, he began laughing and told me that when he was in college, and had practically completely recuperated from his war wounds, he thought he'd face his fears and try to take up driving, since all his friends were. So he shopped around and found an old junker for a couple of hundred bucks. It was going to need a little work, but that was okay since his buddies were going to give him driving lessons anyway in the meantime. Well, he had to have it towed out of the seller's lot to the garage where he was going to have it worked on, so he and his buddies just got a tow rope and decided to pull it. Unfortunately, they put Dad behind the wheel of his car, the one being towed, since it *was* his car. He got the part about easing on the brakes so as not to hit the tow car ahead down pat, but steering, which they considered a no-brainer, had yet to become a practiced art for him, and as they were going around a corner, Dad cut it too short, the car jumped the curb, and just like all those movies you see, he capped a fire hydrant, knocking it clean off with the car, now impaled on top of the broken hydrant, with water gushing out from below the skewered vehicle. They

6

didn't know what to do, but it was going to be bad no matter what, so they just untied the rope, hopped in the tow car, and drove off. The car hadn't been registered yet so there was no paper trail, and although he waited nervously for days to hear the cops come knocking at his parent's front door, they never did. He took it as a sign and gave up on the idea again of learning to drive. And in a big city like Detroit, with plenty of mass transit, he really didn't need to.

The O'Briens

Dad met Mom a couple of years after getting out of the hospital and being discharged, then entering the University of Detroit (U of D) under the GI Bill. He said that when he was officially discharged the Army charged him for the rifle he had lost on Okinawa, something like $45. At U of D he was a Journalism major, having always wanted to be a writer, these being the glory days of Mailer and Hemingway, *True Magazine*, *Field and Stream*, and *Esquire*, among others. Now fully recuperated, he was usually impeccably dressed, and always carried a hundred-dollar bill in his wallet. His first meeting with my mother however, was less than romantic. He showed up at a Halloween party in a woman's wig and lipstick, and was so inebriated that he ended up anointing the bushes outside. Nonetheless, Mom had seen him before, when he was more stylish and less in his cups, and his friends generally had all spoken highly of him. Days later he remembered seeing the fiery redhead at the party, and called her up, apologizing for his earlier behavior, and asked her out. She decided to give him a shot, went out with him, and from that moment on, they were meant for each other, come what may.

Mom's family, the O'Briens, were not so keen on Dad. You see, the O'Briens were upper-class Irish, often referred to as fruit-on-the-table, or lace-curtain Irish, whereas Dad's family literally lived on the other side of the railroad tracks, among relatively ramshackle three and four-story wooden row-houses bounded by alleyways (okay, today we'd call them "tenements"). In an interview I did with Dad shortly before his death, he remembered at some point that when he was very young they lived in the bottom floor of one of these tenements, and the Italian guy who lived with his family above them was a rag-picker and junk man. He had a small horse and wagon, and every night he would walk the horse up the wooden stairs to the second floor and stable it in one of the upper bedrooms, walking it gently back down the stairs in the morning, this being his only means of livelihood, and thus he needed to take care of it. The Brewers were referred to as "brick-throwing" Irish; a description they didn't always disavow, nor were they ashamed of. They were definitely of a rougher cut, fighters and scrappers, and not always eye-to-eye with the authorities, as evidenced by the ne'er-spoken-of patriarch, James (or was it William?).

But Mom's family were very upper crust and well-known in the city offices of Detroit. Originally established in Lawrence, Massachusetts, sister-city to Lowell, another great textile town, they had come by way of the Potato Famine steerage, originally landing in Boston. Their story starts with the two O'Brien brothers, Timothy and Dinty (short for Dennis) from County Kerry, who landed in Boston around 1874, where they found work in a foundry. They worked, slept, and ate together for three years to save enough money to bring over a pair of sisters they had known in Ireland, the Kellcher girls, whom they then took on as wives. These would have been my great-grandparents on my mother's father's side. They all moved to Lawrence, Massachusetts, and I think my grandfather's uncle Dinty became a policeman, but it was his father, Timothy, that had the more interesting fate.

Timothy was a brick mason, and worked in the factories of both Lawrence and Lowell, repairing broken brickwork, mostly on the large furnaces that powered the steam engines that ran the looms for the textile factories. This would involve going in on a Sunday late at night, or early Monday morning before dawn, so the furnace could be shut down for the weekend and have cooled off enough so that he could go in and do the repair work. Well, he was inside the large furnace at one of the factories, working away, and either didn't notice, or wasn't noticed, when the early Monday morning shift came in, shut the door, and fired up the big gas furnace to get ready for the days' work. By the time anyone figured out what had happened, he was gone, literally. They didn't even have a set of teeth to bury. As a result, my grandfather John O'Brien, like his counterpart on my father's side, had to go to work and support the family, unable to consider marrying until the children were all out of the house.

My Mom's father, John Theobald O'Brien was apparently quite a fellow. I never knew him, nor did my father ever meet him, as he had died in 1947, the result of multiple strokes, before Mom and Dad met. He was a fireman before enlisting for World War I. He was also a baseball player, and played on a minor league team out of Lawrence. When he left for the war in France, he was under the command of "Black Jack" Pershing, and plans had been made to stop briefly in Ireland, before final training in England and shipping over to France. He really looked forward to seeing the land of his ancestors, having grown up listening to stories of the Old Country, where both his parents had been born, and where the Potato Famine was now just a bad memory. But the Irish Uprising of 1917 squelched the possibility that a horde of first generation Irish-American soldiers, armed to the teeth, would get the run of the isle. They were all kept on board the troop ships, and he and the others were obviously angry that they were close enough they could see the lights of Ireland, without ever being allowed to land. He eventually got to see Ireland on his way back from the war in France, but the upper hand of the English allies in keeping them at bay and offshore in 1917 was always a sore subject in and around their house.

John fought in France in some of the worst battles of World War I. Mom said he told them about eating rats and dead horses when the going got tough. He was shot at least twice; once just outside the right eye, which just skinned his scalp and was sewn shut by a fellow soldier with a piece of thread while sitting in the foxhole afterwards, and another time in the left heel, a bullet which he carried until he died, just under the skin where it could be felt and rolled around. The worst story I heard and was repeated to me by my mother, was where he spent a night in a foxhole under heavy bombardment all night long. When the shelling finally stopped, he and his comrades dug out from under the dirt piled on top of them in the morning, and they noticed that they were all covered in blood. Each man checked himself and his buddies for wounds until one of them noticed the blood was still dripping from above. As they looked up, they saw that during the night, a cow had been flung up in the now-bare tree above them. Although all the leaves had been stripped, the cow was caught in the remaining overhanging boughs and continued to drop its gore on the doughboys below.

When he came back from the war, he married my grandmother, Mary Elizabeth Hughes, and planned to go back to being a fireman in Lawrence. He'd been promised that his job would be waiting for him when, and if, he returned, and so it was. But when he found out that he'd now be working under a former junior fireman he himself had trained years before, but who had sat out the war, and in the interim had therefore gained seniority, he told them all to go to hell. A friend suggested to him that there were opportunities out West, in Detroit (as if you could consider Detroit "out West"), so he went to check the city out. And it was full of opportunity just as it had been portrayed. He quickly got a position with the Liquor Commission as a "beverage agent" since Prohibition was now in full-swing, and he was a veteran, as well as an Irishman, and for the most part, an oddity—an Irish teetotaler (??). From what Mom remembered of what she'd been told, this was an ideal job in Detroit, since the speakeasies were well-known and tolerated. The only times they had to be shaken down by the beverage agents were during elections, to show the Feds a strong anti-vice side on the part of the city government, or when the speakeasy owners crossed city hall. In the former instances, barrels of beer were 'sacrificed' for the newspaper cameramen, smashed with axes, and the swill allowed to run down the sewers, while cases of aged Scotch and Canadian whiskeys recovered as "operating expenses" were later hand-delivered to the commissioners, electioneers, and party bosses. In the latter case, where speakeasy owners were lax in paying their "taxes," or had otherwise troubled the politicos-in-power, a young sixteen-year-old Greek kid with a nice moustache growing on his upper lip would be sent in to buy a beer, and as he left, the agents would soon follow, shutting the place down, not because of the alcohol sales, but for the moral turpitude of corrupting a juvenile.

John O'Brien was also an avid fight fan, and because of his connections in City Hall and the fact that he was sort of an adjunct policeman (being with the Beverage Commission) he got a lot of free tickets and prime seats at boxing events held in Detroit. He often even took my Mom, who was then only a child, as this was not considered a vile, or even dangerous sport at the time, but just regular entertainment. Mom told me that once, when James J. Braddock, the famous Irish fighter from New York, came to fight at Naven Field (later Briggs stadium, which I remembered as a kid, and now Tiger Stadium), before he became really famous (like maybe 1931), her dad had Braddock and a bunch of other Irish gentlemen over to their house for a men's-only sit-down dinner. Ma must have been about 6 at the time, and her brothers would have been young enthusiastic adolescents.

These were interesting times, and from the family histories I often wondered if my respective grandfathers ever crossed paths. Apparently, my Dad's father, as a working-class Irish descendant with a large family, would supplement his income in the winter by helping to drive trucks of contraband liquor across the frozen Detroit River at night from nearby Windsor, Canada. This was exactly during the same period that my Mom's dad was with the Liquor Commission and would periodically have to bust the truckers if only to show the city's federal compliance with the Volstead Act. In another musing I often have as an underwater archaeologist, I wonder about the many trucks that didn't make it across when the spring thaws arrived unexpectedly and those last few shipments had to be made. How many cases of 100-year-old (and older) bourbon, scotch, and rye whiskey are yet lying buried within hapless trucks in the sediments at the bottom of the Detroit River or Lake Erie today, waiting to be rescued?

My grandmother's family on my mother's side were Scotch-Irish, the Hughes. They didn't have enough money to make the final leg to Boston from Ireland, so they put off on Prince Edward Island, Nova Scotia, or New Scotland. It was here that my grandmother was born and, as a result, subsequent to their move to Lawrence, she always enjoyed dual citizenship. When her parents did finally move to Lawrence, they joined other family members who had already settled there a generation earlier, one ancestor of which was John Patrick Hughes, who was a Union officer in the Civil War, wounded and captured by the Confederates, and spent most of the war years in the infamous Libby Prison in Richmond, Virginia, until released at the war's end, with a pension for life.

I don't know much about my grandmother's family, other than her brother Patrick was a priest, who became pastor at St. Theresa's in Detroit. I know that unlike the rest of the family, my grandfather, John O'Brien, travelled all the way across town to have confession at St. Leo's, because "he was damned if he was going to give confession to his brother-in-law." Once my grandmother married John O'Brien, she became Mary Elizabeth O'Brien, which had been my grandmother on my father's side's maiden name. As a result, when Mom and Dad got married, they had to provide some sort of documentation that they weren't related as cousins.

Mom had two brothers, Donald and Allen. Donald was the oldest, and was evidently quite the intellectual. He went to the seminary right out of high school and was studying to be a missionary to Asia. Unfortunately, when World War II broke out, he was conscripted out of the seminary and into the Marine Corps because he had learned to speak Japanese, and the need for interpreters was paramount. It was unfortunate because his service undoubtedly affected him for the worse, although he served honorably throughout the war during most of the Pacific campaign, and was never (physically) injured. His job as interpreter was to talk reluctant Japanese defenders out of caves, tunnels, or surrounded redoubts, and he must have been pretty good at it, promising them whatever it took to get them to surrender. But more often than not, once they came out, they were summarily executed, the official excuse being that the army on the march didn't have the wherewithal to handle prisoners, other than a few officers. He was on Okinawa at the same time as my father, but this was years before they would meet back in Detroit. Suffice it to say, from what he observed, he lost his vocation to become a missionary and apparently his moral compass was from that time on permanently knocked off its binnacle (more on this later). After the war he was sent to China as part of the U.S. efforts to stabilize the former Japanese-occupied mainland. He spent the post-war years luxuriating, profiteering, and sending back crates of rare and expensive merchandise cajoled from once wealthy, but now destitute, Chinese families and purchased for pennies on the dollar. Not bad for a former seminarian and potential missionary.

Mom's other brother, Allen, was an odd sort of duck. He was christened Allen Larkin O'Brien, after the three Irish Republican Brotherhood "Manchester martyrs." These were men who had killed a policeman in 1867, while trying to rescue two other already-arrested Brotherhood members. They were caught and later hung for the crime. It appears that there may have been at the time some other undisclosed "political" (IRA?) connection with these same O'Briens, besides just the name. In any case, Allen considered himself somewhat of a street tough, but most of the stories indicated it was a lot of talk and not much action. Unlike the rest of the O'Brien family that drank rarely, if ever at all, Allen took to it readily. One story mentions that the police were called one day to the house, where they found the drunken teenage Allen standing atop the family baby grand piano waving a small pistol around and threatening to shoot anyone who came near him. (The family friend who told us this story was the policeman, affectionately known by us as Uncle Jerry, who had answered the call.) The policeman attempted to reason with him, until he got within arm's reach, and then he quickly grabbed Allen's ankles and pulled them out from under him. Allen crashed onto the top of the piano, was quickly disarmed, smacked around a little, and due to the family connections, was let off with a warning.

During the war, Allen volunteered with the Army Air Corps with hopes of becoming a pilot. During training they discovered that his eyesight was below par for a pilot, so he continued training as a navigator. He was in some action, and a piece of flack shrapnel cut his upper lip badly, and the scarring was such that he always had a bit of a sneer, which didn't help either his reputation or his temperament. At some point while recuperating, he got in a fight and struck an officer, and was given a general discharge, since it apparently wasn't totally unwarranted. Years later, after the war, when Dad started dating Mom, one evening Dad came to pick her up and while he was waiting for her Allen sat across the living room, just glaring at him. Finally, he said, "Barney, I don't think I want you dating my sister anymore." To which Dad replied, "I don't really give a shit what you want, Allen." Allen got up, and Dad did too, although Allen was maybe five years older than Dad and at least a head taller; Allen pulled out a leather-encased blackjack, also known as a sap, and waved it in Dad's face, saying "Well, you damn well better give a shit what I want." Just about that time, Mom came down the stairs and when Allen looked up, Dad just reached out and grabbed the blackjack out of his hands and put it in his own pocket. Then he said, "Let's go, Flo" and they went on out. The two men never liked each other after that, and I remembered as a child the blackjack being in Dad's tackle box, where he used it for years to stun fish before taking out the hooks they may have swallowed.

Mom was Flora Therese O'Brien, the youngest, and a contemporary of the Shirley Temple-era, with dark red curls and a cute smile. She was devoted to her father, John, and, bad as they later turned out to be, she was protected virtuously by her two older brothers. Born in 1925, she was almost exactly a year older than my father, and he always referred to her as "Flo." She had led somewhat of a sheltered life at home, as was customary back then, and this became especially acute when her father had a series of strokes, beginning just before the war years, and she became his primary caretaker. Her brothers taught her to drive at 14, and while her brothers were in the service she got a special dispensation to drive alone at 16 because her mother didn't drive, and she had to do all the shopping errands, etc. She went to St. Theresa's Grade School and High School, and had completed a year or two of college when she left to go to work and help support the family when her brothers were deployed. During the early 1940s she was the payroll clerk for WXYZ Radio in Detroit. At the time, WXYZ produced the radio serials *The Green Hornet*, *The Lone Ranger*, and *Challenge of the Yukon* (which later became *Sgt. Preston of the Yukon*), and sold the broadcasting rights to these series to other stations in New York, Chicago, and elsewhere, who would then air them live across the country. She knew all the principal radio actors of these series, and told me once that Tonto was actually an old Jewish man. There was also a little-known family relationship between the Green Hornet and the Lone Ranger, where the Lone Ranger was the Green Hornet's grandfather's brother, but very few listeners ever picked up on the obscure references to the Green Hornet mentioning his grandfather "riding with some Western vigilante." Mom also did a brief stint as a model, and we have a couple of the pictures, but apparently she quit as soon as she realized the lifestyle wasn't in keeping with her upbringing. She never drank, and I don't think she ever had more than a sip or two of wine in her whole life. This aversion was ascribed to some party she attended when she was in her late teens, where one of her best friends had gotten lushed up enough to end up making out with some disgusting louse, and Mom decided that that would NEVER happen to her. It was said that the O'Briens were also supposed to have an "allergy" to alcohol, although I think this was some trumped-up excuse to explain her father's work with the Liquor Commission and Allen's troublesome behavior when under the influence. In any case, no other members of the family, on either side, ever experienced an allergic reaction to alcohol, or any aversion to it. If anything, whatever problems have ever occurred have always resulted from the opposite affliction and/or attraction.

Detroit and "Mudder"

Some of my earliest memories were of downtown Detroit, the slush and snow in winter, women all wearing fur coats (sometimes with the heads and feet of the minks around the collars still dangling), men smoking cigars everywhere and thinking nothing of throwing them down when done, even in places that had rugs and carpeting. And if television shows then were black-and-white, on a small, sometimes round screen, it also seemed that life in the 50s, especially in Detroit, was also in various shades of grey. The stores were big and busy, and I can still see the sparks flying from the tops of the electric buses (or were they streetcars? or both?), in the maze of criss-crossed wires that stretched over the streets. Every so often there would still be a horse-drawn wagon, but by then they were few and far between. One of Dad's best friends, Jerry, the policeman mentioned above who had disarmed my uncle Allen years before, was a mounted policeman in downtown Detroit for over twenty years and had more than a few harrowing tales of car-and-horse encounters, as well as riot control and chasing down felons fleeing on foot down the city streets.

Mom would often take my brother and I to visit my grandmother who lived in downtown Detroit, and it was always an interesting experience. Since Mom always called her "Mother," I also called her Mother, but it came out "Mudder" and that's how she was referred to. She spoiled us, and especially me, rotten. Supposedly, I resembled the kid who played Timmy on the Adventures of Lassie, with blond, tousled hair and wide gaping eyes. Even strangers on the street would comment as much. When we visited "Mudder" of course, Dad never went along. The resentments that had built up over the years were just too much. In 1953 Mom's Mother had lent Mom and Dad the money for the down payment on their first house on Churchill, and although Dad made sure it was paid back promptly, I'm sure she never let him forget it. Between that and the Allen business, Dad wanted nothing to do with Mom's family (although I believe he and Donald would have gotten along if family loyalties hadn't had their sway).

Mudder lived in a huge brick house on the corner of Dexter and Boulevard, within walking distance of the YMCA. One time, I guess I was around five, my uncle Allen happened to be staying at his mother's when we went to visit. He said he was going over to the "Y" to go swimming, and asked my Mom if she wanted me to go along with him. She said it would be alright, except that I didn't have a bathing suit. He said, hell, he's just a little kid, he can swim in the raw. I didn't know what that meant and asked. When they told me, I was appalled and begged her not to let him take me. He just shook his head and left. He was living in the basement, which had a small apartment, with a bathroom, amongst the other storage areas filled mostly with the crates of goods that Donald had sent home from China after the war. The next morning, while Mom and Mudder were drinking coffee, they asked me to go down in the basement and tell Allen to come on up. I went down the dark stairs, and wandered the pitch black labyrinth, which smelled like a Chinese opium den, looking for Allen. He must have heard me, and jumped out of a black side-room with a yell that sent me screaming back up the stairs. He thought it was hilarious, unlike our respective mothers (who gave him a rash of shit), but it stuck with me because I never went back down in that basement ever again, even though I later grew more tolerant of Allen. [Just as a footnote, the "Y" story reminded me that my grandfather on Dad's side said he used to swim with Johnny Weismueller on the YMCA team in Chicago, before he became a famous Olympic swimmer, and later, of course, Tarzan.]

Mudder was always buying us gifts, which usually ticked Dad off no end, and she invariably took us out to lunch at some fancy restaurant in Detroit. Her and Mom would order lobster, whereas my brother Paul and I (he was probably two and I was maybe four) were content with just a huge éclair and ice cream. They took us over to the lobster aquarium and they would pick out which ones they wanted. I remember the waiter lifting out one particularly huge and ugly one, and shoving it into my brother's face, which set him off into a screaming fit. I'm just glad he didn't shove it my way or I would have lost it too—it was a horrendous sight for a couple of suburban kids. On one of these excursions, as we were leaving, my grandmother lost her footing on the carpeted stairs at the restaurant, and fell over. She laid there and cried out in agony. She had broken her hip, and I remember riding in the ambulance to the hospital, sirens blaring and lights flashing. I always wondered if I might have been the cause, as I was always tugging on her coat to get her attention to some ongoing event, or trinket for sale.

She had apple trees in her back yard and they were huge, towering well over the three-story house. The apples were green, hard, and tart, but I loved them anyway, and would stock up on bagfuls before we headed home. Eventually, they'd start to rot and Dad would throw them away when I wasn't looking. After her husband had passed away in 1947, and finally the sons moved out on their own in the early 50s (Allen in the basement, and Donald up in the attic apartment), she decided to rent out some of the rooms, and there was always a constant entering and leaving of these strangers. But there was one who was my favorite, a middle-aged Spanish gentleman, who would always give me a piece of candy or two, after asking my Mother if it was alright. I don't remember his real name, but it was something like Mr. Perón. When I'd see him coming down the stairs to go out I'd run up yelling "Perro, Perro!" It was only later that he told my grandmother that it meant "Dog, Dog!" in Spanish, but he didn't mind, since I was always so happy to see him, and I'd get the candy anyway.

15170 Churchill

As I said, we moved to the house on Churchill, out in one of the new suburbs of Detroit, called Southgate, a good hour drive from downtown. Since Dad didn't drive, Mom would have to take him in to work. This meant that we all had to get up before six, while it was still dark, especially during the frozen winters. Dad would go out and start up the car, warming it up with the heater, and scraping the snow and ice off the windshield and back window. Then he'd come inside and carry my brother and myself, still asleep and wrapped in blankets, and put us in the backseat. By this time Mom was up and ready and she would come out and drive him all the way into downtown Detroit, to the Ford plant, and then we'd turn around, drive back home and get ready for school. In the evenings we'd drive back downtown, and wait for Dad near a large World War memorial on the banks of the Detroit River, and Dad would come out of a nearby tavern at a proscribed time, and we'd all drive back home. We did this for years, until Dad found a neighbor who worked downtown, and began paying him gas money for a ride.

The years on Churchill were great. At the time, it was a fantastic place for kids growing up. We lived directly across from the baseball field of McCann Elementary School and two blocks to the west were a stand of "The Woods," where Dad would take my brother and I for walks in the winter, and we would spot rabbit and deer tracks in the snow, finally settling down on some log and Dad would light a fire and we'd cook hot dogs, before heading home. The houses were all cookie-cutter post-war construction, with every other one red brick and the others grey brick. I remember two instances where I was nearly snuffed out, one of which my family knew and the other I don't think I've ever told anyone. The one I've never told was a time I was down the street at the Meredith's house. The kid my age, Louis, had two older brothers, I guess at the time they must have been six or seven, and Louis and I were probably four. Well, the boys had a pair of roller skates and they were skating down their driveway, which was a little longer and steeper than most. I was amazed by this and they finally asked me if I'd like to try it. I said sure, and they were very attentive about binding these clamp-on roller skates onto my tennis shoes. Then they stood me up at the top of the drive and let me go. I whizzed down the driveway, waving my arms, and stayed upright, but... there was a large car bearing down the street, one of those big, lumbering and rounded 1950s types (I'm thinking a Buick). The kids started screaming for me to stop, which I couldn't do, and the driver didn't see me until the last second as I rolled into the street. He slammed on his brakes just as I slid down onto my back. The car screeched to a stop, and I recall looking up, under the front bumper at the still-hot engine, and the tires just inches from my head and feet. The driver was out of the car as soon as it stopped and ran around to the front. He looked under, and grabbed me by the collar, yanking me out. By now the other kids were standing around, and the driver, shaking from either relief or shock or both, gave us all a good cursing, before climbing back in and taking off.

The other instance I don't remember, but was told to me by my mother... My grandmother, Mudder, had given me a very large, heavy, pure silver Medal of the Immaculate Conception, also known as the Miraculous Medal, on a strong chain. The idea of the design and powers of the Miraculous Medal was inspired by an apparition to some French nun back in the 1850s. If you were wearing it when you died, you got a plenary indulgence of a free ride to heaven, no questions asked. This is the medal that first showed the Blessed Virgin Mary standing on the globe, hands outraised with rays of "grace" shooting out of her palms, and crushing the Great Serpent underfoot. According to the story, the medal was designed by Mary herself, with orders to this particular hallucinating nun to have the medals struck and distributed throughout Christendom, which the Pope at the time duly authorized (Oh yes, and they were generally rather expensive, though usually made of cheap metal, stamped out by the millions). Well, this medal was very special to me, and I wore it everywhere, never taking it off. As I said, the houses on

Churchill were all the same, and the yards were identical as well, they only differed in the landscaping out front, and whether anyone built a garage, or barbecue, or patio in the back. One of the favorite means of getting back home, if you were at a neighbor's house, was simply climbing and jumping the chain-link fences that separated the backyards. One day while coming over the last fence into our own back yard, the chain of the medal hanging out the back of my collar caught on the fence. I hung there, twisting, with my toes just barely touching the ground. Luckily, it just so happened that Mom was in the kitchen doing dishes, some thirty or forty feet away, even though the window over the sink didn't look out over the fence I was hung on. But she heard some gurgling, and looked out the back door to see me dangling there. She ran out and lifted me off the fence just as I was losing color and consciousness. Needless to say, Dad was happy to put that medal where even the BVM herself would never find it. Later, I was given a scapular instead, which is a light necklace made of thread with two fragments of blessed cloth (in plastic!), one for hanging in the front and one for the back, and even though I believe the same deal applies about going to heaven if you die with it on, it was just never the same... and it was scratchy... just not worth it (eternal salvation, i.e.).

Another time a bunch of us kids were racing across the back yards of the houses, clambering over the fences as sort of a steeple chase. Now it was pretty much an unwritten rule that you always wore shoes in Michigan, but one of the neighborhood families was from Alabama, and for their kids the rule was loosely, if ever, enforced. We're running, climbing fences, jumping over, and running on to the next one, trying to see who could get to the end of the block first. One of the Alabama-family kids was a lot smaller, and chubby, so he was lagging behind. All of a sudden we heard this blood-curdling scream, and turned to see this round little kid, maybe four years old, standing there screaming. We hurried over to see what he was screaming about, and saw that he had jumped over the fence and landed with both bare feet on the tines of an upturned rake, the prongs sticking out the top of his feet as he stood there screaming. We lifted him off the rake, and quickly got him home (luckily, just a house away), and they went squealing off to the hospital. We were all waiting for him when they got back, but other than a tetanus shot and a couple of stitches, he limped along for a couple of days and soon was as good as new. Tough little bastard named Tony.

One of my very first "friends" I ever remembered happened to be a little girl who had been badly burned in a house fire. Her name was Alice and she was perhaps six years old, and I might have been four. She had the melted-skin scars and patchy hair that typifies such tragedies, but to me she was just a normal little girl, funny and full of life. I would go to her house, and she would entertain me by pretending to cook stuff, and she would read to me. Her family doted on me, and I'd spend hours at their house, eating meals with them and watching television, since I was one of the only kids who would play with her. I only realized later that she never came outside during the day, and of course, she was pitied by anyone who ever laid eyes on her. I just didn't realize she was different, until others pointed it out to me, and then another bastion of innocence fell to ruin. At some point her family moved away, because I never saw her again after I was five or so.

The following event wasn't related to the little girl above, but it was just about this time, that one spring morning we awoke to the sound of fire engines in the neighborhood. Mom made my brother and I stay in the house and she went down the street to investigate. When she came back, Dad was with her, visibly shaken, with black smudges around his nose and eyes, and you could still smell the smoke on him. He had gotten up early as usual, to get ready for work, and had heard screaming down the street. He ran down with a few of the other men in the neighborhood, and one of the grey houses, maybe six or seven doors down, was engulfed in smoke, with a few flames lapping out a window or two. The screaming had been the mother of the house, who was in her nightgown out on the front lawn, screeching that her children were inside. Some of the men, including Dad, tried to get inside, but the smoke and heat beat them back. Dad and another man hooked up what hoses they could and began pouring it onto the flames. Since this was a new suburb of Detroit, the volunteer fire engines were going to take awhile. The distraught mother could not be restrained and she ran back into the house. Soon a fire engine showed up and they quickly doused the live flames. This was the fire engine we had heard maybe a half an hour previous. The firemen made their way into the house, and one-by-one they carried out the mother and her children, five little girls aged one to six, laying them out side-by-side on the front lawn. This was when Mom had gotten to Dad, and brought him home. When we finally drove by on our way to work and school, the bodies were still on the lawn, but now covered in some green sheets, the house still smoking. What had happened was, the father, who worked at a factory job, had gotten up while it was still dark, had coffee, and smoked a cigarette, tossing the not-quite-extinguished wooden match into the trash on his way out the door to drive to work. He was notified later that morning at work that he had lost his entire family, as well as his house. We only saw him one time after that, when he came to thank the neighbors for their rescue efforts and they gave him a collection of money they had raised to help with the burial costs. I now knew what the term "a broken man" meant, and never needed to ask.

On a lighter note, this was near the time that I discovered the wonders of women. Two little girls down the street had both taken a fancy to me, and they were vying for my attention. One Saturday afternoon we had just gotten back from the library (I was already a voracious reader by six, if mostly Superman comics and Mad magazines, so Dad made it a ritual to go to the local branch library once a week or so to broaden our horizons), and one of the little girls had staked out the house, waiting on our return. She came up onto the front porch and I came out and was shocked to see that she had taken her mom's bright red lipstick and plied it across her mouth. She sat me down along the edge of the porch and began asking me if I liked her, if I liked her better than the other little tart, and if so, would I like to kiss her? I was a bit flummoxed and really didn't know what to do. I didn't want to alienate the other little girl, who I liked a lot, but then here was this little doll, ripe and ready, as they say "a bird in the hand." Maybe it was about time for me to get kissed, seeing as how I was already six years old. Dad must have been eavesdropping just inside the screen door, because just about this time he came out, amusedly looked at this little tramp with the slather of lipstick and told me it was time to come in. She was upset, and headed back up the street, huffing and puffing, but I was secretly relieved. I wouldn't get my first kiss for seven more years.

The summers in Michigan were pleasant and lots of fun, but the winters were brutal, and I imagine they still are. One morning in mid-winter I woke up and was staring out the large-paned front window, looking at the fresh snow that had fallen during the night and trying to peer through the thick fog that had enveloped everything, when a large beast slowly emerged out of the mist, walking toward the window. I yelled and Mom and Dad both came running, speechlessly stunned to see this large red bull unconcernedly standing in the snow on the front yard, not ten feet away, the steam huffing out of his nostrils. Dad put on his big red hunting coat, and went out onto the front porch. My Mom, brother and I stood in the doorway behind him. Out in the fog you could hear bellowing, loud yelling, car horns, and sirens. A couple of men came out of the fog, nodded to Dad, and quietly draped a rope over the bull's head and led him off. But the yelling and sirens got closer, and the fog slowly began to lift. Now we could see a police car or two, red lights flashing, and Dad walked down to the street to find out what was happening. A policeman told him that down the highway at the end of the street a cattle truck had jackknifed in the snow and fog and flipped over onto its side, and the cattle, many of them injured, had wandered off into the neighborhood. Some had tried to jump over fences and were caught straddled on either side. A few had broken legs and had to be shot. He suggested we stay

15

inside. But by now, the fog had lifted pretty good and we could see all the way across the street, where men were trying to lasso the sprier cattle running on the baseball field, and there was a cow bellowing on the neighbor's fence, its stomach torn open by the struggle to get itself free, and policemen standing around wondering how to get it off with the least injuries to it and themselves. Hours later, they got a crane, slung straps under it, and lifted the poor creature up onto the back of a pickup truck with wooden slats, driving it off no doubt to the slaughterhouse. In my mind's eye I can still see the puddles of green poop the frightened animal shat out in torrents as they lifted it off the fence.

Another winter tale occurred one time when we had to ride the bus to school because Mom had pneumonia and couldn't go outside in the winter air to drive us. We bundled up and set out to the end of the adjacent block where the bus was supposed to pick us up. I remember it was a clear winter's day, the sun was out, but it was bitterly cold, and windy. There must have been ten of us, and we talked for a while, stamping our feet and huddled together. At one point, way down at the end of the street where the bus should be coming from, while watching traffic go by, I saw a school bus being towed by a wrecker. What would be the odds that that particular bus would be ours? We all waited, it got cloudy, the temperature dropped, and the wind picked up. Some of the older kids said the hell with this and began to walk home. We didn't want to get in trouble, especially as we had complained so loudly about having to ride the bus in the first place; not waiting long enough would have just meant we were boycotting the whole arrangement. Finally though, it became apparent that we'd waited long enough. Most of the other kids had already headed home, so my brother and I made our way back the two or three blocks to our house. We'd been out there at least three hours. When we got inside, I realized that we had gotten frostbitten, since we couldn't move our stiff white fingers, and after Mom got our snow gear off, and we warmed our hands near the heater, the pain was so bad that we just stood there bawling as our hands and feet thawed. I wasn't mad at the school bus driver, but I was plenty pissed that the school had never taken the time to call the parents when all these kids hadn't shown up for school, especially after the driver had obviously called in that the bus had broken down.

St. Pius

After kindergarten at McCann, the public school across the street, my brother and I went to St. Pius X Elementary in Southgate, which was a relatively new Catholic school built in 1953 and run by the Dominicans. I was just entering third grade when my brother was brought in by Mom for his orientation and admission into first grade. His name is Paul Craig Brewer, but we always called him Craig, a good Irish appellation. People thought he was named for Craig Stevens, the handsome actor who portrayed Peter Gunn, but that show didn't air until 1958, so that couldn't have been the case, since Paul was born in 1954. But now it was 1960, so people just continued to believe it, since Peter Gunn, with its famous Henry Mancini theme music, was probably the most popular adult show on television at the time. In any case, here we were in the Principal's office, and they were filling out all the paperwork to get my little brother Craig into school. The nun asked my mother for his name. "Paul Craig Brewer, but we call him Craig," she answered. The nun looked down and asked "But what do YOU want to be called?" "I want to be called Paul," he coolly answered. My Mom and myself were dumbfounded, staring at each other in horror... "No, no... you can't..." my Mom started. But the nun cut her off with a raised hand, looking down at my brother, "Paul it is then. Whenever you're here at school, you will be referred to as Paul." "No, wait..." again my mother started, and again she was cut off, as the nun directed an aide to show "Paul" to his new classroom. I was then directed to go to my own class, and the interview was over. From that day on, he has been known as Paul, although it caused no end of grief for months afterwards at home, and everybody, friends, relatives, and even mere acquaintances, had to adjust their salutations accordingly. Once in a great while, we'll still run into some long-lost relative that will refer to him as Craig, but as time ticks on they are now very few and far between. I later found it interesting to learn in the history of the New Testament the sudden conversion-initiated name-changing of the prosecuting Saul of Tarsus to the proto-evangelist Paul. As I've done my homework, he has become one of my least-favorite New Testament characters, being quite the self-righteous demagogue, and in my opinion, a bit of a showman.

People often ask me, having been raised Catholic, gone to parochial schools my whole life, and having been an altar boy, if I ever witnessed or was subject to any sexual abuse for which the Church has gotten (and sadly, earned) such a tarnished reputation. My mother once asked my brother Paul, not too many years ago, when all the headlines and magazine covers were at their most unrelenting peak, whether he had ever seen or been subject to any overtures. "What are you asking *me* for?" he said, "David's the cute one!" And although that was always true, I never did see anything "funny" except for one incident while at St. Pius. I was in the boy's bathroom standing at the urinal with maybe two other boys, peeing, when in walked one of the older priests. He took no interest in us boys standing at the urinals, but he noticed that the stalls were occupied. He knocked on one and asked if anyone was in there. "Yes!" the kid blurted out. "Are you doing number one or number two?" the priest asked. I can't remember or didn't hear what the kid said, but the priest moved on to a second stall and repeated his questions. He never tried to open the doors, nor did he make any further inquiries. Again, not taking any interest in us boys standing at the urinals, he turned and walked out. I remember us looking at each other and although we didn't say anything, I know what we all were thinking: THAT was weird. But other than that one strange, and relatively non-threatening, incident, I can honestly say that I never saw, experienced, or knew of any sexual abuse by any of the priests I was ever in contact with. Now, at the same time, I have seen priests drunk, cursing, smoking, playing cards, overeating, farting, and yes, physically assault troublesome high school delinquents, as well as each other. I have seen them reading Playboy magazines, and watched their eyes follow flirtatious and undisguisedly erotic high school girls (and sometimes their mothers) until the beads of sweat on their brows, and the gathering saliva at their mouth corners required mopping with a handkerchief. But no, I have never seen any "unnatural" behavior on the part of Catholic clergy. Nuns, however, well, that's another story…

Ourlando

In 1961 Mom and Dad made the decision to leave Michigan. Dad put out feelers and went out on job interviews to Salt Lake City, Baltimore, and Orlando. He liked Utah, except for the fact that he had to get a license to drink. He thought this was hilarious and carried the card around for years showing it to friends. The mountains were beautiful, he said, but the remoteness of the desert was a little daunting. And there were all those damn Mormons. Catholicism is strange enough, but Mormonism is just plain wacky. We were all for going there, not only because we didn't realize how desolate the desert can really be, but because we were told we might have to ride horses to school, and that was just too cool. But he kept on going to these interviews and the one in Baltimore was with Martin Marietta, the big defense contractor, and they told him they had an opening at their new plant in Orlando, Florida. He flew down to Orlando, shook hands on a deal, and started to work. He said what really cinched the deal for him, before he had ever met anyone in Orlando, or even seen the town, was how the stewardesses, in their southern drawl, called him "Honey" and "Sugar," and that when the door to the plane opened on arrival, the bright sunshine was accompanied by the wafting scent of orange blossoms. Meanwhile, up in Michigan, Mom got the house ready to sell, and made other arrangements for moving out of Southgate.

Martin Marietta was paying the moving expenses, so that wasn't a problem, but Dad didn't want us to drive all the way down from Michigan, so they hired a guy who was heading South anyway to drive the car down, our 1959 brown-and white Ford Fairlane 500. I think they were going to give him $100 and pay for gas. He figured it would take two days and he would leave about the same time we were going to fly out. Ma packed up a few valuables, gave away a few treasured items we'd never use, and we flew out sometime in April 1961 to join Dad in Orlando. He had been staying at the seedy Angebilt hotel downtown, taking a cab to work, until one of his office buddies, who had relatives in Michigan, suggested he stay in a spare bedroom at the house with his family, until we'd arrive, and they could drive in to work together. We got in on a Friday, and Dad met us at the airport, and it was just like he said, sunny and smelling of orange blossoms. We had dinner with the family that Dad had been staying with, then went to our hotel on Colonial Drive, across from Belks. The next morning, my brother and I were up early and wanted to go in the swimming pool at the hotel as soon as possible. Mom got to sleep late. So, Dad took us down to the pool, and we padded around in the shallow end, since we didn't know how to swim, and we laid around soaking up the warm April sun, while he watched us, reading the paper. At some point, I was out of the pool, and my brother Paul was in the shallow end, but bobbing up and down, and he started to slip into water over his head. He started thrashing about, and we could see he was quickly getting into trouble. Dad said "Quick! Get in there and help your brother!" So I jumped in without hesitating, or thinking for that matter, because then *I* was in over my head, and, although I had a grip on him, now we were both going to drown. Dad suddenly got up, ran down to the shallow end and jumped in up to his chest, shoes, clothes and all, and grabbed us just as we were going down for the proverbial third time. He pulled us out, gasping and choking, and was a little shaken himself, since he also had never learned to swim. We stayed out of the pool for most of the rest of the day, while Dad laid his cards and money out from his wallet to dry in the sun. Little did we realize that the near-death drowning incident was nothing compared to what we had to face that evening. Newly arrived from the hyperborean regions of Michigan, where the winter's snows were just melting, and where our pale white arms, backs, stomachs, and legs had not seen daylight for at least the previous nine months or so, we had taken no precautions against the tropical sun, and that night my brother and I lay sobbing in misery as our lobster-red and trembling cadavers were slathered with the anesthetic sunburn salve called Unguentine. Needless to say, other than going out for breakfast, we stayed inside all the next day watching television, and moving as little as possible.

3300 Debbie Drive

Soon the moving van arrived and we settled into a rental house on Debbie Drive, boxes piled high, and furniture placed accordingly. It was wonderful for us, as the neighborhood had lots of kids our age, and the backyard was full of orange trees, already dropping fruit by the minute. We couldn't get over the fact that here were oranges literally rotting in the street, so we tried to gather as many as we could in grocery bags, to "save" them, much to the amusement of our Floridian neighbors. Soon we were overwhelmed and no matter how many gallons of orange juice we squeezed (squoze?), the bags of oranges began to rot in the carport, and we had to eventually give up and use them for mulch. We were quickly taught by the other neighborhood kids though, that the small green and hard oranges (and especially grapefruit, because they had bumps on them) were perfect for large-scale "wars" between adjacent neighborhood kids we might catch passing through on their bikes. Sometimes these "wars" would break out on a large scale, with older groups of boys, and sometimes a tomboy girl or two, coming down the street armed not only with the golf-ball-sized green oranges, but full-grown baseball-sized orange oranges, and some of them good and rotten, so that these major assault campaigns would be declared cease-fire only when a parent would call and a police car or two would cruise through.

Speaking of police cars... we had been in Florida over a week and already moved into a house, and the car still hadn't shown up. Mom and Dad had last talked to the guy who was driving it just before he took off, the day we flew out. He was someone they admit they hadn't known very well, and whom they had actually gotten out of the classifieds in the Detroit Free Press, a guy who was just looking for a means to get south. And they'd given him gas money, and the keys to their beautiful 1959 Ford Fairlane. But now there was no way to get in touch with him, these being the days of rotary telephones, and heck, it was only supposed to take him two days. He seemed like such a nice guy. And here's the rub: nice guys DO finish last. He had made great time the first day, but kind of overextended himself the second day, and so pulled over to get some sleep, somewhere in Georgia. He was awakened by the tapping of a flashlight on the window, and once he was rousted out, he began to explain about the "arrangement" of driving the Michigan-plated vehicle to Orlando, but no, he didn't have a home phone number, he was supposed to call Dad at work when he got in (but now it was the weekend, Dad wasn't working, and wouldn't be until Monday). To make a long story (for him) short (for us), he ended up spending a week on the rural Georgia county prison farm, Cool-Hand-Luke style, until they got verification of the status of the car, registration, "arrangement", et al. I think Mom and Dad gave him an extra $50 bucks for his trouble when he finally arrived.

Once we got the car, everything was grand, and we began to explore the countryside around Orlando. One of the big draws back then was Moss Park, a large lake with a public beach, lots of kids, and relatively safe and shallow. Well, we were going to head out to Moss Park one day, Mom, my brother Paul and I, all in our swimsuits, with towels, picnic stuff, the works. Mom backed out of the driveway a little too fast and just clipped the bumper of a car coming down the street, who also hadn't seen us backing up. They got out and exchanged information, and both agreed that there was no visible damage, but the other driver insisted that a policeman had to be called. So we waited. When the officer arrived, he quickly determined (maybe due to the Michigan plates) that the (very) minor accident was Mom's fault, let the other driver go, and told Mom that she was going to get the ticket. He was a young policeman, obviously a country boy, and very polite, "Yes, Ma'am, No, Ma'am." Mom was upset that he had determined without being there that it was all her fault, since there'd been no damage, and complained bitterly, as well as turning on the water fountain and crying that we had just moved down to Orlando from Michigan, and even relayed the troubles about the guy driving the car down, etc. The policeman was wavering and just wanted to get the ticket written and go on about his business, telling her about how we needed to get the car registered in Florida, etc. She begged to be let off with just a warning, and it looked like he was about to give in, when my brother and I jumped out of the car, what with Mom crying and all, and she saw that we hadn't any shoes on. Now this was a very sore point in Michigan, to be outside without shoes on, and she straightened up, and said "Get back in the car! You look like a couple of hillbillies!" Whether it was a Freudian slip, or just an instinctive reaction, it didn't matter... she knew she had stepped in it. There was only a glance, but as soon as the cop saw Mom quit crying so suddenly, and worse, when the word "hillbilly" came out so readily, the jig was up. He pulled out his ticket book and began writing.

All in all though, we enjoyed our brief spring and summer on Debbie Drive, except for our rude introduction to "palmetto bugs," the large insidious and armored roaches that would pop out at the most ungodly times, like when you were playing hide-and-seek and found a great cupboard to hide in, or might start flying around your bedroom at night in the darkness, finally landing God only knows where, or worse (women tell me it's THE worst), when you turn on the shower and one either slinks out of the drain or flies out of the folds in the shower curtain, again to flit about in some random flight pattern round your nakedness. Dad would say, "Jesus, they're as big as turtles!" thinking of course, of those little green turtles you'd get at the county fair, and in that regard, he wasn't far off. Of all of us, though, Mom showed the least intimidation, and would smash them relentlessly and unmercifully whenever she saw them, with whatever was at hand, and which sometimes WAS her hand. You've got to admire the genius of evolution in them, though, because those bastards were, and are, tough. I've seen many a large cockroach take a full blow, shake its head, and scurry off to plan a retaliatory counterattack. I'm sure you've also read accounts of scientific tests where they've cut off their heads, and the damn things only die days later (not of the beheading, but of starvation, just because they can't eat). They WILL outlast us, nuclear war or no.

Race Relations

There was one disturbing fact about Florida though, and that was its relation to blacks. Now, to be honest, I had very few introductions to blacks in Michigan as well, but the few encounters that did occur were always happy and celebratory. Mom knew a few folks from having lived in downtown Detroit, and whenever she happened upon someone she knew, you could tell that there was some mutual affection. This was a little unusual since she had lived through the race riot of 1943 that lasted for three days before Federal troops were called in to break it up. Her brothers were in the service, and she was taking care of her Dad who had had a stroke, and she told me about the gangs of black kids going through the neighborhood in downtown Detroit, breaking windows and in some instances, throwing Molotov cocktails. But none of this seemed to affect her and like I said, when we met some old black friend of hers she would thrust me up as a baby and they would converse for quite a while. But when we got to Florida things were different. This was still Deep South and segregation was in full force. There were always signs everywhere, "No Colored" or "Colored Only" or, more prominently and more frequent, "Whites Only" (often mass-produced and metal type-faced signs as opposed to hand-scrawled). This would set Mom off, and I can't count the number of stores we were asked to leave after one of her tirades. Dad didn't feel the same sense of injustice and was more pragmatic about it, knowing there was very little to be done on the local, or even State level. He knew it was going to take Federal intervention, and he also knew it wasn't going to be peaceful. After all, he was a product of the tougher side of Detroit, and had helped surround his own neighborhood during the 1943 riots. But both of them taught us that the whole segregation business was the result of ignorance more than anything. And we learned about this ignorance first-hand when stores started selling souvenirs commemorating the centennial of the start of the Civil War, back in 1961. My brother and I bought, or asked Mom to buy us, a couple of blue plastic Yankee caps, as opposed to the plethora of grey Rebel caps with the Stars and Bars on top, that were going out the door. I mean, if they're going to celebrate the Civil War, well then, by God, we'd celebrate it too, seeing as how we (the Yankees) won. Well, jeezuz-fucking-kee-rist, you'd think we'd freed the slaves all by ourselves. It was the first time I'd ever heard the Civil War referred to as the War of Northern Aggression. In fact, it was still so fresh to many of these Southern sympathizers that one old lady still referred to it as The Late Unpleasantness, and I guess this isn't so unrealistic, since a hundred years was only a couple of generations. Anyway, we caught so much shit wearing those silly little hats out in public that it wasn't long before they "disappeared" (I remember finding one of them flattened in the street, run over.) That was okay. I got back at those stupid crackers by drinking out of the "coloreds only" water fountains every chance I got. "Hey! Cain't you read? Tha' water spigot ain't fo' you! Drink out of this one over he-yah! Whassa matter with you?" "Huh?... Oh, sorry," I'd reply, then laugh. Later, when I got a little older, wiser, and tougher, emboldened by my liberal Northern parents, I'd tell 'em, "I'll drink anywhere I want."

2. At Play in the Service of the Lord (1961 – 1966)

St. James

      After a month or so of goofing off and getting acclimated to Central Florida, Mom and Dad decided we needed to get back into school before the year ended, so we'd be ready to advance to the next grade in the fall. So, on May 5ᵗʰ we got dressed up, hair slicked back, and drove to St. James, in downtown Orlando. How did I know it was May 5ᵗʰ? As we drove into the small street that fronted the school and parked, we could see kids, teachers, and a gaggle of nuns thronged out onto the playground. Mothers and other women were carrying small black-and-white television sets into the school. There seemed to be a lot of excitement. We went on in to the principal's office, where Sister Mary Ethelburga welcomed us in while people ran about; she closed the door, and upon our introductions, the very first thing she said to me was "Don't you have the courtesy to pull out the chair for your mother!?," something I'd probably never done for her ever before, under any circumstances, but I jumped to it this time. Then, after looking at the textbooks we had been using in Michigan (I remember the big deal being "fun with phonics" at the time), which she relatively dismissed as some northern folderol, she began to examine us, both physically and orally. "Stand up straight!" "How old are you?" "Now, can you recite The Lord's Prayer?" Well, this was a standard query back at St. Pius in Michigan, so I began… "Pater Noster, qui es in coeli, sanctificeter nomen tuum, adveniat regnum tuum…" THAT shut her up. Now she realized that it wasn't a couple of her regular wannabe-Catholic redneck goobers she was dealing with. By this time the excitement was reaching a fever pitch outside, so Mom asked, "Is something going on out there?" "Oh, just some spaceman is going to be launched from Cape Canaveral today." Oh my God! It was today that Alan Shepherd was going to go up! And that's why everyone is staring to the East, hands shading their eyes, Cape Canaveral was less than fifty miles away—they thought they might be able to see the contrail from here! Even though Mom wanted to go out as much as we did, Sister Ethelberga kept her in there to fill out paperwork, but sent my brother and I outside, seeing how nervous we had become since we realized what all the hubbub was about. I can't honestly say that I saw the plume of that little Redstone rocket through the trees that day, but I sure as hell was standing there facing east out on the St. James playground with everybody else when it went off, thinking I'd seen it.

When we all tramped back into the school, Paul and I found out that our brief moving vacation was over. Sister Ethelberga sent Mom home and had us taken to our respective classrooms right away. I was extremely lucky. My third-grade class of maybe twenty kids was led by (coincidentally) Miss O'Brien, a comely and buxom young twenty-something girl just out of college who was kind and virtuous, and just pleasant to be around, unlike the aged old sour nun my brother got stuck with over in first grade. Back then, the teacher you were assigned to was the same teacher you had all day, switching lessons from History to English to Math to Religion and Geography etc., punctuated by recess and lunch, all at the turn of the hour hand or the sound of a bell, and by a bell I meant a hand-wrung bell down the hallway. Located directly across the street from Lake Eola in downtown Orlando, the old limestone school (built in 1928) is still there, and more full of students than ever. It's now a beautiful school, modern, and well-endowed, and still exhibiting that Florida limestone face and red tiled roof. Back in the early 60s however, the playground was dry and dusty, and the classrooms were hot in the early fall and late spring, without air conditioners, or even fans, and cold as hell in the winter, if you didn't get burned by standing too close to the steam radiators. Students spanned all economic classes, but they were all white, and all Catholic. The first days were a little rough, trying to mix in with kids that had already been together for almost the entire school year. The boys on the schoolyard were the typical groups of roughnecks and eggheads, nerds and geeks, although we didn't have those names back then. I only had one incident where the tough guys wanted to prove a point, and they had surrounded me and were just giving me general taunts, a little poking and prodding, I suppose, to see what I was made of. Now, I was a small kid, always, even through high school, and one of the bigger ones, a kid named George, decided to give me a push, but he didn't know that we didn't take that crap in Michigan. So I hauled off and hit him in the stomach. I must have got him right in the diaphragm, 'cause I knocked the wind right out of him. He doubled over, fell to the ground, and when he finally regained his breath, got up crying and ran off. Never had any more trouble with the bigger guys after that, but I realized that the members of my core group were going to be the smart and sensitive eggheads. If I've ever been chauvinistic, it would have to be in the area of brains. Men or women, friends or foes, they had to be smart; not necessarily educated or even knowledgeable, just quick-witted and intelligent. Within days I had made two life-long friends, Dennis LeFils and Ed Quinby.

First Fridays

I'm not sure I ever realized it before but, not only were the three of us the smartest boys in class (in my humble opinion), but we were also the littlest. This became obvious as the nuns would line us up, from smallest to largest, whenever we had to make the ten-block walk to St. James, the church, from the school. I suppose it was easier to keep an eye on the line and maintain discipline by sizing us up. This trek would occur at least once a month, and oftentimes two or three times a month, and during the Holy Easter season it could happen two or three times a week. I know it occurred at least once a month because the nuns were especially vigilant to see to it that we, the children, would "make our First Fridays." Now I'm always surprised to meet Catholics that don't know what the devotion known as "making your First Fridays," also known as the devotion to the Sacred Heart, means. The story goes that some French nun in the 1700s would have these visions of Jesus talking to her, sometimes on the cross, sometimes not, but invariably having his living, beating, heart exposed, ringed with its own little crown of thorns, and oftentimes shooting out rays of light. This was the origin of the Sacred Heart paintings one often sees in homes, schools, and church. Usually it's just Jesus with a big sad-face on, his cloak open, exposing his tortured heart with its very own crown of thorns and a little blood. And that was the point: that the sins of mankind were black arrows shooting into his heart and making him sad. But Jesus had offered this hysterical young French nun a solution to make him happy, and for the most part this was really just to keep several promises, most of which were just to "be good". But the last promise said that if anyone happened to receive Communion in a state of grace on the first Friday of every month for nine months in a row, they would receive a plenary indulgence. Now a plenary indulgence is nothing to sneeze at. This is a guarantee that you will go to heaven, no matter what—and that means no matter what sins you might ever commit for the rest of your life too. Well, it took this little neurotic nun many years to convince the Church that she wasn't just nuts but really had these visions, which in fact she probably did (have the visions that is, not that they were authentic). Once the visions, and subsequently a miracle or two as a result thereof, had been determined by a Council of the Church to be real, then, by default, the promises had to be real as well. So, our nuns at St. James made it their sacred duty to see to it that we, the children, we innocent lambs of God, would by hook or by crook make our First Fridays, thus guaranteeing us eternal salvation and the pleasantries of heaven after death (and forever). The catch was, you had to make them in a row, without missing any. School started in September, sometimes late August, and it was out by May, so, counting out the months on your fingers, it was evident there was little or no wiggle room. And Fridays were notorious for being a day you might just happen to get sick, or worse, that the relatively godless secular government might declare a holiday on a First Friday just by chance. Under both these circumstances, it was unlikely that you would get up out of your sick bed, or drive into town on a holiday, just to make your Communion (even if, should you begin to recover and feel better on your sick day, you might go out fishing to get some fresh air and sunshine). And even if you did get to school those nine months in a row, and the nuns happened to get us all to the church on time, rain or storms notwithstanding, there was always that nagging doubt that, maybe, just maybe, you, of all people, hadn't confessed all your sins in a timely manner before committing a new one. Luckily, however, you could still receive Communion and technically be in a state of grace if you had only a venial, or minor sin, on your soul. Lying, for instance, or beating up your little brother. To commit a mortal sin as a child, I was later to learn from my dear Jesuit-educated father, was damn near impossible. So for all those unlucky adult and fallen Catholics who never had the nuns herding you like cats to church every First Friday of every month while you were in grade school, so that you could keep your Sacred Heart promise to Jesus and enjoy the fruits of everlasting harmony in the now-content bosom of the Lord, all I can say is, it's gonna be rough.

Tradewinds and the Big Ol' Fish

These were heady days. It was now summer, with plenty of time off, and here we were in Florida, and for a couple of kids, straight from dreary Detroit, not to mention seeing the delight of our parents, this was truly a Land of Enchantment. We had to get out of the house we rented on Debbie Dive, and that summer, Mom and Dad started looking around for a house to buy. A friend of Dad's at work lived in a brand new suburb outside of Orlando called the Isle of Catalina, and although it was considered a ways out of town, out in the scrub, they decided to check it out. They looked at several houses, but took a particular interest in one very rundown but large Florida-style block house on a large lot on a canal. And it had a pool. The problem was the house had been vacant for at least two years, and looked it. The pool was full of large strands of seaweed and algae, the yard was overgrown with weeds, and the house smelled of musty neglect. The fellow who had originally purchased the house, which was one of the model homes built for display in the newly-created "Isle" was a guy named Doctor Crowder. Oddly though, he wasn't a doctor in any sense of the word. His parents had christened him with the dubious first name of "Doctor" in the hopes that he would get a bit of a head start in life as a result. He had bought the house newly-built in 1959, then had a falling out with his wife, who took him for everything he had, and, after entertaining a string of various women in his Playboy-era bachelor pad, who would each leave him in turn when they found out that he was neither a real doctor nor had any real money, he ended his days alone (and possibly by his own hand). The house had subsequently lain up in probate for a year or two, but now, Mom and Dad's interest ignited a frenzy for the developer to get some of his money back out of it. They offered him $21,500 "as is," and he jumped on it. But it was going to be a lot of work to get it in shape. Luckily, Dad was in his mid-thirties, still energetic, and was making a pile of money at his new job, so he hit it with a vengeance. Paul and I were not much help, being only 7 and 9, but we made the most of investigating the neighborhood. One day, while Dad was inside the house painting, and Mom was busy cleaning, we were out back fishing in the canal. Dad had shown us how to use his casting reel from Michigan, but we were constantly creating "bird's nests" of tangled line at the reel, which would take a full five minutes at least to unravel before we could cast the black rubber worm out again. So we took turns casting and unraveling, casting and unraveling. To be honest, at that time, early on, we were then hopelessly pitiful as fishermen, but it kept us occupied and out of Mom and Dad's hair. It was Paul's turn, and I helped toss out the plastic worm, and handed him the rod. Bang! The line went taut, he gave it a jerk, and wham! there was a splash as a large fish cleared the water, shaking his head to throw off the hook. We were both stunned speechless. Being the elder, I grabbed the rod, and told him to go get Dad. He ran into the house, yelling excitedly "Dad, Dad, we caught a fish! Hurry, hurry, you've got to come out!" Dad, who was at the top of a ladder, busy painting, was unimpressed, thinking that we had hooked one of the many small bream that were as common as minnows in the canal. He said he'd come out in a little bit (which meant he wasn't coming out at all). Paul ran back out and I handed the rod back to him, since, by all the rules of fishermen, it really was his catch. While Paul tried reeling it in, I spotted the next-door neighbor, a retired Army Colonel, coming out of his house. I ran up and breathlessly told him that we had hooked a big fish. He ran over and his eyes grew big behind his thick glasses as he helped us land the fish, a huge five-pound-plus largemouth bass. Quickly, he grabbed an empty garbage can and filled it with water, then put the fish in it, its tail sticking out of the top of the large can, twitching. After congratulating us on the catch, he asked where our Dad was, and we pointed to the house. He walked in, went up to Dad, and told him he needed to come outside. Dad thought something was wrong, or that we kids had screwed something up, so he got down from the ladder, set his paint roller aside and followed the Colonel out the back door. Even Dad was speechless when he saw the tail sticking out of the garbage can. It was a magnificent fish, even by today's "professional" standards, so after showing it around the neighborhood, we took it back to the house on Debbie Drive, which we hadn't yet vacated, and Dad cleared out the freezer so we could stuff it in, bent almost double. Well, back then, in Orlando, the old-timers will remember that one of the premier sporting goods stores in the nation, Denmark's, was downtown. On Saturday evenings they had a television show and would highlight the various catches that hunters and fishermen had brought in during the week. So we called and they said yeah, bring it on in, and they would take a picture and put it on the show. Thawing the damn fish took a whole day, and by the time the thing was bendable, it was starting to smell—I think Ma even sprayed it down with Lysol before we packed it up and drove downtown the next day. Now Denmark's was, as I said, one of the premier sporting goods stores in the nation, certainly in the Southeast. It was one of those stores that Hemingway would write about, various stuffed animals in threatening stances (even menacing squirrels and rabid-eyed raccoons), trophy fish on the walls, split bamboo fly rods, large brass reels, guns and ammunition, the whole shebang. The place smelled of leather and saddle soap, and if I recall correctly, it even had wood floors that creaked, and the old men who did nothing but sit in the corner all day, smoking, surreptitiously drinking, and talking. We walked in and, having introduced ourselves, as Mom was so well-adept, they went right about their business and quickly weighed the leviathan, as we had never thought to do—five and a half pounds! Even by those days, a noble freshwater gamefish! They posed my little brother holding this fish half the size of himself, and that was it. By the time we got home the fish was exceedingly ripe and there was no putting it back in the freezer. When Dad got home from work, it was ceremoniously buried in the back yard. We all waited for Saturday to arrive after having alerted the neighborhood kids, and sure enough, among the rednecks who had shot, stabbed, netted, run over, or hooked the local Central Florida fauna that week, there was Paul's picture, proudly displaying the great fish, with the declaration by the co-host of the marvel of it having been caught by this new freckle-faced kid from Michigan, "Cute as Christmas."

Swimming Lessons

That summer we moved into the house in Catalina, freshly painted, with the pool cleaned out and plenty of time to explore. Mom and Dad were worried over the pool and decided we needed to learn to swim as soon as possible. It just so happened that the Orlando Police Department was offering swimming lessons down at the lake, so we gladly joined up. The classes were taught by a young handsome cop and a beautiful girl from the Red Cross. In no time flat my brother and I had proceeded from floating face down to swimming like otters, learning all the strokes: side-stroke, backstroke, treading water, breast stroke, etc. and, of course the famous Australian Crawl. We were so good, so fast, especially since we had the pool at the house, that we eventually quit going to the classes. Nonetheless, one day, the Orlando cop and his young assistant showed up at the house, and asked why we quit coming. We made up some lousy excuse, but they said we couldn't get the cards for completion unless we came for the final swimming "test." Under Dad's direction, we'd been practicing in the pool and had been learning to hold our breath to the point where holding it for two minutes was easy. When it comes to swimming, it's the act of breathing that slows you down. Once you could swim with only taking a breath every so often, you can cover a lot of ground very fast.   So the next day we went down to the lake for the test, and we were so good that we not only qualified for the basic swimmer's card but the advanced as well. I'm sure that the young cop and the girl were romantically involved (how could they not be?), but a year or two later she got engaged to the older brother of one of our neighbors, just after he had returned from a tour of duty in Vietnam. He also was a tall, handsome guy, if a bit cocky, and had bought a flashy red sports car, a convertible, with the money he received when he separated from the service. Unfortunately, just before they got married, he drove that sports car up under a semi that separated his head from his neck. I don't know what happened to that beautiful vivacious young woman, but to be honest, I wished she had married the cop. Although I can't remember her name, strangely enough (or maybe not so), I remember his. It was Robert Strange. His teaching me to swim stood me in good stead later on in life, saving my life, and others, innumerable times throughout the years.

Altar Boy Instruction

Once the summer was over, it was fourth grade, the following school year and, under the incentive of Mrs. Schoffstahl, a short Spanish firecracker who dyed her hair blond, but always had black roots (and to whom was attached no visible German Mr. Schoffstahl), the training for becoming an altar boy began. Once I had volunteered for this honor, Dad got visibly excited, since he had grown up as one of the anointed ones himself, and decided one evening that we should "practice" at the house. We had a very nice wooden coffee table that sufficed to function admirably as an altar, and we dug out the old Latin Vulgate missal we'd carried from Michigan in order to get the Roman rite down pat. Dad acted as the priest and my brother and I became the altar boys, and we went through the motions of two or three Masses before getting bored and tired. The priest who actually taught the newly invested boys at St. James was Father Troy, a young Irish priest. He was kind and delicate, tall, thin, young and full of enthusiasm. But at the time (1961-62) he was just one of the several foreign priests, generally Irish and Spanish, who had been sent as missionaries to the heathenish and heretical Southern Baptist United States, since there was at that time a glut of young men coming out of the seminaries in those countries and Florida was considered a desolate and (considering the ongoing civil rights movement activities at the time) dangerous deployment. His patience and dedication to detail were such that he had us ready for the altar in a week or two. He was less successful with the older altar boys, sixth, seventh, and eighth graders, who had grown slovenly in their approach, but bit by bit, even they came around to his way of doing things, through the shame of being shown up by the younger neophytes, if not by his repetitious gentle reprovals. It's a sad truth that some dozen years later he ended up leaving the priesthood, returning to Ireland to get married and open a bicycle shop. Maybe not so sad after all, for him anyway.

Earlier I had mentioned Dennis L., one of my dearest and oldest friends. We were pals right from the get-go, both of us smaller than the other boys, and smarter by several degrees. Always in the advanced class, we often vied against each other in intellectual contests, with Dennis generally prevailing. He was stronger in math and quicker in reading and comprehension, whereas I was better at remembering history and spelling, and where I grew bored easily and then would fall off on concentrating, he could focus interminably on whatever problem beguiled him. Unlike him, I was a bit of a disciplinary delinquent, and spent many a day with my own desk facing into the corner, banned from interacting with the rest of the class. Then I'd be mortified for having been singled out, eventually begging to be released from confinement, on the often short-lived promise of improvement in what was then referred to as "courtesy." The only instance where I remember being punished for misbehaving paid off was the time my third-grade teacher, the dear young and voluptuous Miss O'Brien made me sit under her desk for an hour—the view was magnificent. I was never hyperactive (we had plenty of those types in the school), but I was easily distracted either through boredom or by the flirtations of those cute little girls, or when my mischievous shoulder-imp would whisper some new irresistible attention-getting diversion into my mind. Spit balls were the preferred weapon, always with a straw, and every election season we'd collect bumper stickers and rub the gum off the back to create mega-snotballs that would stick to anything. These things, sometimes as big as your fist, would stay stuck to the ceiling for weeks, sometimes months, before they would eventually lose their grip and fall unexpectedly during a lesson, a test, or when some celebrity like the bishop would be visiting, often causing even the teacher to laugh at the surprise of it.

Dennis and I would visit each other's houses, often spending the night after playing war games with plastic soldiers, tanks, etc. and riding our bikes to various stores around Orlando. We became altar boys together and, much to the frustration of our parents, often volunteered to serve the 7 a.m. weekday Mass, Monday through Saturday, since no one else ever would. My Dad would get so upset that I didn't have the sense to keep my mouth shut, but Mom was extremely understanding (in fact, a living saint). She would get up at 6, wake me up to get ready, and then she would iron my cassock and surplice in the pre-dawn dark. Then she would drive me into town, dropping me off, and heading back home, to then drive my brother Paul in to school an hour later. She usually gave me a dollar or two, and after Mass, Dennis and I would walk the six or eight blocks back to school, meandering through the shops on the way. I recall the Rexall's Drug Store, directly across from the church, where Dennis and I would get breakfast, one egg, toast, grits, and a coke, for 29 cents. We attracted all kinds of people, from little old ladies who often picked up the tab (having recognized us as the altar boys at Mass), to the Old Man Jesus, who frequented downtown Orlando in the mid1960s. He was a flighty old geezer, short and wizened, with a long white beard and disheveled hair, who wore flowing scarves of bright purples, orange, green and red. Always polite, but still kind of scary in his appearance, he stuck to the story that he was Jesus Christ, returned to the earth to save those who believed in him, and damn to those who didn't. He didn't bathe regularly, had bad teeth (of those that remained), and generally stank. So he was often asked to leave any establishment wherein he might enter to get a drink of water. This was long before homeless people were a common sight, and with his bright colors and wild mannerisms, he was a city street standout for many years. Dennis and I took a wicked delight in questioning his bona fides, since we knew all the right questions, to the point that it became plain that as unbelievers in his divine mission, he'd gladly be holding the door to hell-fire's ovens open for us when the time arrived. He had no idea about the redeeming quality of First Fridays, however. And he's supposed to be Jesus? Give me a break!

By fifth grade, our favorite stopping point on the way back to school after serving those morning masses was Royal's, on the northwest corner of Robinson and Magnolia. Not only was it a drug store with a soda fountain, but the candy choices, jukebox, and pinball machine made the place irresistible, often making us late for school, even though we had left the church in plenty of time to make it by the first bell. And here occurred my first life-changing musical reverberations to the Beatles. Dennis had two older brothers, and an older sister, so he was introduced to these new fads as soon as they were on the horizon. But I still remember the first time I ever heard the

Beatles on the jukebox at Royal's singing "She Loves You" (Yeah, Yeah, Yeah), and the flip side "I Saw Her Standing There." It was magic. Although I'd heard rock 'n roll for years, this was definitely something different. And damn if it didn't strike just the right chords in a young prepubescent's heartstrings. Kids nowadays have no idea what an impact the Beatles were. I have complete sympathy with the breathless expression my Mom used to get when she described seeing Sinatra at the Fox Theatre in Detroit back in the forties, and finally understood those nutty bobbysoxers who screamed and swooned over Elvis when I was much younger. And we were the guys. The young girls at St. James had already homed in on this phenomenon—hell, they already knew the birthdays of the Fab Four, who was married, who was single, and who was available, what their favorite desserts were, everything. It was good timing. As they were edging into womanhood, we guys still had a couple of years to go before we'd be springing to attention, but the idea of romance was well indoctrinated into our pre-libidinous lusting. We knew we wanted them, and they knew we wanted them, but none of us really understood why. Beatlemania filled this void extraordinarily, and with their help (and that of the Kinks, Herman's Hermits, and the Dave Clark Five), by the end of fifth grade we knew where we stood, or more precisely where we wanted to end up when we saw her standing there.

Priestly Health Tips

Fifth grade at St. James meant going upstairs, literally. Kindergarten through fourth grade were taught downstairs, and fifth through eighth were taught upstairs. So moving upstairs meant that you were now with the upper classmen. It also meant that we were being exposed to the ministrations of physically growing up as well. As our bodies developed, all at different tempos, the teachers knew they had to confront the inevitable. Thus began an attempt at "health courses" or what is known today as sex ed. These were pitiful sessions where a priest would gather us segregated boys in the choir room and try to get us to understand the differences between men and women (as if we hadn't already cracked that code by a sudden proliferation and appreciation of dirty jokes and our own observations of the burgeoning brassieres around us). The priest—brought in no doubt for his expertise on human relations—was an older gentleman, embarrassingly inept. He tried and tried to get his points across, hints at menstruation, masturbation, and general maturation, and finally failing miserably, he ended up just saying "Are there any questions?" At which point, and after a few moments of unnerving silence, one of the taller, more developed, and experienced guys raised his hand, was called on, and said "So, Father, is French kissing a sin?" A few of us less-worldly guys looked at each other, "French-kissing (?)," what the hell is that!? The priest stiffened, squinted squarely at the miscreant who had dared to voice this affront to human decency out loud, and exploded: "French-kissing!?! French-kissing!?! My God, son, why, you might as well stand three feet apart and just spit into each others mouth! Yes, French-kissing is a sin! And it's a filthy practice that will cause disease too. French-kissing!? It's disgusting! Where did you hear about French-kissing?" Now, having put the singled-out sinner on the spot, we all wanted to hear, "Yeah, how did you know about French-kissing?" "Well, Father, I have an older sister in high school, and she was telling me about it…" Not only did that end health education as we knew it, but that poor bastard (and I'm sure his sister too) undoubtedly got an earful from his parents after the parish telegraph lines were burned up throughout the school's administration, and the high school too. One of my very first lessons in "Don't ever volunteer, and never ask questions." The silver lining was that by the end of the day we all knew, boys and girls, what French-kissing entailed. Sounded yucky. Why would you stick your tongue in somebody else's mouth?

Serving Mass

These began the golden days of serving Mass at St. James. At the time, the church was not yet the Cathedral, and the bishopric of the diocese was then St. Augustine; the bishop was Joseph Hurley, a wizened old man who looked the very part of a bishop, with his bright red cummerbund and sash against his black cassock, a red skullcap, and that awesome huge ring. We were still doing the Mass in the Latin Vulgate, as this was prior to the modifications of Vatican II having yet been implemented. St. James was a beautiful church back then, with an altar and communion rail made of pink Florentine marble, a huge sanctuary with two adjacent small altars on each side, devoted to St. Joseph and the Virgin Mary, respectively. Even the choir loft at the rear and above the entrance to the church was only entered by going up a mysterious winding stairway. In short, the place was awe-inspiring, as it was meant to be, and to be inside this giant ark on a stormy day, full of people, with a little incense floating around, and being a little woozy from not having eaten breakfast in order not to have "broken your fast" from the night before so that you could partake of communion, all meant that you would be in the perfect state of mind for receiving the sacrament of swallowing a piece of the actual (not figurative, but actually transubstantiated, or "trans-substanced") body of Jesus, the same guy who lived two thousand years previous. And to remind you of the seriousness of the situation, the church had one of the most realistic, life-size, tortured, bleeding, and agonizingly twisted crucifixion statues ever produced hanging right over the altar (which was up against the back wall, with the priest having his back to the congregation then). *Passion of the Christ* be damned, Mel Gibson had nothing on this one.

Besides the 7 and 8 a.m. weekday low masses, Monday through Saturday, there were the full-count Sunday masses from 6 a.m. through noon, with the weekly High Mass at 10. Often, no altar boy would volunteer for the 6 a.m. mass and the priest would handle it alone, or sometimes some old man (since it seems that early morning mass was only attended by old, old people) would volunteer to assist. Once an altar boy, always an altar boy. And then the later-in-the-morning Sunday Masses were always interesting, not only because there was always somebody you knew in the congregation—usually some wise guy who tried to make you laugh by making faces, or a pretty girl blinking her eyes at you, or maybe your current nun/teacher for that school year staring you down straight-faced—but because you got to see all the priests of the parish interacting all at one time, which never happened during the week. They would schedule themselves, some liked early masses, others wanted later masses, and the Monsignor, Father Farrelly, usually had to do the high mass himself, with at least one other priest, sometimes two. As an altar boy, you had to get everything ready, candles, bells, water and wine, hand towels, etc. So when you would go to the adjacent rectory, where all the priests lived, you had to fill the cruets, just like your oil and vinegar cruets for your salads, with the water and wine. When you went in, and made your way to the kitchen, you had to pass by the living room door, and as you peeked in you could see the priests sitting around in shorts, T-shirts and wife-beater undershirts, in their easy chairs and sofa, reading the paper, watching television, smoking, sometimes laughing. It was both fascinating and disturbing at the same time to see these guys, some of whom you knew really did not like each other, relaxing and waiting their turn to "go on." Only when the bishop was in town for some high liturgical holiday did everybody stay formal, wearing both coats and collars at all times. These liturgical holidays reached their peak during Holy Week, from Palm Sunday through Easter Sunday. Every single day was devoted to some obscure neo-pagan Christianized ritual: dousing candles, pouring oil into a tub of water, covering over the crucifixion statue with a purple shroud. Good Friday was somber and black and culminated in the heart-rendering and gory retelling of the trial and crucifixion of Christ through the Stations of the Cross, which generally and coincidentally ended with an afternoon thunderstorm, often at or around 3 o'clock, the hour that Jesus historically ceased to suspire. Otherwise, the Easter Season was a joyous springtime celebration, ending with all the ladies and girls dolled out to the tees on Easter Sunday, everybody gorged on chocolate bunny ears, at the culmination of Lent.

Litany of the Saints

The reason I brought up Advent and Lent was actually to address the awful devotion known as "Forty Hours." Now the Forty Hours devotion has dubious origins, but the gist of it was that, in times of peril, or at the beginning of liturgical seasons such as Lent or Advent, it was a good idea for a priest, or preferably a bishop, to bless a large wafer, or host, thus transubstantiating it into the physical aspect of Jesus Christ, and then to put it on display, in a large and beautiful device called a "monstrance," which is a gold or silver container with a round glass center wherein the large host can be seen. Surrounding the host the monstrance has radiating peripheral fingers, like the rays of the sun, and the whole thing rests on a large cup-like base. Then, for forty hours, the congregation can view the host on the altar and 'commune' with Christ directly, either praying for the peril to pass, or to prepare for the liturgical season at hand. The "40" of the forty hours comes from the sacred Jewish forty of forty days of rain for Noah, forty years in the desert for Moses, forty days in the desert for Jesus, and finally, and conclusively, the forty hours that Jesus lay in the tomb from the time of the crucifixion until the resurrection. (Let's see, that would mean that if he died at roughly three o'clock on Good Friday, he was in the tomb by six o'clock [or before sundown], so twenty-four hours would have been six o'clock on Saturday, and another sixteen hours would have been 10 o'clock a.m. Sunday, the day after the Sabbath, when the girls show up to apply the burial oils and unguents and find him missing—that's your forty hours. I still don't know how you get "three days in the tomb" out of that.) Nonetheless... the forty hours devotion is generally an opportunity for members of the congregation to come in and talk to Jesus one-on-one, but unfortunately, what with the bringing out of the monstrance, and the putting it back, and just to kill a good chunk of time, there is a lot of what we might call, pageantry. This involves several processions, singing of hymns in Latin by the choir, homilies, and sermons, all carried out with lots of sprinkling of holy water, burning of incense, and chanting. This last one, the chanting, is the worst. Why? It involves the Litany of the Saints. A litany, by definition, is a long repetitive list. In this instance, it is the reading of the entire list of known and reputed saints, and it's made even more unbearable in the fact that for each invocation that is made a response is required. And finally, the torture is complete by having to do this on your knees, wearing a heavy (and hot) cassock and surplice on top of your clothes, while you inhale voluminous wafting clouds of frankincense. Oh, and you're holding a six foot staff atop which is a large candle in a red glass with a swinging gimbaled candleholder. I remember going through at least two of these so-called "devotions," both of which ended badly.

In the first, I was a fresh altar boy in the fifth grade. Everything went well, and the devotion went rather smoothly, if overly long. The reading of the Litany of the Saints takes about two hours, what with the responses and singing, etc. For the procession, they needed all the altar boys, from the smallest to the oldest, for a well-formed processional line-up. Being one of the smallest, I was near the front. It had never been my habit to eat breakfast anyway, and you couldn't if you were going to have Communion, so I was used to that, although it probably didn't help. When the Litany was over, it was time to get up, turn around and file out of the church, down the main aisle. If you've ever been on your knees for two hours, not having eaten, and then stood up, you might know what happened. Well, I got up, turned around, and made it down the altar stairs. Somewhere down the middle of the main aisle though, I apparently started to waver, not staying exactly in line. I heard a few whispers from my buddy, Dennis, "psst, David, get back in line," but tried to "stay the course." The next I knew, a black tunnel closed in around me, and apparently some gentleman in the congregation stood up and caught me, and handed my candleholder staff to Dennis, who was right next to me. I went down for the count. When I

29

awoke, I was outside, lying on one of the concrete benches outside the church, they had taken my surplice and cassock off, and I guess I had pissed myself. To this day I remember the pants I was wearing, light green corduroys that luckily didn't show the wetness. But I knew it. And the teachers hovering over me knew it too. I was sure this was it, and that I was ashamedly an altar boy washout. They had me lie there for a little while, and someone offered to drive me back to school, so I wouldn't have to walk the four or five blocks with the rest of the class. While I was waiting, Father Farrelly, the tall broad-shouldered and red-headed Irish pastor (and not yet Monsignor), came out to see me, kind of laughed, and said "Ah, so you took one for the Lord, eh, Brewer?" and his reassuring smile meant everything was alright. I'm sure he'd seen it before. They got me back to school, and I sat in the cafeteria storage room in my underwear while someone washed, dried, and even ironed my pants, and I went back to class none the worse for wear, except I had to describe to everyone what it felt like to pass out. At the time, being young and feeling immortal, it felt pretty cool. Later experiences in life have taught me, however, that it's more akin to a taunting whisper from the Angel of Death.

The next instance was perhaps a year or so later. Again, I didn't know what the initiating rationale for the Forty Hours devotion was, but I think it may have been around the time of Kennedy's assassination. This time it was evening, and we'd already finished the goddamn two-hour Litany of the Saints, so now it was time for a visiting priest to deliver a homily, or sermon, on the perils facing the nation, how we were going to endure, etc. Dennis and I were elected to stand at the foot of the pulpit with our swinging candleholder staffs, facing the congregation (like I said, pageantry). We stood there for perhaps fifteen minutes when I noticed that among the crop of nuns sitting in the two front rows facing the pulpit, one of the younger ones was making goo-goo eyes at me (?!). What the heck? She was obviously trying to get my attention, and once she had it, she started doing one of those ever so subtle head-jerking-to-the-side maneuvers. Oh, Jesus! I then noticed that Dennis had started wavering, and obviously she had seen this coming. I reached around behind him, where no one could see, and tried to steady him, but looking over at him, his face was pale and I knew it was just a matter of time. I looked at the nun pleadingly "What can I do?" She started whispering to the nun next to her, and the whispers started going down the line of nuns toward the Mother Superior at the end. Now all the nuns were staring at me and Dennis. With my free hand behind Dennis, when I wasn't holding him steady, I started waving at the other priests, who were sitting quietly, listening to the sermon, but actually not paying much attention at all. Finally, one of the younger priests noticed my frantic waving and got up and came over. He caught Dennis just as he was going over, and I grabbed the swinging candleholder staff. The young priest lifted Dennis up and helped him off the altar behind the pulpit and into the nearby priest's sacristy, the room where they get ready for mass. The nuns all breathed a sigh of relief, almost in unison, smiling at the outcome. As far as the congregation, unless someone was really paying attention, which I don't believe was the case after the droning litany and the dry sermon, anyone looking up would have just seen where once there were two altar boys standing next to the pulpit, each holding the red candle-staff, now there was only one, holding two staffs. I don't think the priest delivering the sermon not ten feet away ever even noticed.

The Funeral

Not only for the participants, mourners and celebrants alike (depending on their viewpoint), weddings and funerals were always special events for an altar boy. Weddings were invariably on Saturdays, but to make up for a weekend morning lost, you almost always made some money. They were joyous and happy occasions with everybody smiling, cracking jokes, shaking hands, and at the end, you were handed an envelope with cash, anywhere from $5 to $20, which for a kid of 12 or 13 was the equivalent of a birthday bonus. Funerals were a different matter. They were generally held during the week, but it could be a Wednesday, or more often, Friday, and they might be at 9, or 10 a.m., sometimes even 11 or 12 if the deceased was a local bigshot and "arrangements" had to be made. Now this was good for the altar boys because we were allowed to cut school for the service, and the school really never knew when you might be getting back (although we usually tried to make it back for lunch). Unlike the modern style of memorials, which are generally more celebratory of someone's life, back in the 60s these were somber, dismal affairs, with lots of black suits and dresses, veils, purple crepe, tall candles on black stands surrounding the coffin, and of course, clouds of incense—which is why it took three altar boys for a funeral, as opposed to the usual two. The Mass would begin, everybody would settle down, we'd get the main drama done through Act One, generally past the blessing (and breaking) of the host, and then the priest would go up to the pulpit and extol the virtues of the deceased and the benefits of the life hereafter for so gracious and giving a person as so-and-so, who could now cast aside this empty husk and enjoy the company of the glorious saints etc., etc. When the priest went to the pulpit, that was the signal for one of the altar boys to duck into the passageway that led behind the altar, go to the priest's sacristy (his get-ready room), and start preparing the coals that you needed to cook up the incense for the finale. While this particular server went back to fire up a small self-igniting coal and fill another small bowl ("the boat") with incense (and I mean the heavy Graeco-Latin blue/grey hang-in-the-air stuff, too, not the modern-day get-a-whiff crap), the other two were condemned to sit stone-faced in a set of stiff-backed throne-like chairs, facing both the pulpit, and the open door to the priest's sacristy. (Mind you, these are at a right angle, or perpendicular, to the view from the church pews themselves. That is, from their perspective, the congregation, so to speak, only observed our stoic altar boy visages on the right side of the altar in profile, if somewhat saddened by the gravity of the proceedings.) The third altar boy, and a year superior to us by age and grade, was one Joe Bivens. Dennis LeFils and I were the other two. It's only recently that I realized, or rather, remembered, that it was Father Linane who was the actual Master of Ceremonies that day. It just came to me later, by the effort of memory and the shock of his demeanor at the time, when I was jarred into his identity coming back to me.

Father Linane was another Irish missionary priest, I'd say approaching his forties, black-haired but thinning rapidly, and always appearing to have somewhat questioned his vocation, nonetheless plodding on undaunted, like those doughboys you see in black-and-white World War I movies. And short, maybe five-foot four at best, but stocky, like rugby vs. soccer. One of the kindest men you could ever know, though. He had the Christian aspect down pat, he was going to be as good as he could be; for instance, volunteering to deliver communion to the home-bound old and sick, not to mention listening to their (boring and self-indulgent) confessions. So, in retrospect, I suppose he was a short, middle-aged, somewhat repressed balding parish priest in a strange land, far from the green moors of Erin, who carried on the tenets of New Testament Jesus as best he could, considering the circumstances. He was probably one of those elder-son sacrifices to the Mother Church that the (olden) Irish were always so fond of—son-to-seminary equals "I get a Golden Ticket" for Ma and Da.

Anyway, so Dennis and I are sitting there stone-faced and bored when Father Linane goes to the pulpit to administer the elegies. Bivens ducks out and crosses over to the priest's sacristy, where we can see him getting the censer out, finding the self-igniting coal, lighting it, and, after closing the top, give it a few swings around to get the air flowing over it and fire up the coal. Then he goes out of sight and we know that he's filling the "boat," the small brass container for the dry incense that the priest will spoon over the hot coal when he's ready to walk around the casket, sprinkling holy water and shaking the censer. We wait. And we wait. Bivens knows

FatherLinane has only gotten started, and he's got a full five minutes to fuck off before "Requiem in Aeternum" signals the final proceedings and we need to spring back into action.

So he tries to make us laugh. We can see him, but no one else can. And this is standard operating procedure for the coal-lighter: making faces, sticking his tongue out, the usual gambits. But Dennis and I were veterans, so we could sit and wait him out, stone-faced. But then Bivens disappears. He's in the sacristy somewhere, goofing off. We know that. We wait. Father Linane is going on about why death is really just a passage to a better existence… Then Bivens comes into view, walking sideways, with his back to us(?). What the hell? Slowly he turns to face us, and there's something sticking out of his black cassock, just below the waist of his white surplice (?!). A fleshy protuberance, wiggling around, as he danced a little jig! Thank God, it was his finger! Nonetheless, he had taken us by surprise, and pulled off the famous mirage trick-of-the-eye, making you think you saw something that turned out to be something else. We couldn't contain ourselves, and we began to snort and snarf and wheeze with suppressed laugh-pressure. All the while, Bivens is dancing around just beyond the doorway with his finger sticking out at crotch level.

Father Linane stopped talking. The people in the congregation, some half-hidden behind the purple-draped casket on its wheeled funeral home bier, were all staring at us. Father Linane slowly turned to look at us, with a stare that spoke louder than words, "Are you boys out of your minds?" When Bivens saw us glance over at Father Linane, and our smirking smiles turn to flushing red-faced shame, and our eyes dropping to stare into our laps, he knew we were in trouble. He ran back into the sacristy, and got the censer and incense ready for the final blessing. Father Linane, who had lost his train of thought, finished up nicely with his "Requiem in Aeternam" and came down from the pulpit. Out came Bivens with the censer and Dennis and I handed the priest the holy-water sprinkler (the official name of which eludes me right now). We followed Father Linane down to the center aisle of the church, and as we circled the casket twice, he splashed the holy water on it the first round, then we switched over, and he shook the censer as we rounded it the second time, making sure to lightly clang it against the loose chains by which he held it up. I tried not to look at any of the family or other mourners, because I could feel their squinty steely eyes boring into our respective necks. We went back up the steps to the altar, and finished the service. Once it's over, it's over. We walk off the altar and the funeral home guys, acting as ushers, take over, walking everybody out, folding the flag if there is one or the black or purple pall if there isn't, wheeling out the casket, gathering up the flowers, etc. It's a long-standing custom that when we get back into the sacristy, the altar boys kneel down and get the priest's blessing, and from our perspective that's what really signals the end of the business for the day. And that's what we did: we followed Father Linane into the priest's sacristy, and knelt down. And he gave us the blessing, making the sign of the cross over our heads. Then, without a word, he cuffed us hard enough that we did one of those Three Stooges bonk-bonk-bonk as our heads collided in turn one with the other. To add insult to injury, he then lit into us about how unprofessional we had been, and how ashamed he was of us, and how he didn't want to see us again anytime soon, and on and on. We got up and scurried out of there as fast as we could, since it looked like he might give us another clout if we didn't. He was a good priest, and really a kind man, but it took months before he really forgave us and things went back to normal. That damn Joe Bivens!

Sanlando Springs and First Kiss

At the end of the school year, just before they let us out for summer, there was the Choir and Altar Boys Picnic at Sanlando Springs. This was just too much fun. Sanlando was not only clear, beautiful, and cold, it had a huge slide that must have reached at least thirty feet or more off the ground, and lots of walking paths along the spring run. Probably the most fun of all was that in the bathhouse and refreshment stand there were maybe five or six pinball machines. Anywhere else in Orlando, kids were not allowed to play the pinball machines and there were always signs that said "No one under 17 is allowed to play this machine, under penalty of law," but here at Sanlando Springs they were happy to make change all day long for us as we filled those machines with nickels, dimes, and quarters. Once the slide had lost its thrill after climbing those thirty-some steps at least thirty-some times, and the money for the pinball machines ran low, and the clock said we only had a couple of more hours to go, this was my chance to try to get a kiss from J.J. Now J.J. was a petite dark-haired fireball at school. Unlike most of the other girls, she was brash, playful, and just the least bit mischievous. I believe she was the only girl I ever saw who was ever singled out to sit in solitary, and even that was a rarity because, unlike us rowdy boys, and whereas the other girls were too shy and self-effacing to even attempt frivolity, she was usually too smart to get caught acting up. We were all crazy about her, even to the point where Dennis and I decided one day to both take her to the movies, and then spent the entire movie with either his arm or mine over her respective shoulder whenever the other's would fall asleep and he had to move it. Nonetheless, she was just a lot of fun to be around. So I decided, this was my chance to cut her out from the crowd, and I asked her if she wanted to go for a walk, which she demurely accepted. Although I thought I'd been pretty sly, apparently our disappearance did not go unnoticed, as I found out later. We walked along the paths that lined the spring run, and I mumbled on about how I liked her (no response), and finally I got her to sit down on one of the little wooden bridges that spanned the run. After a horrible ten minutes of silence and mounting despair on my part, I just asked her if I could kiss her, and she said okay. So I did. Nothing grand, no, no french-kissing, nothing except a little lip contact for all of two seconds, but I have to admit, my heart did leap, just like all those gazelles that a young boy's heart is inevitably compared to. But then… a loud hurrah, and clapping from out of the bushes, maybe fifty feet away! Oh Lord! We'd been followed and spied upon by a group of altar boys and choir girls led by one of the young coaches from St. James. J.J. jumped up and ran away, gone in an instant, while they crept forth out of the bushes, laughing and pointing at me. Apparently there had been some friendly wagering as to whether or not I was going to triumph in my endeavor. Well I did, but whether or not it was worth the mortification I had to endure, and now poor J.J. went through as well, on the way home, well… hell, yeah, it was worth it! Later, I bought a "friendship ring" and tried to seal the deal, but, again, as smart as she was, she refused to accept it, and I had to go back to Gordon's Jewelers and get my $14.95 back. And even though I had lost the receipt, they gladly gave me my money back anyway. I'd just been in the day before, asked too many questions, and paid for it mostly in change. They'd seen it happen all the time.

Civil Writes

When I was in the eighth grade, nearing the end of the school year, I got caught carrying out some misdemeanor in class and was sentenced to an hour's detention and a five-hundred word essay after school by Sister Mary Lourdes, a long-faced and no-nonsense nun of the Order of St. Joseph; you know, the ones with the long black veil dresses to their toes, capped with that stiff white cardboard forehead piece and then topped off with some more black veils—the standard "penguin suit" made famous by *The Blues Brothers*. [A curious aside: One day back in fifth grade this same nun was walking down the aisles between the school desks, and when she got down our aisle and walked past one of the really notorious troublemakers, John O'Rourke, he stepped on the trailing tip of the headmost veil, and "whoosh!," before you know it, that thing is on the ground and a short-sheared, black-haired Sister Lourdes is scrambling to snatch it up and get it re-attached. I've got to admit, the sight of the Sinead O'Connor nun-pate was one of the most startling things I think I've ever witnessed. Maybe there IS something to that burqua stuff.

Oh yeah, and O'Rourke got off blameless, the dodger; she thought she'd just snagged it on something.] So I've got an hour to kill and a writing assignment for detention—to this day, I can't remember what my infraction was. It must have been a good one, though, to incur that level of punishment, but this WAS near the end of the school year and we all knew we were going to graduate, so we were pushing the envelope. Well, Sister Mary Lourdes tells me I have to write my essay on Civil Rights, always a hot topic for Central Florida Catholics in those days. I thought about it, and just started with a vision of a slave ship, went on to plantations, the Civil War, Reconstruction, etc. and finished up with Martin Luther King, Jr. and the whole Christian perspective of the inequity of segregation and Jesus' admonition about "caring for one's brother, and loving thy neighbor." I'd totally lost track of time… everyone else was gone. Shit! There must be eight pages here! That's way over 500 words! "I gotta go, Sister," and I handed her the assignment and got out of there. I come back to school Monday and she wants to talk to me (this can't be good). But she tells me that she was really impressed with what I had written, and that I should enter it into the school's creative writing competition. Well, that's all well and good I told her, and thanks for the consideration, but in fact, I had written the report as a punishment, and it didn't seem right that I should enter it as something I really wanted to do. She said that she had already talked it over with the committee (whoever the hell they were), and they had agreed that it would be acceptable. So I said sure, okay. It had to be pared down to five minutes reading time, so there's was quite a bit of editing to do. She gave me the paper and I took it home. Since the competition wasn't for another month, no worries. Being a preoccupied pubescent pre-teen, I quickly lost it.

When the competition became imminent, I had to face it, I was going to have to write it all over again from memory. Well, that wasn't going to happen. But I was still going to have to rewrite it. And this time, I only had to write five minutes worth! I sat down and pieced together what I could, trying to tie it together nicely, and finishing on the righteous indignation of "Onward, Christian Soldiers!" Surprisingly, on the day of the competition, held in the chorus room at St. James School, there were more than a few black people in attendance. This was especially evident at what was then an all-white school, and where even in church on Sundays, blacks still sat in the back. Someone (Sister Mary Lourdes?) must have notified the troops, so I suppose I had the deck stacked because everybody loved it. The applause were particularly sweet because on the second rewrite I hadn't really been as swept away in one of those fugues that those young French nuns were always falling into, unlike when I had written the first. This time I was more methodical, and technically more succinct. I still have a nice picture of now-Monsignor Farrelly shaking my hand as he handed me the Creative Writing award. And my good friend and neighborhood public-school buddy Dan Anderson was kind enough to lend me the nice summer seersucker jacket of his that I'm wearing in the photo. You can't go wrong with a good seersucker.

The Spelling Bee

That same year, and right around the same time, the National Spelling Bee was going to take place. Now I'm a good speller, and always have been. Hell, I used to read the dictionary for amusement (besides looking for dirty words). Throughout grade school I could always count on Spelling for an easy "A." At this point in time, however, finishing up eighth grade, and getting ready to graduate to high school, I was failing Spelling. Why? Because I had given up. I refused to do my homework. It had always seemed silly, and now, it was just an insult, so I quit doing my homework. And here's why. The Spelling class workbook, in which one was to do his homework, was simply a daily list of words, and then you were expected to COPY those words five times, and then there might be ten sentences with blanks wherein you were to place the appropriate words. Well, this just burned me up. It was tantamount to simple enforced labor without rhyme or reason. There were no "problems" to work out; there was no question to be answered. It was simply rote reproduction. So I just quit doing it. At the time we had Mrs. Roberts teaching Spelling. Mrs. Roberts was a WWII German war bride, blonde, strict, and vivacious, as long as you stayed on her good side. And she was generally very tolerant, so it took a lot to have her go off her nut. As for the spelling homework, I explained that I didn't do it because I felt it was a waste of my time. Although she was disappointed, and explained to me that for every homework assignment I missed there was a red mark in the book and I would likely fail Spelling as a result, she didn't press it further (and deep down I really think she secretly agreed with me). I didn't care—we'd all been informed of who was going to graduate, no matter what. But the Spelling Bee was coming!

Apparently every school at the time had to participate in the National Spelling Bee, even if it only meant that they had their own in-house competition. Sending someone on to the finals in Washington is always at the cost of the participants, not to mention sending alternates, chaperones, etc. So no one from St. James was going to Washington D.C. anyway, that was for sure. But we WERE still going to have a spelling bee. So they handed out copies of that godawful National Spelling Bee word list with all the Jeopardy-words that describe different kinds of dinosaurs, flower species, or arcane mechanical devices and medical anomalies. They lined up the combined eighth grade classes along the three walls of a classroom, and with three teachers at the front, they started lobbing in from their loaded lexicon. A student could repeat the word, but this was before that time when you could ask one of the teachers to "please use it in a sentence." Hell, even they didn't know what half the words meant, nor did we… it was only enough to spell it correctly. And if you didn't, well, you sat down at your desk. Now as anyone knows, the biggest part of this whole process is luck, whether or not you get an easy word, or for instance, already understood the defining term for say, speaking in tongues ("glossolalia" Today, they would say, "Could you use this in a sentence, please?" "I think I'm coming down with a fit of glossolalia." "Glossolalia, g-l-o-s-s-o-l-a-l-i-a, glossolalia."). Well, at the end of two hours, there's just me and Barbara Bonfield, and damn, she's smart. We went back and forth for a few words before the teachers were looking at each other, and the clock, and the rest of the kids who were now seated, started getting fidgety. They decided to call it. What the hell? We'd gone through this whole gut-wrenching torture session to have it end in a draw? They'd get back with us. Well, after the class let out, Barbara and I broke away from our respective fandoms, girls on her side, and boys on mine, and mutually decided we wanted to finish it. So the next day we presented our case to Mrs. Roberts, who seemed rather nervous about the whole business, and said she'd take our request to the Principal, who I think at the time was Sister Moira, a sour middle-aged short and dumpy grouch of a penguin. Several days later Barbara and I were called to the Principal's Office, where they sat us down and between Mrs. Roberts and Sister Moira, they pummeled us with obscure parts of speech, those arcane medical terms, and rare animal sub-species until all of a sudden, they stopped, Moira looking over her glasses at Roberts, and said that Barbara had misspelled her word, whatever the hell it was. I had to spell mine correctly to finish the business, and again, I couldn't tell you what it was, but I spelled it right. Barbara cried a little, but not too much, it was such a relief to have it over. As they glanced back and forth to each other, tight-lipped, I realized what the problem was. They were going to have to give the Spelling Bee Award for the school to a problematic scofflaw who refused to do his homework, and who was failing Spelling! But there was nothing to be done about it. Once we got back to class and everyone saw Barbara's red eyes, they all knew; but to be honest, I wasn't the least bit big-headed about it, because I knew it could have gone either way, and I told Barbara so. In point of fact, she was much smarter than me and should have won. To put the final nail in the Spelling Bee story, when Monsignor Farrelly handed out the Spelling Award at church (in front of our parents and everybody, along with everybody else's commendations and awards for the school year), he made a special point of mentioning from the pulpit that I had failed Spelling that same six weeks wherein I'd earned the award. He said he thought it was rather curious (Aargh! the shame! At least he didn't invoke the biblical, "Pride goeth before a fall."). Serves me right, though. I think I'll go and have a fit of glossolalia now.

3. Central Florida Catalina Summers (1962 -1968)

Dad had bought a boat the summer of '62, a big behemoth of a heavy fiberglass hulk, only eighteen feet long, but very heavy, with a 75 horse Evinrude. I can still smell the seats, which folded down flat, and the slight whiff of fiberglass and gasoline from inside the hull. It also had a bimini top that came in handy when those Florida summer rainstorms would show up unexpectedly. We took "the boat" out regularly that summer, and eventually named it the *Flora-Su*, after Mom and the dog, Su-Su, a registered Pekingese we had brought down from Detroit. Clear Lake was just beautiful back then, actually clear enough that you could see the bottom in most places, even to the point where you could pick which fish you wanted to hook: "No, not that one!... yeah, that one." The lake was spring-fed (and I imagine it still is, but not noticeably any more) and where the springs came out, the lake had a nice sandy bottom, about 15-20 feet deep, and it always reminded us of ginger ale (Vernor's, Detroit's best). Paul and I were already swimming like fish, completely fearless, and could hold our breath underwater for minutes at a time. We began experimenting with water skiing and had a pair of big red flat double skis to get started with, one of which had an extra boot so you could drop the other one and take a shot at slaloming with just one ski. By the end of the summer we were skiing regularly, jumping waves and cutting back and forth. Mom had tried swimming, and took a lesson or two, but never felt comfortable with her face in the water, so, although she didn't swim well, if she had a life preserver on we weren't worried about her drowning. This was not the case with Dad who, even though he wasn't afraid of the water per se, and would jump in anytime as long as he had his old black truck tire inner tube around him, he had an unabiding fear of death by drowning his entire life. He never tried to learn to swim, not once, while at the same time, as long as he was in shallow water, or holding on to the edge of the pool, he would submerge his head and sit underwater. But free-style swimming? Without the inner tube? Never. Apparently this was the result of his father's idea of early 1920s swimming lessons. Now remember, this was my grandfather who, as a younger man, had swam with Johnny Weismuller at the YMCA in Chicago. When it came time to teach his own sons how to swim, he followed the age-old and insane system of hoisting them up, tossing them in, and letting them make their way to the edge, again and again until they were confident enough to jump in on their own. Well, although Dad was the oldest of the three sons, unlike his brothers, who really did become very proficient swimmers, he sank to the bottom, had to be retrieved, and once the water was rolled out of him, and he came to, decided then and there that as a city boy he'd never need to learn to swim anyway, so the hell with it.

Fear of Drowning

This had a couple of repercussions later on. When he joined the Army in World War II, part of basic training involved jumping into a pool and making your way to the edge. This was easy enough to circumvent: he just got his hair wet and traded places with some guy who had already completed the training, and went on to the next exercise. But later on it got serious when, on the troop ship crossing the Pacific, he was extremely anxious about the possibility of torpedoes, and then, the worst possible scenario played out. It was April 1st, 1945, and they were getting ready to storm the shore at Okinawa. They had already climbed down the cargo net and were in the landing craft when they heard the stories from returning craft where, on hitting the beach, the craft, loaded with men, would hit a sand bar, and couldn't get over. Stuck, they just dropped down the forward ramp and let the soldiers run out. Unfortunately, between these sand bars the water again dropped to 8 or 10 feet before coming up to the next one. Since these guys were carrying 80-pound packs, wearing boots, and carrying guns, grenades, and extra ammo, a lot of them would step off into the deep shoal water and just drown. So everyone was told to check his Mae West, the yellow life preserver named after the old Hollywood legend whom you would all come to resemble when you inflated it fully. Heading into the beach Dad was horrified to find that his, not unlike a few others, had a small tear in it and wouldn't hold air. He started to freak out, knowing this was a death sentence for him for sure. Well, one of the guys next to him traded vests with him, assuring him that he was an excellent swimmer and not to worry, the bullets would probably kill them both anyway. (Apparently though, they received very little resistance on those initial landings; the Japanese had dug in and let the Marines and Army walk right over them, only to jump up and attack from behind later—or so the story goes.) In an odd quirk of fate, Dad accidently met this same fellow some twenty years later in Florida at a VFW gathering, and they stayed in touch thereafter.

One other time, the whole family was out water skiing, and even Mom got up on her orange "ironing board," a skiing device for amateurs that really did look like an upside-down ironing board that had a release-hook on the front of the handle that would throw the line off if you fell. Well, we all decided to take a break, stop at the springs on the lake, have a picnic lunch, and just swim around in the cool bubbling water. Paul and I were already over the side, swimming some distance away, while Mom stayed in the boat and Dad got inside his inner tube. Suddenly we heard Mom yelling for us, "Hurry, hurry!" As Dad had jumped into the water, the inner tube got caught on a cleat, and when he went over the side, it just ripped the inner tube wide open, and Dad began flailing, calling Mom, panicking. Paul and I got right over there and swam up under Dad just as he was going under and lifted him to the surface, holding him there, until he got a grip on the transom and was able to pull himself aboard. We were all quite shaken, imagining what might have happened. But Dad was seriously scared, having seen his life flash before his eyes, and he was especially grateful that we had learned to swim so well, and that, as a result, a tragedy (his) was so quickly and easily averted. We got him another truck tire inner tube right away, but we kept that torn one in the garage for several years afterwards, before it was finally cut up when Dad got nostalgic one day and built my brother and I a set of "rubber guns," which apparently were quite the entertainment for young boys back in the 1930s: the "laser tag" of the Depression.

Skirting Perdition

We still had to serve Mass a few weeks during the summer. At least someone had to. So, every so often we'd get a call from the rectory, and no matter how you wriggled or moaned, or made excuses, it was sometimes just impossible to say no to a priest. He could even shame Mom (but not Dad) into it, if by chance I wasn't home and she happened to answer the phone. It was bad enough to have to get up in the school year, before dawn, and watch poor Mom ironing our cassock and surplices while we'd choke down our breakfast, clean up, and head out, but at least then you knew you were getting up eventually anyway to go to school. But to have to do it in the summer was extra burdensome. It meant a double two way trip for Mom to drive us in and back. And it was always a week-long commitment, Monday through Saturday. Which meant there was no way in hell we were going to church on Sunday. And this led to a bit of an ethical dilemma. You see, the total effects of Vatican II still hadn't kicked in, so for the most part, we were still operating under the old strict Latin system that had been maintained for over a thousand years. And this system, dogmatically codified in the Baltimore Catechism since the mid-1800s, specifically stated that to avoid going to Mass on Sunday, if one were physically able, was, yes, a mortal sin. And what, might you ask, is a mortal sin?

From the Baltimore Catechism:

Besides depriving the sinner of sanctifying grace, mortal sin makes the soul an enemy of God, takes away the merit of all its good actions, deprives it of the right to everlasting happiness in heaven, and makes it deserving of everlasting punishment in hell.

I think it's a bitch that it "takes away the merit of all its good actions." That seems a bit much; you can work your whole life doing nothing but good deeds, then one slip-up and? I digress…, so …"What three things are necessary to make a sin mortal?" To make a sin mortal these three things are needed: 1) the thought, desire, word, action, or omission must be seriously wrong or considered seriously wrong; 2) the sinner, must be mindful (or aware) of the seriousness of the wrong; and finally, 3) the sinner must fully consent to it (and not be sorry for it… ever).

Luckily for us, Dad had been taught by the Jesuits at the University of Detroit, and therefore, he carefully explained why we would not have to suffer the pangs of hell for not going to Mass on Sunday. First of all, after having served Mass all week, Monday through Saturday, would missing one more Mass on Sunday be seriously wrong? Well, no. And poor Mom had gotten up every day to iron our vestments, and then driven us in to town, and then came back and picked us up. After all that service to the Church, and therefore Jesus, and therefore, God, would her missing Mass on Sunday be seriously wrong? Well, no. And as for himself, well, he'd been working all week to pay for the car and gas and food so that Mom could take us in, and we could perform this service to God six days out of seven; so, therefore, would missing a seventh day on his part, a day he considered "a day of rest" be considered seriously wrong? Well, no, but… But nothing, he would say, since the final arbiter was himself, and if he did not consider it seriously wrong, well, by God, it wasn't. And since all three items listed above were necessary to commit a true mortal sin, he didn't even have to consider the other two requirements.

Later, Dad would expand on these themes, and I remember one such discussion we had later in life where he explained just how difficult it was to commit "a really good, solid, and unassailable mortal sin." In fact, he said that the Jebbies (as he referred to his Jesuit instructors) considered it beyond the capability of most mere mortals to actually commit a real mortal sin, since most people don't have the stamina or the intellectual ability, or moreover, the will, to either a) *know* that something was a really serious wrongdoing, with wide-ranging consequences, as opposed to simply a momentary (and therefore, unserious) selfish undertaking (and most people only discover the real seriousness of those consequences after-the-fact), b) *plan ahead*, after realizing the seriousness of the act, since some sort of premeditation is absolutely necessary to make it a mortal sin, rather than simply acting upon an instinctive emotional reflex such as self-defense (like in war) and/or finding your wife in bed with the neighbor, and c) then *actually carry out the act*, or fail to carry out a necessary act (i.e., commit an act of omission)—and this is where most people fall down on the job, because they don't have the will, they're just too scared of getting caught, or they get an overwhelming sense of remorse *before* they either commit, or don't commit, the dirty deed and therefore, they chicken out, and finally d) after carrying out the mortal act, *they have to NOT BE SORRY* for the sin… ever. That means right up until the end, a person has to feel no regret, no remorse, no pity for the victim, and no fear of eternal damnation. Even on his deathbed, even unto his last breath, one must be willing to say "I'm glad I did it… and I would do it again." Most people just can't hold up to these standards, and eventually, either in old age, or after periods of reflection and/or changes in temperament, or worse, becoming reformed, they give in and feel sorry for their misdeeds, most of which never made it to mortal sin status in the first place. So, to commit a real, true, grand and sustainable mortal sin is damn near impossible. God, those Jesuits were good. No wonder they were referred to as "Jesus' Storm Troopers."

Speaking of Storm Troopers, and to help drive the lesson above home, have you ever seen Kurt Vonnegut's play *Happy Birthday, Wanda June*? The title character, Wanda June, is a little girl, perfectly innocent, who is unfortunately run over by an ice-cream truck on her tenth birthday (there's Vonnegut's twisted humor for you). So she goes straight to heaven, being a virginal child incapable of having yet sinned. Well, her best friend in heaven, it turns out, is a tall, young Nazi Storm Trooper. Now what, you might ask, is a Nazi Storm Trooper doing in heaven? As things are revealed, he also is a young innocent, based on the fact that, whether by brainwashing or slowness of mind or both, he truly, and heartfully, believed that the actions undertaken by the Third Reich were not just correct, but for the ultimate good of his fellow man. Therefore, since he too died in a state of (Christian-minded) grace, where else could he go, but to heaven, since his motives were pure and without reservation? None of this gives away the plot of the play, which goes on to dramatize their combined efforts to rehabilitate a still-living Hemingway-esque womanizer, drinker, and rabidly heartless big-game hunter so that he might see the light. In any case, I highly recommend seeing the play if ever you get the chance, and I'm constantly surprised at the number of people, even Vonnegut aficionados, who don't know about it or have never seen or read it.

Giant Locusts, Carnivorous Plants, and Snakes

Yeah, exploring around Catalina during the summer was great fun. Besides the lake, the woods were especially attractive, as they were composed of swamps, dirt roads, and sometimes just foot trails through the scrub. Have you ever seen one of those giant, almost prehistoric, grasshoppers, over six inches long, an inch in diameter, brown, yellow, orange, totally unafraid of humans, and fierce-looking? They could jump six feet at a bound, or fly fifty yards, and if they happened to come your way and hit you, their legs, with those hooks on them, would catch in your shirt, and you'd have no choice but to grab them and slowly pry them off of you, one leg at a time. And they would spit on you, too. Remember the old cartoon grasshoppers that were always "chewin' tobacco" and spitting? Well, these Cretaceous monsters we'd come up on haphazardly on the scorching sand trails were always chewing away on something, and damned if they wouldn't spew it on you when they got upset (like when they got hooked onto your shirt and you had to manhandle them off, as mentioned). Frightening. I remember low wet areas where both the trumpet plant (an insect-eater where some hapless bug would crawl down into the trumpet-like hood and the spiked hairs inside flexed and made it a one-way trip down its gullet to the digestive juices in the bottom) and Venus flytraps, always fascinating, grew wild. Of course, we generally had our trusty BB guns handy, and then woe be unto any small creature that came in range, the legitimacy of minor murders offset only by the ability to study the carcasses up close, just like Audubon did. And then there were the snakes.

When we first moved to Florida, some busybody at Martin Marietta had given Dad a pamphlet on snakebites. Besides describing the various poisonous snakes of Florida (which actually did come in pretty handy), it had all these pictures of people who'd been bitten, mostly children, and the ghastly effects of swollen arms, legs, and purple fingers as big as kielbasas, the results of which we were later to discover were mostly the physiological response to the treatment of the day: put a tourniquet on the extremity until you got to the hospital (if you made it). The pamphlet worked; it scared the hell out of us. But eventually, once you had already encountered a snake or two, most of which were non-poisonous, a young boy's quickness and curiosity would always win out. Once however, I had caught a snake that I couldn't identify. It just didn't look like the pictures in any of the books (or pamphlets). I decided to put him in a bottle and just ask our next-door neighbor, Mr. Gaskins, who was an old native Floridian and an orange-grove trail-rider, since he'd know what kind it was for sure. I figured he'd be home in about an hour, and I was putting this snake into a clean milk bottle, tail-first, when, just as I let go of his neck to drop him in, he turned and bit me on the finger. Bit me good… and it was bleeding. Holy Shit! I didn't know what to do. Even though Mom was home, I really didn't want to initiate an emergency ride to the hospital if it wasn't absolutely necessary. I checked my symptoms: my heart beating a mile a minute (because I was scared), and my finger hurt like hell. Could I feel the poison making its way up my arm? How long would I have before it would be too late? Should I put a tourniquet on? What if they couldn't save my arm? It was my right arm! Would I now have to learn how to write with my left hand? Just as I was sure that I could feel the pangs of cold deadly venom crawling up my arm and heading toward my heart, Mr. Gaskins came driving up into his driveway. He wasn't out of his truck before I was standing there with my bottled-up snake, hiding my soon-to-be-purple-sausage-hand behind me. "Mr. Gaskins… could you help me out here? I caught this snake and I don't know what kind it is… uh, is it poisonous?" He looked at it for a second or two, then handed the bottle back. "No, that's a corn snake; some people call the brown ones rat snakes… but watch out, they'll bite ya." "Yeah," I said, pulling out my finger, "he bit me when I was trying to put him in the bottle." He looked at me, laughed, and said "See, I told ya." With that, I left Mr. Gaskins, rode my bike down to the woods, and let that snake go. Now I know what a corn snake looks like.

Another quick snake story… One day my brother Paul and I were out at the dirt mounds, the leftover dirt piles which they had dug out for the last canal in our subdivision. They hadn't yet hauled the dirt away or built any houses out there yet, but some of the old timers would keep their boats tied up there, to go fishing. We were just walking along, when we spotted a snake on the far side of the canal, on the edge of the water and trying to climb up the canal seawall. It was obviously a big water moccasin. We picked up a couple of dirt clods and started throwing them at it. The dirt clods were exploding to the right and to the left on the seawall, and splashing up water. Well, I'll be damned if that snake didn't figure out where those dirt clods were coming from, and turned and started coming across the canal, swimming toward us. Now this was odd, but we still had the sixty feet of water and another seawall between us, so we just kept pitching out dirt balls. Between us and the snake someone had tied up a small aluminum fishing boat, and in no time flat, that snake had crossed the canal and was now behind that boat where we couldn't see him. And now we had to stop because we couldn't very well be throwing dirt clods into some guys boat, when, wouldn't you know it, up over the gunwale of that boat comes this big, black cottonmouth and, not to put human feelings onto a cold-blooded reptile, but he was mad as hell. Boat or no boat, we let fly with a couple more dirt balls, and we hauled ass, got to our bikes and rode out of there, not slowing down. Even a rattlesnake will turn away if he can, and he'll do whatever is necessary to avoid you, but do not ever tell me that water moccasins are not aggressive. Meaner than a rattlesnake, by far. So when I generally refer to someone, usually an old girlfriend, as being "meaner than a snake," it is generally the cottonmouth water moccasin that I am referring to, as the females are notoriously more ill-tempered than the males. I might sometimes leave out the details as to what instigated the mean streak in the first place, whether it was dirt balls being thrown, or whichever of my many other thoughtless actions, the retaliation of which resulted in their being called one as a result.

The Entrepreneurial Spirit

Sometimes we felt we needed to earn some extra money, you know, for comics and maybe a soda or donut. Now Paul and I already had a pretty good gig going where we would cash in empty soft drink bottles for the deposits. Mom and Dad supported this, since they didn't like hauling out the nasty bottles in the car and standing in line just to get a buck or two. But Paul and I spent many a rainy day out in the garage in what we referred to as our "rain factory" and as the water from those afternoon summer downpours rolled off the open garage doors, we would collect the rainwater in all the empties and this fulfilled several functions. First of all, it kept us busy when we couldn't go out and play or explore anyway. Second, it cleaned out the nastiness out of the bottom of all those mostly-empty Coke, RC, Pepsi, and Nehi (both orange and grape) soda bottles that, having been dormant in the garage for weeks would attract the most vile of insects, flies, molds and general wickedness you could think of, not to mention the dreaded palmetto bug. And third, it gave us a fairly reliable inventory of what was available after the rain factory was shut down of how many bottles we could reliably turn into cash. And believe it or not, the going rate even back then in the 60s was a whopping 5 cents a bottle. The only logistical problem was transportation. We developed all kinds of slings and packs and saddlebags and over-the-shoulder holders, but even at our best we were lucky if we could carry six or seven six-packs of empties between us. Well, this meant our maximum take would be about $2.25. That was generally enough though if we didn't have any "incidents" on the way that might cause a breakage—always a risk to the net profit end of the business.

So we'd load up our bikes with what we could carry and ride up the two-mile entrance road to Catalina out onto Michigan and up to Orange Blossom Trail, making our way eventually to Red's Market. Sometimes we could dump them off at the 7-Eleven that was on the way (one of the first in Orlando, and by default, one of the first in Florida? I'm not sure), but they were always problematic. Sometimes they'd take them and sometimes they wouldn't; sometimes they'd only take a certain kind, or only so many. It just wasn't worth it to stop the bikes, get off, find out what the deal was for the day, and get back on. Best just to push on through to Red's, since EVERYBODY, all the white trash rednecks and trailer goobers, bums, hillbillies, cowboys, and even middle-class Moms and Pops, took their empties to Red's. That was because Red's recognized this as a sizable part of their business. If they were going to sell shitloads of soda pop, then by God, they had to pay the deposit when they got the empties back. There would be grocery carts full of bottles in all sorts of conditions, some half-full, some unopened, some chipped, some full of dirt. I don't think anyone else, except us, ever cleaned out their bottles. So this was a cottage industry for the surrounding several miles of the aforementioned clientele. There was only one trick. You had to be sure that the bottles you brought in were of the same brand as those they sold. If they didn't sell Royal Crown, or RC, then they were not going to give you the deposit for RC. Fair enough. I'm pretty sure we learned this the hard way, ending up hauling half our bottles back home on occasion.

Red's Market

There was another problem with Red's… they had the meanest cashiers in town. They didn't take any crap off of anybody, and they dished out plenty on their own, often unprovoked. These were big buxom broken-fingernail bleach-blond bitches, and that was describing them kindly. Being oversized crackers themselves, they didn't like kids (like us), and they didn't like blacks (which they made clear by their attitude), but they would generally only mutter under their breath most of the time, cigarette dangling, since a large part of the fresh-fruit and vegetable open-air market was supported by the poor and old-fashioned southerners who liked their greens right out of the ground and their fruit right off the tree, and if Red's was known for anything, that was the freshness of their produce. So fresh, in fact, that with the large fans blowing, and the soda pop bottles fermenting in the background, and fruit ripening all around you, and the thick perfume and tobacco-smoke of the surly cashiers, it really was a sort of magical atmosphere to walk into as a kid. That is, until she screamed at you, "You damn kids, how many times do I have to tell you, we don't carry Pepsi any more… now get those damn bottles off the checkout line, and get out of here!" To be yelled at and vilified by an adult like that was an unsettling experience for us, although her own kids at home probably wouldn't have thought twice about it. (I was always amazed at how resilient the "native" kids—as I thought of them—were when it came to countering parental tactics. When I heard some lard-ass harpy screech at her kid [or more likely, some of the other local juvenile delinquents], "You better run! If I get my hands on you, I'm gonna skin you alive!" I'd have nightmares of being crucified onto some wooden kitchen floor in her shack and being pared with a potato-peeler, whereas the local kids being addressed would often just turn around, laugh, and spurt out some epithet like, "Shut up, Fat Ass." For some genteel Catholic boy from Michigan, it was an extraordinary sort of exchange to witness.) But once we got home and told her what happened, Mom jumped to the defense, "Get in the car!" She drove straight down there, and much to our embarrassment, but WAY, WAY, worse for the poor cashier, she lit into her like one of those famous Mama Grizzlies (although I always thought of her as more of a Boxing Mama Kangaroo for some reason), "Don't you ever talk to my boys like that! If you EVER talk to them like that again, both my husband and I will be down here and talk to the owner, and you will soon be out of a job. NOW APOLOGIZE!" Which she did. Hell, she could have been Red's wife for all we knew, but she apologized anyway, with everyone else in the store as silently stunned as we were. When we left, I can tell you, both Paul and I were as sorry for that poor woman as anyone could be... which caused a hitch in our bottle-delivery system, since after that, one of us would have to check the store surreptitiously to make sure that THAT particular cashier wasn't working, and if she was, it meant pedaling another mile or two down the road to another store, that might, or might not, take our haul and give us the deposit. Lesson learned: there's always a trade-off.

Strawder's Pharmacy

Once we got our money from the bottles, Paul and I would settle down at Strawder's Drug Store at the corner of OBT and Michigan and check out the comics to see if any new ones had come in. It didn't really matter, because if no new *Superman* or *Batman* or *Jimmy Olsens* were in, we'd settle for a less serious read such as *Lois Lane*, *Flash*, or even *Archie*. But once we got the comics, we could settle down, enjoy the air-conditioning, and sit at a booth by the soda fountain, and maybe have a cherry or vanilla coke and donut with our leftover change while perusing our loot. I remember once, we had finished our donuts (they were two for 15 cents) but still had some coke to go, and we had eight cents left. So I started to negotiate with the waitress behind the counter, "Uh, excuse me, ma'am... we don't have enough money for two more donuts, can we just get one for eight cents?" She put her hand on her hips (totally realizing we weren't even going to leave our last eight cents as a tip for all the time we had gotten cokes, and donuts, and occupied that booth, making a mess for over an hour) and started in on why they were a two-for-fifteen-cents special instead of the usual price of ten cents each. And she was getting a little loud about it. Luckily, our good friend and neighbor, Mr. Gaskins, had come in for a cup of coffee and to read the newspaper. He stepped in and told her to give us two more donuts on his tab. "Why, THANKS, Mr. Gaskins!" (thus fortuitously avoiding another run-in with the local merchandising support staff). Strawder's later was sold and changed its name to Swan's, after the new owners, and then moved across the street. It was just a coincidence that when Strawder's became Swan's the price of comics jumped from 10 cents to 13, and even though it was clearly marked on the comic-book covers, I always secretly though they (the Swans) had something to do with it.

The Corner Cupboard and Rattails

So, we still needed extra money; now more than ever, with the declining supply of bottles (since Mom was on one of her proverbial "diets," so no more ice-cream floats, ergo, fewer Pepsis). My school-buddy Dennis had told me about selling a small local paper called The Corner Cupboard, a bit of a little advertising vehicle and gossip sheet with maybe one editorial that came out twice a week, like Tuesdays and Fridays. He was having pretty good luck with it in his neighborhood, so I decided to give it a shot in mine. Well, the damn thing only sold for 10 cents, of which I got to keep four cents per paper, and you had to go door-to-door, which was part of the deal. The first week or two turned out okay, with me pocketing a couple of bucks and a buck or two in tips, but it sure involved a lot of walking. It didn't make sense to take your bike, get off, and have to walk back and forth to it, so it was easier just to walk across the lawns. But God in Heaven, here it was, summer, and to sell even the fifty papers they would drop off, I had to hit at least two hundred houses. Think of it as Halloween in reverse, where I'm trying to practically give some rag away for a dime house-to-house, and the homeowners would pull tricks like "I'll pay you twice next week," and then not be there that next trip. Or they might say "Just a minute, let me go see if I can find a dime," close the door, and not come back or answer the bell. Or, they might corner you like you were some Jehovah Witness wannabe, bend your ear for 10 minutes, and tell you in detail why the paper was so lousy. In any case, by the third week it was a disaster. I ended up owing the delivery guy for papers I couldn't sell, so I told him to forget it, I wanted out. But Paul and a friend of his had taken another tack to get money. The city was in the throes of some sort of rat attack, and had offered a bounty in the paper of ten cents for every rat tail that was brought in to the police station. Well, this idea was obviously supposed to support rat extermination downtown, around the food businesses, not out in suburbia, where we lived. Nonetheless, my brother Paul and a neighborhood friend, Bubba Jones, knew we had lots of rats out in the nearby woods, so they borrowed the money for a couple of large rat traps, and began setting these things, dabbed with peanut butter, in the surrounding tropical forest. Sure enough, they started catching rats, sometimes having to dispatch the still-living, but wounded and dangerous vermin with the trusty BB gun. Then they would chop off their tails with a hatchet, put them in a jar, and when they had thirty or forty tails, bring them down to the police station. It turned out to be quite profitable, and soon, even more so. One day, they're walking out of the police station counting out their swag and dividing it up, wondering where to spend it, when, out of the back door of the police station comes the officer presently in charge of rat tail rewards, and they watch as he empties the jar of tails into the nearby dumpster, then heads back in. Quickly, one of those cartoon-like light bulbs pops up in the air over their heads, and within minutes they have hoisted themselves over the edge of the container and scooped up several weeks' worth of rat tails brought in from all over the city, many of which had not yet mummified, but had begun the process of reverting back to ripe organics. A couple of empty jars now filled (to the brim?), they brought them back home but found there was no house willing to store them (or god forbid, consider refrigerating them), "no, not even out in the garage!" So they hid their new-found treasure out in the woods, where the tails were allowed to ferment in the sealed jars. Well, they couldn't show up the very next day with all these tails, because the cops would suspect something after they'd just cashed in what they claimed was a week's worth of work. So they had to wait. After another week however, it was obvious that if they didn't cash them in soon, the results of their marinating mayhem may soon be nothing but maggots. So they took them in and sheepishly handed the jars over to the officer in charge. One crack of the jar lid, and he closed it quickly. "How many?" "What!?" "How many tails you got altogether?" he asked. Oh shit! They hadn't bothered to count them. "About eighty?" they figured. "Well, I can't pay for 'about eighty'" he said, "You'll have to give me an exact amount. Go outside and count them, then throw them into the garbage bin out back."

I think the count came out to more like a hundred and forty, and they made a nice little haul of fourteen dollars to split, but this time, once the rodent remains went into the garbage container, they stayed there. Was it a coincidence that the city ended the rat-tail-reward program the very next week? I don't think so.

A Meteoric Mystery

A couple of years later, one other very strange thing happened during the summer, one of the most interesting and perplexing things to ever have occurred in my life, even now unto my sixtieth year. It was a lazy Saturday afternoon, and I was lying on the living room floor, reading in front of the sliding-glass door, which opened out to the pool and patio. Dad was in the bedroom watching television. I don't know where Paul and my Mom were, but they were out, probably shopping. As I said, the sliding-glass door opened to the backyard pool and patio, and yes, the patio screen enclosure at the time did have a few short ligustrum bushes just outside the screen that partially blocked the view. But only twenty feet outside the bushes was the canal, a glassy brown freshwater expanse of sixty feet in width. We happened to have a boat dock, but now we didn't have a boat under it, (Dad had gotten sick of dealing with it, and sold "the big boat," the *Flora-Su*, to a neighbor, at a reduced price, much to Mom's distress), but we did have a small johnboat with an engine (the *Flora-Su II*) that was not parked under the boat dock at the time but along a couple of tires hanging further down the seawall. So this empty boat dock was less than forty feet away from where I was lying on the floor reading. Sure, I was preoccupied reading, as I said, but it was a quiet, still, clear and sunny afternoon, and had any boat come down the canal I would habitually have looked up to see if I knew who it was. All of a sudden, there was a loud "BOOM," like a sonic boom (NOT a gunshot), but close by, and I jumped up to look out at the canal, from where I had heard the report. I could see that the center panel of the roof of the boat dock, some twelve feet in length and over eighty pounds, had been thrown over on its back hinges into the water. No one had come down the canal. I ran into the bedroom and got Dad, who had been watching the loud TV and had heard the boom but thought nothing of it. When I told him about the boat dock, we both ran outside to look. As we stood outside at the canal's edge, looking at the boat dock, with its center panel thrown backwards, and now resting in the water, a few of the neighbors came out as well, all saying "What was that?" We all looked up and around but the sky was clear, not a cloud, or even a contrail. Then I noticed that there was a tiny stream of bubbles leading out from under the boat dock, clear across the canal, at a diagonal across the canal, leading up to and under our neighbor's boat, which had not moved all day.

Now I can think of an explanation for the bubbles. Had a large turtle or other creature been under the boat dock and gotten frightened by the loud (what I can only describe as an) explosion, it would have taken off in a hurry, and scampering across the canal bottom it would have released a little flurry of bubbles, the remnants of which we witnessed. But what was the source of the explosive boom, the power of which flung over the center panel of the boat dock that several men could not equal? I know this to be true, because Dad and I had to get into the johnboat, maneuver it over to the roof panel, and with the help of several neighbors, lift it up, get under it, and ease it back down into place, taking up much of the rest of the afternoon. Yet it had been flung over in less than a second. Dad just shrugged and didn't make much of it, but it has bothered me numerous times over the years, and I've only been able to come up with one rational explanation: I think it was a tiny meteorite, probably no bigger than a BB. It must have come in at a low angle, just over the rooftops of the houses, and hit the water below the boat dock. The impact would have caused a small explosion that would have instantly turned the water into a ball of steam, certainly powerful enough, like a boiler exploding, which would have flung the center part of the boat dock up (the only section which could have moved, since, unlike the rest of it, was hinged to let you lift it up when you got into or out of any boat under it). Being hinged, it didn't fly away, but was just flung over onto its back, into the water. The steam quickly dissipating, there would have been no other remaining physical evidence. And maybe that tiny stream of bubbles was the trail left as the meteorite particle buried itself along the canal bottom. As I said, I've often pondered this one, but I can't come up with a more rational, plausible answer. No, it wasn't a boat racing down the canal that I didn't see, snagging a dangling rope or line, and pulling the roof section over. And I don't believe for a minute that it was some gregarious (and large) gator (the likes of which we've NEVER seen in the canal in over fifty years) that might have been on the seawall under the boat dock and somehow became surprised, swung his great tail up four feet off the ground to smack the boat dock roof, sending it flying, and maybe that's what I heard, and not a sonic boom—then he jumps in and swims across the canal under the neighbor's boat, never to be seen again (?!?). No, I'm sticking with the meteorite for now. If you can come up with a better answer I'd love to hear it. "There are more things in heaven and earth, Horatio…" As it is, it's one of the only real mysteries I've ever come across that I was directly involved with, and never been able to optimally rationalize.

4. Descent into Adolescence (1966 – 1972)

The Boys and the Bees

      You know, when we were kids, there was always a lot of noise. All of us were always calling each other names: Spazz, Dingle-Berry, Queer, Butt-head. There were few rules about it, and usually they were just the first things that rolled off your tongue, without a thought, although you were always trying to one-up the other guy, without slipping into down-and-out swearing. I can't recall any one of our friends veering off the well-trodden path and going for Ass-hole, Faggot, Dumb-ass, etc., and Shit and Fuck were just not used at all, period, ever, …rarely even by adults. My Mom's favorite curse was "Oh, go to hell," which, as mild as it was (the mildest a Detroit upbringing had to offer), was still unsettling when it came from your own Mother (How could she say such a thing!?). Dad however, was a connoisseur of swearing, but he tried to keep it under wraps except for his business cohorts and other worldly man-friends. Now and again though, it would slip out when he was in a fit of high pique, or lesser drink, or both, and I can still remember neighbors of the Baptist persuasion, their faces blanching and going silent when Dad might let some foul utterance get loose like a loud fart. But for us neighborhood kids, "Queer" was a standard epithet, and as far as we knew, it just meant you were a weirdo. Sometimes you might throw down "Queer-bait," but again, we had no idea. And calling someone a Spazz was pretty much the same thing, you were a weirdo, except we knew enough to keep it in check when someone who really was spastic was in the area. Well, apparently at some point the neighborhood parents began to talk, and decided to "nip it in the bud" as Barney Fife would say. So Mom sat my brother and I down one day, and tried to explain how some people (men) were not attracted to women and they might be called "queer" but it wasn't a very nice thing to say, and everybody was different, and we shouldn't judge people just because they were "different." Speaking for myself, and I'm two years older than my brother, I had no real idea of what she was talking about—sure sounded queer, that is, weird, to me. And within weeks, any adult neighbor who heard a kid call another kid almost any name whatsoever, was called inside, scolded, and sent home. Which then sent us to the dictionary. For instance, I had no idea that a dingle berry was a small clinging clot of dung, or my favorite, "a delinquent partial turd." I just thought it sounded funny. Now it made even better sense, and it was really difficult to keep a straight face when your neighborhood friend's Mom, on the verge of tears, would be telling all of you now lined up in her kitchen that it wasn't funny calling each other Dingle-Berry because it was a very, very serious disease, extremely painful, and which for all practical purposes, was incurable. (No doubt confusing it with beriberi, which is in fact, curable.)

I guess it was about this time that Mom decided that Dad should give us "the talk." I might have been twelve, and my brother was ten or so. Dad didn't want to do it. It was like when Mom would tell him he'd have to spank us for some major infraction, usually for having disrespected her in some fashion, and thus, it had to be done. Though this only happened once or twice, he hated it worse than we did. We'd talk about what we did, or said, or more likely what we didn't do, and he'd say "fine, let's get down to it," and wham, it was over. Not like when he was pretend-mad at us. Then, all he had to do was take off his belt, bend it in half, and SNAP! the two halves together. That would send us into paroxysms of feigned fright and screaming, yet the leather was never actually applied. But now he had to face the music. Mom wasn't going to let up until he told us "the facts of life." He was so miserable about it, that we made it easy for him. As soon as it became apparent what the conversation he was trying to start amounted to, we told him we knew all we needed to know. "What about condoms?" he asked. "You mean rubbers?" my brother chimed in. "Prophylactics," I corrected, "yes, we know." The relief was palpable on his face. If we had already gotten past condoms, he was home free. He still had to kill some time in our room, though, to make a convincing argument for Mom's sake, so soon we were talking about school, places on the globe we might like to visit, a friend of his who was going on a safari to Africa, etc. Once enough time had passed to convince Mom that we'd had the serious manly conversation regarding sexual intercourse, he got up to leave. But before he left the room, with his hand on the doorknob, he turned and said, "About what we were talking about before… just keep it in your pants, okay, you won't have any trouble." Words of wisdom.

Another summer, after sixth grade, while carrying out various explorations, I found a torn-apart pornographic paperback out in the woods. It took me days to organize the pages back into their proper sequence, and then painstakingly wire the pages back into something resembling a book. That piece of fantasy however, kept me occupied most of those warm summer evenings, as I learned what adventures were entailed in climbing the "mounds of Venus" and other detailed intricacies of which that particularly cunning linguist so vividly described. By the time I got back to school in the seventh grade that September, I was well versed in what was ultimately involved when she loves you, yeah, yeah, yeah, and after I wanted to hold her hand.

Pat

As summer drew to a close, on one of my last outings to the lake, I watched the "public school" kids playing around on the dock, splashing around and generally having a good time. They usually gave me and my brother a wide berth, and except for a few really good friends in the neighborhood like Tim and Dan Anderson, we didn't generally socialize with these rowdy redneck kids. That particular day one of the slim bikini-clad girls got up on top of the ladder, standing on top of the wooden uprights to jump off, showing how she could keep up with the boys, but it was wet with green algae and she slipped, the two-by-six beam-end mashing into her right tit, before she dropped sideways, screaming into the water. She cried out, coughed and moaned, and then went limp, and a couple of the guys carried her out of the water, got her in a car and carted her off to the hospital. It was pretty exciting while it played out, but later we found out it was just a couple of broken ribs, and of course, a now-swollen black-and-blue mammary. Sitting around discussing these events in the shade of the old cypress trees, I struck up a sideways conversation with a well-built olive-skinned girl in a small red bikini with short boyish brown hair and a little overbite. She had asked where I went to school, and I told her I was starting into Bishop Moore in September. "Oh, Catholic, huh? Well, I'm a Catholic too." She was going into her last year at Memorial, the neighborhood Junior High School, which made her 13 years to my 14. When she told me where she lived, I knew it was just down the street from us, so I asked her if I could give her a ride home on my bike. She said yeah and sat on the crossbar in front of me while I whimsically (and slowly) made our way down the road. We soon became friendly, and would walk our respective family dogs together in the evening. Sometimes her family would have me over for dinner, and afterwards we'd go sit out back by the canal and make out. This is where I found out why French kissing was so cool. There was a slight drawback however. We both had been fitted for braces that summer, so we had to be more than a little careful of getting into any embarrassing entanglements. Nonetheless…

She and her older brother, Paul Jr., had been adopted when she was an infant and he, a toddler, from Saudi Arabia when her Dad was stationed there as some sort of Government liaison. Now he worked for Martin Marietta, the big local Defense contractor, where my Dad worked too. And even though they were Catholic, they weren't very religious, and there was always a slightly detectable undercurrent of unhappiness in the house. Her Dad hardly ever spoke directly to her Mom, who I remember was very sweet. Later it developed that the old man had outside interests and eventually they divorced and moved away. But for the rest of that summer, she was my first real girlfriend and we enjoyed each other's company a lot, even though we never got much past the French kissing. But she was energetic, and fun, and a bit of a tomboy, and we'd go out in the small johnboat and fish and swim… and make out. When I started to Bishop Moore, I invited her to our first get-together dance and got a lot of eyeballing from my classmates and they're dates—she was an impressive figure of a girl. Things only went sour when one day while riding home in the car we passed her walking down the sidewalk from Memorial and I saw her holding some other guy's hand. She hadn't seen me, but I broke it off quick, and even though she tried to make up, that was it for me. Then she became a bit of a nuisance, showing up at the front door unannounced, calling on the phone, or just walking her dog back and forth in front of our house. But I didn't budge, as far as I was concerned she was out. Besides, high school was now beginning to absorb more and more of my attention.

The Newspaper Business

During the summer before high school, I was still needing money, and once again, my buddy Dennis had told me that he was now doing pretty good with a newspaper route in his neighborhood, selling the Orlando Sentinel. I met a guy in my own neighborhood who had a paper route, and asked him about it. He said it just so happened that his own route had gotten a little too big and unwieldy, and he had to make two runs every morning to deliver them all. He only wanted to have to make one run, so if I wanted, he was willing to give me a chunk of it, maybe fifty subscribers to start off with, and he'd help me get it off the ground. Well, this was great! The only trouble was, the route wasn't really in our own neighborhood, but was maybe two miles away, around Kaley and Orange Blossom Trail. Then the delivery area was up and down maybe ten blocks square, which was another two miles, easy, and then two miles back home. We'd have to be at the dropoff by 5 a.m. when the papers were off-loaded (which meant getting up by 4:30 to ride the two miles to the drop), then fold them, do the route, and be home by 7:30 to get ready for school. Well, hell, I can do this! So I borrowed enough money for a couple of wire saddlebag baskets for my bike and put them on. My neighborhood buddy had a motor scooter, so he had no problem getting around, but I hauled out around 4 a.m. one morning in August to start my first real job. Luckily, I had a headlight that worked fairly well.

The carriers met at a Texaco station, my neighborhood buddy, a couple of black kids, and an old white guy with a car, and the truck pulled up at 5 and dumped several bales of papers out the back. We snapped the bundling wires and divvied up the count, and started rolling the papers, snapping them tight with rubber bands. Now, rolling papers is just like rolling a joint; that is to say, you don't roll papers, just like you don't ROLL a joint—you fold them… nice and tight. Well, I wasn't rolling them—I mean, folding them—very tight, so I had trouble fitting all fifty papers (and a couple of extra, just in case) into my sidecar baskets. My buddy lent me one of those over-the-shoulder bags the Sentinel gave out for the walking delivery boys downtown. With my baskets full and the bag over my shoulder half-full, we plodded out into the pre-dawn darkness, him on his little scooter and me pedaling frantically behind. He taught me all the tricks of throwing it sideways over your head, figuring out addresses that weren't displayed, watching out for dogs, placating those geezers who wanted it placed just inside their screen doors, and most important, if by chance you threw it into the bushes or up on the roof, well, that's why you carried a couple extra. Later, we sat down and he explained the payoff and how you had to go and collect on Saturday mornings, because that was the only time people were home where you could pin them down for payment. And once we paid the distributor, whatever was left was ours, especially tips if you could get them. So now I became rather solvent, had a few shekels in my pocket, and was ready to begin high school. This was great for awhile, but once school began to get serious though, it was getting harder to get up at four in the morning, and I really wanted my Saturdays for myself instead of wasting them browbeating and shaming the slackers on why they ought to pay the paperboy. So I told the paper route manager that Thanksgiving Day, the biggest day of the year for a paper's overall volume, what with ads and all, would be my last. I had grown the route to about seventy-five papers by that time, so there was no way I was going to get those all delivered by bike. I got a friend who had a car, Tim Anderson, to come out with me that morning, a Thursday of course, and we filled his little convertible Morris Minor right up to the window edges with my last day's delivery. As I recall, it was cold and there was a light drizzly fog out that morning, long before sunup. The papers stayed where they landed, and that day none got put inside any goddamn screen door. They may have gotten them free as well, because I never went back to collect. With the advent of high school, both my newspaper delivery days and my days of serving Mass came to an end, and I would now begin a life of semi-secular wakefulness, consisting of, yes, not only dis-illusion, but some dissolution as well.

Bishop Moore

Now Bishop Moore was even further away than St. James, out near Edgewater and Par, north of Orlando between College Park and Winter Park, and those first two years Mom was carting me back and forth every morning and Paul to St. James, so it was beginning to get a little much for her. And I was finding various excuses to stay late after school (pals and girls). But I quickly learned that the city bus went right by the front door of Bishop Moore, and a single transfer later, I was on my way to Holden Heights and let off at Strawder's, my old comic-book hangout. Ten, fifteen, twenty miles for a quarter, you couldn't beat it. Then Mom only had to drive up a mile and get me. Later, when Paul started at old BM, we travelled together until I got a car. But Bishop Moore was an eye-opener. We had to wear uniforms: white shirt, blue tie, grey slacks, and brown or black shoes. In the winter, say from November to March, we wore blue blazers. You could spot a covey of Bishop Moore students from a mile off, and we were often jeered at by "regular kids" riding by. "CAAAT-LIIIIKKERS!" But, to be honest, it was never really that bothersome, since we had a lot of roughnecks in school as well, and the regular kids knew that if they got caught one-on-one, the odds were against them. So, they only chanced yelling and pointing when they were in a car and knew they weren't stopping anytime soon, and I really think the girls were impressed with our white shirts, with blue ties and blazers, whether they were ready to admit it or not.

The first year I was there at Bishop Moore, it was still segregated. No, not with blacks, who were at that time non-existent there, but between the sexes. The girls' school was on the other side of an elementary school, St. Charles, and on the lake, under a grove of towering pine trees. The boys' school was adjacent to Dubsdread Country Club, and partially bordered with the local neighborhood houses along a back road that led out to Par and Edgewater. It lay in the stark sun, and I don't recall any air conditioning unless it was in the cafeteria, which offset the cool with the kitchen cooking, or maybe in the office, which could get hot for other reasons. So we didn't see the girls very often. In fact, only when we had to go to church for some holy day of obligation or another. They would sit the girls on one side of the church and the boys on the other, with a coven of yardstick-wielding guard-nuns constantly on the prowl to straighten up any curious ogling of the opposite sex from either side. I remember coming into the church one day and the nuns were just finishing up with the girls, where they had lined them up and then had each girl kneel in front of the altar rail, checking with their rulers to see that the bottom of the skirts hung low enough to touch the kneeler. If not, their names were taken to be sent home to their mothers for correction. But the girls were way ahead of the nuns and had already learned how they could roll up (or down) the waistband, as circumstances warranted. Only the most obvious and careless little harlots were caught with their skirts above their knees. Ooooh, those skirts, though! Yes, they were plain grey, but pleated, and when you matched them up with the white short-sleeved blouses (often sheer enough to see through, and God bless us if it rained), and the short white socks in summer (sometimes with frilly lace) and the long blue knee-highs in winter, matched up with a pair of saddle oxfords, a couple of pigtails with ribbons… well, a young man's thoughts might often turn away from his scholastic duties. These were also the days of unanticipated and unassailable hard-ons, impossible to predict, and embarrassingly unable to be hidden when detected; a constant source of aggravation.

I guess that's why they had kept us separated for so many years. It just so happened that the second year I was there, 1967-68, they decided to go co-ed. They never really explained why this change occurred (at least not to us), but I have my own theories. I think it had just gotten too heavy on the testosterone, and that they hoped that bringing girls into the classroom (not all classes, mind you, but at least half) would 'civilize' the men. As an example, during the first year as a freshman, when the schools were strictly separated, the upper classmen were notorious for shoving around us "new kids" and it was tolerated, if not endorsed, by the faculty. Every now and then though, some sophomore dick would pick on the wrong guy and get his clock cleaned. I'm thinking here of an incident involving one of our freshman buddies, Damian Palowitch, a broad-shouldered tough from a neighborhood near mine, whose fame as a rough character far preceded him. When sophomore number one fucked with him and got decked, sure, Palowitch had to go to the office and got a detention, no big deal. But when the sophomore assholes decided later that they would take him down *en masse* they really didn't know what they were fooling with. When it was over I can only recall the words of Jim Morrison, screaming "There's been a slaughter here!" This time, however, Palowitch was not going to the office, was not going to apologize, was not going to detention, and was not to be reasoned with by any priestly referee. I believe it was a week before he returned to school, and when he did, not another sophomore ever fucked with a freshman again. And what could the faculty do? To punish him for the defense of a multi-layered and lopsided assault would have been in itself, defenseless.

Ed Mullens

There were other instances that showed the system had malfunctioned over the years. Walking down the outside hall with a friend during my first week of orientation at school, about three classrooms ahead on the left, all of a sudden there's a loud "THWAP!" and out the open front door of the class some kid comes flying out at least three feet off the ground. I swear he didn't even touch the six-foot wide walk of the open hallway, but flew over it and landed in the open grass outside. As my buddy and I walked up, he was rolling in the grass with both hands on his ass, whimpering. We stopped, turned, and looked into the classroom to see a lean, twisted gargoyle, in a short-sleeve white shirt and tie, hunched over, with a hideous half-smirk, standing there with a huge paddle in his left hand. "What are you looking at?" he demanded. Not waiting to answer, we hustled off, giving one last backward glance at the poor miscreant writhing in the grass. That was my introduction to Mr. Mullens.

Although the first week of high school was an orientation of sorts, when the class schedules were finally handed out, there it was…Jesus Christ! I was in Mullens' English class. The first day we all sat in silence, terrified. Just the way he liked it. He seated us in alphabetical order, with the admonishment that that's where we would stay all year, so get used to it. Well, that put me in immediate danger, surrounded by Terry Beatty, Joe Behnke, Noel Bobko, and Greg Bretz, four of the worst troublemakers ever to cross the corridors of Catholic education. Needless to say, we became great pals. And there in the corner, next to Mullens' desk, was a rack of various ass-smackers, paddles that had been made and donated by previous classes who had undergone his instruction over the years. Easily a dozen… from small single-handers with raised little knobs on the attending surface, to medium two-handers with holes drilled through ("to cut down wind-resistance"), to a huge two-by-eight beam that was in fact a joke, yet was ominously unfunny. I believe it was called "The Tree." All had custom-made handles, some wrapped in leather ("for a better grip"), and many with a hanging hole and wrist-sling in the end ("in case I work up a sweat and it slips loose").

Now a lot has been written about Mr. Mullens, and more should be written about him, since there's no doubt that his is an interesting story. So I won't belabor the poor man's memory other than to share a few personal notes. He was a real enigma. As frightening as he was to behold, and his sense of strict discipline notwithstanding, nothing lessened the endearment that every pupil he ever taught ended up having for him when it was over. His right hand and arm was a twisted gnarly hook of an appendage. Apparently he had not let go of a hand grenade fast enough during the Korean conflict. Whether it was one of ours or one of theirs, or what the circumstances were, we never knew, nor would we ever ask. The shock and shrapnel not only ruined his right arm to the point that it was obvious to everyone who ever read his scrawl on the blackboard that he had to re-learn to write with his left, but it also created a permanent grimace on the right side of his face, so you never really knew if he was frowning at you or smiling at some inner amusement. Not quite as bad as Batman's nemesis, Two-Face, but almost. He ran the class like a ship's captain (I'm thinking Wolf Larsen here), stern and tight, never allowing even the most minor misbehavior, and usually cutting off the offender before anyone else even realized a misdeed was in the offing. He nonetheless had the wickedest sense of humor, and the sample sentences that we either had to parse or otherwise edit in some way were often hilarious. Things like "The old broad who runs the candy store down the street smells like a wet camel." Again, this was prior to the classes being integrated with girls.

Now, I never got smacked, except once, and it only recently dawned on me that I was put in that class, not because I needed any remedial English instruction (the nuns at St. James had more than covered that), but because I was grouped in with the roustabouts who needed Social Instruction. That's why I was surrounded by juvenile delinquents! I was one of them! All my more gentlemanly friends from St. James (Dennis and Ed, for example) were in what might have been considered an advanced class, but in reality it only meant their teacher was forgiving, supportive, and emotionally in-touch, none of the qualities which could be used to describe Mr. Mullens. He was, however, quite refined in his own way. He had us watch the movie version of Julius Caesar, with Marlon Brando as Marc Anthony, and then decided each and every one of us would memorize at least the first part of the funeral soliloquy. I think he gave us a long weekend to memorize it, and then, the following entire week was spent listening to it recited over and over in every southern drawl, every stuttering staccato, every hesitant and painful dead space, and every muttering whisper that young men of fourteen could pull out of their ass to destroy the good name of Caesar. But there were a few of us, not many, and yes, I include myself, who understood and appreciated the irony and sarcasm of Anthony, and who were more than happy to bend the ears of our fellow plebes to rub in the shame and folly (and especially the hypocrisy) of the damnable assassin Brutus, who was, of course, an honorable man. When played to the hilt with gusto and righteous indignation, fairly spitting out the name of honorable Brutus, and finally laying our heart in the casket with the most unfairly abused corpse of great Caesar himself, even old Mullens would crack a grin wider than his already-maligned jaw allowed. It was good stuff.

So, the one time I did get smacked was the last day of school. Bobko and I had planned this ahead of time. Noel Bobko (named Noel because he was one of those unfortunates born on Christmas Day) was a greaser from New York. And this is not to disparage him, for he was very proud of it. He acted tough, he swaggered, he bragged, and he was always looking for "pussy." Oh yeah, and he slathered back his longish black hair with what can only be described as petroleum jelly. I suppose he had to put on the role of extreme tough guy to make up for the girly Noel he had gotten stuck with. Sort of like the *Boy Named Sue*. In any case, we came up with the idea that we were going to throw old Mullens for a loop, surprise the shit out of him. As I said, it was the last day of class, the sun was shining, tests were done, everyone just wanted the day to end, so we could all go home and start to enjoy the summer. Well, neither Bobko nor I had been walloped during the preceding nine months because we were generally too smart to fall into any Eternal Truth traps (an "eternal truth" being inviolate rules of English, like "the subject always agrees with the predicate," the breaking of which got your ass-cheeks violated). As far as being troublesome, there were plenty of other opportunities outside of Mullens' class, so why push it. But today we decided to surprise Mr. Mullens and the class in general. While everyone was reading quietly, and Mullens was finishing up his grade book, we stood up, shook hands, walked up to the front of the class, and "assumed the position." There was a light gasp, a rolling murmur, and more than a few chuckles from the class, but Mullens just looked up, slowly closed his grade book, got up and went over to the arsenal and picked out a particular paddle of notorious reputation. Without a word he walked over, took a few practice swings (these were backhanded lefties because of his withered right arm), enough so that we could hear the air above us go "swoosh." And BAM, he sent Bobko flying out the doorway. I gulped, grabbed my ankles hard and looked up and out the door to see Bobko sprawled and rolling in the grass. The next thing I knew, I was flying over the terrazzo breezeway floor, and lying next to him. You know, it didn't hurt the instant it made contact, but as time went on it hurt more and more. Maybe a full three minutes later, we collected ourselves, brushed off the grass and sand, went back in and gingerly sat back down at our desks. Mullens had already put the paddle up, and was back to filling out his grade book. Our classmates were convinced we were insane.

Sophomore Year

Sophomore year yielded the realization that we were going to be sharing classes with the girls. Holy Cow! And they were all beautiful. So there was lots of flirting going on, and school started getting intense in more ways than one. I had gone out for football the previous spring, since I was told that this was the manly thing to do. And I made the final cut too, as a guard. Now anybody who knows anything about football knows that the offensive guard's position is simply to protect the quarterback, which meant you got slammed, you got up, got back in position, and got slammed again, and again, and again. Well, between running laps in full gear, doing pushups and situps, and getting slammed again and again, I decided the hell with that, and did not show up for summer practice. What? And give up a solid month of my joyous, relaxing summer to carry out all that crazy, undignified, and painful waste of youth under the magnified Central Florida August sun? I don't think so. I didn't think it was a big deal, but apparently, having made the Spring Training cut, by not showing up for Summer Practice, even as a crummy guard, I had snubbed the football coach, Harry Nelson. As if he cared (or so I thought). After school had begun, we got ready for our first pep rally in the large golden geodesic dome that has been the icon of the school since it was built through donations from the prominent and wealthy Heidrich family, of orange-grove fame. Now Harry Nelson was a bear of a bull of a man, one of those guys with a flat-top haircut to match his square head, notorious for laying hands on (male) students, and though he only taught mechanical drawing—he had to teach *something* to be a faculty member, besides being the football coach—he was famous across Central Florida for repeatedly leading the Bishop Moore Hornets to State Championships against schools four and five times our size. So he had a great reputation, and following his recent death, he has become a candidate for canonization. I never saw it myself, and always thought he was a bit of a blustery bully, despite being a brilliant football coach, and in my own case, this realization played out at the pep rally. I was sitting with my homeroom class, all boys in our uniform blazers, on the tiered platform benches that lined the inside of the dome, just inside the entrance door. People were coming in and getting settled, and everybody was getting excited. In through the door strode Nelson, scowling, hands on his hips and looking tough, and he began to survey the crowd. At some point, his glance wandered across mine, and he noticed I was watching him, so I smiled. He dropped his arms and stiffened, then he slowly raised his arm, pointed at me, and beckoned me to come on down with his crooked index finger. What was this!? So, I got up, maybe ten rows from the floor, and "excuse(d) me" all the way down until I got to the bottom. I walked over to him, looked up, and before I knew it, he had grabbed me by the lapels of my blazer, lifted me off the floor and stuck his face nose-to-nose in my own, and growled "Don't you ever smile at me unless I smile at you first… understand?" I mumbled "yes, sir," and he threw me up into the stands, four or five tiers up, splayed out right on top of all these (other) stunned sophomores. I made my way back to my seat, with everyone asking, what did you say? Did you do something? All I could answer was, "I smiled," which, as a matter of fact, I did not do again throughout the ensuing pep rally. No, I don't think he knew who I was, or would have cared if he had. Although, if he had put two and two together and figured out I was the guard who hadn't shown up for Summer Practice, I'm sure the outcome would have been much worse. As it is, it didn't matter who I was, he was just looking for someone to get his blood up, and that day I just happened to pick the lucky number. May You Rest in Peace, Coach Nelson.

Soccer Champs

Since I didn't go out for football, I was one of those approached by Father Granahan, who I had known as an altar boy and student at St. James and who was now teaching religion at Bishop Moore, to join a soccer team he was trying to organize for the high school. He really put the pressure on all of us old students from St. James, and even though we didn't know a damn thing about soccer, he got a bunch of us, me, Dennis, Ed, Bill Gilbert, Joe Nursey, Paul Saville, and others to join up. Then we had other stalwart sophomores recruited from Bishop Moore like Frank Francisco and Frank Partridge, and a couple of upper classmen, Bruce Furino, who could run circles around anyone else, and our incredible goalie, Bob St. Lawrence. Father Granahan was a small, wiry, flush-faced black-haired Irishman, and he whipped us into shape in no time, with drills every afternoon and scrimmage games between ourselves, where he and his Assistant Coach, Father John Ennis, another off-the-boat Irish footballer, would join in to torment us with their dribbling, passing, and head-balling. But they got us to the point where we could hold our own, and when the season started, we began traveling across the state and playing all-comers. By all-comers I mean anyone we could play. There was no organized soccer inter-high school program anywhere in Florida in 1968 so, besides playing other Catholic schools with Irish priests pushing for it, like Bishop Kenny in Jacksonville, we ended up playing the Air Force Academy, St. Leo's College in Tampa (alma mater of the actor Lee Marvin, among others), Rollins College, and various "public" high schools, who simply turned their football fuckups loose on us, without recourse to rules, or referees, just rumbling. There was even the incident where Father Granahan, as small as he was, was mistaken for a student player by one of the foul-mouthed public-school gorillas posing as a soccer player, and we all had to step in to keep them separated, and yes, keep Father Granahan from going to blows and discrediting his temporarily-misplaced collar. But we always knew when he was getting frustrated with us. Soccer is, after all is said and done, a game of endurance more than anything, as opposed to a game of scoring, obviously. And when we'd start to wear down, or just didn't show the drive that was necessary to stun the other team into submission, or happened to get near the opposing goal but then passed instead of shooting, we'd hear Father Granahan, both arms raised with fists clenched, red-faced and railing at us from the sidelines, "Kick the flaming ball!" This was as close as he could get to cursing, but it was enough for us to get red-faced too, and "just drive the damn bloody thing home," as Father Ennis would chime in. At the end of the year, it just so happened, we had won more games than anyone else, and by default, we were the State champs!

54

When they had the Sports Awards dinner at Bishop Moore, which was a big damn deal, I wasn't present, as I had a more pressing date, but here's what was told to me that occurred. Coach Harry Nelson was the Master of Ceremonies, and after the food was served, he quickly handed out the baseball, basketball, swimming team, golf team, and tennis team awards and letters (you know, those fuzzy things with the school initials that you sew onto sweaters), crediting the attending coach of each for his tireless endeavors. Then, for the highlight, each and every football player was acknowledged for his singular performance and contributions, with funny anecdotes and reminiscences of various games re-played, as he was given his trophy and/or letter. At the end, the soccer players were just looking around, wondering how they're accomplishment, State Champs, the very first year they'd played, would be celebrated. Nelson reached into the box of letters, grabbed the remainder, all of which were to go to the soccer players who had earned them, including yours truly, and flung them out into the crowd, scattering them across the tables, chairs and floor. Then he adjourned the proceedings. Apparently he didn't consider soccer a sport worthy of formal respect, unlike tennis and golf. He must have caught some shit from the Dean of the School for his attitude and performance because, when we came back to school the next year, and winter rolled around, whenever he saw me or one of the other soccer players wearing a letter sweater with the damn thing sewn on, he would growl, gnash his teeth, and turn away, but he never said a word. He let his flying football monkeys carry on the rude commentaries for him. *Pax vobiscum*, Harry.

Fleeting Early Phases

> *The sway of alcohol over mankind is unquestionably due to its power to stimulate the mystical faculties of human nature, usually crushed to earth by the cold facts and dry criticisms of the sober hour. Sobriety diminishes, discriminates and says no; drunkenness expands, unites, and says yes. It is in fact the great exciter of the Yes function in man. It brings its votary from the chill periphery of things to the radiant core. It makes him for the moment one with truth. Not through mere perversity do men run after it. To the poor and the unlettered it stands in the place of symphony concerts and of literature; and it is part of the deeper mystery and tragedy of life that whiffs and gleams of something that we immediately recognize as excellent should be vouchsafed to so many of us only in the fleeting earlier phases of what in its totality is so degrading a poisoning. The drunken consciousness is one bit of the mystic consciousness, and our total opinion of it must find its place in our opinion of that larger whole.*
>
> William James,
> *The Varieties of Religions Experience*

Although a few of us had dabbled in drinking over the early years of adolescence such as stealing a little of the leftover (and unblessed) wine left in the cruets after Mass, or maybe swiping a beer from the fridge when no one would notice, things took a decidedly different turn during the sophomore year at Bishop Moore. And even though this was 1968, the Summer of Love, the idea of anything more intoxicating than booze was still more of an idea, or more accurately, more of a magazine feature, than for us a reality. Just like all the generations that had preceded us, except for the hip and cool beatniks who had indiscriminately dipped into marijuana and heroin, alcohol was the drug of choice. There was no other choice. During the summer, as a couple of us were beginning to drive, and so began flexing our freedom wings, we had experimented with the overindulgence of beer, most notably Colt 45, and of course Boones Farm and Ripple wines. They weren't hard to get, and more than once were provided to us by less-than-totally-responsible adults, even some parents. But soon we graduated to the harder stuff. And this happened in a very curious way. From my own perspective, I had been friends with a couple of the older kids at St. James, the guys who had taught me to be an altar boy. Now that we were in high school, they were still two grades ahead of me. So they were seniors, and we, my friends and I, were sophomores, and they were in a totally different level of delinquency than we were. We might go to the drive-in, have a few drinks, cruise up and down Colonial Drive looking for cars full of girls to flirt with, smoke a cigarette or two, that was about it… maybe climb a water tower. Like I said, small stuff. These guys however, were working on becoming small-time mobsters; well, okay, maybe just burglars. What they would do is they would tail a liquor truck, until it finally pulled over and had to make a delivery. Inevitably, while the driver was making his delivery, he would leave the back of the truck open, often lining up the next level of deliveries in-line along the back edge of the truck. While he was inside doing his thing and talking with the owner, these guys would lift as many cases of whatever was available as quick as they could, one guy acting as lookout, and then they'd haul ass. Then, on Friday afternoon, they would pull up in the parking lot at school and take orders. If you weren't sure what you wanted, they might pop the trunk open so you could choose, and there would be bottles of different liquor all lined up on a blanket. And it didn't matter what you bought, it was $5 a bottle. We didn't care, we had no discriminating taste anyway. So we generally settled on bourbon, because it went well with coke.

This was not good though, since, as I said, we were all just beginning to drive, and for the most part, we didn't have cars of our own and, more than not, we were borrowing our parents' vehicles, for a night on the town. That's why the drive-in was such a refuge. We could sit, drink, talk, smoke, etc. without bringing down the law. But, eventually, we'd seen every movie at every drive-in in town, and now we were looking for adventure. For instance, there was the infamous night of "Christmas is Over!" sung (loudly, over and over again) to the tune of "Crimson and Clover," where post-Christmas, but pre-New Years 1969 we all got ripped (let's see if I can remember this, I believe it was myself, Greg Toole, Dennis LeFils, Frank Franciso, Billy Gilbert, and oh yes, Kenny Edwards) and singing loudly, we tore down some dead end street in some neighborhood, knocking over garbage cans full of Christmas wrappings, ornaments, bottles, etc. and much to our surprise, at the cul-de-sac at the end of the lane there was a street party, encompassing at least a half-dozen families, with tables of food, and music of their own, who all stood staring at us, since they had heard us coming a half-mile away. We made a quick U-turn just before we'd have been knocking over the tables, with either Gilbert or Edwards or both, yelling "Fuck You" while hanging out the passenger's side windows front and back. We had not gotten out of the subdivision before we were pulled over by a policeman, rousted out of the vehicle, and lined up, heads down and now very humble and submissive. "You boys will go down that street, pick up every piece of trash, put the cans back, and when you get to the end of the street, you'll go up, and apologize to all the families having their barbecue, and anybody else you meet on the way. I'll be waiting here," he said. And we did so, gladly. When we got back to the policeman, guarding the entrance to the subdivision, he got us out of the car again, determined by question-and-answer who was the most sober and therefore, the driver-designate, and told us to go straight home. Which we did. On other occasions, I recall a policeman following us home, then obligingly driving off. Those days are now gone, probably forever. We were young, stupid, and lucky, but for Orlando in the late 60s, we weren't criminals. Not yet.

The drinking was always excessive. Or so it seemed at the time. A fifth of Ancient Age would do four of us nicely, but then we were young, and our livers were fresh so it didn't take much, and besides, we were immortal. But there was plenty of puking out of car windows, on couches, hugging toilets, and more than many instances of impromptu wrestling. Then there were the hangovers. One night I came in rather late, bleary-eyed and soused. Dad was in the Florida Room watching television, and I was too drunk to be smart enough to avoid him and so I asked what he was watching. He looked at me cock-eyed, and said "Horatio Hornblower." This was long before I'd ever become a fan of C.S. Forester and the entire Hornblower saga, and I don't think I'd ever heard the name before. It was the perfect sobriety test. I couldn't repeat it to save my life. "Horsey Blow? Horashee Haarbler?" Dad squinted at me, "Have you been drinking?" "Just a little bit," I said as I swayed back and forth, no sense in lying. He just sighed and said "Go to bed. We'll talk about this in the morning." And in the morning, he got me good. He waited until about 9 o'clock, just as the summer sun was getting hot, came into my darkened bedroom, and rousted me out, "All right hotshot, time to mow the lawn." No amount of begging, crying, moaning, or wimpering would sway him. Back then, a self-propelled lawnmower was still a Popular Science pipe dream, and our lot was so large that, the only time we attempted a record by tag-teaming it as fast as we could, my brother, my Dad and I still took 45 minutes. Now I was condemned to do it alone.   To this day I don't think there is a more diabolical torture than pushing a heavy roaring lawnmower (with small wheels) through a savannah of lawn in the broiling heat while poisons are slowly squeezed out one's pores, with an axe-splitting headache, hangover, and a mouth feeling full of cotton... Waterboarding is for sissies, and in this particular instance would have been a welcome relief.

Then Came Virginia

One day out of the blue, standing in line at the school cafeteria, getting plates and trays and silverware, I looked up to see behind the serving line the most beautiful girl I'd ever laid eyes on. Blond, big blue eyes and luscious red lips, smiling and laughing, I lost my concentration and appetite altogether. Walking out with an empty tray, I started asking friends who she was. She's a sophomore, the same as us, in a couple of the girls-only classes. Got a boyfriend who drives a motorcycle, Mark something. Oh hell, I know who he is: big good-looking guy, yeah, with a motorcycle, but dumber than dirt. Shit! What a waste. But I started keeping an eye out for her, and it got to the point that I could spot her in a crowd a half-mile away, always amazed that all these other guys weren't chasing after her. But eventually they broke up. She'd been riding on the back of the bike and burned the inside of her left calf on the tailpipe, caught some shit from her folks, and I think came to realize this guy wasn't all he appeared to be. And, worse, he was from a broken home. Then quickly, too quickly, she's on the arm of a big goofy guitar player who sings to her over the telephone "Virginia" to the tune of "Gloria," stretching out the V-I-R-G-I-N-I-AAY. (Eventually, this son of a fried-chicken magnate becomes a State Senator.) Well, she tosses him over for his cousin, a cute Justin Bieber-lookalike, and they become a regular item for six months or so. Then moves in a new student from up north, well-to-do family, good-looking (must have been, since all the girls were swooning, including Virginia's Mom), and sophisticated smart. His name's Jack Duval and she drops everything to take up with him, the dog. They go along for a couple of months as the school year wears on. It's coming to an end, and soon, summer will be upon us. Well, I get invited to an end-of-school party where a number of the older students, Juniors and Seniors, were going as well. The party was being hosted by a well-known party girl, one of the infamous Kelly sisters, and she in turn had made invitations to all the girl friends she could think of, so it was going to be a bash. She lived on a lake with a big yard, and the word was that her parents were out of town. To top things off, I was driving around by then, and they asked me if I would pick up Virginia and her girlfriends and give them a ride. Boy, would I!

I got all dressed up, even putting on a tie, and Mom and Dad let me take out the Ford Galaxie, 426 cu. inches of engine, white with blue interior, and a convertible to boot. I picked up

Virginia's friends first, since I didn't know how to get to her house, and we made our way to her parents' over near Lake Holden. When she came out she looked gorgeous. I insisted that she sit by me up front, the hell with her girlfriends. On the way to the party I remember I got so distracted looking down at her legs that I nearly rear-ended some pickup truck on Orange Blossom Trail, coming to an emergency squealing stop inches from his back bumper. That would have changed my whole life (as I suppose any other decision I made that day or any other would have). We arrived at the party safe and sound, and it was already rocking, people dancing in the carport, as dusk settled in over the lake. She went off with her friends and I saddled up to a couple of my older friends, who were freaking out over the music being played by some guy named Jimi Hendrix. It was wild, and normally I would have been drinking with the rest, but tonight I wanted to have my wits about me in case Virginia showed up again (not to mention promising Mom and Dad I'd be careful with their car). And sure enough, there she was, standing alone and a bit uncomfortable. I don't think she'd ever seen a party like this before, and although I really hadn't either, I felt completely at ease. I started talking with her and found out that her boyfriend, Duval, couldn't come, and from the way she spoke it was obvious that she didn't mind him not being there at all. Apparently, he was his own greatest admirer. After a few minutes, one of my older altar boy delinquent booze-mobster friends called me over. He asked me who my girlfriend was. When I told him she wasn't my girlfriend, he said that he was going back to his house to pick up some more beer for the party, and he was taking one of Virginia's friends with him, a girl nicknamed "Rabbit," and how about I ask Virginia to go along with us. Well, this was perfect. I didn't have to drive, and we could get away from the party alone, and shit, we got the back seat to ourselves! Virginia was glad to get out of there too for a while, so off we went.

I had just gotten my braces off a month or so earlier, but I still had that damn retainer in my mouth. So when she wasn't looking, I took it out, and stupidly slid it into the seat crack instead of just putting it in my pocket. Now, Jerry, the older former altar boy, and Rabbit were comfortably nestled up in the front seat, and he would give her a little kiss at every stoplight. When we got to his house, he asked if we wanted to come in. Although Rabbit was gung-ho, Virginia got a little nervous then and said, no, she wanted to stay in the car and wait. I said, of course, that I'd stay with her. They weren't gone three minutes before Virginia and I were lip-locked, and we stayed that way until they came back about fifteen minutes later, toting the beer. I suppose it sounds naïve, but I was sure we were smitten with each other. On the way back to the party I asked her if I could take her out, if this wasn't interfering with her boyfriend business. She said she'd love to and the boyfriend was on the way out anyway. So we began seeing each other that summer between sophomore and junior year, and I think we both fell pretty hard, at least I know I did, and we soon became inseparable. Oh, and I'd forgotten that goddamn retainer in the back seat of Jerry's car. Well, I'd been warned not to lose it since all the money Mom and Dad had put into the braces would be wasted if I lost the retainer and my teeth started returning to their old chomping grounds. And the cost of a new retainer? Well, let's not go there, as this would have also involved a confession as to what happened to it. In any case, I called him up a couple of days later, made my way over to his house, and retrieved it from the crumbs and coins and gum and hair that had also made their way down the crack of the back car seat cushions.

Shoe Fair

After school had started and I'd given up the newspaper (delivery) business, it became apparent that if I was going to maintain any kind of lifestyle, dating, drinking, or otherwise I still needed some sort of a job. We were down at the local Orange Blossom Shopping Center when I noticed that one of the empty storefronts was moving stuff around inside. The front door was open so I went in and met the proprietor, a middle-aged woman with some sort of German-

Austrian accent, big, broad and blond. She immediately told me she'd hire me, and could I start right away? Sure, I said, what's the pay? $1.25 and hour, straight up, no Social Security, no taxes. I shook her hand and started moving boxes. Now this was my first real job, and I threw myself into it. By the end of the first week, I'd knocked out maybe twenty hours between the weekend and after school. And then the lessons began to sink in. She had hired two other teenagers, just a little older than myself, maybe 16 or so, and they were the typical juvenile malingerers when she wasn't around, but beaver-busy while she was. I always worked at a steady pace though. So, when she was around, and they would frantically get moving, all of a sudden it looked like I was the slacker. And she started cheating me on my hours, since we didn't have a time clock. She'd record that I came in at five, when I knew I was there at four; and she'd put down that I left at 6:30 when I helped close at 7. So I quickly learned that she couldn't be trusted, and when I told her about the differences, she'd say she'd make it up to me the next week, and then hope I'd forget about it. But eventually my talents bubbled to the surface. They had a pile of wooden shelves that had to be put together, angled downward to show off the shoes, with a little lip on them so the displayed shoes wouldn't fall off. And they not only had to be assembled, they had to be painted too. Well, the two lazy idiots that she had previously hired were not up to the job by any stretch. I assembled shelves like a madman, always keeping mine separate from theirs and showing them to the old frau every time she showed up, so she knew who had done what. After two weeks of this, she let the lesser of the two evils go, and, although I didn't get any more money, she became somewhat more honest about my hours, and told me that I would be a salesman as soon as all the shelves were dried and stocked with shoes and we could open the doors for business. Well, this sounded pretty good.

A week or so later we opened up, and now as salesmen, she wanted us to dress up. For me this was no problem at all, since I was wearing a white shirt, grey slacks, and navy blue tie every day as part of my BM high school uniform, and as the weather got cooler, I started wearing my navy blazer. My shoes? Why, penny-loafers, of course. The pace at the store had taken a decided turn downwards. Often no one would come in for hours, and she couldn't think of enough things to keep us busy—you can only vacuum the floor so many times, and other than stacking shoes and entering inventory (which you didn't have to do very often unless shoes were really moving), there was really no need for two shoe salesmen. So she began to hint that if things didn't pick up she was going to have to let one of us go. I had told Virginia all about the goings-on at the Shoe Fair store, and she had talked to her Dad, then a young and handsome ex-Marine (I know, no such thing as an ex-Marine) who worked as a metal designer and fabricator at a plastics factory down in Kissimmee. He told her they'd hire me there as a laborer for $2.50 an hour. I drove down there, filled out an application, shook hands on the deal, and thanked Virginia's Dad for the good word. Then I went in and told the old bitch that I had gotten another job, and congratulated the poor bastard who got stuck with her. I was overjoyed, since I had now doubled my pay, and they wanted me just to work on weekends and holidays, or whenever I was free from school, to give some of the older family men a break. And I could wear whatever I wanted, the dirtier the better. Now I should say that, at the end, I did enjoy selling shoes to the ladies, and even though I never developed the proper fetish, holding their delicate foot in your hand, and slipping on a couple of pairs of heels for them to walk around in, all while kneeling on the floor in your shirt and tie, and seeing the beaming smile on their face when they'd been assured of how attractive they were in their tasteful and most stylish choice of footwear,well, this almost made it worth only getting a buck and a quarter an hour. And no, I do not have any upskirt Penthouse adventures for the more prurient of cads out there. After all, this was still the late 60s, and I was only a Catholic high school kid, not yet sorely twisted by the ways of the world. Sorry, it just didn't happen yet. Maybe later.

Better Plastics

In the summer of 1968, down in Kissimmee, Better Plastics was a hellish place. It had twelve or fifteen of these cast-injection-molding machines, eight foot high and maybe twelve feet long, in two long rows on the concrete floor of an open fan-cooled but hot metal-roofed factory. One woman at each machine tended the monsters that all went deafeningly "BAM! HISS! CLACK!" three times a minute and spit out a variety of plastic flower pots, confection and deli containers, and even clear plastic glasses. These women were white, strong, redneck housewives for the most part, often related to each other, whether by birth or marriage. Other than the floor manager, a slight, wiry guy with a bad temper named Harold, who always had a dribble of chewing tobacco hanging at the corner of his mouth, the men were either the two or three executives, salesmen and owners, who worked upstairs and wore white shirts and ties, or the metal-workers in the machine shop downstairs who either fixed the machines or made parts or new design molds for the machines. Then there were the five or six general laborers like me, who loaded trucks, stacked the warehouse, mixed the plastic, and drove the trucks. The place ran twenty-four hours a day, in three shifts, where the late shift might be manned by black ladies. When a machine went down, they would send that woman home, and once it was fixed, they would call her back. The women really did work hard, climbing up a small metal staircase and loading the hoppers with raw plastic by the bucketful, gathering up the products as they were spit out and boxing them up by the count, stacking the boxes, etc., all while listening to the completely unsynchronized slamming and hissing of the mechanical mayhem going on about them. Not to mention, the plastic was being melted continuously before being squirted into the molds, so it was always a hot and dangerous place, and when the mechanics were working on a machine they would sometimes spew out puddles of molten plastic to clear the nozzles, leaving white and green cream-like turd sculptures hardening on the floor. Like I said, hellish.

I started out by sopping up the oil the leaking hydraulics on the machines were constantly leaving in puddles on the floor. I mopped it up with rags, and spread that oil-soaking kitty litter stuff on the spots, and then went on to the next machine. Usually, by the time I'd cleaned up the floor around the last machine, the first was ready to sop up again. But I got pretty good at it, and started using some of the reject plastic food containers to catch the really bad leaks, and within a couple of weeks I had it pretty much under control, and the floor manager liked the idea that we could actually recycle some of that oil I was catching that had previously been going out with the trash. They even had a centrifugal oil-recycling tank system that hadn't worked in years, so me and one of the mechanics took a look at it and we had it up and running in no time. Then they bought one of those liquid-sucking vacuums, and soon the whole oil-leaking machine problem was manageable, and they were getting half their oil back to use again. This also solved the perennial problem of the women slipping and falling, since they had to manhandle the large 50-gallon-size cardboard barrels full of the raw plastic from which they each fed into the uppermost hopper of their respective machine. Every so often, as they were moving these 80 lb. barrels with the hand truck, one of them would hit a slick spot and wham, down they'd go. I don't recall any serious injuries other than a sprained wrist or two, and more often than not it was just an excuse for some tension-releasing laughter. Besides, these women were glad to have the factory job since at this time Kissimmee was nothing but a little cow-town, and OSHA was still years down the road. I do remember getting chewed out by the yapping floor manager Harold for being too helpful by bringing the barrels out to the ladies when I could, and "they were getting spoiled and now they were asking the men to bring them out for them." It was also a well-known secret (!?) that he was banging one of the loudest factory women, a blue/black-haired harpy twice his size, who now figured that this was how the operation ought to be carried out, and he decided that apparently this was all my fault for starting the whole business of helping them out in the first place. She started a refusal campaign as to wheeling out these large barrels, and he knew that if he put his foot down, his balls would soon be as blue/black as her hair. Mad as he was, even he started bringing out the barrels eventually. And production picked up.

Soon I moved up to mixing and dyeing the raw plastic. I quickly learned the difference between polystyrene (hard, for small green flower pots), polypropylene (pliable, for large black flower pots and clear food containers), and polyethylene (pliable and clear, mostly for food container lids). We received the raw plastic as tiny pellets or beads in either big brown bags or large crates of cardboard containers, delivered in train cars. Unloading these large crates with a ramp and truck and forklift was always a dangerously comical affair, and more than once ended up with a ton or two of plastic granules in a pile next to the freight car, which meant scooping it up in buckets or with big coal shovels. Once we got back to Better Plastics it ended up in big open piles, separated by the types listed above. These big open piles were fun to run and jump and roll around in, except plastic would get in everywhere, every crease in your shoes and socks, every crack in your skin, down the crack of your ass, etc., and yup, every so often you'd cough up one of these tiny plastic granules, or dig one out of your ear. I often wonder if I don't still have one or two lodged in me somewhere.

The guy who taught me to mix the plastic was named Red, because he was a tall skinny ex-truck driver with a headful of bright flaming red hair. I liked him, and he was friendly enough, but he had a bad drinking problem, and the most horrific badger of a wife a man could ever be saddled with. Many a morning I came in and found him asleep among the bags of raw plastic stacked to the ceiling, rather than go home. I'd let him sleep, even punching him in on the time clock, while I went to work. When he'd wake, he'd help me out and we'd get caught up and ahead in no time, and then he'd tell me his adventures out drinking the night before, maybe show me the pornographic playing cards he always carried in his back pocket. Then he'd go back and lay down among the bags. Sometimes he'd be there for days and nights on end, because he just didn't want to go home. Then when payday came, he'd usually be gone. That's when his wife would show up, demanding his check. It was always a scene. She'd swagger in and start screeching at the floor manager, "Where is he!? Where is that goddamn sunuvabitch!? You better give me his fucking paycheck, otherwise he's going to spend it on drink! Do you hear me!? He owes me that money and I'm not leaving until I have his paycheck!" The floor manager would try to reason with her, telling her that he wasn't authorized to give her the paycheck without his permission, but eventually she got so unreasonable, even tearing at her own hair and screaming, that he would threaten to call the police on her. And sometimes he did. And it was all old news to them. They'd drive down to the local bar and either they brought Red back, or more often, they'd bring back a written note from him to let the manager give his wife his paycheck. What the cops never did was to take his wife to the bar where he was at. They were at least that sympathetic to him, and probably under strict orders from the barkeep as well, to keep her at a distance if at all possible. True peacemakers back then. It even got to the point where it was agreed to print up a check for the wife to get, and pay him the remainder in cash. Then one day Red just disappeared.

The guy who replaced him was George Putnam, a little old man, sixty-five years old, bald, with a little pudge gut, who couldn't have been five-foot-four. The sweetest man you could ever meet. He had a real soft spot for his wife too, who was in constant declining health, overweight, with some sort of heart disease so she couldn't breathe very well. Just talking about her, he might start crying, and it would just break your heart. But damn, could he work. We would load trucks together, just him and me. And when I say load trucks, I mean semi trailers, forty feet long, stacked to the ceiling. They'd bring the forklift, with a pallet full of boxes and by the time we got one pallet loaded the second one would be waiting, each box forty pounds, twenty to a pallet, forty pallets to a truck. We might go two hours without stopping, in the hotbox of a trailer, sweat pouring down off of both of us. I'm 16; he's 65. When we were done we could of course take a long break and drink a couple of cokes, but the sweat would still pour for another half-hour or so, and I remember my heart beating so fast I thought it would pop. I can't imagine what his must have felt like, and more than once I thought he was going to have a heart attack for sure. After Red left, George and I took over the mixing of the plastic together, when we weren't loading trucks. He also got me started on the forklift, and soon I was moving things around in the warehouse. One day they told him to take me out in the big straight-axle truck (like the largest U-Haul you might rent) and show me how to drive it. Later I found out it was because they wanted him to make a delivery up to Georgia, but he tried to beg off because he didn't want to leave his wife, even for a couple of days, so he volunteered to show me how to drive the truck. I got familiar with it in just an hour or two. The next day we loaded it up for the delivery of some polystyrene flower pots to a nursery in Thomasville, Georgia. It was a Friday, and I left Kissimmee immediately, figuring I could get four or five hours in before dark. Here I was, 16 years old, driving a large truck full of merchandise, on an out-of-state delivery. I was in heaven, a knight of the road, a highwayman. They'd even given me spending money for gas and meals and a hotel for one night. Other than the gas, for which I needed receipts, whatever was left was mine to keep, so George told me not to get a hotel room, but just sleep on the front seat of the truck—good advice! I made it upstate about three or four hours to Perry before I got in any trouble. But in Perry, I was starting to get real hungry, and once I spotted a restaurant it was too late to pull over and I passed it. Rather than just turning right and going around the block and coming up behind the restaurant like I should have, I decided just to make a U-turn on Highway 27. Well, this was crazy on many, many levels, but I didn't know that yet. First of all, you can't just turn a big truck around like that, even across three or four lanes, so I ended up making a three-point turn that blocked both lanes of traffic while everybody was honking at me for being such an idiot. This attracted the notice of the local law enforcement officer, who pulled me over in front of the restaurant, once I'd finished causing the traffic blockage, and found a parking space. He was very kind considering the violation, and after I'd told him the whole story about it being my first trip in a large truck, how hungry I was, and no, I didn't realize it was illegal to make a U-turn across two yellow lines on a state road; he let me off with a warning and the strong suggestion to get out of town as soon as I'd finished eating. The worst of it however, was once I went into the restaurant, packed with families (and just my luck, a bunch of truckers), all having dinner on a Friday night, and all of whom had witnessed through the broad plate glass windows of the establishment the U-turn, the traffic stoppage, the cop with lights flashing, the dressing-down by same, and all now staring at the unkempt and hungry hangdog teenager walking in the door. Luckily, there was a seat at the counter, so I only had to face the waitress, but the hum of conversations in the whole restaurant was only resumed finally after a series of chuckles, snorts, and few muffled laughs. I ate quickly and quietly and, when I got back to the truck, took the cop's advice to heart.

Stopping at a truck stop before crossing into Georgia, I slept on the long front seat just as George had suggested, and pocketed the hotel room cash. In the morning I finished up the drive and got to the Thomasville nursery by 10 o'clock. I soon met the two owners, who were surprised at how fast I'd made the trip, and we threw up the sliding back door of the truck. It wasn't quite fully loaded, and there were stacks of open flower pots lying about, with boxes of smaller ones stacked in the back. One of the owners climbed in and picked up one of the flower pots and crushed it in his hand. It crumbled like a cookie. He fuddled around and got one from another part of the stack, squeezed it, and the pieces fell from between his fingers. Then he picked a box at random, cut it open and pulled out one of the smaller green styrene pots. Crushed it too. "We're not accepting these," he said. "What do you mean?" I countered, even though it was obvious what the problem was. "We're not taking these," he said, "take them back." Well, this threw me for a loop; what was I supposed to do? I told them I needed to call the office. Could I use their phone? No problem, they said, but nothing was going to change their minds. I called Better Plastics, which I knew was open on Saturdays, and explained my predicament to the floor manager, who told me I needed to talk to the Sales Representative, and he gave me his home phone number. I called the house, and the guy's wife answered. He was out at the golf course. He'd just left, and he'd be gone all day. No, there was no way to get in touch with him. Well shit, I thought, this is just great. What could I do? I thought about it a minute, and decided that as a representative of a business that had inadvertently sent an inferior product, I should just take the high road, so I apologized for the crummy (and crumbly) flower pots and told them someone would get back to them to make it right on Monday. They seemed to be happy with that, shook my hand, and we closed up the truck. I headed back south, this time taking my time, since I had almost two days, the rest of Saturday, and most of Sunday, to get back. I got back Sunday afternoon, backed the truck into the loading dock, got in my car and went home.

The next morning when I got in and punched my timecard, George and the floor manager were standing in front of the open back door of the truck. "You didn't make the delivery?" "Well, I made the delivery," I said, "they just didn't accept it." Then I took one of the flower pots and showed them how the thing fell apart when it was squeezed, even with the smallest pressure. They looked at each other long and hard, then they looked at me, shook their heads, and the floor manager walked off. George took my arm and led me aside, telling me "This ain't good, son. There's going to be trouble." "Well, shit" I said, "they sent me up there with a load of crap! What was I supposed to do?" Then the floor manager showed up and told me the Sales Rep was coming in soon and wanted to see me when he got there. I sweated for about an hour, and fifteen minutes after he arrived and went upstairs, he called me in. On the way I picked up one of the styrene flower pots. I'd never been up the stairs before, and cutting through the machine shop the guys all gave me a sad kind of look, but I went up and found that it went straight into his office, no outer anteroom or secretary or anything. The Sales Rep was a big man, white shirt and red tie, and he looked up and did not invite me to sit down. He started yelling immediately, "Goddammit, Brewer, why didn't you make that delivery!? Jesus Christ! We gave you money, and trusted you with that truck, and you just bring it back full?! You cost us 900 bucks! What the fuck's the matter with you?" I admit that I'd been scared, and I was really afraid that I was going to be fired for sure, but at that last one, like, What's the matter with ME? I got pissed and just pulled out the flower pot and crushed it in my hand, fragments falling all over his desk and the floor. "They wouldn't accept them," I said. He looked at the broken pieces falling out of my hand, and it was then I realized he knew this was a shitty load of pots all along. They just wanted to dump them on some hick nurserymen in Georgia, and figured they'd use me to do it. His voice mellowed and he said, "Why didn't you call me?" I told him about calling the factory, getting his home phone, and talking to his wife, who told me he'd be gone all day and there was no way to get in touch with him. Then I tried to turn the tables on him and asked, "Did you go play golf on Saturday all day?" He ignored me and said calmly, "We might have had them delivered somewhere else." "Well, I'm sorry," I said, and I reached into my pocket and pulled out the $35 I'd pocketed for not staying in the hotel. "Here's the hotel money. I didn't use it. I slept in the truck." I dropped it on his desk and walked out. Then I went back downstairs, through the machine shop, and through the factory, and went back to working with George, mixing and dyeing the plastic granules. Somebody else unloaded the truck and later I saw some of the women putting a box at a time into the grinder that chopped up the factory seconds and imperfections, with the resulting ground-up plastic fluff to be gradually shuffled into the raw mixed barrels, dyed and then re-cast. I wasn't fired, and no one spoke about the incident again, but I also never got to drive an out-of-town delivery for them again either.

63

Virginia and My First Car(s)

That summer of 1968, once I'd turned sixteen, Mom and Dad were pretty good about letting me take the family car, the white convertible Ford Galaxie 500 mentioned before. This was because I'd been driving since I was fourteen with Mom at my side, and she knew I was a very good driver, having learned from her. Dad was not so keen on this, since he had just started driving himself, so we had bought another car, a small green Mustang, generally recognized to be Mom's car until he started taking it to work, and unless there was some pressing errand, I was pretty much free to use the Galaxie. So this was great for dating Virginia. Since we had started by making out in the back seat of a car, it just seemed natural to keep on doing it, and this thing had plenty of room to sprawl out in the back. We might go out for pizza or a movie for a date, but there were always still a couple of hours to kill before we had to go home, and I would pick these out of the way parking places, and we would crawl into the back seat and just make out for hours. One of our favorite getaways was along the golf course at Dubsdread, near Bishop Moore, since I knew the lay of the land there, and it was adjacent to a decent neighborhood, not to mention the moon shining over the fairways. One time though, I drove up on the other side and behind "the girls' school" so we could get close to the lake, parked the car, and we got a blanket out and, instead of crawling into the back seat, we went down and lay by the lake. Damn if some nosy neighbor didn't notice the parked car and called the convent, which was between the girls school and the gymnasium, a couple of hundred yards away. As we lay ever so still, we could see the shadow outline of the principal, a strict old penguin, saunter across the school grounds, go to the office, and goddammit, flip on the hall lights. We didn't move and she walked up and down the halls, probably looking for vandals, or thieves, or what have you. She walked down the sidewalk toward the lake, and we were on a small incline just below the sidewalk, so we held our breath, and I swear, she stopped and looked out at the lake right over the top of us, close enough I could smell her. Eventually, she gave up, turned off the lights and went back to the convent. Had she caught us, it would have been a serious breach of school policy and the parents would have been on their way within the hour, pregnancies being a particularly popular scourge at the school at the time. For the most part for us though, it was innocent canoodling, and for the first year I never got past second base, which was okay, if frustrating (for me), and I have to admit, Virginia was very cool about where to draw the lines, which were generally below the thighs and above the navel, in the front. But as long as we were happy together otherwise, and she was my girl, it was no big deal to me. I'd take care of the rest of the business on my own time.

Then one night, we were heading home from being out on a date, and we had maybe an hour or so before we HAD to be home, so I got the bright idea to pull into a construction area where they were building a new subdivision across from the one where Virginia lived. This way it was close by, and we could make out right to the last minute. As I pulled down the unfinished dirt road between half-built houses, I realized I was getting into some pretty soft sand. Shit, I thought, I better turn around before I get stuck. And sure enough, in the act of turning around, I got the damn car stuck right up to the chassis, and sideways across the road. No fucking way was it coming out without a tow truck. Luckily, there was a gas station just up the road, maybe a half-mile. We still had some maneuvering time, it must have been around 10 p.m., so Virginia and I walked up to the gas station. (As an historical note, most, if not all, gas stations in those days were full-service, with tools on the wall, a mechanic or two, a lift for the car, the works, and they might be open until midnight, or in a few cases, 24 hours.) When we got up there I talked to the mechanic and luckily, they had a tow truck. I told him it was just right up the road, and asked if he could help us out. The greasy bastard just kept staring at Virginia while I was talking to him, licking his lips and pulling on a cigarette. "Fifty bucks," he said. "Fifty bucks!" I moaned, "I don't have fifty bucks, all I have is ten." "Sorry," he said. "Wait a minute… I have this," and I took off my class ring, which the school had made us buy in our sophomore year, and because I had bought mine from an outside jeweler, and not the school-sponsored purveyor of class rings, and it was white gold, it was easily worth over a hundred dollars. "Will you hold this until I can get you the fifty bucks tomorrow?" He looked it over, glanced up and down at Virginia again, and said, "Let's go… get in the truck." We piled in, and as soon as he started shifting gears, Virginia scooted over against me because his hand was a little loose on the shift knob, and he kept glancing up against her leg. When we got to the car, he looked it over, and said "no problem," then scrunched down in the sand under the front of the car and started to hook up a winch line from underneath. Then he got up, flipped on the winch, and the wound-metal wire slowly tightened. And it tightened. The car gave a little sideways nudge, and then stopped. The tow truck started digging backward into the sand. And the wire started to groan. The tow truck dug in some more towards the car, and the mechanic stopped the winch. Then he eased up on the line, and went back down in the sand in front of the car. I figured he had to adjust the tow cable, to get a better grip, or hook it up differently. But he just unhooked the wire, went back to the tow truck, and reeled it in, hooking the end to an eyebolt on the back of the truck. "What are you doing?" I said. Without a word, he climbed back into the tow truck and started to pull away. "Hey!" I yelled, and started running after him, "What about my ring?" In the shadow of his headlights pulling away, I saw his arm come out the window, and luckily, I saw a small black orb fly out of his hand into a pile of sand along the roadside. And he drove off, leaving us in the dark. It took me a minute or two to find the ring and dig it out of the sand, but now we were no better off than we had been an hour ago. I knew I was going to have to face the music on this one. So I told Virginia that I'd walk her home, and when we got there I'd need to use the phone. Her house was another half-mile walk in a different direction, and when we got there it was almost midnight.

I called Dad and gave him the slightest of details and directions to the car. He said he'd get a wrecker and meet me there in a half hour. So I said goodnight to Virginia and hoofed it on back to the car. When Dad got there, and we were waiting for the second tow truck, he just looked at the car, buried to the bottom of the door, and said "How did this happen?" "Well, I took a wrong turn and when I felt it get sandy I tried to turn around." He looked around at the dark sandy street, and the half-built houses, not a block away from a regular well-paved road, and he knew Virginia lived just a half-mile away. "Took a wrong turn, eh?" Then he said "Open up the trunk." "What!? What for?" I stammered. "Well, maybe we can jack it up and put something under the tires" he said. I popped the trunk and there was the sandy blanket I kept there when Virginia and I would go out. The jig was up. He just looked at the blanket and closed the trunk. The wrecker came, and it was a big one and easily pulled the car out. I followed Dad home, where Mom was waiting up, and he just gave me the proverbial "Go to bed, we'll talk about this in the morning." And in the morning he informed me that I needed to buy my own car, because the Galaxie wasn't going to be so convenient any more. Well, after working at Shoe Fair, and now, Better Plastics, I had put a little money away, so I was overjoyed, as Dad had generally resisted this until now. Obviously Mom had gotten to him. In the paper I found an old 1963 Renault Dauphine for sale for $450. The owner even offered to bring it over When I saw it I fell I in love with it right away, light blue, leather seats, big trunk. The only weird thing about it was that it had a push-button gear shift on the left hand side of the steering wheel. Yeah, push buttons! So you pushed a button for each gear, and there was just the slightest delay before it kicked in. But it was a great little car. I'd had the car maybe four months when Virginia and I decided we'd take up going to church on Sunday, and we had my brother Paul in the car, too. A light drizzle had come up, and going down Orange Avenue, when I tried to stop in traffic, the damn thing, light as it was, slid a half-block into a stopped car. It was just a dented fender, but between the push-button gearshift, and how small and fragile the car now seemed to be, I decided to go for something bigger.

65

Besides, the back seat wasn't big enough to stretch out in. I put an ad in the paper and within two days sold it for $450, just what I paid for it, bent-up fender and all.

Old Blue

The next car was also from the paper, and Mom and I drove up to Winter Park to look at it. It was a light blue 1966 Ford Fairlane station wagon, with a standard shift on the steering column, commonly referred to as three-on-the-tree. A standard shift, especially the three-on-the-tree, was no problem for me, as I had learned to drive my buddy Frank Francisco's Valiant, which had the same setup, as well as the truck at Better Plastics. The guy wanted $800 for the car, I offered $700, and we settled at 750. Mom wrote him a check and I agreed to pay her back out of my savings. We went home, leaving the car there, because Dad wasn't going to let me drive it until I got insurance (which, for some reason, had gone up as a result of the fender-bender with the Renault), and the guy needed a day to get the title ready for transfer. Another curious thing was, when we got home and told him the name of the guy we bought it from, Dad said, "that name sounds familiar." The next day when he came home from work, Dad was talking with Mom when I walked into the kitchen and they both shut up immediately. "What's the matter?" I asked. Well, Dad was a pretty high-level executive at Martin Marietta back then, but at the time they were experiencing some serious layoffs. Luckily for our family, Dad was one of the guys who made those decisions, and not necessarily one of the guys on the receiving end. Dad had recognized the name of the guy I had bought the car from, who happened to work at Martin, but Dad had learned that apparently, he wasn't going to be working there much longer. The check for the car hadn't even cleared yet, but Dad swore us both to secrecy, as this was top confidential employment stuff, and he said he was sorry, but there was nothing he could do about it. We went back a couple of days later, after the check cleared and the insurance had kicked in, and it was very difficult to sign the title transfer, shake hands, get the keys, and smile at the guy, who was extremely nice, yet was going to be out of a job in a week or so. When we got home, Dad expressed some concern when he saw that I had gotten a standard shift, which meant he wouldn't be able to drive the car, even if he wanted to, or needed to, since he was just learning to drive himself, and an automatic was absolutely essential for him. I offered to teach Dad, but he didn't think much of the offer, and testily declined. Tell you one thing though, when you put that back seat down, there was puh-lenty of room back there. Probably the best car I ever had. Certainly the most fun.

Walgreen's Summit Meeting

Virginia and I went on to enjoy each other's company, and by junior year we were a solid item. We were fooling around more seriously now, and experimenting while practicing our own physical education. For the most part however, it all came down to tribadism, simply rubbing up against each other to get off, you know, like lesbians do. With my new car, I started taking her to school in the morning, and had my brother in the car as well. Soon it became apparent that her folks were usually gone by 7:15 to get to their respective jobs, and we didn't have to be to school until 8:30. Allowing fifteen minutes to get to her house, and fifteen minutes to get to school, that left roughly 30-45 minutes we could fool around in the morning, before we had to go. Mom and Dad were really surprised at how fast I'd get up and out in the morning, dragging my little brother with me. I soon found out though that I couldn't just leave him in the car while I was helping Virginia "get dressed and ready for school." He was 14 now, and had gotten his learner's permit, so I began to show him how to drive my stick shift station wagon. When I'd get to Virginia's I just let him have the keys and told him to "go practice"; which he did with a vengeance, the car lurching, and gears grinding all the way down the street. Soon though, he bought a motorcycle, a little Suzuki 50cc and then he was independent. In the afternoons, when I didn't have soccer practice, we got to her house by 3:30 and running repeats of the *Ben Casey, M.D.* television show started at 4. We'd lay on the floor to watch them, but I don't think we ever saw a single one in its entirety. Her Mom, who was very nice, blonde and long-legged, would get home about 5, smile at our obvious playing around, and then I would generally beat a hasty retreat. I'm sure Virginia kept her generally apprised of our progress on the sexual scale, and as long as we didn't cross into any dangerous territory, I think both her and her Dad were very tolerant. Not like my own Mom and Dad. And this probably had its origins in the generations, if not the geography. My own parents were children of the Depression, teens of World War II, and in their twenties when they married, all in industrial Detroit under rigid Catholic strictures. Virginia's parents were teenagers when they met and married, growing up here in the South, where Catholicism had a much looser bondage on the spirit of the young. And they were a young couple, vibrant, expressive, still having fun, maybe seven or eight years younger than my folks. One day I came home late one afternoon, and when I walked into the living room, Dad was sitting in one of the large comfortable chairs, still in his suit from work, which was in itself unusual, with his tie loosened, but just sitting there, staring ahead. He was upset about something, and not just upset, but mad. Normally, he would have changed out of his suit right away, as soon as he got home from work. When I said hi, he just grunted and shot me a stare that made me know I was the object of his wrath, although for the life of me I hadn't done a thing I could think of to warrant it. Mom came out of their bedroom down the hall in a house dress. Again, this was odd. Mom always wore slacks, or shorts, or even a bathing suit, unless it was all-the-way formal for church or a funeral. They both looked at me, and Mom said, "Stay here, we're going out, we'll be back later." Okay (?!). After they left, the phone rang. It was Virginia. "Your Mom and Dad are going to meet my Mom and Dad up at the Walgreen's," she said, "your Mom found a note in your pants pocket while doing laundry about us going to confession." Oh shit, I thought. This isn't good. "How did you find out about this," I said. "Your Mom called my Mom. I've already talked to my folks about it. I think it'll be okay," then she hung up. Shit, shit, shit... no, I didn't think it would be okay, not the way they were looking at me when they left. And I still wasn't sure about what I'd written or why. I sweated for an hour before they came home, and when they did I had to play dumb until they finally sat me down and told me what (they thought) had happened. Then I had to pretend to get mad (but not too mad), as well as be thankful (but not too thankful). Here's what actually happened.

As Virginia and I had gotten more intimate, we also became more confident, in the sense of confidential, as opposed to brave. It was obvious we were approaching some sort of high-water mark in our relationship, if you get my drift. She finally let it be known that she had already crossed that Rubicon with the infamous prior boyfriend, Jack Duval., and said that it hadn't been that pleasant an undertaking at the time, much of it having occurred under pressure, if not duress. I was furious; I wanted to kill the bastard. No, she told me, because, although it may have been pressured, there was at the same time that, you know, overriding curiosity, so she was not entirely innocent. And she did feel bad about it, but mostly for my sake. Well, I was calmed considerably by her honest appraisal of the situation. Thinking on it later, during some class, I penned a note to her not to worry, and that, if she really felt bad about it, just clear it up by way of the convenient act of confession, and we would no longer speak of it. After reading the note, she just handed it back to me, with a look that made me feel like a stupid and foolish juvenile, but then I stupidly and foolishly put it back in my pocket, there for Mom to find while prepping the family laundry. In her eyes, this was the smoking gun that Virginia and I had crossed the divide, and she let Dad know probably before he had gotten home from work. By then she had also called Virginia's Mom and set up the meeting at Walgreen's. Luckily, however, Virginia's Mom had simply sat her down as soon as she had gotten home from school, and wanted to know what this was all about. Virginia handled it majestically and simply said that she had let the bounder,

Jack D., fondle her breasts at some point while they were dating, and she had told this to me, and she felt bad about it. Simple. I, however, had written that silly little note, and now, things had gotten blown out of proportion. And this was the message that Virginia's Mom (and Dad) carried to the meeting with my folks at Walgreen's restaurant. There was supposedly some communication as to whether we should be allowed to see each other anymore, but by this time we were so tight they all knew this was an impossible request, so they decided to caution us strongly about seeing each other in our respective houses ALONE. When Mom and Dad came back from Walgreen's, that was the gist of the summit meeting delivered to me, and why I had to pretend to be mad, but not too mad (for invading my privacy and the reading of the note), and to be thankful (which I was, because we could still see each other relatively unbridled), but not too thankful ('cause now they were all watching us). Once things calmed down, and by that I mean once Dad calmed down, because he really did like Virginia and knew she was at heart a great girl, he took me aside and gave me some advice: "Don't ever put anything down in writing that may come back to haunt you." I've done what I can through the years to follow that advice, but have not always been successful, as this testament may prove to be the pudding thereof. And of course, back to the point, what they were all afraid of was an unexpected grandchild, which up until then would have been an improbability anyway (on my part).

5. The Adventures Begin (1969 – 1972)

I Give You the Boy…

Then the day arrived. Strange, we'd been playing around more and more until it really was becoming unbearable for both of us. I remember a swimming date at her house one night. It was a full moon; her parents were out; her grandmother (whom everyone considered a bit daffy, if not demented, and this was long before "dementia" was popular) was the sole adult at the house. And SHE was waiting for her boyfriend, Frank, to show up since the Mom and Dad were out for the evening. Frank was an odd egg. Skinny old geezer, you'd see him downtown walking the streets aimlessly—but he always wore a suit and tie, if loosened, and of all things a hat…. a fedora. He smelled bad, and had bad teeth, and I mean really bad (obviously from neglect). But he was hot for Grandma, and she took to it like rolling off a log. One time I was asked to help "fix the bed" after one of their trysts—they had knocked the mattress right off the underlying supports. So Virginia and I were swimming in their new pool, it was dark, and of course, we were kissing, hugging, and playing around, when she got it into her head for us to go inside, into her parents' bedroom, which opened onto the patio, and then into their small bathroom. I admit I was scared. Jesus, if the parents came home there'd be no escape, and her old man was still a young and muscular ex-Marine. She lay a towel down on the floor, and we both quickly discarded our wet bathing suits. She pulled out some K-Y jelly, and obviously knew what it was for, and we took our luscious time to bring each other off manually. But technically, after drying off and getting dressed, I was still a sixteen-year-old virgin (Y'know, it still doesn't seem like the right word for a young man. Girls, sure, but for guys I'm thinking something along the Prince Valiant or Sir Perceval-type of innocence. It'll come to me. Maybe something like describing a virgin forest: "up to this time unused, untrod, unworked, undiscovered, etc.").

Give Me Back the Man

We'd just gotten out of school for the summer, finishing our junior year. My birthday was June 8, so now I was seventeen and all was good. We were in love. Then, one Saturday morning, it must have been 9:30 or 10 a.m., she called me and said, "Get over here right away!" No explanation; none needed. When she said come over I went. I recall I threw on a pair of long pants and, wouldn't you know, they were a pair of gold-colored checkered golf pants, really goofy-looking. When I got there, she didn't waste a minute. Her parents had gone out grocery shopping; her little sister was watching TV. Grandma was still in bed. She pulled me into her Dad's recreation room, where he had a really nice professional-size billiard table. She put a towel down, lay me down on the towel, underneath the billiard table, unzipped the goofy golf pants, pulled me out, and straddled me. It was all over in about a full minute. I zipped back up, gave her a kiss, and she told me I'd better go, just in case. Apparently she had figured the timing out, because there was just a single small drop of blood next to the zipper. I got in my car, and as I started to pull out of her subdivision and out onto the main road, I looked in the rearview mirror and realized I was not the same guy I'd been fifteen minutes earlier, and I never would be again. So, when it comes up, I can honestly say that I lost my virginity underneath a pool table. I usually leave it at that, so that whoever is asking can imagine the worst: how I got there, what were the circumstances, was this in a bar, who was the woman, was it a woman, etc. In fact, it was the best way it could have happened and I was very lucky, having heard some of the more unseemly initiatory horror stories of many of my acquaintances over the decades.

Virginia and I lasted another two years. During my junior year I had played another season of soccer, but hardly ever showed up for practice, just the games, much to the frustration of not only the Irish priest coaches, but my fellow teammates as well. But we were pretty good, and I recall we had a number of injuries, which I was lucky enough to avoid. We had a great soccer team, but by this time, other schools started getting their acts together, and we placed only second or third. The reason I didn't go to practice was so that Virginia and I could spend that hour or two after school and before her parents came home to go on our voyages of exploration. She and I put that Falcon station wagon to good use going to the beach, double-dating, etc. Often we'd go to the drive-in, and I would pull the car in with the rear facing the screen. Then we could throw down blankets and watch the movie out the lowered back hatch. Better Plastics was steady enough and once I'd worked that summer of '69, I was pretty flush. I guess I got a little too big for my britches when Father Granahan took me aside at the beginning of my senior year and laid down the law. "Look, Brewer, you're gonna have to make up your mind. It's either you'll be playing football [soccer] and go to practice or you're gonna take up with that girl. You're gonna have to make a choice. What's it gonna be?" I don't think ten full seconds passed before I said "So long, Fadda." What's a young man going to say? But this may have been the beginning of the end. We were both working at Better Plastics on the weekends now, and without soccer practice or soccer games, maybe we were seeing too much of each other. So I'd go off drinking with my buds on Fridays (which she disapproved of highly) and end up showing up with a hangover at the factory on Saturday mornings. At one point in our senior year, she wanted to "take a break" and I found out that she was seeing my old arch-enemy Duval, who had joined the soccer team (as my replacement?)! I went into a blue funk and started drinking more. Luckily, she quickly realized what a narcissist he was and why she had broken up with him the first time. We were back together in plenty of time for the prom.

Lake Lawsona

Having graduated from high school and earning steady good money at the plastics factory, and with my eighteenth birthday approaching, it was time to leave the nest, or so I thought. Looking around for an apartment, I came upon a basement unit that was perfect, if a bit rundown. On the backside of an old Orlando house, it opened onto Lake Lawsona, one of the many downtown lakes surrounded by brick-lined streets with large reaching live oaks. It was going to take a lot of cleaning to get it livable, since it hadn't been occupied in a while, but the landlady was very nice and supportive, glad to have someone move in and make the place habitable again. It had a low ceiling, maybe 6 foot, which was fine for me, but later gave some of our taller pals a bit of a neck twist. Since there were two bedrooms, I figured I'd share the place and save on the rent, so I called up my friend Ed, who also had no problem with low ceilings, and asked him if he wanted to go in on it with me. I also had an ulterior motive of course. Ed and I both had the steady girlfriends, and we knew how it was always a challenge to find a place to get away alone together, so this was going to solve all that. Ed said sure, he'd go in on it, but he probably wouldn't be living there, just using the place when he could. Well, this was perfect! I was going to get a place of my own with help on half the rent. I made arrangements with the landlady to start cleaning the place that weekend and come by on Monday to give her the deposit.

Ed and I cleaned the place over the weekend, and Monday was my birthday. Now turning eighteen, I planned on telling Mom and Dad that I was moving out, leaving home, that is, after we had cake and ice cream when Dad came home from work that evening. On Monday, I had to work all day down at the plastics factory in Kissimmee, then meet the landlady, give her the deposit, get home for the ice cream and cake, and then work myself up to tell Mom and Dad. That was the plan. So, on the way home from work, I stopped at the bank, drove straight to the landlady's, gave her the deposit, and headed for home, since Dad would be home any minute. When I got there, Dad was already home. Walking into the kitchen, there was the cake with the candles as yet unlit, and sitting around the table were Mom, Dad, and my brother, all staring at me, scowling. "What's the matter?" I said. "Why don't *You* tell Us" said Dad blankly. "What are you talking about?" I asked. "Your landlady called," said Mom. Oh shit, busted before I could even start warming up anybody up to the idea. Damn, I hadn't left the woman more than fifteen minutes earlier. "What did she want?" "She said you gave her five dollars too much on your deposit," Mom said, "When were you going to tell us that you were moving out?" I hemmed and hawed, stammering out a half-assed rationale. The fact was, I'd been completely blindsided, and rather than being able to sit down and ease into it, now I appeared to be nothing but a sneaky self-centered snot. "Happy goddamn birthday" said Dad as he got up from the table and walked away. Mom tried to explain how ungrateful it made me appear, wanting to get out of the house the day I turned eighteen, after all they'd done for me. Even my fifteen-year-old brother was upset that I hadn't taken him into my confidence about my new place. Suffice it to say, the candles stayed unlit.

But families will heal their rifts eventually, and I even got a solid nod from Mom and Dad when I eventually showed them the place and they saw how hard I'd worked to clean it up. They still weren't happy about it, but they were also glad it wasn't worse than they had imagined. And it really was a nice location, opening onto the lake like it did. So Ed and I began to enjoy our new-found freedom. One of his first additions to the apartment was a large carboy of grape juice with a balloon on top as his experimental foray into winemaking. Now, later we would all become very proficient at the art of fermentation, and we'd make wines and beers galore over the years, but this was strictly a first-time effort, with canned grape juice, baker's yeast, and that infernal balloon, which would inflate, and deflate, then inflate again (as temperatures rose and fell), but Ed wouldn't let us drink it until the balloon eventually gave up the ghost and went limp. We had a few friends over, with their girls, and we siphoned out a couple of gallons, and before we knew it, we had the first of one of our many housewarming parties. In the morning bodies in various forms of undress were found on and about our living room couch. Only years later was it revealed to me that apparently more than one cherry (both pit and stem, respectively) had been de-natured on that now-anonymous and probably Good-willed piece of furniture. We never locked the doors. Back in Orlando in those days it would have been a silly piece of business. (I suppose it's still a silly piece of business, as probably anywhere across America, if someone wants to get in your house, a door lock is the least of their concerns.) So the place became a hangout of sorts, and more than once I had to throw people out when I came home from work and just wanted to relax.

The Door to Deception

One night I was doing just that, relaxing alone, reading, when a friend pulled up. This was Dick Shanahan, a great guy who also happened to be the President of our senior class at graduation. He will go down in history as the fella who had the audacity, when handed his high-school diploma, in full regalia at the local co-cathedral, to reach up and pinch the bishop's cheek after shaking hands when he received it. To this day I can still see the shock and utter disbelief on the bishop's face (not to mention the stunning effect on the congregation), but Dick jauntily walked off the stage after a quick wave to everybody before anyone could recover their bearings. Dick and I were good pals, and on occasion we had shared more than a drink or two, him being a good Irishman, but we really hadn't hung out a whole lot together over the years. He was more of a serious academic than I was, and he had that class president stuff to deal with. But now my place had become a house of refuge for those wanting to get away for the evening, and since I was bored I was glad to see him. He wanted to know, would I like to smoke some pot? He held out a little tin of dental powder residue, with what looked like some grass clippings and a couple of rolling papers inside. Apparently he'd gotten it all from his older brother. Well, I'd heard of this stuff, read about it, and knew that some of my friends had tried it, but the reports I'd gotten did not signify that it was any kind of substitute for a stiff drink. So I said sure. We went to the bedroom at the back of the house. As he rolled one up, I asked why the dental powder tin? To keep the police dogs from sniffing it out. Oh, really?! He lit it up and we each took a couple of puffs, sat back, took a few more, stared at the ceiling, took a few more and then finished it. We sat there for a while, and finally he said, "What do you think?" "Well, Dick, I got to be honest, I don't feel a thing." "That sometimes happens the first time for some people," he said quietly. I was still waiting for Something to occur, after all the hubbub that had been spouted about this stuff. Maybe it wasn't the real stuff; maybe it had gone bad; maybe the dental powder had affected it somehow… Anyway, he said he had to leave, he had just needed somewhere to go to smoke. "Hey, here, you want the rest of it? Go ahead and keep it, I've got more." Why thanks, as the little dental powder tin of pot headed my way, I caught it easily.

Walked him out the front door to his car. It must have been around 9 or 10, and the apartment floodlight for the parking area was shining out onto the lake, maybe ten or twenty yards out. There was some noise and splashing going on out there. I looked out and there were these three or four young kids, and I mean really young, like two or three years old, and they were naked and splashing around in the shallows and laughing. I got a little upset, since this looked very, very dangerous, especially at this time of night, with no one watching them (for God's sake! There might even be a gator out there!). "Hey!" I yelled, "What're those kids doing out there?!" Dick stopped with the car door open and looked at me across the top of his car, "What kids?" "Those kids!" I yelled at him, and I pointed back towards them. Dick looked at me, smiled, and said, "Those aren't kids, they're ducks!" I looked back, and sure enough, there were three or four of those large white Peking ducks you always see in the lakes, and they were quacking, and splashing about (possibly mating!) under the light shining into the water. "Don't feel a thing, huh?" Dick laughed as he got into his car. I just stood staring at those ducks until he pulled out of the driveway. My first encounter with the dreaded Mary Jane, and she had got me good. Snuck up on me and turned a covey of ducks into some playful cherubic sex-ridden water sprites, and then changed them back. What a trickster.

Vaya con Dios, Virginia

That summer after graduation from high school Virginia and I enjoyed the freedom to relax at my apartment, but we were also working together almost every day down at Better Plastics in Kissimmee. She had become one of the ladies on the machines, and although she was probably the youngest, and certainly the best-looking, because we saw each other all day and then still tried going out at night, it began to put a strain on our relationship. Then, the Other Guy showed up. Just back from Vietnam, they hired this 24-year-old to help out as an auxiliary floor manager. So he got to spend a lot of time helping out the ladies, including Virginia. He was nice enough, but definitely had an eye out for her. He drove a Camaro, which was the hot car of the day, and also had a motorcycle, which was old even then, that he wanted to sell. When I heard the motorcycle was for sale, I told him I was interested. This set into motion a series of circumstances that I couldn't foresee and which in retrospect were inevitable, considering how both fate and karma work. Virginia had been showing a considerable interest in children. We'd had a couple of close calls ovulation-wise, which she seemed to take in stride while they scared the be-jeezus out of me. Although we'd talked about getting married, I said I wanted to wait until we were at least twenty-one, but that was now a good three years away. She even suggested that as a lark she'd stuff a pillow in the front of her dress, and we'd go visit the baby-room at the hospital (and we did it), whereas I was getting more and more used to stretching out on the old sofa in my bachelor apartment and enjoying some down and alone time. So the day came to get my motorcycle. It was downtown at the repair shop getting tuned up and ready to go. We all drove down to the shop together in the Camaro, with Virginia in the back. When we got there the Other Guy told me the title was at his house back in Kissimmee, so why don't I ride the bike and follow them back? Okay… Only now she's sitting up front with him in the Camaro, and I'm following, and it's a good hour drive down (got the picture?). When we got down there, we signed the papers, played a game of pool, and had a beer. Virginia and I left, and we rode the motorcycle back to Orlando and her house, her hands clasped from behind and around my engines. Within two weeks she wanted to break up. Within six weeks they were engaged. It became unbearable, and I couldn't stand to be around and seeing them at Better Plastics any more, and besides, the summer was running out and I was starting college at Florida Technological University (now the University of Central Florida) in the fall. So I quit Better Plastics, then couldn't afford the apartment on the lake any more, and moved back home. At least I had the motorcycle.

It was not good at school. Virginia was now going to FTU as well, so I'd see her almost every day on campus, and since we really didn't know anybody else, we'd sit and have lunch and talk between classes. She was still the flirt, but now she was engaged to the Other Guy. So I was still distracted by her; I could look at her, and smell her, laugh, joke, and even reminisce, without the freedom to touch her. And then there's a fairly remarkable thing about going to college: you don't have to go to class if you don't want to. This was amazing to me. I already had the books, so all I had to do was read them and show up to take the tests. But then I had other books too, like *The Hobbit*, and *The Lord of the Rings* trilogy. And I kept that little dental powder tin half-full too. Needless to say, the grades began to suffer. And it was my own damn fault. I chose a major in Zoology (what was I thinking?!), and that meant, besides the easy first-year prerequisites of Speech, History, etc., I had to take specific prerequisites for the major, like Organic Chemistry and Botany, of all things. So, now I wasn't showing up for Speech and History classes, and I was getting stoned for Organic Chemistry and Botany. But I sure as hell was keeping up with Bilbo and Frodo as we trod toward the Mountains of Mordor. The first quarter I got a "D" in Organic, which meant I had to take it (and Mom and Dad had to pay for it) again. The second quarter I took it, I got a "C-." The third quarter, well, I got a "B", but I was damned if I was going to take Organic Chemistry II (where the "II" means twice as hard), which was still required for the Science majors. Forget it. In the end, I killed a whole year literally stewing in my own juices over Virginia (the only girl I'd ever 'known'), following wizards and fighting orcs, riding my motorcycle, getting rippled on weekends, and smoking pot. A typical first year of college, I suppose. Bottom line, Virginia was a beautiful girl, a perfect steady girlfriend for three years, whom I'd watched turn into a beautiful woman. I just wasn't ready to settle down, physically, mentally, or emotionally. Hell, I was still a kid, and as far as I was concerned, I was just getting started. As the first year of college wound down, she and the Other Guy got ready to get married. That was it. I wasn't going to be seeing her again, probably ever. I sent a dozen red roses to the wedding and wished them the best of luck.

Jill

The only real good that came out of the wasted 1970-71 school year was when I went up to visit my good friend Ed in Gainesville that spring. He said if I came up he'd have a "surprise" for me. Turned out to be two surprises. I had decided to ride my motorcycle up, since this would be a nice day run, and when I got there and found his dorm room, he said that first we were going over to his girlfriend Ann's and her roommate's apartment for a little wine and dinner. Well, this sounded fine. When we got there, although I already knew Ann from high school, and she had been dating Ed most of the time I'd been with Virginia, I was pleasantly surprised to meet the roommate, Jill. Not hard on the eyes, she was a little taller than me and well-proportioned, a light brunette with a knowing smile, and though initially a little shy, after a couple of glasses of wine, and the conversation flowing smoothly back and forth, it was almost painfully apparent that this was one brilliant girl. Where I had been spending time reading *The*

Lord of the Rings, she was reading Nietzsche's *Thus Spake Zarathustra*. In school she was studying pre-med and had every intention of becoming a doctor. Later I was to learn that this wasn't necessarily *her* intention, but had been her mother's since she was just a little girl, and as such, she was fulfilling someone else's dreams and not necessarily her own (unless those dreams were to make her mother happy). We all had a nice little dinner, and it became obvious that this had been a pre-arranged setup to get Jill and I together (probably due to my whining to Ed about the loss of Virginia). It worked. We could both well appreciate the intellectual banter that ensued, with input from Ed and Ann of course, and we made plans to stay in touch.

But it never worked out. Though we tried to see each other, even to the point of my driving down to meet her parents (and her giving me an impromptu haircut before they got home from work), we just could never move forward in tandem. She was an inveterate letter writer and she pummeled me with long treatises on poetry, philosophy, and her own dark mood swings. I liked her a lot, but probably respected her more, and was constantly urging her to let her hair down and relax, enjoy life a little. She thought there wasn't enough time. And she was right. Even after I brought home a later girlfriend (Lisa) and there was Jill, unexpectedly and awkwardly visiting the house and Mom, and we parted ways still pals, Mom and her continued to visit and write letters to each other for years. She eventually got a doctorate in Anthropology, became relatively well-known in the field, and ended up teaching at Appalachian State University, marrying one of the professors there. They didn't get along (for long), and after divorcing, she drove her car down the mountain one rainy evening to go to the store, slid off the edge and was killed. Though there was some question about her death, considering the mood swings and the recent divorce, she had left some tea warming on the stove and she was obviously out of catfood (empty bag), and being the letter writer she was she would surely have left a note, so we were all sure it was an accident. Tragic, because of all her brilliant potential.

Meeting Mescalito

The second surprise happened later the next day, Saturday, when Ed told me that he had been given a little dose of mescaline by one of his "artist" friends. Want to try it? Well, this was now entering a new level of psycho-exploration. I'd read a lot already about hallucinogens, but it still sounded a little scary. What the hell. I was with Ed, whom I could trust explicitly, and we were in a safe environment, the campus of the University of Florida, where we could walk everywhere and so wouldn't have to drive. And we'd already fulfilled our social obligations with the girls, so we had a free night out. "Let's do it!" We split the little blue capsule, washed it down with a little apple juice and sat in his dorm room, waiting for it to kick in. The sun was just going down. A half an hour later it was dark, nothing had happened, and we were getting hungry. The campus is surrounded by little burger joints, bistros, and bars, so we decided to head on out and get something to eat. We were cutting across the open grassy perimeter around the campus, when we bumped into some of Ed's art history friends. As we stood there, Ed talking to them, I had the first rush of "Whew! What was that?" Ed didn't seem to notice. He said bye to his friends and we continued our trek across the green space, which seemed to get longer and longer. Then we came across a bronze statue of some University benefactor or forgotten professor. Amazing. Astounding. Incredible. We circled it once or twice, and I could see Ed's eyes widen (the eyes of an artist, mind you). We plodded on. We crossed the street to one of the greasy-spoon burger joints, went in and sat down. We both ordered a burger, fries, and a coke. The place was full of students on a typical Saturday night, loud, boisterous, and laughing. When the coke came, I took one sip and bang! I was in another world. I started laughing at the absurdity of it all: the people, the food, the plastic seats, even the waitress (who was sweet, but was taking her job way too seriously, I thought). Ed just smiled, but I was getting hysterical, laughing uncontrollably, until tears rolled down my cheeks. Luckily the rest of the place was so loud that no one really noticed. The burgers came. I took one bite and put it down—there was no way I was going to be able to eat it now; I could actually see the ground-up cow in it. Even the little curly fries were what I could only describe as ridiculous. So I just sat there, laughing, giggling, and crying, until I could convince Ed to get out of there. The coca-cola however, was particularly delicious, bubbly, and nose-tickling.

Next door was a little bookstore that sold other knick-knacks, incense, and other stuff. Normally, I could kill an hour easy in a store like that, but again, it was just too overwhelming, and although Ed was still functioning relatively normally, looking over a few of the comics and statuary, I again begged him to leave. I had to get back to the grassy open areas. But crossing the street this time wasn't the simple operation it had been coming over. It was dark, and the headlights were moving way too fast. We had to cross at least four lanes and it looked impossible to me. Ed didn't have to hold my hand, but he did have to hold on to my shirt to get me across. In retrospect, I'd forgotten that these surroundings were all familiar to Ed, whereas I'd never been to any of these places before, and under the circumstances, I was at a particular disadvantage for maneuvering around. When we got across street into the grassy campus, we both lay down on our backs and just stared at the stars. When we finally got up, we stumbled upon a Frisbee, one of those glow-in-the-dark ones, and spent a solid hour putting it under lights to brighten it and then throwing it back and forth. Finally we wore ourselves down and sometime after midnight made our way back to his dorm where we fell into an exhausted repose. The next day, after a decent breakfast at the now-not-so-awesome burger joint, I said good-bye to Ed, Ann, and Jill, and headed south on my motorcycle, little leftover visions of mescaline madness making the road home hum in my head melodically.

Maine-lining

Meanwhile, as the spring quarter at FTU ended, a good friend of mine, Frank Francisco, asked me if I wanted to go up to Maine with him for the summer. His Uncle, Ardeen, helped build roads up there and they were always looking for a couple of strapping young men to help maneuver the large blocks of cut granite that they built the curbs out of. We'd make some decent money and get to see the country on the way. Perfect thing to take my mind off of Virginia. Again, it was the beginning of summer and my birthday was coming up, and even though Mom and Dad weren't too happy about the grades, they knew how broken up I'd been about Virginia, and they also knew this trip to Maine would be good for me. So, Frank and I both bought a couple of ten-speed bikes for some off-road riding, his was orange and mine yellow, and we hit the road in my '66 light-blue Ford Falcon station wagon, bikes strapped on top. We stopped briefly in New Jersey, just outside New York, and spent an evening with a pair of his cousins who owned a Graeco-Italian restaurant. I would never suggest that it was a mob place, but they could easily have filmed *Goodfellas* there without missing a beat. We got to South Portland on a weekend, and Ardeen (a big, barrel-chested mountain of a man, like a lumberjack), got us put up in a small one-room cabin three or four miles from Old Orchard Beach, a seaside tourist haven on the southeast coast of Maine. He told us to be ready to go to work on Monday, and let us know where to show up. Since we had a day or two, we jumped on our bikes to ride down and explore the ocean town. It was a quick ride on our new fast bikes, and very picturesque, if a bit grey. But for a couple of Florida boys, it wasn't really what we'd call a beach. Oh sure, it had the ocean, and waves, and salt breeze, but there wasn't a lick of sand. Just rocks. Big rocks, little rocks, round rocks, square rocks, various sizes of trapezoidal rocks, and lots of pea gravel. The water was dark grey, almost black. And even though this was now summer, the height of the vacation season, there couldn't have been two dozen people as far as the eye could see. We went down and put our feet in the water, and it was freezing, middle of June. That night we had to pull out blankets to sleep. We'd left 90-degree-plus weather in Florida, and now were shivering at night. Rocks and cold, and apparently it was always so cold they could only work four months out of the year. First impression, this was a strange place. And that was before we met the Canucks and the crazy ladies.

But by Monday we had warmed up when we were put on the tamping rods. To build the curbs on the tree-lined roads, they first dug a trench along the roadside. The trench was cleaned out with shovels, and then a front-end loader (which is what Frank's Uncle Ardeen worked) would bring in a several-ton slab of granite that had been smoothly cut across the top to form the curb edge. He would slowly lay that slab of cut rock into the trench, and then, under the direction of a keen-eyed foreman, a group of maybe six of us would go to work jockeying the slab around with these long, heavy steel rods with a blunt square of metal welded to the end, while at the same time tamping gravel in and around it to hold it in place. The foreman would be constantly checking to see if the slab was level and straight in-line with the last one and the string that showed where the next one coming down the line was going to go in. Meanwhile, we would furiously tamp and tamp and tamp, until he said enough, and by that time, the next slab was being brought down the street. Later, they would partially fill the trenches with more gravel and cement so that the slabs would stay put. On both the tamping and the shoveling crews, there were a contingent of French Canadians, or Quebecois. They were lean, muscular, with bad teeth but all had a certain *joie de vivre*, a "joy of life." They worked happily and had lots of fun with us Florida boys, while sipping their beers and wine at lunch, and rattling off to each other in that French-Canuck gibberish that even the old-timers who'd worked with them for years couldn't understand. And no woman in sight was safe, even if she only peeked out from behind her front room window curtains. "Whoo, whoo!" they would shout, "Don't you want me to come and fuck you!? I am very fine at fuckeeng, really I am!" Then they would laugh, blow kisses, wink, take off their shirts and flex their arms. When a boss came around they were back to work, seriously bent over their shovels, chattering away in their thick French patois. It was especially awful if a grown woman walked down the street, but they would raise such a hackle that any woman in her right mind turned a half-block away, and went around the block rather than pass even on the other side of the street. But because it was summer and school was out, there happened to be a gaggle of teenage girls who took a particular delight in teasing the workers, and although they started out hiding behind trees and running between houses, eventually they came right up and sat on the lawn as the workers tried to get the stones set while the boss was around. When he wasn't around the Cajun-Canucks hooted, and grabbed themselves by the crotch, flexed, and stuck their tongues out. The girls were told several times to stay away from the workmen, but eventually they would show back up, and a few of the braver ones even sat just out of reach during the lunch break, laying back and listening to the Frenchies testing out various Anglo-obscenities.

Dexey's Daytime Runners

Then one day Frank and I were put on a detail cleaning up driveways of excess sand and gravel. We'd not only have to remove whatever excess had been piled up inside the driveway itself and pile it up on the side of the street, but we had to actually shape the driveway so that they could later cover it with cement without too much extra modification. We would make it conform to the slope of the yard, build up the sides, leave a little gutter along the road edge, level it at the sidewalk, etc. It was detailed work, and it became apparent to the foreman that he couldn't trust the Canucks on their own, not in that neighborhood, and it took a little finesse that only a couple of smart college boys could handle. We'd knock out four or five driveways a day, which was just fine by the foreman. We were working on one of these driveways one day when out of the nearby house stepped a young lady with shoulder-length auburn hair, rather plain, but friendly, maybe twenty-three or four, a little older than ourselves. It was nearing lunch time, and

76

after a few opening questions, she asked us if we'd like to come in and have something to drink. Why, sure we would. She got us a couple of beers and put on Paul McCartney's second solo album *Ram*, which had just come out. I remember hearing "Uncle Albert/Admiral Halsey" for the first time, and all three of us talking about what a shame it was that the Beatles had broken up. Well, we had to get back to work before the foreman came looking for us. "Maybe these could help you out," she said, as she shook a couple of orange football-shaped pills out of a small envelope onto the kitchen counter. "What are these?" "Dexedrine, high-class speed, generally for middle-aged housewives who want to curb their appetite and lose weight," she said matter-of-factly. Turns out her name was Sharon and she was the only daughter of a doctor, and she'd been intercepting all the free samples the pharmaceutical companies were constantly sending him in the mail. She had the PDR (Physician's Desk Reference) and she was very knowledgeable in her own right. "How many should we take?" "One each ought to be plenty for the rest of the afternoon… why don't you come back at the end of the day and we can have a few drinks." Okay, see you then.

Too Hot

We knocked out ten driveways that day. When the foreman showed up, he had to tell us to stop working, and even he was surprised at how many we had done and told us we needed to slow down and pace ourselves. Back at Sharon's house, she let us in, and now she had a girlfriend with her, Susan, a very thin girl with short black hair. We started drinking cocktails, gin and tonic, and before long we were dancing and we'd quickly paired off. Frank had taken to Sharon, so Susan (who was nice enough) and I sat together. After just a few drinks and some initial making out, Sharon's Dad came home, so Frank and I made a quick departure. The next day an interesting thing happened. We were working away, back on the tamping, shoveling excess gravel, and moving granite slabs with cant hooks (wooden pikes with a large cantilevered hook on the end, usually used for rolling logs). It was only about 10 in the morning and Frank and I were just hitting our stride, aided and abetted by our little orange footballs. All of a sudden, the foreman comes down the road and tells everyone to pack it up for the day. "What's the problem?" we asked, and then noticed everyone sitting down, mopping their foreheads. "It's hit 90 degrees, too hot to work, pack it up!" Hell, Frank and I hadn't even noticed, and even if we had, it wouldn't have made any difference to us; 90 degrees in Florida in June/July would have been a pleasant workday. And it was a Friday; our first payday! We got our checks and hoofed over to Sharon's house. She grabbed a handful of pills, and called her girlfriend Susan. "Let's go to your place down by Old Orchard," she said, "and we've got to pick up Susan on the way." We hopped in the car, got our checks cashed, picked up Susan, a pizza, and a case of beer, and got to the cabin by two or three o'clock. After a beer or two, a couple of joints, and listening to some records (Melanie, Cat Stevens, James Taylor, and Carole King were all big back then), we asked them what they wanted to do. In the vernacular of the day, Sharon stated bluntly "We want to ball you," with Susan gleefully nodding alongside. Frank and I just grinned and led them off to our respective blanket-covered cots. And between that and a couple more beers, and getting up to change the records and/or smoke another joint, that's how we spent the rest of that day.

Hubba Hubby

The next morning it was time to move on, and since I was the designated driver, having the only car when…, oh, yeah, Frank and Sharon wanted to "sleep in," it being so cold and all. But Susan was in a hurry to go, so, okay, let's go. We had one more round at tilting, and then, we showered and I got her out into the car. "I gotta be home by 10 o'clock," she says. "Okay," I told her, not asking why, "we'll make it." I drove up to the house as she directed me, and there was a small group of people standing on the raised sidewalk along the street: an old lady, a couple of kids, and some tough-looking Hispanic or Italian guys, one with his arms folded. "Uh oh," she said. "What? What's the matter?" I asked. "That's my husband and his brothers." (!?!?!?!?) "Your husband! You never said you were married!" I was freaking out. We pulled up, and they were standing on a stoop along the street. "Good luck," I said as she got out, and as soon as the door closed, I pulled away quickly. All I saw were several pairs of trousered legs, and luckily, no one bent down to look into the car. But I could hear the noise start up as I pulled away, and looking into the rear-view mirror I saw the guy whose arms had been folded grab her by the upper arm and lead her into the house, the other guys following. Only the older woman watched my car as I wheeled down the road and turned the corner. Apparently this had occurred before. When I got back to the cabin, Frank and Sharon were up and about, so I had to ask "Goddamn, Sharon, why didn't someone say something about her being married?" "She doesn't like her husband," she said flatly. "Nonetheless…" I looked over at Frank, who's looking at Sharon, and he says to her "You're not married, are you?" She looked up and laughed, "No… not anymore."

Saint Blazes

Needless to say, I didn't see Susan any more, even keeping a watchful eye out the cabin window for some car full of guidos to show up and take the place apart. Even Frank got a little weary (and wary) of Sharon (she had too many pills and ate them like candy) and soon we had moved on down the neighborhood setting curbstones and cleaning driveways, and we weren't on the same street, so the attraction gradually wore off. One Friday Ardeen invited us out to a farm he and his wife owned so we could meet the family and enjoy a bit of real-life rural Maine hospitality. Well, this was one of the first home-cooked meals we'd eaten in weeks, other than our spaghetti, pizza, and macaroni and cheese that we'd cook up at the cabin, leaving dishes that the young housemaids dutifully cleaned up even though we told them not to—a couple of really underage and attractive girls, maybe 15 or so, that obviously had a crush on us, but which, thank God, we were smart enough to keep at arm's length. The next day we got to the farm and they were having a cookout, with a large outdoor spread of various side dishes, and desserts. I can still see Ardeen, as old and as big as he was, running across the fields in his overalls and hat, with his dogs howling behind him. The main course was brook trout, which someone had caught by the dozen, and grilled to a tasty sizzle, still tender and delicious. We dove right in, and they kept loading our plates as we emptied them. Now, I've eaten a lot of Florida fish, mostly saltwater, with a few fried catfish and mullet, and they all have decent size bones that you can easily feel with your tongue, and most of the time the ribs and smaller bones stick to the backbone anyway. But trout were a new experience for me. They were small, so you had to eat a lot of them to get full, and the bones were like tiny bristles, or coarse hairs that you could try to pick out, but hell, half the time they went down without you even noticing. But I got one stuck in my throat. It wasn't bad; I mean, it wasn't going to cut off my breathing or anything like that, but it was just annoying enough to be scary. First I tried not to let anyone notice. Then I coughed, and coughed again, hoping to loosen it. Finally, I was gobbling down big hunks of bread, washed down with beer, figuring that would do it for sure. Nope. It wasn't going up or down. I told Frank, who passed it on, and I got a couple of back slaps, but again, since it didn't seem life-threatening, I just treated it as a major annoyance and told everyone not to worry about it. But it scared me. Scared me enough to recall the once-a-year ritual where the nuns dragged us down to St. James to "get our throats blessed." Here, the priest would take a pair of candles, crossed with some red ribbon and place it athwart each of our necks while intoning the watchful power of God through the assistance of St. Blaise. This is the ancient tradition attributed to a third-century (and therefore, early) doctor/bishop who was martyred by the Romans with small red-hot clawed rakes used for combing wool. I guess they just scraped the meat off of him. Apparently, as a physician he was renowned for fixing throat problems, especially crap getting stuck in the gullet (which must have been a more common event in the days before processed food), and not just for people, but animals too. Even when he was being led off to his martyrdom, some woman came out crying in the street and begged him to clear an obstruction in her choking kid's throat, which he took care of wham-bam. But the cold-hearted and idolatrous Romans were not impressed, and mercilessly hot-combed him anyway (you'd think they would have choked, hung, or garroted him, wouldn't you?). So I prayed. "Please, Saint Blaise, if ever there were a time to get to work and do your thing, it was now, because this fucking fish bone is not moving, and if it does move, and moves the wrong way, I'll be so ashamed to have passed on in such a frivolous and senseless manner (not to mention the embarrassment it'll cause Mom and Dad and my brother), and especially at such a young age, before I have really tasted the many and varied joys of life, seeing as how I've only been with two women so far, and it'd really be nice to have kids someday." The damn thing stayed there all the rest of the day. We drove back to Old Orchard and the cabin and went to bed. In the morning, miraculously (or was it because I finally relaxed?), it was gone. Hopefully, this little recounting of the saint's wondrous ability will add to his further glory and get some other recalcitrant Catholic down to church on February 3rd to "get their throats blessed." *Deo gratia, Sancto Blas*, that's one I owe you.

Goodbye Girls?

The summer of '71 was ending in Maine and we made plans to head on home to Florida. A couple of buddies, Ed Quinby, Greg Toole, and Bruce Dacey called us and said they'd like to take a road trip, drive up and visit us, see the country, and we could follow each other home. They drove up in Greg's little Karmann Ghia, with poor Ed riding all the way in the tiny backseat. We were delighted to see them, especially because they brought a stash of pot, which we had run out of weeks before. While we were showing them around South Portland and Old Orchard Beach, where we worked, and told them how we had helped build the roads, we ran across the young neighborhood girls who had teased the Canucks. It being Saturday, there weren't any Frenchies around to hassle them and they were now very friendly and outgoing. They also took a shine to our new buddies from Florida and invited us to a party that evening at one of the girl's houses, kind of a going-away bash. Later, we planned our itinerary that would carry us through New Hampshire and the White Mountains, down to New Jersey and New York City, and then down Interstate 95 all the way back home. For now though, we got ready to go to the party. We stopped and got a case of beer, but when we got there, the girls had already broken into a couple of bottles of wine, music was playing, and they wanted to dance. They all looked to be about 16 or 17, and for us 18 and 19 year-olds, the age-ratio seemed ideal. The parents were away, and we had the run of the place. Surprisingly, although there was a lot of groping and kissing, and fondling, no one ended up in the sack, and I have to give the girls credit for that, because they were very aggressive about what they wanted and to what limits they were willing to go. This was probably from dealing with the Canucks who crossed over from school and needed strict handling, whereas we were good Catholic boys who only needed the touch of the spur and not the full-fledged horsewhip. The festivities continued to nearly dawn. In the morning, the place looked as if there had been a tragic train crash, bodies in various states of undress sprawled across the floor, couch, and chairs. I got the boys up and we bedraggled ourselves out the door, hopped in the old station wagon and made our way down to the cabin at Old Orchard. After cleaning ourselves up, and doing a half-assed job of putting the cabin in order, we hit the road and headed for New Hampshire, again with the bikes strapped across the rooftop. Two hours later, we were setting up camp in the White Mountains, smoking a doobie and cooking hot dogs over the open fire. Then, inexplicably, Greg told us that he was heading back to South Portland (!?). The girl he had sidled up with the previous evening apparently had made him an offer he couldn't refuse if he'd come back the next evening. Well, what's to be done? Ed offered to go with him and next thing we knew, they were gone, with promises to return the following day.

White Mountain Races

Bruce, Frank and I slept well that night, and the next day went exploring. We'd camped near an old hiking trail which twisted and curved down the mountainside, and after coming back to camp for breakfast and a joint, I decided that I'd give it a try on the bike. Cresting a small hillock near the campsite, it was all downhill from there, the trail weaved back and forth, getting steeper by degrees. I twisted and started squeezing the handbrakes, but since it was still morning and having cut through the dewy grass, the tire rims had gotten wet, the rubber brake pads wouldn't get a grip, and with the steepening decline I picked up speed despite squeezing the brakes as hard as I could. Going into freefall, I finally hit a rock and catapulted head over ass into the brush. I was lucky; other than a few scrapes and a couple of bruises, neither myself nor the bike were much the worse for wear. I had to walk it all the way back up however, because it was just too steep to ride. A half-hour later I made it back to the camp and relived the excitement of the ride with Bruce and Frank. And sure enough, Frank said he was going to try it now. Over the hillock he went, but he was back, panting and covered in weeds in only fifteen minutes. It was tougher than he thought, and more dangerous than I had described. Despite my protests, of course Bruce also had to give it a try. Frank said there was no way Bruce was going to use his bike, and so, reluctantly, with lots of warnings and threats, I let Bruce take my bike over the hill and down the trail. After an hour had passed, Frank and I started to get worried. So we did what anyone in our place would, we smoked another joint and waited. Another half an hour and we could hear Bruce coming over the hilltop. Huffing and puffing and limping, he was carrying my bike over his shoulder, the front wheel bent to hell. He was cut up pretty bad, but I gave him a rash of shit anyway for my poor bike. But he looked so pitiful I couldn't stay mad and we all ended up laughing at what was certainly nothing more than a case of infectious stupidity brought on by thick-and-stoney-headedness.

Joisey Tomatoes and the Big Apple

By the time Greg and Ed got back it was already dark, but at least they brought some beer. We traded adventures, and it appeared that ours turned out to be more exciting than theirs. [Note to self: the bird in the hand is always better than the promise of bush later.] We hit the sack, and in the morning, refreshed, we headed for New Jersey and Frank's cousins' restaurant/hotel, with plans to invade New York City *en masse*. We got to New Jersey by mid-afternoon, and the cousins were extremely hospitable, giving us both a hotel room and dinner. It wasn't going to be a totally free ride, though, and we asked what we could do to help around the premises. Well, it just so happened that the entire lot surrounding the parking lot was choked by tomato vines six to eight feet tall. Tomato seeds from discarded sauce residues (and I believe some overflow septic tank sludge) had taken root early in the summer and now they were in full maturity, with hundreds, if not thousands, of tomatoes, both hanging and deposited on the ground, which of course couldn't be used for food because of their dubious origins. They asked us if we would clear the surrounding lot of the tomato vines, and in return they would let us occupy the hotel room as a base of operations and give us meals until we left. The next morning, armed with some large kitchen knives, a couple of rakes and a machete, we attacked the killer tomato vines. By the end of the day, we'd made a sizable dent in clearing the lot, but we were a mess. Tomato vines are really not that easy to cut, as they get woody, and sometimes you have to end up just sawing through them. Especially these, as they had obviously gone wild; and although it was fun to squash them underfoot, and lob a few at each other throughout the day, the tomatoes were everything from hard green marbles to rancid, stinking, and worm-infested mush balls. (As an historical side note, when tomatoes, which are a New World fruit, not a vegetable, were taken back to Europe, they were considered not just inedible, but poisonous, for several generations, until some adventurous Spaniards started cooking them and then the Italians turned it into an art form. Probably because they are [closely] related to the deadly nightshade.) We made plans to finish the next day so we could go into New York City and carouse. The next morning we hit the tomato field with a vengeance, and by noon we had cleared the surrounding lot, and disposed of the vines and rotten tomatoes in a large dumpster in the corner. The cousins were happy with our work, so we cleaned up quickly and caught a bus into the City. As my first foray into New York City, I was disappointed on the ride in. The rundown factories and empty lots of northern New Jersey were depressing. But once we entered New York City itself, the busy-ness and grandeur of it all sank in. We were let off at the Port Authority Terminal, and we made our way into the City via the subway. It was already mid-afternoon, so we made as much of a tourist stab at it as we could: 42nd Street and Times Square, Madison Square Garden, St. Patrick's Cathedral, and quick drop-ins to various porn and food shops. We were delighted to find out that the drinking age in New York was only 18, so we availed ourselves of a few cocktails, but soon found out that the price of such an indulgence was prohibitive to our low economic standing, and our tight-fisted tipping generally got us a lack of service that sent us wandering again. We finished the evening with a Russ Meyer Film Festival down in Times Square; the perfect venue for the artful appreciation of lots of big tits, soft porn, and gratuitous violence.

Sleepers

When we got out of the movies it must have been around 11, so we got on the subway and made our way back to the Port Authority Terminal to catch a bus back to Jersey. When we got there it was past 11:30 and the last bus for the night had already left. Shit. We didn't know what to do. The next bus wouldn't be heading out until 8 the next morning. We didn't have enough money for a hotel. But the City That Never Sleeps was still awake. Hell, if it came down to it we could ride the subway all night. Which is what we did, nutty as that sounds. At first we were going to just go back into the City and kill a few hours, but once we got on the subway and saw there was no one else on board, we stretched out on the seats and laid down. Soon however, it became clear that the train was still going to make its stops, and every so often a couple of ugly dudes right out of *Taxi Driver* (i.e., uglier than us) would come on board and give us the eye. By this time though, the five of us looked pretty rough, after camping, working on the tomato-clearing, and already having spent the better part of a day walking the streets of Times Square, so no one messed with us. Nonetheless, we decided to post watches so the others could sleep (no mean trick on a moving subway that stopped every five to ten minutes, doors whooshing open and close). And that's how we spent the night, riding from one end of Manhattan to the other, back and forth, two guys up and three guys down. When the day crowd started coming on board around 7, we got out at the Port Authority and coddled ourselves with coffee, beer, and bagels. Catching the 8 a.m. bus back to Jersey, we were back in our hotel beds by noon.

Marvel-us

Ed and I got up before everyone else, and he said he wanted to back into the City one more time before we left (!?). What the hell? Well, it just so happens that Ed is a graphic artist, and has been one as long as I've ever known him (since third grade). He draws in a very broad, dynamic style that evokes action, movement and quickness. Unlike myself, who has been a devoted DC Comics fan since forever, Ed sipped from the Marvel Kool-Aid cup when they made their big breakthrough in the mid 60s with Spider-Man, Thor, Doctor Strange, Fantastic Four, and the other hobgoblins that tried to upstage Superman, Batman, the Green Lantern, Flash, Wonder Woman, etc. among the pantheon of *real* superheroes. So, Ed had worked up a set of demo pages that he wanted to submit at Marvel Headquarters in downtown Manhattan. It had been Saturday the day before, and now it was Sunday and the other guys were resting. He wanted to go back in on Monday, while businesses were open, and there to locate the office, and hopefully, to deposit on the desk of one Stan Lee (editor and supreme magus), a sample of his talented efforts to show his fealty to the Marvel "style." Okay, I told him, I'd go with him. The other guys had had enough and didn't want to see the City again, so Ed and I once more caught the bus on Monday morning and went into New York. This time it seemed so much different; I suppose because it was a workday and it was really bustling. The weather was beautiful, bright and sunny, and we set about our mission right away. Ed had the address, so it was just a matter of finding it. This took an hour, and we soon learned about buildings having multiple addresses depending on which street that particular entrance faced. Once we figured it out though, we were in the elevator heading up to the great man's floor. Ed had his portfolio ready, and we walked into a large secretary's office that had both her desk and the credenza behind it stacked with envelopes, papers, books, and correspondence. She asked if she could help us. Ed muttered that he had some sketches that he'd like to drop off, and she said fine, took the package and tossed it on one of the large piles on her desk. Anything else? Nope. (We were suddenly finished with the delivery to Marvel.) Thanks for your time. It was over in a minute. I don't know what Ed was expecting, but I thought we'd get to see some guys hunched over a drawing table, or at least some large posters of the forthcoming issues, maybe an inflatable Spider-Man. And you mean to tell me that Stan Lee is sooo busy that he doesn't have the time to come out to the front office and shake hands with a couple of young men who have come all the way from Florida (by roundabout way of Maine), one of whom could change the way comics are drawn forevermore and establish a whole new Renaissance of graphic arts for the final quarter of the millennium? Well, he'll never know what he missed that day or how the culture would ultimately suffer for the lack of it.

Dopes Dealing

Our business finished, Ed and I decided to enjoy some refreshment. We found a little alleyway that opened into a small café, with tables and surrounded by tenements, but peaceful and shady. The best deal for the money was a pitcher of sangria, full of floating fruit, which we sat and enjoyed while listening to the New Yorkers' bantering among themselves. After enjoying the sangria, and now with a glow from within, we again took to the streets, and must have given our own selves away as out-of-towners as we stared skyward at the impressive and monumental buildings surrounding us. A young tough in a tight t-shirt, jeans rolled at the cuff, and boots spotted us and crossed the street. Then he asked, "Hey, you guys wanna smoke a joint?" Why, what an extremely hospitable effort on this homeboy's part to welcome a couple of strangers into the Big City! Sure. So he pulls out this doobie, and we light up and smoke it, him keeping an eye peeled. It was good shit! Either that or the sangria was kicking in… not to mention, damn, those buildings are really big! He asked us where we were from, we talked briefly, and then he asked if we wanted to buy some. Well, how much? $30 a bag. Ed and I looked at each other— hoo, hoo… this was an opportunity to get some real good NYC stash, and we'd look like heroes to the boys back in Jersey. But we were hesitant to give him the money up front, smart as we were. No problem. "I'll get the stuff and you guys can pay me after I bring it back, how's that?" Well, we couldn't argue with that. He told us to just walk around and he'd find us in about ten or fifteen minutes. Cool. It was only when he turned to go get the dope that I jabbed Ed in the ribs with my elbow, raised my eyebrows, and made him look. This guy had a straight razor tucked into the back of his jeans. Oh shit, what are we gonna do now? Well, there were still two of us and only one of him, but what if he comes back with some buddies? Shit. Shit. Shit. We'll just stay out of reach, okay? We walked back and forth, not sure what to do, when, damn, here he comes, all by his lonesome. "Okay," he says, "but I can't just hand it to you on the street, we got to find someplace." What the hell?! He leads us across the street and right into one of those large and busy office buildings. There's a set of carpeted stairs leading up, and other walkways leading around, with people constantly coming in and out of the building. He sits on the stairs and invites us to do the same. Then he pulls out of his pocket two big bags of pot and hands them to us, people still coming in and out of the front door in plain sight not ten to twenty feet away. They'd glance at us, register what was going on, turn, and keep going. We quickly stashed the bags in our pockets, pulled out the sixty dollars, and counted it out to him. "I hope you don't mind," he said, "but I rolled one out of each bag as my commission. Here, I'm only gonna smoke one…" and he handed me the other one. In a moment he was up and heading out the doorway, "Thanks, guys, enjoy your visit to the City," and he was gone. Scared to death someone was going to bust us, we got the hell out of that building and just started walking, fast. Now, here we are in New York City with pockets full of pot, a little high, and a little more than anxious from this fortuitous yet frightening encounter. It was time to get another drink. We picked a quiet, dark little joint and sat at the bar. I don't remember what Ed ordered, but I think I was just dumb enough to order a "Manhattan" because I'd never had one before, and it seemed appropriate, considering the locale. It was awful, and it was very expensive. Finishing our drinks under the wrothful glare of the bald and surly bartender, we decided it was time to head back to Jersey. Not until we got off the subway and back to the Port Authority terminal and boarded the bus did we pull out our loot, the two bags of pot, and start getting a good look at it. Damn, it looked funny (and not in a humorous way). And there was a large amount in each bag, which would have been unusual anywhere, even in Florida, but New York City!? They should have been smaller. Uh oh. It didn't smell right, either. But wait, he'd given us that other joint that he said he rolled out of the bags, and he'd kept one for himself. Hell, he wouldn't do that if the stuff was fake. I took out the joint and just unraveled the end of it. Goddamnit, it was brown. The stuff in the bags was green. Shit, shit, shit. He had gotten us stoned, and even laid another real joint on us, figuring we'd smoke it and be happy, but the two bags were just not right. It became painfully obvious that we'd been duped, badly. Once it was clear this stuff was probably catnip, we made a pact not to tell the other guys so as not to look like the real dopes. Getting back to the hotel in Jersey, we held out for about an hour before they wormed it out of us, and even then, when we pulled out the "dope" they had to roll up two or three fat ones themselves and puff away, before they too admitted that we'd been cat-nipped in the butt.

Nolin and Tally-trekking

Our adventures finished in New York, we headed back to Florida, with Greg and Frank heading back to Tallahassee and Florida State University, Ed to the University of Florida in Gainesville, and Bruce and I back to Orlando, where I was still going to Florida Technological University in Orlando. Now that previous year that I'd been at FTU, besides generally flunking out of school, and blue-funking over Virginia, I began spending a lot of time with a good friend from my last year in high school, Bob Nolin, always called Rob by his parents, a true iconoclast if ever there was one. They were first generation Boston-Irish Catholics, with the thick Bostonian accents and intellectual stamina, despite the die-hard Catholic devotions. It always amazed me how his dear mother would solicitously make sure he had his cigarettes as we headed out, "Rob, have you got your cigarettes? Have you got enough?" Whereas my parents, although they both smoked since long before I was born, would have been horrified if I had picked up the habit at that early age (even though my brother did, on the sly). Coming from a good upper middle class Catholic family, he had three younger brothers and a youngest sister. That last year at FTU, we went out a lot together, generally just going to drive-ins to watch Clint Eastwood movies, smoking cigarettes and pot, listening to music, talking philosophy, and drinking various Ripples and Boones Farm wines. We just needed to kill time since all our buddies were either in the

83

service, were off to college in either Tallahassee or Gainesville, or were preoccupied with a girlfriend. The drinking age was still set at 21 so any wine we got we either had to talk some drunk or homeless person to buy for us, usually at some cost, like one for them as well, and on more than one occasion the fellow would go into a package store and just go back into the lounge and have a seat and drink on us. If we were pissed off enough to eventually follow him in we were immediately told to get the hell outta there, and then we'd have to find another location and do it all over again. After the drive-in movie and having finished our bottle of wine each, we'd get a little mischievous and cruise Colonial Drive looking for girls, or scout out some other troublesome entertainment. For instance, one night we got the wild idea to drive up behind the funeral parlor on Lake Ivanhoe and pull around back to the big oven where they cremated bodies. Opening the door to the now-cooled cooking slab, we scooped out a handful of white bone fragments and put them, where else, in the ashtray, where we could look at them, fondle them, and eventually just pitch them out the window at the end of the night when they lost their morbid allure and got too worrisome.

Probably to curtail our unexplainable excursions, Nolin's Dad bought the house a pool table, and thus we began hanging out there, out in their garage, where we could smoke, drink, play pool and listen to music to our hearts' content (Neil Young was an oft-repeated favorite). But this only heightened the fact that there were too few of us old high school "adventurers" left in Orlando, and we could only ever muster up three or four at a time. Since Nolin could practice with his brothers and his Dad, who was a fine player in his own right, he constantly had the rest of us racking 'em up. So, to break up the routine of beer, billiards and boredom, we would plan weekend trips to visit our buddies in Tallahassee, often stopping on the way to pick up Ed in Gainesville, when his high school girlfriend, Anne, let him off the leash. Usually, I drove the old blue Falcon station wagon, but if it was just Nolin and myself, and we were bypassing Gainesville, we'd take Nolin's little Volkswagen Beetle. Invariably, these trips involved drinking on the way, and sometimes we'd even measure the trip by the number of six-packs, as opposed to mileage or landmarks. At FSU in Tallahassee Greg Toole and Dennis LeFils shared a dorm room on the tenth floor of Kellum Hall, an all-male dormitory known for excessive behavior. When we'd get there, 6, 7, or 8 p.m. they'd be all pissed off that we hadn't waited to start drinking, as they had, in the misguided belief that that was the right and proper thing to do, so that we'd all start out the gate at the same time, I suppose. We'd have already had ten beers each, with two left in the cooler, and have smoked four or five joints already. They'd have a fresh bottle of bourbon, cokes and ice at the ready, and woo woo, let the games begin.

About those joints—one time Nolin had procured a bag of pot to take with us up to Tallahassee to share with "the boys." Not wanting to get caught with it, should we get pulled over, he decided to hide it in the little heater vent alongside the drive train that ran up the center of the car between the seats. Ingeniously, he stuffed it in there but made sure that the corner of the plastic bag was caught in the little closing door of the vent, to be easily retrieved if needed. After an hour or so, it was time to twist up another doobie for the ride, but when he opened the little floor vent, there was nothing left but the little corner of the plastic bag. "Oh shit," it was all gone! Who knows where? The rest had been ripped out, probably out the exhaust or under the car, back down the highway fifty miles or so. Oh well, nothing to be done about it. Damn. We had a couple more beers. It was mid-autumn, and it was starting to get dark. We still had an hour or so to go. It started getting cool. We're listening to the radio, buzzing along old Highway 441, heading north, and it starts getting pretty cold. Up go the windows, and Nolin turns the heater on. A Volkswagen heater is a wonderful piece of work, it kicks right in, the warm air coming out the mid-dashboard vent right above the radio. After a minute or two, the car gets comfortable, but there's just this smallest certain hint of something smoldering. Goddamn, maybe the car's on fire; it's been known to happen to Volkswagen's before. Then the heater starts making funny noises, the fan is rattling. The stink gets worse, the rattling won't stop, and now, little pieces of flotsam are starting to fly out the vent, little pieces of dust, or bug parts, or… or… Jesus! Little flecks of pot are flying out of the heater vent! Not a lot, just a few now and then, with the unmistakable smell of burnt rope mixed with burning plastic. Oh great! This is just great. Nolin turns off the heater, but then nothing happens, and there's no way we'll be able to get into the heater vent. So, there's nothing to do but turn the heater back on and sit there while little flyspecks of marijuana sporadically flit out the heater. Hopefully, there'll be enough to pick up in the dust and hair of the car floor and seat cushions to make it worthwhile, and we're not pulled over, with the car smelling like a head shop on fire. At the end of the ride, and going through the dirt on the floor the next day when we could see clearly, there was barely enough for two joints to get us home, and even they were pretty rough. So much for VW's *farfegnugen* ("driving pleasure"). [Now Dennis tells me that this happened to him and Nolin when *they* drove out west in Dennis's VW van. Could this have happened *twice*? Well, yes, it could, and rather than modify my own memory, we'll let it stand.]

Ah, but those visits to Tallahassee were inspiring. Dennis and Greg would give us the grand tour of campus, and we'd lay around their dorm room smoking pot, drinking, and reading underground comix (yes, underground "comix" as opposed to comics, really dirty and completely depraved graphic rags such as *Zap Comix, featuring Mr. Natural, Zippy the Pinhead*, etc. and starring Captain Pissgums and His Perverted Pirates, Flakey Foont, Oat Willie, and of course, the Fabulous Furry Freak Brothers). I recall they had a poster on their ceiling of all the Disney characters in various pornographic poses: Snow White and the Seven Dwarves, Mickey and Minnie, Cinderella and the mice/horsemen, with Prince Charming wanking himself while looking on, etc. It was pretty raunchy, and I knew that Dennis's parents, who were very staid churchgoers, had come up to visit the weekend before, "So, did you take down the poster when your folks were visiting?" "Naw, they'd never look up there." (Wanna bet?) Then there was the night we brought up Ed. Sure, we'd had a couple of beers on the way up from Gainesville, but now Greg and Dennis had prepared if not a full bar, at least some choices. We were also introduced to a couple of wildcards from down the hall, Bob Tirelli and Steve Trowbridge, who had their own stash of liquor they were willing to supplement the gathering with. Something also tells me that this was the time that Greg and Dennis had somehow finagled enough money to buy a WHOLE POUND of pot, Columbian, for $160 (true). The business plan entailed dividing the sixteen ounces into sandwich bags to be sold for $20 each, and thus, doubling the original investment, which still had to pay for textbooks. So we settled down to helping divide up the pot, weighing it carefully, taking out some (but not all) of the seeds and stems, and bagging it up, while rolling up and smoking a couple of extras and sipping various off-the-cuff cocktails. We were all hitting it pretty hard and Ed exceptionally so, since this was a special treat away from Gainesville and the girlfriend Ann's critical oversight. Tirelli and Trowbridge were popping in and out to smoke and bring in samples of music and their own potent alcoholic concoctions for us to try. Soon we were all blotto, and the music was blaring out into the dormitory hallway, and Ed started to nod out. The final straw was when we went out into the hallway and began an Olympiad that consisted of sliding on our stocking feet, an impromptu soccer game, and finally mattress-jousting (running from each end of the hallway at full-tilt carrying a single twin mattress and trying to un-horse, or knock off his feet, the oncoming champion).. The clamor got the attention of the RA, the resident advisor, who personally cared little about drinking and dope-smoking, but let us know that it had also got the attention of Campus Security, who were on their way.

Uh oh, time to move. This meant quickly hiding all the booze, and especially the dope, and making the room somewhat presentable. As far as the other guys down the hall, they were on their own. By this time, not only was Ed passed out, but he had urped on the 6-by-9 foot Oriental rug that Dennis had brought up from Orlando to decorate the room. [Fom Ed: "I was less of a lightweight and more of an idiot then. I didn't pass out early at all, but settled down after drinking and smoking copiously when most were doing the same finding spare floor space to sleep. I woke not long later to see Nolin and, I think, Tirelli who I didn't know at the time, sitting opposite each other at a small table with a bottle of clear liquor between them. Each was daring the other to upend the bottle and drink it down. Back and forth it went for quite a while. I got tired of it and thinking also that I was immune to everything decided on a grand gesture to end the argument. I took the bottle, said "Either do it or don't." and swigged down about a quarter of the fifth. Nolin responded, "That's the way to do it, Quince." I went back to sleep and soon woke to experience my liver erupting bile-vomit, which probably saved my life or at least worse repercussions. Sorry about the rug. The rest is accurate history though and Nolin will back this up-- if he remembers the '70's at all that is."] There was no way this was going to be cleaned up quickly (and Ed's condition improved upon), before the gendarmes arrived. We could already hear them coming down the hall, knocking on doors, and demanding entry for inspection. Quickly, we rolled Ed up into the rug Cleopatra-style and slid it under the lower bed of the dormitory bunks. The booze was hidden and the windows had been opened for good measure. When they got to us, while the rest of us pretended to be reading, Greg opened the door and politely answered all their queries ("No, sir, no one's been drinking here." "Yes, sir, we did hear the noise, but we didn't open the door." "Yes, sir, we'll keep an eye out." "Thank you, sir."). When they were gone, we pulled Ed out and rolled him out. He was a mess. What are we gonna do with him? We stripped him down to his underwear, so we could rinse his clothes, as well as the rug. Luckily, the dorm floor's bathroom, with a series of adjacent showers, was right across the hall. Then we carried him in and deposited him on the floor of one of the showers, and turned it on. (Remember Martin Sheen in the opening scene of *Apocalypse Now* when the MPs come to get him and toss him in the shower? Well, there you go… we did it first… alcohol-poisoning triage.) He jumped up immediately, but we kept him in there until he was properly soaked. Then the strangest thing happened. Ed wouldn't get OUT of the shower. We turned the water off. It didn't matter. He just stood there, leaned against the tiles, and held the front expandable band of his now-wet underwear out away from his stomach with his thumb ("It's too tight"). As he fell into semi-consciousness, he would lose his grip on the elastic band and it would snap, also snapping him awake, where he would again thumb out the elastic, holding it away from his stomach, until the process was repeated over and over again. He would not come out. He wouldn't lay down. We couldn't even dry him off. This lasted for the better part of an hour before he relented. I can still see Nolin, who refused to leave him, sitting on a nearby toilet seat, smoking a cigarette, waiting for Ed to come on out of there on his own, which, eventually, he did. Being young and resilient, we bounced right back the next day, said goodbye to Dennis and Greg, dropped Ed back off in Gainesville, and drove back to Orlando. But Orlando wasn't getting any better. In fact, it was getting much worse.

6. Tallahassee Prime (1972-73)

Juniper Drive

It was official now that all that land that had been bought up southwest of town years ago was under construction, and Disney World was coming. Opening October 1st, 1971, this was greeted by many as a wonderful thing, but not by everybody. Starting my second year of college, the grades weren't getting any better, and except for Bruce, who had bought a bike of his own (after mine had been repaired), all our other friends had moved on up to Tallahassee, going to Florida State, and were sharing a house now. That was Dennis, Greg, and Frank; even Nolin went up there to go to school. Bruce and I, down in Orlando, would kill a Friday or Saturday night riding our bikes all the way up to Winter Park, often partying with kids from Rollins, although we were really never part of the group. Between that, and the oncoming cloud of Disney rolling in over the horizon, we decided to head on up to Tallahassee too and see if we couldn't make a living up there. Mom and Dad weren't too happy about it, but they saw that I'd been idling at school, and the trip to Maine that summer had shown that I could survive in a different environment if need be. Besides, I'd started growing my hair long, and Dad and I were not seeing eye-to-eye on Vietnam, and soon the kitchen debates began to get ugly. It was time to go. I packed up the old blue Falcon wagon, picked up Bruce, and we headed on up to Tallahassee. The boys were all glad to see us when we got there, but it soon became apparent that the house was gonna get a little tight. They'd rented a four-bedroom house at the corner of Juniper and Crabapple off of West Pensacola, and although four bedrooms sounds like a lot, we were now part of a six-person (all male) household. Dennis let me share his room with him, and Bruce shared one with Greg. Nolin and Frank each had their own. The first (and really only) source of tension centered on food. Though there were certainly shared expenses for groceries, there were also certain "favorites" that were bought out of pocket by individuals, to be sequestered away for private consumption. Most notably, Cheez Whiz and/or potato chips. But in a house full of young men, often stoned and subsequently suffering the debilitating effects of mind-numbing munchies, sometimes these caches were discovered and pilfered, which often led to brief but bitter strife. Luckily, I was never a party to these burglaries and besides generally acting as an arbiter, or rather referee, when these trespasses became evident, I had the lone talent of being the one guy who was able to cook worth a damn. So there were lots of meals where spaghetti, macaroni and cheese, tuna noodle casserole, etc. were featured entrees, as well as breakfast on the weekends, when we weren't eating Domino's pizza or Whataburgers. To reduce the potential for conflict a couple of rules had to be established quickly, including 1) whatever was IN THE REFRIGERATOR was fair game for anyone—there could be no "secret stash" in the refrigerator; and 2) if you cooked (and I was the only one who did, other than hot dogs or canned goods), you didn't have to do the dishes—which still left the five of them to fight over it the next day (it was always the next day), even though we had a dishwasher (the first I'd ever really had experience with, and which constantly overflowed because the next-day dishes were never properly rinsed and thus clogged the drain in the bottom)   Nonetheless, life progressed at Juniper Drive rather smoothly, considering the close quarters.

Greg and Dennis had made the acquaintance of a slightly older graduate student, Doug M., who was a bit more worldly than the rest of us because he, in turn, had older siblings who had already graduated, and thus he was already exposed to the variety of music, drugs, and the inevitable progressive ideas that college life produces, which he generously shared with us and we lapped up eagerly. During the Spring break, Greg got a few small barrels of Orange Sunshine from Doug and we all planned a road trip to inaugurate the opening of that particular door to higher learning. Steve Trowbridge, our good friend from the dorm at Kellum, had a family cabin up in North Georgia, and he said we were welcome to stay there for a few days to use as a base of operations, just across the state line from Great Smoky Mountain National Park and Asheville, North Carolina. Greg and Frank had gotten it into their heads that for this initiatory experience we really, really, had to go and tour the Biltmore Castle, the ostentatious (and what I refer to— though I know it's not the correct stylistic term— as) Rococo 250-room largest home in America, built by one of the Vanderbilts in the late 1800s, which was located just outside Asheville. Although I wasn't keen on touring a gargantuan mansion for this *ad hoc* intellectual excursion, I still wanted to befriend Lucy in the Sky with Diamonds, so I was stuck. Besides, I had the only large car that would hold us all. So, Dennis, Greg, Frank, Bruce and I decided to make the trip and gathered up our camping supplies. Nolin decided to stay home since he was avidly bird-dogging the young teenage girl next door, and with us gone he'd have more freedom and room to carry out his nefarious plans. He needed the ability to operate on various fronts and from different angles, with the option to adjust accordingly, because somewhere along the line her father had discerned his ultimate intent, and was unamusedly wary and on alert.

Truckin

So us boys headed out one morning and by the end of the day we were at the cabin just before dark. A rough and rustic piece of handiwork, the cabin was set just off a dusty dirt road in a little glen that had a small creek running through the back edge of the property. It had a small upstairs loft for sleeping, and gaps between the wooden floorboards below. Even though it was cold outside, considering the body heat from five of us, a small fireplace, a bottle of bourbon, some pot, and our sleeping bags, we were very comfortable. The plan was to get a good night's sleep, get up early, and get to the Biltmore by the time it opened at 10. Waking, we jumped in the car for a day of adventure, and as we headed to the Biltmore Estate, Greg handed us each our little orange barrel-shaped hits, figuring it was going to be 45 minutes or so before it kicked in. The anticipation was growing, because in effect, we were going to visit a real American palace, the closest thing to Versailles in this country ("They say even the doorknobs are gold-plated!"). We followed the signs, Greg dutifully navigating from the passenger seat, until... There it was! A long winding drive that led to a mansion, outbuildings, and gardens that could be seen in the distant valley. But wait! The large iron gates, palisaded on either side by massive brick columns, were closed. No other cars were going in, or even approaching. There was a sign posted. "Closed for repairs." Uh oh, and the first shudder of an approaching mindstorm coincided with the realization that not only was visiting Biltmore out of the question, but we had made no other alternative backup plans. Shit. "What are we gonna do? We can't sit in front of the gate—we gotta get outta here." "Quick, before somebody sees us." "Goddamn, I'm starting to trip!" "Where are we gonna go?" "I don't know, but let's get moving!" "I'm not sure I'm gonna be able to drive much longer!" "How come you didn't know that it was gonna be closed?!" "Shut up! Let's just get outta here, quick!" I pulled out of the entranceway and just started driving. I had to get off the main highway as soon as possible, as my driving ability was quickly coming unglued. Near a small gas station I saw a sideroad leading up the mountain, and took it. It wound and warped and climbed, up, and up. Now everyone is silent. The acid is kicking in and we're just looking out the car windows, admiring the grand view. I'm trying to stay attentive to the road, twisting and turning, anticipating other vehicles coming in our direction, while glancing over the road edge to valleys thousands of feet below. We continued to climb for many minutes and many miles when, all of a sudden, the car just stopped running! Luckily, we just happened to be near one of those touristy lookouts on the road edge and I was able to pull in. What happened? I looked down to see that, in all our excitement and anticipation, we had simply run out of gas. We got out of the car and stood looking over the precipice and away to the forest and mountain vista laid out before us for at least a dozen miles. We stood there amazed, now seriously feeling the lysergic acid coursing through our vitals. As we stood there in awe, the cool air blowing about us, we began to hear the far off low hum of a truck struggling up the mountain from miles below, the driver shifting gears constantly to make it up the incline. We watched that truck for perhaps half an hour, aching for the poor gearbox as it ground and pulled its cargo up the twisting snakeskin of asphalt, gaining its way slowly uphill. "RRRhhhnnn, ruh nnn, rurrrhhhnnn, rhrun,,,, rrrrrhhhhunnnn, rhunnnnnnn, rrrrrhhhhnnnn…"

MadDonald's

Once we broke out of that particular wave of consciousness, we had to figure out how we were going to get some gas. Hitch-hike? Dangerous when straight, crazier still when you're taking your first real hallucinogenic roller-coaster ride. Then I remembered the gas station at the bottom of the mountain road… and it was all downhill! The boys pushed the car around so it was facing down the road, we all piled in and free-wheeled it all the way down, silently gliding from side to side down the road, using the gearbox to ease the braking, finally coasting up to the gas pump with just the slightest crunch of gravel under the tires. After filling her up, now the crew is hungry, sullen, and still trippin'. "Let's go over there to McDonald's and get something to eat," someone suggested. We traipsed in and gave our orders, fiddle-farted around with paying and making change, and finally settled down into a booth, when the next wave of loosely shaken delirium came coursing through… Once one of us started laughing we all became hysterical. Here we were in a McDonald's in Asheville, North Carolina, and instead of the golden doorknobs of Biltmore that we had been anticipating, we were surrounded by the bright-colored plastic red, yellow, and orange fixtures of the basest forms of Americana: cardboard cutouts of Ronald McDonald, huge golden (they're really yellow) arches, a bright orange tabletop with ketchup packets and other condiments, where even the cups and containers were bright orange, red, and yellow. It was maddening. And we were maddened. One bite of the Big Mac revealed that it, too, was plastic. The Coca Cola was cool icy liquid plastic. The noise of the restaurant was that of the plastic factory that I had spent two years in, with the slamming of the fryers, the clanging of the cash registers, and the loud hum of the crowd. And all my dear friends were laughing, crying, eating, choking, laughing, hiccupping, crying, snorting, and again laughing themselves silly. I believe that was the last bite of a Big Mac I ever took. Now that's not to say that I never walked into a McDonald's ever again, because I've been on field trips where the group inevitably, and by group demand, HAD to go to McDonald's, and even my oldest son spent time behind the counter at one in Tallahassee as one of his teen jobs, and I would stop to visit him there, but I never again purchased or ate a Big Mac hamburger, and I can't drive by one without looking at the mindless hordes lined up at the drive in without smiling. Cattle devouring cattle in a bright psychedelic plastic abbatoir. They have no idea.

We made our way back to the cabin and spent the rest of the day tramping about the mountainside, following the stream, crossing it at intervals, and laying about in the open fields. It was probably the best way to finish the day safely and in the most pleasant of settings. The next day we drove back to Tallahassee, keeping the interior of the car enclouded in a blue haze of marijuana. The only divergence was when we all fell asleep, except Frank, who was driving, and when I finally awoke and asked him where we were, he admitted he had no idea, concentrating instead on the music out of the old eight-track. A quick reference to the map and road signs revealed we had been heading west on backroads into the depths of mid-Georgia, an hour out of the way, and it'd take an hour more to get back to get on track. So much for higher consciousness. Once we got back to Tallahassee, we found out that Nolin, whether or not he had accomplished his objective with the young girl next door (he being very coy about the results), was nonetheless barred by the dad from crossing the adjoining property line, and so he, Nolin, generally stayed indoors that winter, at least during the daytime. Bruce and I, since we weren't going to school, and funds and credit running low, decided it was time to get to work. So, Monday morning we went downtown and made our way to the Personnel office for the State and began filling out applications. I got lucky right away, and was directed to the Parks and Recreation Division, where I met an old lady who said there was an opening at the local state park, Maclay Gardens, but she warned me that before I went I'd have to cut my long hair and facial fuzz. Bruce got lucky as well and was sent to some bureaucratic paper-mill downtown, where he got the same advice, "Cut your hair and you can have the job." This put us both in quite the quandary, since long hair at the time actually established your place in society: rebellious, free-thinking, liberal, anti-war, intellectual; whereas short hair showed an affinity with conservative herd mentality (passivity, as opposed to "pacificity," which was the long-hairs' credo), gullibility (when listening to Nixon), and generally aggressive and right –wing politically (unlike we "bleeding-heart pinkos"). So, Bruce and I talked and argued about this (standing up for your rights, or getting a paycheck), and we discussed it with our buddies as well. Then we took different tacks. I felt it was no real big deal, and I could always grow it back if the job didn't pan out. But Bruce, well, he did the unexpected. He went out and bought a short-hair wig. Yes, a SHORT-HAIR wig. Bet you didn't even know they had such things.

Hi Ho, Hi Ho…

So Bruce got his short-hair wig, and I got my hair cut and shaved my Jesus-beard. But Bruce had thick, dark curly hair, and lots of it, almost a frizzy Afro, so he ended up spending a good half-hour every day, putting in bobby pins to hold back the stray strands of hair sticking out, and fastening the wig itself into place. If anybody bumped it, whether at the house or the office, he had to start all over. Mine was certainly the more interesting gig. As a novice park ranger at Maclay Gardens, my main duties were to help anyone who asked. My first assignment was helping an older, obese and lazy maintenance ranger repair and paint all the picnic tables. This entailed us picking them up, bringing them to the work shed, then sanding down all the rusty spots and splintery surfaces, tightening all the bolts and replacing any rotted planks, and finally spray painting them a bright forest green. At some point he became "sick" and quit coming to work (plainly due to drinking) and I had to manage on my own with one of the black laborers, "Custis," who was big and strong, a bit slow-witted (to the point where he drooled ever-so-slightly when he either exerted himself or thought too hard), but nonetheless a sweet human being. What had taken the old white guy and me a month to do, Custis and I knocked out in a week, and they had to come up with something else for me to do. It was simple… winter was coming on, so we were expected to pick up all the Spanish moss and pull it out of the hibernating trees when we could get at it, so as to make the Park a wonderland of camellia gardens and (not-so-quite) natural environs to present it as more of an early 19th century plantation, which is what it was. There were only four of us maintenance guys now, three blacks and myself, and unless we were called off for some other duty we were the labor team for the park. Let's see, there was Custis, then an older gentleman called Mr. Otis (a sullen but tiny wrinkled old black who could care less if I lived or died, or for that matter, ever existed), and a tough middle-aged black guy around 35-40 yrs old named Jason. Now everything went well, the black guys and I walking the length and breadth of the park each day, picking up Spanish moss by the wheelbarrow-ful with pitchforks where we could reach it, and ladders where we couldn't. Yes, they often scolded me for being too energetic about scarfing up these wads of air-filter bromeliadic fungi, "They'll be plenty more tomorros… (they never said my name)." It was always "psst," or just a grunt, with a purse of the lips and a slight jerk of the head, eyes lifted, and sometimes just the eyebrows, or even one eyebrow alone… I don't know… the biblical implications of invoking the name of

90

David? I have no idea, but I never insisted, although at the same time I sure as hell learned a lot about non-verbal communication. [Later I learned these were cultural traits and tricks handed down from slave-days, and long before that, silent African hunting and gathering signals.]

3805 Ballard Road

Once Bruce and I had started earning some money, as little as it actually amounted to, and considering the close quarters that we boyz-2-men inhabited, it only seemed fair for the tribe to split, and move on and out to bigger and better venues. Summer was approaching, and we had been going out to the sinkholes south of town to swim, risking life and limb riding atop Doug M.'s big white van, smoking pot by the handful, and laying about listening to the wondrous meanderings and reverberating inanities of a strange new band called Pink Floyd. On one of the trips heading south and amid the surrounding scrub forest, we spotted a "For Rent" sign on Ballard Road and pulled in to check it out. The family was still home and we met the dad, a guy named Robert Ballard (*not* the guy who found the Titanic), and he told us yes, the land all around had once been in his family, and thus the name of the road. His kids were growing up, so he and his wife finally sold the old homestead to a pair of developers who eventually wanted to turn it into a trailer park subdivision. But this particular house was a cinder-block four bedroom, two bath (with a shared shower), that had five acres of surrounding land, and the developers wanted to rent it out until they put their trailer park plans in action. This was perfect for a group of troublesome post-teenagers, or rather, responsible young college men. Greg and I met with the developers and signed a six-month lease, the two of us looking the part of earnest young fellows, he with his short hair and me, not only with short hair, but also in my park ranger shirt with bright Florida Park Service patches on the top of the sleeves. I think the rent was originally $180 a month, and they said the house would be ready by the time summer rolled around in a few weeks. The developers were a couple of sleazy real estate tycoon-wannabes who were actually the sons of some Tallahassee State legislator who bought the land just to keep them busy. I can't remember their names, but I'm sure Greg would, as he carried on a running feud with them for a span of eight years or more. So Greg, Frank, Bruce and I made plans to move into Ballard, while Dennis and Nolin jumped ship early and found a place closer in-town, and nearer to the University, on Duval Street; actually the left-hand-side of what is commonly referred to as a double-barrel shotgun house, where the two halves of the house mirror each other, with a living room at the entrance, a bedroom with adjacent bath, and then a kitchen in the back, adjoining a small porch. Back in the 30s when these were built, the two families would share a common kitchen and bathroom at the back of the house, but these had now been modified since the 50s for college student rentals, so they each had a kitchen and separate bath. They were referred to as shotgun houses because apparently, if you needed to, you could clear out one side of these straight-line wooden frame houses from the street to the backyard with a single shotgun blast straight through. When they were side-by-side as a duplex, it took a double-barrelled shotgun to get the job done.

Just Us

We cleaned out the house at Juniper and moved into Ballard (as it came to be known) sometime in the late spring '72. It was just about this time, I got pulled over for some minor infraction that required an appearance in Traffic Court. I called in to Maclay Gardens and told them I'd be late one day, and showed up at Traffic Court wearing my grey Florida Park Service uniform top with the stiff shirt, name tag, and bright patches on the sleeves, and my short hair, and was called up before the judge after the first two or three cases were (interestingly enough) summarily dispatched with set fines. He politely asked me my name, where I worked, and how I was to plead. Well, c'mon, you always plead "no contest" unless you're downright innocent, so

91

that was that. I then noticed however, that my fine was substantially lower than the couple of cases ahead of me, which were similar in degree, and I was dispensed with. No matter, I was glad to get out of there and made my way to Maclay Gardens to get to work. I get to the park and I'm picking up moss for about an hour, when I get a message that "The Lieutenant", wants to see me. The top guy, Lieut. Durban, was an old ex-military double-dipper who just wanted to ride out his years, watch the camellias and azaleas and crape myrtle grow, and listen to the Spanish moss wistfully drop out of the trees. Grizzled, buzz-cut, and stiff backed, he nonetheless had more than adequately adapted to his position as caretaker of a little piece of quiet paradise, and he didn't want to be bothered by details. I went to see him in his small, yet comfortable, wooden cabin of an office suite, all by his lonesome, and he sets me down in a chair in front of his desk (I remember it was cold, first time we'd met face–to-face, and there was only a small space heater for the whole damn building), and he began to ask me how the work was going —"Great," I thought, "did you see that all the picnic tables are done?"—and told me I was an exemplary employee, everybody enjoyed working around me, they couldn't think of enough good things to say about the quality of the work we'd accomplished.... then his eyes dropped, he coughed, took a big sigh, looked up and said "Were you in court today?" (Obviously he knew, so there was no hedging the truth...) "Why, yes sir, I was... but it was only for a minor traffic incident, a bad taillight... and the fine was only $35!" "Yeah, well, I got a phone call from the judge. (What!?!?) He said he went easy on you, because you were a State employee. But he didn't like seeing the Florida Park Service uniform in his courtroom either. If you ever get pulled over and have to go to court again, you change into civilian clothes before you go, understand?" "Yes, sir, sure, of course... I didn't realize..."

"And another thing, as long as I've got you in here... I hear you've been eating lunch with the black workers in their shed..." "Yes sir, I'm a laborer too, so..." "Yeah, well, I'd prefer it if you'd eat over here with just us, ...and they might prefer that too." (?!?!?) Well, now I was at a loss. Was he TELLING me not to eat with them, or was he suggesting that maybe they didn't like this white boy sitting in on their free-time lunch, listening to their conversations, and not being able to speak to each other as freely? Before getting my hackles up, I figured I'd have to get that straightened out. "Did they complain about me eating with them, sir?" He looked at me stiffly and said, "No, but I'm telling you they might prefer it that way, and I know I would too." "Well, I'll see what I can do, sir," and I got up and walked out. It was close to lunchtime, so I got my lunchbag and went into the worker's cabin with the three black guys, and just laid it out: "The Lieutenant said I shouldn't eat here with you guys any more. Do you guys mind me eating with you?" They just looked at each other, and the old man said, "You ought to do what the Lieutenant says." Well, hell, this was as roundabout a statement as what the Lieutenant had said. I took my sandwich and apple and went out the door, but goddamn if I was going to go over and eat lunch with the white guys, with whom I had nothing to talk about. From then on I just went out walking during lunch or, when it was bitter cold, sat by myself in the machine shop. It didn't matter much, because soon I was assigned to the picnic shed at the lake and was told that was going to be my standard duty for the foreseeable future.

This was a great assignment. My duties included emptying the garbage cans, making sure the toilets and changing rooms were clean, checking the walking trail and picking up Spanish moss and branches when I wasn't doing anything else. All of which I could accomplish within an hour of arriving to work at 8:30 a.m. The rest of the day I was alone, unless someone came up to check on me, or, now that winter was settling in, the lone chance of someone coming to visit occurred. So I got a lot of reading done. For some reason (conscientious objector, duh) I was really into the peaceniks back then and I remember reading a lot of Gandhi, Rheinhold Neibuhr,

92

Bertrand Russell, Robert F. Kennedy, and others. Then sometimes a couple would pull into the deserted parking lot, and upset to see this truly Lone Ranger sitting there reading, since what they really wanted was to be alone, they would venture out along the walking trail that extended maybe half a mile along the edge of Lake Hall. When this happened, I'd wait the requisite twenty minutes or so, before I'd follow, generally finding them screwing just off the trail, or sometimes smoking pot. They were always scared to death to see a guy in a Florida Park Service uniform, thinking I had some sort of law enforcement status (which I hadn't) but I never made a big deal out of it, just apologizing for disturbing them. Otherwise I enjoyed the solitude, and not having to report to anyone. When the weather started to warm up in the Spring, I would often see ten and twelve-foot gators slowly swimming back and forth across the lake. Once in a while I might chase a water moccasin out of the brush along the lake's edge, raccoons and possums were a constant nuisance around the trash cans, and there were several incidents when deer would just walk through the picnic area, grazing, and as long as I didn't move, they didn't even notice I was there. Yeah, there were a few times I'd bring along and fire up a joint, meditating on the North Florida landscape, quiet with cool breezes whispering by, broken only by a pine cone dropping every so often either on top of the picnic shelter or out near the tables. These were my first real experiences with open-eyed meditation, as opposed to my early school-day daydreaming.

Ballard Deco

We moved into Ballard Road, and I slept on a mattress on the floor of the smallest room in the house, with my head tucked into the open closet. Frank got the large master bedroom with direct access to the shared tub/shower bathroom, the other entrance coming in from the hallway. Greg took the other large bedroom at the end of the house and Bruce the one closest to the living room. Mr. Ballard was kind enough to leave two of his ratty old couches in the living room, and I had brought an old green recliner from Juniper. A bean-bag chair and a coffee table made out of cinder blocks and orange crates finished the furnishings in the living room. We were short of a kitchen table (which is always the center of attention in any house), so I pilfered a large cable spool from the side of the road and, spending a Saturday morning on it, I tightened it up and covered the top with an octagon-shaped yellow formica top, perfect for sitting around, eating, drinking, talking and (most important) playing cards. A couple of folding chairs and we were in business. The kitchen also had one of those formica-covered "islands" with shelves at the end, which made for a perfect impromptu bar, or platform for fixing large meals. It took the first week for us to figure out that there was going to be no garbage pickup in the neighborhood, what with us being out in the rural county, so I would take a few bags in to town on my way to work to drop in large waste containers out behind stores; but the garbage was so awful, nasty, and haphazardly packed, spilling out on the way, that I soon had to boycott that duty, or I'd have been stuck with it permanently. The solution? We paced out about ten or fifteen steps out the back door into a large open space, and set about digging a pit. The ground was pure sand so this wasn't so bad. We took turns going round and round with a pair of shovels and in a couple of hours we had a hole eight feet across with a large berm of sand around the upper edge, and deep enough that it was impossible to get out without two or three strong arms on the end of a rope, six or seven feet deep. Trash would go in, and maybe once a week we'd set it afire and stink up the neighborhood with black sour smoke for an hour or two. Although it sounds terrible, our neighbors all did the same thing. When I think now of all the toxic materials that went into that hole and its general proximity to our well pump (maybe twenty-thirty yards away) I shiver with ecological regret. To finish our decorating, someone had found a medium-sized naked plastic baby doll (the kind that had the roll-up eyelids when you tilted it) and we ceremoniously made a small noose and hung it by the neck at the entranceway to the house along the dirt drive, an homage to Alice Cooper's *Dead Babies*. It hung there for years drawing a few comments from visitors. No telling how many Jehovah Witnesses it kept at bay. (Yeah, I know, it's sick, but if you ever go down to Capt. Tony's Saloon in Key West, they used to have a large wooden plank leaning up against the inside of the bar with one of those small bright yellow in-your-car diamond-shaped signs that says "Baby On Board" at the top and below there was a similar doll nailed up on the piece of lumber crucifixion-style. Now, that's sick… and still funny.)

Sally the Pig

There were a couple of young girls down the road and one day they came riding their horses up to the house, rearing them up just in front of the large plate glass living room window. One was Jackie, a tall blonde with a ponytail, a bit of a tomboy, and an excellent horsewoman, in jeans and T-shirt. The other was a small brunette, a little younger, named Susie, with a tiny frame and buck teeth and braces, yet who could also handle a horse without any problem. They had been coming over to the Ballard's (who also had horses) on a regular basis, so this was just their normal stop when out riding in the surrounding scrub oak sand hills. They had come to check us out. Unfortunately, they were still in high school, and even though they were welcome into the house (one time Jackie actually rode one of the horses through the front door into the living room, just to show us she could, before we shooed her out), we were smart enough not to get into any compromising situations, although flirtations based on discussions of animal husbandry were fair game. We may have smoked a little pot with them, but that was as far as we'd go (this is speaking from my own personal perspective, however). For my part, I took up a little animal husbandry of my own and bought a small piglet from Jason, the middle-aged black laborer I worked with at Maclay. When I found out he raised pigs and sold them I asked how much for a piglet ($40), and how much might I get at full weight in four months or so ($140). Well, this seemed like a great investment scheme to me, so I drove out to his place, got the piglet, and brought her home. Ballard had an adjacent acre or two ringed with barbed wire, and inside one field there was a small tin-roofed lean-to surrounded by hogwire, with a watering trough. I put her in there and named her Sally. Then I soon learned the difficulty of being a pig farmer, even with one small pig. Jason gathered food scraps in large fifty-gallon barrels from restaurants all over town to supply his own herd, whereas the boys and I, being young men in our twenties, never left enough scraps of food to scrape off a plate, despite all the other toxic garbage we managed to produce. So I tried feeding Sally poke salad, which grew rather abundantly around the property perimeter. But poke salad is only edible when it's new; that is, only the new shoots, or tips, were good for forage, the rest being bitter and indigestible, and gathering enough of the new tips, even on a daily basis, was damn near impossible, considering the energy to be expended and the appetite of the ravenous piglet. Soon I was buying pig pellets, like dried dog food, at the farm supply store. Well, hell, at $5 a bag, which might last a week, I saw that my projected profits were going right down and through the little oinker's belly, and as she got bigger, she ate even more. Another problem was she was too damn smart. Long before pot-bellied pigs as pets were the rage, we let Sally roam through the house on occasion, and I even taught her a couple of tricks: sit, beg, lay down, oink… which was not a good thing, because now I was getting attached to her, like a pet, and the prospect of a nice barbecue in a couple of months appeared a little grisly. And she was always escaping. At first, I found her digging under the hogwire, and that was easily remedied by laying a strand of barbed wire along the bottom of the fence, so if she tried digging she would hit that barbed wire quickly with her snout and stop. But then she continued escaping and I couldn't figure how. I walked along the perimeter of the fence, and couldn't find any holes, and the gate was tight and secure (??). If I sat out there and watched her, she would stay inside the pen, but if I happened to go into the house, she'd be outside the fence and running off into the woods in no time. Luckily, I would follow her tracks as far as I could and then calling out "Sally" and whistling, she'd come running back and follow me right up to the

94

pen gate, which I'd then open and let her in. One day I hid behind the house where she couldn't see me and watched for over a half an hour, when I saw her walk along the fence, testing it at various places, and then she pushed open one of the hogwire squares that had come unwelded. She pushed it open, squeezed (squoze?) out, and the wire sprang back into place, appearing closed. Aha! It was easy enough to entice her over to me with a couple of oreo cookies, and I got her back in the pen and wired the gap closed again. One day, however, I came home from work, she wasn't in the pen, and even though it was getting dark I followed her tracks for maybe half a mile through the woods, before I couldn't see any more. I called and called, and whistled, but she never came home. And that was the end of Sally

Now the boys have said it was because of the LSD. I don't agree. Yes, there was a day when we partook; and yes, there was a little fragment left over; and yes, okay, I agreed that, since we were all dosing ourselves, shouldn't we all, all of us? So the last fragment went to Sally. We goofed and flopped around, and sat on the roof to watch the sun go down, but before retiring for the night, we checked in on Sal, and the worst we heard were grunts and snorts – not much different than what we had already heard from each other all night. I'm sure she was more freaked out by the assholes staggering towards her pen with flashlights in hand at midnight to check on her, than she had been, sitting looking at the stars and listening to the swine-herds laughing and falling about in the nearby cinderblock house. Look, I'll be the first to say that it wasn't right or moral, or ethical, and of course, it might be considered cruel and thoughtless (which of course, it was, one of many thoughtless, or rather, ill-conceived acts for which I shall surely incur a great karmic debt) but…, clawing at the best rationale I can muster, at the same time, in a different place, the great and esteemed Dr. John C. Lilly, at the behest of the Department of Defense, was injecting dolphins with lysergic acid diethylamide to see if they were cognizant or not (the results being dubious). We were just dosing a pig; her ultimate fate almost, if not somewhat, predetermined. Nonetheless, it was almost a month later that she finally ran off. Perfectly pig-normal in the interim, with no visible signs of either short or long-term porcine-psychosis (and you can quote me on that). So you can put me down as not supporting the pig-dosed theory of her running away, UNLESS you want to pursue the idea that, as a result, she had reached a higher level of consciousness, and decided that, before becoming pulled-pork, we could go fuck ourselves and she was going to take off for good and see the world… now THAT I could believe!

The Root Man's Magic

The job at Maclay began to get tiresome after the lone winter, where reading and changing trash bags, when not picking up moss, began to turn into real work once families started showing up in the spring to have picnics and frolic about. One day Custis let it slip that Mr. Otis, the older black gentleman, who had worked there for many years, was what they called a "Root Man," and that meant not only that he knew the various forms of herbal remedies for the region, but that he practiced other mysterious arts in the rural black community as well. Well, curious as I was, I tried saddling up to him and asking questions. At first, he just rebuffed me, curtly saying that he didn't know of any such things. But eventually, he would point out a bush, or plot of weeds, and tell me their name and what they were good for. That's how I found out about poke salad, made famous by the *Poke Salad Annie* song ("She'll get your granny!"). One day when we were walking alone, I pressed him for something more "you know, magical." He turned and looked at me, and said, okay, he'd tell me a spell, one spell, if I promised not to bother him further. Okay, says I, sure. He slipped down into a whisper so I had to bend down close to hear him, and said "You know how when you with a woman, and you want to stay hard, sometimes… if you really like that woman, it's sometimes difficult, and you'll go off too soon?" "Yeah," I said, and told him, "I try to think about baseball, but it doesn't always work." He whispered

"Wey'll, all youse got's to do is put a dime under your tongue. You'll be fine, you'll be able to go all night long with her, long as you keep that dime there." Now THAT was an interesting concept! And not like anything I'd ever heard before. Sure sounded like some sort of black magic (pardon the pun) that just might work. But, being the busybody that I am, I had to push it further… "So how, Mr. Otis, does that work?" And there went the magic. "You be so worrisome about swallowin' that dime, it'll keep you occupied so you don't get off. When you ready, you jus' spits it out, or swallows it."

Maclay Away

Later that spring, it began to get busy, and then the picnic area near the lake would get pretty crowded. They hired another maintenance "ranger" and he turned out to be a real asshole. One of those guys who, if you give him a uniform, all of a sudden becomes a fascist. Guy named Brad, he was 45 or so, ex-military, blond/grey-haired, and insane. He would take it upon himself to direct parking, telling people exactly where and how to park, and throwing a shit fit when they didn't do it exactly the way he wanted. I just went around helping people get set up at their tables, listening to them commiserate about what a jerk he was, emptying garbage cans, and then spent repeated performances cleaning up the bathrooms that they all seemed to trash on the hour. One day while Brad was out there directing parking there came a lot of yelling from the lake. Way out in the middle someone in a small sunfish sailboat had overturned. From the sound of it, the two people hanging on to the boat couldn't swim, because they just hung on yelling for help. I went down to the lake edge and gauged the distance, maybe a quarter-mile. No other boats on the lake and by this time Brad was coming down beside me. He decided that he needed to go for help, call the fire department, and off he went. I thought about it for a minute, took off my shirt and shoes, stuffing them with my wallet and keys, and went on in. It really wasn't a bad swim, although it felt like it took forever, and they kept yelling for help the whole time, even when I got up close to them. And they had life jackets on! As a kid on Clear Lake my old buddy Dan Anderson had one of these sailboats, so I knew how to right it quickly; trouble was, I couldn't get them to let go of it and just float there for the minute or so it would take. I finally got them, a couple of teenagers, a boy and a girl, to just float there hanging on to each other, shut the hell up, and give me a minute with the boat. I had it up and ready to go, sail flapping with the wind, in one full minute. I helped them climb aboard one at a time, and damn if they didn't just leave me there, and sail back to the boat landing. I swam back, and by the time I got my shirt back on, sitting in wet pants and pulling on my boots, the fire engine had showed up and the kids were already eating at their family picnic table. Brad gave me shit about going out there alone, but the firefighters were very nice, shook hands with me, gave me a knowing sideways head-jerk toward the asshole Brad before leaving, and I went and laid out in the sun to dry off. Brad got to Lieutenant Durban before I did, and I had to get mildly chewed out again for "unnecessary risk-taking." That was a Saturday, and by Monday morning I decided I was finished being a maintenance park ranger at Maclay Gardens. Summer was coming on, and the traffic and problems were just going to get worse. I still have the bright State of Florida patches I eventually cut off that old grey shirt, but it was the first of many lessons where I learned that "no good deed goes unpunished."

City Cab

Having cast off the uniform and demeanor of a staid and upright park ranger, I was now free to begin exploring life on a completely different level, as well as let my hair and beard grow. Friends of mine had taken up driving taxicabs in Tallahassee, and apparently the company was looking for more drivers. So I got my chauffeur's license (a relatively easy extended written test at the time), and went down to City Cab. Now there are innumerable stories, as one might expect, that came out of City Cab in Tallahassee in the early 70s, just as there are innumerable cab stories anywhere else over generations, and still being generated today; all I can do is give you a few of mine, and I'll try to keep them to the most interesting. I wasn't hired as one of the company drivers, but was given over to one of the private owners, a guy named Simpson, a real tightass who wanted the car washed every week, by hand, and had peculiar ideas about how and where to go and make money. He already had a night driver by the name of Patrick, and so was willing to give me a try as the day driver. Patrick was a slim hippie, with a halo of wispy grey-black hair, and a quick smile, with a long high-pitched Midwestern drawl. He giggled a lot, and had delicate mannerisms, but hung out with some of the roughest bikers in town. He claimed the darkness. I don't doubt that he was probably weaponized too. Now everybody knew that the night drivers made more money, since they got the evening and nighttime bar trade, and usually knocked off only after sucking up the morning getting-to-work rush-hour runs, but this was okay by me, since I wanted my evenings free, and the night run was also known as sometimes risky business. I was happy just to be a free knight-errant plying the roads of Tallahassee, and wasn't particularly grasping or greedy at that time in my life, or very ambitious either, for that matter. For me it was the adventure, not the money. And starting off green I didn't know the tricks of the trade anyway, so I was willing to watch and learn.

The Admiral's Widow

One of my earliest lessons was when a call came over the radio asking if anyone was willing to "visit the admiral's widow." Even more intriguing than the request itself was that no one was willing to take it, even though I had been sitting among a line of cabs none of which had moved in the previous hour. I got on the radio and said I'd take it. "Are you sure, Number 3?" croaked Otis, the surly dispatcher. "Yeah, I got it," I said. "All right, but leave your meter running, and be out of there in an hour," he replied, and gave me the address over on the edge of the Indian Head Acres subdivision. Well, this sounded interesting... as I pulled out, the other drivers were smiling and laughing at me (what the heck?). When I got to the house, I went to the door and rang the bell. After a minute a tousled grey-haired, overweight, and obviously tipsy old lady in a house dress answered the door. "What do you want?" "You called a cab, ma'am?" I asked. She brightened up and said, "Just a minute." She came back and handed me a twenty-dollar bill, "You know the liquor store over on Lafayette?" "Yes, ma'am." "Go get me a fifth of Canadian Club," and she closed the door. So I hopped into the cab, turned on the meter, and headed to the liquor store, calling in my 10-20 (location and destination). "Did she give you a check?" asked Otis. "No, a twenty." "Well, when you get back, you leave that meter running until you leave, you hear me?" he growled. I went by the drive-thru window (where back in those days we could get a drink handed out already mixed in a plastic cup), and got the CC, and made my way back to the house. When I got there, I forgot entirely about Otis's orders, turned off the meter, and went to the door. She finally opened it and I handed her the bottle in a bag, and tried to give her the change. "Keep it," she said. Well, hell, this was when a bottle of Canadian Club wasn't but seven or eight dollars. Considering the delivery fee of maybe five, this was still quite a nice little tip. Then, out of the blue she said "You know how to play chess?" "Yes, ma'am." "Well, then, come on in." And in I went. There was the chess board on the dining room table, the pieces all askew. "You set it up," she said, "You want a drink?" Damn, I had to think about that one. Not that half the drivers weren't tippling all day anyway, often with a pint under the front seat, but I was getting a little nervous under the circumstances. Pictures of the dead admiral were lined up in the pantry, with various battleship pictures, flags, commendations, swords, guns, and what-have-you hanging on the walls. What the hell! "Sure, I'll have one." By the time she came out of the kitchen, I'd had the board all set up. She mixed it deadly strong with just a dash of ginger ale, and... damn! I had forgotten about the meter. I decided to come clean about it, rather than just run out and turn it on. "Ma'am, if I'm going to play chess, and have a drink, I hope you don't mind, but I have to go out and turn on my meter." "Shit, I don't care," she said… "Who's the dispatcher?" "Otis." "Fuck Otis," she laughed. I ran out quickly and turned on the meter. Then ran back inside, sat down, took a draw off the glass in front of me, and we began to play chess. The first game went down pretty fast. She was good, but obviously impaired. The second game plodded on slowly, and I was into my third drink when the doorbell rang. "Goddamnit," she said, and got up to answer it. In came one of her older neighbors, a bald guy with a moustache, who just happened to be carrying a brown paper bag. I could guess what was in it. He gave me a sour nod, and pulled out the bottle of Canadian Club. She went in the kitchen to fix another drink (even though she still had half a one on the table), and he started giving me the third degree. "Is that your cab out there? Did I see the meter running? You know, you shouldn't take advantage… How many drinks have you had? blah, blah, blah" Well, it worked. I decided I'd better get out of there, since I quickly sensed that he wasn't there just to play chess. When she came out, I lied and said that my dispatcher called and I had another run, and even though I'd like to stay, I had to go. She was very nice by then, and sad to see me go, so she said she'd get her checkbook and would I let her know the fare? I ran out and checked it, and even though I'd been in there maybe two hours, the clock running by itself alone doesn't ring up that much, and the rate only gets way up there fast on the meter when you're moving, so it came to something like thirty-five dollars. I went back in where the old bald guy was just glaring at me, and she asked me to write out the check for the fare with a ten dollar tip. So I wrote it out for forty-five dollars, and it took her all of two minutes to sign the damn thing, her hands were shaking so bad. I took the check, said goodbye, and as I was leaving, getting into my cab, damn if there wasn't another old guy neighbor, this one, pudgy with a shock of white hair, also giving me the stink-eye, going up the walkway to her front door with, yes, a bottle in a bag under his arm. I had a brief vision of the two geezers getting into a drunken brawl in her house, or even worse, her entertaining a post-menopausal *ménage à trois* (the horror!). And that wasn't the end of it. When I called in to the dispatcher that I was leaving, Otis sputtered out, "Did you get cash or a check?" "I got a check," I said. "Go right to the bank and cash it right away!" When I got to the drive-thru window at the bank on which it was drawn, they informed me that there was a hold on the widow's account (!?!). The hold wouldn't be released until the first of the month, about ten days away. Apparently, her kids had made arrangements with the bank to give her so much spending cash at the beginning of each month when the admiral's pension (and I suppose her Social Security) kicked in, and checks were to be drawn against that amount. I was out of luck for at least ten days and had to pay my share of the fare, about 40%, out of my own cash in hand. Between that and filling up the car with gas at the end of the shift, as we were all required, I ended up broke for the day. All the drivers waiting in line at the bus station got a real kick out of that, and even the ill-tempered Otis got a chuckle. Now I knew why it was standard operating procedure not to dally with the admiral's widow.

Specs

Then there was Specs. One morning, slightly before dawn, I got woke up with a call from my night driver, Patrick, to tell me that he was coming out to the house at Ballard. He had a special fare, and he asked if I had any pot. Yeah, I got a couple of joints worth, I told him. They were on their way. I got up, got dressed, and put a couple of doobies in my shirt pocket, and sure enough, here they came up the old dirt drive. I got in the passenger seat, and there in the back was a little white-haired balding old man maybe 75 years old in a short-sleeved white shirt, who couldn't have been five feet tall and maybe a hundred pounds or less. He had on a pair of goggle-glasses that made his eyes appear huge and owl-like, and Patrick introduced me, "David, meet Specs," (for the spectacles). Patrick had picked him up at the bus station about ten o'clock the previous evening, and they had spent the whole night going from bar to bar, with Specs picking up the general tab, buying drinks for various women Patrick introduced him to, and dancing, not to mention, paying Patrick for the separate cab fares between trips. The bars had closed down around four, even the old late-night bring-your-own bottle clubs, and now Specs had said that he wanted to try some marijuana, since he had heard a lot about it but had never tried it. But… where to go to try it out? Well, hell, we could have stood outside the car at Ballard and smoked the joints right there, but Patrick, always mindful of the meter, wanted to "go somewhere" where we could enjoy it, and insisting that we couldn't smoke in the car because of the tight-ass owner, Simpson, who'd smell it. So I suggested the Ochlocknee Bridge; it was a ways away, secluded, and peaceful, and we could park the car under the bridge so as not to draw any attention from any police that might be out at that early hour. Patrick thought this was a great idea. As we drove along I asked Specs a little bit about himself, but other than saying he was from Bonifay, several hours west of Tallahassee, he didn't want to talk about himself much. When we got to the river, Patrick pulled down the old boat ramp road and quietly eased the cab under the bridge. We all got out and I suggested we take the little foot trail down along the river, til we could find a little spot to sit on a log somewhere and smoke, that way we wouldn't be near the car, just in case. I led the way and Specs followed me and Patrick brought up the rear, having locked up the car, but leaving the meter running. We hadn't gone maybe fifty yards along the river, flowing noiselessly beside us, with the light just coming up along the tops of the trees and putting out the stars, when all of a sudden, Specs dropped to his knees, put his face in his hands, and began sobbing uncontrollably, letting out pitiable little choking cries. Patrick and I looked at each other, scared that he was sick or something, and I said, "Specs, Specs, what's the matter? Are you okay?" and he said, "Oh please, boys, please, please don't kill me… I know that's why you brought me on down to the river here, but please don't murder me and throw me in the river… I got family…" Patrick and I looked at each other over the top of this poor pitiful sobbing creature… and then we both started laughing. Patrick started in on him first, trying to help him up, "Now Specs, stop that. We have no intention of killing you… we're just gonna smoke a little pot, okay?" "Yeah, Specs," I chimed in, "you're a great guy, we're not going to hurt you, don't worry." "You're not…, you're not… gonna kill me?" he said. We laughed again, "No, of course not." And just like that he was on his feet, smiling, chipper as can be, wiping his big bug eyes under his coke-bottom lenses, "Well, thank you, boys!" We couldn't help it, and had to keep chuckling at this, it was so surreal. Luckily, there was a tree down nearby, right there along the riverbank, edging out into the water, where we could all sit side-by-side. I pulled out a joint, we lit it, and started puffing. After half an hour or so of silently stoned watching the muddy little river roll by and hearing the birds singing and chirping to each other as the light of dawn got brighter, we got up and slowly made our way back to the cab, and Patrick headed us back to town. Specs told Patrick that he was out of money now, so we took him straight back to the bus station (since he had bought a round trip ticket) and I gave him the last joint I had in my pocket so he could enjoy it later. I dropped Patrick off at the cab stand, which back then was at the old Oil Well gas station down on South Adams Street, and started my day shift. A couple of days later, Patrick told me that he had found out from one of the dispatchers that Specs had run away from an old folks home in Bonifay that his family had put him in, taken a couple hundred out of the bank, and just decided to go on a spree in the big city of Tallahassee, but that his family probably wouldn't let that happen again. Apparently the cops in Bonifay had called all the cab companies in a hundred miles and had been told to keep a lookout for him. Poor Specs, all he wanted was a little taste of freedom before they locked him away for life, and then he was old, and they beat him to it.

The Pastime Tavern

One of the regular pickup spots, if not a favorite hangout, for the cab drivers was the Pastime Tavern down on Tennessee Street, across from the Florida State University campus. Going strong by the mid-60s, it was once noted for several years to be the most beer-consuming bar in the State of Florida. Owned by Jim Gregory, who supposedly got it from his Dad, the main draw was Miss Kitty, who, not unlike the famous Miss Kitty of *Gunsmoke*, was a just-past-middle-age matronly barmaid with a questionable background, tough-as-nails and a heart of gold. The place was famous for the billiard room in the back, always beshrouded in a hazy fog of smoke, where the main table, closest to the pass-through half-door to the bar, was for the serious (i.e., gambling) players, surrounded by a small gallery of theater seats, and strictly overseen by Howard, one of those ageless skinny-armed, black-hair-dyed, and pot-bellied pool hall managers who never drank, but strictly and scrupulously watched over the goings-on, and barely ever spoke a word. He dished the balls out for the remaining dozen tables or so, all regulation-sized, and collected the money at the end of the play. How he kept track of everyone and how long they played, I could never figure out, 'cause he didn't write anything down, but if ever he erred, it was on the side of generosity, once he got to know you, and I never saw him get mad, even when the occasional drunk and boisterous player would swing his pool cue around too much and break one of the overhanging fluorescent bulbs, sending small shards of glass and neon dust crashing down onto the felt. He'd just get out his little whisk broom and dustpan, walk over, sweep it all up quickly and efficiently, and stare down the culprit until they'd put down their cue and step away from the table in shame.

Miss Kitty

Early on, I got a call to pick up some guy at the Pastime, so I went on down there, parked the cab out back and walked in… my first time there. I asked for the fellow who needed the ride, and he happened to be working on finishing up a game of nine-ball at the main table. He told Miss Kitty to give me a beer on him while he finished his game, so I went and sat at the bar, enjoying the ambience. I say this because back then the State of Florida was fiddling around with the idea of lowering the drinking age, as some other States had already done, since a goodly number of young men were fighting in Vietnam, but couldn't buy a legal beer when they got home. The drinking age in Florida however, was still twenty-one, and at the time I was only twenty. The long hair, beard, and cab-driver's badge had been just enough to cloud Miss Kitty's usually perceptive intuition, and I relished the idea of being a part of the men's club. I continued in this trend quickly and again and as often as I could, being amicable and gaining Miss Kitty's confidence and personal acquaintance, so that after the first couple of beers she never ever thought to ask me for identification, even as I saw her throw out any number of sneaking no-good poseurs for not having the requisite age-verification, some of whom were dear friends of mine (and were sometimes there at my invitation). Almost a year later, I walked in one afternoon, and asked her, "Hey, Miss Kitty, is it true that you guys will give a guy a free pitcher of beer on his birthday?" "Why, yes, it is, hon," she said, "is today your birthday?" "Yup." "Well, Happy Birthday! How old are you?" she asked, smiling. "I'm twenty-one." The smile dropped like a turd out the ass of a hunched-up street dog. She threw down her bar rag, "You son-of-a-bitch! You've been coming in here drinking for a year! We could have lost our license… get out! Get out of here right now!" her jiggling flabby underarm and ring-laden finger directing me to the way out. "But… but…" I stammered, but there were no "buts" about it. She could see my obvious dismay, and I must admit that the sudden loss of her highly-valued good graces as a result of my prolonged (but what I had considered harmless) subterfuge nearly brought me to tears. She didn't relent, but she lowered her voice, still scowling, and sternly said, "Come back tomorrow." The next day I went in, tail between my legs, apologetic, and thoroughly chagrined.

She came up to me smiling, as if nothing earlier had ever occurred, and said "Well, hi, birthday boy, what'll you have?" She was so nice that I brightened up, and asked "Can I have that free pitcher now?" "I'm sorry." she said, "but your birthday was yesterday... today you'll have to pay full price..." and she uproariously laughed in my face.

Snookey

My last cab story involves a young girl named Snookey, one of the only female drivers (oh yeah, besides Snapper, the middle-aged redhead semi-pro). She was a perky little thing with a cute face (which is what a girl is called if she's not stunningly beautiful) and a bit of a bowling-pin figure, a little wanting up top with a little extra on the bottom. She had a mop of light brown curly hair and a bubbly personality (at that time). She would sit and work the daily crossword puzzle and started asking me for a little help. Well, it got to the point where I'd be sitting up close next to her and we'd pore over the thing together. Nothing came of it and although I was infatuated with her, as was every other cab driver, she really showed no inclination towards any of them, and they could be a dogged bunch. The obvious conclusion was that she had to be a lesbian. I was unconvinced and undeterred. Some three months later, I was down in Orlando and came into an insurance settlement (more on that later). It wasn't much, $350-$400, but my brother had just gotten back from a short vacation in Jamaica, and told me what fun he'd had and that the round-trip tickets were going for $125. So, being an idiot, I called Snookey and asked if she wanted to go to Jamaica for a short 10-day trip. She said sure, and hopped a bus down to Orlando. I picked her up at the station, brought her to the house and introduced her to Mom and Dad (Dad was NOT impressed, and kept asking her what "Snookey" meant, to which she was adeptly evasive). The next day, Mom drove us back to the bus station and slipped me another fifty dollars for the trip. We took the bus down to Miami, where Snookey had some friends we'd stay with for a night and who'd drive us to the airport the next day. It turned out that this was some warehouse that her best girlfriend and the attached boyfriend had converted into a motorcycle paint shop, as well as having several levels of adjacent living-area lofts. The best girlfriend wasn't there, off on a trip somewhere, but the boyfriend was very cordial, despite being one of those "cool" artistic and well-built long-haired rich boys that everybody envies until you get to know them, sort of a smug Fabio asshole. Well, he pulled out a couple of bottles of wine, showed us his various painted gas tanks and designs, and then we all settled down, and they began talking about the old days, old friends, the missing girlfriend, and what they'd been up to, etc. I was not going to be a part of the conversation, so, tired as I was, I asked where we were sleeping. He showed me to a little tuckaway up in the loft that had a mattress on the floor. I lay down and was soon fast asleep.

I woke to the sound of someone exercising, maybe wrestling, maybe fighting... oh, god, no! It didn't take long to figure out what it was..., goddamn, I peeped out the divider and there was Fabio with Snookey, her face-down in a pillow, ass-in-the air, grunting and moaning, and him hammering her from behind. They must have been going at it for some time already, because he finished rather quickly. Damn, damn, damn... yeah, I was mad, but hell, what was I going to do? Run out there and play the affronted cuckold? I don't think so. They had a history (although I'll bet the absent best-girlfriend wasn't aware of it). If anything, I was the outsider. Besides, nothing had been either discussed or romantically broached between me and Snookey, (hell, I was counting on the trip to turn the matter) and if I was going to be the true sensitive man of the 1970s then I had to "turn the other cheek" and let her "express herself" (like motorcycle-painting Fabio had been doing? I wish.). Still, I was fucking mad. I lay back down and fumed, feigning sleep. Eventually, she came in, lay down on her side, and fell asleep. In the morning we packed up quickly and Fabio took us to the airport. Even though I was starting to get a little cold-footed about the trip, she was still being cute and nice, and at the same time was wickedly smart enough to wait until we got on the plane before she told me, "Y'know… you understand, don't you, we're just traveling as friends." "Huh? Oh yeah, I knew that." Well, I sure as shit knew it now—but had I known it when I asked her to go three weeks earlier, I could easily have found another travelling companion who would have been twice as entertaining. We flew over the western end of Cuba and landed at Montego Bay, MoBay for short.

Jamaica Me Crazy

It was late afternoon, and we were going to need a place to camp since we had decided to "rough it" and not waste money on hotel rooms. We headed down the runway fence until it gave out, and then there was a large expanse of open ground with the bright blue ocean lapping at the shore, all darkening as the sun was going down, so up went the tent, out came the sleeping bags, and soon I had a nice driftwood fire going. Maybe this wasn't going to be so bad after all. Now we could relax. While we were talking, out of the darkness, a duo of dark Rasta-boys came walking in. Nice guys. Curious. Where did we come from? Welcome to the island. Not "the island", THE ISLAND. "Want to smoke a spliff? Some ganja? Here, we got spliff, mahn." And they fired up a wad of pot, we partook, and life was grand. We were talking small talk for a half an hour when one of them said, "So now you got to pay for the ganja, mon." I wasn't sure I heard him correctly. "I'm sorry, but what did you say?" "You got to pay for the ganja, mon." "Well, you didn't say anything about paying for it… you just offered it." Snookey and I looked at each other. "How much do you want for it?" I said. "How much you got?" (!?!) Uh oh, now it was gonna get ugly. All of a sudden, Snookey got up and said, "We're not putting up with this shit! I'm going for help," and she just up and walked off into the darkness. Well, this not only took me by surprise, but both the Rasta boys too, who looked at each other and were obviously freaked out, wondering what to do next. After a second or two, one of the guys jumped up and went after her, off into the darkness. So now it was just me and one guy. He gave me a look, dove right into the tent, and started rooting around in our stuff. I took the opportunity to grab a piece of firewood, and started yelling at him, while pulling at the leg that still hung out the tent. He backed out, and I held the piece of firewood threateningly, but we ended up getting into the clinch immediately, and started rolling around on the ground. I soon realized I wasn't going to beat him, he was that strong, and we were both getting desperate now. So I maneuvered him over by the water, where I knew I'd have the advantage, and we splashed on in. I was right. It scared him and he totally broke loose and started running. I started after him, and finally flung the firewood piece at him as he outran me. Now I was a hundred yards from the campsite, in pitch black, soaking wet, and wound up tight as Tom's hatband with the adrenaline pumping. I thought about Snookey and whether the other guy had gotten to her. I started yelling. "SNOOKEY!... SNOOKEY!" I listened… and way off in the distance I could hear her calling back. I figured the direction and even though I couldn't see in the darkness, I started running. I was picturing this Rasta boy manhandling her, maybe even beating her, or even raping her, so I poured on the speed, running full tilt. I ran and ran and ran and … PRAAANG! I didn't even see the three strands of barbed wire stretched across my vector, and now I was strung upside down, wrapped twice, cockeyed and tangled in it. After a few seconds, when I realized what had happened, it slowly took a minute or two to get myself loosened bit by bit, but I'd been torn up pretty good. Once I got free, I called for Snookey again, and I could hear her not too far off now, so I hobbled in that direction as fast as I could. I came up on her in a few minutes; she was fine, all alone, and just walking along nonchalantly making for a set of lights in the distance.

The lights turned out to be a small marina, with maybe a half-dozen small wooden fishing boats tied up. In any case, it appeared safe, being well-lit. So, I left her there and walked slowly back to the camp, packed up everything, and carried it back to the marina, all while punctured with barbed–wire holes like a stigmatized St. Stephen (who was actually stoned and not shot through with arrows, as usually depicted). When I got back, we lay down on the wooden dock, and tried to get some sleep. An hour or so later, the sound of footsteps on the dock woke me and here comes a drunken stumbling old black fisherman. "Whashoo doo-in?" he asked. We told him about almost getting robbed and trying to sleep on the dock. He pointed at one of the larger, closed-cabin boats. "Thass mayn," he mumbled, "You can shleeep dere." We pulled the line in and climbed aboard, laying out on the front deck. He staggered on board with us, and eyeing Snookey, said to her "You come sleep down here, wi' me" motioning for her to go below deck. "No, that's not gonna happen," I said, and she seconded the motion. He got mad, and made his way back across the deck, cursing, and stepped back onto the dock. "O'll be back in a hour," he slurred and again staggered down the pier from the direction he had originally come. As soon as he was out of sight, we let the line out and dropped the anchor some twenty feet from the dock, then lay down once more and tried to sleep. He showed up as he had said, about an hour later, and saw that he couldn't get on the boat. He started yelling and cursing at us, but we just pretended to be sleeping and not to hear him and soon he slid down onto a rickety old wooden bench on the dock and fell fast asleep. When we got up in the morning, I used the anchor as a kedge, tossing it again and again, pulling us to the dock. Once there, we tied her up and made our way towards town, leaving him cooking in the morning sun. All that happened the first night we got to Jamaica.

We camped out everywhere we could to save money, and the second night I unwittingly pitched the tent on a large pile of fresh pig shit. The pile had dried to a crust on the outside, but once we got in the tent and started moving around, we spread that shit all over the bottom of the tent and then it really began to stink. The next morning I did the best I could to wash the bottom in the nearby sea, but it stank the rest of the trip, especially when exposed to the sun. One morning we awoke to a set of black faces staring down at us through the skylight screen, when we had camped in a public park in Kingston, and later that day, while Snookey went tourist shopping, I remember reading the paper while I enjoyed a Dragon stout and couple of patés, the cheap local spiced meat turnovers I had developed a real taste for. The inside article was concerned with the latest news item that 65% of the patés sold on the street and tested by the government had been composed of dog meat. They tasted fine to me. And apparently we were following the filming of *Live and Let Die*, the latest James Bond movie, because everyone kept telling us, "Oh, you should have been here last week while they were filming," and there was evidence of it with prop elevators in some of the shallow caves, and two-dimensional building sets built and deserted. We camped a week out at the Seven-Mile Beach at Negril, and that was back when the beach was seven miles of sand without a hotel in sight. One afternoon I walked the whole seven miles south along the beach. On the way, there was a little tiki hut with a few young people hanging around, some music playing, and the smell of ganja wafting down to the beach. I thought I'd check it out, and as I got to the hut, there were a few guys and girls standing around smoking pot, all watching one of the guys screw a young black girl quite vigorously. I took a couple of puffs and continued on my way. Hours later I reached the end, with a deserted-looking island just offshore, then sat down to watch the sun set. Out of a nearby bungalow, this beautiful woman in a bikini emerged and began stretching. Then out came a photographer, and she started posing while he shot away, island and sunset in the background. After a while, the girl whispered something to the photographer, and he walked over to me, told me he was doing a Sports Illustrated shoot, and asked me if I'd leave, since the model was somewhat intimidated by me sitting there watching them. "Well, no," I told him, I was there first, and I had just walked seven miles and was resting. They were both mad at me, scowling and cursing under their breath, but kept shooting. Once they quit I got up and wandered off toward the island. Too many sea urchins on the coral heads, so I was never going to make it, but as I picked my way through the shallows I was surprised to see an octopus arm, and then another, lifting out of the water and obviously pulling himself along over the coral. Darkness setting in, I made my way all seven miles back to Negril and the campsite, where Snookey sat unhappy because no one was paying any attention to her, and I hadn't been around to entertain her. Too bad, but she had been somewhat of a snot ever since Miami.

The Deal

Then one night we had made our way by train to the Blue Mountains (where all the famous expensive coffee is now being grown), and hopped out at this small one-street town that was celebrating some holiday or another and there was quite a little carnival going on. We walked along the street, bought a beer and looked at the vendor stalls, while horses and donkeys rode past with costumed cavaliers and other celebrants. Out of the crowd a young black man with his hair pleated in very neat cornrows, and of all things, wearing a full tuxedo, less the cummerbund, walked up to us, and addressed me specifically, "Excuse me, sir, may I speak with you for a minute?" I'm thinking the guy must be an extra from the James Bond movie, it was just that absurd. "Alone, if you don't mind." "Sure," I said, and looked over at Snookey, who was now obviously pissed off, so we walked off out of earshot, some five or ten paces away. "Is this woman your wife?" he asked, as we both looked over at her, arms folded, shifting her weight and ticked off. "No, we're just friends, traveling together." "So, she is not your girlfriend," he stated matter-of-factly. "No, like, I said, we're just friends." (Now I was getting suspicious.) "I'd like to make you a proposition," he said. "Yeah?" "If you would step away and leave her alone, I will promise to have her back here within an hour and a half; she will be fine and happy, I guarantee, with money, and in the meantime, I will see to it that you are entertained by two very beautiful Jamaican girls…with rum…and ganja…" I looked over at Snookey, standing some twenty feet away, scowling and pissed, and remembered the night at Fabio's in Miami. "No, I'm sorry, but that is not gonna happen," I said, as she began tapping her feet in frustration. I looked back at him, angry. Smiling, he shook my hand, and said. "I understand. Thank you for talking with me." And he walked off into the crowd. I eased on over to Snookey, who jumped me right away, "What was THAT all about?" I hesitated for a minute, and thought what a rash of crap I'd have to listen to if I told her what he really wanted… Did I consider it? For about two seconds. If I told her though, then she would have taken off down the street after him to read him the riot act. It would have been ugly no matter what, and, for my part, wouldn't have settled down for days, if ever. So I lied, "He just wanted to sell me some pot." She huffed and said, "Well, you should have done the deal…" I thought about it, and you know, maybe she was right.

7. Orlando Inter Alia (1972 -1974, Roughly)

I had gone back to Orlando before going to Jamaica with Snookey because driving the cab in Tallahassee wasn't pulling in enough money to keep up with the bills. Driving the cab, I was wearing rags (which didn't impress the clientele), and the only meal I could afford every night was the $4.99 all-you-can-eat fried chicken at Tucker's, located at Four Points where the Crawfordville Highway intersected Woodville Highway, and the drive-in theater sat on the east side of the road. You couldn't beat it though. To compensate for the frazzle-haired, toothless, thin, white-powdered, and lipstick-smeared old waitress, Rose, there were unlimited bowls of rice, black-eyed peas, cole slaw, sometimes corn, and always, layered and delicious buttered biscuits (with honey!), and gallons of either sweet or unsweet iced tea. Not to mention the best oil-dripping yet crispy fried chicken parts on this side of the State Line.

Even worse than being poor, having been out of school now for over a year, and it being 1972, I became eligible for the draft. When the numbers were pulled I was number 83, and that year they were going to induct everyone below something like 135. Fuck!

Bye, Old Blue

The final straw was the car, my beautiful blue Falcon station wagon that had carted me around for years, and in which I had caroused with Virginia, driven to Maine and North Carolina and back, and back and forth from Tallahassee to Orlando a dozen times at least. The poor bitch was finally giving out. I told the boys at Ballard that I was heading down to Orlando to deal with the draft board, and since I was taking the bus I'd leave the keys in the old blue wagon, and if I never saw it again, I sure would miss it, but it had outlived its prime and was giving up the ghost. It was insured, so, if anything happened to it, let me know, and I would make it up to them. They got some fun out of it, riding around the sandy scrub forest roads round the sinkholes south of Tallahassee, and eventually let it go, parked in the woods. A few weeks later I got a call from the insurance company that they were sending a check for $300. I argued that it was worth more than that, but that was all they'd pay. When the check came, I called Snookey and made plans for Jamaica. The boys reminded me of my promise to make good, but it was either them or Snookey at the time. I also saw it as my last hurrah before the draft got hold of me. So, to be honest, I took the money and went to Jamaica with Snookey instead. Just before we left, the insurance company called, said they'd found the car, and wanted their $300 back. I told them that as far as I was concerned they'd already bought it. To this day the boys still remind me about not sharing that $300, some 35 years later (which would have amounted to less than $75 each at the time). Believe me, I've done penance for that sin a dozen times over. To show my good forbearance, I will spare you and my friends the details of the events that preceded the five or six of us standing on the beach at New Smyrna one late night the previous summer, a set of headlights pointed out to sea, and the waves crashing over the hood of Sandy Patterson's mother's Mustang.

In the Navy

To keep the draft off my back, I had looked into joining the Navy, which had a six-month delayed enlistment before you had to show up for induction. Then I immediately began working on a deferment as a conscientious objector. The war in Vietnam had been going badly for several years, and no one, not even President Johnson, or now, Richard Nixon, could explain the rationale for our presence there, nor the goals, nor how or when or why we'd ever get out. Nixon had gotten elected with a "secret plan" to end the war that remains secret to this day. He continued

Johnson's bombing of the North, then extended it into Cambodia, and then Laos. It didn't matter. The "Vietnamization" of the war was a failure, not because the South Vietnamese wouldn't fight (they fought extremely well, considering), but because their leaders were all corrupt, their officers inept, and the U.S. began cutting back on the money. As the spigot closed, the North Vietnamese got better and better at infiltrating the South, and the handwriting was on the wall. The general population of the United States realized that this was an immoral and unwinnable war.

> *"...In our opinion, and from our experience, there is nothing in South Vietnam, nothing which could happen that realistically threatens the United States of America. And to attempt to justify the loss of one American life in Vietnam, Cambodia, or Laos by linking such loss to the preservation of freedom, which those misfits supposedly abuse, is to us the height of criminal hypocrisy, and it is that kind of hypocrisy which we feel has torn this country apart..."* John Kerry, Vietnam Veterans Against the War, to the Senate Foreign Relations Committee, April 22, 1971

Six months passed quickly and I got the notice to show up for a bus to Jacksonville, where I'd then get shipped back to the Orlando Naval Training Center. I went, amid tearful goodbyes, handshakes, and backslaps. As far as I knew, I was going into the Navy. After spending a night in a seedy hotel (The Heart of Jax), getting physicals, and taking the oath (yes, I took the oath – there was no choice), they separated us into various groups, and I found myself alone sitting outside the recruiting commander's office holding my file and waiting for the bus to take me to Orlando. I sat and thought, and had maybe two hours to think. Then I got up, went to the commander's office, knocked, went in, and told him I'd changed my mind. "WHHHAATT?!?" he roared, "You can't change your fuckin' mind!" "But I never wanted to join up in the first place," I told him. "Then why'd you join the fuckin' Navy?" he was livid by now. "Because you had a six-month deferment for enlisting…" He looked at me, stared at me for what seemed an eternity, and I could see the wheels rolling behind his eyes. "Gimme that fuckin' file!" he snapped, and I gave it to him. He opened it, looked at it briefly, then tossed it into the wastebasket next to his iron-grey desk. He opened a drawer, pulled out a small pad and began scribbling. While he was writing he growled at me, "You fucking little prick! I'm sending you back home to Orlando, only because I have to, and when the draft comes after you this time, you won't have a choice where you're going to serve… and if they ask us, we're going to recommend Vietnam." He threw the paper at me, which was a ticket for the civilian bus back to Orlando, and told me to get the hell out of his office. Needless to say, when I got back to Orlando, friends and family were surprised, and my poor Dad, who had already told all his friends I was joining up in the Navy, was most sorely disappointed—he wouldn't talk about it, and they must have all thought I was 4-F, physically unfit. (You gotta remember, he was working for Martin Marietta at the time, the manufacturer of the Bullpup missiles—the first successful air-to-surface guided missile, full of napalm and god-only-knows-what-else, used to bomb military targets in North Vietnam—as well as the Pershing inter-continental ballistic missile, which kept the Russians awake at night and on their toes.) I imagine I earned an FBI file by then.

The Argument

Now before anyone goes off and starts to give me a rash of crap about not following through on the enlistment and/or taking the oath and then abandoning it, you should first consider the times. It was 1972, and up until then both Lyndon Johnson and Richard Nixon had lied to the people about not only why we were there, but if and when and how we were ever going to get out as well. Meanwhile, we were carrying on an obviously racist and imperial war of aggression in

North Vietnam, using some of, if not THE MOST horrific weapons of war ever devised by the mind of man (to wit: napalm, Agent Orange, massive aerial carpet bombing, torture, assassination, etc.), and WE WERE NOT WINNING. In fact we were not winning in South Vietnam either. Not only the general U.S. populace, but the politicians, whose sons were now being drafted as well, even our returning soldiers and the other veterans, had turned against the war. It had to end. An oath taken under duress, or more correctly, not freely given, is not binding.

I decided, while sitting in that recruitment waiting room, that I was going to take a stand, and it had to be against the war. The commander made the mistake of letting me sit for two hours, to think (worst mistake ever, to let a man think). In matter of fact, I have an old friend who happens to be a lawyer and he maintains to this day that, because I took the oath, the commander probably no longer had the authority to let me go, and since I then followed the only order ever given to me, to go home and wait, I'm probably eligible for back pay and benefits. I don't think so, but I like the argument.

Conscientiousness

Yes, I considered going to Canada, but that really wouldn't solve anything, and would have made things worse by far, for me and everybody else. In fact, that really was just running away. No…, better to stand up as a conscientious objector, even if it meant going to jail. But this took a lot of preparation. I had to get letters of support from everyone I knew, and although it was easy enough to ask friends and my immediate family (yup, even Dad wrote one), it was harder to ask people I hadn't seen in years, old teachers, priests, nuns, and relatives. One day during Spring Break, when I knew they were having a teachers' planning day (but the students were off), I drove out to my old high school, Bishop Moore, to see if I couldn't get a couple of letters from some of my old teachers. After checking in at the office, I was given free rein to wander the campus. I went to see Father Bluett, a large hulking ex-prizefighting priest born in Ireland, with a ready wit and large smile, but nonetheless, someone you didn't cross or even trade verbal jabs with, much less physical ones, except at your immediate peril. He had taught us Latin during that first year in high school, and he didn't put up with the old ploy of passive resistance either. I once saw him lift a teen off the floor by his sideburns when the fellow decided to play the mute rather than simply admit he didn't know the answer to some mediocre Latin translation.

[A little side note: one time we were on an altar boys' picnic at the beach some five or ten years earlier, and Father Bluett was sitting in a car with his identical twin brother, who was also a priest, and they were somewhat preoccupied, so a gang of us, four or five, snuck up behind the car. As we looked over their shoulders, over the front seat, we could see that they had a Playboy magazine spread out to the centerfold, and they were admiring this intriguing form while drinking beer. They yelled at us and jumped out of the car, but by then we had run and gotten to the water and mingled with the other altar boys, and they had to give up on the chase. We thought it was hilarious and only later did it dawn on me, and I thank God it hadn't been the case, that they could just as easily have had their dicks in their hands instead of a couple of beers. THAT wouldn't have been so funny.]

Anyway, I went to Father Bluett's office, and he was very glad to see me (we had always gotten along pretty well and growing up I had served Mass for him many times, even making sure to give him the "extra" splash of wine when prompted with a wink). After telling him why I was there, he took the time, the better part of an hour, to ask me all kinds of questions about my feelings, the war, my feelings about the war, my feelings about war in general; and if I recall correctly, we finished up with a general discussion about Man's Inhumanity to Man. He was sincerely interested in my motives and the depth of my understanding about what was involved as a conscientious objector. At the same time I freely admitted that if I felt we, as a country, were threatened, or that I might have to defend myself or my family, I probably could turn on the violence gene like anybody else. In the end, he said he'd write the letter, asked me who to send it to, and told me he'd send me a copy. We shook hands and said goodbye. It was probably the last time I ever saw him, although I hear he's still out there somewhere, and still a priest.

Walking down the breezeway, the same one I had walked so many years before on my first day there, I glanced in the old classroom, and there was Ed Mullins! A little more grizzled, a little more hunched over, and looking smaller than I remembered, but when I said hi, he gave me the old gargoyle grin, and we shook hands (me being smart enough to use my left hand, which he appreciated). I told him why I was there, and he was very blunt. He didn't believe in being a conscientious objector; when your country called, you answered, and you answered "yes". Oh shit, I should have known better. Here I am, asking a guy who got his right arm, face, and most of his right side blown to hell fighting a stupid "police action" in Korea, to write a letter on my behalf so I wouldn't have to serve. What was I thinking? To be honest, I hadn't considered asking him in particular; it just so happened that, after seeing him in the old English classroom, I couldn't help going in and saying hi (I was still in awe of the old bastard) and once he asked me why I was there I just let it out. However… he surprised me again. He got very serious (in my mind, dangerously so). Even though his didn't go for all that "peace" crap, and he still didn't believe a young man (especially a young man from Bishop Moore) should shirk his duty, he also did not agree with the war. Not only was it an exercise in futility, no matter what we all felt about it in 1966, '67, '68, etc., but it was quickly becoming apparent by now that this was an immoral war. And that was what concerned him. There are reasons to fight, and maybe we had one early on, and maybe once you're there you need to finish the job. But by this time we were already pulling the bulk of our troops out (while at the same time we still were sending others in), and attempting to hand it over to South Vietnam through the "Vietnamization" of the war, but now, we had flown bombing raids over into Laos and Cambodia, and even though Kissinger was carrying on talks in Paris, there was still talk of a possible limited nuclear strike at Hanoi to bring it to a close, like we had done to Japan. No, Mullins knew, and he let me know, that, even Korea was a "just" war compared to this one. He said he'd write the letter. Asked me where to send it, and no, he would not give me a copy. Sorry. I took a long gulp, thanked him, shook hands again and said goodbye.

An Objection

Well, so far so good. Thought I'd ramble on over to what use to be known as the Girl's School, but later became the Upper Classmen's School. It was pretty quiet over there, and much as I wandered around, it seemed deserted. But then, just as I was getting ready to leave, I noticed one class door open. It was Miss Redmond's classroom. Now Miss Redmond was a sour young dump of a woman, who had obviously had a rough time growing up, no doubt as a result of her bad attitude, which was reflected in the acne-scarred complexion she sported. But I remembered that she had been the instructor in our Principles of (or was it supposed to be *Problems in*?) American Democracy class, commonly referred to as P.A.D. There'd been a lot of Civics stuff, the various branches and makeup of Government, the role of Congress, how to make laws, etc. You know though, I don't ever remember us ever discussing the Vietnam War, not once… anyway, considering how smoothly things had gone with Mullins and Bluett I figured, what the hell, being the Civics teacher she sure as hell understood what was going on. I went in and she just stood up from her desk and asked what was I doing there, no hi or how've you been, though it'd been two years since I'd graduated. I laid out my case as plain and as clear as I could. Her eyes narrowed behind her horn-rimmed glasses, her face flushed, she started to sputter, and then she lit into me. For not using any curse words, she was nevertheless very adept at insult, as well as innuendo (although she didn't really know me, or anything about me) and the attempted inducement of guilt ("coward", "peacenik", and "shirker" were some of the kinder epithets she slung my way). I stood there, took it, didn't respond or argue, and when she finally slowed down to catch her breath, I told her thanks anyway for her concerns, and turned for the door. I should have known better than to have assumed everyone was going to see the world my way. She didn't stop, but she was slowing down, realizing that other than stating why I was there, I had offered no rebuttal, or even a comment on her venal attack. It was okay, it was going to be part of the deal, and I may as well get used to it. I was a bit flushed myself, having just weathered her broadside, but all I could offer was a glare over my shoulder as I left. Later I learned she was an Army brat, and that explained a lot. Apparently one of the Chemistry teachers later took a fancy to her and they got married and she mellowed out considerably after that. Nonetheless, if that poor bastard ever got on her wrong side (and how could he not eventually?), I'm sure he would have rather considered a lifetime commitment with a carping harpy from hell a preferable alternative (as if he hadn't already made that choice). Maybe some things were worse than going to Vietnam.

Blodgett Gardens

Since I was in Orlando, working on the conscientious objector business, I needed work and my good friend Frank, who I'd gone to Maine with, suggested that I might work at his family's nursery business (which just happened to be right next door to Bishop Moore High School). I went and talked to his Mom, Frances, and she said she'd love to have me work there, one of the reasons being that only she and her Dad, Mr. Blodgett, were there during the week. The other kids dropped in when they had a chance from their other jobs, and school, and lives; and they'd be there on the weekends, so I could have my weekends off. Mr. Blodgett was getting on and was in his early 80s and lived on the property, so a good part of my duties were to help him out around his house, as well as just to be there if something heavy needed to be moved or planted. Otherwise, I could help around the nursery with general duties, including sales, potting plants, weeding, spraying, etc. The only trouble was, she could only pay me $85 a week off the books, which was only about $2.12 an hour, but she'd buy me lunch every day, and she'd bring in donuts and coffee in the morning. This was okay by me, and she was very understanding when I had other things to attend to, or was late, or was hungover. Frances, or rather Fran, Francisco was a tough, wiry, and smart tomboy of a mother, and at that time ran the nursery off the cuff, quickly adjusting to conditions as they arose. She wore jeans and flannel shirts with rolled-up sleeves, and always, always, had her pruning shears in a little leather holster on her belt. I always called her Mrs. Francisco until several months in when she told me "Look, we're all grown-ups here, call me Fran." Mr. Blodgett, her Dad, was tall and thin (as most 80-some-year-old men are), with watery blue eyes behind thick glasses, thinning white hair, and a quick perfect-plated denture smile. He always wore short sleeve shirts, even in wintertime, and although it never seemed to bother him, he was always cold to the touch, being thin and old, and we'd have to work hard to convince him to put on a sweater when it got really cold. His house on the grounds of the nursery was always dark, and slightly unkempt (I should talk), but comfortable, and I would often fix lunch for him when Fran was away, and we'd sit and talk. He was the most fascinating conversationalist, and you never knew what subject he'd bring up next. He could switch from talking about life in Orlando in the 1930s and 40s, to religious concepts of life after death, to the mysteries of women (always with a twinkle in his eye), and all this in a matter of a half-hour. The only time he'd get tongue-tied and choke up is when he started talking about his departed wife, and then I'd have to divert the discussion, because even I couldn't take it to see him like that. Bottom line however, he was a nurseryman *par excellence*. He knew not just the common names of plants, but the Latin species and sub-species, and each its individual requirements: how much sun, special nutrients, seasons of blooming, seeding, pruning, when to (or whether to ever) transplant, their medicinal qualities, pests, etc. Whereas Fran was the brains behind the business end of the nursery, Mr. Blodgett was the soul of the place, and there were dozens of people who would show up to either ask him advice, show him some project they were working on, or beg some slips or cuttings off of one of his many exotic floral experiments. I learned a great many secrets of nature from him, and one of my favorites was where he would go shopping at the local grocery store, pick out the biggest, brightest, and most flavorful fruits, bring them home and surgically remove the seeds as we relished gobbling down the carcasses. Now you can't do it with every fruit (most citrus products have to be grafted, and other fruits often need the shock therapy of a winter cold snap or even a hard freeze), but some, like avocados, peaches, plums, even a few apples, can be grown right from the seed, or pit. What he was doing was taking all the effort the big companies out in California had put in developing these various strains, and putting them right into his own little backyard mist beds, to propagate some of the best fruits and vegetables in Central Florida, and three or four months later, sell them right out of the nursery. Not just evolution in action, but a brilliant piece of business acumen as well. They were always good to me, and I'll always remember my days at Blodgett Gardens fondly.

Mom Cared

While I was biding my time in Orlando, and pursuing the conscientious objector status, Mom convinced me to sign up as a volunteer for We Care, a local suicide and drug-prevention telephone hotline that she had been associated with for a number of years already. She thought it would do me some good, keep me out of the local bars in the evenings, and it wouldn't hurt the pursuit of the conscientious objector status as well. It was a strange thing, really, that none of us in the family really appreciated or understood, but in retrospect, Ma should have been given provisional sainthood just for that stint alone. She had suffered from insomnia for years while we were in high school, and this was exacerbated by Dad's drinking, which did get bad there for a while, although he never lost a day's work because of it, nor did I ever see him even once suffering from a hangover. But things at Martin had gotten pretty bad as the war in Vietnam began to wear down, what with a lot of layoffs, and guys who had been close and trusted pals for years had to make choices for job survival that often tore them apart, him often having to help make the decisions as to who stayed and who went. The layoffs could destroy whole families at a pink slip's notice, and the tension was palpable throughout the community. As a result, Dad started hitting it pretty hard when he got home from work, and there were more than a few resulting riotous altercations between him and me and my brother, and worse, with Mom, who loved him dearly. [Dad once told me a story about one of the older guys who had gotten laid off rather abruptly. The guy was never going to get another job to match the one he'd just lost, and he knew it. During the final week of his last two weeks' notice, while he was still covered, he just drove off the Interstate into the median and crashed into one of the concrete bridge pylons that held up an overpass. No note, no forewarnings, and no reason, according to the traffic report. But since it was an accident, and fatal at that, his family got double indemnity from his maxed-out insurance, and they were set for life. Dad said he knew the guy, and how the layoff had affected him, and he was convinced it was no accident.]

So Mom was doing this We Care suicide hotline most evenings, which often included her having to go out to really nasty parts of town late at night, often alone, to "save" some distraught and hysterical (almost always a) woman from offing herself (on more than one occasion, the next

110

morning she would show me some handgun that she had talked someone into handing over, and there were many nights she stayed at the hospital while some poor girl got her stomach pumped). I went in and signed up for the telephone counseling end of it, and it was pretty cut and dry stuff. They started me off on the Teen Hotline, and this consisted for the most part of young jilted girls crying and bitching about their boyfriends. All I had to do was listen sympathetically, agree with them that they were better off without the bastard, and ask them if they needed any followup counseling by any of the other referral agencies at our disposal (which they never did, *unless* they were pregnant, and then that ratcheted things up a notch). Later I moved on up to the adult We Care suicide-prevention end of the business, and even though I didn't go out on any runs (these were handled by trained interventionists, of which Ma was one), it sometimes got very tense with people who were obviously depressed for any number of reasons, many of which were undoubtedly physical in nature. But again, a sympathetic ear, an empathetic conversation, and an offer for followup counseling (which in these cases was often sought and given), and the phone call, which might last as long as an hour, could often be terminated without regret. Never did I have anyone kill themselves over the phone, nor did I ever hear of it happening, although threats of it, crying jags, cursing, and hangups were quite common. Usually, there were two of us on a shift, which might run from 8 to midnite for me, and we would sit across from each other, at two facing desks, each taking a call as they came in. So if you weren't on the phone with your own "client," you might very often be sitting across watching the other phone counselor's face, and from that you could tell just how serious the situation was that he or she might be dealing with. They also had rookie police officers go through the phone counseling training just to warm them up as to what situations they might expect once they got out there on patrol.

A Sympathetic Ear

Well, one night I'm sitting across from one of these new cops, a detective-in-training, short-haired, in civilian clothes, we're talking for a little while, getting acquainted, and I've already decided he's one of those full-of-himself self-righteous born-again assholes, when my phone rings. I answer it and there's a female voice on the other end and I give the normal intro "We Care, how may I help you?" She says "Well, I really don't have a problem, I just want someone to listen... would you be willing to listen to me for awhile?" "Sure," I says, "that's what we're here for... but you said you don't have a problem..." "Well, the only problem I have right now is that I'm really horny..." (!?!?) Whoop, whoop, whoop... my alarms start going off. She goes on, "I've got this big old sausage I had in the refrigerator, and I've warmed it up, and I just want to use it to get off... but I'd really like it if you would listen to me while I do it, would that be okay?" Holy shit! I look across the abutting desks, and the detective wannabe is looking at some of the magazines they had laying around. "Yeah, sure, I can listen to you, like I said that's what we're here for... but if I get another more serious call, I'll have to take it, okay?" "Sure," she says, and then goes on, "I've taken off my pants and underwear, and I'm sitting here with my legs up on the kitchen table, and I'm rubbing this big, thick sausage between my legs right now..." and she went on, her voice getting huskier, and her breathing getting more rapid. I looked across the desk and there's police-boy looking at me, looking around the room, looking at his watch. Finally, his phone rings, but it's someone he knows and it's just a short message and he quickly hangs up. He gets up and fixes himself a cup of coffee. Meanwhile this girl is going at it, I'm trying to keep a straight face while she's moaning, saying, "Are you listening, can you hear me, oh God, it feels so good..." and I'm flushed and answering as steadily as I could "Yes, I hear you, uh huh, go on..." Finally, she lets out a panting groan, and after about thirty seconds of heavy breathing, says "Oh, man, that was good. I really needed that. Thank you so much for listening to me. I hope you don't mind, but I've got to go now." "Okay, bye," I say and gently hang up the phone. The dickhead detective says "Was it serious?" seeing the shock on my red-flushed face and how quiet I am. "Yeah, pretty serious," I said, "but she worked it out all by herself. Just needed someone to listen to her." He replied laconically, "Those are the best kind." "Yeah, you're right," I agreed.

GOP Miami '72

As the summer of '72 waned, an old cab-driver friend of mine, Bill Rehberg called and said he was going down to Miami in late August to demonstrate at the Republican National Convention. He was passing through Orlando, and how would I like to go along? Well, this was perfect! All the paperwork was in and I was just waiting on a determination of my conscientious objector status, what better way to express my objection to the war than to demonstrate at the unchallenged GOP nomination of Richard Nixon in Miami. [Does anyone remember CREEP, the Committee to Re-Elect the President? Serious as a heart attack, I kid you not, and the Nixon cronies were proud of the acronym!] So Bill showed up in late August, left his car at my parents house in Orlando, and we hitchhiked down to Miami. We both had long hair and beards by then, so sometimes it was an hour or two between rides, but I remember the last ride we got on the turnpike was from a van with a couple of biker-types, and these guys were smoking pot and drinking beer all the way. When we got to the outskirts of Miami, they took us to their dirty little cinder-block "pad" in a crummy neighborhood, with sheets for drapes, overflowing ashtrays, empty beer cans on the tables and floor, and a couple more big and ugly bikers, and one thin and quiet straight-haired biker-chick. Bill and I bought a couple of six-packs of Colt 45 tallboys to stay on their good side, but after sitting around for awhile it became clear that they weren't going to take us any farther, even though when they picked us up they said they'd take us all the way to Flamingo Park (staging area for the demonstrations). Soon the beers were disappearing fast, all the joints had been passed around, and it looked (and sounded) like the bigger biker boys were taking turns with the girl in an adjacent bedroom. At some point it was suggested that maybe Bill or I would like to participate, but we were getting very nervous by this time and the bikers were already starting to argue amongst themselves (never a good sign), so Bill and I thanked them for the ride, and made a hasty retreat. We got to the main road, and a guy in a truck picked us up and deposited us within two blocks of the park, where we quickly found a plot of ground deep inside the park alongside the handball court walls and established our presence among the disparate and motley hipsters and their granny-gown girlfriends. The entire park was enclosed by a wall several blocks square, and from the inside the organizers had established guard-like watchtowers to observe those coming and going. They also could see outside the walls and across the adjoining streets where there were large numbers of "business" men in short-sleeve white shirts and ties, some in nondescript black cars and some walking about just watching, constantly watching. They looked like a phalanx of Mormons.

The demonstration staging area inside the park was well-organized, and after getting a bite to eat at one of the food kitchens, we settled down and met some of our neighbors just as the sun was going down. There was going to be a concert that night down on the baseball field, and people had already started painting their faces and making impromptu costumes. We had a small hit of orange sunshine, so we split it and headed down to the field to get a good seat. It was a raucous good time, sponsored by the Zippies, a theatrical offshoot of the politically-radical Yippies, the Youth International Party, which had been in existence since the Democratic Convention in Chicago in 1968.

[Forgotten little known fact: the 1972 *Democratic* National Convention had already been held in Miami only six weeks earlier, with little public (or revolutionary) fanfare, even though the inside maneuvering had been highly contentious between the avowed anti-war peaceniks Hubert

Humphrey, Eugene McCarthy, Edmund Muskie, and the eventual nominee, George McGovern—all of which is chronicled in Hunter S. Thompson's *Fear and Loathing on the Campaign Trail '72*. The Republicans, however, moved their convention site from the original site in San Diego to Miami on short notice in May because muckraker Jack Anderson had discovered an attempt by International Telephone and Telegraph to bribe the U.S. Justice Department by donating $400,000 to the San Diego bid as the site of the GOP convention in return for a favorable ruling on an antitrust suit. As the YIPpie protestors out West started to get organized, the San Diego mayor promised that if they showed up he'd crack heads worse than what had occurred in Chicago in '68, so the Republicans quickly changed venues at the last minute to avoid the bad press. This way they could also avoid most of the many bad-natured, well-organized California protestors, in favor of the fewer and more laid-back Florida ones. It didn't matter much though in the long run, since it wasn't going to be a convention per se, but actually a coronation. CREEP had done their homework.]

Although I don't remember much of the rally concert that evening, I do remember one band playing a scurrilous sing-along song with the chorus "Bozo Rebebo Makes Love to Tricky Dick" (Charles "Bebe" Rebozo being Richard Nixon's flashy Cuban-exile pal who often stayed weekends with him at the "Florida White House" compound on Key Biscayne) and another song by a Grateful Dead-takeoff band with the title "Eat the Rich!" extolling the practical aspects of feeding the fattened well-to-do to the burgeoning welfare roll have-nots. Later, we stumbled back to our campsite to catch some sleep before the next day's big march.

When we awoke they were handing out donuts and coffee. This was great! The march wasn't scheduled to begin until noon, so there was plenty of time to walk around and explore, and the park was not unlike a grand carnival with all kinds of long-hairs, half-dressed women, and painted faces amid a congress of tents, lean-tos, tarps, blankets and firepits. Around one of these tented campsites there was a serious discussion going on among both the wild-eyed firebrands and a few middle-aged and graying older gentlemen in short-sleeve shirts, so Bill and I sat in to listen. It was a sober discussion of how the demonstration needed to be carried out. There were those who felt signs needed to be made, but what would they say? No to Nixon? Well, he was going to get the nomination anyway, no matter what, so that was a waste of time. End the War? Hell, we were already pulling our troops out and the peace talks in Paris had finally decided what shape the table was going to be, and now they were actually talking, so the war *was* ending. They decided that signs were okay on an individual basis, just as long as they weren't offensive and didn't say "fuck" or "shit" and didn't try to establish some sort of theme for the demonstration as a whole. The people watching their TVs knew why we were here. In the end, the only sign I ever saw was one that said "Eat the Rich!" from the song of the night before. Even that one was considered offensive by some of the more timid protestors, because it espoused violence, if not cannibalism.

What if the police start getting violent? Could we defend ourselves? Should we carry things like sticks or clubs? That's when one of the clean-cut middle-aged grey and balding men stood up and soft-spokenly said, no, if you carry anything, having something in your hands would only encourage a violent takedown as an excuse to "prevent violence." No, a peaceful demonstration didn't mean YOU wouldn't get hurt, it meant that you wouldn't hurt anyone else, or destroy any property. And as long as we were peaceful, we had the Constitution on our side, and the public would be sympathetic, if not supportive, of this demonstration against a sitting President and "Four More Years!" He was very persuasive, and I later learned that this was the famous long-lived intellectual and anti-war protestor David Dellinger. We had an hour or two before the

113

march was setting out, so we went back to our campsite to rest up. We had just gotten there and laid down when this scrawny hippie with long blond hair and no shirt came walking up carrying a yellow plastic bag in his hand, half full. "Hey you guys, you want some 'ludes?" and he held out the bag. We looked at each other, and said, "Sure, man," and he said "take all you want…" (All we want?!?!) We were polite though and only took two or three each. Then he wandered off, handing out these Quaaludes like candy to everyone who was in the area. Quaaludes were methaqualone, a central nervous system depressant that makes you very groggy for several hours, and was a common recreational barbiturate at the time, although they usually went for something like $5 apiece. Luckily, we didn't take them right then, but just put them in our backpacks for later. Not ten minutes passed when another long-haired hippie, taller and older, and somewhat frantic, ran up and yelled "Anyone seen a guy handing out Quaaludes?" "Yeah, he just came through here…" He started jumping up and down, and then he cupped his hands and started yelling loudly to anyone in hearing distance "DON'T TAKE THE QUAALUDES! DON'T TAKE THE QUAALUDES! IT'S THE CIA! THEY'RE HANDING THEM OUT SO YOU CAN'T MARCH!" He asked us which way the guy went, and we pointed out the direction, and he ran off, but then you could hear him again yelling further on. Bill expressed my sentiments exactly, "Well, I'll be gawd-damned."

We started to line up around 11:30 and it was very well organized. We were all pretty excited and a few of the older hipsters with bullhorns were both working us up and passing along sage advice at the same time. "Four No More! Four No More!" and "Don't take your ID, leave your things here and they'll be guarded! Go to the bathroom now! Here, drink some water!" And then it was time. As we literally marched out the main gate two and three abreast, we were met outside by a gantlet of the short-haired and short-sleeved white-shirted guys with ties and we had to march out between them as they were taking pictures and carefully looking to see what we were carrying, if anything. I didn't see anyone get pulled out of line, but you definitely got the impression that they could have done so if they wanted. Then, all of a sudden I saw a familiar face. It was the dickhead detective wannabe from We Care! He didn't recognize me, or pretended not to, and I couldn't help but point him out to the crowd as we passed by "Hey, I know this guy! He's a cop from Orlando!" He ducked down and scurried off, as if we didn't know that all these guys were law enforcement of one kind or another. Onward, we pushed on into the streets, stopping traffic just by our presence, walking between the cars. A few horns were blasted, and a few curses were flung out, but generally, the people in the cars and on the sidewalks were smiling, and more than a few were flashing the "V for peace" hand sign. I remember passing close by one car with a cute girl sitting behind the wheel and she was smiling, and her window was down and I said, "Why don't you join us?" She said, "I'd like to, but what would I do about my car?" and I told her "Just lock it up and leave it." She laughed and flashed me the peace sign.

So here we are, walking (as opposed to "marching") down the streets of Miami Beach, traffic at a standstill, between and among cars trying to get either home or somewhere else, and around the corner comes another contingent of demonstrators (latecomers!) and who is at their forefront? Allen Ginsberg! (Which is why they were late since, being devotees, they had to wait on him, being fashionably late for the demonstration.) As our two groups converged and began moving up one of the main avenues, it just so happened that I ended up right next to him. We were all singing, chanting, and yelling when someone raised their hand, and we all got quiet as we heard a "TRAMP, TRAMP, TRAMP" coming from far off, but getting louder. "Here they come!" someone shouted. And around the corner, to the left of us, came an organized troop of black-suited police with helmets, batons, riot gear, and the whole surreal darkness of the ghosts of Kent

114

State. No one was laughing or happy now; these guys were scary. Once they'd swung around the corner in unison, they moved out of their tight formation and started to widen their presence, effectively closing off the street, from sidewalk to sidewalk. Then around the corner to the right, "TRAMP, TRAMP, TRAMP" another cadre of armed cops, this time Highway Patrolmen in helmets, came down the street and cut us off from advancing. We were surrounded. Should we make a break for it, and try to get through their lines? Ginsberg, right next to me, said "Now's the time, lock arms and sit down!" and I locked one arm in his and the other in Bill's. Everyone locked arms and we sat down in the intersection. One of the black-op cops stepped forward and got out his bullhorn, "You are ordered to clear the streets immediately! If you do not, you will be arrested for obstructing traffic!" This seemed just a little ironic since they had us surrounded, and they themselves had blocked off the streets and also blocked any way of leaving. I suppose though, if someone had unlocked their arms from the rest of us at this moment, gotten up, and said, "The hell with this, I'm going home," they probably would have let him or her pass through. But no one did. After a few minutes, the guy with the bullhorn announced, "This is your last chance, if you do not clear the streets immediately, you will be arrested!" Well, apparently they had prepared for this and had cleared one of the sidestreets of cars by rerouting traffic. Now down this same sidestreet came a convoy of rented trucks, the large single-axle moving van type you might rent from U-Haul. The cops got the other cars in the street gently moving around the seated demonstrators and then the trucks backed up in a line some twenty feet away. They threw open the back doors, and started lifting people up off the street and sidewalk and depositing them into the back of the trucks. Then the demonstrators in the truck would stand up and start shouting curses at the police, while helping load their brethren. The trucks had all been rented from a single company, and on the side of each was the painted slogan "Dietrich Rents Trucks!" This quickly became a chanted mantra of "Dietrich Rents Jails! Dietrich Rents Jails!" When they got to us, and they lifted him up, Ginsberg started yelling "Be careful, I have a hernia!" and in fact, they carried him gently to the truck, with at least eight of them raising him up and then setting him gently onto the rear of the open doorway. I decided just to walk on over and jump up there myself since they weren't being nearly as considerate when lifting up us younger troublemakers, often giving them the old heave-ho that sometimes didn't quite always make it up and onto the waiting platform, with the poor lump dropping to the pavement.

They were pretty smart, those cops. Once the truck was full of maybe 40 people (and they separated them by sex as they loaded the trucks), amid the now loud cries of "Dietrich Rents Jails!" with fists in the air, yelling in unison, the back hatch was slammed shut. Banging on the inside of the truck walls, and immersed in total blackness, the truck began to move. Well, we all knew where we were going: to the Dade County Jail; but hell, it wasn't that far away, just right across the river, maybe ten blocks, so the banging and yelling kept on for awhile, until we realized, simply by the motion and speed of the vehicle, that this thing wasn't just weaving in and out of city traffic, but had pulled up onto a highway (not really on the scheduled route). One must remember that this was August in Miami, and with all the banging and yelling we had forgotten that there were no air vents coming in. We couldn't even get some sunlight to peek in under the hatch door in the back. The driver had pulled up and onto I-95 to take a little detour until we settled down. What should have been little more than a fifteen-minute delivery turned into a 45-minute rolling sauna roast. Luckily, because we had Allen Ginsberg, the Voice of Reason, with us, we quickly explored the benefits of an impromptu lesson in meditative contemplation and controlled breathing. Other truckloads in the caravan must have experienced sheer terror and/or panic, if not loss of consciousness. Nonetheless, when the door finally rolled up at the jail, we were all not only soaked in our own and others' sweat, but we were silently, seriously, and somnolently subdued. There'd be no more trouble out of us, that was for sure.

Ginsberg was the first off the back of the truck, and the first in line for processing. The rest of us just milled around, gasping like fish out of water, until we were directed into one of several lines. When we got to the head of the line there were a couple of shirt-sleeve cops, and they would take each of us, back you up against a concrete wall, and take a Polaroid photo. Then you and the photo were escorted to a nearby foldout table, where another cop had you ink your right thumb and put it on a piece of paper to which the Polaroid was stapled (I recall smearing mine ever so slightly, but the cop didn't notice, or didn't care). Then came a set of questions, beginning with your name. Bill and I decided to play the John Doe card, and then refused to answer any more. "Fine," the cop said, with a smirk.

Once we got a drink of water and a baloney sandwich, the 50 or so of us stuffed into a cell that would normally have held maybe twenty, and were entertained by Ginsberg, using a metal tabletop as a bongo drum as he sang Buddhist chants, recited poetry, and answered questions about himself and the Beats. But it didn't last long; he was the first one out the door, after maybe two hours. Over the next twelve hours they would call people one at a time, and the ones who had lawyers (and/or money) were released first. By the next morning there were maybe the twenty the cell would normally hold, and we were the worst, the down and out, the resistant, and the unclean. Those who gave them a name began to be released, and believe it or not, because we stuck to the John Does, Bill and I were the last ones let out of that particular holding cell. It was late afternoon by the time we got back to Flamingo Park and retrieved what little belongings we had. There was no rest for the weary, and we were told by the cops (who now occupied the park) to get out of town as soon as possible in no uncertain terms, preferably by dark. I remember standing at the toll booth on the Turnpike just as the sun was going down. There were enough returning truckloads of demonstrators heading north, however, that we had no trouble getting a ride in the back of a pickup. We slept all the way to Orlando. You've got to admire the Founding Fathers, young and as naïve as they were: that saving the country from tyranny stuff is a lotta hard work, besides being a royal pain in the ass.

8. Tallahassee Redux (1973 – 1975, or Thereabouts)

Recycling

Since I was still spinning my wheels in Orlando, working at the nursery, Blodgett Gardens, and waiting to hear from the draft board on my petition as a conscientious objector, I bought an old Ford pickup truck for $450, one that had obviously been recently repainted a bright red and white. It ran rough but was otherwise dependable. As winter came on, and Nixon got re-elected after proclaiming "Peace was at hand," and despite Watergate, which was heating up, things slowed down at the nursery and I decided I'd move back to Tallahassee and await the draft board decision up there. I packed what meager belongings I had, drove on up to Tallahassee, and jumped right back into my old bedroom with the mattress on the floor and my head in the closet at Ballard Road. It felt like home. Now Dennis was living there, with Frank and Greg. I got a job at a nearby paper recycling plant, which was within walking distance if I cut through the woods. It was a strange operation, where it was my job to bundle these broken down cardboard boxes into a hydraulic smasher, and once I could smash no more, I'd leave the hydraulic on the high end and run these large long wires around the bundle, twisting them taut, and then release the pressure, and push the bundled cardboard block out the end. Then I'd pick it up with a forklift and stack it in a truck trailer parked on the property. I did this with good white paper as well, which paid ten times the cost of cardboard when they could get it, but that was a rarity. Although they had guys all over town who would drop off truckloads of cardboard and other paper for a couple of bucks, the owner had a system that gave him a constant supply He had one of his foremen stand out on the road and flag down garbage trucks that were heading out of town to the city dump past the plant which then existed out Springhill Road where the airport runway now lies. He'd have these trucks just dump the garbage-laden filth on the flat concrete floor. Then the foreman would scoop up a load with the forklift and a metal catchpan on the front that they had welded together just for that purpose. He'd lift it up and shake it onto a conveyor belt that sloped upwards, and a gang of maybe four or five black ladies would sort through the swill and toss off whatever paper products, boxes, notepads, or newspapers, etc. they could lay their hands on (and these were not days of sanitary rubber gloves either, although it was so nasty that sometimes the women would bring their own heavy thick dishwashing gloves from home). But the garbage, trash, waste, and offal that those poor women had to contend with was just awful. There were dead animals, leftover food from restaurants, medical waste, grease, oil, used tampons and sanitary napkins, and any kind of imaginable tripe, vermin, and rot you might expect to find in the city's refuse. And when the ladies would get fed up, or a paycheck was late, or they just couldn't stomach it any longer, guess who would have to go up those greasy metal stairs and help go through it. As the conveyor belt went up, there at the top the non-paper remnants of garbage would finally drop into the large bed of an old dilapidated high-sided truck, and once it was full, or the day ended, I'd have to drive the truck out to the dump (the garbage's original destination), and dump it into the landfill. The truck didn't have any kind of tarp or cover, and one day when I was driving back to the plant, a sheriff's deputy pulled me over and read me the riot act. Pointing back along the road, he showed me that scraps of garbage had blown out of the back of the truck and had littered both sides of the road. He gave me a ticket for a bad taillight ($110) and told me that unless I walked up to Capital Circle and back on both sides of the road and picked up all the loose pieces, he'd also give me a ticket for ten or twenty counts of littering, at $25 a pop. So I walked those two half-miles and picked up every piece, and when I got back to the shop, I told the boss that, no matter, I wasn't going to pay the $110, since the taillight wasn't my fault, and if he didn't like it he could go ahead and fire me. He paid it. I was making pretty good money, but it really was a disgusting job. So much so, that I'd wear the same clothes all week and wash them only on the weekends, since it didn't make sense to en-filth a different set of jeans and shirt every day. But every night I scrubbed myself in a hot shower trying to get the smell and grease off of me before pulling on some more comfortable duds. Then, in the morning, cringing, I'd pull the stiffened work clothes back on before tromping off down the dirt paths through the woods to work, loosening them up with the walk in the morning dew before I got there. It wasn't so bad at the factory once winter kicked in and the cold kept down the stench and the flies (and their progeny, the various-sized and mashable maggots). When I came home from work, oftentimes I smelled so bad that the other guys wouldn't let me in the house until I'd taken off my clothes and boots outside, then I'd have to go inside in my underwear and shower and change before I could hang up the dirty clothes in the carport to air out before putting them back on the next day.

A Little Litter Later

Luckily, just about this time, one of the paper suppliers decided he could do as good or better job than what was going on at the Springhill factory, and he opened a paper-recycling plant of his own over on Woodville Highway, right along the railroad tracks, so he could load directly into rail cars. The manager and I jumped ship at Springhill and went right to work with nice clean office paper and cardboard, and no more of that sorting through garbage business. Trouble was, even the new owner had trouble getting access to enough real quality paper to make it worthwhile, having gained the enmity of his former partner, and he was subject to all the rancor that the old man on Springhill could muster and have flung his way with over twenty years of contacts all over town. So it soon became apparent that this was going to be a losing proposition and eventually we'd have to close up shop. At one point however, as a last gasp measure, I asked to borrow his truck with its open-bed plywood-built trailer attached, and make a go of it to try and gather a couple of loads of paper on my own. He said sure, and I picked up a good friend of mine, Charlie Gear, who had just moved to Tallahassee with his new young wife, Rosie, and needed work, and the two of us went behind every State building, restaurant, and office we could find, and even though we spent a whole day scouring the city, all we could do was fill the trailer maybe a third of the way, hardly enough paper in weight to pay for the gas. Done and finished, we headed back to the recycling plant, driving down Apalache Parkway, when a car pulled up next to us and began honking his horn continuously, lights flashing. When I rolled down the window to find out what the driver wanted, I was met with tumult of curses and castigation. What the hell? He started screaming "Look behind you, goddammit!" continuing his tirade of abuse. We pulled over, got out and looked behind us and there, down the entire length of Apalache Parkway, leading up to the Old Capitol building itself, was a confetti-strewn path of paper on both sides of the highway, cars flinging up pages of memos, typing paper, and IBM cards as they passed. While driving, the back door of the trailer had come unlatched and we had lost half of the third of a load we had spent all day collecting. Having experienced this before, I knew that there was no way we could pick up all that paper, certainly not without getting killed on the highway or attracting the law, or both. Hanging our heads, we secured the trailer hatch, and quickly got off the main road. Gradually, by back roads and diversions, often slinking in behind a store or other enterprise to hide on the way, we slowly and circuitously made our way back to the paper recycling plant and I handed the owner the keys to the truck. "Sorry, Jack, it ain't gonna work out. Take care." I was at the Pastime that night having a beer when it came on the news (with the television reporter standing out there and papers flying about behind her as cars whizzed on by) that some itinerant and obviously uncaring litter-mongers had thrown hundreds of pages of paper, some involving State budget allocations, etc., all over Apalache Parkway. The case was "under investigation."

Lisa

     As luck would have it, one fine and crisp winter day, it snowed. It must have been a Saturday, because I wasn't working, and I'd decided to go into town and visit my old pal Bob Nolin, who lived a block up from the Governor's Mansion in the left barrel of that double-shotgun on Duval Street. When I got there, Bob was entertaining his new girlfriend, Celia, and her roommate, Lisa, with some wine and pot. Bob and Celia decided that to really get an eyeful of the white stuff, rare as it was, we needed to drive up to Georgia, where weather reports had said it was blanketing the countryside. After smoking a little more pot, we all piled into Nolin's old green Rambler wagon, him and Celia up front, and me and Lisa in the back, and we headed north up Old Bainbridge Road. And it really was beautiful. We careened up the old canopy road, through the overhanging live oaks, and then the stands of pine trees and winterized pecan groves, right on up to the Georgia Line, some 12 miles away. At some point we decided to pull over and walk up to a field we could see that was pure white, without a footprint, or any grass poking through. We parked the car on the side of the two-lane highway, trudged through the borderline woods to where we could stand along the hogwire and barbed-topped fence that surrounded the field and admire Nature's handiwork. After ten minutes or so of silent awe-fulness, and then another five minutes of snowball fights, it was time to go. As we walked back to the car, I noticed Lisa was flagging a bit. Apparently, she had worn pretty lightweight shoes, and she was really very, very cold! I helped her along with an attendant arm, which I believe she was grateful for, and by the time we got back to the car there may have been a different tone in the air. Then again, it may have just been me. Let's just call it romantic. We rode back to Nolin's and spent most of the rest of the day sitting around smoking pot, drinking, and comparing notes.

Bob had met Celia a couple of months prior, just before school started and while he was still driving cab. Celia was hitchhiking (not unusual at that time, in Tallahassee anyway, even for a girl), and he picked her up and gave her a free ride, neither of them realizing what that free ride was going to cost eventually. She was an art major, daughter of noble Cuban émigrés displaced by Castro after the fall of Batista. Lisa was a purebred Italian, second generation off the boat, from a working class family, and she and Celia had gone to high school in Lakeland together before teaming up to go to school at Florida State. Lisa was an English Lit major, and both were straight-A students and of course, New Age hippie chicks and recovering Catholics. Brilliant coupla girls, really. Lisa and I hit it off right away. I asked her out (alone) the next Friday and we went to dinner and had pizza and beer. It was a memorable first date for several reasons, one of which was that I'd forgotten my wallet and she had to pay for it. (I really did forget it, and I had a helluva time convincing her that I hadn't done it on purpose. I'd changed into nice clothes and left it in those stiffened up old work clothes hanging out in the carport at Ballard.)

Big brown eyes, a quick smile, a figure to die for, and a hearty laugh as well as a thick black Italian mane of hair, with a small mouth and slight overbite, a touch of the Arab showing in her royal nose, she was quite interesting. I guess I was too at the time, a tousle-haired cavalier and as dedicated a liberal as she'd ever encountered up til then (I'd imagined). She was sophisticated in her taste and broad in her artistic and literary knowledge, and I was constantly learning cultural phenomena second-hand from talking with her about her classwork, things that I'd never before been aware of, much less exposed to: a lot of the European stuff, you know, the Renaissance, the Baroque Period, Rembrandt (who I came to love), Goya, Titian, Bosch, and other artists, more Shakespeare, and the classical musicians: Beethoven, Bach, Berlioz, etc. It was eclectic and exciting, and soon we were all meeting, Bob and Celia and Dennis and Greg and Frank, et al, on a regular basis down at the Pastime to discuss both these historic and other world-changing matters.

She and Celia had long been planning a European backpacking and Eurrail-hostel summer trip for the Summer of '73 and had saved the travel money from their part-time day and night and whenever jobs as waitresses at the old Western Sizzlin' on Tennessee Street. Since she wasn't going to be around all summer I decided to go back to Orlando for a few months and tidy up loose ends with the Selective Service and maybe work and save up some money before they got back. The prior spring, while she was in heat, her dog Toto had climbed a tall fence, paw over paw, to get into a yard of a large black Labrador to get knocked up and when Lisa and Celia had gone backpacking to Europe that summer (while I was in Orlando), I happily accepted the responsibility, for Lisa's sake, of seeing Toto through her late stage maternity and parturition. I think there were nine pups, all born healthy, and I kept them and Toto out on the breezy back porch where I slept in the apartment I shared in Orland with two old high school buddies, Bill Gilbert and Brian Hurst.

Frankly, I Give a Damn

That summer (1973) with Gilbert and Hurst was the summer of Alice Cooper's *Billion Dollar Babies*, more Pink Floyd, Credence Clear Water Revival and Goose Creek Symphony. Speaking of Pink Floyd… they had scheduled a concert as part of the Dark Side of the Moon Tour at Tampa Stadium for June 29, so we put together a contingent to head on over. Besides myself, there were at least six others, my brother and a friend of his, Gilbert and Hurst, Frank Francisco and Bruce Dacey. We all piled into my red-and-white Ford pickup truck and to accommodate those in the back we put a large sofa in the pickup bed. We piled in around four o'clock so we'd have plenty of time to get there and get a good seat, and we smoked pot and drank a few beers as we went, but we saved the psychedelics for the show. It was a beautiful afternoon drive and when we got there the place was already filling up, so we ended up sitting near the top, nosebleed seats, which wasn't so bad for the panoramic effect. It was a fantastic show, especially enhanced by the psychotropes, but finally, it was time to go home. We all got into the truck, three up front and four in the back, and headed home to Orlando. It was a nice, clear, summer evening, stars out, and a little cool; the marijuana softened the edge of the last whispers of LSD, and we all were happy from the music and lights display (they even had the large helium flying pig and cow balloons). We were maybe an hour out of Tampa and an hour to go, when all of a sudden "WHAM!" We all jumped, and I looked in the rear view mirror and saw that the tailgate had fallen open. Whew! That was scary. I pulled over onto the shoulder of I-4 and latched it back up, hopped back in and we kept on going. Maybe five minutes later, one of the guys in the back tapped on the window, "Hey, where's Frank?" WWWWHHHAAATTTT? I whipped on over to the side, we all jumped out, and I pulled down the tailgate. We counted heads real quick—Frank was missing! Oh shit! Oh shit! We looked back down the highway… He must have been leaning up against the tailgate, and when it fell open he just tumbled out. Oh God, Oh God, what'll we do?!?!? "We've got to go back and look for him, no matter what!" "You're right, you're right!" "Oh, God, what am I gonna tell his parents?!" I latched the tailgate back up, and we got moving again. I was sick. Poor Frank! He's unconscious lying in the middle of I-4, probably getting run over and over again like some awful Sasquatch roadkill! Another tap on the window, "He's here! He's here!" I pulled over again and hopped out. There's Frank, sitting on the sofa with the other two, Bruce and Brian. "What the hell?" I asked. "I was cold from the wind, so I crawled up under the sofa and fell asleep. When you stopped and latched up the tailgate it woke me up." I guess I was still tripping, I was so glad that Frank wasn't killed, I wanted to cry, I wanted to laugh; I was still tripping, so I did both.

120

Air America?

One song that made a big impression that summer was Don McLean's *Bye Bye, Miss American Pie*. Why? It had already been out for over two years so it was rather old hat, even by then, but Hurst, who had started dating some barmaid/stripper he just met, decided that they were going to go to New Orleans, just so he could "take my Chevy to the levee." All-righty then. They headed out on a Friday, and were supposed to be back at work on Monday. Monday came and went; so did Tuesday Wednesday, and Thursday. They got back the following Friday and announced that they had continued on from New Orleans, went to Las Vegas, and were married! They moved out together and I haven't heard from him, or about him, since. (What are the odds he's still married to her?) While Hurst was gone, one afternoon my brother Paul was over visiting and, since it had been raining a lot, he and Gilbert and I decided to go hunting for psilocybin mushrooms. Where to go? We decided to head down to Taft, south of town, where in fact, circus trains would spend their winters and you could sometimes see giraffes, camels, and elephants grazing in the pastures. But since it was summer, they were on tour, and most of the pastures were turned over to cattle farmers. And it was far away from everybody, so we shouldn't be bothered, and it would be a relatively uneventful excursion. Or so we thought. Once we got down there we drove around a little and finally chose a nice broad green pasture, where we could see the cows congregating at the far end. For mushrooms of the right disposition, you needed dairy cows, brown and white Guernseys, even Brahmans, but if you stuck with the old black Angus beef cows, you'd usually end up empty-handed. Usually, one person would drop off the others, then continue driving around, returning in roughly fifteen minutes to pick up the pickers. But this time, we hadn't seen a car since we got out there, and it really did seem rather remote, so we decided to just park the truck and cut the time with three of us fanning out. It was now late afternoon, July 25th, 1972. (I'll tell you why I knew the date in just a minute.) After sweeping back and forth across the pasture, and not finding anything, we got closer to the cows at the far end, and damn, saw that they were beef cows, Angus. So we turned and headed back to the truck. As we walked we could see from a distance that there was another truck parked behind ours, and a guy in a cowboy hat standing near a fencepost. We dropped the plastic bags we had in our hands, and eventually started to approach the fenceline. Up swung a double-barrelled shotgun, pointed our way, and the cowboy, an old geezer neatly dressed, told us to "Put up your hands!" just like they do in the movies. With our hands "reaching for the sky" we tried talking to him, "Hey we were just looking around… we didn't bother the cows… we'd just like to leave… would you mind not pointing that gun directly at us like that?" But he was unbudgeable, "Shut up! You're trespassing! A sheriff's deputy will be here in a minute. Just stay put." And maybe ten minutes later, a sheriff's car pulled up; he got out, put on his hat, talked briefly with the cow farmer, and had him put the gun down. Then he invited us back over the fence. There wasn't much discussion, since we were caught dead to rights, although empty-handed, thank God. The deputy tied each of our hands behind our back with their new plastic zip-ties, which work extremely well, and put the three of us into the back seat of the patrol car. The farmer drove off in his pickup truck, and the sheriff's deputy called in on his radio, saying that he was going into the field to see if he could find anything. He then clambered over the fence, and we watched him go walking around the pasture. The sun had already gone down, and it was getting dark now. Over the car radio, we could hear him talking over his hand-held. After about ten minutes, he requested a helicopter with lights to help him scour the pasture. Holy Cow! In another ten minutes, the helicopter was radioing Orlando International Airport, which was maybe three miles east of us, for permission to enter the flight paths to assist the deputy. In another minute, permission was granted. The air traffic controllers agreed to have all approaching flights make another pass or two, and they'd hold up any departing flights too, while the helicopter crossed over to the pasture. They had held up all traffic in and out of the airport so that the helicopter, with its bright lights shining down, and sweeping back and forth, could hover over the deputy in the pasture as he scoured the area for "evidence!" We were astounded by the tenacity of both the cowboy and the sheriff's deputy, and wondered what the taxpayers, much less the passengers aboard the now-circling flights, and those stranded on the runways, would think about the wisdom of this turn of events.

After another ten minutes, the helicopter was cut loose, the Airport was put back to normal operations, and we were on our way to the jail downtown. We were booked for trespassing, and my brother spent his 18th birthday (July 26) in jail. In the morning, at our arraignment, we pled *nolo contendre* to trespassing, and we were fined $50 each, with time spent, and then they cut us loose. In another twist of fate, we had just walked out of the old City Hall building into the morning sunlight, when we heard a car honking. There was Mom driving by, and she had spotted us standing out in front of City Hall. She pulled over and rolled down her window, "What are you doing out today? Shouldn't you be at work?" We said we were taking the day off to celebrate Paul's birthday, and she said, "That's right, be sure and come by the house to get your presents." Apparently, Freedom's just another word for "Happy Birthday!"

Papa Joya

I was working again at Blodgett Gardens and when Lisa and Celia got back from Europe, I drove over from Orlando to welcome her back at the airport, and finally met her family, who were also there, though I hadn't really expected them (duh). Her Mom was sweet, short, and friendly; whereas her Dad, although small in stature, was that solid brick of an Italian father who was unimpressed, if not disappointed (and pissed) at the unlikely specimen that his daughter had chosen to take up with (a lowly, Irish-bred peasant, and even worse, a long-haired and unshaven hippie at that). I got to stay over at the house (in a spare bedroom), and when I awoke (or rather, when Lisa woke me up) her Dad was already working on her car outside. After a quick breakfast, both Lisa and her Mom made it clear that I should probably go out and help him (probably MY duty now to work on her car in the first place??? Italians! Lisa hadn't been home twelve hours yet, and I hadn't been awake more than an hour. [These are the rants of someone who is only looking at it in retrospective; at the time I just shrugged my shoulders and didn't care much one way or the other.]). Well, he didn't want or need any help, he was fixing the driver-seat-positioning mechanism that had gotten stuck and knew exactly what he was doing, whereas I hadn't a clue. He made it clear that it was a one-man job. That's okay. But then, going back into the kitchen with Lisa and her Mom, since I wasn't to be privy to their Mom-Daughter conversation (no doubt about me), and because I worked in a plant nursery (when I worked), you know, wouldn't it be nice if I trimmed the bushes in the back yard (!?!). Okay. Which I did for the better part of an hour, just to stay out of everyone's hair. It didn't matter; she was coming back to Tallahassee with me (by way of Orlando, to pick up the mutts.) Her Dad knew it, her Mom knew it, and I knew it. I have to say however, that even though I knew her Dad didn't like me (and never did), I liked her Dad. Perhaps because of it.

Back to Ballard

We left Orlando in two cars, my red-and-white Ford pickup and her old brown Dodge Dart sedan. She was almost overwhelmed by the puppies, who were now weaned and fat, and had clambered over any barrier I could devise and were all over the back porch, shitting everywhere. She decided to keep one and give the others to good homes. But we were all going to Tallahassee in the meantime, to stay at Ballard Road. Now that fall was arriving, Frank and his girlfriend at the time, a sweet blonde and buxom earth-mother named Hannah who had a wide smile and an infectious laugh, decided to move out of Ballard and get a place of their own. So I

122

asserted my rights and claimed the large room, with access to the shared bathroom and shower, by explaining that Lisa and her dog, Toto, a Benji-type mutt of exceeding, almost extraordinary intelligence, were coming as well (Toto too? Yes, Toto too!), and we'd need the larger room, with the bathroom, her being a girl and all. I got rid of the old red-and-white pickup and bought a small Ford Econoline van, the idea being that someday we could go camping. We moved Lisa out to Ballard, I moved my stuff from the small room across the hall, and Dennis took the other hallway room, Greg stayed put in his comfortable "office" at the end of the hall, and Bill Rehberg, whom I'd gone to Miami with, moved into the small room I'd left. So we had one nice happy, big family. When Lisa moved into Ballard, as I said, she actually brought along the aforementioned Toto and her puppies. The one Lisa kept, right from the beginning, was the large and ungainly son, with a pelt of soft black hair, appropriately named Pozzo, after one of the characters in *Waiting for Godot*. I say "appropriately named Pozzo" because I always though it meant "Crazy" in Italian, but now I find out that it actually means "well" as in an oil well, and that the correct Italian for "Crazy" is actually Pazzo, "to be crazy about something" like falling in love. Nonetheless, it was still an appropriate name for this large, but gentle beast in that he was, like Pozzo in the play, a hapless impulsive. Frank was kind enough to leave his waterbed, the first I'd ever seen, and Lisa and I had a lot of fun chasing bubbles. It's a weird thing though, as I'd never had back trouble in my life up until then, but after a week on that damn bed, I'd have to sleep a night on the floor to get my spine "stiffened" again. And it would suck the heat right out of you, even in summer if you didn't have a few insulating blankets underneath you. And then there were the dog claws invariably punching holes in it, and other causes of leakage. Otherwise though, it was great fun. Until it wasn't.

Lisa and I enjoyed the rest of winter and part of the spring together, and I even took a class at Florida State with her: Shakespeare's Later Plays, which were generally the darker ones, and we'd sit up talking about the characters, motives, and sub-plots inherent in *Othello*, *King Lear*, *Macbeth*, and *The Tempest*, which are the plays I remember us concentrating on. Of course, she got an "A" and I got a "B," even after giving it my best shot. On another front, I hadn't heard from the Selective Service in awhile and I wondered why. Then, it just so happened that the headlines in the paper, as a result of the signing of the Paris Peace Accord, declared that Melvin Laird, the Secretary of Defense had suspended the draft! It was January 27, 1973. I was free! The draft would formally end on June 23rd. If I had done anything different, I'd have been inducted for sure.

K-Bar Shucking

What could a fella do to keep "things right"? Well, I suppose one of those things would be personal safety. One Saturday afternoon we all decided to meet at Nolin's place downtown, sit on the back porch, and eat some oysters. Oysters were really the thing back then in Tallahassee, as they are even now. There were competing oyster shacks all over town, and they were always having contests to see whose shucker could beat the others. At one point, the contests got so serious, that one of the oyster houses that catered to the State legislators hired the former world champion shucker, a middle-aged gray-haired old German woman, named Heidi. She was really something to watch too. People would line up outside the oyster bar just to watch her shuck oysters lightning fast. And the strangest thing about it; she shucked them from the hard-to-open lip end, not the butt-end, like everybody else in the world. She was truly amazing. Well, that Saturday, when Lisa and I got to Nolin's, they'd already started, but there was only one oyster knife, so it was a slow process, waiting for each one of us to use the oyster knife in turn. So I asked Nolin if he had any other knives I could use (not having learned at that point that a screwdriver is probably as good or better than any oyster knife). Nolin went inside and brought out a Marine Corps K-bar knife, sharpened to a razor's edge, and handed it to me. [Nolin's always very helpful like that. Reminds me of the time when Celia asked him one night if he had a flashlight, so she could go check the water in the car battery, which had been giving them some trouble. "Here, just use this," he said as he handed her his lighter. The bandages around her eyes came off in about a week.] I start to work on an oyster, and yes, before you ask, we'd been drinking a few beers. I opened one or two, but the damn knife was large and unwieldy, and sharp. Just about the third oyster, I'm trying to manhandle it, and SWIP! Well, shit, I knew that I'd stuck it into my palm by the way I was holding the oyster shell, so I just turned my hand over to see if it had come out the other side. Yup… goddamn, there was a line of blood forming where the knife had come out the top of my hand. No one else had noticed, so I grabbed a cleaner one of the rags we had, wrapped it tightly around my hand and nudged Lisa. She looked up at me, and I leaned into her and whispered "We have to go to the hospital." "WHAT!? Why do we have to go to the hospital?" Well, now everyone looked up at me and I said, "Because I just put that knife through my hand." Lisa's going, "Let me see. Let me see." I said, "No, I already know that I put it through my hand. I need you to drive me to the hospital." "Lemmee see it first," she insisted. "Fine," I unwrapped it and opened it quickly so they could see the palm, the worst part. "Oh, shit!" Then she said, "we've got to get to the hospital." We got up, and quickly left the group. It didn't really hurt that bad at first, probably because of shock, and because I kept the rag pulled tight. We got to the emergency room, sat down, and waited. But it wasn't a long wait, maybe 20 minutes, when they called me in, and Lisa came along. A young intern in green scrubs sat me down, unwrapped the rag, looked at my hand and said, "Been shucking oysters with a knife, eh?" I hadn't said a word to him. "Yeah, how did you know?" I said. "See it all the time," he said as he put a couple of shots of anesthetic into it, and started to clean it out. When he was finished stitching it up, five in the palm and three on the top of my hand, he gave me some antibiotics, and told me that no matter how good he cleaned it out, it was still going to get infected, oysters being as nasty as they are, and the hand would swell up, and I might get a little fever. He said to just keep taking the antibiotics til they run out, rinse it in hydrogen peroxide once in awhile, and in a week, I could take the stitches out myself. And everything he told me happened just as he said. I think the whole business cost something like $60, which I gladly paid. Ahh, there's nothing like good old-fashioned universal health care; today that would have cost the taxpayers $600, if not $6000 or more.

The Running of the Geese

The puppies grew up rather fast, and we found good homes for them all (except Pozzo, of course, who grew up large and fast, eventually topping 75 pounds). The trouble was that we had *too* much room at Ballard and we couldn't fence it. So we'd let the both Toto and Pozzo out and they'd have acres and acres to run around in, and although they were pretty good about coming right back when called, every now and then they wanted to stretch their legs, and they'd have a go at it. But apparently that wasn't enough as it usually is with the rest of us. It just so happened that at the end of the old dirt road, adjacent to a block of trailers scattered in the woods, there was an old lady who raised gamecocks. That's right, fighting roosters, meaner than hell, each tied by a chain to its leg to a pine tree (to keep them from getting at each other), and a fifty-five gallon barrel upended nearby that they could perch on. She must have had fifty of them. No, no laws or even any agricultural regulations against it back then (1973), 'cause we were in the county, and even though we knew about these roosters, we weren't worried about the dogs getting at or even near them because they would jump up and spur anything that came near, and getting hit once, the dogs would steer clear of them. But we hadn't counted on other people raising fowl, and apparently one of the trailer residents had a gaggle of geese that he would periodically let out to forage in the woods round the trailers, they being naturally smart enough to stay away from the

124

fighting cocks. As luck would have it, one day while the dogs were out running, this guy had also let his geese out, and supposedly there was a wild free-for all with Toto circling them like a sheepdog and Pozzo cutting in and pouncing on the stragglers.

Lisa and I were sitting out front on the couch at Ballard when we heard the howling, a screamlike howl that just kept getting louder. Down the road, and up the dirt drive came Pozzo, running as fast as he could, "Owoooo! Owoooo! Owooo!," with Toto running alongside licking at his face. There was blood everywhere, and his lower left jaw just hung like it was barely attached, Toto lapping away as fast as the blood would run, him howling and crying. I was sure he'd been hit by a car. We picked him up and put him in my van, told the house to call the vet and tell him we were on our way. When we got there, the vet immediately gave Pozzo a shot to put him out, and after examining him told us that it looked like he'd been shot with a shotgun. He said that it didn't look life-threatening, but there was nothing we could do, and just to leave him there and let him work on him; he'd get back to us. When we got home I went down the road and knocked on a bunch of trailers, but no one would open the door, even though I knew they were home and could hear the televisions going inside. Finally, some woman opened her door, and when I asked if she knew anything about any shooting that morning, she just pointed at a certain trailer and closed her door. I went on over, put on my pissed-off face and knocked. I waited, and knocked again. Finally, the door opened and this skinny acne-scarred redneck in a T-shirt and shorts stepped outside, "Can I help you?" "You know anything about anybody shooting a dog out here this morning?" "Yep, I do, I shot that dog, 'cause he was killing my geese. Had one in his mouth, so I got my shotgun, walked up and shot it right out of his mouth. You want to see the dead goose?" Well, he had me there. It was a no-win situation. In the end, neither of us had our pets or livestock penned up, and if the dogs were killing the geese, well… "Did you have to shoot him?" I asked. "I'm sorry, man, I really am, but I didn't know what else to do," and he really did look like he was sorry. All I could do was leave with an empty threat, "This may not be the end of this…" And I knew it was an empty threat because, when it came down to it, I also knew exactly on which side the sheriff's office would land. "All right," he said and went back into his trailer. Some twenty years later, long after Lisa and I had gone our separate ways, and Pozzo had been dead at least ten years, I ran across this guy at a formal function being held at FSU. He was in a suit, and had cleaned up considerably. He had a drink in his hand, and when he saw me he came up and stuck out his hand, "Hey, I know you! Where do I know you from?" I didn't take the handshake, and just said, "You're the guy who shot my dog." You could see the recollection cross his face like a dark cloud blowing across the sun. He put his hand down, turned and walked away.

When we finally got Pozzo back, his jaw had been wired together and we had to clean it several times a day with hydrogen peroxide. The vet gave us a small handful of shotgun pellets, and a couple of teeth that had to come out, but otherwise, considering how young Pozzo was, and the attention we gave him, he recuperated fairly fast, and the wires came out in a couple of weeks. Meanwhile, we couldn't let them out, except on a leash, and it soon became apparent that even Ballard Road, as homey as it was, was getting a little crowded. Lisa and I were getting along pretty good; good enough in fact that we decided we were going to move out of Ballard and live in sin together. She was cruising along in school, so what the heck. We started looking around, checking out neighborhoods and places marked "For Rent" somewhere with a fenced in yard for the dogs. We were in the backyard of a house on Lewis Blvd, over by Palmer's Meat Market off of Woodville Highway, considering whether to go for it or not, when a pudgy little old man in a T-shirt and baggy pants, stocky, short, grizzled with a head of messed up white hair and a mouth full of snaggled teeth came over to the fence from the house next door and called us over.

"Looking for a place to rent?" We were a little wary, but he seemed harmless enough. "Yeah, we might take this one here," I said, pointing over my shoulder. The old guy asked "How much does he want for it?" Lisa and I looked at each other and figured what the hell, it's not a secret, "$250 a month." "Well, how would you like to stay over here for $150 a month?" he said, "no deposit." Now his house was twice as big as the house we were looking at, which in fact shared its lot with another house. And his yard was huge, he had a large garden in the back, chickens penned up alongside a rustic wooden workshop in the back, and it was all fenced in, which was a plus, considering the dogs. "Why don't you come on over and look at it, we'll talk it over, and then you decide," he suggested. Well, why not? So we walked on over.

Herb and Roy

His name was Herb Odel and on entering his house the first and most forceful thing that hit you was the smell. It smelled like a little old man who might live with a menagerie of animals, and who hadn't really cleaned his kitchen (or taken a bath) in ages. And sure enough, that's what it was! Besides the little one-bug-eyed Chihuahua that followed on his heels nervously dancing about, there in the corner of the living room was a tall cage wherein (no shit) sat a monkey, I'm pretty sure a macaque. After we did a quick walk-through to look at the various rooms, he let her out of the cage, and she bounded around the house, finally settling on his shoulder as he sat on his vinyl couch and invited Lisa to sit next to him. The monkey's name was Lottie, and she immediately began to pick at Lisa's hair, which was disconcerting to say the least, but so intent and gentle was the little simian, that soon Lisa just let her have at it. At least it kept her (Lottie, not Lisa) occupied while we talked. "So how did the little Chihuahua lose his eye?" "Oh, one day he growled at me and I gave him a smack on the back of the head, and his eye just popped out on a little string. I just pushed it back in and he hasn't been able to see out of it since." (?!?) Now the house was a bit ramshackle and had obviously been built from scratch, if not from leftover materials, but it was sizable, comfortable, and cheap. Herb had built it himself some thirty-five years earlier, and raised a family there, adding on various rooms as the family grew. His wife had died five or six years earlier, and he was getting lonely (one reason for the monkey and the dog). He told a fascinating story of growing up with Roy Rogers back in Ohio before Roy'd became famous. Told me Rogers' real name was actually Leonard Slye (which I found out was true), and that as far as he was concerned, the kid was nothing but a troublesome juvenile delinquent, but he could strum a guitar, so he packed up and went to Hollywood, divorced one, and then met up with his young wife Dale Evans, and the rest is history. No, he was never a cowboy, but everyone back then rode horses, and there was more than a little gunplay going on as well, which may have been one of the reasons for his leaving Ohio. Then, while we were comparing notes, Herb told me that he too, had grown up Catholic, and to prove it he lit right into the Confiteor, in Latin, and wouldn't quit until I told him, okay, okay, I believed him. And here was his proposition: we could have the large master bedroom in the back, and he'd move into one of the smaller "kid's" rooms down the hall. He loved dogs, and was happy that we'd be bringing two; he had chickens for fresh eggs, a large freezer on the back porch that we could stock with whatever we wanted, and all he wanted was $150 a month and the company. Well, we'd have to think about it, and we'd get back to him. Meanwhile Lottie finished preening Lisa's hair and gave me a sly sideways glance. "She doesn't cater much to men, except me," he said. Just as well, I didn't want that thing groping through my hair anyway.

Well, we decided to make the jump. In fact, I think it was the money ("money" not "monkey") that made us take the jump, but there was no doubt that it was going to be an adventure. We started off on a sort of trial basis, and he was ever so accommodating: friendly, funny, and even a bit wise for all his rough edges. He had a bunch of chickens, and we'd go out every morning and get half a dozen eggs or so, and his garden area was huge, maybe sixty feet long by thirty feet wide. Having worked at Blodgett Gardens and spring just coming on, this was going to be a lot of fun, so I helped Herb put in a crop of small red potatoes. The henhouse was attached to the side of his open-ended workshop, which was completely run down, but there were still lots of old-time tools for woodworking, pipefitting, electrical work, etc. hanging on the walls. Lisa insisted that he and I clean up the kitchen for human use and I was surprised to find he didn't have any detergent, or cleanser of any kind. "How do you clean the stuff out of the iron skillet here?" He went out the back door, threw a handful of sand in the thing and rubbed it around, then went back inside and rinsed it. I was down to the store and back in an hour with all kinds of cleaning supplies, and then I finished the job until Lisa was satisfied. It was only then we met Bertie. She'd come over to lay claim to her regular share of the eggs, and she walked right in the side door, never a knock or even a how-ya-do. A tall, half-bent, sort of broad old woman, she was maybe 70 or so (roughly the same age as Herb), with mussed-up greyish-white hair full of bobby pins, thick glasses, a bit of a limp, and an arthritic talon of a right hand, her underarm dewlaps flapping, and dressed in a plain, flower-patterned linen house dress. She stopped cold when she saw us. Herb introduced us and she just touched our outstretched handshake with her hand. "Glad to meet ya," she said. She gave Lisa the once-over, but she didn't really know what to make of me, long reddish-blond ponytail, a face full of fur. I don't think she'd ever been this close to a real live hippie before. But the real icebreaker was due to the dogs; she loved Toto and Pozzo right away, especially Pozzo. She took him with both hands by the muzzle and cackled happily as she shoved her mug right into his, reveling in his dog snot and slobber as he licked her face, a ritual that was repeated several times daily for as long as we knew her.

Bertie Jones

Alberta "Bertie" Jones was a Florida cracker woman the likes of which you rarely ever see any more. She lived across the street in a small two-room wooden shack with cracks in the floor, cracks in the wall, cracks in the ceiling, and at least six little black toy poodles that I swore were puppies the whole six or seven years that I knew her. She sat in a rocking chair that was always threatening to crush one of the pups, but never did. Although the floor in her living room, which couldn't have been ten feet square, was worn and wooden tongue-and -groove, she had it covered in newspapers upon which the little black bastards pissed and shit and ate all day and all night long, week after week, month after month. They might come out onto the porch when the weather warmed up and she'd sit outside, but I never saw them venture down the steps into the yard, ever, and I don't think she encouraged it anyways, "Too many rattlesnakes around." Although if I were her I'd have been more worried about the hawks in the neighborhood that were always dropping down unannounced and unanticipated, carrying off either some hapless squeaking squirrel, rat, snake, or small chicken. She dipped snuff behind her lower lip and was always spitting into an already-half-full coffee can. She ate Campbell's soup, cooked some great biscuits from scratch (though you'd never want to see her making them), and watched the television all day long, when she wasn't walking over to Herb's house to argue with him over one thing or another. All her garbage, empty Campbell's soup cans, snuff tins, shat-upon newspapers, rags, eggshells, etc. went right out the back door in a broad fan-shaped pattern depending on how far she could throw it that day. Once every month or two, when the weather got dry enough so she could pick up the scraps, she'd pile them into an empty fifty-five gallon drum and set it afire. Roaches? Oh gawd… what with all the dog shit and spilled dog food, the roaches were everywhere, and they were those nasty little German ones too, even though we all lived under the beautiful spreading live oaks that harbored the big palmetto bug ones as well. Sometimes, when things got quiet, you could hear them rustling behind the cardboard paneling in her house.

Oh yeah, her arthritic right arm? Oh, it was arthritic all right, but the reason it was claw-like was because it had been broken some thirty years earlier when her husband tried to beat her with an axe-handle, and she had fended off the blows with her right arm. "It was just never set right. He was not a very good man; bad drinker." Luckily, I suppose, they never had any children, and although she had a few relatives down in Woodville, they hardly ever came by to see her, and the closest thing she had to family was Herb (and now, us). Now Herb was a real go-getter and he'd be up before dawn, finish his "chores" and be off most of the day. He and his son, Bob (the good one), would earn extra money by going catfishing with a trotline down the Ochlocknee River, which ran near Bob's house. A trotline, for those who don't know, is a long piece of 100-pound nylon twine, maybe a quarter of a mile long, with hooks placed every yard or two. The idea would be to tie off one end of the line, then bait and drop the hooks as you went downstream. You'd let them sit overnight, and in the morning you rowed or motored your way back upstream, pulling up the hooked line and dropping catfish into the bottom of the boat. Then you'd go home, clean and strip the catfish, and then sell them to some local fish store for the going rate per pound. To keep the line from tangling, you usually placed the hooks in notches all around the edge of a square wooden frame, where another frame sat on top, and another, then going down the inside of the frames with the line piled up in the center as you baited them and tossed them over. And what did they use as bait? Ivory soap! They'd get five or six bars of Ivory soap and slice off dabs or small chunks and use them for bait. Apparently, being 99 and 9/10ths pure (lard), it was cheaper than any other bait going, with the advantage that it would float just off the bottom where the catfish liked to roam. In a single night of fishing and a half-day of cleaning they could rake in a couple hundred dollars, then they'd celebrate with a bottle of whiskey after taking Bob's family out to dinner. When this was going on, sometimes Lisa and I wouldn't see the old man for days.

Concrete Products

So now, back in Tallahassee, in a new house, it was time to get another job. I hadn't planned on anything in particular, but when I checked out a small concrete plant and asked if they needed any help, they asked me if I could drive a concrete truck. Well, I still had my chauffeur's license from driving cab, and this entitled me at that time in Florida to drive just about anything I wanted, but I had to be honest, "no, but I've driven other large trucks with a single axle, and I'm willing to learn." Good enough. They handed me over to one of the best drivers, a short chubby black man named Carless. [I asked him if he meant his name was Carlos, but he said no, his Mama named him Carless because when he was born they didn't own a car. Go figure?! Later in life, I met a guy in the Virgin Islands, another black guy, who worked on fixing the 'gypsy' taxicabs, who told me his name was I-ran. I said "do you mean Ihr-Ran, like the country?" "No," he replied, "my name is pronounced Eye-ran, and my Mama told me it was because when she was pregnant with me, she had to run from the police, and when she got away without getting caught, she was so happy that when I was born she named me I-Ran, and it's the one I'm stuck with."] Anyway, Carless took me under his wing and after riding with him for a week, I was ready. If I recall correctly, those things had twelve gears: six low, just to get the damn truck moving, and then six high to keep you going. When driving, you had to plan way ahead, because once the truck was loaded with nine cubic yards of liquid concrete (one cubic yard being roughly equivalent to a pickup truck load), Newton's First Law of Motion kicked in, and that truck was going to keep going in the direction intended until something acted on it to either change direction (steering), or slow it down (brakes), and the brakes were air brakes that built up pressure in an air tank as you drove, but if you used them too much or too often, and the air pressure dropped below a certain limit, well then, you had no brakes until you built that pressure back up over several minutes of driving again (other than a hand-emergency brake that was next to useless). Then there was the rotating drum that always lent a certain centrifugal pull to one side

128

or the other as it spun around while you drove along. It was an eerie feeling you had to get used to, especially when changing direction, but the cement had to be kept in motion, for as soon as it stopped moving it would begin to set, and the worst thing a driver could ever do was let a truck full of concrete set up inside his drum.

[It's actually a chemical process, put in action by the ingredients, but kept at bay by the agitation of the one aptly-named ingredient, quick-lime, which is nothing but burnt shell or limestone. It just wants to get back to its original form once water and sand is added, as "quick" as it can, with a little gravel, rock, and pebbles added to stretch it out a bit. It's not just that the concrete needs to dry out, like most people think occurs with a sidewalk under the sun, for instance. That's why concrete can be poured even under water; it will harden nonetheless, it's a chemical process! One other last fascinating feature of concrete: it gets harder the older it gets. Apparently some of the first modern concrete from the 1890s (the Spanish-American War stuff) is harder than the stuff we make today, given a set of comparable ingredients, although today we have more sophisticated methods of measurement for consistency, not to mention re-enforcing bar, commonly known as re-bar. It's a general rule of thumb though, that the older concrete is, the harder it is. Even Roman concrete is still pretty damn hard.]

To incur the cost of removing and replacing a drum full of hardened concrete attached to your truck (they'd just lift it off with a crane and bury it; they didn't even try to save the drum.) meant you were fired for sure and your reputation would follow you wherever you went, so that driving a concrete truck was never going to be a likely option again. Not so with "dropping a truck," what they called it if you rolled over, which happened a lot, considering how top-heavy those bastards actually were, or if you took a sharp turn to avoid an accident and the drum, loaded with frothy concrete might come loose, disengage, and go rolling down the highway spewing grey milkshake and rock-laden shit out the back hopper, hopefully coming to rest before (God forbid!) killing someone. No, this was a fairly common occurrence, and after the mess was cleaned up, and where there were no injuries or fatalities, the driver was just assigned another truck and he went right back to work. That's because the other drivers on the road, the ones in those quick little boxes of thin bent steel and overcompensating engines called cars, could never understand the might nor the maneuvering related to driving a concrete truck and they constantly and unwittingly either challenged that might and maneuvering, or otherwise acted thoughtlessly in the face of it. Rarely, if ever, was a driver at fault in one of these situations, and a ticket for a moving violation by a driver was unusual, if almost unheard of. Let's just say that the police were sympathetic to what the truck drivers had to put up with out there.

Mmmm, Sausage

Now, no matter how well you cleaned your truck, little by little some concrete would harden up inside along the crevices. So this meant that once every two months or so, you had to crawl inside the drum (with the truck turned off of course), and beat out any built-up accumulations with a small sledgehammer and chisel. Since I was still a wiry, slim kid back then and the other drivers (all black) were generally a bit older and stouter than me and couldn't just slip down the hopper like I did, they would have to work hard for an hour or more just to loosen and unlatch the "access port" that you can still see on the sides of cement truck drums today, this before they had any hope of "squeezing on in." So, they would pay me $10 or $20 to go into the drums on their trucks and bang out the buildup for them. The banging out wasn't so bad, except it was loud, like sitting inside a bass drum. No, the real danger lay in the blades. Each drum has two counter-spiraling blades welded into the inside of the drum to keep the concrete turning over and over again, and these blades were maybe 18 inches high. From the constant turning of the concrete, gravel, and sand, they were continuously honed to a razor-sharp edge. They were so sharp that you couldn't touch them, and if by some fluke you were to fall against one of them they would have sliced you in half just from the weight of your body's meat laying across the razor's edge. I'd had no idea how dangerous those blades were until I had to go into those drums and bang out the residue and saw them for myself. Then one day I had a delivery out to the FCI, the Federal Correctional Institution, out on Capitol Circle, a large federal prison that held white–collar criminals for the most part, but a few of the dangerous ones as well, either awaiting trial in Federal Court or a transfer to one of the other Florida prisons. I drove up the long drive, under the barrels of the machine guns in the watchtowers, and was directed by radio to go around the back, where an automatic rolling barbed-wire-topped gate opened and let me drive on in. They were fixing some underground utilities and I backed in and slowly regurgitated my load into the finished trench. Then I hosed off my truck as a couple of the working inmates smoothed off the slab, got one of the guards to sign the work order, climbed back into my truck and headed for the fence. This time the gate didn't roll back though, so I stopped, and a guard carrying what I could only describe as a machinegun came out of a side door. He asked me to get out of the truck, but leave it running, and open the hood so he could see the engine. Meanwhile he walked around the truck and had a mirror with a handle on a set of wheels so he could look under the truck. I finally got the hood unlatched and opened it so he could look inside. I asked him if he thought an escapee could possibly hide on top of the running engine, and he said it had been done before with a guy who threw a carpet mat over the engine and laid atop it until he got out beyond the fence and down the road. "Well, what about that drum? That could hold a dozen prisoners," I said, "Don't you want to climb up there and look on in?" "Nope," he said, "Just give it a good spin." I told him "You know, there's some pretty sharp blades in there, and if anybody were in there they could get hurt pretty bad…" "I know," he said, "Spin it!" So I gave it a good empty spin, way too fast for anyone inside to hang on and live. Then he asked me to reverse it slowly. You see, it's when you reverse the drum that the concrete (or whatever else might be in there) is brought up to the top and then rolls out the hopper and goes down the chute. Luckily, nothing came back out. I still didn't feel comfortable with the idea that he had me spin it just because he was too lazy to climb the ladder and look down into the drum. What IF some prisoner had climbed up and in there when nobody was looking? There'd have been nothing but a pile of raw sausage on the pavement… and damn if both the guard and I wouldn't have both ended up in the headlines, possibly ending up inside those very same gates for good; him for being a lazy and world-weary prison guard, and me for just following (could you call them "Nazi-like"? How about just "fascist"?) orders. At the time though, I've got to admit, under the circumstances "it seemed the right thing to do, I was just following orders..." So much for Free Will, sticking it to "The Man," and Conscientious Objectivity.

He Rises!

Then there was the Capitol Building. Unbeknownst to me at the time, one of the reasons they had hired me to drive the truck was that the company owners knew that construction was soon going to begin on the new Capitol Building on land behind the old historic Capitol. For years, legislators, State Senators, and lobbyists had been fighting among themselves to move the State Capital from Tallahassee to Orlando, where it would be more centrally-located. But the old-timers, the real boys behind the power, didn't want any of that. Orlando already had Disney World, and the opportunity to get away to Tallahassee for four months out of the year and play around as they had for decades, under their own rules, was way too enticing. Hell, if they moved it to Orlando, you might have to take your family! So legislation was quickly passed to build a new Capitol Building, and they broke ground before the plans were even finished, so that they could stop any further talk of moving the Capital. To get the fence-sitters on their side, the size of offices, each with a view of the surrounding countryside, an increase in staff (and pay), and a city ordinance stating that no other building would ever rise as high to block that view cinched the deal. The construction fences went up, and the excavations began. To accommodate a parking garage below the chambers, some four stories of earth were removed. Then, one day everything stopped. We got a call. Start sending trucks, one after another, full loads, and keep 'em coming. And it wasn't just our company; it was every company in town.

While digging the parking garage, and then pounding pilings into the substrate to support the planned superstructure above, at some point one of the pilings just disappeared down a hole, a cavern, where a great emptiness was encountered. Now it was well-known that the area planned for the Capitol Building was riddled with Fuller's Earth, which is a type of clay that fullers (workers who used to soak fabric to make it more "full") used to use for de-colorizing and cleaning wool, thus "Fuller's Earth." It's also the main ingredient in cat litter and that stuff they throw down in garages to absorb oil (the same stuff I used back at Better Plastics under the leaky injection-molding machines). This Fuller's Earth had to be removed because it will shift and flow over time with the absorption of water, and you don't want that below a twenty-two story building. So they were removing the Fuller's Earth when they hit this gap. Well, the underlying limestone karst formation is also known to be riddled with gaps, but none had been anticipated here, atop one of the mighty seven hills of Tallahassee. Although we were told not to talk about the discovery of this surprising abscess, and I don't remember the newspaper ever picking up on it either, it led to all kinds of speculation about underground tunnels, escape routes, or secret treasure caves under the old Capitol to be used in the event of attack or invasion during the Civil War. One after another the trucks waited in line, then we each drove down the earthen incline into the excavation area, and backed up to a prepared off-loading ramp. Extending the chute as far as we could, we flung the entire 9-yard load down into the maw of what-we-figured was a bottomless abyss. To see an entire truckload of concrete, and then dozens more, emptied in a matter of minutes was an impressive sight. The loads in the hole were allowed to set overnight, and after two or three days of constant dumping, the thing finally began to fill, and the emptiness was conquered. I'm still amazed at how many other people don't remember this, or how few ever even knew about it. Some things are just so extraordinary that you can't make them up, and if you did, people would say "I don't believe that, it's just too strange." I still like to think that what it was may have been some sort of secret Masonic underground meeting hall for the old-time Antebellum legislators, with an escape route tunnel down near Cascades Park to the east.

Labor Lost
This was just the beginning though, because now the construction began in earnest. The powers-that-be also decided to begin construction on a new Department of State building, to be entirely crafted out of concrete, so we were running full days, every day, between the new Capitol rising in the sky and the State building two blocks away. Now though, you emptied three loads each into 3-yard buckets that were hoisted by ten and twenty-story high cranes to be dropped into pre-cast forms for pillars, stairs, walls, or what-have-you. It was a very exciting time. I guess I drove for about four months before it started to slack off, and then the inevitable happened, although I hadn't seen it coming. You see, I was the youngest driver, the only white driver, and the last driver hired. But I was good. One day, after the headlong rush of pouring the Capitol and then the Department of State had eased off, as we were all sitting around eating lunch on the loading dock of the warehouse, this white guy in a long-sleeve white shirt and tie walks in off the street, went around to all the drivers and handed out a handful of cards. We looked at them, and they were union sign-up cards. Actually, they were cards that you would fill out and if more than half the drivers sent them back, signed, then an election could be held that would allow the

drivers to organize or not (i.e., join the union or not). To be honest, back then, for all my liberal tendencies, I wasn't a fan of the unions one way or the other. Jimmy Hoffa was only recently released from prison (1971) in a plea deal with Nixon, so I didn't like the implied association. But the black guys wanted to know my opinion on the matter. Although I threw my own card away, I told them that "for you guys, this would probably be a good thing. But you either got to stand together or let it go, 'cause if only a few of you do it, they'll probably fire you." Well, an hour hadn't passed before one of the more timid drivers, in a show of company loyalty, went in and showed the card to the owners (and probably re-iterated what I had said). Damn if the next day they didn't announce that we were all to be evaluated for our driving skills, and they placed a bald white mechanic's assistant (not a driver, just an ass-kisser) in charge of making the evaluations. And stranger still, he only rode with me. Even though I'd already been driving for over four months, in some of the scariest and troublesome locations in town, and never had an accident or "dropped my truck" (although I'd had some close calls), now I could do nothing right, and this guy was put in my truck just to harangue me it seemed. And indeed it was so, since a week later I was given my walking papers, although it was made very clear that I was being laid off, and not fired (which I would have raised a stink about). Well this was fine with me. As long as I was laid off, I was eligible for unemployment, so I could sign up. Now I'd have the freedom to plan a real strategy for my life. Right.

The Red Bird Café

Just before they let me go at Concrete Products, I was really getting along great with all the other black drivers, even the old-timers who didn't like me at first. They knew I had given them good advice regarding the unionization, even if it wasn't what I was going to do. Sometimes on a hot day I'd bring in a cold watermelon from some roadside vendor, and share it with everybody during lunch, and they always enjoyed that (even while I was kidded about the white boy supplying the darkies with melon, and they always made it plain that I was the one who had to clean up the rinds that they would just fling to the ground when they were finished). In the afternoons, when it got slack and we'd be waiting on orders, they'd be throwing craps up against the back of the warehouse, and they showed me how to play So, during the last week I was there, when they all knew I was leaving, they asked me to come out with them for drinks on payday, Friday. "Sure, where we gonna go?" "We're taking you down to Frenchtown and going to the Red Bird." First of all, this is 1973 or '74, and despite what anybody might say, antagonistic race relations had only been quelled by the self-imposed voluntary separation of blacks and whites for years after the assassination of Martin Luther King in '68, even in Tallahassee, the home of historically black Florida A&M University. Frenchtown was the lower-class black section of town, just off of Tennessee Street, that housed juke joints, whorehouses, bars, and backroom gambling halls. It was called Frenchtown because it had been originally settled by free blacks and Creole Cajuns (like the French who settled New Orleans) soon after the Civil War. The Red Bird Café was a large unpainted wooden saloon on the northwest corner of Virginia and Railroad that had been around since the 40s and had been the venue for such famous jazz notables as Nat and "Cannonball" Adderly, Dizzy Gillespie, and many others. Even though the place was showing its age by this time, it was still the prime gathering place for blacks and black musicians in Tallahassee, especially on Friday and Saturday nights. The whole surrounding neighborhood though, was rife with nothing but guns and drugs and trash and broken bottles. It was not a safe place for a white long-haired hippie with a pocketful of payday to be going at any time, day or night, and I expressed my apprehension. "You just stick with us, we'll take care of you, and you'll be fine," they told me. So, in we went. They picked a large table in the very middle of the floor, and although the place didn't quite come to a standstill as I was escorted in, there was a marked downturn to the Friday-afternoon payday hubbub, and all eyes followed the

132

auburn-haired hippie to the seating. Lots of comments were whispered back and forth, but the boys at the table took special pains to surround me with friendliness and drinks. Eventually, drinks started coming in from afar, "for the white boy" and though I tried to reciprocate and buy a round or two myself, there was no keeping up. The noise went back up to its original level and after a ten-minute interval with my pals, I was relatively ignored. Old Carless, who had been my mentor, stood up and gave me a left-handed toast: "We're sure gonna miss you, Davey," and then, while lifting up my long reddish-blond ponytail, to the other truck drivers at the table, "You know, he was so pretty, that when we was alone in that truck I thought once or twice about takin 'im out to the woods and fuckin' 'im." And although I was shocked and embarrassed, they roared with laughter, and another round of drinks was brought to the table. When all is said and done though, I'll bet there aren't a dozen white people alive in the world today who can say they were entertained inside the Red Bird Café in Tallahassee, Florida, before it was torn down.

Pastime Peanuts

Nixon was fighting against the Watergate hearings, layoffs were happening all over Tallahassee, and Lisa and I had just moved into a new house; it was a good time to take a break. To fill in my days at the Pastime, and having learned my lesson from the K-Bar, I started to (carefully) shuck oysters in a little counter they had set up opposite the bar. The oysters cost the customer a mere10 cents apiece, and I didn't get paid at all, except for tips, which in turn paid for my beers. They had another job offer at the time, but I politely declined, as I wanted to keep my evenings open. This was the beginning of that silly craze where bars offered roasted, salted peanuts where you shed the husks and dropped them onto the floor, the idea of course being that the salted peanuts would get the customers to drink more. I'm not sure it ever really worked out that way though, because you could get so full off the free peanuts, soon swollen in your gut by the cheap beer you'd guzzled, that you often ended up sometimes leaving earlier than you originally intended. In any case, the unanticipated consequence of having these half-eaten and crushed-underfoot peanuts all over the floor was a plague of rats from the attic, basement, alleys, and nearby surrounding neighborhood. To combat these determined vermin, they tried a lot of different techniques: the tried-and-true spring-loaded rat traps, the old sticky pads that would fasten themselves almost always to a still-living and writhing rodent, even poisons of various toxicity and delayed reactions. None of these worked, and they actually ended up scaring the customers as half-smashed, partially glued, and sick dopey rats were encountered here and there accidentally by the public. So, someone suggested, and the management acquiesced, that if a person were to be allowed to stay in the bar all night, and after the general spread of husks were swept up, he could put a small pile of uneaten peanuts down on the floor, with a spotlight centered on it, then when a rat would approach the pile, he could decisively assassinate the little bugger with a plink from a pellet gun, dispose of the remains, and be ready for the next in a minute's time. In this way, the rat problem could quickly be whittled down to a semi-monthly nuisance. It was a wonderful plan. All he wanted for pay was free access to one of the cheaper beer taps. Needless to say, we can foretell where the flaw in this particular plan developed. In the morning, when they opened the doors, the soused sniper was asleep at the bar with his head on his folded arms atop the pellet gun, the pile of peanuts scattered about with only the husks remaining, and the rodentia having left nothing but a pile of turds as their calling cards. The body count was nil. That was pretty much the end of the free peanuts at the Pastime (I've seen this roasted peanut phenomenon rise and fall at many other places over the years, but of course, rat traps and poisons are so much more unobtrusive and effective these days, so you rarely if ever have to see their hideously twisted, panic-eyed and contorted little corpses). I often wondered why didn't they just get a cat or two?

Go West, Young Men

Since I was between jobs, had a little money, and a little time, Nolin and I talked about taking a road trip out west, maybe see the Rocky Mountains (the movie *Jeremiah Johnson* having made a great impression on all of the boys-to-men in our group, and still relatively fresh in our heads, psychologically). I got my van tuned up, oil changed, checked the tires, and he and I loaded it with what little camping gear we had, a goodly stash of pot (which we kept hidden in our coffee pot), a bottle of rum, a few mushrooms, and, after kissing the girlfriends goodbye and promising to stay out of trouble, we were on our way. We decided to make the mad dash for it right off and, taking turns driving, we passed New Orleans the first evening and got into Texas before finally stopping and pulling out the sleeping bags and spending the night by the road at a large rest area in or near Beaumont. The next day we kept on going west, but knew we'd have to turn north soon, if we were going to eventually make our way to Denver, where an old friend of Celia's said that she'd put us up for a couple of days if and when we ever showed up. So at some point we jumped off of I-10 near Houston and headed north, again, tag-team driving, and I remember seeing the skyline of Dallas that evening as we took the bypass around it. Another night sleeping on the ground and in the morning we headed for Amarillo and New Mexico. About 10 a.m. the next day, in a small sleepy little town called Quanah (ancestral home of the right-wing billionaire Koch brothers), a cop car pulled out as we slowly passed through the main street, and he followed and we watched; we watched and he followed. As we approached the city limits heading west, he put on his lights. Pulling us over was a young (our age? older by a couple of years, maybe?) policeman, definitely Barney Fife in nature, with one over-sized eye that looked off and up to the sky, whose name tag said "Lonnie Pritchard." Why'd he pull us over? He had pulled us over because, as we had left town, the van's tire had "touched the centerline." At least he was smart enough not to tell us, well, in all honesty, here was a van, with two bedraggled long-haired hippies, cutting through the Texas hinterlands, and if we weren't carrying a little dope, then no one was. He got us out of the van, put us in the back of his car, and asked us if we had any marijuana with us. Of course not. Well, would we mind if he took a look? What if we DID mind? In that case, then, he would have the van towed back to town and he would get a search warrant, and they would take the car apart. And if we let him search the van, and he didn't find anything? Why, then we'd be free to go on our way. The choice seemed clear. Go ahead, have a good time. We watched as he sidled up to the van, threw open the two side doors, and surveyed the situation. Then he looked back at us before rolling up his sleeves and setting to work. It was our only hope—the van was a wreck inside; we'd been on the road for three days now, sleeping and eating in it, changing shirts, but little else, and the back of the van was covered with open sleeping bags, food scraps, trash, empty beer and liquor bottles, and old clothes. It stank, even to us, and we figured there'd be little chance of him eventually making his way to our little camping coffee pot that held the stash, hidden in the food cabinet, before he'd get disgusted and give up. In he went, and out came the sleeping bags, out came the trash, out came the dirty clothes, out came the food scraps, out came the empty beer cans and liquor bottles. He hopped out and again looked at the two of us, who watched him, while trying to maintain a pair of straight and unaffected facial expressions. Back in he dove. Out came our remaining foodstuffs. Out came our good clean clothes. Out came the cooking gear. Out came the little Mason jar with the mushrooms. Uh Oh. Finally, out stepped Lonnie, holding our little coffee pot, with the top open. He looked over at us, looked down into the little aluminum urn, looked back at us, and smiled a big broad grin. And believe it or not, he then did a little dance, a jig if you will (think Walter Huston in *The Treasure of the Sierra Madre* when he's telling the boys what idiots they are for not knowing gold when it's under their feet). Nolin let out a deep sigh as I looked out the window. I remember seeing a tractor two or three miles away, kicking up a big dust cloud as it went plowing across a sky-wide field, and thinking "Texas. Marijuana. Life sentences for possession. Take a good long look, you may never see a tractor plowing a field again."

Pulling Rawhide

He took us into town, to the 3-cell jailhouse, and had us change into white jumpsuits. Oh yeah, we got a shower, too; our first since we had gotten on the road in Tallahassee. Back in the cell, Nolin began a routine of pushups, obviously anticipating a long stay. I sat and pondered what we would have to say to the girlfriends, much less the families. Next to us, in the adjacent cell, on the other side of a solid wall where he couldn't be seen, we could hear someone pacing about. Eventually, hearing us, he began talking. I can't remember his name, but apparently he was a young cowboy who had gotten into trouble after getting drunk in town, either a fight or drunk driving, or both. He'd been in over a month, and hadn't seen a lawyer or a judge, or anyone else for that matter, other than Lonnie, who passed him his food, but otherwise wouldn't talk to him. He did have a Bible, and found some solace in that. He said he "polled" calves for a living. I hadn't heard this term before, nor had Nolin, and I asked him what it meant. The way he explained it, while riding the range (nowadays in a pickup truck), when he and another cowboy, or sometimes just him alone, would come upon a very pregnant cow, soon ready to give birth, he would throw a rope over her head, and tie her to the back of the truck. Then, he pulled a fencepost out of the back of the truck and with a posthole digger, would plant this post some ten feet behind the cow. Then he would reach up into that cow, grab the calf-to-be by the legs or head or whatever he could get his hands on, and pull until something stuck out the back of the cow. He would then attach what is commonly called a come-along, which is a hand-held winch, to the post in the ground, and the other end to a rope tied to the projecting calf-part, and then, despite the cow's loud and mighty protestations, he would winch that calf right on out. Unhitching everything, removing the post from the ground, and tossing it all back into the pickup truck, the heifer would already be licking the calf clean, and he would move on down the range to find another one. Supposedly this was safer (and faster!) than natural calving, where you might lose both the cow and the calf should some unforeseen difficulty arise during the normal cow-birthing process, which is a long drawn-out and risky business anyway, especially out on the open range with coyotes and other predators always lingering about. So that's the story he told us, and I'd heard of this process since, but many years later I learned that a "polled" cow, steer, or bull, is simply one that has had its horns trimmed short. In retrospect, I think he might have been saying he "pulled" calves, whereas I had heard "polled," at first thinking he just counted them. The other thing I remember about this young cowboy was that he would cry at night. He didn't moan, or blubber, or even make much noise at all, but nonetheless, in the middle of the night you could hear him sobbing and whimpering piteously, shedding tears he couldn't hold back. It was rather unsettling, and for our part, did not seem to bode well for our immediate future.

King Pong

But then again, Lonnie took a special interest in us, since we were a couple of oddities as far as he was concerned, a couple of college hippies, just traveling the country for the hell of it, and he was happy to have someone other than the cowboy to talk with. Then when he found out we could play ping-pong, he was positively overjoyed. Let the games begin! He let us out and we went into the police station garage where a ping-pong table was set up in one of the car bays. We played a few practice rounds and it became clear that he had been practicing for years with any prisoner he could get to challenge him. Now Nolin is a helluva billiard shot, having mastered the requisite skills while playing in his own home garage pool parlor (not to mention the many hours we had all put in at the Pastime), but without rubbing my own shining brass lamp too bright, I'm a formidable table tennis maven, having developed my own eclectic style from various tables associated with schools, bars, neighbors, and recreation centers over my best teenage years. So it fell upon me to give Lonnie our best. We spent the better part of a day going back and forth, and he gave as good as he got. After a few hours, it was pretty much a draw. When I'd get tired, I'd let Nolin play him just so Lonnie could revel and skip about in triumph over the college boys in his custody. But Lonnie was indefatigable. He wanted to play more. Hell, as much as I enjoyed playing, I was getting to the point I just wanted our baloney sandwich and coke, and to lay down on the jailhouse cot. "Why don't we make it intrestin'?" he finally blurted out. Nolin and I looked at each other. "What do you have in mind?" Nolin said. "Well, I don't know," said Lonnie, "why don't you think of something?" There was nothing we could offer: he'd taken all our belongings, even our clothes. For that matter, there was only one thing he could offer. "Tell you what," I said, "let's consider a best-out-of-five tournament. If I win, we get our clothes back, you give us the keys to the van, and we'll be on our way. Whaddya say?" He was so geared up and heated from playing that I believe he actually considered it for a moment. Looking down, he finally shook his head and said, "Naw, I can't do that…" He really looked disappointed. "Let's just play for fun," he said. "Nope. I'm finished," I said. "Aw, c'mon, just one more game," he was almost whining. "Nope," and we were led back to the cell. Later that day we got a chance to make our one phone call and let the girls back home know that we were incarcerated in the Lone Star State in a little shithole called Quanah, but we didn't know what the outcome was going to be until the next day when we were set to see the judge. They were more upset than we were, since it was well-known that in those days there really were people in Texas who were serving long prison sentences simply for possession of marijuana.

C Note and See Ya

In the morning Lonnie came and got us, and as we were headed out the front door of the police station he led us past what looked like a storefront display case of various trophy pipes, roach clips, bongs, and other paraphernalia associated with dope-smoking. Apparently Lonnie had been busy over the years. He walked us across the street to the little three-story brick courthouse, and we went up the steps, through the large wooden doors, and into a little chamber where an older man in a short-sleeve open-collared shirt sat at the head of a shiny wooden table. "Boys, this is Judge Samuels," said Lonnie. The judge looked up, but only said, "Have a seat, gentlemen." We sat there silently with our hands folded in front of us, like good Catholic schoolboys. He shuffled through some papers, then looked up and said, "You understand what you're being charged with?" "Yes, sir." "How do you want to plead?" Well, there was no getting around it, no beating around the bush, or waffling. Lonnie had caught us dead-to-rights, so we both said "No contest." The judge said "100 dollars each, and time served," signed the papers, had us sign the papers, and Lonnie told us it was time to go. We hadn't been in there five full minutes. Somewhat stunned, we thanked the judge, got up and walked back across the street in our white jumpsuits with Lonnie "guarding" us. We were allowed to call the girls again, and luckily they had already taken up a collection from our friends, so they wired the money, with a little extra, and within two hours we were cut loose and down at the garage where the van had been secured. The inside was a wreck, with everything just thrown into a big pile in the back. But we didn't want to take the time there to straighten it out; we just wanted to get out of town. We got in, pulled out onto Main Street, and eased our way back down the road to the highway. We had thought of heading home, but hell, we were more than halfway to Denver by now, so we decided to forge on. As we left the city limits and then passed the spot on the highway where Lonnie had nabbed us, I reached up under the driver's seat, where I had stashed a pint of rum that Lonnie had missed, pulled it out, and was pissed to see that half of it was gone. The goddamn mechanics at the garage had gone through our shit! Ah well… I took a pull off of it, and handed it over to Nolin—who was firing up a joint! "Where the hell did that come from?" I asked. "I had it with me," he grinned, "I smuggled it into jail… had it with me the whole time." "Oh, give me a break!" I said, surprised, "how did you 'smuggle' it into the jail…Lonnie searched us." "I rolled it up into my sock," he said, "He looked in our shoes, but he didn't unroll our socks, and when he gave us our shoes and socks back, I just kept it there in my sock." "Well, I'll be god-damned!" I said surprisingly; I had to admit, it was pretty ballsy.

Amigos en Amarillo

We headed northwest towards Amarillo, and when we got there it was already dark. To calm our nerves from the road hum and the previous several days of lockup, we decided to stop at a nice dark bar on a sidestreet downtown. When we went in, the place wasn't so dark inside as we expected and it was half-full of cowboys and cowgirls, rednecks and hippies, even a small band playing Allman Brothers songs in the corner. We fit right in. Like any bar though, it had its watchful regulars, and it was soon apparent that we'd never been in there before. Some short-haired friendly redneck finally asked us if we were new in town, and when he found out we were from Florida he invited us over to a table with his friends. When they heard our story of being tagged in Quanah, they insisted on buying all the beer from then on out, just to show us how wonderful Texans really are, and that we shouldn't judge the state by the likes of Lonnie Pritchard. After a couple of hours and many, many pitchers of beer, we said we had to go look for a place to park the van and crash; did they know of any out-of-the-way spots we could park and get some sleep? Well, sure they did! And they'd even take us out there and show us. So we followed them out of town, down a side road and (from what we could make out in the headlights) it was a large empty sort of asphalt parking lot, out in the middle of nowhere, like one of those park-and-ride lots. We all shook hands, what a great bunch of guys. They left us and we crawled in the back of the van to go to sleep. Then it began to rain.

We were awakened by a loud rapping on the window. I looked up to see a uniformed cop staring in, tapping on the window with his knuckles. We got out and the policeman asked us what we were doing out there. We explained about being on the road, getting tired, and pulling over to sleep (leaving out the bar part). He looked around, decided we were harmless, and told us in a nice way to get back on the road. Unknowingly, we had parked in a bit of a depression in this flat asphalt lot, so that all the dust and sand from the surrounding area had pooled up around the van in a big, wide, but not-too-deep mudpatch from the rain. As we tried pulling out, the tires began to spin, and the cop had to back off and get around behind his own car so he wouldn't get hit with flying mud. But it was obvious we were sliding and getting stuck. Just then, up pulls a station wagon, and the four guys we'd been drinking with the night before piled out. They talked to the cop and said we were friends, and told him they'd get us out. The cop seemed to know these boys so he said okay and drove off. We were so glad to see those guys, because the cop had put the fear of God in us that we might end up pulling another Quanah gig. The guys said they were just coming to check on us, 'cause they were worried. But we didn't have a tow rope, how are we going to get out of there? No problem, said the boys, and they waded ankle-deep right into the mud and started to push. With the tires spinning, and mud flying all over them, slipping and sliding and pushing, we eventually hit a hard patch and we were free. They were a mess however, covered with dark gray and black sticky silt; but they didn't care, and laughing, they told us to follow them back to one of the guy's houses. When we got there, we all went in, and they stripped off their dirty clothes, put on some shorts and T-shirts and started doing laundry, putting on some music, turning on the TV, and cracking open a few beers out of the refrigerator. Then, after firing up a big joint, the guy whose house it was asked us all if we'd like some breakfast, and started cooking up bacon, eggs, and potatoes. This was incredible! As it was, they were all either between jobs or on some sort of unemployment or receiving service benefits and

137

they found it comforting to hang out together during the days until things brightened up. The guy who owned the house, and was cooking breakfast though, was adamant that he had to have the house cleaned up and everybody gone by the time the "old lady" showed up from HER job, around four that afternoon. No problem. After breakfast, and having gotten a few of our own clothes washed and dried, we all just sat around smoking dope and drinking beer until about noon, when Nolin and I decided we'd better get going. After handshakes, pats on the back, trading phone numbers, and offering our truly heartfelt thanks, we got back on the road. I cannot say enough about how friendly and helpful and gracious these guys were; they made an impression that has countered my overall disdain for Texans in general as depicted in the news and popular press over the years when I've recalled just how unselfish and good-hearted they were to perfect strangers on the road (and self-confessed jailbirds at that).

Amazing Spiders, Man

The Texas-New Mexico state line from Amarillo heading west is just 50 or 60 miles away, but we weren't going to be stopping any more in Texas, that was for sure. So we made for New Mexico, and fueling up at the state line, we decided to skip all the tourist sites: Roswell, Albuquerque, Santa Fe, Taos, etc, and just head on up through the desert and hook up with I-25 to make Denver in a day or so. (Had we had more time, and paid more attention to the map, I'm sure we would have stopped in Tucumcari, not too far out of the way, just to have a look-see, considering its affiliation with the Clint Eastwood movie *For a Few Dollars More*, the whole Spaghetti-Western series of which we had been fans of back at the drive-ins in Orlando.) Nolin took the first shift driving while I tried to tidy up the mess in the back of the van. At some point after sundown, we stopped, ate dinner and bought a bottle of cheap rum. I took over driving while Nolin tried to catch some sleep in the back. Driving along was fine, music on the radio, headlights on the highway, no other vehicles either ahead or behind, yes, it was somewhat hypnotizing. The rum probably didn't help either. Looking back, though, it was probably beautiful desert country that I didn't get to see since it was so dark. Just as the false dawn was making itself evident, that barely discernible change in darkness coming over my right shoulder to the east, I was quite mesmerized from driving all night when I heard a pop. Not loud, just a little pop, then another one, then a couple more. I sat up alert, scared to death that something was going wrong with the van, maybe the tires. The popping not only didn't die away, it got more persistent: pop, pop, pop-pop-pop. As I looked down onto the road, in the headlight beams still lighting the way, I could see dark spots on the road. Pop-pop-pip-pop-pop-pip-pop-pop-pip… I slowed down and stared—the spots were moving! Oh shit, I know what that is! It's crabs! I slowed to a stop and Nolin woke up, "What's the matter? Why are you stopping?" "Shit, there's crabs all over the road!" But as I rolled down and looked out the driver's window, even opening the door, I was amazed to see in the dawn's early light, that they weren't crabs at all… THEY WERE TARANTULAS! Thousands of tarantulas were making their way from north to south across the highway, and I had been smashing them for miles. We looked out the windshield, and there, stretching for miles ahead, were multitudes of black and red tarantulas crossing the highway. No, we didn't exit the van to check them out. I eased the van back into drive and as the sun came up we slowly crushed hundreds more of the big front-legs-a'waving arachnids for another mile or two before the morning migration finally eased and the highway was clear again. I was now straight-up sober and clear-headed, but now it was Nolin's turn to drive. Besides, we were coming onto Colorado.

High Plains Drifters

We barreled on up I-25, straight up the High Plains, making directly for Denver, and stopped somewhere near Colorado Springs in mid-afternoon to take a rest. We noticed a broad field backed by an evergreen forest, with the distant mountains as a backdrop to the northwest. Pulling the van over at a roadside stop that had an empty old green pickup parked there, we could see a broad mountain stream winding its way through the field, and it came near the road, so we stopped and got out to stretch and rest by the water. We hadn't been there maybe ten minutes when we heard laughter, feminine laughter, coming from just inside the evergreens. We sat up, and here, through the waist-high broomstraw came running a couple of young girls, naked as jaybirds, laughing and being chased by a slender (and somewhat effeminate, and also nude) young man. They spotted us just as they got to the opposite side of the stream, and without any hesitation or inhibition, plunged into the water, half-swimming and half-trudging their way across, and lay down in the tall yellow straw alongside where we sat watching. One was a tall, thin brunette, with long arms, hairy armpits and legs and that wondrous thick patch of pubic hair. The other was a shorter strawberry-blonde, a little stouter considering her stature, also sporting the requisite hippie-chick hirsuteness. The guy? I don't think we even noticed him; it was obvious that he was a tag-along, and something tells me he may even have been a cousin to the taller girl. They lay in the sun, sprawled out, and started asking us where we were from, where we were going, etc. Then they started chiding us to go in for a swim. At first they were playful about it, but soon they saw that they'd have to resort to friendly innuendo concerning our status as real men, "Are you afraaaaiiid? Is it too cu-cu-cooooold?" Well, it WAS too cold, we could tell that not only from just feeling the water, but by staring at their skyward-pointing nipples, and the goose-bumps that still hadn't settled down after five minutes lying in the sun. But a man's ego is a very tremulous piece of business, and so, in the end, we had no choice. We stripped on down, and I took just long enough so that Nolin had to jump in first, so I could gauge his reaction. It didn't seem too bad, so in I went. Great God in Heaven! This was no doubt snow-melt that had worked its way down from the white caps on the mountains in the far vista. Freezing was putting it lightly. Painful (and probably deadly to a couple of Florida boys) is a more accurate description. Suffice it to say we did not linger, and the shrinkage factor was in full force. Now it was absolutely necessary to lay in the sun and gather what warmth we could. They thought it was hilarious. Luckily, we still had a half-bottle of rum to take the edge off, and we passed it all around. After warming up, we got dressed and they pulled their hidden clothes from out of the bushes, and invited us back to their place to smoke some dope and relax. The taller girl asked Nolin for a cigarette, and after lighting it, she began a hacking cough.

We followed them to a ramshackle little wooden house in the woods, a typical hippie hangout with no heat other than a small fireplace, clothes and trash laying all around, and the whole thing tucked back into a little copse of trees shading everything and lending a dark aspect to the whole place, even though it was a bright and sunny day elsewhere. By the time it took us to get there, maybe a half an hour later, the taller girl was coughing very deeply, and now she was shivering. The dip in the icy water had done her no good. They fired up some pot, and we finished sharing our rum, but the poor quaking creature she'd now become was distressing to watch, hacking away and wheezing betweentime. Finally, she took to the bed, and even from there she continued to periodically cough loudly and spasmodically. There was no doubt that she had bronchitis, and untreated, it would develop into pneumonia. We offered to take her to the doctor, but they all passed on it, preferring to ride it out. Although we'd considered staying the night, it was time to go if we were going to make it to Denver by dark. Wishing them the best, and giving them a rather sad goodbye (I really think the girl was in a bad way), we left them to their own devices. We made it to Denver just as the sun was going down that night, and as we came up over the surrounding edge of the "bowl" that surrounds Denver, I was surprised to see how the smog of the day's traffic had settled in over the city. After calling Celia's friend, she said to come on over, she and her roommate had been expecting us. They seemed a little shocked at our

139

appearance when they opened the door to their brownstone, and I suppose we were a sight by then: a week on the road, bedraggled and long hair all a-muss, having slept only in the van or by the side of the road, with several bottles of rum and numerous joints consumed, not to mention the two-day stint in jail.

They encouraged each of us to shower and in the meantime cracked open a bottle of wine. Then, each in turn as the other washed up, we attempted a little conviviality and becoming acquainted with these prim and proper girls, and they were very nice, considering. When I mentioned the smog cloud I had seen, they said that this was a regular thing, and overnight it would clear out and we'd be happily surprised to see the city clear by morning, but then again, as the day went on, the warmer smog-infested air would again settle during the day, filling up the large "bowl" in which the city sat. But it had been a long trip and we were really tired, the road having finally caught up with us. They had a couple of sofas already prepared with bedding and pillows, and they were just too tempting. Perhaps we could talk more in the morning. When we got up they already had breakfast cooking and a pot of coffee freshly-brewed. Refreshed, we were ready to give them our full attention as they told us about their lives in Denver. They were teachers, grade school and middle school, home for the weekend, and the friend of Celia's was excited to show us her several dulcimers and a small harp, all of which she played expertly. I'll be honest though, you can only listen to a dulcimer for so long before the wide-eyed marvel and approving smile on your face begins to get heavy and forced. I'm sure Nolin felt the same. They were very nice girls, if somewhat unexciting, considering our usual fare. Nonetheless, they took very good care of us, and laying around quietly all day Sunday, I even got to pick up a book, which I hadn't done since leaving Tallahassee.

By Monday morning however, as the girls went off to teach, Nolin and I had to come to grips with the realization that our funds were drawing slim, and we'd be hard-pressed to carry on. So we went on into town and found our way to the Unemployment Office (not to register for unemployment, but rather, to pick up some quick day-labor). This proved to be a waste of time, since we were not even residents of Colorado, much less Denver, and the lines and paperwork were more daunting than working would ever have been. We stopped into a little hole-in-the-wall bar to get a couple of beers and weigh our alternatives. I decided to make a plea to my Mom in Orlando for enough money to get us the gas we'd need to get home, and after calling her, we made our way to the Western Union where I was delighted to find that she had thrown in some extra as well. I think Nolin may have called Celia also, because I remember that all of a sudden we were flush. We looked at the map, counted our money and found that we had enough to forge on to nearby Rocky Mountain National Park, before turning for home. Now that we were solvent we also thought well, hey, maybe we can get a little pot before we get out of town, the better to enjoy the great mountain vistas. There was a nice dirty little porno shop next to the Western Union (as usual) so, what better venue to look for some marijuana in a strange town? Inside, while rummaging among the magazines and sex toys (this was even before VHS tapes), we met the clerk and let him know our request. He said no, he didn't have any, but there was a stripper (and sometime whore) named Red who lived just a block away, up a couple of floors in a tenement, and she might be able to help us (maybe in more ways than one). We found the building, climbed the stairs, and got to the right floor, but there were no numbers on the doors. This was going to be awkward. We listened at various doors, hoping to get a clue as to which might be hers, but ended up just pacing the hall. Suddenly a door opened and a thirty-some-year-old red-headed rough-looking woman in a fur-lined dark green coat walked out and locked her door. It had to be her, so we asked if she were Red. She just looked at us and snarled. She then went over to the elevator, keeping a close watch on us the whole time. We tried again, "Excuse us, we just came from the porno shop down the street and the clerk said you might be able to help us?" "Oh, he did, did he?" she said, "You tell that asshole to go fuck himself." As the doors to the elevator closed all we got was the finger and a loud "Fuck You!" It was probably a good sign that it was time to get out of Denver.

Rocky Mountains, Hi!

In the morning we bade an early bye to the teachers and got back on the road. Making our way north up I-25, we stopped briefly in Boulder to see the University of Colorado campus, walk through the Student Union, and have a snack before turning west and heading for Rocky Mountains National Park. We camped just outside the park, and spent a freezing night huddled round a small fire, sleeping fitfully (at least I did). But the sun came up bright and warm and we made our way into the park, climbing constantly and stopping only to fill our cups with snow to mix with rum. At some point the traffic on the mountain road was backing up, and we found out it was because a ranger ahead was letting each car know that the road was going to be closed the next day, possibly for the rest of the winter season and it was advisable to consider whether you were going on for good or whether you'd rather go back. Well, we decided that the Continental Divide, which marks the height of the Rockies, was only a few miles ahead, so we'd at least make for that before we'd decide. When we got to the sign marking it, we pulled over just past it, got out of the van, scooped up another cup of snow for a drink, and just admired the view and the quiet. The other cars had passed, those that were forging on ahead, and there we were alone, at the top of the United States. After half an hour or so, the cold began to settle in, and the sun was at its apex. It was only going to get colder and darker from here on out. We weren't going to head further west into the park. To do so would mean days of freezing weather and no going back the way we'd come. No, we'd reached as far as it was possible to go on the money and supplies we had. It was time to go home. At least it would be downhill for the first hundred miles or so, all the way past Denver. We got back in the van, turned around and headed for Florida.

I could tell you all the adventures we had going back, except that there weren't any, not one. We had only one destination and that was home. So, other than stopping for fuel and to check the oil and tires, and taking the same opportunity to empty our bladders, we tag-team drove that van all the way back to the Sunshine State, one sleeping in the back while the other drove, and believe it or don't, we crossed into Florida within 24 hours of standing at the Continental Divide, and three hours after that we were back in Tallahassee. Two regrets: that Lonnie hadn't taken the chance to play me for our freedom (which, in the long run, turned out all right), and we hadn't taken a camera.

Cancun, Can We?

You'd think I'd had enough of travelling for awhile after that, and you'd be right. But after a few months of wintering over at Herb's house, which was as draughty inside as it was without, and saving some unemployment money along with both of us getting a nice income tax refund, Lisa and I decided to take a vacation together. Still trying to be practical, we looked at the various alternatives: I'd already been to Jamaica (and didn't want to go back), the trip out West with Nolin was precarious at best, and almost a near disaster, and wouldn't we like to try something exotic and yet inexpensive? Round trip flights from Orlando to Cancun were something like $125, and the peso was sitting at 12 to the dollar, so we decided to go to Mexico. Lisa spoke a pretty good Italian-Spanish pidgin, and I could cover the basics of who, what, when, where, and how much, so the language barrier didn't seem to be insurmountable. Under Lisa's direction we planned our itinerary and travel route, which would involve flying into Cancun,

141

bussing down to Belize, then west to Guatemala, and then back again, for some 10 days or so, backpacking and staying in cheap hotels all the way. We made arrangements, drove down to Orlando in Lisa's new Ford Pinto, left it at my parents' house and flew out to Cancun. At the time, Cancun was not yet a major tourist area, and in fact, the first major tourist hotel had only just begun construction. We stayed in a sleazy pink hotel on the mainland, a few blocks from the ocean where we could see the new hotel grounds being cleared for construction.

In the morning we could see that Cancun was just a bustling dirty little city, and the beaches were neither near nor inviting, especially with the building going on. But someone told us about Isla Mujeres, an offshore island frequented by young Americans, both cheap and accommodating. It was an idyllic Caribbean getaway accessible by ferry, where you could rent a hammock in a protected thatched-roof hostel on the beach for 8 pesos a night (roughly 75 cents at the time), and the sand was clean and the water was clear, not to mention the many, many beachside lean-to bars. That sounded like what we were looking for, so we caught a taxi to the ferry, and within two hours we were on the island, set up in our hammocks, and ready to have a Margarita. For two days we enjoyed the sand and the sun and the bars, but even heaven can get a little boring without a challenge, so we decided to stick to the itinerary and make our way down the coast. Back in Cancun, and refreshed from two days on the beach, we caught a bus south and made for Chetumal, the last major town in Mexico before entering Belize. On the way we passed Cozumel, which we could just see on the horizon out to sea, and we stopped for maybe ten minutes at Tulum, the waterfront Mayan ruins, to both deposit and pick up passengers, but not given enough time to explore the ruins themselves. From Tulum, we took the Benito Juarez highway (it was a dirt road, you couldn't really call it a highway) to Chetumal, a nice four-hour bouncy ride with peasants, crying children, cages of roosters, baskets of fruit and vegetables, and the guy sitting in front of us with a shotgun precariously shouldered, the end of its open barrel gently swaying back and forth between Lisa and myself as the bus careened down the road.

At one point, the driver's barreling down the dirt highway, I suppose making up for lost time, when we round a corner and up ahead is another bus heading our way, also kicking up dust. Between us is a small (and narrow) stone bridge, dropping to the left (our side) maybe a hundred feet into a small jungle-runoff chasm. Who's going to slow down and let the other pass? Not missing a beat, not slowing down, not even touching the brakes, the two buses slide into the stone bridge mouths on either side and scraping the three-foot-high rock and mortar wall on our side and the other bus squeezing along the hillside on the other, they jammed together to a halt, throwing down baskets, chickens, and a few passengers, including little old ladies and children who hadn't seen it coming and didn't brace themselves. Rocking back and forth between forward and reverse, metal screeching as they worked themselves loose, once they freed themselves, they continued on as fast and reckless as they had earlier.

Belize It or Not

Chetumal was a quaint and beautiful little white-plastered town, typically Mexican with overhanging porches and high arcaded walkways, except that it sat on the edge of the sea. We got a room that night when the bus unloaded us, and, although it was already dark, there was a festive bustle on the streets as the heat of the day gave way to the cooling sea breezes, and people came out to enjoy their evening promenades. We hit the sack early, being tired from the bus bounce, and in the morning enjoyed some pastries and café con leche, before checking out and getting back to the bus station for the next leg. Then we found out that we'd have to wait for the same daily bus that deposited us the afternoon before, as only a single run occurred per day. So now it was roughly noon and we'd have to wait until almost five o'clock for a bus to carry us

142

across the border into Belize. There was nothing to do except go back to the waterside, read a book, drink a beer, kill time (something the Mexican psyche seems well-adapted to). At some point for a handful of pesos we convinced the landlady at the hotel to let Lisa use a room to take a nap, but I just stayed out on the waterfront watching the sea, reading, and walking about and taking in a beer at the closest cantina.

Sitting there, all alone and taking in the blue-green water and the quiet, I got a little hungry and asked to see a menu. Other than tacos and tortillas and enchiladas, it was all Greek to me, although I recognized *pollo* and *bifstek*. But what's this? They got tortuga on the menu... cheap too! Well, I figured I'd try some, and ordered it. As I sat starting in on my second cerveza, this large man comes out of the kitchen with a bat. He wades out knee-deep, reaches over a set of wooden stakes I thought were just part of the scenery, lifts out a small 2-3 foot turtle by the flipper and tosses it into a nearby wooden boat. He climbs in, and the next thing I know, he's raining down blows on this helpless marine reptile, which is flailing right and left while he's waling away. I sit up, thinking "Holy Shit!" Then he pulls out a large knife from a side holster, and in less than three minutes, he's setting the carapace over the side into the shallow waters, which start boiling with small ravenous reef fish, steps out of the boat carrying several large bloody steaks in his hand, rinses them in the water and walks back into the kitchen. I hear a loud sizzling and smell a savory scent. In five minutes they're setting down a plate of two fried green turtle steaks, some beans and yucca, on the table in front of me. It was delicious. Almost exactly the texture and taste of what rednecks gobble down as "chicken-fried steak." I may have forgotten to tell Lisa about having lunch without her.

When the bus finally came, it wasn't but an hour down the road that we crossed over into Belize, and were let off in the border town of Corozal. A quick review of our passports and we were on our own. Now, however, it was night, and there must have been a half-dozen of us American touristas that needed somewhere to sleep, with no hotel in sight. While negotiations were being carried out about letting us put down our sleeping bags in a nearby church, I noticed someone filling a bucket from a water spigot. We had been warned about drinking any water, but after three days drinking only beer and drinks, I was just dying of thirst. It was coming out of a spigot, and we were out of Mexico, I figured I'll just rinse my mouth out. But it was so good, I just let one drop slide down my throat. Within the hour I was literally spewing shit out behind the church that had eventually let us Americans stay for the night. This was not good. In the morning we left Corozal on the early bus to Belize City. The bus ride was most unbearable for me, since there was no stopping and I just had to pucker up my ass for an hour or two until we got there, and when we did I was the first one off the bus, and after making hurried inquiries, was directed to my first real third-world public shitter. In fact, before you went in (and you could see the feet of all the "customers" from the street), you had to step over the raw sludge running down the gutter from inside to a nearby canal that eventually ran down to the sea. Cleaning up as best I could, which was as difficult as taking the running shit itself, I made my way back to the bus. Just before I got to it, there was a small roadside stand selling fruit, cigarettes, and other goods, and I noticed they had bottles of Old Belize rum for $2 a bottle. Hell, maybe I could just clear out my system by sipping on the rum for the rest of the bus trip. We were heading out the Western Highway to the Guatemalan border and it was going to be another 4 hours easy. If anything, it would make the ride more bearable. Getting back on the bus and settling in next to Lisa, I began to feel normal. As we pulled out onto the roadway, I unscrewed the cap to the rum, took a sip, as did Lisa, with the silt of cane silk still visibly floating within, and, as I tried to reseal it, came to find that the screwcap was of a design that could only be opened once; there was no manner of tightening it back on. So I spent four hours with the bottle between my legs before

143

devising a cork to seal it where I could put it into my pack and not worry about it spilling out. They deposited us at the Belize side of the Guatemalan border, but we were told that we wouldn't be able to cross until morning, and we spent the night in a shack that a farm couple used as a feed barn. There was little or no sleeping however, as goats ran underneath banging their horns against the wooden joists underneath, and after it got very dark late at night the rats came out, crawled under the door jamb and scurried along the walls, surprised that a couple of foreigners were laying in the middle of their feed lot.

In the morning, after my diarrhetic dump, we made our way by foot to the small steel and wooden bridge that crossed whatever river acted as the boundary between Belize and Guatemala. On the Guatemalan side there was a little blockhouse of wood to one side and a little red-and-white banded vertical-swinging road gate, like the kind you see in the movies at third-world border crossings. Standing around were a half-dozen mean-looking uniformed Guatemalan Army guys with machine guns strapped over their shoulders with their hands at the ready. We walked across the bridge and entered the wooden blockhouse, which had only a long table and a desk at one end with another uniformed Army officer sitting behind it. Rather than dealing with each of us individually, Americans and other touristas, peasants, and merchants, as we came in they took all our passports and papers at one time, and the Army officer at the desk perused each of them slowly and laid them in a pile to his side. Then he got up and walked out the door and over to another building on the other side of the road, where he went in and closed the door. It was easily a half an hour before he came back out and entered the blockhouse, and I'm sure it was just to see if anyone would lose their temper at being made to wait so needlessly. But no one did. During the half hour we talked with the other people waiting, and found out we could catch a bus right there in the bordertown of Melchor that would take us to Flores, an island-town in the bottom part of Lake Peten Itza, which was a regular taking-off point for tourists going to the Mayan ruins at Tikal. But we quickly made acquaintance with a young rich couple who had rented a jeep and were planning on leaving immediately to go to Tikal. I didn't even get a chance to relieve my bowels. So I suffered for three more hours of bouncing up and down rough-shod roads called highways, and speeding at that, to make the park at Tikal by dark as well as to quickly bypass bandits that were known to be preying on any unlucky vehicles they could waylay. This was right in the middle of the twenty-some-year "war" with underground Commie guerillas fighting the oppressive U.S.-backed military government, and there was also still some lingering tension resulting from threats that same military government had made against Belize, which, being a recent British protectorate, were answered by Guatemalan-Belize border flyovers of British jets, usually three at a time twice a day.

Tikal Me Pink

We arrived just as the sun was going down, and it was wonderful. You could see the tops of the temples sticking out of the canopy, but most welcome was the hostel, a real place, with real food, real cots, and best of all, real bathrooms, with toilet paper and everything! After shitting, taking showers, and freshening up, changing clothes, etc. we got a great cafeteria-style meal of chicken, beans and rice, and plaintains. Even some safe-to-drink bottled water and coke I could mix with my leftover rum. Hitting the rack early, we were exhausted, and the cool jungle, with its attendant animal sounds, provided a soft serenade to sleep.

The next morning found us rested and relaxed, ready to face the ruins. The towering kapok trees with their huge buttressing roots and broad canopies lent an idyllic aspect to the whole scene, and even a few tiny deer didn't mind passing through quietly and cautiously. I was feeling much better, and after breakfast we made plans to go out and look at the ruins. Looking out the front of the hostel breakfast and gathering room, we faced the dirt and grass runway where small planes full of rich tourists would be flown in. At the end of the runway, off to the side were maybe three wrecked and twisted and rusting hulks of vintage and some other not-so-old planes. They sent along one of the Guatemalan cabin boys to keep us company since things were still a little skittish in the countryside and we were just a little ways out there as far as civilization was concerned, but since he didn't speak English, he would just point at things, and otherwise just kept an eye out. It was magnificent! We walked about and looked at the interpretive signs that showed the layout of the exposed ruins, all cut out of the jungle some twenty or thirty years prior (and apparently still being cut out). At one point, as I explored on my own, I came upon a hole dug into the backside of one of the smaller pyramids. Later, years after I became an archaeologist, I learned that this was what was professionally described as a "looters hole," while, in fact it was an attempt by the local indigenous population to supplement their meager and/or non-existent wages by pilfering the ruins, mining into their interiors with picks and axes in hopes of finding some long-lost "treasures." All I found was a long hand-carved tunnel dug into one of the monuments. Gulping against trepidation, I entered the hand-hewn cavern, until light gave out and at the same time I reached the end of the tunnel per se, since they'd only gotten so far. On my way out, I noticed a beam above my head that must have been laid down at the beginning of the very pyramid's construction and the pilferers' pikes had knocked a wedge or two loose, so reaching up I snatched a small piece of wood, no bigger than a piece of the True Cross worn about a Templar's neck, and scarfed it into my pocket. Again, I would learn later, that according to the tenets of True Archaeology, this would have been a mortal sin. But yet, as both an ignorant and an innocent, I was nonetheless pure in my misbehavior. Somewhere this indistinguishable fragment of Mayan forestry lies in my billet, amongst another hundred unidentified artifacts.

Then there were the large stelae, which are those five or six-foot high and three foot wide stone monuments that have the Mayan pictographs and odd writing on them. We even saw the ball court, with stands on both sides and the ring on one side wall replaced—this being the "no-hands soccer-basketball" do-or-die ballgame where the young warriors, clad in wooden-pleated kilts and shinguards would try all day to get the fist-sized rubber ball through the little-more-than-fist-sized ring on the wall. Supposedly, they were as rabid about this game as we are on our own sporting spectaculars, and bets could be made that would involve not only treasures and servitude, but generally culminated in somebody, and sometimes whole teams, getting complacently whacked with large obsidian-bladed axes. Some scholars have argued that the teams played for the honor of being sacrificed and it was the winning team that bit the bullet. This has always seemed a bit counter-intuitive to me, and would ultimately result in more and more mediocre games and fewer "gladiator-hero-sports stars," which certainly would be antithetic to any and all physical contests ever described in cultures throughout the world as well as throughout history. No, I'm fairly sure that it was the losers who were ceremonially dispatched.

Temple IV

By far the most impressive pieces of architecture were the temples, and of these the tallest was Temple IV. Back then they'd let you climb the things, but neither the guide nor Lisa wanted to scale it. I had to go. As I climbed it was strange to note that the steps were larger than an actual step up. By that I mean that you actually had to stretch your legs to reach the next course… and they were very steep. Once I got to the top, where the temple platform lay, it was all so evidently clear what (some of) the functions were The temple platform was just above the canopy of the highest trees, so you had a broad vista from which you could scan 360 degrees as you walked about. Besides being able to lord it over everybody by looking down onto the plaza below, which would have been filled with shops, houses, and administrative buildings, you could see for a five or eight mile radius in each direction. You'd be able to see distant smoke fires (which may or may not have been used for communication), and you could see other temple tops just barely poking above the forest jungle (from which you could certainly have communicated by either mirrors or fires, or lamps at night). But there, as plain as can be, was the feature that lent that aspect of foresight and wisdom to the temple priests that was gained by simple observation: several miles to the southwest a set of cumulus clouds was building, and from the look of it, would be hitting us in about an hour, maybe 45 minutes. On what appeared otherwise to be a cloudless and sunny day, if I were a temple priest, all I'd have to do is make my way down to the plaza and blithely tell a few of the temple guards and/or messengers to spread the word that I think the shops ought to close up since I believed we'd have a nice thunderstorm ("a terrifying gift of the gods", as per my communication therewith) arriving in about twenty minutes or so. In this prescient announcement alone, there must have been an extreme amount of awe engendered by the masses. Add to this the noted perambulations of the stars and planets and moon at night, plainly visible above the canopy (as opposed to the visibility afforded the grounded), to further develop that most famous and accurate of calendars, and the literally elevated role of the knowledgeable priest becomes perfectly understandable.

Speaking of the astronomical observations of the night, Lisa and I were invited on an evening tour of the ruins on our second, and last night, since there was a full moon and the ruins were supposedly quite magical when bathed in lunar luminescence. It was a small group, maybe eight or ten of us, and it was exceptionally beautiful and wondrous to see these towering limestone edifices reaching up towards the bright orb above. While half the group wandered about the plaza, Lisa and I sat on one of the lower structures with the guide just staring up at the moon. After a bit, I figured I'd try a little Spanish out on him and see if I couldn't get some kind of response out of this otherwise silent sentinel. Pointing up at the moon (and these were the days when we were sending Apollo missions up there on a semi-regular basis), I said "Los astronauticos de las Estados Unitos estan a la luna." He looked up, then looked back at me, and shrugged. Then he said, "Cuidado, esta la muerte." I wasn't sure I heard him right, or what he had said ("Careful, there's the death"?). I looked at the moon again, thinking he was talking about our guys possibly dying on the moon, or maybe that the full moon may be some strange Mayan portent of doom. Again, he said "Cuidado" and then turned on his flashlight and shone it at a spot near my left elbow, upon which I was leaning. Not six inches away, and approaching, was this huge multi-colored tarantula. I jumped, yelling, "Jesus Christ!" It was twice as big as the ones I'd seen in New Mexico, and rather than the dull red and black coloration of those same New Mexico "pet" tarantulas you now see in stores, this one was a bright red, white, and blue, with a black undercarriage and legs waving around. It scared the shit out of me. "La Muerte," he said stoically, and, me clutching Lisa, we scampered off to join up with the rest of the evening tour.

De Hydra

When we left Tikal, we caught a tour bus heading back to Flores and the border with Belize, all of which took the better part of a day. Not having to wait at the border to get OUT of Guatemala, we even got a ride quickly to Belize City, and were in a room in a nice small, wooden, and wide-porched tourist hotel before dark. Although I was feeling much better and no longer had the running shits, all of a sudden once we had stopped moving, I developed a crushing headache. Now, I never get headaches, other than those associated with over-indulgence the night before. I mean seriously, I probably haven't had five headaches in my entire life, and in this instance, we hadn't had any alcohol in three days. But what I only came to discover years later is that this is a serious symptom of dehydration. Considering that I had been diarrhetic for damn near a week, and been traipsing up and down pyramids and temples in the tropic heat, and only had some coca-cola at meals in the meantime, I was now staggering from this monumental migraine, and took to the bed as soon as I could. I remember laying there in agony, while on the broad second floor porch just outside our door, the hotel management was showing a movie about the wonders of the Great Belize Reef. I could hear the narrator describing the underwater scenes, and even though I really wanted to go out there and watch it, and encouraged Lisa to go ahead without me, I just couldn't even lift my head from the pillow, with another across my face to block out what little light shone through the blinds. I don't know how bad off I was, but by morning I felt fine and after buying some bottled water I was as right as rain. Thirty years later I found out just how dangerous dehydration can be when, while I was in the Virgin Islands, I had one acquaintance die from it and a good friend end up in the hospital for three days. The acquaintance was a co-owner in a bar, and he was a gruff old man of about 63 or 64, in good health; but he'd been drinking nothing but beer all day and was working on his boat, sanding, cleaning, painting, etc. That night around midnight he called a friend of his and asked him if he wouldn't mind taking him to the hospital in the morning for some scheduled surgery. Well, this friend of his was close enough to know he didn't have any scheduled surgery and asked him what was going on. In the ensuing conversation it became clear to the buddy that this guy was delirious, so he drove over to his house, found him semi-comatose, and got him to the hospital. When he got there, they did everything they could to revive him, including intravenous saline solutions, the works. But apparently, once your kidneys shut down they don't accept any water no-how. He was dead by 3 a.m. after coming to briefly and saying goodbye to a couple of friends. (Now, I won't go into the level of quality to be expected at a Virgin Islands hospital at that time, other than to say that I knew people who would fly to Puerto Rico just to have a broken arm set, rather than go to the emergency room in St. Thomas, but that's another story altogether.) The other fellow, a very good friend of mine, was working outside on St. Croix, near the ocean, clearing brush, and working on some concrete. Now, he grew up on St. Croix and knows the danger inherent in the tropic sun, but he just wanted to finish up a certain section of what was going to be a tank for a small fish hatchery before he took a break. He was 43 at the time, healthy as a horse, and of strong French Caribbean stock. And he just passed out. Luckily, friends were nearby and got him into a truck, and they hauled him off to the hospital. He was there for three days. Just like the other guy, they couldn't get the fluids to go into him except drop by drop, until his kidneys kicked back in and started accepting water again. So, word to the wise: drink water when in the tropics, even when you're not thirsty; don't over exert yourself, and don't think that beer is a substitute or even a palliative, because it's not. And always remember the cowboy-with-a-canteen's advice when he finds you face down in the desert, "Don't drink too fast! Here, just have a drop or two at first…"

Making our way back to Mexico, we got stranded in a little wayside town in a rainstorm, and had to sit it out in a little two-table cantina where we had some wine and beans and rice. Once the rain stopped and I made some inquiries in my broken Spanglish, we found out we'd have to hire a cab to take us to Chetumal, the beautiful seaside town that led us back to Cancun. While we were waiting for the cab, Lisa decided to try to rinse off her shoes that had gotten muddied when the rain caught us. There was a puddle some twenty or thirty feet away, but as she made her way to it, carrying the shoes she wanted to rinse off, she ended up getting mired in more mud. It wasn't a serious situation, as the mud never got even ankle-deep, but it was that sticky red clay-mud that makes big clod-hoppers of snow-shoe-like aggregates on your feet. The locals were quite amused, watching from their doorways, and as the cab pulled up I called out to her to just forget it, and come on back. I mean, I wasn't going in there after her or we'd both have been entrapped, or at least en-mired. When she got back to the cab, I guess the amusement on my own face was evident as she tried scraping the big globs of goo off of the holiday sandals she had started off with, and then the boots she strapped on to carry out the intended mission. She didn't think it was funny at all, and somehow I was supposed to have done something to remedy the mess. But I didn't, and we rode to Chetumal in blustery silence. At Chetumal, we stayed in the same little hotel we had stayed in on the way out, and the next day got us back to Cancun.

Conch Beat 'Em

There was one day left before we had to fly out, so we decided to go out on a boat skin diving the next day. We found a boat going out, it was relatively cheap, and they would feed us, and the water was clear and bright and beautiful and blue. Getting back on board, the mate told everyone to sit and wait and he'd be back in a few minutes with our lunch. Then he dove overboard and swam away. As we waited, the boat just rocked and rocked, and soon Lisa said she was getting seasick. I'd been on the water enough to know that one of the quickest ways to alleviate the malady, especially when it first came on, was to get back in the water, which we did. After a few minutes, even though the seasickness had passed, we were getting cold, having already been snorkeling for an hour or two. Luckily, the mate came back about then with a large bag full of conch, and we all got back on board. It was a quick run back to the beach, and under a modernized tiki hut, he quickly disengaged the large snails each with a single thrust of his knife, then sliced them up into small pieces that he mixed in a large bowl with lime juice and coconut water, while we watched, sipping our Coronas. Properly "cooked" by the lime juice acids, a few other fruits were added and we each got a nice bowlful, although the conch was still pretty tough (and always will be unless you mash it with a meat hammer, or pressure-cook it). We were satisfied and tired, and asked him if we could take the big beautiful pink and yellow conch shells home with us. Sure, he didn't care, take as many as you want; so we took four each.

The next day, preparing to fly out of Mexico, we had to confront the Customs officials. No problem, we hadn't smuggled anything. Nothing we could think of. They passed us on through. On arriving in Miami though, now coming in from Mexico, they once again asked us if we had anything to declare, especially as to any food, agriculture, or meat products. Well, yes, we had eight conch shells that we had been allowed to take. Open your bags. No problem… until we pulled out the plastic bags that they had so carefully been wrapped in. You see, when the dive boat native guy, or any native guy for that matter, kills and cleans a conch, he does it with one swift punch through the otherwise impenetrable shell at a secret (for me, but well-known to him) "sweet spot" somewhere between the third and fourth axial turn from the end. In fact, he is severing the muscle from the rest of the brains, guts, and other vitals of the true living snail, which remain in the end-point of the large carapace. When we removed the conch shells from the plastic bags, now two days after death and dismemberment, and aromatically enhanced by the several hour unrefrigerated airport exodus in Mexico and the subsequent plane trip, the U.S. Customs official coughed, blanched, and told us to "Pack 'em back up and get the hell out of here!" which we and all the other people awaiting their turn in line were glad to have done as quick as possible. Only when we got back to Orlando and dropped the shells into some buckets of bleach-water were we able to appreciate their beautiful colors (which you shouldn't compromise by putting them in bleach-water, ever, but we didn't know any better at the time, although it sure cured the immediate problem).

Once we got back to Tallahassee, things weren't quite the same between us, and although we stayed at Herb Odel's house for another six months, I'm afraid the handwriting was on the wall. Things were going to change.

9. Cracker Box Carpenters (1974 – 1976)

Aldo

One morning Lisa and I had just gotten up, we're having coffee with Herb, and an old friend of his showed up. He was a tall, broad-shouldered redneck with a flat plain face, baseball cap with a "Red Man" logo, khaki pants, boots, and a striped short-sleeve shirt. He must have been about fifty-eight at the time. He was an old carpenter named Aldo Bonifore and he'd come by to see if Herb would help him out on a job he was getting ready to start. Herb and he talked briefly about the job at hand when Herb suggested that I ought to come along too, because he and Aldo were too old to be moving a lot of the lumber and heavier stuff around. Aldo thought that was a great idea, and offered to pay me a 20% cut of the profits. Hey, I was just beginning to enjoy living off the dole, and I really wasn't too keen on spending my days out in the woods busting ass with these old coots, but it was money off the books that wouldn't affect my unemployment, and one look from Lisa and I could tell she was already tired of me spending my days down at the Pastime, and wanted me to at least pretend to be productive. So I said sure. Little did I realize which door of fate I had just opened and was getting ready to walk through. They say that opportunity knocks, but that isn't always the case. Sometimes it just beckons with a wink and a nod (and even a tempting whisper of prosperity). And you know, an opportunity can be all those things it promises: dangerous, exciting, even inspirational, but it's not always, or let's say not necessarily always a positive thing. At the same time, you'll never find out until and unless you answer. So I got on my steel-toed boots, jeans, and a heavy shirt, and off we went.

The three of us sat up front in Aldo's truck, me in the middle of course, and we hadn't gone a mile before Aldo said he had to stop at the store. He came out with two tall boys of Budweiser, put one under his seat, popped the other one open between his legs, sipping as he drove. We headed down US 27 towards Perry. After a half-hour of driving (him and Herb talking about old friends of theirs I didn't know, who were either dead or should have been), and both Budweiser cans gone out the window, we turned off the highway down a dusty little dirt road, then another, and into a dirt driveway that led to a small open field with a trailer adjacent to it. On the edge of the field was a large pile of lumber, pressed-board siding, cinder blocks, cardboard boxes of nails, rolls of tar paper, and bundles of shingles, all under a plastic sheet. You see, Aldo's trade was building Jim Walter houses. Anyone who has ever lived out in the woods, probably anywhere in the United States, especially the South, knows what a Jim Walter home is. We used to call them "cracker boxes," with all the dark sarcasm attached. The original intent, however, was a rather noble one, that just happened to make Mr. Jim Walters a very rich man. He wanted to provide a way for a poor family to have its own house, and this is how he did it. If you owned a piece of property outright, say five acres, you could put up the deed on that land and Jim Walter Homes would drop off all the material needed to build the shell of a decent ranch house, of which they had maybe a dozen different designs. He also provided the construction crew (us) to whom he sublet the work on a contract (Aldo) basis. Once the shell was finished, the doors were hung, and the county inspector had signed off on the building permit, a check was cut for the construction crew, and then Jim Walters would let you know where your next job was going to be. The landowner would then make payments on the house to Jim Walter Homes for a period of say, twenty years, and after that, the landowner would get his deed back. If he failed to make the payments, Jim Walter not only got the land, but the house as well. We only built the rough-frame shell of the house; it was up to the discretion of the owner how much more they wanted Jim Walter's to do (electrical, plumbing, sheet rock, painting etc.), or whether they'd try to finish it on their own. You'd be surprised how many young redneck couples never finished their house like they planned, argued over seeing this empty shell of a house in their yard outside their adjacent trailer windows, get in serious fights over it, and ended up getting divorced, leaving it all to Jim Walters to finish up and sell later on. Sell the trailer too.

But that wasn't our problem. No, our problem was that we didn't get paid a nickel until the house was framed-in, the keys were in the locks, and the building permit had the county inspector's signature on it. This might take three weeks or a month, depending on how hard and how fast we worked. So we started off great guns. Both Herb and Aldo knew all sorts of tricks that made the work go quickly, but with just two old men and myself, who had never before swung a hammer in earnest, it was hard, hard work. And Aldo soon let it be known that since he held the contract, and he was the Master Carpenter, Herb and I were therefore the grunts, and he wasn't going to move any heavy stuff unless he absolutely had to. Then he and Herb started arguing, arguing over Aldo's drinking. Besides the two tall boys Aldo drank on the way to work in the morning, at lunch he'd buy a six-pack, and generally downed four of them over the afternoon. By the third afternoon beer though, he was useless as a carpenter, and we'd end up breaking off at about 3:30, so Aldo could get us home relatively intact. Well, hell, it wasn't a week in, we'd just got the floor done and started putting up walls, when Herb decided that he'd hurt his back. Now he couldn't lift anything. They got in a big argument and that was it, Aldo gave him a hundred bucks, and Herb wasn't coming back. When we got home, I asked Herb what he wanted to do, and he said he was moving out to his son's land, that his son had an extra trailer out there, and he just wanted to lay around and catch catfish from now on. This wasn't surprising; I think Herb was getting tired of living with us, and I know Lisa was getting tired of his slovenly ways. So, he left us alone in the house, moved out to his son's place, and I called up an old friend of mine, Bill Cummings, to see if he wanted to come and finish the house with me and Aldo. Herb left the goddamn monkey though, which I wasn't too happy about. One day I came home, Lisa was downtown working the dinner shift at the Western Sizzlin, and as I came in I heard a ruffling sound coming from the kitchen and saw that the monkey cage door was open. As I peered round the corner into the kitchen, there was Lottie on the kitchen table dusted white like one of those Japanese snow monkeys that sit in the water in the National Geographic, up to her elbow in a bag of flour, with flour all over the table, the chairs, the floor, everywhere. I let out a "Hey!" and she looked up out of that bag and screeched at me, baring those canine fangs of hers. I yelled at her to get out of the flour, and damn if she didn't come at me! Luckily, there was a kettle-top laying on the table and I quickly whipped it up to fend off her advance. Then I chased her around the kitchen, with her screaming and knocking glasses and dishes off the counter as she scrambled to get away from me, until she finally took refuge in her cage, and I slammed the cage door closed. Goddamn, I did not like that fucking monkey.

What Ifs?

We picked up Bill on Monday morning, and Aldo went through his routine of buying a couple of Bud tall boys, popping one, and putting the other under the seat. I'd already told Bill about him so that was no surprise. No, the surprise came when he had finished the second can before we were halfway to Perry, and decided he needed to stop at a solitary little wooden grocery/gas station by the roadside and get some more. This was breaking the pattern. We pulled in and all got out of the truck, and he asked if we wanted some sodas. Sure, what the hell. We also got some sardines and crackers for lunch. After grabbing his beer, he sauntered up to the register, and there was this frumpy middle-aged old woman, with glasses and graying hair, in shirt and jeans and boots, and Aldo starts talking with her, "Hey, honey, how are you today? You alone? Must get real bored working out here all by your lonesome…" She brightened ever so slightly, just from the attention, and told him she lived in the house out back, and her husband

150

was back there. He kept on, even with Bill and I awkwardly standing there, waiting to pay for our sardines, "What you say you and I don't go back there in the cooler and heat things up a little bit? Your husband'll never know a thing," giving her a little wink. Now she wasn't smiling. "You better get along, mister," as she rang up his beer and looked over at me and Bill. "Suit yourself, don't know what you're missin'" said Aldo, straightening up, and he walked out to the truck. "Sorry about that," I said as I paid. "That's all right, honey, looks like he's had a couple a beers already this morning." When we got back to the truck, Aldo was sipping on one of his beers, and we climbed in. I had to say something, I just couldn't help it. "Goddamn, Aldo, what were you thinkin' back there? Jesus, she wasn't even young, or good-lookin', or nothin'." "Yeah," he says, "well, those are the ones that want it the most. I was just feelin' a little frisky, and thought she might want to go for a trot. Those older ones aren't worried about getting pregnant, so they're more likely to jump when given a chance." He put the truck into gear and we rolled on out of there, and we drove out to the worksite. This was the first I had ever seen of this type of behavior (although it wouldn't be the last, by far), and it was rather disturbing. I started playing "what if" in my head. What if she had said "okay, let's go." What if the husband had come on in the back door while they were in the cooler? What if the husband kept a gun under the register, like any normal country storekeeper does? What would Bill and I be doing? What if the husband figured we were accomplices? This was just the sort of thing you read about in the papers all the time: *Store Owner Shoots Suspects*, where people say to themselves, "I wonder what *really* happened out there that day?"

Yeah, Aldo was a horn-dog, and a bad drinker, but he was a crackerjack carpenter. He'd say the damnedest things too, and you never knew if he was joking or not. At one job site, we showed up on a Monday morning and the young skinny redneck girl who lived in the adjacent trailer, and who Aldo had been flirting with whenever her young redneck husband left to go to work, came out with cups of coffee for us. Sure, it was cold out, but she had always stayed in the trailer all day while we worked, never coming out, because when she did, Aldo would be leering at her and making smacking sounds with his lips, trying to engage her in conversation, which she coldly rebuffed. But this morning she came out with the coffee, talked with us briefly asking how the construction was coming, and then went back in the trailer. Me and Bill commented on how unusual this was, but Aldo just sat there smiling to himself. Then, out of the blue, he said, "I came out here this weekend." Bill and I just looked at each other, and I said, "What do you mean you came out here this weekend?" "I came out here on my own to see if I couldn't get a little extra work done," he said. "Her husband had gone off hunting, so she was all alone. We ended up taking a shower together." (!?!?!?) Now this was just unbelievable. Aldo was a sixty-year-old man. True, he was tall, and not in too bad a shape, but he was just a gnarly old cracker, nothing to look at. She was skinny, like a lot of trailer girls are, with long straight black hair, fairly plain-looking, and couldn't have been twenty-five at the time. The thought of him getting into that trailer, much less taking a shower with that girl was well, preposterous. Still, she had come out and given us coffee, even talked with us, which had never happened before, and there sat Aldo, unusually quiet, sipping his coffee, smiling. Later, when she came out and got in her car to go to the store, Bill and I were up working on the rafters, and although I watched ever so carefully, I didn't see the least bit of eye-contact or even a hint of whimsy on either her face or Aldo's. In fact, Aldo never even looked up from cutting the ends off those rafters. To this day, I don't know if he was just jerking us around or not. If anything, the fact that they did NOT look at each other at all, especially Aldo not ogling her as she went to the car, as was his habit, made me wonder even more.

151

I, Surgery

Another time we were working on a different job, down in Ivan, near Crawfordville, and Aldo had had his usual four beers by noon, but was still working, and while cutting one of those really hard 12x6 yellow-pine rafters, a splinter flew up and embedded itself in his eye. It wasn't that big, maybe a quarter of an inch, but it was stuck right in the white of his eye. We drove up to what we thought was a small hospital, but it turned out to be an old folk's home, and they said they couldn't help. The nearest hospital was in Tallahassee, some thirty miles away, and it was bothering him so much that he didn't want to wait. Well, I told him that if he'd let me, I had a very fine-tipped pocket knife, and I thought I could back that thing out real quick, but he'd have to trust me and hold still. He thought about it and said sure, give it a try. Now it happened that on that particular house, both Bill and Nolin were helping out, so I disinfected the knife tip with a match, let it cool, and had Aldo lay back with his head in my lap, so I could see down into his eye. It wasn't going to be too difficult, because I could see the splinter clearly and it wasn't all the way in, so all I had to do was catch the end of it and back it out slowly. But between his drinking, and the nervousness of me holding this thin-bladed knife just over his open eyeball, he started twitching, and squirming, just as I'd catch hold of the splinter-edge. I told Nolin and Bill, "Quick, hold him tight so he doesn't move around", while I had his head gripped tight between my knees, and his eyelids peeled back with my left hand. They held him hard, I got the end of the splinter, and it came right out, no blood, no vitreous fluid, nothing. I held it up on the knife-tip and smiled; and Aldo fainted dead away, passed out cold. We let him sleep for an hour or so, and put all the tools away, before we woke him and called it a day. He was very thankful, not having had to go to the hospital, and he bought us our very own six-pack for our troubles. This wasn't the only time I ever did eye surgery with that pointy pocket knife; the next time I did it on myself.

The Wrecking Rue

Aldo finally hooked up with one particular lady, Thelma, who was a small and wiry widow, a country-fried type of woman, initially tolerant of his drinking, who fed him good home-cooked meals, and finally just had him move into her house, where she lived with her thirty-something-year-old son, Matthew. After a few months of putting up with some of his off-the-wall drinking bouts however, both Matthew and Thelma laid down the law: either he quit drinking or he'd have to move out. Well, by this time, Aldo had really fallen for Thelma, to the point that he wasn't even looking at other women, and so he decided to go on the wagon. He'd always smoked Camel non-filters, but to take the edge off of his craving for drink, he asked me to get him some pot. That was easy enough in those days, and I got him a few joints now and then. He seemed to be happy, admirably quit his drinking, and we were building houses like nobody's business. He even renewed his interest in a small farm he owned up in Cairo (pronounced Kay-Ro, like the syrup, as opposed to the capital of Egypt). So he and Thelma would drive up there on weekends where he was trying to get it back in shape after years of neglect. Well, one Friday evening, as they were driving up to Georgia (how can it be said without invoking the word "ironically"?), a drunk ran a stop sign at one of the many rural side roads and slammed into the left front driver's side of Aldo's pickup. I got the call on Sunday from Matthew, who told me his Mom, Thelma, was pretty busted up, her head had cracked the windshield, she had a couple of cracked ribs, a fractured arm, and was going to need a new set of dentures, but otherwise she was very lucky, and had already been sent home from the hospital after a night and a day of observation. Aldo, however, was in much worse shape. He had caught the steering wheel, breaking it off straight across his face, and the steering column had crushed in his chest. He also had multiple fractures all along his left side, where the impact had taken place. The only thing that had saved him from being completely impaled was that he had been wearing his seat belt.

He was in Intensive Care and they weren't sure he was going to make it. The drunk who had hit them was, of course, unscathed.

We were finishing up one of the houses at that time so I waited about a week, and then realized if I was going to keep working and get it done, so we could get paid, I'd need Aldo's tools and a crew. Once Matthew let me know that Aldo was out of Intensive Care, but still in what they called Critical Care, I made plans to visit him at the hospital to ask him about using his tools, and just check in on him. Bob Nolin said he wanted to come along too, so we drove on up to Tallahassee Memorial, and they started to give me a load of crap about how only family could visit. Therefore, I suddenly became his nephew on my Mom's side, and once they let me in, Nolin just followed. They said it would be a minute or two, why don't we just stand there while they figured out which one was Aldo. As we stood there next to the door we looked at the nearest bed and there was some swollen helpless pathetic monster, tubes going in and tubes running out, a respirator huffing away, and yellow blood-soaked gauze wrapping it up like one of Dr. Frankenstein's failures. Truly, it was a hideous sight. "God, I hope Aldo's not as bad off as that poor bastard," I said. The head nurse came back with a clipboard in her hand, looked at the clipboard attached to the foot of the bed of this wretched grotesque we had been staring at, and said, "Here he is."

Jeezuz-Fucking-Kee-Rist-in-the Morning! It didn't even resemble a human being, except for the fact that it lay prone on a bed. There was no face to speak of. I say that, because although swathed in bandages, it didn't even have the contours of a face, with a large gape of ooze sopping through the bandages where a nose and mouth should be. Only one eye was visible under the wraps, and even that one was closed. His body was at least twice its normal size. It was ghastly. Then the eye opened. Wet and rheumy, it glanced one way then the other. I leaned over and gently said "Aldo?" It looked around before settling on my face, not eighteen inches away. He looked at me, as if for the first time, and finally realized who I was. I don't think he ever saw Nolin, standing on the other side of the bed, that eye being covered. He tried to say something, but it just came out a gurgle, and he gave up right away. I tried to say some comforting things, told him that Nolin was there, that we were sorry for what had happened, that we'd check in on Thelma, the usual babble when one sees someone in that condition. He lifted his right arm, the one closest to me, and apparently the only one functioning, which made sense if they were hit on the left side. He crooked it and touched his heart area. I looked up at Nolin and we didn't get it. He kept touching his heart area. Nolin came around to my side of the bed, where Aldo could see him. He pointed at Nolin's shirt pocket, where he was carrying a pack of Pall Malls. Did he want a cigarette? That was out of the question, and he couldn't have smoked one even if he were out of the hospital, having no face any more. He must be delirious. The drugs have addled him. We couldn't stay long and I knew they'd run us out soon, so I wanted to ask him about using his tools. Then it dawned on me! He always kept the joints I gave him in his cigarette pack in his shirt pocket. Was that it? "Are you worried about the pot? The joints in your cigarette pack?" He relaxed. That was it. "Okay, we'll take care of it. We'll check in with Thelma and figure it out. Okay?" He blinked his eye and tried to nod his head, but it barely moved. Finally, I just blurted out, "Listen, Aldo, would you mind if I used your tools to finish up that house we were working on?" He raised his right hand and gave me the okay sign. "Okay, pal, just take care of yourself, get better and get out of here. We'll see you in a coupe of weeks." We shook his one good hand and left. It was a sobering experience that had to be washed away as soon as possible. We headed down to the Pastime to shake off the willies.

I went and visited Thelma and Matthew, and she was healing up pretty fast, except for her broken arm. I let her know that I had visited Aldo with Nolin, but I sure as hell didn't say anything about how he looked. They already knew. She told me the whole horrid story of the wreck. How they didn't see the truck until it was on them. That when she came to and saw what a crumpled wreck the truck was, steam and oil and gasoline hissing, that she was sure that Aldo was dead, and she couldn't even make out where his head was as to where the crushed-in truck top, door, and steering column began. How it took something like an hour for an ambulance to get to them, and the fire rescue trucks had to cut Aldo out of the car. But she did remember him reaching over with his right arm, pulling out his cigarette pack and dropping it behind the seat. She did remember that. And she was glad I was going to take his tools and finish the house. Matthew told me where the truck had been taken, and said there were some tools still in it so he was glad that I was going out to check on it. Bill and I drove on up to Thomasville to the junkyard where the wreck of the truck was stored, and after a little talking at the gate the guy let us in. It was very, very bad. I got the tools out first, since they were in the back of the pickup and easiest to get to. Then we had to pry the passenger side door open to get to the front seat, and there were great brown stains of dried blood everywhere. I couldn't lean the seat forward as it was meant to go, but after digging around and pulling shit out from under the seat, I eventually found the cigarette pack, and shook out four cigarettes and two joints, all with brown stains scattered on the paper. Bill and I fired one up right away, after getting back in my van and heading back south to Tallahassee.

Sub-Contracting

We decided we'd finish the house ourselves, since all it needed now were the shingles put on, and the doors hung. Nolin wasn't available, since he was finishing up his schoolwork, and still driving cab part-time. Now, Bill's the real carpenter, a strong, solid, and bespectacled steady hand, so he was going to hang the doors, which is trickier than it sounds, since you've got to do it just right, hang them correctly on their hinges so they fit snug, but swing freely, drill the holes and install the locks so they line up just right with the lockplate, etc. I'd handle the shingles, which is pretty rudimentary. But I needed help carrying up the bundles. Bill and I carried up a few, but there were something like 50 bundles that had to be carried up a tall 12-foot ladder, and each one weighed nearly 80 pounds. Well, after 2 or 3 each, I decided I'd just hire a couple of friends to come out and spend a day just hauling shingles. I was going to have enough of a time just nailing them down on the hot tar-papered roof. Of all our friends at the time who happened to need the money, and were willing to come out though, there were only Greg Toole and Jimmy Gear. Greg was out of school, living at Ballard Road, and just needed some spending money; hell, always slender, he couldn't have weighed 150 pounds back then. Jimmy had just come to Tallahassee to join his two brothers, Charlie (of the paper-recycling fiasco on Apalache Parkway) and Barry, Nolin's old cohort in crime since high school. Jimmy had yet to establish his nascent empire in Tallahassee, so he was just looking for a little rental money. But Jimmy was then sitting at right around 280, and chain-smoking unfiltered Camels, like Aldo, one after another. I showed them how it needed to be done: lift the bundle up toss it onto your shoulder, and climb the ladder using your other hand, cross the roof, then gently lay the bundle down, and then you'd climb back down and get another. I went up the ladder and started nailing the shingles down, by myself. After finishing the bundle I'd just carried up, I waited, but no shingles were forthcoming. So I crawled over to the roof edge and looked over to check on them. I had to laugh, they were so pitiful. They couldn't even pick up the bundle, much less sling it onto their shoulder, so there was no going up the ladder, and thus, no shingles. "Okay," I yelled down to them, "You can break the bundles open, and then carry HALF a bundle [40 pounds], but then it's going to take twice as many trips up the ladder." This they were willing (and able) to do. But now, instead of 48 trips up (and down) the ladder, it was more like 96. It was going to be a long day.

Payoffs

Once Bill and I had finished the house, I called Jim Walters, who had already heard about Aldo, and they told me that they were prepared to change the contract over to me. I could come in and they'd give me the check as soon as I'd gotten the building permit signed by the county inspector for the framing. Damn, I'd forgotten about the building inspector! But I did remember that Aldo always had a pint of whiskey under the front seat of his truck when he was expecting the inspector. So we went and got a pint, called the inspector, and waited. When he finally showed up late that afternoon, I went up, shook his hand, and he started right in looking over the house. He pointed out this board and that board that needed moving, this header over a door that needed changing, some hurricane clips that needed to be put in, and finally, he didn't like the set of stairs that were on the back, so they would need to be re-done. What the hell? Most, if not all of that, was done while Aldo was working with us, and the inspector had never ever asked him to do things over or change anything. At least he hadn't found anything wrong with the doors or the shingles, the only parts Bill and I had really done all by ourselves. As he made these notes on the permit hanging on the power pole, I walked over to the van and got out the pint of whiskey, walked over and handed it to him, "Here, Aldo said I should give you this." He took it, looked at me, shook his head, smiled, and said, "You should have given that to me before I did the inspection, son… might have saved you some work." (Of course…I couldn't believe I had been so naïve, or really, so stupid to think he'd ask for it, or that we'd be openly bartering—you give him the pint before he even gets out of his truck—what a moron I was!) "You still gotta take care of those things," he said, "but next time you call, I'll sign it." So we finished up everything the next day, called the inspector, got the permit signed, and the following day drove over to Jim Walters and got the check. I'd replaced Aldo on the contract, and now I was officially a carpenter sub-contractor for Jim Walter Homes. I paid off Bill, Jimmy, and Greg, gave Thelma half the money for Aldo, and paid Lisa back for money I'd borrowed, and we celebrated in grand style.

Mick the Dick

The next job was already underway, and the Jim Walter contract manager asked if Bill and I couldn't help out one of his contractor's who was in a bind. We drove out there, and met the remnants of an unhappy crew, working under the screaming dictates of their sub, a guy named Mick Elmhurst, a tall, gangly piece of bad attitude, with not only the hippie ponytail, but a long Hatfield-McCoy beard. It just so happened that my buddy Bill knew this guy, as they had been rough-frame carpenters on some apartment complex way back when. Later, Bill would fill me in on what an asshole this guy had been, but now, on our initial introduction, I was already seeing it firsthand. He wasn't happy that we had been assigned to "help him out" and he made it clear that he was going to keep the lion's share of the payoff. His crew of two were already at their wit's end dealing with him, and when they saw their shares dwindle on the introduction of Bill and myself, that was the last straw. They picked up their tools and left. Well, Bill and I tried working with this guy Mick, we really did, but for all his bluster, he was semi-competent at best, and it looked to me like he'd never built a Jim Walter house before in his life. Having worked on a couple already, I had picked up more than a few tricks from Aldo and Herb (and Bill), so I would offer suggestions on how to do something quicker and better, despite the plans, but this guy Mick was just too hard-headed and arrogant, and we ended up taking too much time as he pondered over what the plans "meant," as if they were some slab of hieroglyphics, instead of what they were meant to be: a plan. In short, the guy was an idiot. We got the floor done, and had just put up the first wall when the owner came home from work, a nice black guy who happened to be a mechanic that fixed Tallahassee city busses, and asked if he could talk with us. He noticed that the living room window was on the left side of the house, whereas he had wanted it on the right side of the house, and had been told by Jim Walters that this was not going to be a problem. In the end, what the owner wanted was a mirror image of the house presented in the plans, and since this didn't affect the structural integrity, of course, Jim Walters had said it wouldn't be a problem, just tell your sub-contractor. Well, this was just too much for Mick, who didn't get it, and he went into a tirade about how this was too difficult (it wasn't), and that we'd have to get extra money for changing the plans (we wouldn't), not to mention re-doing the work we'd already done (not much, considering). At the end of his hissy-fit, we picked up our tools, and drove to Mick's trailer, where he was going to call Jim Walter's and give them a piece of his mind, as well as demand more money.

We got to his trailer and there sat his wife, Tanya, one of the most beautiful women I'd ever seen, a black-haired beauty of Mediterranean extraction. Meanwhile, the place smelled of old diapers, and they obviously had suffered from Mick's lack of productivity, or at least his inability to provision the place. Tanya was overworked and coping as best she could, but living with this jerk couldn't have been the least bit pleasant, at any time. Wonder what she ever saw in him? Oh yeah, I forgot… those tall arrogant assholes are supposedly good in the sack, as attested to by the squawling kid, and that she was willing to put up with his bullshit. In any case, he called up Jim Walters and talked with the construction manager, who told him that under the terms of the contract he ought to just shut up and get back to work. Well, we were done for the day, so I suggested to Bill that he and I make our way to the Pastime. Then Mick started in on Tanya, giving her a rash of shit for no apparent reason, and I pushed Bill that we had to go (before I said something we'd all regret). The dickhead made some suggestion about coming along, but I was adamant that I wasn't coming back that way, so in effect, he was not invited. When we got to the bar, I told Bill that I wouldn't be able to work with this guy, no matter what. Mulling it over while we drank our pitcher, I came up with a plan. I'd already usurped a contract once, when Aldo had gotten into his accident; why couldn't I do it again? Only this time it would be before Mick might befall some accident. First of all, I called Jim Walters and asked if they'd give me the contract for the house if I could get Mick to agree to hand it over. The manager said sure, but from his experience in these matters, it was probably going to cost me. How much? That was between me and Mick. I sat and figured quickly on a napkin how much work had been done already, and how much was left, as opposed to the percentage of money the contract was worth. I figured $200 was a fair price to buy out Mick. I called him up, and damn if the sunuvabitch didn't want $400! No, no, and no, and I countered that he had already lost his crew, and if he didn't take my offer, he wasn't going to have me and Bill either, and he'd have to find another set of hands. He'd get back with me. An hour later he called back and had apparently figured the bird in the hand was worth the none he'd get in the bush. $250? No! $200! Okay, he'd do it. We'll meet you down at Jim Walters tomorrow at 10 o'clock. Now I had a real problem. I didn't have $200.

I was going to have to ask Lisa for a loan. Even though I had started going back to school a little bit, and Lisa and I actually took a class on Shakespeare's later plays together, our relationship was getting somewhat strained, after spending all my extra money on the risky road trip with Nolin, the less-than-romantic trip to Mexico, my passing time at the Pastime, and that she had to carry the load anyway until I'd get paid at the end of a job, sometimes three or four weeks apart. And she was sick of living out at Herb's house at Lewis Blvd. The place was icy cold in the winter, and although she'd done wonders to make it homey, it was still a rathole, and the palmetto bug ("big roach") population never seemed to go down no matter what preventatives I applied.

Finally, even though Lisa loved her, she was getting gradually unnerved by Bertie Jones walking in on us in the mornings, plopping down on the edge of our bed and rudely waking us up, especially on Saturdays, screeching "GET UP, YOU ALL! It's already 8 o'clock! How can you sleep so late?" (Yes, we sometimes locked the doors, but Herb had given her a key years before, and if she were locked out, she'd just bang on the door or the windows til we got up and let her in.) Lisa was looking for another place to live, and was wisely saving her money for that eventuality. Me? I liked Herb's place, I liked building Jim Walter houses, and Bertie didn't bother me at all. If anything, I found her to be a humorous diversion. Lisa finally found a place, it was a nice middle-class home under a sprawling live oak, in a nice neighborhood, with hardwood floors, and new (used) furniture. Once we moved in I had to put up a fence for the dogs (with a gate), and when the move and the fence were done, Lisa's affections noticeably lessened. It was all my own fault, and she was outgrowing me by leaps and bounds with her concentration on university studies. But I asked her for the $200, and she graciously loaned it to me.

I paid the bastard Mick off with the $200, and we changed over the contract. Bill and I were going to need some help now, so we recruited Nolin, now out of school and no longer driving cab, who was also living hand-to-mouth at the time, since moving into a small little wooden house near Ballard with his girlfriend, Celia. All three of us were what can only be kindly described as down-and-out. We had to get this house done so we could cash in and get back on the good foot. I couldn't ask Lisa for any more money (especially for any beer money), and we needed gas for the van as well. So I devised another plan. I remembered that Aldo had once had us load up all the leftover wood into his truck after one of our jobs, and he took it up to Cairo to store at this farm. So I had Bill and Nolin count every piece of lumber that was under the plastic tarp, while I went through the plans step-by-step, and counted exactly how many pieces of each length and dimension that we would need to complete the house. Then we loaded up all the extra boards into the van, and headed south. The plan was this: when I had been finishing my stint at paper recycling, it just so happened that a fellow opened up a lumber store right next door, and not just any lumber store; he was processing his own "pressure-treated" lumber after having purchased a large boiler-sized pressure cooker in which he would add all these noxious chemicals that made the run-of-the-mill #2 yellow Southern Pine impervious to termites and other pests, wood rot, mildew, fungus, etc. We heard that he was accepting good lumber which he would buy, and after pressure-treating it, would turn around and sell for three to five times the price he paid. I believe the guy's name was Roscoe.

Van No Go

All was proceeding smoothly, we had a van full of lumber, a ready buyer, and a beautiful day ahead of us. Driving south down Crawfordville Highway, we were already contemplating the division of the spoils, when, stretching our luck, the van sputtered, and ran out of gas at the top of the hill that is the home of Florida A&M University. As we coasted a half-mile down to a final stop, we got out and started scratching our heads, "What to do now?" Unfortunately, and unknown to us at the time, we had glided to a stop right in front of the city-owned mechanic's shop for the Tallahassee bus lines. Out walked the guy whose house we were supposed to working on, rubbing his oily hands with a rag; the same house from which the lumber now loaded in the van had been, to put it nicely, purloined. He looked at us, looked at the van, looked at the lumber sticking out the back door of the van, and said, "Hey, boys, what's goin' on?" I jumped right in, "Hey, Mr. Brown, we've got a quick job down at Woodville Highway that Jim Walters wants us to take care of." "That wood's not from my house is it?" he asked. We all shook our heads, "Oh no, no, not at all." "We'll be back at your house tomorrow if we finish up this job down south today," (well, we would!). "So, what's the problem?" he asked. "We ran out of gas… could we borrow a gas can?" "Hell, I got some gas, hold on a second," and he went into the shop, coming out with a five-gallon can that had at least three left in it. He poured it in, I started the engine right up, and we thanked him, jumping back in the van and telling him we'd see him tomorrow. He still had a funny look on his face as I watched him in the rearview mirror, watching us drive off, shaking his head.

Lumbering Along

So we get to Roscoe's lumber yard on Woodville Highway, appropriately named the Woodville Lumber Company, and go in to see him. It's a nice quiet weekday, and this big blustery cowboy is sitting in his cool air-conditioned office, boots up on he desk, hat tilted back, smoking a cigar, and he says, "Howdy, gentlemen, what can I d o for you?" "Well, we heard that you'll buy lumber, and we've got some outside. Are you interested?" "Let's see what you got," he said swinging his feet to the ground and getting up. We led him out to the van, where the boards were sticking out the back doors, tied together. I untied them and swung the doors open so he could get a good look. "What's all in there?" he said. I gave him the list, something like six 12-foot yellow pine 2 by 8s, six 10-foot yellow pine 2 by 6s, and maybe a dozen 8-foot white fir 2 by 4s. He looked at the ends of the boards which were clearly marked "Property of Jim Walters." "You boys didn't steal these boards, did you?" he smiled. "No sir, we're working on a job and these are leftover," I said. "It don't matter," he said, "it'll disappear when they're pressurized… come on inside." We followed him in and he sat at his desk, still munching his cigar, both wet and smoky, and started banging away at an adding machine. Then he looked up and said, "I'll give you $75 dollars for all of it." We looked at each other and brightened up… hell, that was $25 apiece! When you could buy a tall-boy Busch in the can at the Pastime for 55 cents, this was a godsend. "Unless you want to make a deal…" he said ever so quietly, almost whispering, as he leaned over the desk. "What kind of deal?" I asked, looking at Bill and Nolin, wondering where this was gonna go. He stood up and reached into his pants pocket, then pulled out a large coin in his hand. "I got this silver dollar here… here, take it… look at it," handing it over to us to have a look at it, "and I'm willing to flip this coin with you boys for double or nothing. You win, I'll give you $150… but if you lose, you just give me the lumber and we're still friends. Whadda you say?" Oh shit! This really threw a monkey wrench into it! We'd seen that money in our hands, the beer already being poured as we celebrated, and now, an opportunity for twice as much! We could go for weeks on $50 each, and even have a meal or two for lunch instead of sardines and crackers. And gas for the van. Or we could end up bust, worse off than we were. "Could we go outside and talk this over?" "Sure, boys, take all the time you want… uh, can I have my silver dollar back?" We went outside and began the discussion, but it was over before it began. No, we were not going to flip a coin double or nothing, we were going to take the $75 and split it, we were that desperate. Sure there was an imaginary scenario where we won the toss and capered off with extra money out of our pockets, but reality was nipping at our ankles, and we'd already had a close call with the house owner, no, it was time to settle down and take the original offer. So we marched back in, and let him know and he handed over the $75 already sitting on his desk. Then he pointed out the window and showed us where to unload the wood. That wasn't the end of it though, we were to see Roscoe the Lumber Guy several times after that.

Back to work on the bus mechanic's house, we went at it with a vengeance, and even though we were relatively new as a working group, and he had wanted a mirror-image of what the plans actually displayed (which took a little getting used to, and meant we had to be extra careful, now that the wood was rationed), we knocked it off in about three weeks. This time the celebration was both short-lived and bittersweet. Our celebration on finishing the job was at our usual hangout, the Pastime, of course, and we were surrounded by friends. One couple was a friend of Lisa's named Maggie, and her boyfriend, also named David. Nice couple, and they got along well. It just so happened that when we moved out of the house at Lewis Blvd. David asked if he and Maggie could have the monkey. We asked Herb Odel and he said he was tired of her anyway, and if they'd give her a good home, they were more than welcome to have Lottie the monkey. This was perfect! The strange thing was that Lottie the monkey had reversed her sexual discrimination regarding men and just loved this guy David. So I guess it was a match made in heaven. In any case, there was a new face in the crowd that night, a guy I'd met briefly a week before. He was studying Law and was new to town and looking for some friendly folks to hang around with. His name was Craig, and he was well-groomed, thin and smart, with an engaging personality that I'm sure would add to his lawyer credentials later in life. I made the mistake of introducing him to Lisa.

Such Sweet Sorrow

While I played pool with the boys, he and she compared notes and apparently my status as a boyfriend was reviewed and found wanting. Later in the week, I noticed that she was coming home later and later, and eventually, a week or two after, sitting home one Saturday night with the dogs on the couch watching Saturday Night Live (which was still fresh with the original cast and which we had always enjoyed watching together), I realized something was amiss and Lisa wasn't coming home anytime soon. Not being able to enjoy the skits, since my mind was now preoccupied dancing with the green devil, I went and did one of those things that you always regret but which, in retrospect, was for all practical purposes, unavoidable. I went into the bathroom, opened up the medicine chest (which I'd always considered public property, as long as I lived there), and I popped her diaphragm container (which probably wasn't considered public property), and found it empty. After she finally got home, and subsequent to all the yelling back and forth, I began sleeping in the guest room.

None of this is to imply that I was either an innocent prior to these proceedings, nor actually that I didn't deserve getting cut loose. These were the 70s for chris'sakes, and we were all of us, then in our early twenties, pushing the envelope when it came to experimentation, infidelity, philosophy, and intimations of mortality. I had not been as attentive to Lisa as I should have been, and probably took her for granted, considering how tolerant she'd been. And my prospects at the time were not looking all that bright either. If anything, I was turning into a North Florida redneck, what with all the skinny-dipping in the sinkholes, swinging a hammer for a living, beer-drinking, dope-smoking, and general unkempt and uncaring hippieness, while she was getting more sophisticated, better educated (she was even invited to become a Phi Beta Kappa), and looking forward to a fulfilling and productive career. So, it wasn't that much of a surprise that we were heading in different directions and, though I regretted it later, at the time it appeared to be an opportunity for independence.

East Call and Mindy

I rented a little upstairs apartment on East Call St. within walking distance of the Pastime, in a nice shady neighborhood across from Leon High School. When I say little, I mean there was a living room of maybe ten feet square, half of which was taken up by the climbing stairwell, a kitchen half that size, and a single bedroom of maybe twelve feet square, with a bathroom again a third that size. I remember the rent was $90 a month. In the apartment below me two young girls moved in, just out of high school, and it was quickly established that they were not just roommates, but mates; and though these were days when that sort of thing was still rather unusual, especially living together and snubbing their noses at the world, they were very protective and caring of each other. At first, they didn't know what to make of the hairy carpenter-man who lived above them, but after sharing a couple of beers and bowlfuls, and carrying on portentous world-changing discussions on religion, sex, and politics, we reached a plateau of understanding that grew into a long-term friendship. I was somewhat attracted to the blond, muscular one, Mindy, who was obviously the alpha-bitch, if that's not putting things too harshly, only because she showed a particular penchant for philosophy and mysticism, and although she wasn't that well-educated, she had a very incisive and sharp intellect. The other girl, Ruth I think her name was, was the earth-mother submissive wife, and even though we got along pretty good she hardly ever came upstairs, and never without Mindy, although Mindy would come up and sit and talk sometimes for hours by herself. And that was it, just talk, even though I did let her know that if she ever wanted to take a stroll down the straight and narrow, I'd be happy to oblige.

The Owlets

I had maybe a month of solitude, and was in fact, enjoying it, and we were still slapping together the Jim Walter houses, when, I couldn't explain the why or wherefore, but Nolin and his girlfriend of long-standing, Celia (Lisa's best friend), mutually decided to separate—what are the odds that after comparing notes, the girls decided they were better off without these anchors around their necks? So he moved in with me. There was only one bed in the bedroom, my room, so, he either slept on the couch in the living room, or when the weather was nice, he liked to crawl out the back window and sleep on the slightly sloping roof that covered the girls' downstairs kitchen below. We never let on, but from their kitchen roof, at night we could peer down from above right into their bathroom shower, but they never showered together, so there wasn't any action, and you can only watch someone wash themself so much, even a girl, without any other activity going on, before the thrill is gone. Now before we hear the lecture on how perverse and prying (and wrong) this activity might be, let me first explain that it wasn't a planned voyeuristic endeavor anyway, but came about incidentally while smoking some pot out there on the roof, watching the stars and otherwise contemplating the universe. Nonetheless, it reminds me of another story that occurred many years later, when a neighbor of ours from across the street one day came over all upset, because she came home from work, as per her usual routine, and while she was taking a shower, she looked out the window, and up in a tree, some fifty yards and two house lots away, she saw there was a guy sitting in a tree, in the bower of a couple of branches, with one hand grasping a set of binoculars through which he was looking, and the other, well, let's just say, NOT grasping a branch (of the tree) to steady himself, his legs otherwise tightly managing the requisite safety grip. She saw him, let out a loud yelp, and he saw through his binocs that she had seen him, and as she quickly escaped and toweled, he scampered down the tree and made off. Before coming over and telling us, she had already called the cops, who came out and saw that he had actually prepared his prying eyes owl's nest by putting a set of tree-house-type 2-by- 4 steps up the tree trunk, and had probably figured out her routine by timing her arrival home and her need to bathe and change into non-work clothes. A quick canvass of the surrounding houses and duplexes proved fruitless. The board-steps were removed, and he was not seen again, apparently learning his lesson. She was somewhat nervous from then on, looking out the window that was now curtained whenever she was showering, but she had a boyfriend from Guatemala who was something of a gangster and promised her that he would have the guy murdered if they ever saw him again, and this seemed to make her feel better— ironically, her full-time job was to gather evidence for death-row appellants. Unlike us bumbling dopers, that was a dedicated Peeping Tom!

160

Poverty Struck

So, Nolin, Bill, and I were building these Jim Walter crackerboxes and trying to struggle along without any money until the next inspector's signoff, so we could get paid. It was a tough time, and we had to pull out all the stops. For awhile, even Bill was staying at the little apartment too, since we were attached to one another as being a working crew, and sometimes it was just easier to let Bill stay over, rather than him going home and us having to drive out and get him in the morning. How to get money? First of all, we needed to have gas to keep my van moving to the jobsite, since it was loaded with all our tools, and during the day, was our only mutual means of transportation. We turned to larceny, and in the evenings, made surreptitious ventures into the various State parking garages, where we employed a four-foot length of hose, also known as a Georgia credit card, to suck gasoline out of some of the State cars parked there. It was an awful business. Nolin was the lookout, since he refused to suck out the fuel, because whoever did it always got at least one mouthful of gasoline, and he being a smoker, loudly claimed it ruined the taste of his cigarettes for hours if not days. Thus, Bill and I would take turns filling a five-gallon gas can, which might entail hitting two or three cars at a time, before we all made off in the dark of night, later filling the van from the can in a more remote and safer locale. (I know, I know, gasoline at that time was under a buck a gallon, but we were so strapped we couldn't even afford the $5 needed to drive around for a week.) When the next visit to Roscoe's Lumber Yard proved disastrous—we had decided to go for double-or- nothing, and after the silver dollar hit the floor, bouncing once, we ended up loading the lumber out in the back of his shop and driving away without even our pride intact—Bill and I took to selling plasma for food and beer; another undertaking, so to speak, that Nolin refused to participate in, and therefore, although he may have partook of our shared victuals (socialists that we were), he ended up having to buy and roll his own cigarettes. No, Nolin otherwise assisted me in another altogether illegitimate but harmless scam that never did pan out, even though the planning and performance were almost perfectly aligned.

Off at the Races

At that time, Winn-Dixie, the chain of southern grocery stores, had a bit of a sweepstakes going, and the gist of it was this: they would give a card to every paying customer, and this card was of the scratch-off variety which are so common for lotteries nowadays; the area scratched off would reveal the number of a particular horse that would run in one of five heats shown on a select sponsoring channel on Saturday nights at 7 p.m.; the winning horse in any of the five races yielded a $100 payoff, which you could redeem at your local store. Well, we knew of course that these weren't actual "races" and that they were reruns of some old track races wherein the folks at Winn-Dixie absolutely knew the outcome, thus projecting the distribution of prizes across the State via the one-per-customer handout of these scratch-off tickets. Nonetheless, as we noted after a few turns casing out the checkout lines at our nearby store, the place was practically empty on late Saturday afternoons, some two hours before the broadcast. So, as I would purchase say, a pack of gum, smiling, flirting, and distracting the cashier, Nolin would walk through the empty line next to hers, scarfing up whatever pile of these tickets that had been leftover from the earlier part of the week. Then he would pick another cashier, with an empty line next to her, and buy his Bugle Boy tobacco to roll up his cigarettes, again making conversation with the checkout girl while I went through the adjoining empty line picking up what piles of leftover tickets I could find (these were again, in a time when cameras were not as prevalent, or rather, as ubiquitous as they are today, where to attempt such a thing now would be nothing but a fool's errand). Once we got home with maybe a hundred tickets, we'd scrape them clean and stack them in piles by the numbers. The larger piles were guaranteed losers, and were discarded, as were most of the smaller ones; but when there remained only one or two tickets left for each race, the odds were now in our favor. We would get all worked up, have a drink (if available) and sit back to "watch the races." No gambler at the track, whether it was Charles Bukowsky or Damon Runyon, or dear fictitious Sam Spade, was as nervous when the horses rounded the last turn and neck-and-neck came tumbling home! More than once this ended in a photo finish, where we would have to wait another five minutes, and sit through another goddamn Winn-Dixie commercial, to find out the results. We did this maybe three weeks in a row. For all the hours we had put in, for all the risks we had taken, we never won… not once.

Lum and Dumber

Soon we got a contract on a house out near the railroad tracks on Woodville Highway, not far from Herb Odel's old house where Lisa and I had lived for two or three years, and started building sometime in late October. It started getting cold quick, so we worked harder and faster, again selling any extra lumber to Roscoe at the nearby Lumber Yard (but no longer gambling, lesson learned, just selling it outright). The old guy we were building it for was retired, and he came out every day to check on our progress. His name was Lum Hartsfield, and he was a grossly obese old retired white guy, huffing and puffing as he ambled out from his pickup truck. He'd been retired for many years, and now that all his children were gone and grown up, he wanted a nice little place for just his wife and himself to finish out their days. He'd watch us work for an hour or so, and then get back into his truck until we saw him the next day. We always let him know if we were going to take a day off, so he wouldn't have to drive out if we weren't going to be there; but since the weather was getting colder by the day, and we were still dirt poor, we decided to work as much as we possibly could, even weekends. We'd gotten the floor finished and most of the walls up, when a bad rainstorm set in for a day or two, and then the cold front behind it froze the whole town solid. Going out to the house site, we found that, because we had done such a great job of putting together the floor, nice and tight, and put up all the outside walls, but hadn't yet cut out the "plates" for the doorway entrances, where later you'll put in a nice door jamb of hard oak, we had, in effect, created an ice rink, where the floor was frozen solid with ice an inch-or-so thick up to the edge of the two by fours. At first we thought this was marvelous, and we ran back and forth and slid around for awhile, before Lum drove up with one of the Jim Walter contracting managers following behind him. Lum had gotten worried because we had been gone two days, even though it was obvious we weren't going to work in the rain. So he called Jim Walter's who sent out their construction manager to check up on us. After looking things over, the guy took us aside and said that he thought we had done a good job so far, except that, because the floor was so tight, when the ice melted he was afraid the standing water would cause the floor to buckle. We should have left some space between the plywood sheets that made up the floor, so that air could circulate, and water could drain out. Well, how the hell were we going to fix that? He said we'd have to take the saw and run it down the adjoining edges where the plywood sheets met—that would open up a quarter-inch gap that would let the water run out and everything would be fine. Except for one small detail. Someone was going to have to use the circular saw to cut through the inch of ice (thus turning it into water), and for another three-quarters of an inch to penetrate the floor. There was no chance of talking either Nolin or Bill into doing it: Nolin didn't operate dangerous machinery, and Bill had already had too much experience in the construction trade for me to convince him it wasn't all that risky. Besides, it was my job site, my fault, and my saw. So I tried a test cut, and it worked just fine, but at least I had sense enough to figure out that, rubber-soled boots or not, I would have to be un-grounded to be certain of not getting electrocuted. Thus I ended up perched on a couple of wooden blocks, with the extension cord raised off the ground, and cutting as fast as I could before the sun turned the ice to a puddle that would have been impossible to negotiate. Nervously, I knocked it out in about half an hour as Bill and Nolin stood near the breaker box ready to pull the cord (and hopefully, administer CPR) if they spotted me going into electro-spastic slobbering convulsions.

Lum was still pretty happy with us and the progress on the house, and he'd tell us every day how his wife was looking forward to moving in. He even brought her around one day after we had gotten the siding up and the windows cut out so she could get an idea of what it was going to look like after the roof was on and the yard cleaned up. She was an overweight old redneck just like him, though not as obese, and whereas he was in his mid-sixties, she was probably in her early to mid-fifties, graying, chubby, and friendly. It was getting near Thanksgiving, but by now, all three of us were bachelors, unattached and uninvited to any big dinner going on, so we decided to go ahead and work on Thanksgiving Day. We were starting to put up the rafters, which is a tricky piece of business, and Lum came out early, since he and his family were planning a large dinner early in the afternoon and then to watch football later. He was exuberant and beaming: the house was almost finished, he was going to be with his family all day, his wife was happy, and he was retired and ready to start afresh. We wished him a Happy Thanksgiving and got back to work on the rafters. Funny thing, he didn't show up to check on us the next day.

On Saturday, Lum's pickup truck rolled up, and out of the passenger side came his wife. She waddled up to us all teary-eyed and sobbing, holding a kerchief to her face and told us that Lum was dead. He had a heart attack right there at the Thanksgiving Day dinner table, and before the ambulance arrived he was gone. Needless to say, we were stunned, and just stood there, tools in hand and looking hang-dog, not knowing what to say. It doesn't affect the house though, she said, everything was switching over to her and we should just keep on and finish it as fast as we could, although if we wanted to take the rest of the day off, she understood. Well, that sounded like the right thing to do, so we started pulling up our cords, and saws, and other tools and putting things away. As we did so, the driver's side of Lum's pickup opened up and out stepped a tall thin middle-aged redneck in jeans, rolled-up sleeves, and cowboy boots. He looked to be about forty-five and he had that pomaded pompadour hair that those kind of guys think looks good. He walked on up to Mrs. Hartsfield and put his arm around her. She looked up and smiled. Before we had finished packing up the van, she was already in the framed-up house, roof half on, showing him how it was going to be, room by room. As we pulled out of the job site, they were standing out front, his hand on her ass, staring at the soon-to-be-finished house. It's still there to this day, and when I drive by down Woodville Highway, I always mutter a little prayer, "Poor Lum."

The last house we built was down in Woodville and it was for Aldo's nephew, Bobby Bonafore. This was sort of strange because both Bobby and his father were professional carpenters who worked for the county, but, although Jim Walters would let anyone finish their own house, they insisted that the shell (that is, the rough-framing) be put up under their own direction. So we began putting up Bobby's house, and it was the middle of summer, and it was hotter'n hell. Plus we had Bobby and his dad coming home from work every evening and checking over our work. In their defense, they weren't pushing us to have it done fast, they just wanted it done right, so there wasn't going to be any cutting corners or any more trips to Roscoe's Lumber Yard. We worked under the scattered pine trees, which, no matter what anybody says, don't offer much shade, but they sure do cut down any breeze coming through. Because it was so hot, we'd take long lunch breaks, pick up some sardines and crackers, or bologna and bread and mustard, and visit the nearby sinkhole, which for us was the one known as Power Line Sink. This was because it was situated immediately below some large power lines right along a stretch of an inspection road between two of the tall supporting metal erector-set towers. There were two entrances to the

163

sinkhole cave. You could either walk on down a slippery, greasy clay hand-carved stairway (this was also the only exit), or you could just jump maybe ten or twelve feet down through an eight-foot-round hole at ground level and hope that either no one was below you or you didn't hit the projecting limestone sides. Once you were in there though, there was a small cavernous shelf on which you could sit along the cool water's edge that seeped up from the rocky aquifer below, with the entrance hole just above the center of the pool. It was truly magical—cool, refreshing, and semi-dark with light reflecting from the hole above that shimmered along the walls, just like an underground swimming pool.

Since it was summer, it was sometimes occupied by the local redneck rough-and-tumble teenagers and their wet t-shirt and Daisy Duke girlfriends, but more than half the time we ever went there we had the place to ourselves. One time, we pulled up, got out of the van, and could hear voices whispering up and out the hole. When we jumped in we surprised a guy and his girlfriend who were just getting ready to start messing around. They quickly departed... and as we were sitting there on the ledge, cooling off, I spotted a head-sized green round thing maybe twenty feet down on the bottom, on the silt pan where the water entered from unknown depths below. I dove down to see what it was and ended up retrieving a more than half-bottle of Matus red wine. Obviously the guy and gal had brought it down with them and, trying to keep it cool in the water, it had gotten away from them while they're frolicking, but still had enough wine in it that it didn't float, but sank. We sat there and passed it around, toasting our good fortune and enjoying the idyllic ambience. Once we'd cooled off, eaten lunch, and taken a quick little siesta, it was time to get back to work.

This was the house that was going to end it all. I'd gotten tired of the grind, the stress, the late payments, the goddamn busting ass and just being poor all the time. I'd also picked up the bad habit of chewing tobacco. No, I hadn't done it long, but I found out that the benefit of having a "chaw" in the pocket of your cheek meant that you were so worried about swallowing even a drop of juice that your concentration was often centered to the task at hand as well, and time would fly by, not to mention the rush the half-digested nicotine was delivering from your buccal glands to the brain. And the added benefit was that same one discovered by the Spanish when they first were introduced to the nicotinic drug five hundred years earlier: you could work like a motherfucker and not get either hungry or thirsty (since the nicotine suppressed your appetite, and the overindulgence of saliva kept your mouth constantly watering, which is why, ergo, you spit constantly), and, you got all this energy while keeping your hands free so you could hammer and haul lumber. But it wasn't good for your teeth, or your gums, or for that matter, your love life (and here I was in my mid-twenties), not to mention, you really had to clear out the pipes before you could start drinking any beer in earnest. I quickly gave up that bad habit once I'd decided to give up the other, building Jim Walter homes.

An Epiphany

Bill and I were finishing up Bobby's house down in Woodville, again with Bill doing the doors and stairs, and me on the roof. And like I said, it was hotter that bejeezus. Bill had helped me put on the tarpaper, and snap the chalk lines that showed where every other line of shingles was to be aligned. And we'd both carried up at least twenty bundles of shingles, so there was plenty to work with. I was up on that goddamn roof, and it had to be 140 degrees (just like... what was it they called that last desert they had to cross to get to Aquaba in *Lawrence of Arabia*? Oh yeah, the Devil's Anvil!). Anyway, out of my nail apron, I was pulling out roofing nails, which are short, maybe an inch long, with large heads, and what you have to do is, once you've laid the shingle down in place, you hold the nail between the index finger and middle finger of your left hand, with your thumb on top, set it down where it's supposed to go, move your thumb and tap it twice with your hammer (a sixteen-ounce roofing hammer, not a regular framing hammer) to set it upright, then slam the thing home with one large swift blow. By now you've already got the next nail in hand, ready to set, tap, and slam. So the sound you hear is generally "tap, tap, BAM! tap, tap, BAM! tap, tap, BAM!" with at least three (or is it four?) nails in each shingle, before you slide the next one into place (hell, they don't even use hammers anymore; now they use pneumatic nail guns and staplers). It's a funny thing though, what happens to your brain as you sit atop a blackened tarpaper-covered roof in North Florida in the middle of the summer, during the late afternoon. Soon you'll notice that it's hard to carry out simple addition in your head, say, with fractions (what's 2 3/8 inches plus 1 and 3/4?). Then, when you're doing a repetitive task, like banging down shingles, your mind begins to wander while the blood in your head gets hotter and hotter (hell, even Lawrence almost fell off his camel). Then you do something stupid. Tap, tap, BAM!; tap, tap, BAM!; tap, tap, (did I move my thumb?) BAM! (No, I forgot!). Dropping my hammer, I grab my thumb and squeeze it, trying to squeeze the pain right out of it, Oh God, Oh God, Oh God, it hurts! When I finally get enough nerve to look at it, the blood has already piled up blue under the nail, and I can feel each beat of my pulse as it throbs where the pressure has already started to build up. You want to cry (but that would be a bit unmanly now, wouldn't it?); and you want to laugh at the stupidity of it (but it just hurts too fuckin' bad). So, what's to do? You sit for a minute, rocking back and forth gripping it… and then, once you've regained your composure, you slowly reach into your nail apron and very gingerly take out another roofing tack, ever so carefully holding it between your left index and middle finger, and you slide your now poor and misshapen thumb over the top and steady it, then moving it aside, you lightly tap the nail twice, pulling your hand much farther away than you really needed to, and BAM!, you drive it home. Where you were knocking in maybe eight to ten nails a minute, now you'll be lucky to knock in two. Unfortunately, the heat hadn't lessened, and the shingles still had to go on. After a while, the throbbing lessened to a mere pulsing ache, and I started resuming a little bit of the steady routine. But God it was hot. As I hammered, tap, tap, BAM! I started to think about how things were going along, tap, tap, BAM! Aldo was out of the hospital, living with Thelma and her son. I'd gone to see him and it was awful, tap, tap, BAM! . He was in a wheelchair and needed help even in the bathroom, but that was only temporary. He could just stand up, and they were encouraging him to try and start walking. But his face, (tap, tap, BAM!), his face was grotesque, and I mean that in a kindly Quasimodo way. Imagine if you had a full swing, as with a baseball bat, but used a crowbar instead, one of those heavy ones, (tap, tap, BAM!), and then hit someone right below the eyes, right in the nose, but instead of blood splattering and bone shattering, it just smashed in the meat of his face. Well, that's what Aldo looked like. His eyes looked downward, as his sinuses were gone, and there was no nose to speak of, just an inverted almost cartoonish pushed-in puss that he had to dab with a handkerchief every few seconds. His lower jaw seemed relatively intact, but the upper jaw just sank into the nose-hole. He would mumble, but I didn't understand a bit of it. Thelma and Matthew translated, and although he was glad to see me, he was asking if I'd bring his tools back (tap, tap, BAM!). I told him about finishing up his nephew Bobby's house and as soon as we were done, in just a day or two, I'd be happy to bring his tools back and I really appreciated him letting me use them (tap, tap, BAM!). So I was going to stop building houses soon anyway, and realized to myself that, to be honest, it was rather a dead-end sort of existence, and I needed to start thinking ahead (tap, tap, BAM!). The other thing Thelma told me was that Aldo had gotten a large insurance settlement, since the old drunk who had hit them was in fact, well-covered, as was Aldo in his own right, and that the plastic surgeon had told Aldo that they were going to reconstruct his face pretty much any way he wanted (tap, tap, BAM!). She even showed me the book they had given him, full of pictures of various handsome men, from which he was supposed to pick out the features that he wanted to live with the rest of his life (tap, tap, BAM!). Well, I'd been thinking of going back to college before I got too old and too far removed from it. I was now 25, so I needed to move in that direction soon… I'd even gotten the application for Florida State and student loan forms, I just hadn't filled them out yet. What I needed was a little incentive. Tap…. Tap… (did I move my thumb?) Oh, shit, no!… BAM! The blood spurt out from under the now-cracked nail… that dark purple kind of blood too, not just the plain old red. I dropped the hammer, but knew enough that it wouldn't do any good to grab it, so I just stared at it; besides, other than feeling a little faint, and maybe a little nauseous, it really didn't hurt that bad at all. It was, in fact, like my arm from the elbow down had suddenly grown rather numb. I lay back on the roof, and had to laugh. That was it, the sign I was waiting for (I'd say that I'm not superstitious, and things like Friday the 13th and black cats and broken mirrors don't bother me in the least, but I do take notice of omens—if you get up in the morning and break a shoelace, you can pretty well be certain that the day is not going to progress smoothly: it already hasn't). I eased my way over to the ladder and slowly crawled down, holding my stricken left thumb up high to keep the throbbing at bay, went over to the ice water bucket, dipped in a plastic cup, filled it, and stuck the smitten digit in the cup of icewater. Then I went and checked on Bill, who was finishing up, and suggested we call it a day. That evening, rather than go to the Pastime, I sat up and filled out the application for Florida State and the student loan forms.

When we finished the house, well, that was it for me. I took Aldo's tools back to him over at Thelma's, and they were getting him ready for the first round of plastic surgery, reconstructing the bones in his face. I never saw Aldo again. Or maybe I did and I didn't know it. I ran into Matthew, Thelma's son, some two or three years later, and he told me that Aldo had gotten much better under Thelma's care, she had gotten him up and out of the wheelchair and he had been walking well on his own. But after the final surgery to repair his face, and subsequent to the finer operations reconstructing the facial sinus bones and his upper jaw, sometime while he was wrapped in bandages with the new face that he had picked out from the picture book, he disappeared. Took the insurance money, and without a goodbye or thanks-a-lot, left the State, left his farm, and just went away. Thelma was mighty troubled over this, especially because she had taken such good care of him when he needed it most, not just at the end there, but even more so early on when he'd been drinking heavy, and it just broke her heart that he really turned out to be the rotten bastard that she had met so many years earlier. For a long time afterwards, when I'd be sitting in some small-town North Florida or South Georgia redneck bar, I'd look around and wonder if any of the older good-looking country gentlemen might possibly be Aldo, enjoying his new-found face and freedom. Thought I might recognize the eyes. But after five or six years, I didn't worry about it anymore.

10. All the Young Dudes (1975-1977)

Lazy Bones

It was right around this time that one Friday night a bunch of us were all down at the Pastime, but it was getting late, and Nolin said he'd give me a ride home. We pulled onto Tennessee Street in the old green and yellow Rambler station wagon he had bought, and he turned right to stop in at the old Mike's Beer Barn (then at Raven and Tennessee) and get a pack of cigarettes, and I bought a six-pack of beer. As we pulled out, not halfway up the block, here's this long-legged redhead in jeans and an open-collared shirt, a little tipsy, standing there with her thumb out. We pulled over. "Where you headed?" asked Nolin. "Out Old Bainbridge," she said. "Hop in." I got out and opened the back door for her, and off we went. Now Old Bainbridge was then more of a long and lazy flowing road, heading north out of Tallahassee to Bainbridge, Georgia. It now ends at the large highway that surrounds Tallahassee, called Capital Circle, then it crosses Highway 27, before picking up again, going north to Havana and up to Bainbridge. The road is designated a "Canopy Road" for the overhanging live oak branches meeting overhead from both sides and the many beards of hanging Spanish moss, and we'd often drive it both during the day and the night just for pleasure, usually stoned, because it was so hypnotically beautiful, and just plain fun to drive. Throw on a little music and it was a fantasy trip away from both time and temperament. But tonight we headed up the dark and snaking two lanes, with just headlights showing the roadway below, the curves to either side between the roadcuts, and the moss hanging like cobwebs above. We drove on for awhile, the radio playing, until Nolin turned it off and asked "how far?" "Just keep on going," she said. I asked her what her name was. "They call me Lazy Bones." Well, that was interesting… "And why do they call you Lazy Bones," I countered, and she started humming the old song "Lazy Bones," at that time recently made popular again by Leon Redbone, who sang it in a slow monotonic bass baritone. Then she started singing it, whispering slowly, "Lazy Bones… how you gonna get your day's work done… sleepin' in the noonday sun… Lazy Bones… Lazy Bones…" The trouble was, those were the only lyrics she knew, and being a little drunk, she just kept singing them over and over. At first it wasn't so bad, and I think we even sang along with her for a bit. But hell, we didn't know the rest of the lyrics either. At last, we reached the end of Old Bainbridge at Capital Circle. There's a big old oak tree with a turnaround at the end there, and I asked Nolin to pull over, I had to take a piss. "Yeah, me too," he said. We pulled over and he and I got out, going over by the big old oak. Suddenly, she starts wailing loudly, the windows down, before we'd even unzipped our flies. "Oh God, no, no!" she cried, her head in her hands, and we stopped dead, and said, "What's the matter?" "You're going to drag me out and rape me, aren't you," she yelled. We looked at each other, and Nolin said, "Hell no, we just had to take a piss!" She abruptly sat straight up, and said, "Oh yeah, me too!" and jumped out of the car, ripping down her jeans and, squatting there right between us, taking a long and luxurious pee. We all zipped back up and got back in the car, but by now Nolin was getting a little vexed, as they say in the Islands, since she wasn't able to give very good directions, and him being an old cab driver, this was somewhat frustrating. Finally he wormed it out of her, "I told you I lived out Old Blountstown Highway!" "Goddamnit! You said Old Bainbridge." Well, hell, Blountstown's a whole different road entirely, but luckily, on the same side of town, only four or five miles from where we were, and we couldn't leave her there in the dark, could we, now that we'd taken her this far. "I'll make it up to you," she said wickedly, and this struck a chord of adventurism that got both our attention.

So we finally get to Blountstown Highway (aka Hwy 20) and after a few wrong turns she finally finds her own damn house, which is a bungalow duplex. She invites us in and, as she goes back into a bedroom, she tells us to make ourselves at home and grab a beer from the fridge and she'd

167

be right out. We grab a couple of beers, look around a little bit, and settle down. After a minute or two, she comes out in a see-through negligee, just standing there. She's still humming "Lazy Bones." She goes to the middle of the room, throws down a blanket, and spreads herself out, opening the negligee. Nolin and I are both smiling at this point, especially now that she's singing the words again, "Lazy Bones... lying in the noon day sun... Lazy... Bones... how ya gonna get your day's work done..." We get down on the floor at her level. Now she closes her eyes and starts rubbing herself, gently (yes, down there). In a minute or so I reach out and touch her ankle. She sits upright in a flash, "No... sorry... the deal is, you can't touch me... do whatever you want, but don't touch me!" Okay, okay... She lays back down, closes her eyes, and starts rubbing herself again, gentle, and is now both humming and singing, but still the same two lines, of "Lazy Bones," over and over again. Nolin and I look at each other, shrug, and sip our beers, watching Lazy Bones. I noticed that there was one of those instant Polaroid cameras sitting on the coffee table. I picked it up, aimed it at Lazy Bones, and snapped a picture ---ZZZZ, and the picture slides out of the bottom of the camera. She opens her eyes and says "What was that?" "Nothing," I reply, hiding the camera behind me. Every minute or so, when she gets involved with herself and loses touch, I snap another picture, to which she opens her eyes, looks around, and then goes back to pleasuring herself. After maybe fifteen minutes, she's finishing up with herself, we're out of beer, and the camera's out of film. She sits up, brushes back her hair, and says, "You guys better leave now, my boyfriend is going to be home any time now..." WHAAAATT!?!?!? "Yeah, and he won't be very happy to see you here, he'll probably get really mad." She didn't have to ask twice. We left as quick as we could, after thanking her for the interesting evening. As we left, going down the stairs, she asked, smiling, "What about the pictures?" "Pictures? I don't know what you're talking about?" Smiling back at her, I patted my shirt pocket, and off we went.

I'd say that was the end of the story, but it wasn't. A couple of months later, I ran into her and one of her girlfriends sitting at the bar at the Pastime. She remembered me and I just remembered her as "Lazy Bones," which threw her girlfriend for a loop, wondering where that came from. I think her real name was Sandy. In any case, after relating the story of our first meeting, which didn't seem to surprise the girlfriend at all, the three of us all laughing about it, and now finding out there never was any imminent boyfriend coming home that night (she just wanted us to leave), she got serious, "Really, I'd like to have those pictures back. You see, I'm getting married at the end of the month, and I just don't want the chance of those pictures getting around." I promised I would never do any such thing and that they were securely locked in my desk drawer back at the apartment. But she wouldn't let it go, and even the girlfriend started getting all over me about it, so, okay, I told her, you can have the pictures back. We drove to my apartment, and I dug the pictures out. There were maybe five or six photos, all of her lying on the floor of her apartment, spread-eagled and laying back with her eyes closed, hand in crotch. The girlfriend was now slightly shocked, but giggled anyway, agreeing that it was a good thing that I was willing to give them back. Even though they were all pretty much the same, I said there was one, a little closer view than the rest, that was my favorite. "You can keep that one," she said. Anyway, we left the apartment, went back to the Pastime, and she was so happy she bought me a pitcher of beer, and I got to keep that one picture (where it is now, I have no idea). But two months later I ran into the girlfriend down at the Pastime again. I hadn't recognized her alone, but she remembered me. She told me that while driving on the turnpike on the way back from their honeymoon, Sandy and her new husband had been run up on and crushed by a semi. She said she still thought it was very gentlemanly of me to have given her back the photos without a fight. Another tale of dead girls that we have known.

The Empire Strikes

Jimmy Gear hit Tallahassee like a large meteorite (an ass-teroid? no, that wouldn't be fair; Jim was a man of character, if anything, although he would have enjoyed the pun), crashing in with crater-creating impact and a social sonic boom as well as an overall contagious awe of the universe at large. He arrived with his brother Charlie of whom I spoke earlier, by way of first, New Orleans, and then San Francisco, both towns upon which he and Charlie had made their indelible mark and nearly conquered in their own right, before being drawn to Tallahassee by their oldest brother, Barry, whom I'd gone to grade and high school with, and who was a bosom buddy, if not dynamic duo-diabolist with Bob Nolin. Once they hit Tallahassee, along with a few other family members, they all settled into a large house at Pensacola and Wahnish Way, also known as Railroad Avenue, and set up household there. Charlie and his new Panamanian-born model-wife Rosie, however, quickly set up their own household over near 7th and Boulevard (originally named for Simon Bolivar back in the late 1800s and then bastardized to "Boulevard Street," which didn't make a lick of sense). This however, is not their story, but mine, so I will leave it to them to tell their own. The rest of the tales given however, are relations of my own experiences with the brothers Gear, and thus I consider free to relate between thee and me. I have no doubt however, that if Charlie (and especially Barry, for that matter) were ever to put their own adventures to pen, there would be plenty of experiences to curl the finest straight (even ironed) waist-length tresses into the tightest of nappy dreads.

Nevertheless, Jimmy quickly became a power to be reckoned with, starting, as we all had, as a cab driver. He soon had Miss Kitty at the Pastime wrapped around his little finger, and was quickly offering advice to bar and club managers up and down the Strip, based on his Orleans-Frisco and even earlier bar and restaurant management experiences. So, though I'd already been around Tallahassee for five years or so, and Jimmy had been in town only a single circum-ambulation around the sun, whereas I might know who the owner of a bar or club was and maybe might have said hi once or twice over the years, Jimmy was now having lunch with these guys on a regular basis and telling them what they ought to do to improve their businesses. And they were listening! Oh, he knew his stuff, that's for sure. For instance, he was counseling both sides in the parking-lot wars that had broken out between Jim Gregory, the owner of the Pastime, and Jim Smith, the owner of Poor Paul's next door, both of whom shared a large dirt parking lot out back, but got to arguing when customers would indiscriminately frequent both places. Thus, there occurred hand-stamps, windshield stickers, warning signs, parking fees, parking lot attendants, license plate trackers, even a tow truck or two. Hell, you couldn't even go out back and smoke a joint out there for a stretch. Between the avenging owners and their hired hands, the wannabe cops, and the real cops, it really wasn't safe to go out there at all, much less an hour or two after you'd had your beer quota and then some. True, it cut down on the "Oh yeah, motherfucker, let's step outside" fist-fights, but otherwise it affected business detrimentally for both bars. They finally settled it with a nominal exchange of money, but it was ugly for a year or two. I'm pretty sure Jimmy was instrumental in bringing the two sides to the bargaining table. I know he was in negotiations at the time with Jim Gregory, the owner of the Pastime, to make use of the open space downstairs as a late-night after–hours club, which, in fact, opened to great success and which developed a nighttime following all on its own, the Pastime Downstairs. This became the scene of one of our very few altercations.

The Prince of Tallahassee

One night, it was early, maybe six or seven in the evening, Jimmy and I were sitting downstairs at the bar there, which was manned by a guy named Joe, who I always called Fu Man Chu, because he had long black straight hair, small eyes, a mustache and long goatee also of straight black hair, and being thin and quiet, he always reminded me of a Chinese mandarin. Had he worn a kimono, instead of the standard long-sleeve shirt and jeans, anyone in the world would have agreed with my description. Anyway, Jimmy and I were having a beer or two early on, long before the usual crowd came in, and Rosie, Charlie's then-still-girlfriend-wife was there as well (flirting and getting free wine coolers from Joe, aka Fu Man Chu). It was just the four of us. After a few beers, the conversation happened to turn to, of all things, who was The Prince of Tallahassee, myself or Jimmy (I may have declared myself the same and was abruptly challenged by Jim). I defended my long-term associations with Ballard Road, cab driving, the sinkholes, the Pastime, and, of course, Miss Kitty (whom I adored as much as Judge Roy Bean ever worshipped the talented and admirable Lillie Langtry). But NOOOOOO! Jimmy put forth the argument that he was a power to be reckoned with, and no mere passing fancy, nor was he just an itinerant roustabout carpenter like me, but was changing the face of Tennessee Street as we spoke, and in fact, here we were in a place that he had helped create from nothing, with nothing. We engaged. As we grappled, arm in arm, it went back and forth, "I'm the Prince of Tallahassee!" "No you're not! I'M the Prince of Tallahassee, you bastard!" "The hell you are!" "Oh yeah!?" "YEAH!" We knocked over a couple of tables, and a few glasses left over from the night before went flying, shattering on the floor. Rosie and Joe were laughing as Jimmy and I did our faux wrestling dance of alpha-dominance. Now, in all fairness, Jimmy was sitting right around 300 pounds back then, and I was, although in my prime, maybe 165. He flung me to the ground, and with one of my legs pinned below me he jumped down on top of me and I heard a "SQUINCH!" My left knee was popped out of its socket like a barbecue chicken wing you separate midway. "All Right! All Right! Goddammit! YOU're the Prince of Tallahassee," I loudly proclaimed. I couldn't get up, and was definitely crippled. He and Rosie helped me to a bar stool and after a couple more beers, it didn't hurt near as bad, but there was no doubt it was damaged. I made it home that evening, but in the morning I knew I had to go to the hospital. Rosie was kind enough to drive me, and after the x-rays, the doctor told me I had one of those football-type injuries where the ligaments on one side of my knee had been torn apart. What do I do? Well, you let it heal, that's what you do, and then be careful, but "If you were a big-time football player, we'd operate on you and tie them back up." In the meantime, he gave me a soft splint that I could take off whenever I took a shower. I limped about and had to wear the damn thing for six weeks. Over the years, the knee would go out every so often (usually when I did something stupid, like jump over a fire), but generally it has never bothered me too much. Funny thing though, we never even asked or wondered, since we were fighting over which of us was the Prince of Tallahassee, who was the King?

Ova Argenta

[This story has been told at various times by various individuals, and I understand that Nolin even offered a version at Jimmy's memorial service, of which I was absent. I'm sure everyone has their own perspective, which we can chalk up to "the Rashomon Effect." This is how I remembered the incident in question.]

Barry (aka "FinBar") had been on one of his notorious benders one late Friday night, and while walking his way home from the Strip down on Tennessee Street the great hunger set in as he meandered homeward, so he stopped in at the local Steak 'N Egg that used to sit on the corner of Monroe and Brevard. He went in and sat at the counter, ordered up his two eggs, sausage and toast, "No…, no coffee, just milk," keeping in mind his sometimes sensitive and tricky gut. Before the order came, he had to take a leak, so he went around the end of the counter, down the short hall, and made a quick stop in the men's room. As he came out, he noticed the cardboard boxes of eggs stacked in the hallway, each holding the requisite 12 dozen by 12 dozen gross.

When he got back to the counter, his food had arrived, and as he ate, the little Chequered Daemon that often accompanied him on these late-night jaunts started to whisper inside his head and a pleasantly wicked idea began to hatch.

He finished his meal, paid the bill, and made his way back to the men's room again, scouting out the egg boxes in the back hall. The back door was right there. In fact, they were almost stacked against the door. He touched the door latch bar and pushed it open. No alarms back then, nothing but the cool night air. Looking around, he only took a second to decide, and quickly lifted one of the cases onto his shoulder, pushed the door open, and stepped out the back door, letting it quietly close behind him. A mad dash around the back of the building, out from the bushes, and he could see all the way up and down Monroe Street, deserted at 3 in the morning. He quickly trotted across the four-lane road, and scurried down the darkened bush-lined sidewalk to Duval Street, two blocks west, where he was currently living with Nolin. Setting them down on the kitchen table, he chuckled to himself as he lit up a cigarette. After putting it out, he trundled off to bed.

The next morning around 9 or 10 he awoke, and while fixing coffee, stared amusedly at the carton of eggs on the table. What the hell? He started to fry some up. The smell and noise awoke Nolin, who came out and could only laugh at the situation as he lit his own cigarette and sipped his coffee. "And what, pray tell, inspired you to steal a dozen dozen eggs?" he asked. "They were just there… they talked to me… and they asked me to liberate them." "Well, Jesus Christ, Barry, there isn't even enough room in the refrigerator for them all." "Yeah, I know… so we better start eating them… how many would you like? Maybe give some away. I'll call Jimmy, he'll know what to do."

Soon Jimmy arrived and after looking over the situation, he said, "Okay... here's the deal... We gotta boil 'em… hard-boiled… not too fast, but all the way through. That way they'll keep longer. You got any big pots here? Here… here's one. Now put them in with warm water, a dozen at a time, no more… bring it up slow, and once there's a slow boil, let them go for another five minutes. Rinse them in cool water, not cold, and then start another batch. I'll be back in an hour… keep'em going until I get back."

I'm sitting at home in my little apartment on Call Street, finished breakfast and coffee, having just smoked a joint, and was just sitting down on the couch to read my new issue of Omni, when Jimmy pulls up in his famous large white (and beat up) pickup truck. "Hey, David, I'm going down to the Pastime, you wanna come?" "Damn Jimmy, it's not even noon yet… I think I'll just take it easy here, thanks." "C'mon… I'll buy you a beer… I need you to come with me." Well, that was a dealmaker right there, as we were all poor, all the time, and a free cold beer before noon on a Saturday was just the ticket. "All right, lemme get my shoes on…"

Having parked in the parking lot behind the Pastime, we walked up the old steel-grate back door stairs and entered the venerable old pool hall. Passing the sour urine-smelling men's room we came into the pool hall proper, already awash with floating cigarette smoke, balls clacking, and beer flowing. There were only two or three tables occupied: the professionals' table, which we never went near, but which was occupied from nine a.m. to closing every day of the week, and a couple of others just fooling around. We headed to the bar and greeted Miss Kitty in our usual cordial way. "Good morning, Miss Kitty… a couple of cans of Busch if you'd be so kind… tall boys." As we sipped our cans of beer, Jimmy tells me a little bit about some eggs at Nolin's place, but I don't really get the connection. When Miss Kitty strolls by, he nonchalantly

171

addresses her, "Hey, Miss Kitty, if you don't mind me asking, how much do you pay for this large [it was a gallon] jar of spicy pickled hard-boiled eggs here?" "Oh, I think we pay four dollars a jar, and we give them the empty jars back," and she walked off again. As he looked at the jar, turning it round, he said "Looks like there's maybe two dozen eggs in here." Besides the commercial label on the front, there was a hand-written index card taped onto the side of the jar that read "Whole Cooked Boneless Chicken, 50 cents!" That was cute.

I could see the wheels turning in Jimmy's head, he was making the calculations not just for the free eggs now boiling away at Nolin's place, but way off into the future as well, maybe even on a grand corporate level, with thousands of workers boiling millions of eggs all over the country. Back then (1975?) you could buy eggs for 50 cents a dozen (cheaper if you shopped around or bought wholesale). If they weren't large eggs, but rather medium, you could easily fit two dozen in the same gallon jar. At 50 cents apiece, the Pastime could make 12 dollars, minus the 4 dollars of cost, for a profit of 8 dollars, whereas now they were only getting a profit of 6 dollars per jar. For 4 dollars per jar, Jim could buy four dozen eggs for 2 dollars, and with an extra dollar per jar pay for the spices, cooking, labor etc. for two jars, with a clean profit of a dollar a jar, and the next jar already paid for, a grand profit of roughly 5 dollars for every two jars. And that was if he was paying for the eggs! He could use the free eggs now being boiled to get the whole operation moving, sort of like seed investment capital. He called Miss Kitty over, leaned across the bar, and started whispering to her, while I wandered off to go play the pinball machine. When I got back he was smiling that Cheshire cat grin of his and we finished our beers to go. When we got to Nolin's place, everybody was dutifully boiling, rinsing, cracking, and de-shelling eggs under the direction of Nolin's girlfriend, Celia, who had dropped by and took over from the kitchen-challenged Nolin and Barry (Barry, however, later became an excellent cook under the direction of the kitchen manager at the old Subway Station).

As Jimmy laid out his plans, explaining the deal he had made with Miss Kitty, Charlie showed up and was recruited immediately. While Nolin and Barry were boiling eggs a dozen at a time, and I helped Celia peel the shells off, he was going to Publix and get the ingredients for a Cajun-style hot and spicy egg-pickling sauce that he would whip up when he got back. Meanwhile he asked Charlie to go to the hardware store and get a container large enough to hold the gross of eggs and "make sure it was clean" so that the pickling process could take place over maybe a week or so. When Jim got back the eggs were dutifully boiled and unshelled, and he set to work creating his own basic pickling sauce. I recall the gallons of vinegar he used as a base, because as they heated up, first the entire house and then the whole neighborhood reeked of hot vinegar. There were all kinds of other 'secret' ingredients, and Jimmy knew exactly what he was doing, never at a loss around a kitchen. When Charlie showed up he had a brand-new small garbage can, shiny, with a tight fitting cover. The hot and steamy vinegar-based secret sauce went in first, then the eggs were carefully added individually by hand so that they didn't break up. It was hot to the touch, but would cool eventually, and according to Jimmy no refrigeration would be necessary since the pickling sauce was a natural room-temperate preservative. But he didn't want anyone opening the can for at least a week, and I think he even got out some masking tape and taped the lid on so that no one would chance a peek. The can was set out just inside the back porch, and we all retired to the Pastime to celebrate and let the house air out from the vinegar stench.

The week went by slowly, but finally the next Saturday arrived. I couldn't get over there until later, and when I pulled up and went inside I came upon a funereal setting, several abject and disappointed faces sitting around in silence. "What's the matter?" "Go see for yourself." I went out onto the back porch and there was the brand-new garbage can, still shiny, with the top now just set on haphazardly. I lifted it and looked in. The eggs were all there, just as we had left them, intact, and now, undoubtedly quite pickled. But they were silver! A dull dark tarnished silver for sure, but silver-gray nonetheless. What had happened? Well, the garbage can was indeed new, and shiny, because it was freshly galvanized, which is to say it was electro-plated by the galvanic process of putting an electric current through the metal while it was hooked up to a zinc plate, which gave it the bright and shiny metal patina both inside and out. By placing the acidic vinegar (especially warm heated vinegar) back into the can, the process was reversed, and whatever had been placed inside the can, whether it was eggs or silverware or a tire iron, would come out with a fine skin of zinc plating. Suffice it to state the obvious: Hard-boiled? Yes. Pickled? Most assuredly. Edible? Well… no. Any one of us should have seen this coming, but caught up in the hysteria of hard-boiled capitalism at work in the laborious birth of free enterprise right before our very eyes, we were blinded by everything but the science. It was a tragic blow. Especially to Jimmy. None of the rest of us had anything invested in it, except maybe Barry, but at least he and Nolin had gotten a breakfast out of it. Jimmy was out the cost of the pickling ingredients, and the garbage can too, which he had given Charlie the money to buy. I think he'd even bought a half-dozen large clean glass jars at Ashmore's down in Frenchtown and may also have been working on his own set of labels too. But worse, he'd have to face Miss Kitty—after convincing her to drop her pickled-egg purveyor and promising two jars full of Jimmy's special Cajun-spiced eggs within a week.

But there was a more immediate problem: what to do with the silver-gray galvanized eggs? No, they weren't going in the garbage, which wouldn't be picked up for days. And here was a perfectly good, brand new garbage can that Jimmy wanted to take home, since it was his already. At one point we talked about pouring them down the storm drain out on the road, but this idea was nixed as having too unpredictable an outcome; besides, the Governor's mansion was only a half-block away, and there was no telling which direction the culvert led. So, a big old plastic ice cooler used for fishing excursions was found under the house, and the eggs were poured into it, filling it nearly to the brim. The top was closed and the plastic latch secured and for now, the whole damn thing was just slid back under the house to be forgotten. Jimmy had to avoid the Pastime, at least the upstairs part, for a week or two. After he thought maybe Miss Kitty wouldn't remember the whole deal, he ventured up there one afternoon, and she lit right into him, considering the sales pitch he had made, and now the pickled-egg supplier was mad that after all the years he'd been supplying them he'd now been asked to hold off. But Jim was good at mending fences if he was ever good at anything, and it wasn't long before he was back in Miss Kitty's good graces, and the original pickled-egg provisioning had been restored. All was well, and the great silver pickled egg caper was over. Or was it?

It must have been about nine months later, and I'm pretty sure it was Charlie who was organizing a major fishing trip to Sikes Cut out at St. George Island. These were always generally successful trips, and the take-home pay of reds, trout, whiting, and maybe a small shark or two were well worth the two–hour drive each way. So he was scouting about for a large ice cooler in which to carry the ice, bait, and beer on the way out and the fish on the way back home. Lo and behold, there under the house over at Duval Street was an old large blue-and-white Igloo ice chest. But as he pulled it out, it was obvious that there was something inside. He pulled it out anyway, and popped the top. Jumping Jehosophat! The eggs, after nine months (just long enough for Charlie to forget they'd ever been stowed there), had absorbed most of the Cajun spicy pickle juice and had congealed into a semi-solid 2-foot- by-one –foot-square hard-boiled brick; and it still smelled to high heaven! We each got a glance at it, before the lid was once again clasped down, but now, what to do? Nolin said, no, it was not going back under the house. Again, what to do? It must have weighed sixty pounds. It would not fit into any garbage can we knew of. And just putting it on the side of the street would have caused no end of grief to anyone who opened it, and surely, the law would have eventually gotten involved. There was the solution—underneath the porch were two old shovels. The offending cooler was dragged to the very back of the yard, and after a half an hour of intensive double-digging, it was interred into the welcoming pit, and a sepulchral mound was raised over it, patted down, and there it lays entombed, as far as we know, to this very day. This is now under the parking lot of the Associated Industries of Florida, one of the largest business lobbying groups in the State of Florida. (I later became a functioning archaeologist, and I often wondered then what the archaeologists of the future will think when they dig that cooler up and find the giant silver-gray consolidated giant egg-cube inside. Undoubtedly, they'll associate it with the 20th century pagan Spring solstice and fertility ritual where we color hard-boiled eggs that supposedly come out of rabbit butts in celebration of the death-defying resurrection of a 2000-year-old Jewish mystic who was executed by the Romans for sedition... But they'd be wrong now, wouldn't they?)

The Smuggler

Once Bill and I finished up Bobby's house, it was time to look for a new gig. Nolin had moved back in with his girlfriend Celia, and they were thinking of moving down to New Smyrna Beach. In the meantime, I'd been approached by old Herb Odel to move back into his house at Lewis Blvd. He'd let his bad son, Howard, move in after Lisa and I had left, and Howard had abandoned it, leaving town without notice, or paying the utility bill. Herb said he'd consider it a favor if I'd move back in, just to have someone in there, since he knew I'd always liked the place, run down as it was, and, by the way, Bertie missed me. I said sure, I'd love to, but the rent was going to be a trial for awhile. He didn't care, "Pay me when you can." Howard had let the place go to hell, and hadn't paid any rent, and was on the lam anyway, because the law was always after him. He was a cigarette smuggler, which meant that he had this old Chrysler that he had ripped the back seats out of, and he would drive up to North Carolina and load the trunk, and both the front passenger and backseat area, right up to the windows, with cartons of cigarettes covered with a blanket. Then he'd drive back down to Tallahassee and in the outlying rural towns of Quincy, Perry, and Marianna he'd sell them to disreputable retailers at a considerably lower price than they'd normally pay, since now he'd cut out the taxman, besides buying them at the lower North Carolina wholesale rate. So if he bought two hundred cartons in North Carolina for say, $3 a carton back then, and sold them for $6 a carton in Florida, he was doubling his money, and could pay for his gas and a hotel room and still pocket almost $500. But he wasn't very smart about it, or anything else for that matter, and he had a bad attitude, so he was always getting in arguments with his retailers, and when they'd had enough of putting up with his crap (and once they'd sold all their tax-free cigarettes) they'd just rat him out, so there's was always an arrest warrant out for him. He showed up at the house one day, not realizing that I'd moved in, and wanted to stay there for the night. As a disguise, being a "fugitive," he had dyed his hair (from its normal light brown) with black shoe polish, and as he stood there trying to convince me it was only for the night, the sweat ran down his cheeks in dark gray Addams Family rivulets. I told him to come back later, and when he left I called Herb, who came out with the good son Bob (Howard and Bob were half-brothers), and they were waiting when he got back and gave him refuge for a day or two. Last time I saw him.

Chicken Feed

I was still plenty mad at Howard myself, because when he had left Herb's house and had the electricity turned off, he had never taken the time to empty either the refrigerator, or worse, the freezer. When I got there and opened up the refrigerator, the stench drove me out of the house. But, as I said, the freezer was worse; it was nothing but a solid mass of large crawling brown-ringed inch-long maggots. Part of the deal for moving back in was that I had to clean it all out. Once I'd gotten the refrigerator cleaned out and sanitized (and especially de-odorized), I had to figure out how I was going to deal with the open-top chest freezer. I couldn't drag it out, it was too heavy, which meant I was going to have to stoop over and scoop out the goddamn maggots by hand with a dustpan. At first, I thought I'd kill the damn things with bleach, but then figured I wouldn't be hanging my head over and into that poison without some dire consequences, and I'd still have to dispose of the dead filth somehow. Luckily, the freezer was out on the back porch. There were still a few chickens left out in the hen house, so I let them loose into the yard, and then started scattering maggots with the dustpan in a large fan out the back door of the porch. The chickens went wild, running back and forth gobbling down the crawling horrors as quick as I could toss them out. In no time flat, the chickens and I had neatly disposed of ten pounds of writhing larval parasites with little or no after effects. Now I could get out the bleach and start the disinfecting and de-odorizing. I have always had a strong stomach, and it really takes a lot to get me to retch, but both the refrigerator and freezer at Herb Odel's are unforgettably and olfactorily etched in my memory as each of them in their turn nearly brought me to my knees. Later however, that Irish iron gut of mine would serve me well in its stead.

Hung Up

I didn't last too long at Herb's house, maybe six months or so. I was dead broke, so my old buddy Dennis, who was about to enter into a large contract hanging wallpaper for a new Villa Cortez apartment complex over on Jackson Bluff asked if I'd lend him a hand. Dennis's oldest brother, Sonny, had taught him the trade and since these were new apartments, there wasn't going to be a lot of prep work, the paper just needed to be hung as quick as possible. Dennis would handle all the thinking part, and all I had to do was paste the sheets and get them to him in a timely manner so that he could get them up. I'd also lend a hand going ahead of him when a wall had to be smoothed down and/or sanded, or a hole had to be patched, but generally I just pasted and carried sheets, and watched Dennis do his thing, which in itself was rather amazing. Hanging wallpaper is tricky business; matching patterns and slapping it up on the wall sounds easy, but those bubbles can be a real headache sometimes, and when the sheet-rock hangers have not put the walls up straight or matched the ceiling dead-level, it quickly becomes apparent when looking at the finished wallpaper, which then has to be redone (a lot of it is simply fooling the eye, which is one reason you have the constant repetitive patterns). Then there were the damn windows, but Dennis knew how to make them come out looking good, no matter how screwy the window frames had been put in. More than once, when Dennis asked me, "How does it look?" (especially after a difficult set of double-cuts), I was amazed enough to respond automatically with the old adage that Aldo the carpenter had taught me, "Fits like goat's lips!" to express admiration for a tight seamless fit (next time you get a chance, look at a goat's lips; they fit together like your fingers when your hands are clasped say, in meditative thought). We always tried to get in the unfinished apartments before the plumbers did, so that the paper could be put up on the flat walls and then the plumber could cut his own holes. If the plumbing was already in, Dennis had to work around the sinks and toilet and all the pipe entrances. The only real trouble was that we had started in late October or early November and it got very cold very quickly. You're dealing with water, sponges, and mixing paste, so you're always either wet or very damp. The apartments weren't yet heated; hell, they didn't even have doors or windows half the time. So it was always cold and miserable, but we kept up our spirits by listening to rock and roll and smoking dope. Dennis was quite the perfectionist, and I have to admire him for that, although at times he'd get frustrated when the paper just wasn't working out, or the damn sheet-rock guys had fucked up, or the plumbers had beaten us into a bathroom, and he'd let out a yell as if someone had stabbed him in the heart. Other times, he'd be concentrating so hard on fixing some screwup (and I'm sure the numbing cold had something to do with this), that he wouldn't even notice that he'd sliced his finger with one of the many razor edges that he used to trim the paper. But he was always very good about sharing the money with me and paying me a fair wage. At one point, after I'd watched and helped him for awhile, we decided to tackle apartments separately to try and speed things up, and it worked somewhat, although he could always knock out two apartments to my one. After the weather warmed up in the Spring and we finished Villa Cortez, Dennis got another contract for the sister complex, Casa Cortez, and I'd had my fill of paper hanging, so Dennis and his new girlfriend, Maria, took that one on. As aggravating as I found it to be, learning to hang wallpaper turned out to be a blessing when I had to fall back on it for some relief later on.

Buckling Swashes

Myself, Nolin, Dennis, and a few of the other boys had been enamored by the resurgence of *The Three Musketeers*, the first of the modern movie re-makes in probably forty years. This was the one with Richard Chamberlain, Michael York, Oliver Reed, and that other guy (Frank Finlay), which in my opinion was always the best. Oh yeah, and it had Raquel Welch too. In any case, I had taken up fencing as a result, since I was dabbling at Florida State anyway, and they offered it as on of those Continuing Participant Education (i.e., free, community) classes. The teacher was Jan Delaney, a respected and well-known fencing instructor with the requisite dueling-type scar across his cheek. After a few weeks of instruction, he foolishly gave each of us a foil that we could take home and practice our exercises with, supposedly in front of a mirror. I never went back. As a matter of fact, I was nosing around Mike's Pawn Shop on Tennessee Street a week or two later and there was a fencing helmet, and an épée, which is a stouter piece of steel, having three edges as opposed to a foil's four sides (thus, less likely to turn, or bend, when pressed against an opponent). This was a piece of hardware that might be used to kill your adversary (i.e., "run him through"), rather than the foil, which was only meant to give him a good prick, or maybe drive home a point or two. Suffice it to say, when the Capulets and the Monatagues went at it, they were using épées and not foils. Ditto with the Three Musketeers. I think I got the helmet and the épée for something like 5 bucks.

So began a series of impromptu fencing lessons and swordplay among all us young men, on porches, up and down stairs, through houses, and even out in the street (always with an eye out for the law, just like the real musketeers). Even though we'd try and have at least one person wear the padded helmet, the loss of visibility was always a problem, so it was discarded more often than not. We were young and stupid and invincible, and it's a miracle that no one ever had their eye poked out, though there were plenty of scratches, slashes, and jabbed ribs. One day, after hanging paper all afternoon at Villa Cortez, Dennis and I were back at Lewis Blvd. and I don't know how it came up, but we decided to have a little friendly fencing match. Me being the "trained" individual (what, maybe five lessons in all?), I let him have the épée, which was longer and, as I said, stouter. It also had a much larger handguard, a bell that encompassed the entire hand and wrist. The foil, which I was using, is much lighter, though not much shorter, and the handguard barely covers your knuckles. At some point (pun unintended) it must be discussed: what type of tip was on each of the aforementioned weapons? The foil had a small little flat button, a little bigger than a BB, from which a groove ran down the inside of one of the blade edges. This groove was to accommodate a small wire, attached at one end to the button that would electronically signal a "hit" in actual tournaments. The épée, again, a much stouter weapon, did not have this groove for the wire (although it did have a blood groove, so that, in an actual serious duel, a bodily puncture would not be stopped up, and this groove would allow the blood to disgorge freely). Its tip, which had been at one time deadly pointed, had been hammered down to a blunt jagged-edged knob about the size of the very end of your little finger.

We went out to the back yard and crossed swords; we parried, we thrust, we spun around, we parried some more. Click, click, clank, click, clank clank… the blades clashed again and again. At one point, I thought I had him on the defensive, which I did, as he was backing up. I pursued. Click, click, clank. As I leapt forward, he turned his head away, but thrust back directly into my advance. The foil flew from my hand; I'd been disarmed! Worse, though, I'd been dis-armed… no he hadn't cut my arm off, but the jagged point of the épée had skipped over the top of the knuckleguard of my foil and the point had entered between my ring-finger and middle-finger knuckles and the blade had run a little over a foot up into my right arm, not quite exiting just below my elbow. Luckily, he (or I, or both) had yanked it back out immediately, because I wouldn't have been able to do it consciously afterwards. Other than a small dribble of blood between my knuckles, the blood groove had only opened up an apparent tributary inside my arm. It began to swell immediately, so we drove to the hospital as quick as we could. While Dennis sat in the Emergency Room waiting area, they took me in and x-rayed the arm. No broken bones, of course, and the blade had missed the artery, thank God, but the meat had been ransacked from my fist to my elbow, and the internal bleeding was going to cause a lot of swelling. The doctor said that it was a shame that the blade hadn't pushed all the way through the arm by my elbow, because if it had, he would have been able to run a wire like a straightened coat hanger up the wound and out the other side, reaming it out with antiseptic gauze. That, and a little caustic, would have made the whole injury a lot less traumatic. As it was, other than a tetanus shot, and a whole lot of antibiotics, there was nothing else he could do. Even the entrance wound between the knuckles had already closed by itself and would have only taken a stitch or two anyway. But it was going to swell up considerably, and it was going to hurt like a motherfucker (my words, not his); it was also going to get infected, no matter what, so the antibiotics were heavy duty and there were lots of them. Pain pills? Other than the injection he'd already given me, no, he wasn't going to give me any pain pills. "This way, you'll know when it's getting better, when it stops hurting. Maybe two weeks. Otherwise, keep it elevated as much as you can." Thanks, Doc.

As I recuperated, I got word that Herb Odel wasn't doing so good, his health had taken a bad turn, and his son Bob let me know that if anything happened (which was already imminent), as nice as he was, Bob was going to turn me out of the old homestead on Lewis Blvd. I'd been behind on the rent, but had made improvements in the house; nonetheless, that wasn't going to change the inevitable outcome. Meanwhile, I'd had Bill Cummings move in to help me out, but between the two of us, any small carpentry jobs we had were eaten up by utility bills, food, pot, and beer. We even spent a good chunk of our own money helping put in a new floor and re-setting the toilet for poor old Bertie Jones across the street when she showed us how her toilet was so wobbly she had to hang onto the sink to keep it still while she used it, and then use the sink as a safety handhold in case it fell through the floor in the meantime. Nonetheless, I knew I'd have to leave Herb's place soon. It was also right around this time that I found out that Lisa was getting married to her new older boyfriend (who all my "good" friends said looked a lot like me), so that was another chapter closing. As a mental and emotional purgative I spent that day, aren't weddings always on a Saturday of course, lying on the old couch in the Lewis Blvd. living room, tripping on LSD, contemplating the universe and wondering where I'd end up next.

Summer in Smyrna

I got a call from my old pal Nolin, who by this time *had* moved down to New Smyrna with his girlfriend, Celia, and they had an extra room, what about coming down and visit for awhile? I thought, "What a wonderful way to emigrate from a Tallahassee that had turned sour and start afresh." He even suggested he might be able to get me onto one of the deep-sea fishing boats that regularly ran out of the quiet little Atlantic coast port town. I packed up what clothes I had, including a few essentials (the épée, a couple of books, and some wallpaper-hanging tools), hopped in the van and drove south. Bob and Celia had gotten a nice little upstairs apartment not 500 feet from the beach. Since it was upstairs you could see the ocean from the living room and kitchen windows, and the porch, which they shared with the other upstairs apartment provided both a panoramic view and seabreeze scents-uality. They had a small guest room, with its own adjacent bathroom, and so I took to the life of a beach bum according to the best instructions that Nolin could muster; for instance, only two pairs of shorts were needed, so you always had a dry pair to change into; no shirts necessary, but you carried a T-shirt with you (with a pocket: for your dope, or cigarettes, or whatever) in case you had to enter a public place off the beachfront; no shoes, always; canvas tennis shoes, sometimes; and real men never wear flip flops. We took to fixing long tall stiff drinks (rum and coke, rum and tonic, rum and fruit juice, rum and anything), rolling a couple of doobies, and slowly cruising up and down the beach, stopping just every so often to jump in the ocean and cool off. Celia was working at a flower shop, and although Nolin was supposed to be looking for work, he wasn't looking very hard. Not at the beginning of the summer anyway. We swam, we fished, we drank, we cruised, we explored, we swam some more, we drank some more, we ate when Celia came home. She was very tolerant; and at first, I think she was glad that Nolin had someone to hang around with during the day while she was at work. I think she was priming him for marriage and knew that my acting as a diversion would keep him off track thinking about the possible ramifications, which he'd be apt to dwell on if they were just living alone together and if he were home alone during the day. Despite all this, Celia and I had always gotten along well and she knew I thought highly of her.

I tried picking up some wallpaper-hanging jobs, and since there were only two decorating shops in town, it was a quick search. I met the old woman who owned Williams Decorating, out on the causeway between the mainland and the beach-side, and she said she'd be willing to give me a try. So she tossed a couple of jobs my way and, after the initial rough spots, they were generally very pleasant. At first though, it was a kitchen or two in some residential houses, which were always a pain in the ass, because inevitably, there would be a lot of prep work: tearing out old wallpaper, patching the walls, working around appliances, etc; all with the homeowner watching you like a hawk so you didn't wander off and steal anything, or otherwise talking at you incessantly out of (their) sheer boredom. But later, I got orders to go to some of the many tall condominiums to do either a kitchen or a bathroom, or both. These were great. They were always empty, so I could open the sliding glass windows overlooking the beach and ocean, turn on the stereo to whatever station I wanted and as loud as I wanted, raid the liquor cabinet (they all had one), fix a drink and settle down to work. The old battle-axe, Mrs. Williams, always wondered why these jobs took me so long. To shut her up, I'd ask "Were the owners happy with the quality of the work?" knowing already that I did a top quality job. Hell, I might have been slow, but I was good. "Yes," she grumbled, "they were very happy with the work," as she handed me my check.

But these jobs weren't bringing in much money, and they were intermittent. I was also getting underfoot around the small apartment, when I'm sure Celia wanted more time alone with Nolin. So I ended up going out in the evenings to the local hangouts, not always arriving home in the clearest frame of mind. Sometimes we'd all go out together, but I was always the third wheel and, being single and prowling at that, it wasn't necessarily a happy triumvirate when we got home. This was about the time that the idea of going out on the fishing boat came up again.

Call Me Fishmeal

So Nolin pointed me in the direction of the Sea Harvest, which was the local seafood dealer and small restaurant where the fishing boats off-loaded their catches, always surrounded by injured and beggarly pelicans and crumb-snatching seagulls. I went down and there was a nice long green-and-white wooden-hulled boat, soon ready to go out again, the *Charley Boy*. With only the cook aboard, he told me that the captain was down at the local Winn-Dixie buying groceries for the next trip, and yeah, they could use another hand, why don't you go on down there and talk to him? (It only dawned on me later, wouldn't you think the cook would be buying the groceries? But what the hell did I know about fishing boats?) I drove over the bridge, and found the Winn-Dixie, and after checking out the aisles, it was soon obvious who the captain was, shopping for groceries with his first mate in tow. "Captain Benton?" I asked. "Yeah," he looked me up and down, "whaddya want?" "I heard you're going out soon and maybe you could use an extra hand, any chance I could go along?" I asked. "Ever been out commercial fishing before?" "Oh yeah, sure," I lied. "All right, be down at the dock at 9 tomorrow morning," he said, and then, "how much beer you want?" I told him a case would do, and I'd see him in the morning.

I packed up what little gear I had, a change of jeans and a t-shirt, hat, and some cigarillos. Nolin lent me a small set of binoculars, and other than that, I was all set. I slept nervously, but woke up and was ready at eight. Nolin got up, fixed some coffee, lit a cigarette, and said, "Now you don't want to get there too early. There's a lot of work just getting the boat ready, and if you wait you won't have to get caught up in all that shit." Well, I was getting nervous and by ten til nine, I was itching to go. "Hell, they always leave late, don't worry about it," said Nolin. Finally, at five to nine, we get in the car and head on over the bridge to the Sea Harvest. We pull in and I hop out of the car... but... no boat! There's an old fisherman sitting on a barrel nearby, working on a piece of line. "Hey, you seen the *Charley Boy*?" I asked. "Headed out about five minutes ago," the old man said, pointing, "there it is goin' under the North Bridge." And sure enough, about a mile away, you could see it just going under the drawbridge that had finally raised its center, so the boat could go through.

I went back to the car, and started to give Nolin some crap, "Goddamn it, they always leave late? Right! Well, they left on time today! Jesus Christ, Nolin, now I've missed the boat!" Get in!" he said, "I'll get you there!" I hopped in, wondering what the hell he was talking about. He spun out of the gravel drive, took a right, and in another minute, we were crossing over the North Bridge the boat had just gone under. There it was a half-mile up the Intracoastal Waterway, leaving maybe a ten-knot wake. After crossing the bridge, he took a sharp left onto Peninsula, the road that parallels the Intracoastal, heading north. "Keep an eye out for the boat," he said, and as he drove, I could just see it between the gaps of the well-to-do houses that lined the waterway. We gained on it, and finally passed it. He drove up another quarter-mile and whipped into the drive of one of the large waterfront houses. "Get your stuff!" he said. I grabbed my pack and we jumped out of the car, and ran between the houses. Luckily there was a large wooden dock sticking out into the Intracoastal, and here was the *Charley Boy* coming up from the south. I got out onto the end of the dock, started waving, and they spotted me. The captain backed down on the throttle, and she slowly rolled up to the dock. I stood up on the handrail of the dock and as the front deck of the boat eased on up, I tossed my bag up onto it. I was committed now. I jumped up and grabbed the gunwale, and the first mate grabbed me first by the shirt, and then by my belt, and pulled me aboard. There was a loud sickening "CRUNCH!" and as the captain backed off from the private wooden dock, there's Nolin standing there, and the dock now has several boards cracked, broken, and askew. I yelled, "You'll take care of that, won't you?" laughing, because I knew he'd just get out of there as fast as he could and hoped no one had seen him, as would we. [In retrospect, I think the reason Nolin got ass-fired-inspired to catch the boat was because if he had ended up bringing me back to the apartment as a result of his own lackadaisical tardiness, Celia would have given him an earful.] "So long!" I waved, and turned my attention to the new-met crew. The captain throttled up, and we headed for Ponce Inlet, that would lead us out to the sea.

The first mate, who had pulled me aboard, and who I'd seen with the captain shopping the day before, was a tall and lanky biker-type fisherman, tattoos and a baseball cap with his sleeveless Harley Davidson t-shirt, jeans, and dirty white rubber boots. His name was Phil, and although he was friendly enough, he still made me a little nervous. The cook was Moe, a little older than everybody else. Maybe fifty-five, and he was short, balding, and had a slight paunch. The captain, Benton, was also short, maybe five six or so, in his mid forties with slick black hair and a broad face. He was mean-looking, and I got a feeling it wasn't accidental, but that he wore that look on purpose; I suppose so everyone would recognize his authority. When I shook hands and thanked him for picking me up, he was smiling, but it still wasn't a smile that you would call friendly. He told me to get with Phil and get squared away. Phil was already making up a dozen set of leaders, so I watched him for awhile, asking questions. Even though I'd fished for years, and felt comfortable around boats and lines, he realized within five minutes that I'd never been on a commercial fishing boat before. But rather than just give me a rash of shit about it he was quick enough to show me a few things I was going to need to know, since we were going to be on the boat together for a week. There was only one way to tie a line to a hook, only one way that was acceptable. There was a different method for splicing the piano wire that the electric reels were wound with, and the wire was to be kept taut at all times; if it got loose, and a kink developed in it, the kink would have to be cut out, and the wire spliced again, since, if the kink were allowed to stay in the wire, it would inevitably break under pressure, usually with a large fish attached. It was a big damn deal to lose the tackle on the end, which was composed of a large triangular wired rig, the bottom of which carried a 5-lb weight to get it to the bottom, the top to which the piano wire was attached, and the jutting out third angle of the "coat hanger" to which the leader, with hook and bait was attached. If you lost that, *and the fish*, there was gonna be hell to pay (you might lose one or two rigs by circumstance, but if you lost a third or more, well, that was your fault, and then they were coming out of your pay). Leaders were cheap and expendable however, and there was plenty of heavy 100-lb test monofilament and boxes of hooks. Phil gave me my own set of multipurpose pliers, which I was going to need, told me to keep a close eye on it, and to give it back when we got off the boat. There was also an extra pair of (very dirty) white boots, and while you're fishing, that's what you're expected to wear, "so get used to it."

We turned east and headed out the inlet, past the rock jetties. It was odd seeing the jetties and the inlet from this perspective, since I'd always seen them before only from the shore. Other boats were going out with us and just a few were coming in, and between the wakes raised by the boats, and the tide running along the jetties, the water got visibly rougher. I wasn't bothered by seasickness though, as it took a lot rougher water than this to set my inner ear off course. That's not to say I haven't had my share of *mal de mer* over the years, and anyone who says they *never* get seasick, in my opinion, just hasn't been in the right circumstances. You go down below in a rough sea to work on a diesel engine, even if you're just holding a light or handing over tools, or better still, sit for a half-hour on the deck of a boat in a full wetsuit with a set of doubles strapped on your back, in the middle of summer and your only view is below the gunwale so you can't see the horizon, and I guarantee you will never say never again. As we got past the end of the longer north jetty and entered the open sea, the breeze sprang up and the captain opened the throttle, and we started out into the Atlantic.

The *Charley Boy* supposedly was a 38 ft former PT Boat, converted to a fishing vessel. I found this fascinating, since I thought I knew all about PT 109 and JFK in WWII, having seen the movie several times (and then there was always *McHale's Navy*). It really was a marvelous boat, long and sleek, with the bow sticking up maybe eight feet off the water and the gunwales sloping down to maybe 2 to 3 feet above the waterline, with a nice broad square stern. Doing a little research I've come to find out that it probably wasn't a real PT Boat, but more likely a prototype gasoline-powered boat built in the 1920s or 30s (a lot of them in Florida); PT boats developed for WWII ("Patrol Torpedo" boats) were usually 70 foot or better in length, whereas the *Charley Boy* couldn't have been but around 40 feet. Since this was the mid-70s, that seems about right, because the boat wasn't part of the fishing fleet 10 years later, and a boat's lifespan rarely exceeds fifty years (let me put it his way, the *Charley Boy* was already old when I was on it in what, 1977?). We had two electric reels amidships, one on each side, and two off of the stern, again one to port and one to starboard, although the ones in the stern were drawn in a bit on each side, and not directly mounted on each corner. Up front was the captain's forward cabin, and it soon became very clear that we weren't welcome down there, ever. Luckily, a roof had been added that went from the helm all the way back to the stern, and this kept off the wicked, wicked summer sun, and allowed us to stay relatively dry when it rained. I say relatively, because you were always wet for one reason or another. You were either wet from sea spray, when the boat was at full throttle, or when it was your turn to raise the anchor (being the newbie on board, it was always "your turn," but hell, I was young and strong and didn't care, and they knew it, so there you go). But the captain had this uncanny method where he didn't give a damn about pulling it in every time we stopped, and we'd hook a float to the anchor line that would slide along it and lift the anchor up off the bottom. Then he'd drag that anchor and line, the anchor hanging some twenty feet below the surface and two hundred feet behind the boat, and he'd go another five miles or so before he'd back off the throttle, the anchor would slide back down to the bottom, and he'd tell you to once again drop the remainder and tie her off. Of course, he was always watching the depth sounder carefully, and consulting his secret "black book" of fishing holes that every captain kept. Usually what he was looking for was some aberration in the smooth sandy bottom, like a reef, or some anomaly, say a wreck, or maybe some weird geologic feature that might attract fish and, once he'd found it and circled once or twice, then we could drop the anchor safely off-site upstream, and drift back over whatever it was and spend several hours fishing. We'd sometimes spend up to half an hour making sure the anchor was set at a proper distance off-site, that the tide was right, the anchor held on the bottom, and there was enough scope let out so the boat would ride smoothly and only then would he feel confident enough to shut off the engine.

That first afternoon we parked over the wrecksite of some shrimper that had gone down many years prior, and I was soon indoctrinated in the rules of fair fishing. Every fish had to be marked with a knife somehow by the individual fisherman: top fin, bottom fin, nose-skinned, something like that; some defining mark that you made on the fish to indicate that that particular fish was one you had caught. Of course, the ones with no mark were the captain's. We started catching amberjack and a few snapper right away, and I soon found out that, if you got too caught up in the excitement of fighting and landing these large and gregarious fish, why, you might just forget to mark every one you caught, thereby making an unconscious contribution to the captain's tally. Having marked one of the amberjack, I was then surprised to see the first mate grab it up off the deck and start sawing away at it with his knife. "Hey, that's my fish!" I protested. He looked over at the captain, who was of course, sitting in the captain's chair already into his second beer since we stopped, and they both laughed. "Jack ain't worth shit," the first mate said, "it's only sold for catfood. Out here it's worth more as fresh-cut bait" and the captain nodded in agreement. The mate then handed me a half–dozen four-inch long and an inch-thick purple and red meaty slabs I could use to put on my now bare hook, and you know what, the fishing picked up considerably after that.

I quickly learned another couple of things. The captain hated sharks. Why? I don't really know. Yeah, they'd take a bite out of a fish if you were too slow bringing it to the surface. But other than that, they weren't even a real nuisance. Not as far as I could see anyway. He claimed that hell, if there was one, there'd be a hundred, and the fishing would go to shit unless you taught them a lesson. If you hooked a shark and the captain found out (sometimes he was down below in his cabin, sleeping, or passed out, and then we just cut them loose), well, out came the guns. He had a .38 snub-nose, which quickly came out of the damnedest places, out of his pants, out from under the captain's chair, out from his cabin below; and he had a double-barreled 12-gauge shotgun, that generally came out from his cabin when the .38 wasn't enough. But usually the .38 would do the trick, and he would shoot two or three holes in the shark's head, big gaping white or grey flesh-exploding holes, making sure it was not going to live, before he'd cut the leader loose and let the dead fish sink away into the deep.

Now I was not a complete innocent in all this mayhem, and in fact, once the captain saw the interest I took in his unrepentant malevolence, he'd let me shoot a shark or two, even letting me blast 'em with the shotgun once in a while, of which even the cook and first mate took notice, but of which they generally didn't approve. After all, these were just dumb brutes following their natural inclination (the sharks, not the cook and the mate… then again…). At the time, however, to me, they were just fish, whether we were dragging them on board, gutting them and throwing them in the ice chest, or chopping them into bait to entice other fish, or dispatching them into oblivion because they weren't considered a commercially economical species, they were just fish, and any we sent to the bottom were just going to end up feeding more. I only turned away in guilt from the general blood lust when one day, it just so happened that we hooked two sharks at the same time, and both off the stern reels at that. The cook was on the starboard reel and the first mate was on the port, and they were trying their best not to let the lines get tangled and crossed, or they might lose the tackle. The captain bounded off his chair at the helm and dashed back to the cook's line. "Gimme that," he demanded, and snatching up the bottom tackle, he quickly cut the monofilament leader loose and hanging onto it he told the first mate, "Cut that goddamn thing loose and give me the leader line!" The first mate did as he was told and handed the captain the end of the leader to which his own shark was hooked (each of which was maybe four or five feet long). The captain quickly tied the two leaders together, and cast the two leaders, sharks attached by maybe ten feet of line together, off the stern, laughing loudly (and if not maniacally, well, disturbingly). I was on the midship port reel and stunned at what I'd witnessed, and even the cook and first mate, who had gone out with this captain many times before, were speechless; they just got out another couple of leaders and went back to fishing silently, while the captain went back to his chair at the helm and drank another beer, chuckling away. It's one thing to shoot holes in a shark, and let him drift to the bottom to feed the other denizens of the deep, but setting loose a pair, otherwise unhurt, but now attached by ten feet of filament to which, in this life, they would never again separate, just showed a level of sadism that simply pared off another layer of innocence of which in my young adult life I was acutely becoming aware no longer existed.

There was only one shark that the captain let off the hook (literally). One day we were fishing on what are called "the steeples" which are some sort of geologic feature where these sharp mounts rise up off the seafloor for maybe eighty feet in two hundred feet of water off of Cape Canaveral.

Anyway, if you can sit over the top of one of these mounts, apparently you can get a lot of fish as they seem to congregate around their summits. We were doing so-so, when the captain, who was on the starboard midship reel, hooked something. That was not unusual. But once he'd got it to the surface, he called us over to take a look, and that *was* unusual. There on the end of his line, was a shark, a typical grey, maybe five or six feet long, but it didn't have any fins! He lifted it up out of the water, pulled it over the gunwale onto the deck, and let it flop around. It had been finned, and then set loose again. This is where fishermen, having caught a shark of any decent size, cut off the one dorsal fin off the back, and the two side fins on either side. A captain can set aside these fins, not selling them to the fish house, or even telling anyone he's got a dozen or so, and then sell them under the table to some Japanese restaurant for a sizable sum, say $3 a fin back in '77. Now I'd always been told, and everybody thought (and still thinks), that this was the kiss of death for a shark and they couldn't live very long afterwards, not being able to keep their balance, swim steadily, or be able to hunt effectively, etc. But the captain got a pair of pliers, held that shark's tail with one hand, and kept its head down with a foothold, and twisted that hook right out of its jaw. Then he lifted it up and dropped it over the side, and damn if that shark didn't swim away as if it were perfectly normal. Tough sons-a-bitches, and maybe that's what saved this particular fish from the captain's typical wrath: I think he admired its uncomplaining and stoic survivability.

I wanted to prove my worth, as well as enhance my paycheck, so I was always the first one with a line down in the morning, and the last to give it up at night. Since we weren't allowed down below in the captain's cabin, the first mate and I would sleep on top of the large ice chest, four-foot high, ten-foot long, and five-foot wide that took up the center of the amidship deck. (the cook liked to sleep on the raised platform on the port side opposite the captain's chair). Sometimes at night I would doze lying on the gunwale, with a hand touching the wire, and my line down, trying to catch just one more fish. This wasn't very safe, being only two or three feet above the water, but we had lights on all night (so any tankers out there wouldn't run us over) and I kept one foot on the deck. I wasn't really sleeping, but like I said, just dozing, when one night I'm lying like that and I hear a light "woosh." I sit up, look around, everything's quiet, the boat is still, the mate's asleep on the ice chest, and there's no lights on the horizon, so I lay myself back down and close my eyes. A few minutes later, another "woosh!" louder this time, wakes me right up. Alerted, I look over my shoulder, and not three feet from my outstretched hand, is a porpoise, his blue-gray head half out of the water, looking at me with his shiny black eyes. Scared the shit out of me. He gives another "woosh" of air out his blowhole, then he just turns and swims away, off and down into the dark, dark water, his tail disappearing as the lights shone deep into the water following it. I thought ever so briefly what it must be like to be a lone dolphin in that big damn dark ocean at night, and I pulled in my line and got off the gunwale, and from then on spent my nights on top of the ice cooler with the mate.

We'd been out maybe three days and doing fairly well, when we hit a dry spell and didn't catch anything other than a huge pink stingray that must have been eight feet across, and which the captain blew two large shotgun blasts through before cutting it loose. We tried several different locations before the captain announced that the mate and I had to pull in the anchor line, all the way in, and secure the anchor on top of the bow. We were heading out to deep water, straight east, where he knew we could fill the cooler with some tilefish. We got the anchor secure, and he throttled up and headed east, watching the depth sounder as we went. He even let me take the helm; told me to head 90 degrees, don't run into anything, and let him know when we were in 800 feet of water. Then he settled back into drinking the beers.

183

Tilefish are a strange sort of fish. They get their name from the patterning of their scales, which are set diagonally, like tiles, and shimmer in a variety of different colors when brought to the surface. They're supposed to be able to change color, like a chameleon, although I never saw any evidence of this other than that all fish change color when they die. These are the Great Northern Tilefish, also known as Golden Tilefish, and weren't even identified until 1879. Just four years later, in 1883, for some mysterious reason (later found to be a change in deepwater sea temperatures from the Gulf Stream moving offshore) they disappeared completely for almost ten years. Then fisherman started catching them again in 1892, and they came back strong. The fish live at incredible depths for large bottom fish, 300 to 1200 feet, and what I find most fascinating is, they live in holes that they burrow into the bottom, where they sit with just their heads poking above the bottom surface, waiting for something to swim or crawl by. They're generally two to three feet long and weigh anywhere from 12 to 35 pounds and are delicious (the cook made a big pot of tilefish stew that first night we were out catching them, and calling the taste lobster-like is not a far stretch). One odd thing about them though, that I never heard anyone else ever comment on, was that when you reached up into their gills to lift them aboard, it felt (to me) like reaching into a handful of wet cotton (maybe this was some sort of evolutionary adaptation to living in burrowed silty holes, where sand and such needed to be constantly filtered out—I don't know).

We couldn't put out the anchor because it was too deep, so the captain and mate rigged a drogue, or sea anchor, like a parachute you drag in the water, that let us drift slowly as we fished along the bottom. Considering the depth, to drop a line down to the bottom took almost a full minute, and if you weren't sure you'd had a strike or not, and therefore needed to check your bait, well, that was another minute and a half to bring it to the surface, and another minute to drop it back down again. If you did hook a fish, well then, it might take you ten minutes to bring him up fighting all the way. Despite the time involved, we brought them in continuously for two days, as we drifted along.

We had been out about six days now, and the thing that drives a boat back in to port is not running out of gas, although of course, you have to watch the fuel levels. Nor is it running out of bait: you can always cut up one of the smaller fish you've already caught, so you've got plenty of bait. It isn't even the running out of patience, having been stuck on board a floating jail cell with three other bad-smelling and ill-tempered men, with nothing for entertainment all week but guns and knives, hooks, blood, and beer. [In this regard, I'd been rationing my case of beer to make it last the whole trip, when now, near the end of the week, I noticed that, despite my care and counting, my beers were for all practical purposes, consumed. I asked the captain about it, since he was the only one who always had a beer in hand. "Did you buy that beer?" he snarled at me. I said, "Well, no, but apparently I've got to pay for my groceries when we get back in, so I figured they were mine." "Well, you figured wrong... they're all mine," he said, "I just let you guys drink some of them… sometimes."] No, the thing that drives a boat back into port is when you run out of enough ice to have all the fish covered when you come back in. Nowadays, some boats actually carry along ice machines while they're out, but we just shifted the ice we had loaded when we started back and forth until the captain looked in the chest and said, "We gotta go back." If you get stopped by the Coast Guard and your catch isn't completely covered with ice, you've got to toss out enough fish so that it is. And if the fish house finds out, you're going to have to take a big cut on the overall price of the fish, if they don't refuse to buy the whole catch altogether. So, it was time to head home. We set a course for Ponce Inlet, and the captain opened up the throttle and we all took turns at the helm until the Ponce Inlet Lighthouse came into view the next morning just before dawn. By the time we got back to the Sea Harvest, unloaded all the fish and separated them by type, had them weighed, and had cleaned up the boat, waiting on the captain so as to get paid, it was around 1 o'clock in the afternoon. The captain finally got his check, went to the bank, came back and paid us each individually off to the side, under an old live oak, by a picnic table, where no one else could hear. My take home pay, after groceries (including beer, and even though I don't remember eating anything other than coffee, Spam sandwiches, and dishes of fish that we'd caught), for seven 12 to 18-hour days of fishing, was $65. I think it was a Saturday. The captain said if I wanted to go back out, be at the boat by 9 a.m. (sharp!) on Monday (fat chance!). "You did okay," was the only compliment I was going to get, forget about any thanks. By now it was 2 in the afternoon, hotter'n Hades, and I had to have smelled like old roadkill. But I wasn't going to call Nolin and ruin his and Celia's weekend right away. The first thing I wanted was a cold beer and a sandwich, sitting in a nice dark quiet air-conditioned bar. It was a long walk to town along the north causeway, and I remember having trouble keeping my balance, since I hadn't yet got my land-legs back, and I was stumbling forward and sideways like a drunk, so I quickly stopped in the marina next to the bowling alley first, just to get some ice water and a beer, and get steady. They were used to seeing fishermen coming back in like that, so there I wasn't so strangely out of place. Later, by the time I got to the bridge, and crossed it, I was feeling better except for that godawful thirst and now my growling stomach. I went in to the Tradewinds and sat down at the bar. I suppose worse than the smell was probably my appearance, because of the look of unmitigated disgust that the barmaid gave me, besides the upturned nose. My long hippie hair and beard were practically matted (long before dreads on white people were cool), and my clothes were caked with fish guts and dried blood. With my small backpack and unkempt couture I'm sure I looked like a destitute homeless person (which were few and far between back then, pre-Reagan). But I had some money, so after downing a beer and ordering my food, I went to the restroom and did my best to clean up and at least change into a clean t-shirt.

Once I'd gotten a drink and been fed, I called Nolin and invited him and Celia down for a drink. When they showed up it was dark, and it was obvious they'd been talkin' about what to do with me when I showed up, and that was fine and not unexpected. The funny thing was, there was now a job involved. The landlord couple, Mr. and Mrs. Simpson, who owned the whole building Bob and Celia lived in, had asked if they knew of anybody who could paint, patch, clean up, and make pretty one of the downstairs apartments, which was a large two bedroom they wanted to rent at a high dollar figure, being right on A1A and a block from the beach; it just needed some major sprucing up so they could charge more for it. Bob and Celia said they'd be happy to take on the job, and they even knew someone who could do some wallpapering in the bathrooms. But it was implied, if not made relatively explicit in our discussions that evening, that when we finished and got paid for this particular job, I was expected to leave. And again, this was rightfully so, as I'd been a freeloading beach-bum (taught by one of the best) and it was otherwise time to move on.

Since the job for the Simpsons became a paramount endeavor with a nice payoff at the end, Nolin and I lit into it with an energized fervor, for maybe a week. There were even some flashes of flirtation between Mrs. Simpson and myself when Mr. Simpson wasn't around, even though she was in her mid-forties. Knowing what I know now, I'd have been more daring and it really could have gotten dangerous. Then, one day, Nolin got called up to answer an employment opportunity (having been prodded earlier by Celia to apply thereon) as some sort of copy writer at the Daytona Beach (Volusia) County Court. Never the shy one, they had relegated him to a table in the rarely used courtroom, and he quickly commandeered the judge's bench. But if he was working all day, on another job, how were we to figure out how to split the proceeds, once they eventually developed? Well, hell, I owed Bob and Celia a lot for the hospitality they'd shown me all summer, so I didn't care about working on the apartment alone sometimes. I had the free time, and when Celia had a day off during the week, just for fun we'd chase down some hints that the local radio station was putting out on a scavenger hunt around town that paid out some cash (but we never found any of the secret stashes). She also helped in painting the apartment downstairs, realizing that she was putting in some of Nolin's time, and the quicker we got it done, the quicker we'd get paid, and I'd be heading out. I understood all of this and was quite ready to go back to Tallahassee. I'd had my summer in Smyrna, and I was recharged and ready to start back to college.

11. Tally and Beyond the Pale (1978 – 1981)

Becoming Sub-versive

Having finished the job, we got paid, and I packed up my stuff (except for the épée, which I left for Nolin), shook hands with Bob and hugged Celia, and booked on up to Tallahassee. When I got there, the Gear brothers let me sleep on their couch for a couple of days until I found a nice little white house to rent at 410 North Bronough. Joe Gear, the youngest of the Gear boys, moved in with me and we set up residence. Jimmy had by this time risen from breakfast manager of the old Subway (not to be confused with the modern chain of Subway sub shops) on the corner of Dewey and Tennessee Street, to the overall manager of the Subway Station, its upscale cousin-restaurant round the corner on Raven Street. Jim said he'd give me a job as a short-order cook "behind the line," as it was termed. This involved making slices of New York style pizza, and various sandwiches, soups and salads. The place was very popular, and was packed every night. His brother, Charlie, was working as a waiter, when he wasn't wooing waitresses, and Barry was working in the main kitchen during the days getting the prep work done while sipping Scotch and milk. (Before you squinch up your face and wince, first, admit, ever try it? Of course it sounds horrible, but the old black jazz players from the 30's on swore by it, and once challenged by Barry to taste it, I had to admit, that was damn good! Probably *good for you* too, supposedly offsetting ulcers.)

Blues Brother

As manager, Jimmy was what he liked to call "cock of the walk," hiring and firing as he pleased. The place was so popular under his imperial sway that there were lines out the door, reservations to be made, and celebrities to be entertained. One night after a major concert downtown, who came in with his entourage, but the famous Muddy Waters! I had not yet developed the taste for the blues that I only came to appreciate later (you've got to "earn" the blues), and was therefore, under-impressed. Jimmy and Charlie, however, having almost conquered the French Quarter in tandem, and thus knowing New Orleans and its history and truly appreciating its own peculiar dark glamour, were awe-struck. Once the great man (and his followers) had been duly dined, wined, and desserted in undisturbed post-concert peace and tranquility, Jimmy gracefully introduced himself as the manager, and having pressed his *bona fides* as a brother of the blues, asked one quick and forgivable favor. Knowing that Mr. Waters had many times in his career been only allowed to enter through the kitchen of certain venues he had played over the ensuing decades: would he be kind enough to allow a photograph of himself and the staff be taken in the kitchen? Wouldn't take but a minute, and it would make everyone very, very happy. "Of course," the venerable bluesman assented, "just let me know when." The staff was quickly coalesced (the hell with the rest of the public rabble), and Mr. Waters came in, and stood in the back of the kitchen, ringed on both sides by the Subway Station staff, and the photo was taken. Thank you, he shakes hands, "wonderful to have met you, food was delicious, service was impeccable," and he was off. I have seen the picture several times. I might even have a copy of it somewhere stashed in my files. I am not in the picture, however. I took it.

Pink Venusians

We had quite a tight crew working at the Subway Station: even Bill Cummings, my old carpentry partner, decided to take the plunge, so between myself and him on the line, Barry in the back during the days (and sometimes on a busy Saturday night), Charlie heading up the waiters, and dear strict, but devoted and always laughing Lori Cohen acting as Assistant Manager (and as we all know, the Assistant Manager does 90% of the work such as payroll, ordering, scheduling, etc.), Jim was free to exercise his authority with relative impunity, as long as he kept the costs down. The actual owner of the place, Dave Rhodes, a rich, quiet and shy, but otherwise friendly flamer, was busy with his own grand project, planning a huge disco club to be built at the other end of the block, so otherwise he let Jimmy do as he pleased. Again, to keep costs down, Jim would hire some of the local street people on an *ad hoc* basis ($5 here, $5 there) to do odd jobs around the restaurant, like pick up litter, sweep the sidewalks, and empty the garbage cans. One early afternoon Jim comes out of the manager's office, and he's looking for Tom, the street person on call that day. "Where's Tom? Anybody seen Tom?" The barmaid at the time was getting the bar set up, and said "Yeah, I had him take out all the empty bottles from last night to throw them out in the dumpster out back." "Okay, thanks," Jim goes out the back door, where there's a small enclosed area for storing cleaning supplies, hoses, mops, buckets, and where the garbage cans could be taken out and cleaned. Sitting there on a box, is Tom, intently and diligently pouring the last dregs of each and every liquor bottle into one single half-gallon, which he's got damn near half-full. Jimmy says, "What are you doing?" Tom looks up, a little embarrassed, and says, "Well, before I throw them out, I figured I'd pour off the remains so me and some of the boys could have a little snort tonight. No sense in throwing out good liquor." Jim blows his top, and says "Goddamn it, I'm not paying you to sit here and empty bottles… gimme that… now go on and throw out the rest of these, and come in and get your pay, you're through here!" Then, standing there, looking at that half-full bottle of mixed melancholia, as Tom started gathering up the boxes of empties and carrying them out, a light bulb went off in Jim's head. He went back in and told the barmaid, "Here, take this bottle, finish filling it with strawberry daiquiri mix. Keep it separate from the other liquor, and keep the money separate from the drawer. Anybody orders one, you free-pour an ounce-and-a-half over ice and blend it. The tips are yours." That evening there appeared on the bar these little hand-scrawled advertisements: "For a limited time only! Pink Venusians! Secret ingredients! $4 each" They were a big hit! By the end of the night they were gone, Jimmy had a hundred dollars extra in his pocket, the barmaid was happy with the extra tips, and the public was clamoring for "More Pink Venusians!" I guess it was about three days later, I came into the place early; I needed to talk to Jim about a slight discrepancy on my timesheet. No big deal but I wanted it to be cleared up by the next one. He wasn't in the office, even though his truck was out back. He wasn't in the bar. Nor was he in the kitchen, or even the freezer, where we would often step in to have a quick toke. I went out the back door, and there, sitting on a box, was Jimmy, who looked up and smiled as he was intently and diligently pouring off the last drops of all the different empty liquor bottles into one large half-gallon. Damn if it wasn't nearly half-full.

Amy

I had just gotten back from New Smyrna, sleeping on the Gear brothers' couch, when I was re-introduced to Amy, their youngest sister. She had just come up from Orlando, after graduating high school, and Jimmy promised her a job working behind the bar at the Subway Station. While I'd been gone to New Smyrna for the summer, I'd asked Jimmy and Charlie to watch my boxes of books—I've always had a box of books following me around, ones I can't let go of, but they change with the years; some though, I've had forever, since I first picked them up—and apparently Amy had gotten into the boxes, which was no problem (I'd encouraged the Gear brothers to read them at their leisure), and she claims to this day that she fell in love before ever meeting me because of those books. I don't believe it, but it makes for a good story; not mine, but hers. In any case, the first night we met we stayed up practically all night talking about life, love, philosophy, the universe, etc. We even walked around the block at 3 a.m. just to keep moving, and back in Tallahassee at that time you could do that without the least worry, and it might have been the only time there ever was when you could walk around undisturbed at that time of night. No, I did not seduce her that night, or even attempt to, but our discussion laid the groundwork for a lifetime, unbeknownst at the time to probably both of us. She was wide-eyed, inherently intelligent, if not over-educated (due to a public, as opposed to private-school education), and enthusiastically optimistic. Maybe being eighteen and just out of high school, and now in a friendly college town practically run by her brother, there may have been some reason for such an open-ended view of life. Well, we hit it off right away, but… she already had a number of other suitors, I didn't want to settle down, and the age difference of 8 years was a minor problem that initially had her brothers looking at me slightly askance. I had known her older sister, Molly, just one year my junior, back in high school, where she was a cheerleader and very popular. Then I went on one date with her other sister Sally, six years my junior, a few years earlier, and although we got along, the sparks really didn't fly. Besides, Tallahassee was open for all kinds of relational opportunities, so there was no sense in getting tied down. Plenty of fish in the sea.

A Slice of Life

But Amy had the biggest brown eyes. And a serious inquisitiveness for consciousness expansion, just for the answers alone; not on how they needed to be applied, which was every other seeker's search, even my own: i.e., how can I use this information to further my personal advancement? No, she just wanted to know things for their own sake. Refreshing. So, even though I tried to remain aloof and unencumbered, we got along pretty good and despite her many other male attractants, I was entranced by her and could always elicit a special notice when needed. Like the time she was working the bar, which I could see from all the way across the restaurant, and I saw that she had ordered a slice of pizza. So I dished up a nice thick one with lots of everything, what you'd call a "supreme" nowadays, must have been an inch thick, all melted together with a nice overture of mixed cheeses. I heaped all this on, even though she'd just ordered a regular cheese slice, because I knew she'd like it, she could eat half, and take half home. Her only reason for the original meager order was because Jimmy was on one of his many cost-cutting kicks, where we were shaving down sizes, cutting portions, and counting individual pepperoni rounds while cutting them thin enough that you could see through them. (The place was so popular, that we could get away with most of this, and if anyone complained, we'd jut toss on another scrap or two, re-heat it, and that'd usually shut 'em up.) I put it in a to-go box and had one of the waitresses take it on over to Amy. But it never made it. Jimmy just coincidentally happened to be making one of his pass-through inspections and stopped the waitress. "What's that?" he said, and she dutifully replied, "A piece of pizza for Amy." Lemmee see it," he said, and when it was opened, he wailed as if he'd been stabbed in the eye with a hot fire poker, "AAAUGGGHH!" Shit, I saw the whole thing happen, and quickly pretended I hadn't. First of all, he went over to Amy and showed her the unforgivable extravagance in the to-go box in his hand, and began to berate her mercilessly. She was an innocent in all this however, having only ordered a piece of regular pizza, so she defended herself admirably. Realization of what had occurred dawned on him, and the steamy wrath of Jimmy slowly turned my way and I just looked down and pretended I was busy as I could feel heat from the red-coals glare from across the seating area. He tromped on over to where I was "working," blocked my passage out of the short-order food prep line, and then gave me what for, turning the air blue with his well-placed obscenities, none of which I must say were ever directed at me, *ad hominem*, personally, but rather at the situation, and the need for frugality, how every little bit counts, the total attention to the receipts necessary to maintain the operation versus the costs of ingredients and the workforce, etc. I've got to hand it to him, I was almost ashamed. "But she's your sister," was my own pitiable defense. "All the worse!" he shouted, then damning me and the whole ungrateful lot of us for *all* that he had to put up with, who *all* had no idea how much he had to work and sacrifice, in order to keep us *all* employed, how hard he worked, and what little thanks he got... Then, having vented his bile, he turned, walked into the manager's office with the to-go box still gripped in his meaty paw, and gobbled down the giant slice of pizza. All of it.

That's All, Volks

Then there was the time we stole the car. I was by now somewhat actively chasing Amy, enamored enough to ask her one day if she'd like to go for a picnic out in the Old City Cemetery, which was right off of Tennessee Street and Bronough, across from the round Holiday Inn. Bill happened to be around that day, and I don't know what I was thinking, but I asked him if he wanted to come along. He said yes, instead of begging off, like I expected a gentleman might. No matter. So the three of us go over to the old Wine and Cheese Cellar and Bill and I bought a loaf of French bread, several different cheeses, Edam and Brie and Roquefort, and a bottle of San Gría. We hoofed on over to the cemetery, wandered around for a little while looking at the old graves, one of which is that of Napoleon Bonaparte's nephew, Prince Achilles Murat, a monarchical French wastrel who hung out (hid out?) in Tallahassee and spent his money entertaining the Territory of Florida's social elite in the early 1800s, even becoming mayor in 1825. We planted ourselves on some big flat knee-high tomb and spent the better part of an hour just enjoying the scenery, the conversation, and the wine and cheese and bread. It was a wonderfully pleasant afternoon diversion. On our way back to my place at 410 N. Bronough, and as we were walking past the Western Sizzlin' I noticed a very nice almost new, tan-colored Volkswagen. What caught my eye were the seats inside, with gaudy black and red and white vertical stripes. Glancing in as we walked past it, I noticed that, although the windows were up and it was locked, the keys were in the ignition, just hanging there. That's interesting, I thought, and let it go. Well, a day or two goes by, and I'm walking back from the Pastime, cut past the Sizzlin' on the shortcut back to the house, and there it is! It hadn't moved. I walk up, look inside, and the keys are still hanging there. I go back to the house and later mention this to Bill, who had moved into one of the double-shotgun duplex apartments across the driveway. Now I'm watching every day to see if it moves. After a week, I thought, damn, that thing is either abandoned or stolen, or both. Hell, pretty soon the cops are going to notice it, put a sticker on it, and have it towed off. I wonder if it'll start? Bill and I got a coat hanger, and yeah, I was the one, who eventually, after ten minutes of jiggling and maneuvering, and twisting, and re-twisting the goddamn wire, finally popped the lock. We hopped in and "vroom!" she fired right up; full tank of gas too. We drove all around town just to make sure everything worked. Other than the clutch being a little on the loose side, she drove like a champ. When we finally got back to the house, we put her in the hideaway garage next door, just in case. Well, now that we had it, what are we gonna do with it? Driving it around town was probably not a good idea (as it eventually turned out). Why not a road trip? Bill's Mom still lived in Orlando, and I hadn't seen my parents and brother in awhile... let's go. We headed south and it was a smooth ride. It was only when we were just getting to Orlando that the clutch got even worse, and we realized this was the reason it had probably been parked in the first place. Still, we were both adept at double-clutching in synch with the engines rpm's, so it wasn't yet a big deal.

This was one of those quick trips to Orlando, where I actually spent more time with my brother Paul, after the obligatory hour or two with Mom and Dad around the kitchen table discussing life in general, politics, the scene in Tallahassee, and then the inevitable, "So, how's the situation look for getting back into school?" "It's coming, it's coming," I'd respond, before going out. Paul lived near Hoffner, down in Edgewood, at the south end of Orange Avenue, and his local hangout (within a walking block or two) was the Alpine Inn. It was neither Alpine, nor an inn, but a sleazy stinky little beer bar that catered to the cheapest of locals, the old men who'd get there when it opened at 10 a.m. and stay all day and all night. Before I went in the first time, Paul handed me a baseball cap, advertising Caterpillar Diesel, and said "put it on." But I don't wear hats, I protested. "Put it on," he insisted. Maybe because of my long hair and beard, the place might be a redneck hazard I figured, so I put it on and we walked on down. On entering, he said hi to all the regulars, and introduced me to the barmaid, a chunky peroxide blond. She shook my hand, reached over, and took the hat. What the heck? Then she puts it on the end of a broomstick with some sort of tack on the end and pins it to the ceiling, which I now notice is covered with a various and sundry assortment of haberdashery. That was their "thing"; when you walked in the first time you were there, and if you happened to be wearing a hat (as most cowboys, truckers, and rednecks do), they took your hat and pinned it to the ceiling. Once you had one up there, and could point it out, they left you alone and wouldn't take the next or any more. There were a lot of arguments, gripes, and near fistfights (not to mention the loss of a lot of potential customers) over that stupid gambit of theirs, but once it was done, you were welcome and considered one of the family. Luckily, I had no attachment to the Caterpillar Diesel ball cap, and Paul knew it would be entertaining.

After a day or two I picked up Bill and we headed back up to Tallahassee. By now though, the clutch was shot, and we just did our best to leave it in fourth, double-clutching whenever we had to shift gears. We made it back, put it in the garage, and wondered what to do next. "Well, first of all, let's sell the goddamn seats out of it; that black and red and white striped velour had to go, and certainly there was someone willing to pay for them." Once we sold the seats there'd be nothing left to do but sell the thing for parts. Fortunately we had friends who were mechanics at the Volkswagen repair shop right down the street, so this was going to be relatively easy. Bill and I had a few drinks, he went back to his place, and I decided to take her out for one last spin before we started chopping her up. Buzzing around town, I'd just made it to the overpass on Pensacola Street, right where it overlooked the Seminole's football arena, Doak Campbell Stadium (this was back when Pensacola ran to the north of it and before it got wrapped in brickwork, so it still had that naked steel-girder erector-set look). Just as I got to the top of the overpass, the blue light came on. I immediately pulled over, got out of the car and leaned against the door, already pulling out my driver's license. They were two Tallahassee cops, one older and one younger, and they were very nice, not giving me a load of crap for getting out of my car, like they would now. "Do you know why we pulled you over?" said the one. "No sir," I said. "You were doing 40 in a 35 mile per hour zone." I shrugged. The other one called the first one over and whispered something to him. He came back, and asked "Have you been drinking, sir?" even though we were roughly the same age, or maybe he had a year or two on me. I fessed up immediately, and now we're exchanging 'sirs,' "Yes, sir, I've had a couple of drinks, I admit it, but I'm heading home right now." He asked where I lived, and when I told him, well, he knew that I was heading directly away from where I lived, and therefore, had told him an untruth. He and the other, slightly older cop, started whispering again. He came back and said, "If you don't mind, sir, we're going to take you in for a breathalyzer test." "Sure," I said, "let's go." The older cop asked for my keys, and volunteered that he'd park my car in the stadium parking lot. "Okay," and I handed him the keys to the unregistered, uninsured, and oh yeah, stolen, vehicle. I got in the back of the police car, and the young cop and I followed the other one down to the stadium parking lot, where the older cop parked it, got out, got into the passenger seat of the cop car, turned around, handed me the keys, and said "You know, that clutch is just about gone, you ought to have it looked at." "Yeah, I know," I said.

They took me down to the station and I blew right at .1, which was the limit back then in Florida. It was stupid and silly and I was damn lucky they never ran the plate on the stolen car—that probably would have been the end of it for me. With my one phone call I called Jimmy, since he was the only one I knew with any money, and he came and bailed me out. Hell, back then the bail was only $400, and he put it all up rather than go to a bail bondsman. He dropped me off back at the parked VW and I drove on home. Bill and I put an ad in the paper to get rid of the seats, and by that weekend we had sold them. As far as the drinking and driving, to grab the bull by the horns, so to speak, and not having dealt with this sort of thing before, I did the one thing I probably shouldn't have done. I went to the prosecutor's office. They handed me over to a young lawyer, the youngest and newest on staff, and I told him what had happened and asked him what I could do to make things go easy. At first he was surprised, since no one ever came to the prosecuting attorney, ever. And then secondly, they never admit to the crime, which I had just done. He pulled out the file, saw it was my first real (serious) offense, and both taken aback by my honesty, and impressed with my hutzpah, he agreed to the least charge he could muster, which at the time was driving with an illegal blood-alcohol level, known then as DUBAL. This was not the same nor near as serious as a DUI, and meant only that you had registered an illegal blood alcohol level, not that you were driving while impaired, and carried a much less severe fine (they don't even carry DUBAL on the books any more, considering now that you are automatically impaired). I agreed to a plea-bargain right then and there, and to save both of us an appearance in court, I signed some papers, went down the courthouse hall and paid a $150 fine with the cash I'd made from my share from selling the stolen car seats. They gave me a receipt so I could go and get Jimmy's $400 bail money, and by that afternoon it was all over but the crying. Like I said, silly and stupid (am I not a man?).

Well, by now it was getting into early 1979, and things were settling down at the Subway Station and it was losing some of its prestige. Jimmy had made most of the money he was going to squeeze out of it—he was doing so well there for a while that he'd have Amy do his laundry and told her she could have whatever money she found in his pockets; but when he found out that she was making a couple of hundred dollars a week, he quickly changed his mind and said she could keep all the "change" she found there, but the bills had to come home to Poppa. It was time for a new adventure, so Jimmy and Charlie decided to open a bar of their own. They staked out the underground storage cellar on the block of businesses on Tennessee Street below Ken's Tavern, leveled out the dirt floor, and had a concrete slab poured for the new barroom floor. They got a friendly electrician to wire up lights in the ceiling, which was the wooden floor of the barrooms above, and Charlie practically single-handedly hung the sheetrock for the ceiling and the air-conditioning ductwork. Everything was then spray-painted black as per Jimmy's knowledgeable insistence that a bar should remind one sub-consciously of a womb, and consciously of a cave, so that the patrons would naturally feel secure, safe, and "at home." At the conclusion of the spray-painting session Jimmy and Charlie could have easily passed as Amos and Andy had they wandered down to Frenchtown.

Eye Declare

As the paint dried, plans were drawn up for the construction of the bar, bathrooms, furniture, and walk-in cooler. Bill and I had agreed to handle all the carpentry labor for the nominal fee of free beer for life. I had a contractor's account at the local lumber yard, from my earlier work with Jim Walters, so a lot of the wood was charged off the cuff, to be paid back monthly on the charge account once they started making money. After the bathrooms, the first we had to put in was the cooler, since it was the largest compartment backing up the bar-to-be, and had to be big enough to store many kegs and cases of beer. Somewhere Jim got several large partitions of insulated walls, wooden and styrofoam in the middle, with both an inside and outside skin of aluminum. After several trips in his old beat-up white pickup truck, loading and unloading the cooler walls, we were ready to install the thing. It had to be trimmed to fit though, so here I was cutting through this goddamn aluminum-sided styrofoam wall with my circular saw when "tic!" I felt this small fleck of something fly into my eye (Safety glasses? We don't need no stinkin' safety glasses!). When I finished the cut, I went into the men's room (which we had already put together), and looked in the mirror. There was a small sliver of aluminum stuck in the white part of my right eye, luckily just off to the side of my pupil. Shit, shit, shit... I really didn't want to go to the hospital. Well, dammit, I'd done it for Aldo, I suppose I could do it to myself. I got out my trusty (and thankfully not rusty) pocket knife with the long pointed edge, applied a match to the end of the blade on both sides, let it cool as I steadied myself against the sink, and stared into my eye up close in the mirror. Using both hands to keep steady, I slowly put the knife point to my eye and got the edge of that sliver of aluminum and eased it back on out. There was a slight red line where it had been, but nothing came out, no water, no blood, nothing, although both my eyes had teared up from the now-relieved stress. I took it easy for the rest of the day, and within two, even the slight red scratch was gone. Meanwhile, I took the time to go down to the hardware store and buy a pair of safety goggles for a buck and a half.

Cool and the Gang

Before we got down to building the bar itself, there was a little piece of business we had to attend to. The ductwork was all in place, the electricity was on, summer was quickly approaching, and it was getting hotter'n hell down there in the middle of the day and no air circulating. Bill and I had gotten the bathrooms done, and constructed the massive front doors, built like the entrance to a small gothic cathedral (even with the ability to put a crossbeam in place from the inside when closed, making it nearly impregnable to assault). Well, now it was time to face the air-conditioning conundrum: how big, how expensive, where to get it, who'd install it? Once we'd gotten the beer cooler built, the refrigeration guy said he could install the air conditioning too, but he didn't know where to get one the size they needed for the price Jimmy and Charlie wanted to pay. Dave Rhodes, the shy and retiring fey entrepreneur who owned the Subway Station, and was building a big disco next door, came to the rescue one day as he came in to look at the progress of the building of the bar. He took Jimmy aside and whispered something in his ear. Jimmy asked us if we had any sledgehammers and crowbars, which we did, and soon we had a small caravan heading out to the local roadway known as Jackson Bluff, just south of the stadium. Apparently, Dave Rhodes had been partners in a business (a juke joint) with a local pawnbroker. The place was popular for awhile, but there had been a falling out, and Dave and the owner parted ways, with the pawnbroker owing Dave a pile of money. The place was closed down, had been closed down for several months, and no one was interested in re-opening it, and the pawnbroker wasn't letting go of his share of the business interest, so they had reached a stalemate while the place lay fallow and boarded up. Out in the back, however, stuck halfway into the cinder block wall, was a large green industrial air conditioner. "We got to move fast," said Jimmy, and laying into the cinder block, he struck the first blow. In a half an hour the air conditioner was in the back of Jimmy's truck heading back across town, a gaping hole left in the back wall of the former honky-tonk for the raccoons, the bums, and I imagine, eventually the police, to enter. Within two hours the industrial unit was back at the bar-to-be and spray-painted a bright yellow, with nary a speck of green showing. By the following afternoon, we were working in the wafting breeze of the dark semi-subterrranean cave of what came to be known as The Lucky Horseshoe Bar. It was so cold we could work with the doors wide open. Anyone walking by in the parking lot out front would feel that cool breeze coming out the door and it would draw them in like the scent of a sandalwood spring-fed oasis on a sub-Saharan afternoon.

The Lucky Horseshoe Bar

The Lucky Horseshoe probably deserves a book of its own, but again, it's really not my story except in how I was involved, things I witnessed, and its legacy. Therefore, I will plunge on ahead undaunted and anyone who wants to take up the mantle and fill in the details is more than welcome to do so. Anyway, besides the money they'd socked away from managing the Subway Station, Jim and Charlie took out a small family loan, and had already convinced Mr. Peavey, the crotchety old owner of the block of businesses on Tennessee Street above, that they could really make a go of this formerly dirt-floored storage area. It was a great location, since it opened onto the parking area that everyone had to use for all the businesses upstairs, and thus, everyone who parked their car back there had to walk past the entrance, as mentioned above. It was to be named The Lucky Horseshoe in a nod to the bar of the same name that their *pater familias*, Barry Francis Gear, had opened when the family first moved down to Kissimmee/St. Cloud from Ohio back in the fifties. I'm not sure how long this original watering-hole lasted before he gave it up and became a postman in Orlando, but it was a couple of years anyway. So now the boys had gotten the place started, the cement floor was down, the ceiling and ductwork were in, the bathrooms were done, and even the beer-storage cooler and air conditioner were up and running. Now it was time to build the bar proper. They wanted a real horseshoe-shaped bar, with enough seating for about eighteen. Bill and I sketched it out on paper, pulled some tapes, and snapped a few chalk lines on the floor, and soon, with a little adjustment here and there, we had it all laid out. From there it was easy to figure out how much wood and what various types would be needed (me being an expert on figuring out just exactly how much would be needed from my Jim Walter wood-selling experiences). We started right in and with a little help from a friend who was a finish carpenter and added a few decorative touches, we were done in about three days. We decided on the proposed height of the bar by having several people of various statures sit on a barstool with a beer in their hand, afterwards asking which was most comfortable, then we averaged it. It was some odd number like 43 and 3/8 inches, but no one ever complained. Once the top was laid down, a thick slice of plywood with a nice finish on one side, Jimmy walked around and laid down several packs worth of cards, face up, to ring the inside edge of the bar. Then one of the decoupage-artist chicks got out a gallon of clear epoxy and laid a nice layer on top, sealing the whole thing forevermore from water, beer, and any regurgitated fluids that might end up decorating it later. Finally, the guy who owned a leather shop upstairs volunteered to pad the entire outside edge with a leather armrest that he could stitch together with scraps from other jobs he'd done, and he sealed it with some special saddle soap to make it waterproof. When finished it was beautiful; and how many bars have you ever been to where the armrest on the edge of the bar was made out of genuine padded leather? Not many, I'll bet.

We had one small incident that we never told anyone about, when Bill and I were finishing up and putting in the footrail for the bar. We had rented a nail gun because we had to get the nails not only through the 4 by 4 pressure-treated wood, but down into the hardened concrete floor too. Neither pneumatic nor electric, this was a hand-held, wide-bore gun where you put in a .22 caliber blank cartridge, then slipped your hard-forged cut nail into the barrel; and when you pressed it against the surface of whatever you were shooting the nail into, it was armed. Then, when you pulled the trigger, the .22 cartridge would fire and drive the nail right up to the head into just about anything, including concrete Well, after we'd finished the footrail, we still had a few .22 cartridges and some cut nails left. I decided that I'd like to see if we couldn't shoot a nail through a metal garbage can out back. We set the garbage can up out the back door, maybe thirty feet away, and I used the edge of the door to arm the gun, pushing against it but not blocking the barrel. "BAM!" I fired it. We went out there and looked but there was no hole. It hadn't hit the can at all. It must have flown over the top of it. Only then did dumb-ass me realize that beyond the garbage can was an apartment complex wall. Oh shit! Bill and I ran on over to the apartments and started looking along the wall, and there, about an inch and a half below a bathroom window, there was a thumb-sized fresh chunk of concrete taken out of the window sill. Had it hit that window, the nail probably would have passed all the way through the apartment and gone out the front door. Was anybody home? I don't know, and Bill and I scurried back into The Horseshoe and waited and watched, but nobody came. My guardian angel had once more put in a little overtime that day, and racing faster than a speeding nail-bullet, had gotten out in front of it and ever so slightly diverted its path so that it hit that concrete window sill and didn't plug some poor college student in the skull sitting on the toilet or eviscerate his girlfriend as she stepped out of the shower.

The bar opened with a grand fanfare: bands played, people were dancing, and the beer flowed like a mountain stream. There were lots of toasts and shaking of hands and back-slapping; lots of clandestine dope-smoking in the beer cooler too. One of the premier bands playing that day was Crosscut Saw, with the lead singer and harmonica-playing great, Pat Ramsey (now sadly deceased), who had backed up a couple of Allman Brothers tunes on various albums. But there was also a new kid in his band, a young 16-year-old blues-guitar-playing wunderkind named Julian who has gone on to become famous in his own right over the years. It wasn't the wondrous Julian who caught my attention that day though, it was his girlfriend. She was rather handsome for a girl, but had long dark legs, and she was buzzing around in a pair of very short yellow pants and an orange tube-top that accented her well-proportioned teen-aged figure. I say she was buzzing around because she was on a pair of roller skates and was skimming in and out of the crowd, when she wasn't practicing her pirouettes on the broad slab of concrete out the front door. She obviously made an impression on me because when I met her again some 28 years later, although I never knew her name, and hadn't seen her since, I had the opportunity to remind her of that day, while she just thought I was making a pass at her. But that's another story (see Chapter 19). One of the lesser-celebrated local bands that played for the grand opening party was Flat Zapper, named after a band member's cat. It so happened that, living down in Wakulla, one day the cat was missing, they couldn't find it anywhere. They were pulling out of the driveway to go practice and still trying to think of a name for the band, when, as they turned onto the highway, there was the missing Zapper, who had been run over repeatedly throughout the day, flat as a pancake.

Just before Jimmy had signed off as the manager of the Subway Station, he had taken up dating a tall and stunning brunette, Nancy Smith, whom he had hired as a cashier. Jimmy had many, many talents, but we never figured being a Don Juan was one of them. Nonetheless, between his gift of gab and his plucky insistence, he and Nancy became an item, and once The Lucky Horseshoe got going full steam, he asked her to marry him. It was a typical Tallahassee free-form casual wedding, the ceremony carried out in the backyard of their house, and except for the inappropriate interruptions of manic giggling by the drug-addled and mentally-deranged Bill O'Bryan (Bill-O), for which he was properly escorted off-property, it all went off with the required hitch. After a quick reception at the house, we all decided to move the festivities down to The Lucky Horseshoe where we could cut loose in proper fashion. When we got there, the place began to fill rather quickly so, Barry, Amy and I grabbed the best seats in the house which were on the far side of the bar, facing the door. Being on the far side, you didn't have people walking in and out around you, or muscling their way to the bar to order beers. The only things behind us were the pinball machines (Missile Command, Defenders, Asteroid), and some foldup metal chairs lined against the wall and propped up against a few unoccupied booths. The music was playing, everyone was celebrating, and it wasn't long before we were all in our cups.

Whenever there was a break in the music, a set of toasts to the new couple would ring out, some sentimental, some bawdy, and some downright raunchy. At one of these toasts, Barry, who was sitting on the other side of Amy from me, raised his glass a little too fast and a little too high, and (I can still see it in my mind's eye) the beer lifted right out of the glass, hung for an instant, and then splashed down onto the top of Amy's head. "Goddammit, Barry!" she shouted, "You spilled beer all over me!" In a typical oldest brother rejoinder I'm sure he'd used many times over the years he said, "Oh, shut up, you big crybaby!" "Hey!" I jumped in, "You can't talk to her like that!" "I'll talk to her any way I want, motherfucker!" he said. "Wham!" We were in the clinch. We grabbed each other's arms, shoulders, neck and shirt collar, and started twisting this way and that, round and over. We were pushing back and forth, and finally, we careened into the folding chairs lined up against the wall, first sending them crashing into a large pile of metal on the floor, and then sending the booths along the back wall into a giant domino tumble-down. By this time Charlie, who was pouring beers, jumped over the bar and grabbed the two of us, pulling us apart. All of a sudden, out of nowhere, another guy comes crashing into the three of us in a flying tackle (!?!?). What the hell? He knocks us all down, then jumps up and wants to fight, putting up his fists. "Whoa, whoa, whoa" the three of us shouted, "What the hell is the matter with you, and what are you mad about?" "The baby" he says, still steamed, panting and pissed. "What baby" we asked. "My baby… we put it to sleep on the seat of the booth." Then we looked over to see the distraught mother, ten feet away, holding a squawling baby in her arms, trying to be both consoling to the kid while looking mean at us at the same time. They had noticed an unoccupied booth, and the baby, despite the music, had gone to sleep, so they set it on the seat of the booth while they stood next to it, with their pitcher of beer and glasses on the tabletop. Barry and I in our wrestling around had crashed into the chairs, sending the booth seat tumbling, and the infant was dashed to the floor under the falling debris of booth seat, table, pitcher and glasses. We quickly did our best to rectify the situation, apologizing profusely, offering to replace the beer, pleading ignorance, blaming each other, and apologizing profusely some more, especially to the mom. By the time we made the peace, the baby had quieted down, and then we made it back to our seats, Amy had rinsed out her hair in the bathroom, and after one more apology to her from Barry, we were all back on track.

Floor Polish

Then there was the incident with the bikers. Now Jimmy and Charlie started off with the premise that this was an open bar, everyone was welcome, and no intolerance was to be tolerated. This worked for awhile, but then it became apparent that despite the good intentions, they were paving a road straight to hell. Some people just don't get along well; for instance, hippies and rednecks; rednecks and blacks; bikers and hippies; bikers and frat boys… you get the picture. Or sometimes they get along okay, but business might suffer if one group or another gets the upper hand and the others feel, if not obligated, but more comfortable, to leave *en masse*. So they started running "Special Nights" like Frat Nights, Punk Nights, Gay Nights, etc., with beer/wine specials catering to each. This allowed certain groups to congregate on their own, with their own friends and their own music, and helped fill those slow weekday nights when nothing else was going on. The bikers, however, liked to come in early in the afternoon (most of them on some sort of disability compensation: whether Vietnam, drug addiction, mental issues, et al., or else they had a working wife/girlfriend who brought home the basic bacon). Then they'd stay on into the night, which was fine, but it being summertime, they were often well-lit before the sun went down around seven or eight. One afternoon, the local biker gang, the Iron Ravens, were inside drinking it up, when one of them went outside and got it into his head to ride his motorcycle into the bar (I always though it was the one-legged biker named Beak, because I was certain that it wasn't Buzzard, but I've been told by friends that it was altogether a different one, whose club name I can't recall right now). Anyway, this idiot drove his bike through the wide open double-doors, spun a big rubber-burning donut on the floor and peeled out, going back outside into the lot and re-parking his bike, then returning back into the bar, fairly proud of himself for his brass-balled bravado. Jimmy was out running errands, but was back soon, carrying in groceries. He walked in, smelled the burnt rubber, saw the black treadmark on the newly-painted grey floor, and asked what happened. Once informed of the details, he calmly walked over to the president of the club, asked who the daredevil was, and once the fool was pointed out to him, he told the president that, although they were welcome to stay, *that particular individual* had to leave, and was barred from coming back in until such time as he was given a half-full can of leftover floor paint and a brush, to be provided by Jim, and got on his hands and knees and paint over the skidmark. The president looked over at the troublemaker and said, "You heard the man... you gotta go." The jackal started bitching and cursing, saying there was no way he would apologize (which Jimmy never asked for) or ever paint the skidmark over... and he didn't feel much like leaving right then. Well, you got to hand it to those boys, they got discipline. They all stood up, backing up the president, and the troublemaker was gently, but firmly, escorted outside, without anyone having to lay a hand on him. He sat outside on his bike in a funk while the rest of the gang finished drinking. This continued to occur for well over a month, with the gang coming in and drinking on Biker Days, while this guy had to sit outside, resting on his bike, waiting until they finished, with someone sometimes carrying a beer out to him in a plastic cup. Finally, one day he came in, asked to see Jimmy, and after getting down and painting over the burnt-rubber skidmark, was once again welcomed into the fold. I think Jimmy even bought him a beer... on the house... another Horseshoe miracle!

Were we not men? No... we were Devo... D-E-V-O! Devolutionary. There was no one arguing with that. We had Blondie blasting on the stereo, the videogames Defenders blasting from the back wall and Missile Command witnessing the destruction of our Western Civilization because you simply could not keep your beer-sotten shit-concentration together as the atomic bombs rained in, faster and faster... We congregated at The Lucky Horseshoe every day, for most of the day, and into the night. By this time, Joey Gear had moved out of my place, and my brother Paul had moved up from Orlando, after quitting his job printing checks for the famous John Harland and Co. All of us were serving beer as stand-in barkeeps when there was no one else to tend bar, and the pay was always the same: no pay, but you got to keep all your tips, while infrequently tipping a glass or two of draft. Meanwhile, Bill and I were making the most of our free beer for life ("as long as it was Budweiser"). But Amy had moved back down to Orlando and we were dating long distance; I'd see her when I visited down there, and once in a while she'd make a trip up to Tally for the weekend, and it was getting serious, so I'd call her often from the payphone across the street in the basement of the round Holiday Inn. One afternoon after calling, I'm walking back across the street to my house, and as I step into the crosswalk at Virginia St., a small red convertible sports car with a tall blond football frat boy and his equally tall blond girlfriend, whips by me and the punk yells out "Get a job, hippie!" Relying on a lesson taught to me by my father, I flip him a bird, and he immediately pulls into the Holiday Inn parking lot, jumps out of his car, and starts berating me, "Goddamn you, you sunuvabitch, I'm gonna kick your ass," putting on quite a show of macho monkey-screeching manliness for his admittedly stunning sorority slag, who's now egging him on. Well, I'm already across the street by this time, in the parking lot of my house, when I turn, and shoot him both fingers straight -up, laughing at him. He's screaming, turning apoplectic, and starts coming around the fence that set off the Holiday Inn parking area, when out of the house comes my brother, who's about a head taller than me, and who had heard all the ruckus, and asks me what's going on. The frat boy stops dead in his tracks, seeing now that there's two of us, but he continues yelling vile obscenities and spewing loads of spittle nonetheless. Paul and I just look at each other and nod, knowing what the other is thinking. We turn our backsides to the screaming-meanie and drop our drawers, shaking and wiggling our bare asses in his general direction. The girlfriend is appalled, and somewhat frightened at our brass-assedness, and she grabs him by the arm. He shakes his fist in the air and swears retribution, still yelling back at us as they walk across the parking area and into the back door of the Holiday Inn.

Butt Nekkid

Going into the house I find that my brother had been entertaining our good friend Bob Tirelli, who had recently graduated from law school. Tirelli had not yet made his claim to fame during the Mariel Boatlift of 1980 when, as a young defense lawyer in Miami he was assigned to quickly bone up on immigration law and being the ever-resourceful one, got the appellants to answer the three basic questions of something like persecution, allegiance, and economic status, down to an assembly line that paid him roughly $100 a head, all day, every day (from the Justice Department, besides his regular Miami day-to-day pay) for the roughly six months of the exodus, as quick as they could answer "Sí, sí, no… Sí, sí, no," sign the papers, and walk out the frigging door. He almost made enough to retire before he was thirty. But this was early on, long before that, and Paul and he had been sitting in the house, talking, smoking pot, drinking homebrew, and watching out the window while I had my verbal altercation with the frat boy, before Paul stepped out. While we're recounting the cause and effect of the whole incident, as well as the shock and wondrous awe of the frat boy and his blond at the divestiture of our white and pallid patoots, sure enough, maybe ten minutes later, up into the parking lot of the house pulls a Tallahassee Police Department squad car, and a young, portly policeman gets out, tightening his belt and straightening his hat, before advancing. Quickly, Paul and I walked outside before he got to the porch steps and door and smelled any pot smoke residuals. "Good afternoon, gentlemen," he said, "we received a call that someone here has been exposing themselves. Do you know anything about that?" Paul and I looked at each other and shrugged, but luckily, just inside the house, Tirelli had heard the policeman's enquiry and he came bounding out and off the porch. "Don't answer that!" he said to Paul and me, and, to the cop, "Excuse me, officer, I'm a lawyer representing these young men… I'll answer your questions from here on out." Well, this took the cop completely off-guard, as it had Paul and myself as well. So now, the cop was directing his questions to Tirelli, who quickly parried with the whole "you mean, the ALLEGED incident, don't you, officer?" routine, and "IF THAT WERE THE CASE, who made these allegations?" and "Exactly what, sir, if anything was SUPPOSEDLY exposed?" Well, the cop got so exasperated, he finally just gave up, and said, "If we hear any more about anybody exposing themselves around here in public… y'know this is a busy street right through town, people driving by here all the time…, there's gonna be hell to pay!" He then got into his car and left. We went in the living room and thanked Tirelli for his quick actions, and it was then that he told us that if we had admitted anything, even indirectly (which we probably would have done, not realizing the legal implications), we would have both been sitting in the back of that police car right that minute on our way to the station. It was a damn lucky thing he was there. "Whoo, Hoo! Let's go to The Horseshoe and celebrate a win for the home team! Beers are on us, Tirelli!"

A Religious Diversion

The period between Joey living with me and Paul moving in, which might have been the better part of a year, were some of my favorite bachelor days, and taught me how to live on practically nothing but rice, beer, eggs, and pot. I had even picked up the study of Buddhism when I purchased W.Y. Evans-Wentz's translation of *The Tibetan Book of the Dead* (the *Bardo Thödol*) from the dusty old used-book store run by P.V. LeForge that was nestled between Ken's and the leather shop, above The Lucky Horseshoe on Tennessee Street, and then I continued those studies with everything I could get my hands on (and been doing it ever since, now 33 years later). The basic philosophy and psychology of Buddhism made so much more sense than the superstitious prattle of mainstream Christianity. I'd kept up my studies of the New Testament as well, more with a jaundiced eye toward the historicity of it, and I found it much more interesting and exciting when you left out the hyperbole and silly divinity claims of the later gospels, and especially that rabble-rousing megalomaniac, Paul of Tarsus. The guy was a showman who created his own Messianic church (using J.C. as his godly foil), and developed rules and dogma as he made them up. He was always challenging and back-stabbing the original surviving apostles, most notably James and Peter, because he couldn't make the claim to have ever really set eyes on Jesus, except in his own epileptic seizure-visions and auditory hallucinations. Poor Jesus, if he could see what Paul started and what has been made out of his very personal mission and the Church that has been created over the last two thousand years, not to mention what that Church has been partner to in those two millennia, as well as the absurd belief systems it has created, well, he'd be spinning in his grave. Wherever the hell that is. I hold to the theory, espoused by Dr. Hugh Schonfield, a well-respected scholar of first-century Jewish–Christianity history and development, that Jesus did not die on the cross, but rather, was drugged and carried to the tomb by confederates of Joseph of Arimethea, including "the beloved disciple," sometimes referred to as John (of which there were many), who was present at the crucifixion, unlike the other disciples, and to whom Jesus relegated the care of his mother. This was probably the same mysterious young man who had his garments snatched at the arrest in the Garden of Gethsemane and ran off naked, probably the same angelic (i.e., peaceful, undisturbed, and informed) presence the women encountered when they came to anoint the body and the stone was rolled away, with just this individual sitting there in white linen (the habit of an Essene) saying, "If you're looking for Jesus, he's gone. Tell his disciples he'll see them in Galilee." This was also probably the same young rich fellow who much earlier is quoted as having asked how to get to the kingdom of heaven and was admonished to sell all that he had and follow, whereas he was greatly disturbed by this (probably thinking there must be another way to use his resources), and when he walks off, thinking about it, Jesus comments that "it's easier for a camel to pass through the eye of a needle than a rich man to get to heaven." (In point of fact, one of the smaller gates to enter Jerusalem was for foot traffic only, and was called "The Eye of the Needle." Difficult for a camel? Yes. Impossible? No.) This young man continued to follow Jesus nonetheless, and probably provided the ass Jesus rode in on, and the Upper Room where the Last Supper took place and where the apostles hid out for forty days after the trial and crucifixion. Regarding the Upper Room, the events there are the best evidence that Jesus didn't die on the cross, because when he came to visit shortly after the supposed "resurrection" (and how do you surreptitiously enter a locked room? You knock, whisper your name, and they open the door, let you in, and lock it behind you), the first thing Jesus says to the frightened and fugitive apostles is that he's hungry, do they have anything to eat? They feed him some leftover fish, before they start falling all over each other to get back in his good graces, marveling over his wounds and the fact that he's not dead (of which he repeatedly assures them that he is not). Resurrected spiritual beings, especially divine ones at that, care little for the sustenance of a couple of leftover fishsticks. Go ask Osiris.

School's In, Forever

Back to Tallahassee, and speaking of age differences, Amy and I were getting serious, and the travels between O-ville and Tally were getting more and more numerous. I'd finally gotten started back to school in the winter of 1980, now 28 years old, and generally one of the oldest students in whatever class I was in. But now I was motivated. There was something like a two-week delay between when I received my student loans and grant money, and when tuition had to be paid after classes had started. I quickly learned to parlay the money into buying up a pound or two of marijuana, then dividing the same into individual strictly-weighed three-quarter-ounce baggies, and then hitting the streets, the Pastime, the Lucky Horseshoe, wherever, and if I played my cards right, didn't make any mistakes, and didn't dip into the stock too much, I could double my money, then pay tuition, buy books, and still have enough left over to carry me for three months into the semester. That first term I was searching for a major and ended up taking an Intro to Anthropology course (which would change my life), a Narrative Techniques writing course, the requisite Western Civilization course, and a World Religions course. The writing and religion courses were a snap, based on my private-school upbringing and my already-blossoming interest in comparative religions. The Anthroplogy course was taught by a teaching assistant, a graduate student by the name of Fred Gaske. He was very, very good, being both thorough and enthusiastic. He always came in wearing a tie, which was impressive, and because we were nearly the same age, and I was never afraid to ask questions, we often ended up having impromptu "discussions" during class time, always on-topic, but nevertheless more in-depth than he was probably prepared for in an Intro class. But he was patient, concise, and by his demeanor, authoritative. We became good friends later on, even though I couldn't do better than to squeeze a "B" out of him for that class, partly based on the term paper where I discussed the cultural use of hallucinogenics, but laid out some of my personal theories, which of course, couldn't be referenced elsewhere—in an Intro course you're not expected to expound, you're expected to listen and pick up the basics. But I had gotten the basics, and my eventual decision to choose a major in Anthropology (and thus set my life's trajectory) was in large part due to Fred's influence, by far.

I loved studying these various subjects, but I learned very quickly that, if you studied while stoned, it didn't help very much if you took the test while you were straight; since you were in a totally different frame of mind. So, I could study stoned, and then have to get stoned for the test, or I could study straight and then take the test straight. I eventually opted for the study straight / test straight mode; it was easier than having to get stoned for a test at 8 or 9 a.m., and it conserved pot, which I could always smoke recreationally after the tests. Years later, when I got into graduate school, I discovered that being stoned was actually an effective stimulant to class, since we generally sat around discussing wild ideas that sprang up from whatever readings we were currently engaged in. More than once we primed ourselves for that night's class by getting stoned beforehand, sometimes with the professor! But right now I had to get more hours under my belt, so as to hurry up and get my Bachelor's. I took Oceanography (which I loved), and International Politics, the latter taught by a wheelchair-bound Vietnam veteran who was erudite in the subject (probably the only time I've ever used that word in my life, but it seems more appropriate, at least for him, who carried it with a bit of nobility, than the synonyms of learned, scholarly, knowledgeable, etc.). Sure, he had the usual tragic Vietnam psycho-scars, but he also had a very funny, biting, and ironic sense of humor, most of which was lost on the kids just out of high school, but which he noticed I picked up on throughout every day's lecture. My favorite thing about him was that he made us choose for a term-paper topic some piece of international history that we admittedly knew little or nothing about, do our research, and write it up. I chose the Berlin Airlift. Didn't know shit about it. Knew it was a big deal at the time. Had no idea how close it came to causing World War III. Hell of an operation. Only the United States could have pulled it off, and only the Russians would have made them do it. I may not be an expert on it, but at least now I sure as heck know what it was all about, how it started, what caused it, and how it was resolved. But more than anything, it taught me how to do research. Had a couple of beers with him later on, but he tried to stay rather aloof from his students, and that seemed appropriate as well.

Burrowed Away

I also took a playwriting course called Drama Workshop, from the famous Janet Burroway. At this time, Florida State was one of the premier English-major schools in the country for writing, literature, poetry, you name it. Burroway already had a couple of books under her belt, and was well-known, so I felt privileged to be in her class. She was recently divorced, in her late thirties or early forties, and dripping with excess sexuality. She was dating some foreign-looking Lothario at least ten years her junior, but no matter, she was fascinating to watch, listen to, and smell as she walked by. The other students were by and large diehard English majors and had been whipping that racehorse for years on their way to getting their degrees. I was a novice and knew very little about drama, which is a whole different animal when it comes to literature. But she was relatively encouraging, and we would write our scenes, with stage directions, etc. and we'd use the class to act them out, with the writer acting as the director, and Burroway jumping in as she saw fit to criticize, suggest line changes, or applaud. Although I was not too bad as an actor, reading lines and emoting, at least good enough so that they'd choose me again and again to read leading parts, when it came to the writing, I was awful. I couldn't build the suspense; my dialogue was stilted; when I tried to be funny, it came off sadly, or not at all. My play was based on the fishing trip out of New Smyrna (that's where "Call Me Fishmeal" comes from), but, other than getting the scenery right (a cutaway view of the deck with just the farther, starboard, three-foot-high gunwale blocking the stage rear portion, where people and fish could fall overboard, water splashing up and onto the deck, no icebox, and the captain's chair stage left, with the hidden cabin entrances below), I just couldn't make it work. At the end of the term, I was so embarrassed, that I ended up taking an "Incomplete." It took a year for me to finally finish it and replace the "I" on my gradesheet; luckily, she remembered me and replaced it with a "B," which surprised me no end, but was apparently based on my class participation as opposed to my dramatic writing talents. I did, however, learn to watch stage productions from a different perspective, and I can truthfully say that I even enjoy reading a good play (stage directions and all) now and then, *Night of the Iguana* and *The Iceman Cometh* being two of my favorites.

After a brief fling with considering a major in Biology (which became my minor), I went back to taking classes in the Anthropology Department with a vengeance. I wanted to formally declare it as my major, and this involved first, discussing your intentions and motives with your academic advisor in the department, and then getting the required form signed by the Chairman. Well, I was assigned an academic advisor by the name of Professor Rowland, so I went to see him. But his office was empty. I asked when I could make an appointment to see him and was told that they couldn't say. Apparently, a few days earlier, he had fallen asleep in his office, and leaning back to stretch out, his chair rolled out from under him and he fell against the wall and broke his neck, although it didn't kill him. Well, that's interesting, I thought, and I made it a point to go back to his office one more time to look at the chair and note the ding and scratches in the wall. What would I like to do? I'd like to see the Chairman about declaring a major in Anthropology. No problem, have a seat. The chairman's office door was right there, not ten feet away. The secretary walked in and about five minutes later he buzzed and she told me to go on in. The Chairman was Dr. Edwin Cook, a tall gregarious, gray-haired scholar who specialized in the ethnographic study of tribes in Papua New Guinea. He'd been hired out of the prestigious University of Chicago Anthropology Department on high recommendations, specifically to be Chairman of the Anthropology Department at FSU. Later, Florida State found out that those high recommendations were in large part so that Chicago could cut themselves loose of this brilliant, yet problematic, free-thinking and outspoken professor. I walked in, with my long hair in a ponytail, my then-red beard, dressed in jeans and red t-shirt (with a flying Mighty Mouse—not Mickey, mind you— emblazoned on it), and he asked me to have a seat. I had to sit up straight because his desk was piled so high with papers and books that I had to stretch to look over them to talk with him. I explained about wanting to major in Anthropology, that I had learned about my academic advisor's mishap, so I'd need some counseling, and I wondered if he would consider letting me into the department. He listened intently, and then his phone rang. I watched as he groped around, shuffling papers, looking for his phone as it continued to ring, something I'd up til then only seen in the movies or on a situation comedy. He took the call, hung up, and started right in, handing me a little folder. "First of all, you don't need an academic advisor, here's the list of required courses and your electives… take as many as you need to get the degree. We'll be happy to let you in the department, just keep up your grades. Give the secretary your information and I'll send in the form this afternoon." "Why thanks," I said, this was going to be easier than I thought. Then I remembered something, "But I'm supposed to have my Academic Advisor fill out the counseling form and sign it… should I get another advisor?" "Naww," he said, "just fill it out yourself." "But what about signing it?" "You sign it," he said. And that's what I did for the rest of my academic career, never getting questioned about it, not even once. Ed Cook and I became very close friends over the next several years.

In the Fall of 1980 I was now in the Anthropology Department and took three classes that would change my life. One was Introduction to Archaeology. It was the last class taught at Florida State by Kathy Deagan, who, although she was already well known for her digs at St. Augustine, has since become famous as the preeminent Spanish Colonial-period archaeologist in the Southeast United States. I thought her class would be a snap; hell, it was an introductory course, how bad could it be? Once I looked at the book, I said to myself, well, this looks just like doing carpentry, only you're going down instead of going up; same basic tools: a level, strings, shovel, and a trowel instead of a hammer. No problem. And that's how I went into it, with my head up my ass. Deagan was tough, and she covered a lot of territory, and she covered it fast. I hadn't taken into consideration all the detailed survey techniques, remote-sensing systems and dating analyses, artifact identification, interpretation, and technical writing. In effect, I didn't take it serious enough, and when it all came down, I ended up with a "D" in Intro to Archaeology. How embarrassing! First of all, you can't have a "D" in your major coursework, so I was going to have to take it over again. And second, although I didn't know it at the time, I was going to spend thirty-some years of my life as a professional archaeologist.

I took another class in Underwater Archaeology however, where I was so fascinated that I excelled. Admittedly, it wasn't as difficult as Deagan's, since it was composed mostly of a set of readings and grasping concepts. It was taught by a thin, gray-haired, and softspoken fellow in his late forties with a slight paunch, no ass, and a big curly-cue handlebar moustache. This was George Fischer, who was one of the group of three or four senior archaeologists at the National Park Service's Southeast Archeological Center, a central station of the Park Service that catered to the archaeological needs of the national parks in the Southeastern United States and which had been moved from Ocmulgee National Park in Georgia in the late 60s. George had come directly from Washington though, where it was suggested the transfer was to break up the troublesome team of George and his buddy Zorro Bradley. How could the Park Service separate these two as far from each other as possible? So, they sent George to Florida, and Zorro to Alaska. George was known unofficially as "the Father of Underwater Archaeology in the National Park Service," as a result of some early underwater explorations at Montezuma Well out west, and he had also been one of the founders of the national Advisory Council on Underwater Archaeology, which sponsored the annual Conference on Underwater Archaeology.

We had to do readings from Keith Muckelroy's *Maritime Archaeology*, Mendel Peterson's *History Beneath the Sea*, and some generic UNESCO book on Underwater Archaeology. All these were supplemented by handouts of various other articles, and the entertaining lectures by Fischer. The lectures were entertaining because George would be smoking the whole time (you could do that back then in the classrooms, offices, lounges, restaurants, …everywhere, even students), dropping matches and ashes, and he couldn't let a joke he'd heard that day go by without repeating it, no matter how dirty, and he cursed a lot. More often than not, however, he would stop in the middle of a lecture to recount some story, adventure, prank, or practical joke that he had either initiated or witnessed during his Park Service career. For instance, I remember him telling us about the time he met Mel Fisher, the famous treasure hunter. Because they had the same last name, with George's spelled with a "c," they were often confused on the programs, or by fans who got them mixed up. But philosophically, they were leagues apart, as well as being at ethical loggerheads, with George proselytizing for strict preservation and scientific research on historic shipwrecks, while Mel was out for the gold and made no bones about it. One night at one of the early conferences, the professional archaeologists are in the top-floor hotel penthouse bar, having drinks, George among them, discussing the day's seminars, et al, when in the door walks Mel Fisher, a big grin on his face, and says "Hey!" The archaeologists, sitting at the bar, get quiet and look up at him as he reaches into the breast pocket of his jacket, and pulls out a larger-than-a-hockeypuck disc of pure gold. "You guys can talk all you want about science and preservation," he declared, "but I'll bet you don't get to see many of these," and he slid it down the slick bar to dazzle the professionals. Now these conferences are always held in January, and this particular one was somewhere up north, Chicago, or Cincinnati, I'm not sure, but it was snowing outside. He had slung it with just a bit too much pompous bravado, the bar was wet, and that large and heavy gold disc flew down and off the end of the bar, and punched a neat little hole in the safety glass before it flew out into the darkness beyond and ten floors below. "Oh shit!" he yelled, and immediately turned and ran out the door. Maybe a half an hour later, after digging through the snow drifts outside the front of the hotel, he came back up into the bar in disarray, wet and sweating, with his gold disc in hand, to the resounding laughter of the drinkers, and the warm glow of his own embarrassment. And that was just one example of George's many stories that made the class so entertaining.

Academic Diving

The last course I took that term that changed my life forever, was one put on by the Academic Diving Program (ADP) of Florida State called Diving to Research I (because it was a two-semester course and therefore, there was going to be a D to R II in the fall). The instructor was young and blond, somewhat chunky in his mid-thirties, with sharp Nordic/Irish features, effervescently enthusiastic, a post-graduate biology student/teacher named Gregg Stanton. He always wore a blond beard that made him look Amish. But Gregg's boyish looks and bright outlook were somewhat of a screen for a hard-driving, detail-oriented, professional diving instructor. As a scientist with a capital "S" he always insisted to the point of satisfaction that the data hadn't been tampered with, that it was clean and clear. You know, I was slow to realize until later a lot of what he was trying to show us all along. A good man, a great scientist. I owe a lot to Mr. Stanton; he really was one of the best—sometimes damnably frustrating when you'd bring him a problem, and even if he could see the solution, he'd make you figure it out for yourself (that's how I became adept at what is known as "logistics"). His teaching assistant at the time was Rich Johnson, a former Vietnam war vet who was taking graduate Interdisciplinary Studies, and who I'd see later in the Anthropology Department and the Park Service, working with George; though he did, however, carry a remnant of the aura of that unfortunate conflict with him sometimes. Not bad; good. Rich was tall, also blond, and slightly balding, and just like Gregg, bounding with enthusiasm and encouragement so that the two of them really taught us how we could operate far beyond our perceived boundaries. The first part of the course was to get us all up to snuff on the standard (and then intricate) principles of diving with SCUBA, with an emphasis on safety, and an eye to the application of doing scientific research underwater. In fact, the course became part of a larger program called Scientific Diving Techniques. We had people from all over campus: biologists, psychologists, archaeologists, sports medicine nuts, criminology majors, geology, you name it, although generally from the sciences as opposed to the arts. I had gotten certified to dive as a sixteenth birthday present way back in1968, but admittedly had not done any diving in the twelve years since then, other than free-diving with fins and snorkel. But I could still swim like a fish, and I took to the coursework like one as well. This was a "practical" class, unlike anything I'd ever experienced before; there were very few readings, but the lectures were detailed and had just about everything to do with, if not life and death, then getting the job done, collecting the data, and getting everybody home safe and sound. As far as life and death however, we trained in cardiopulmonary resuscitation, emergency evacuations, Coast Guard communication protocols, open-wound and trauma treatment (First Aid), and recognizing the symptoms of covert decompression sickness (and the difference, as opposed to the overt "bends"), fatigue, heat stroke, dehydration, nitrogen narcosis, and even the detection and treatment of diabetes-induced events. There was an explicit policy that if you didn't want to dive a particular day, or a particular dive, for any reason, you didn't have to, no questions asked, and other times the safety officer for the dive might have someone sit a dive out as a precautionary measure, again, with no repercussions whatsoever. We learned to keep explicit records: logs of dives with time in, time out, depth, air pressure in, air pressure out, who was present (and what were their duties), the mission, location, etc. and we were required to make some sort of conclusionary statement, in our own words, of how the whole operation went, with any observations and recommendations. THEN, we would have a sit-down meeting, or "debriefing," face-to face, while events and short-term memories were still fresh, and usually while we were still dripping wet in the cabin of the FSU Marine Lab boat, the R.V. *Tersiops* (that's Research Vessel "Dolphin," before they re-named her—always a bad idea—the "Lady Seminole"). When it came to getting the job done, this sometimes meant going back in for another dive when you were tired (not too tired), because someone else couldn't, wouldn't, or somebody else had decided they shouldn't; as well as keeping watches during the night; staying down that one minute more even though you'd been warned about getting chewed out if you went below 500 psi. But if you got the job done in that last minute, it was worth getting chewed out, because, by God, you had gotten the data, and finished the job.

Dolphinity

My very first project with Academic Diving was trying to locate an artificial reef made of tires off the Ochlockonee River Shoals. What had started out years earlier as an experiment as a fish attractor was a half-ass reef made out of tires that had been wired together, maybe four or five at a time, and then dropped overboard to settle on the bottom, both in a pile and over an area of maybe a hundred yards. We knew where they were, since they were marked on the local nautical charts, sitting in maybe twenty-five feet of water. The theory was that these tires, with their interior concavities, would attract a lot of small fish, and then larger ones would begin to congregate as well, and the fishing would improve considerably. But, it was later discovered that between intermittent flooding of the river, and subsequent storm surges, the tires had gotten overly scattered, sometimes getting turned up on edge and rolling along the bottom for miles.

Also, by this time, now 1980, the whole concept of using tires for artificial reefs was recognized as environmentally unsound, so our job was to go out and find the scattered tire reef and mark its extent, so that other divers (the local dive clubs) could come out and retrieve them to be hauled off to the dump later. Being the youngest, a mere student, and considering that I needed more "experience" Gregg and Rich dropped me off the back of Gregg's small runabout, and they began towing me back and forth across the area known as the Ochlockonee Shoals. I had a ski rope with a flat board on the end that I could use as a dive plane to either go deeper or veer side to side. They were pulling a little too fast for my tastes, making it not only harder to hang on, but I couldn't turn my head to see to either side to scan the perimeter, or my mask would get pulled off. And, as everyone knows, the water coming out of the Ochlockonee is like tea, with all the tannin in solution, but I was lucky as here it mixed with the Gulf and cleared somewhat and I could see maybe fifty feet ahead and down along the bottom. I'm also wearing a set of double-steel 72 cu.ft. tanks, the standard in those days for all our ADP diving, before aluminum tanks became all the rage. So I was good for an hour at least. As I'm flying along, maybe twelve feet above the bottom, which I can see clearly for fifty feet ahead in an iced-tea henna-colored tint, I thought I saw something briefly in my peripheral vision ten feet over my shoulder. I tied to turn but my mask quickly filled with water from the sideways pull. I cleared it quickly and concentrated on the bottom ahead. A minute later, I spot a shape now over my left shoulder. I dive down to near the bottom and notice two large shadows from above following me. Then the line goes slack (???). I slowly rise up from the bottom, looking around in all directions, but now see nothing. When I get to the surface, I yell to the boat, "What's going on?" Rich yells back, "If you see some big shapes following you, don't worry, it's just a couple of dolphins!" "Great!" I yelled back "Hey could you ease off the throttle a little bit?" I went back down and grabbed the tow rope and diving plane just as it grew taut. As we started to move, the dolphins came back out of the dark brown gloom and began swimming to either side and in front of me, where I could see them clearly, back and forth, and though I still kept an eye out for the damn tires (which we found eventually later that day, when Rich was being towed), I felt much better having them for company. Especially when I thought about it later that day, with a quick shudder, how being towed behind a boat like that, legs dangling behind, might present itself as a nice piece of quick snatch-bait for some roaming tiger or bull shark, both of which are notorious for frequenting river mouths that have limited visibility and biting first, only swallowing later.

It was a damn tough course, lectures two evenings a week, Tuesday and Thursday, 7 to 9 p.m., and often running to 10. Then we had our field exercises all day Saturday, starting at 7 a.m., usually driving down to the FSU Marine Lab, a 45-minute drive each way, loading the boat, and heading out into the Gulf, sometimes not getting home until 9 that evening. Looking back, maybe it wasn't so surprising getting a "D" that term in Intro to Archaeology, since I got an "A" in all my other courses. I even took Elementary Spanish that term to start the whole three-term-required language requirement. The whole point of re-hashing this back-to-school odyssey is to point out that a *bardo*, a change of life, or even a change of focus, can occur in a moment, a day, a semester (they're happening all the time), and when it does, and it takes, you are now on a completely different path than the one you had been trodding even a moment earlier, and there's no telling where it might lead eventually. Sounds rather trite and schmaltzy, but it's true. Life is not like a box of chocolates, it's more like a branching tree, or rather, it's more like choosing branching paths in the midst of an otherwise overgrown (and dangerous) jungle, at night, in the moonlight (wearing nothing but a loincloth, like Tarzan), without a knife, naked and afraid.

Respiration vs. Inspiration

It was on one of those "shakeout" cruises we had while working out our routines, that I ever actually ran out of air (at eighty feet!). We went out on the M.V. *Wolf*, a boat that somehow Stanton had squeezed out of the DEA, a lobster boat that had been apprehended smuggling dope, and now belonged to FSU by right of sovereignty, and the good graces of the Feds. Great boat, lots of room, but a bit of a juggernaut, and the thing was even less sea-worthy after Greg had a diving platform, winch, and derrick installed on the back deck. It was a tub, to put it mildly. But, short, squat, and round-bottomed as she was, she was a champ, a little diesel tug of a boat that carried us to hell and back, and in the meantime, when anchored, wiggled like an exotic dancer. The mission that day was to get a core sample from the bottom. Sounds easy, doesn't it? There had been reports that off the coast, I don't know, some twelve miles off of Cape San Blas, a sport diver had seen a grove of large cypress stumps sticking out of the seafloor for a mile or so. Well, the only way this could occur, according to our geological and botanical experts were if, at some point in the remote past, the sea rose in an extraordinarily fast manner, like days, weeks, months, or a couple of years, not even a decade or centuries. To inundate still-living large cypress would have entailed either a rapid rise in the sea near the shore, or an even more rapid deflation of the shore itself, both of which would be large and unusual seismic events, especially for that part of the Gulf Coast. We were also hoping to get a piece of wood that could be carbon-dated to give us an idea of when this event may have occurred. Once we got out there to the position given though, the depth sounder gave no indication of anything sticking up off the bottom. Since the report was many months old, and they'd never been reported by anyone before, there was a good chance that this was some transient exposure of these cypress stumps, and they may have been covered over again by the shifting seabottom sands.

They sent me over the side with a tall, statuesque beautiful body-builder blonde, her name escapes me right now, and being the male, I carried the "heavy bag" with the 15 lb. sledgehammer, rebar stakes , and PVC pipe and caps. She carried nothing but a marker buoy. An eighty-foot dive. After swimming maybe fifty yards off the stern of the R.V. *Wolf* onto a marked buoy line, we dropped the air in our BCs, (or "buoyancy compensators" a.k.a. "life vests attached to your SCUBA tank to either add air from your tank so you'd rise, or drop air so you'd sink," but draining your air tank when used nonetheless), and we dropped slowly down to the bottom, holding hands (for safety's sake) in what can only be best described as an ocean of pea-green soup diluted by half with sea-water. After swimming to the drop-site, carrying all the heavy equipment, and then making the descent to eighty feet, once we dropped onto the sand bottom with a soft "bump" (with nothing but that goddamn turquoise-green as far as you could see, and then only maybe fifteen feet in all directions at that before your eyes just gave up), it was time to check and compare our gauges. Shit! Where we both probably started off roughly the same, at 2100 or 2200 psi, she was showing 1800, whereas I was sitting at 1500; and we hadn't even gotten the fuckin' job started yet! I'd already lost a quarter of my air just getting there. She'd only lost 15%. I handed her the 2"-diameter PVC tube, sharpened at one end , one-meter long, showed her where to stick it, and let all the remaining air out of my BC as I stood flat-footed on the sea bottom. I've got to give her credit, she held that PVC pipe, steadily and fearlessly, and I raised that sledge over my head and we began to hammer it in. Five minutes of hammering, gaining maybe an inch a blow (hey! try it on land, instead of 80 feet below the ocean surface!) and the meter-mark was finally reached. Now we just had to cap it, pull it out, cap the bottom, and get it to the surface. Got to check the gauges again (just for safety's sake). Shit! After all the hammering, I was down to 500 psi. I pop my "J" valve, which allows you access to that last 500 lbs. She was sitting at 750. I reached down, grabbed a hold of the PVC tube, now capped, and gave it a pull... not a budge. I tried twisting it... nothing. I motioned for her to pack up the

206

dive bag and get ready to go. Then I hunched over and pulled with everything I had... it wasn't coming. Goddamn it! We were going to have to leave it. The next thing I know, she wraps her legs around my hands, and squeezes them tightly into her noticeably warm crotch with her thighs, looks across at me, mask-to-mask not eight inches apart, and we both pull... I was adrenaline-inspired... it starts to move, and then, ah, comes sliding smoothly out of the sandy bottom. We cap the end of the tube (now ten pounds heavier since it's filled with sand), pick up the dive bag, hammer, and other crap, look around, and "zzzzpppp" I pull my last breath out of the tank. I signal to go up, and we begin our ascent. At eighty feet, considering how hard I'd been working, if we went up too fast, there was a good chance of a decompression incident ("the bends"). I knew that the fastest we could ascend was one foot per second, and even though we hadn't been down that long, considering the depth, we probably should have had a planned decompression stop, just for safety's sake. All this was going through my head as I slowly exhaled, ever so slowly letting the bubbles just burble out while that last breath of air in my lungs expanded as we rose, because I needed to hold on to that air for a minute twenty. I closed my eyes, went meditative, and concentrated on going up slowly. About halfway, she tapped me and I opened my eyes, and she signaled to me if I wanted to buddy-breathe off of her regulator (this was before we dove with extra 'octopus' regulators, which is now common practice). I signaled "no, I was okay, let's just keep on ascending." It was nice of her to offer, and actually the right thing to do, but I didn't feel we had reached any real emergency status yet, and sure didn't want to initiate one with us fumbling around, pulling our regulators out of our mouth, especially with all the equipment we were carrying, and besides, now we were in reach of the surface. As we broke clear, I was happy to see that the boat had let a retrieval line trail out behind with a float on it. Seas had picked up, maybe three to four feet, so they were watching out for us. They let out some more line, and when it reached us, both of us exhausted, I quickly tied the dive bags to the line, told her to grab it too, so they could pull her in, and rolled over on my back, cradling the PVC pipe (the data!), took a few large breaths of free life-enhancing ocean-enriched air, and kicked my way back to the boat. We found out a couple of weeks later, after it had undergone analysis in the geology department, that they couldn't tell a damn thing from it, it was all just sand to them. A tube of sand.

Fort Frederica

Later that fall, in the last Academic Diving "class project" of the semester, we were all going to Fort Frederica on St. Simons Island, one of the offshore barrier islands along the southern Atlantic Coast of Georgia. Fort Frederica was one of the first of the English coastal forts, built in the early 1700s under the direction of James Oglethorpe himself, during that period when the English were asserting themselves into the New World, pushing down from South Carolina toward Spanish La Florida, when the Spanish hegemony was beginning to wane. The fort was really the center of a small palisaded town along the banks of the Frederica River and surrounded by salt marsh. A lot of the fort had eroded into the river, and although there had been extensive archaeological excavations in the late 1940s, the eroded and now-submerged portions had yet to be mapped. That was our mission. It was mid-November and the days were okay, but the mornings and nights were cold. We got there on a Friday afternoon, looked the place over, and developed a quick game plan on how to approach this thing the next day. This was a National Park Service-sponsored (i.e., paid for) project and the resulting information was for park planning and interpretive use. The Magazine and a portion of the Barracks were just about all of the original fort still in evidence, but we knew the fort walls had surrounded everything and the remnants of some of them, leading up to the water's edge could still be discerned at ground level. The fort had been constructed of tabby, which is a mixture comprised of one-third burnt oyster shell (which yields "quick lime," the binding agent), one-third sand, and one-third water (preferably fresh), then a bunch of whole oyster shells are thrown in to give it some filler and provide an aggregate to bind to. The stuff had lasted two hundred and fifty years, and one of the reasons so little of the fort and walls were left was because it was soft enough you could saw up blocks of it with a long two-man handsaw and cart it off to use elsewhere, which is what the later island residents did. Tabby is really a wonderful building product except for two things: the only place you'll find a big pile of empty oyster (or clam) shells on land is usually in large "Indian mounds" (also called "middens," which is what they are, large garbage dumps), which therefore, are "mined" to be burned in makeshift lime kilns, thus destroying their archaeological significance; and the second problem is that, because of the shell edges, they are sharp and can cut you very easily, especially underwater, after your hands have gone numb from the cold and then gotten swollen up and wrinkled from the extended submersion. First of all, we had to determine the location of the submerged walls, the fort's breastworks, which we did by just swimming around in the tidal creek until we bumped into them, and then putting buoys on the wall corners. While the professional guys were measuring the height, thickness, and width of the walls and mapping them in, the rest of us volunteers were told to go out into the creek and conduct "circle sweeps," where we dropped a weight with a line attached and then swam in ever-widening circles along the bottom looking for loose objects (cannons, swords, bottles, cannonballs, just about anything, though we found just about nothing) until we either ran out of line or bumped into one of the adjacent submerged walls. This was all blackwater diving, zero-visibility, as we kicked up the black sediments and tidal muck. It was so bad that it was better to keep your eyes closed; if you tried to see, all that was in front of your mask was a brown-black swirling that would get you disoriented quickly. With your eyes closed, you knew which way was up from your bubbles, and by feeling your way along the bottom, one hand on the line, so that you concentrated on what you felt, what was real, not what you *thought* you saw. As we swam around feeling around in the mud with our bare hands, eels, catfish, and other loathsome creatures slithered out of the way, and we'd come across natural well-fastened oyster beds, sharp enough not only to cut your hands, but slice through your neoprene wetsuit as well when your legs and arms brushed across them. Then there were clouds of mosquitoes. They were so bad that when you came to the surface, where you would normally switch over from your regulator to your snorkel in one quick move so that you could conserve the air in your tank, the mosquitoes were so bad that we were choking on them sucking them down our snorkels, so we'd switch back and breathe off of our regulators, the hell with saving air.

When we finally finished for the day, we were cold, cut up, hungry, thirsty, and exhausted. And as we dried off and changed into our regular clothes, before we could get to the repellent, we became mosquito bloody-marys-on-the-hoof and they were all lined up three-deep at the bar, so that by the time you were dressed and finally got sprayed, the welts were welts on top of welts. We sat in shivering misery waiting for George, who had left in the van a couple of hours before to supposedly go get some (hopefully) hot food and drinks. When he finally drove up, he had a case of cold coke, and a large fruit bowl. (A fucking fruit bowl!) We drank our cokes, packed up our gear, and got ready to go. As I was picking up trash and empty cans, I picked up a can of Sprite that was nearly full that George had set down at the base of a tree. As I began to pour out the contents, I noticed the pungent odor of Crown Royal. There was very little Sprite, if any, in the goddamn can. That's where he'd been… sitting in some local bar while we were floundering in the mud, with the mosquitoes in our throats and the oysters shredding us to ribbons. I was pissed and only later learned that this was not only the usual turn of events on these projects, but was regretfully expected. Later, after a warm dinner at some local chicken house, with a few beers to wash it down, the cuts drying up, and the welts merely red dots across our faces, all was eventually forgiven. Nonetheless, this routine was to become a recurring problem over the years, although it allowed us up-and-comers to practice a lot of autonomy and to make decisions on the fly to keep a lot of the later projects afloat. It was a hyper-speed method of education on the run. Think of the old days where pilots learned to fly by the seat of their pants. I came to love and admire George, and I learned a lot from him, but a lot of the other, important, stuff I learned was purely self-directed study and application, and a lot of that was the result of the push-and-shove of Greg Stanton and Rich Johnson. Funny, it was a wonderfully synergetic combination, George, Gregg, and Rich, and later, joined by Russ Skowronek, Ken Wild, and myself, that yielded an interesting functional unit greater than the sum of its parts. This was when the Program in Underwater Archaeology really began at Florida State University.

Home Brewers

So now I was back in school, older than most of the regular students (28) and making progress towards a degree. Paul and I had started making beer under the tutelage of the local brewmeister, an old hippie named Billy Chuck, who was president of the local beer-making club and sponsored great get-togethers at his house where we lined up dozens of our various concoctions in those small 3-gallon cylindrical soft-drink Coca-Cola dispensers, all hooked in-line to a large CO_2 gas line that drove the whole system. The house was equipped with a huge cargo net extended between the broad limbs of a giant live oak in his back yard, that oftentimes after one of these homebrew bacchanals would be strung the next day with what appeared to be a nest of limp chimp bodies hanging in the morning sun. He also worked at the local Food Co-op, and pointed out that as a student I was eligible for food stamps, and, although you couldn't buy beer with the stamps, besides your regular meat and potatoes, the ingredients for *making* beer (barley, hops, dextrose, even the yeast) were all food products and could be legally purchased on the government dole. Soon we had cabinets full of capped bottles of homebrew and after only a few initially minor explosive events when were experimenting with various recipes, the house became a regular stopover for friends driving by. Soon we had them making beer as well to reciprocate, and whereas I was experimenting with such things as cinnamon beer (for the holidays), our good Italian lawyer buddy Tirelli was exploring such seemingly forbidden territories as garlic beer and onion beer, all of which sounded horrible, until he invited us over to his place for a spaghetti-and-sausage dinner that revealed the combination as deliciously exquisite. Then winter dropped on us like an overweight Jack Frost wrestler coming off the top ring ropes. We woke up one morning to find that a huge ball of ice had edged itself out of the pipes during the night, and there, hanging on, and encased in it was the kitchen sink spigot. I fired up the gas heater in the living room, and we huddled around wondering what to do next. As we sat huddled under blankets, smoking a joint and getting stoned, waiting for the living room to warm up, in about ten minutes there was a loud shotgun-like blast and the sound of a firehose letting loose in the kitchen. The huge ball of ice had thawed enough that the water pressure behind it blew it across the floor, and now there was an arcing torrent of water gushing straight out from the wall. I ran up facing it, as it pushed against me, drenching me from head to toe like a situation comedy or an episode of *I Love Lucy*, while I fumbled around to discover that the spigot was gone with the ball of ice and there was no way to shut off the gusher. Finally I just pushed a rag up against it and held it at bay as it sprayed out from behind my hand. Paul was standing behind me and I told him to hold the rag while I went outside to find the shut-off valve. He must have held it for ten minutes as I finally found the valve but then had to find a wrench with which to turn it off. By the time we got the water cut off, it was two inches deep in the house, and both of us were completely soaked. Luckily, the gas heater continued to work, because it was still at or below freezing outside. We swept out the water as best we could, used every towel in the house to mop it up, sat down on the couch in the now-heated living room after changing clothes, popped open a cold homebrew and had a good laugh. Tallahassee was always a surprise.

Like a Horse and Carriage

Well, as the winter progressed, the pipes got fixed, and I was getting ready to start a new semester. But we wouldn't be diving during the Winter Semester and the next Diving to Research Class wasn't until Spring. And I was missing Amy something terrible. We had gotten close ever since the previous summer when I had fallen in love and lust with her after watching her swim in the crystal-clear water at Wakulla Springs in her see-through white terry cloth bikini. And we'd carried out a lot of long-distance driving dating, and many long-distance phone calls to boot. Since we were living in separate towns 250 miles apart, and I'd just seen her over Christmas, I knew that if I didn't make a move soon I'd lose her. So one night in mid-January I'm expressing all this to my brother as we sat over a couple of beers, and I told him that I was thinking of asking Amy if she'd marry me. He asked me, "So what's stopping you?" Well, I just hadn't felt the right time had happened yet. "When's that gonna be?" he asked again. Well, I don't know. "How about right now?" he said. What!? He reached into his pocket and pulled out a dime, and pushed it across the table to me, saying "There's a phone right over there." This was in the time when pay phones hung on every wall in every establishment, as well as on every pole down the street, and swear to God, you could make a phone call for a dime and talk all day, local of course. Not a long-distance call, though, for which I had to change out a couple of dollars for a pocketful of quarters on my own, but the dime was a nice challenging gesture. I called her up, and luckily she was home (I think it was a Friday night), and we talked briefly before I told her that I'd been thinking about things and wondered if she'd consider us getting married. Yes, she'd consider it... and that was it. Now, the stories get pretty diverse here. I did call my parents later that evening and told them that I'd asked Amy to marry me, and apparently Mom called Amy to verify it and let her know how happy she was. Amy's Mom and sisters were ecstatic and very happy, hoping this would occur eventually. But Amy tells me, and correctly at that, that what I had asked was whether she would CONSIDER getting married. This is her excuse for telling me and everyone else that she was horn-swaggled into it, and that once the word had gone out, there was no opportunity for her backing down. (As you wish, sweetheart.) The best trick I had pulled on me was when I drove down a week later to make it official, and then sat down with her Dad to formally ask for her hand in marriage. "Nope," he said, "sorry." "What!?" I asked, after all the rest of the family's celebratory merriment at even the mention of marriage, "Why not?" I queried. He wryly mused "You can't have her hand in marriage unless you promise to take the rest of her as well." We shook hands and became very dear friends, as well as golf buddies. He had, however, expressed concern to Amy, not about our age difference (8 years), but the fact that, despite going to school full-time, I didn't have a job. We set the date for August 15, and although the Gear family were strongly attached to the parish of St. John Vianney out on SOB Trail, my family and I insisted that it be held at St. James Cathedral downtown (my old altar boy haunt). Amy came up to Tallahassee about two weeks later around Valentines Day and we went down to the pawn shop and picked out a nice engagement ring and celebrated with all our friends. Then she went back down to Orlando to finish her semester at Valencia, and I didn't see her again until May 25th. My dear and favorite Uncle Tom, my Dad's youngest brother, the handsome one, had once taken me aside years earlier, put his arm around me, and in a manly private conversation said, "Son, if you can remain a bachelor until you're 30, you'll find that the whole world will have been opened up to you and you'll never have any regrets." I made it to 29. What do you want the girl to do? Or me, for that matter? There were larger forces at work.

12.   New Beginnings (1981-1982)

Dr. Dailey

Back in school for the Winter Semester, I was finishing up my remaining days of bachelorhood at 410 N. Bronough St. and had to take classes related to my now-declared major in Anthropology, so I ended up taking two from the same professor. One class was History of Anthropology, a fascinating survey course on the development of the discipline, actually a fairly recent phenomenon, and which entailed all the fabulous famous stories of Schliemann and the finding of Troy, Howard Carter and Tutankenhamen, and the cultural anthropologists Franz Boas, Margaret Mead, et al., (and how about the "Great Belzoni" who, doing archaeology, was reputed to have found so many 'average' mummies that he sold them to the Egyptian railroad to use as fuel in their steam locomotives—I kid you NOT!). The other class was Social Organization, which concentrated on various kinship systems throughout the world and across various cultures. Besides covering monogamy, exogamy, polygamy, and such, the course discussed matrilineal, patrilineal, and avuncular descent, not to mention phratries, moieties, and even fictive kinship (like a shaman having his protegé as a "son"). Not only was it a snoozer, but it was goddamn complicated as well, and we had to learn to draw relational charts, a royal pain in the ass. But it was a required course, so there was no getting around it. The professor was Robert Dailey, always "Doctor Dailey," an amazing man who lectured for hours off the cuff without looking at a single note, and after the first week knew everyone in the class's name, always addressing them as Mr. So-and-so, or Miss So-and-so. He was by then in his late fifties if not early sixties, Canadian by birth, educated at Toronto, and had done his fieldwork working with alcoholic Indians in the Northwest Territories. What had brought him to Tallahassee, Florida and Florida State University was that at some point early on he had developed a good, philosophical, and professional friendship with Hale Smith, the founder of the Department of Anthropology at FSU, who invited him to come down and teach, and from there on, they were pals... until Hale dropped dead of a heart attack (a couple of years before I had entered the department).

On the first day of class I noticed that Dailey gave the same stern warning to both classes:

> You don't want to take this course. It will not help you in any of
> your later studies, or in your everyday life for that matter. It is a
> very difficult course, and I am an exacting and strict teacher who
> grades harshly, and I can tell you right now that there will be
> very few "A's" and "B's," and many "C's," with several "D's."
> I'm telling you this today so that you still have time to withdraw
> and choose another course. Don't say that you haven't been
> warned.

It was extremely daunting, bordering on cruel. I had no choice but to take the classes, since I was an Anthropology major, and sure enough, by the next class, the enrolment was cut in half. And it was all a bunch of hoo-hah; he was a wonderful teacher; very kind and thorough and never minded stopping to discuss and explain any difficult concept or complex question. He was not a harsh grader either, although he was objectively fair, and he'd give you that edge of credit for attendance and class participation. Later, when we became less professional, and actually close friends, I asked him why he made that speech, almost identical, to the two opening day classes. He said it was to weed out all the non-Anthropology students who were looking for an easy class, and it made all our lives (the students who stayed, as well as his, as Instructor) much simpler in the long run since we were going to be together for at least three months. And he was right.

Besides being older than the rest of the students, and having long hair and a beard, I made an impression on Dailey one day when he was in the middle of one of his lectures in History of Anthropology and was discussing the early 18th century argument between evolution (Darwinism) and the inheritance of acquired characteristics (Lamarckian theory). It just so happened that I had recently finished reading a book that had caught my eye by Arthur Koestler called *The Case of the Midwife Toad* that told the story of a young brilliant scientist, Paul Kammerer, who had spent years raising and studying these midwife toads and was all set to present to the scientific community the evidence of some acquired characteristics that he was sure had been passed down, when someone snuck into his lab and fiddled with the results, and when it came out in public he was unfairly blamed for fudging the results and hounded to the point of committing suicide. In any event, Dailey was discussing the argument and mentioned the book by Koestler, but he couldn't remember the title. I raised my hand and when he called on me I told him the title and he asked if I'd explain the book to the rest of the class, which I did, and with such flourish that I even got some applause. Dr. Dailey, who was never surprised by anything, was surprised that day, and from then on we became very close professionally and over the years I considered him not only a mentor, but a close friend and confidant.

Early SEAC

During this period, I started making moves to get a job (in anticipation of getting married and satisfying my father-in-law's only real, justifiable, concern.). So I started pestering George Fischer about working for the National Park Service, at the Southeast Archeological Center (SEAC), having no idea how difficult it might be to actually pursue a U.S. Government job. Unfortunately, there was only one position open for an intern, which is to say, a part-time minimum-wage (temporary, without benefits) position, and Ken Wild, my buddy but now my friendly rival, had more college hours down and done from the University of Tennessee than I had at FSU, and being a diver-archaeologist as well, he was chosen. And rightfully so. About a month later, however, while I was sweating bullets, quietly heading towards the end of the semester and the guillotine of marriage, George called me in and told me, "Miracle of miracles!" *another* minimum-wage part-time 'student-intern' position had opened up. Miracle of miracles! Spare me, Jesus! Now I could go forward and let the Unfaithful, (all the Doubting Thomases) know that I was not only working, but I was working for the Feds (I might have left out the part that it was only as a part-time student-intern "minimum-wage" earner). Dad asked me one day (prior to my upcoming long walk down the aisle) what my Grade-Service (G-S) level was (since he had worked in the Defense Industry for over twenty years, and knew all about that shit). I told him I was a GS-4 Archeological Technician. He thought about it for a moment, and then said, "I didn't know they went that low."

My very first assignment for the Park Service was also one of the most unforgettable. Not because it was fascinating in any way, because it wasn't. But because of who it was for. George called me in and told me that, while on a fishing trip in Everglades National Park, who but the one and only Joe Dimaggio, there on vacation, had hooked an old anchor. The fishing crew pulled it aboard and brought it into the park headquarters. It wasn't very big, and it wasn't very special, but Joltin' Joe was curious about what we could tell him about it. The park wrote to the Southeast Archeological Center, sent a few pictures, and because George was the underwater guy, he got the assignment. Then he gave it to me. I traipsed over to the FSU Library (these were in the days before computers) and did some research. From the description I could tell that it was probably made in the late 1800s or early 1900s, but when it was last used there was no telling (you've got to remember, that you just keep using an anchor, over and over, until you finally lose it). But from the size I could guess how big a boat it would have been useful on, and that would have been a small skiff, or maybe a small steamboat like the African Queen. It was an Admiralty-style anchor, the kind Popeye would have tattooed on his arm, simple yet effective. That was just about all I could tell them. So I wrote it up in a memo that I couldn't help but label "Information on the Yankee Clipper Anchor." A misnomer in more ways than one, but the office let it go, and somewhere in the Government files that memo still exists today. My first assignment. I was now a professional (paid) underwater archaeologist.

SEAC was a very special place back then. It was a lot like a family. There was the Chief, Richard Faust, who everyone referred to as "Pete" (a nickname picked up in childhood). He was a stern and stocky guy with white hair and a moustache who smoked a pipe, and took everything deadly serious (until you really got to know him well). He was rather intimidating behind his big (and usually clean) desk, and he would lose his temper when things went badly. George and he had been equals when the Center was at Ocmulgee, but when the first Chief, John Griffin, retired, and they moved the Center to Tallahassee and made Pete the Chief, George got all pissed off and they never saw eye to eye after that. The truth be told, they made Pete the Chief because he was serious almost all the time, whereas George could never be accused of seriousness even in the most dire of circumstances, and Pete never missed an opportunity to give George a dressing-down and remind him who was on top. I could say they hated each other, but really it was more of a disdain for putting up with each other's crap. As I said, Pete was rather intimidating, and for the most part, Ken Wild and I, the two new interns, tried at that time just to stay out of his way. It was probably six months before Pete ever said anything to me, even a hello or a good morning, and another six months before I ever saw the inside of his office. Besides Pete as Chief and George, the other Senior Archaeologist was Jack Walker, a tall soft-spoken and soft-bodied intellectual who was such a perfectionist in writing up his reports that they rarely ever got done. Again, this was before computers, and although there were a couple of secretaries outside Pete's office to handle the typing, Jack would edit his own stuff by typing a strip of text, usually on yellow paper, cut it out with scissors, and tape or glue it onto the page, overriding his own original, edited text. Sometimes a page would have as many as fifty of these strips, some overlapping three-deep, the page almost completely covered with Scotch tape. Jack Walker was also a talker. When he wasn't editing his own stuff, he'd walk on down the hall until he found an occupied office and then he'd walk in and start talking… and it could be about anything: his dogs, the weather, some obscure archaeological finding, his dogs, the wife, politics, and oh yeah, his dogs. At first this was rather bothersome, since I was gung-ho to make my mark and I resented the interruptions. But one day Rich Johnson was visiting and he taught me to relax. Jack walked in, and Rich just sat back in his chair, put his feet up on the nearby credenza, with his hands behind his head, and he just listened. I tried to work while Jack was yammering away, but Rich just listened, never saying a word. After about forty-five minutes, Jack ran out of steam and walked on out. I asked Rich how he could stand it, and he told me "Hell, I'm getting paid to sit here and listen! Why would I let that bother me? Now Jack's told me everything he could think of, and I even picked up a small bit of useful information there in passing when he told me about an upcoming project. And now that he's talked himself out he won't have any reason to come back here for at least a week." Later, I adopted Rich's attitude, and it really did make life much easier than earlier when I'd get frustrated and have to tell Jack that I was busy three or four times a week. Jack was a gentle soul, and smart; he just needed someone to listen to him once in awhile. And Rich was right about picking up a little nugget of valuable info every so often, if you listened with half an ear, while you let the waves of doggerel and verbal flotsam wash over you.

But George and Jack's days of doing any sort of manual fieldwork were long over by the time Ken and I came on board. Most of their efforts were put to writing reports, developing policy, or making judgment calls (what we refer to as "compliance review"). To carry out the strenuous fieldwork that really needed to be done periodically (surveys, shovel-testing, reconnaissance, etc.) they used a fellow archaeologist who'd come out of the Midwest, John Hardinger. John was a short, likable guy, maybe five years older than me, who would mount these large expeditions by hiring students temporarily and part-time for the duration of a project, cutting corners by camping out and cooking over fires out in the woods. The projects that he took out became famous for their good-old-boy raucous drinking and carousing and some of the archaeology students would fight over each other to go out on these trips. He led one or two excursions each to Canaveral National Seashore, Everglades National Park, Big Cypress, and his favorite, Cumberland Island. Since he generally came in under budget, and upped the number of archaeological sites discovered, all while having a great time, he became a rising star in the Southeast Regional Office, situated in Atlanta, where he was eventually picked up to head the "external program" which dealt with interagency issues between the Park Service and let's say, Bureau of Land Management, or the Army Corps of Engineers, for example. Unfortunately, it later developed that a lot of that fieldwork he and the boys carried out had to be re-done when it was impossible to relocate some of the sites, and it came out that others had just been plotted on maps as a result of hearsay, or sometimes copied verbatim out of other archaeologists' old reports. Then there was also some dissension in the ranks when he made promises that either he wasn't authorized to make, or knew he couldn't fulfill in order to keep some of the harder workers hanging on and insure their continued loyalty; things like offers of a permanent position with the Park Service, a rarity bordering on hardly ever. Then, as I said, he went to Atlanta and began the serious climb up the Government corporate-clone ladder. Though we didn't see much of John for the next ten years, when we did see him again, he'd be the new Chief of the Center.

So that was it at SEAC, for the most part: Pete, the Chief, George and Jack as the Senior Archaeologists, John as the Field Archaeologist, and other than Wilma, the tough-as-nails Administrative Clerk (and then there was always a fresh-faced rotating typist), that was about it. Now there was another section, the Collections (also known as Curation), but other than the single "Curator" (who happened to be Ellen Hardinger, John's new wife, who was a tall, thin, and friendly brunette), it was manned entirely by student interns who changed jobs with each semester. But Kenny and I had made a pact that we were going to stick this thing through and we really wanted to become long-term, permanent, National Park Service Underwater Archaeologists. Ken was maybe two years younger than me, thin as a rail, with a long country drawl, and spikey blond hair that he'd cut himself while looking in the mirror. We became close friends, and friendly rivals, and because we were the underwater guys, they referred to us as "the bubbleheads" and later, when we acted as crew chiefs for some of the underwater projects they'd call us Frick and Frack, because we were practically interchangeable. Our individual talents, however, soon began to emerge: Ken had already worked on a few archaeology projects at his former alma mater, the University of Tennessee, and he could draw real well, so he was very good at recognizing and describing the material culture (ceramic sherds, Civil War stuff, bones), whereas I could write and I had a particular talent for logistics (getting boats and supplies ready, building things like airlifts and floating screens, working out transportation and lodging). Where Ken looked at things with the eye of an artist ("Well, it could have been this, or they could have used it for that"), I was the pragmatic utilitarian and always applied Occam's Razor to the question at hand (The simplest answer is usually right: "Well, it looks like one of those," and 95% of the time that's what it was). Together we made a formidable team, and besides being fearless in the water, we were both comfortable around boats. He was married to a sweet, little, petite blond who was very nice, and although they always appeared to be happy, apparently there was some underlying unhappiness. I was now affianced to Amy and the summer was approaching.

Diving to Research II

During the Spring semester, 1981, the second Diving to Research class took place, and this one was going to be a doozie. In the first class we had learned all the basics, honed our skills, and went on a couple of shakeout projects. This time, we were expected to create, and run a project, and we would each be the director of our individual projects, and use the class participants as the crew. There was some small support money available for travel and to get us on the water, but other than that, we were on our own. The projects of course, were expected to reflect our particular discipline (this was actually a graduate-level course that a few of us, myself included, had to get a special dispensation from the dean to take). The first couple of projects were interesting, if relatively simple in concept, but a quick rundown will give you a taste of what we were doing. The first was by a Sports Medicine major who wanted to measure the effects of hypothermia (debilitating coldness) vs. various body types. So, she measured each of us by weight, height, girth, body fat, etc. in our little red speedo swimsuits, and then we went out into the Gulf on board the RV *Tersiops*, and wearing only the speedo, mask, fins, and buoyancy compensator (no wetsuit) we went over the side with the standard set of doubles and dropped down about twenty feet, hanging on a line, and the clock began to run. She wanted to see how long you'd last. Now this was early Spring, say March, and the water at twenty feet in the Gulf is cool enough even in the summer, but now it was damned cold. With a set of double-steel 72s on your back, in normal summer, with a wetsuit, you could stay on the bottom (less than 30 feet) for two hours. Now we were shivering in ten minutes. We'd do bicycle pumps with our legs, and swing our arms around to keep the blood circulating, that is, when we weren't bundled up in a tight ball to conserve what heat we had left. Of course, for safety's sake, there was an observer nearby, bundled in a wetsuit with clipboard in hand, just to make sure nobody went stiff and sunk out of sight, but otherwise, you were expected to make your own decision when to give up and go to the surface, where you knew there was a cup of either hot coffee or chocolate waiting for you. Because of my penchant for beer, I lasted longer than most, but there were some portly fellows, real trolls in appearance, who lasted longer than a half hour. Eventually, even the toughest of nuts cracked, and would come back on board with blue lips, a white and pallid face, shaking uncontrollably, get their pulse, blood pressure, and inner core body temperature checked (in your armpit, not the other place), then sit down to enjoy a nice cup of java or cocoa.

When she presented her results they weren't all that surprising: thin people didn't fare as well as thick; but there were some other interesting results: women held out as long or longer than men, when considering relative size (probably due to subcutaneous fat distributed fairly evenly, and a generally lower metabolism); and then there was the relatively un-measurable factor of "motivation," a serious piece of business for Sports Medicine folks. Apparently, some of those body types that were expected to last longer, didn't, and even some of the thinner ones just gave up too easily. Did they just not care? Were they purposely trying to skew the results? Maybe they didn't consider the study worthwhile. Some people just don't like being uncomfortable, and if they don't have to be, why should they (even though we all knew what we were getting into). But all those concerns were psychological. Which brings us to the second example of the Diving to Research II class projects, and this one, was by a psychologist. Quite a bit older than the rest of us, maybe by ten years, Mike Pomerantz was an already-successful psychologist, but he had the diving bug and had gone back to school and soon became a strong supporter of the Academic

215

Diving Program. His project was again, simple, but with a serious application that he could probably write up in a professional journal. He made arrangements for us all to go to Panama City, where the Navy trained a lot of its divers, and where they have one of the largest decompression chambers in the country. The idea was to put us into the chamber, take us down to the equivalent of something like 300 feet, where we would most assuredly feel the effects of nitrogen narcosis, also known as "rapture of the deep," and then we would undergo various psychological, perceptual, and coordination tasks, all while being observed outside the chamber and responding to the interviewer's questions. Now my penchant and predilection for smoking pot came into play. While most if all of the other participants rolled around, laughing, making faces, and ignoring the interviewer, I sat and worked crossword puzzles, played chess, and talked with the interviewer until they finally let us out after maybe an hour. No big 'ting, mon.

Bowles and the Fox

My personal project was born out of the previous Fall Semester's class in Underwater Archaeology, the one taught by George Fischer, where we had been encouraged to write an original research paper at the end. At the time, a very odd thing occurred. I had gone to the State Library downtown in the R.A. Gray Building (one of the buildings I'd helped pour the concrete for several years prior), because I knew it had a lot more local history packed away in it. At the time there was also some sort of policy at FSU's Strozier Library that all "Florida" resources were considered to be part of the Special Collections, so you had to know specifically what you were asking for, then make a formal request for the library assistant to retrieve it for you, and then sit in the Special Collections room and hand it back before you could ask for another. Well, that just didn't make a lick of sense to me—I wanted to roam around and see where things would lead me, so that's why I had gone down to the State Library, a resource that most students at FSU were unaware of and where I could just walk among the stacks, and then check out as many books as I wanted (okay, maybe seven was the max) for three weeks at a time. I came across a reference to the pirate Billy Bowlegs (who was fictional, but based on William Rogers, one of Jean Lafitte's crew, who was reportedly very bow-legged, as most sailors were), which led to Billy Boleks, a Seminole Indian war chief, which led to William Augustus Bowles, a fascinating character. He was a British soldier, sometime actor, and Creek Indian sympathizer, self-ordained war chief, and independent organizer, who in September of 1799, carrying guns and powder to lead a Creek Indian insurrection against the Spanish, was wrecked in a British schooner just off of St. George Island, near present-day Apalachicola, about 90 minutes west of Tallahassee. This was perfect, an historical shipwreck in my own back yard; and one on a mission that could have changed the history of the country, especially these new and United States of America, had it been carried out successfully. As a matter of fact, the surveyor sent by Thomas Jefferson to establish the border between Georgia and Spanish Florida, a guy by the name of Andrew Ellicott, who happened to be in the area at the time, heard about the shipwreck from the Indians and went over and spent nearly a week with Bowles and the survivors encamped now on St. George, but he refused them any assistance since that would have been diplomatically unsound, considering the circumstances. The vessel that carried Bowles and the munitions meant to induce (read "bribe") the Creeks was HMS *Fox,* a small British schooner of approximately eighteen guns, and which had been lost because, during a gale, the pilot refused directions from Bowles to skirt to the east of the St. George-Dog Island channel (where the water is deepest), and which is in fact the entrance to Apalachicola Bay even today. She ran aground and it took them two days to get off the stores and some of the guns and powder before the vessel broke apart. They camped over on St. George Island for two weeks until the storms abated (this was when Ellicott visited them) and they could finally get passage across the bay and up the Apalachicola River. Bowles reconnoitered with the Creeks, but now without most of the promised guns and powder, he then

216

boldly declared himself their "Director-General" and leader of the now-sovereign State of Muskogee. The Indians were unimpressed and he was snatched by some of the wavering warriors and ransomed to the Spanish, who had a hefty bounty out on him. From Pensacola, he was shipped in chains to Morro Castle in Havana, where he was fed rotten oranges until he died of starvation and neglect.

It was a wonderful story and I was planning a project to go out and look for the wreck, since I thought I had an idea where it might be located (in the middle of the passage [of 1799] between St. George and Dog Island, since the pilot had refused to hug the eastern side and probably shot for the middle, where deep water would normally have been expected to run). The aforementioned "odd thing" that occurred happened one night while I was in Poor Paul's with some members of the Underwater Archaeology class, and one of the class members started talking about the *Fox*, and how it had been lost off of St. George Island. The guy's name was Henry Paul, and he was a smart, tall, good-looking, intelligent and well-to-do History major and pre-law-school student. Aww, shit, how did he know about the *Fox*? After a little while I sidled up next to him at the bar when no one else was around and asked. He was very circumspect and wouldn't tell me. I told him I knew all about it, and I was thinking of writing my research paper on it. He said he was thinking of doing the same thing. Fuck, fuck, fuck... this was going to be trouble. The next day we both went in and told George that we were considering the same research project. He knew this was going to be problematic so he separated us, asking us each how we had come up with the idea. Only later did I figure out where Henry had gotten his inspiration. It turned out that he had taken a History class at FSU that was taught by J. Leitch Wright, a well-known Florida historian and the author of *William Augustus Bowles: Director-General of the Creek Nation*, which undoubtedly he had either told the class about, or had them read. Well, George asked us each if one or the other might consider some alternative research topic, but neither one of us wanted to give it up. So, after consulting with the Chairman of the Department, he came up with the worst possible solution: we'll work on it together. After fiddle-farting around with a draft back-and-forth for about two weeks, it was obvious this wasn't going to work. Now, Henry was a good writer, I have to hand him that, but he was very secretive, and so he was trying to get the upper hand; plus, he had the History professor, Leitch Wright, funneling him information. So, I did the one thing I knew I could do under the circumstances, for which I knew I had the edge. I said the hell with the historic background, which Henry was pursuing avidly. Instead I concentrated on developing a project management approach to finding the wreck, a research design and scope-of-work, if you will. At the end of the semester, we slapped the two documents together and handed them in. George was duly impressed, and then passed it around to some of the faculty, who stuck their noses into it, tossed out their two cents, and then there was more trouble. They wanted to specify exactly who wrote which section, since he now had to hand out two grades. Well, we sat him down and showed him who did what (although I thought it was fairly obvious), and there may have been a little disagreement over portions in the beginning where we had worked originally side-by-side, but eventually we shook hands on the deal and said it was a fair co-authorship. He gave us both an "A," but it was my first lesson in "Don't ever share a project if you can help it; it always ends badly."

Surprise!

Interesting enough, Henry never pursued Diving to Research, didn't follow up with History, and just went on to law school, and the project became mine by attrition two semesters later. So now it was Spring again, and I already had the project outlined for the most part. What I had done was to take an old 1700s navigational chart of the entrance to Apalache Bay between St. George and Dog Island, as well as one from 1835, one from the 1930s, and a modern one, and then hand-drew them in different colored inks all to the same scale on onionskin paper (no computers back then) and overlayed them. It was fairly evident that the ends of the islands had topographically changed quite a bit over the years, but the offshore sandbar and entrance channel hadn't changed much at all. If they had shot for the middle of the pass, as the records indicated, instead of the eastern channel along the west end of Dog Island, then the vessel would have struck somewhere on the large sandbar guarding the entrance, probably in eight or ten feet of water, considering the schooner's draft. Since there'd been no loss of life, and since they even got to salvage some of the guns and powder in the ensuing couple of days, this seemed a likely possibility and the best place to begin the search. It was still a large area to survey though, and it was going to take a lot of logistical planning. First of all I was going to need a boat with some remote-sensing capability; specifically, a magnetometer (a wide-scanning super-sensitive metal detector) as well as someone who could operate it. At the time there was only one real guy available and he was at Florida International University, out of Miami. His name was Harold Moffitt, and lucky for me, he was an FSU alumnus and a graduate of the Academic Diving Program's Scientists in the Sea course, the precursor to Diving to Research. So he was amenable to bringing up FIU's mag and running it, and had friends in Tallahassee he could stay with. To guide the boat, I figured we'd need two transits that we could set up on a baseline on the beach, and with radio controls between the transit in operation and the boat we could guide it in on a straight line course inward across the sandbar until it got too close to the beach and then the captain could turn her about and go set up for the next run. I needed two transits so the second could triangulate off of the straight-line vector of the first, and once a transect was completed the first transit could leap-frog down the beach ahead of the other one and get set up before the boat was ready to carry out the next straight-line transect. In theory, it was damn near perfect. Then again, I realized that theory and reality hardly ever agree on their first introduction; it was also what might be referred to as "overly ambitious." Nonetheless, I set up the use of the boat with the Marine Lab, got Harold to agree to a weekend, explained the plan of action to the class, got permission from St. George Island State Park, which we'd be operating from, and even induced Charlie Ewen, a graduate student in Archaeology, to give my crew a hands-on tutorial of how to set up, level, and take readings with an optical transit. Everything was falling into place. It was Friday evening, May 24th, 1981 when I finally got it all together. All I had to do was to make sure that everyone would show up early the next morning at 6 a.m. so we could drive down to the coast and get to St. George by 8 or so. Besides Moffitt and the boat captain, course instructor Gregg Stanton, and myself, I had to get a verbal commitment from at least six more participants. The first four were easy and ready and willing to go. But I couldn't get the other two on the phone. Well, after all, it was (only) 10 p.m. on a Friday night, and where am I but using the pay phone at the Pastime between beers. I'd give it another hour before I'd have to leave to catch at least a couple of hours sleep myself or else. I got one of them by 10:30, and just as I was getting ready to leave, I got the other at 10:45. As I was hanging up the phone, there was a tap on my shoulder. I turned around and who's standing there, smiling, with a twinkle in her eye? Amy! (Amy in Orlando?!?) "What are you doing here?!" I said. "Aren't you glad to see me?" she asked, "A friend was driving up just for a day, so I thought I'd come along and surprise you." "Of course I'm glad to see you... it's just that, you know, tomorrow I have that big survey project off of St. George... I gotta be at ADP by 6 in the morning." She said, "Well, I've got to leave tomorrow afternoon, so why don't we have a quick beer, and we'll go back to your place?" When we left the Pastime it was midnight. Needless to say, there wasn't much sleeping done that night, and by 5:30 I was getting up and getting dressed. It was gonna be a helluva day. Before dawn's right hand was in the sky I kissed her goodbye; she wished me good luck, and I let her lie. Every crew member but one showed up, and even that one showed up later. We were on-site and set up by 9 a.m. and waiting on the boat to show. It came round Dog Island from the Marine Lab about 10 and we started the survey. Of course, no project ever runs smoothly, but except for a few glitches with staying on course, leap-frogging the transits, and developing an off-the-cuff radio protocol, we finally finished up around 5, hot, tired, sunburnt, thirsty, sandy, and famished. The van stopped at a Wendy's on the mainland , and the crew got out to get something for dinner, but, having been up for well over 36 hours plus I fell asleep in the backseat instead of eating. The project was considered a relative success. Even though we hadn't found the *Fox*, we'd sure as hell gathered a lot of data to look at.

Surprise! Surprise!

Speaking of a lot of data to look at, two weeks later, when we were talking on the phone because she had called to wish me a Happy Birthday (my 29th on June 8th), Amy mentioned that she was just the least bit worried because she hadn't started her period, which apparently was as regular as The Mailman (her father was a mailman). I told her not to worry about it since it had only been two weeks. By *her* birthday though, the 4th of July, what with the Gear-girls telegraph lines running overtime, it was obvious that the fireworks had been lit. She came up to Tallahassee and we talked things over, and we both decided what the hell, we were getting married in a month anyway, we'd just tough it out. [Our oldest son, Robin, was born nine months and two days after May 25, on February 27th. Amy and I hadn't seen each other for at least a month on either side of it… so that pretty much cinches it, as long as we're speaking of data.] That summer, the whole Academic Diving and Underwater Archaeology crew were planning a large project down in the Dry Tortugas, 70 miles west of Key West and the home of Fort Jefferson, the largest of the Civil War-era brick forts and later known as the prison that held Samuel Mudd, the unfortunate doctor who had set John Wilkes Booth's leg and was thus branded a Lincoln conspirator. The project, however, was a survey of the remains of the *Nuestra Señora del Rosario*, one of the 1622 treasure galleons lost off the Tortugas in the hurricane of that year. Damn, I really wanted to go; and they really wanted me to go too, but it just couldn't happen. My best-laid plans, set in motion earlier that year (and now encouraged by Amy's condition) made it mandatory that we pull off "the wedding of the century," (oh sorry, that was Charles and Diana's, with whom we were competing that summer—they got hitched on July 29, two weeks prior to our nuptials). Hey, we were going to have more fun getting married than those guys were gonna have diving on a shitty old treasure galleon, anyway. At least that's what I told myself. And it sort of turned out that way. They spent most of their time in the field just trying to relocate the wrecksite, since most of it was broken up and scattered over acres on shallow reef that had shredded it over the centuries, and where any remaining structural components had been encrusted and absorbed into the reef itself (think of a plane wreck after three hundred years). Once they found it, it was the following year exploring it that was going to be more exciting and that project I did get to go on. Meanwhile, the wedding of the decade was moving toward fruition in Orlando, The City Beautiful.

The Penitent

One of the New Age prerequisites for getting married in the Church (note the capital "C") was that Amy and I had to take a little course in what to expect out of married life. It wasn't so bad… a lot of propaganda about birth control (too late) and mutual respect. I think the instructor (a married lay person, thank God, and not a nun or a priest) even had us draw up compatibility lists. Not something I'd recommend. Although Amy and I did fine, by their scores some of the other couples probably should never have ever met, much less thought about getting married. Another requirement was that we go to Confession, so we'd be in a state of grace (Graceland?) when the big day came a month later. Well, hell, I hadn't been in a church since high school, ten years earlier, and I'd done a lot of living and learning since then. It went pretty much like it did for Nolin as he had explained to me when he got married to Celia. I had to make an appointment at the Rectory, and when I got there the priest was in an old golf shirt (not like Nolin's who wore a wifebeater t-shirt). He invited me in and we went into the common study, and he invited me to sit down. What? No getting down on my knees? No, it wasn't necessary. How long had it been since my last confession? Well, let's see, that would have been roughly eleven years. Had I committed any grievous sins in that time? (Certainly none I considered grievous, but I had lived with Lisa for about two years without being married, so there was that.) "Adultery." (Then there was the stolen car.) "Stealing." (More than one occasion of over-indulgence, what was that called? Oh yeah…) "Gluttony." (There was that incident with my brother and I shaking our asses at that frat boy and his girlfriend. But that wasn't very grievous, it was more of a lark, and what would you call it anyway? The cop called it indecent exposure. Hell, it wasn't even a sin as far as I was concerned, the punk deserved it. But I got to give this priest here something… I know…) "Pride." The priest just sat in his chair with his hand holding his forehead, listening, and once in a while he'd shake his head slightly after he'd press for details. That just about covered it. "Is that all?" he said. Even I was surprised at how little I had to give up. "Oh, yeah, Lust," I said, "lots of lust." Even though his head was bowed into his hand, I could see him smile at that. "And I've used the Lord's name in vain many times." "How many times?" he asked, which threw me off guard because he hadn't really asked how many times for any of the other stuff. I thought about it a minute, and figured, well, over eleven years, "maybe a thousand." I half-expected him to jump up and say, "Jesus Christ! That's a goddamn lot of taking the Lord's name in vain!" But he didn't say anything, except, "For your penance, you'll say ten Our Fathers," and, smiling, he looked up and said "and you'll cut back on some of that lust, okay, at least until you get married?" Now he had me get on my knees, make the sign of the cross, and patiently walked me through the Act of Contrition. Now having imbued me with the sacrament of Penance, he gave giving me the final once-over sign of the cross blessing, and told me, "Go, and sin no more." I shook his hand, thanked him, and got the hell out of there before I remembered any more sins, or he changed his mind about the penance. If he had said I had to go to the hospital and wash bedpans, or massage old people's arthritic feet with Mentholatum deep-heating rub and clip their encrusted talon toenails, by all the rules I would have been obligated to do so before he'd let me get married. In the old days it would have been sackcloth and ashes… maybe even a little flagellation… at least a couple dozen rosaries. As it was I thought I got off damn lucky.

Things were moving along pretty good. Mom and Dad sponsored our Rehearsal Dinner party upstairs in a private dining room at Rosie O'Grady's, a very fine restaurant and make-believe Western-style tourist saloon in downtown Orlando. The owner, Bob Snow, used to fly over Orlando on clear blue-sky days in his red biplane and skywrite advertisements for Rosie's, or either leave inspirational messages and draw some clever picture, like "Have a Nice Day [smiley face]". August 15 was a Saturday, naturally, and a beautiful day at that. My brother Paul was my best man, with Dennis LeFils and Ed Quinby rounding out the groomsmen. Funny thing, I can't remember who the priest was. Amy's brother Charlie played the violin for the entry march, and Amy was escorted down the aisle by her Dad. It all went very well, and smoothly, with a short Mass attached. Pictures afterwards. Our reception was held at Carlton Arms over on Rio Grande, a high-class apartment complex in those days, but now fallen on hard times. I remember me and Amy, driven over there by Paul, smoked a big doobie, and one of the pictures of us coming in to the Reception shows the red eyes you can't blame on the flash. There was a big three-tiered cake made by Amy's sister's mother-in-law, flowers, music, and lots of booze. After Amy and I danced the first dance, she danced with her Dad. Then I danced with my Mom, then her Mom, and then it was a free-for-all.

[At least I hadn't suffered the shock a friend of Paul's got on his wedding day a couple of years later. Paul was again the best man, and he and the groom, Mike, were waiting in the priest's sacristy for the priest to show up and get dressed, when Mike's Dad came in and asked Paul if he could talk to Mike alone. Paul left, and five minutes later, the Dad walked out and Paul walked back in to find Mike ashen white, gripping a countertop, breathing heavily, nearly fainting, and in obvious shock. "What's the matter?" Paul asked. "My Dad just came in here and told me that he'd wanted to tell me before, but now that I'm getting married and all grown up, I ought to know that I was adopted." Paul said he went through the whole ceremony in a daze, and had to be guided throughout, even to the kiss. I'd call that bad timing.]

I was out back drinking with friends, when Amy came out and told me we had to go. "Why do we have to go?" I asked, and she told me about the fact that the bride and groom have to leave early so they can get started on their honeymoon, and everyone can see them off. "But I don't want to go!" "Too bad," she told me. After eating a piece of cake, we grabbed a large cannon of champagne, jumped in the rental car and headed out to Cocoa Beach where we had reservations at the Holiday Inn. It was probably for the best that we left when we did. We barely finished the champagne by the time we got there and we were in no shape to do anything but go to bed. By the way, while walking into the hotel, Amy looks down and finds a twenty-dollar bill in the driveway: a propitious sign.

We moved up to Tallahassee and with some of the wedding present money we rented a house at 214 W. Brevard, right behind the Governor's Mansion. After that, though, we were dirt poor and determined to make it on our own. To show you how poor we were, there was a day when all we could afford was a package of Hamburger Helper and one-half pound (not even a full pound) of hamburger, and that was going to be it for the both of us. Amy was browning the hamburger, as you're supposed to do, stirring it and talking to me in the other room, working on some schoolwork. The cabinet door just above the stove was halfway open [When is a door not a door? When it's ajar.], and Amy had her head turned my way, talking as she stirred. When she turned back to the stove the corner of the cabinet door caught her forehead, just above the eye. Surprised and angry, she slammed the cabinet door shut, and the thin glass pane that was in the cabinet door frame shattered into exactly 1.4 trillion fragments of tiny broken glass shards and dust particles and dropped readily and completely into the still-sizzling frying pan. I rushed in to first and foremost (of course), make sure that Amy was all right, though the fact that she was cussing a blue streak seemed to indicate she'd survive, and only secondarily to see if the meat were salvageable (ix-nay on the eat-may.) There was no putting that omelet back in the eggs, so to speak; the sheen of the fat from the frying hamburger sparkled even more brightly from the kitchen light glistening off the million slivers of glass embedded therein. It all had to go in the trash. After delivering a slight lecture on the futility of losing your temper with inanimate objects, and the karmic hazards involved, (a lecture, by the way, that did me no good whatsoever, and did nothing to soothe Amy's battered brow), we ate the Hamburger Helper without the hamburger, just the helper. The meal was consumed in silence: our first marital spat, if you don't count the incident where I didn't want to leave the Reception because I was having so much fun. No, let's not count that, whad'ya say? She got me back though. When her friends would ask her what happened to her eye, she'd tell them with a straight face that I clipped her for getting out of line. They'd look at me in horror…, and believed her!

DISC Village

It was between semesters at school, so I couldn't be a student intern, Amy was very pregnant, and I needed a job pretty bad, and it just so happened that my old buddy Frank, whom

I'd gone to Maine with, was working for a large halfway house and farm that had juvenile delinquents, kids from broken homes, abused kids, and druggies, and the place was looking for a rough-frame carpenter. They already had a finish carpenter, really a jack-of-all-trades, but he'd been around so long they asked him to become a vocational teacher of sorts and get the kids doing some hands-on "projects" that he would oversee. Meanwhile they were expanding the place, so they still needed someone to just build stuff, renovate a building or two, and interact with the kids as well. So I dragged out my old carpentry tools, strapped on my leather tool belt and hammer holder, and they hired me. It was a long drive down to Woodville and then several miles further down Natural Bridge Road, a place called DISC Village. Natural Bridge is just what the name implies, where a section of the St. Marks River dips below a natural limestone bridge that crosses it about fifteen miles south of Tallahassee. It's the site of one of only three or four battles fought in Florida during the Civil War. The Yanks had decided to disembark near the mouth of the St. Marks, and march up north, crossing the "Natural Bridge" on the maps, and then continue up the Woodville highway and take Tallahassee, the Capital. A volunteer company from the Tallahassee boys' seminary, along with the local militia, marched south and camped at Natural Bridge, setting up something of an ambush on the high ground overlooking the crossing. Though there were several mad charges by the Yanks on the narrow road that crossed the natural bridge, the boys and the militia held them at bay until the Bluebellies decided finally to give it up and head back to the boats. It's still celebrated every year as a Confederate victory, and rightly so since the Capital was saved from capture (the only one in the South that was), but the number of re-enactors who now scream, shoot, run, fire cannons, and fall into the water, or lay "dead or wounded" each year probably outnumber the actual combatants by three or four times the original.

Once I started working at the Village, they assigned me a couple of the older boys to act as helpers. One was a kid named Jeff, tall, red-haired, and freckled, whose left arm and left side of his chest had been blown apart by a shotgun blast during a botched drug deal, and put back together as best as the doctors could do. He still had it, but, now lacking a few muscles, it hung rather limply, and his hand was twisted into an opposable claw. Sometimes he'd go into a funk over his arm and his misfortune, all brought on by bad decisions, and we'd have to joke around with him until he came out of it. He was an excellent amateur electrician, having worked as an apprentice with some company in his home town, before the "accident." The other kid was named Manuel, or "Manny," and he was a light-colored, kinky-haired rubio from Columbia, but out of Miami. Nice kid, enthusiastic and always upbeat. He took to calling me "Tiger Man," and when I asked why he said it was because of my long auburn hair, and big red beard. Well, I didn't get it, thinking "tiger" meant "striped," and although I'd been told that I looked like a lion sometimes, no one ever compared me to a tiger. He explained that "tiger" or *tigre* was really a catch-all term for South Americans when referring to all big cats, whether pumas, cougars, panthers, tigers, or lions. Anyway, "Tiger Man" stuck, and even though I'm not usually too keen on nicknames, that one wasn't so bad, and the kids all liked it (and it was easier and more friendly than calling me "Mr. Brewer") so I let it go. The whole time I worked there I was "Tiger Man," or just plain "Tiger." Odd, but true. My old pal Frank, who was an office guy and had gotten me the job, when he'd come outside to see me, and the kids walked by calling out "Hey, Tiger Man," he'd look at me sideways and just shake his head. Coulda been worse.

Since the place was way out in the woods, the kids were always escaping—all they had to do was walk off. Then they'd try to hitchhike out to Woodville, and then either north to Tallahassee or south to the coast. They hardly ever made it very far; the cops were on the alert, as were the local population, so if anybody saw kids walking on the road, they called the Village and there'd be a headcount and anyone shows up missing, the sheriff's deputies were on their way. But every so often some kid would disappear for months, if not forever. More problematic than running away, however, was that they were always setting up secret rendezvous' and fucking like rabbits, even the homosexuals. They'd go out in the woods, up in an attic, on a roof, in the laundry room, under a building… they were very inventive. So there was always that risk of pregnancy, I suppose, but I think what worried the administration the most was when one of the counselors would go renegade. It happened at least a couple of times: some just-out-of-college male psychology or sociology major, running either one of the group sessions, or even the one-on-one counseling sessions (always with the door open), would develop a relationship with one of the teenage Lolitas, girls from broken homes who, consciously or not, knew all the tricks of seduction and just wanted to get the hell out of there and start over. Almost invariably, when they were finally hunted down, the counselor would swear undying devotion, whereas the young girl would usually just pick up where she left off, unless she was already pregnant and they were married. In any case, his career was finished before it had even really started.

There was one instance when I got called in and chastised (and no, not for sex). We, my crew and I, had been renovating an old cabin to turn it into a small eight-bed dorm. The boys had a blast during the demolition phase, as we took out walls, sheet rock, flooring etc. Bracing up new walls was easy enough, and we even re-wired the damn thing with Jeff's electrical know-how (although one day he was up in the attic wiring up some light fixtures and one of the other boys at the circuit box got his signals mixed up, and suddenly we heard a loud simultaneous "SNAP" and "YAWP!" and he flopped around a little before we could get him down and check him out). Then we had the bathroom plumbed and I finished up building the toilet stalls, which took a couple of days. All was done and freshly painted, and they let six of the older kids, plus my two helpers, move into the new dorm. About a week later, I dropped in to see how everything was going, and when I went into the bathroom, one of the bathroom stall doors was just hanging there on one broken hinge, all askew. I asked my guys what happened, and they said one of the new kids had been swinging on the door and broken it, but no one had wanted to say anything. I asked them who did it, and even though they didn't want to rat him out, they were more loyal to me than him, and told me who it was. Later that day, I cornered the kid by himself, and told him, "I'm gonna go back in there and fix that bathroom stall door, and if you ever break anything I've built here again, I'm gonna hunt you down and kick your ass!" Then I went in and fixed the door. It must have been the next day that they called me in to the Administration Building, really a set of strung-together trailers, which I never went in except to get my check. The Director called me into his office, and Frank was there, and the Director asked me if I had threatened one of the kids. "Oh, the kid who broke the bathroom stall door? Yeah, I told him that if he ever broke anything around here again, I'd kick his ass… big kid too." They were surprised that I wasn't somewhat remorseful, but then immediately tried to impress upon me that, as a counseling halfway house receiving grants, etc. we could never, under any circumstances, threaten one of the "clients." "But I'd never *really* lay a hand on him," I mildly protested, "I just wanted to scare him." Didn't matter, it had to be as undone as best as we could muster, and as quickly as possible. I had to go apologize to him. What!? They were adamant, and I could see that this was serious business, although I hadn't taken it as such. Still, it galled me no end that I had to apologize to this punk who had vandalized my work, and work done for his benefit too. "Okay," recalling the Golden Rule from a lecture long past, I said I understood, and I'd go do it right away. The "clients" were having lunch, and I always ate with them, so once I spotted the kid finishing up, I followed him out and told him I wanted to talk to him. We sat on the back of an open pickup truck tailgate, and I apologized for telling him I'd kick his ass if he, well, you know. He knew I'd been angry the day before, but now he knew that, despite the apology, I was calm and serious and me and the

223

others would be watching him. That's all it took, and it was the right thing to do. My guys stood nearby, trying to listen, and they knew it was hard for me to be nice to the kid. Afterwards they came up and shook hands with me, because I'd treated him like an adult, not a punk. The kid actually turned out to be okay, eventually becoming a helper himself, and I'd like to think that me and my guys had something to do with helping to straighten him (his ass) out. Now newly married, with a little Pillsbury dough-boy in the oven, I was going back to school in the Fall. I wouldn't be able to work full-time any more, and needed a job that would let me work and go to school at the same time. So George offered me another part-time job with the Park Service ("Intermittent" is what they called it), and I gave notice to DISC Village. It had been a great experience, but a dead-end job. Still, I was thankful to Frank for having made it available, and I knew I'd miss the juvenile delinquents. ["Tyger, tyger, half so bright, Like one dim star out at night; With only mortal eye to see, Did you frame by carpentry?" Why yes… yes, I did. Thank you, thank you very much.]

Storage Whores

Amy and I were enjoying our little white house right behind the Governor's mansion during the winter of 1982, and she was getting very, very pregnant. We had a fireplace and, although the place inside was really tiny, only two small bedrooms, it was on a very large lot and we had practically half a city block to ourselves. The landlord's name was Mr. Funderburk, and he was a tall, slender old born-again Baptist who was one of the Andrew Jackson re-enactors that led the Springtime Tallahassee parade every year. He came over periodically to mow the yard and take care of his aging mother, who lived in a house on the corner. I don't think we ever set eyes on the older Mrs. Funderburk, she never came outside, and eventually he had to move her out to a nursing home. We were still very poor and didn't have much in the way of furniture, and one day my brother Paul and Bob Tirelli show up and say they are going out to bid on some abandoned storage sheds, would I like to come along? Sure. We pile into my big old Suburban wagon that I'd bought off of Amy's brother Joe, and we headed out to Pensacola Street. It was a lot like the TV show, *Storage Wars*, except that you could go in and look around at the stuff first. We watched a few auctions before jumping in, but Paul and Tirelli got excited over one that had obviously been used to store some fraternity crap, so they bid on it and won. For something like 65 dollars they ended up getting a stuffed boar's head (tusks and all), a shotgun, and a few beer advertising signs that eternally filled glasses of beer with yellow bubbling liquid as long as they were plugged in. I got interested when the door to one shed was thrown open and I could see it was stacked to the top with packed cardboard boxes. There was a crib in the back, all taken apart, but hey, I was going to need one of those soon anyway. And what really caught my eye was a ten-speed bicycle hidden back in the recesses. Why that alone was worth maybe 75 bucks. So I started bidding and soon it was down to me and one other guy, 65, 70, 75… he started slowing down, but he went once more to 80. All I had was 85 bucks, but I went for it, and the guy backed down. Well, hell, now I had a load of stuff, and it took us the better part of an hour to load it all up. But I had gotten lucky, because there was a lot of furniture, including a bed and a dining room table, besides the bicycle and the crib. Then there was one box I opened just to check it out, and it had an army helmet, some boots, a machete, and a set of fatigues. This was going to be interesting. When we got back to the house, Amy was impressed with Paul and Tirelli's stuffed boar's head and their shotgun and flashing beer signs. She asked me if I got anything good. Yeah, I said, and showed her the army helmet, the boots, and the machete   She was less impressed with this and asked me how much I spent. "$85" I beamed. She thought I was crazy, and was about to give me what for, when I fessed up and told her about the other stuff. . (The only thing I didn't show her was the "grenade simulator"— marked in green on the side of this large white paper tube— which the guy had probably pocketed off of some training range. It was the equivalent of a small stick of dynamite, a black-powder firecracker 10 times as large. The thing was as big around as your, well, let's just say it was three fingers thick, and maybe six or seven inches long, with a ready-to-light green plastic fuse just like we saw on our now-below-average but previously impressive M-80s). Paul and Tirelli helped me unload all the boxes and furniture before they left, and Amy and I spent the rest of the day unloading boxes and putting together furniture. It was quite a haul, a whole household load of crap, best $85 I ever spent. From the looks of it and a pile of personal papers, apparently some black guy right out of the army had broken up with his wife, put all their communal stuff in storage (must have had kids too), and after a year or so, just let it all go. I set all the personal papers and photos aside and later made a few phone calls trying to track the guy down (again, before computers), and when I couldn't find him, I packed it all up in a manila envelope and dropped it off at the newspaper, the *Tallahassee Democrat*, figuring they would have better luck or know what to do. Nothing ever came of it, but we furnished our little place with all that stuff, and got a lot of baby junk in the meantime.

The Boy Wonder!

By now we knew it was getting close to the birthing business, and Amy's sisters came up one weekend to "attend" to us. After a Friday evening of drinking and commiserating with the girls and their brothers, they (the 'midwives') decided that the birth probably wasn't going to happen that night, so they all decided to go out on the town and whoop it up. They hadn't been gone an hour when Amy started feeling "things." What kind of things? "I don't know, something's going on." Oh shit! We called the doctor, the famous Dr. Alex Brickler, tall, thin, black and delivering babies in Tallahassee for over thirty years. It was now about 10 or 10:30. He said to start timing the contractions and he'd meet us at the hospital around midnite. About 11:30, we headed out to Tallahassee Memorial; it was a bitter cold night, and the frosty vapors came out with our breath as I parked the car and we slowly walked up the front entranceway, Amy stopping every ten steps or so as a contraction would nearly double her over. We got to the front door, and there was a big white sign saying "Under Construction, Please Use Other Entrance." There was no arrow, and we couldn't see any other entrance, so we just started walking around the building, with Amy huffing and puffing and groaning every ten steps or so. When we got to the Emergency Room entrance in the back, they said no, this wasn't an emergency, and we should continue around the outside to the alternate entrance. We had already traversed halfway around the hospital, so there was nothing to do but plod on. When we finally reached the "alternate" entrance, having walked all the way around the block, we discovered that it wasn't but 50 feet away from the one with the Construction sign. Had we gone right instead of left, we'd have seen it immediately. Dr. Brickler later told us that it was a good warmup exercise he would recommend for all the expectant ladies, but they'd never go for it. We'd killed the better part of an hour, and now the contractions were coming on steady, so they got Amy prepped and ready, started the whole monitoring business, and what with the breathing exercises from our Lamaze class, a little grunting, groaning and cussing on Amy's part, Robin was born around 2 or 3 a.m. But he wasn't Robin yet. We hadn't quite decided on a name and thought we'd see what he looked like first. I didn't want a David Junior, though I did like the name David, so in the meantime he just got Boy Brewer on his wristband. The nurses were pretty adamant about getting a name picked out soon though, for the birth certificate, and they gave us a deadline of 48 hours. After holding him and seeing to it that Amy was going to be all right, I headed home, getting there just as the sun was coming up, the drunks all passed out at various makeshift beds around the house. I had a beer for breakfast and was too wound up to go to sleep, so I waited until they started getting up, and then we all made plans to go to the hospital.

It still took Amy and I a day or two to settle on Robin. It was the only name we could both agree on. She liked it and wanted it, and Robin Hood had always been a childhood hero of mine, so Robin it was, with David as his middle name. Only later did it dawn on me that Robin, the Boy Wonder, was Batman's protégé. A couple of months passed, and he began to develop quite a personality. The movie Annie came out in May, and I still can't explain why, but I started calling him Punjab, not necessarily after the big black bodyguard of Daddy Warbucks, I just liked the sound of it, and for some reason it seemed to fit him (for a little while anyway). So it was either Punjab, or sometimes Punjabi-Boy, but Amy finally laid down the law and broke me of the habit, and I'm glad she did—wouldn't that be a terrible nickname to be stuck with? It was just about this time that Robin met the Governor. Bob Graham had been governor since 1979, and he liked to jog around the nearby cemetery. To get there, he had to run by our place with his bodyguard running alongside. I would walk up to the nearby Minit Market on Sundays to get a newspaper, and sometimes I carried Robin with me. We were waiting at the light behind the Governor's mansion one Sunday, when he came jogging up and stopped to wait for the light as well. So I said hello, and introduced my newborn son, telling the Governor that he was a lifelong Democrat, at least for the last three months since he'd been born. The Governor shook hands with Robin, the light changed and we said good bye. Not quite the same as the time later that summer when we were sitting on the front porch with some friends, drinking beer and smoking pot, and hadn't realized the Governor was coming down the sidewalk with his bodyguard until he was right there, marijuana-smoke wafting across his jogging path. We all sat quietly, hoping he'd just run on by, but Amy had to yell out and wave, "Hi, Governor! Good to see you!" He looked over as he trotted by, waved, and had the slyest grin on his face, unlike his stern and unforgiving bodyguard, but at least they kept running.

B.S.

Now back in the sling of school, I had to do certain things to qualify for my degree, and that was to take all the damn classes that I needed to finish up my minor, which I'd never even thought about. Well, between all the courses I started off with at FTU ten years earlier, the whole zoological crap, and those god-awful Organic Chemistry courses, etc., the Registrar said my best shot was to go for a minor in Biology. Hoo-Hah! Sounded easy enough, but then the reality sank in when I saw what was required... and sonsabitches, I had to take the whole upper class biology course roster, as well as another class in Chemistry (with a lab). It cost me a whole semester's worth of tuition, books, and time, but when I was done I'd finally get my Bachelor's. One silver lining was the one and only biology elective I was allowed to take and that was Oceanography and the teacher was supposedly some world-renowned scientist in the field who helped put Florida State on the map as an oceanographic school. His name was Dr. Marisol, and the class was fascinating; the guy really knew his stuff, and even made it interesting. Had I taken that class two years earlier, I'd probably never have gone into Archaeology; I'd have ended up plying the high seas, (and the higher latitudes) collecting water samples and counting plankton by the square inch. But I did it, took all my courses and finally finished. I wanted to graduate in June, exactly thirty years after Dad, but at the last minute the Registrar told me I was 3 hours short, so I had to sign up for a Directed Individual Study (where you get to pick what you want to do and you and a professor agree on it) with Glen Doran (the professor who had taken Kathy Deagan's place) and all I had to do was read some classical archaeology text and do a report on it. Trouble is, he had gone out of the country for the summer and when I finished I had a helluva time getting hold of him so he could get a grade in on time for me to graduate in August. Then, the Registrar threw one more at me: you have enough hours accrued now so you can qualify for either a Bachelor of Arts or a Bachelor of Science degree, so what's it gonna be? I thought about it for not even ten seconds and told them "I've had to put up with so much bullshit to get this goddamn degree, make it a B.S." I was thirty years old.

Dry Tortugas, 1982

Well, the second trip to Fort Jefferson in Dry Tortugas National Park had been scheduled for the summer, and now I was ready and rarin' to go. Since they had spent the better part of the previous summer just finding and marking the limits of the galleon wrecksite, now there was some serious mapping and test excavations that needed to be done. We had a crew of maybe twenty, supported by FSU's Academic Diving Program, the Anthropology Department, and the National Park Service. It was a logistical nightmare, what with our personal luggage for a month-long stay, groceries, dive gear and support equipment (including compressors, because we had to fill our own tanks), dredge pumps (for test excavations), and emergency supplies. Then there was the severe warning of "No Drugs Whatsoever!" with the threat of dismissal and deportation back to the mainland, not to mention expulsion from the University. We spent one night in Key West, after driving 16 hours from Tallahassee, and still managed to get in a couple of hours at the local hangouts. The next morning, all hungover, we loaded the gear, groceries, and personal luggage on board the NPS Research Vessel *Activa*, the 45-ft Park Service boat, captained by Cliff Green, that ran the waters between Key West and Dry Tortugas once a week, carrying off trash and rock-happy residents, and bringing back fresh food and water, ice, and other supplies to maintain the NPS crew that manned the fort. After loading at the Navy Station in Key West, it was a six to eight hour trip, depending on the seas, and we were all glad to finally see Fort Jefferson come up on the horizon around three that afternoon. Off-loading took another two hours, and at one point, we're handing over a Team Leader's suitcase from the boat to the dock when the bottom fell out and two cases of beer fell into the water, with the owner jumping in right behind them and rescuing them with a flair. I'm standing next to George and said, "I thought you said 'No Drugs Whatsoever'?" He looked at me dead-panned and said, "Alcohol's not a drug." I replied testily "Well, hell, goddamit, I would have brought my own beer if I had known that!" Asking around, I found out that I wasn't the only one led to believe that beer and booze were on the forbidden 'drug' list. Two weeks later, halfway into the project, the Team Leaders had greedily swilled all their beer and most of their liquor, and everyone was by now starting to get a little tense. Early one morning it was my turn to fuel up the dive boat with diesel while everyone else was eating breakfast. I walked down to the dock just as the sun was coming up, hooked up the hand-pump and hose to the boat from a fifty-five gallon barrel on the dock and began pumping. I was just finishing when a small rowboat with two guys in it came ambling toward me from one of the offshore sailboats sitting at anchor in the harbor. They pulled up near me and called out, "Hey! Is that diesel you're putting in there?" "Yes, it is" "Well, we need a little bit to get back home when we're not under sail; do you think you could spare a couple of gallons?" I looked in the drum and saw that there was maybe two gallons left, and I'd have a hard time getting them out with the hand-pump anyway. "Well," I said, "I don't know…" I hesitated. "We'll trade you a case of beer for each gallon; we got plenty of beer." "Well, let's go!" I told them. They left their gas can with me and rowed back to their sailboat. By the time they got back, I had deposited the two leftover gallons into their can, and was waiting for them on the dock. When they pulled up, they had three cases of beer, all Budweiser in the familiar red cans, and they said they were so thankful they threw in the extra case for free. I gave them the gas can, we shook hands, and I trotted back to the breakfast room with my three cases of beer on my shoulder. When I walked in everyone stopped talking, stopped eating, and just stared at me as I sat down, picked up a big felt-tip pen, and started writing my name on each and every can in big bold black capital letters that could be seen no matter how you held the can, and consecutively numbered each one on the bottom. "Where'd you get the beer!?" they all clamored. "None of your goddamn business!" I said, "And anyone tries to steal any, there's gonna be trouble, but anyone who wants to barter for one, or buy one, or take one of my shifts filling tanks, come see me." I put two in the refrigerator, and put the rest in plain sight on a window sill next to my upper bunk in the casemate (gunroom) we were using as the boys dormitory. I never filled another tank the rest of the project, and I made a lot of friends, and even a little money.

Fort Jefferson is a huge brick-built offshore fort, the largest of the coastal defenses planned under Jefferson to support the fledgling United States Navy. It hadn't quite been completed when the Civil War broke out. And when the "War of Northern Aggression" did break out, they could no longer get the red bricks they needed from Mobile, Alabama, and had to complete the last few tiers with more yellowish bricks from Pensacola, which the North had occupied. It was well-manned during the War, with some 200 guns mounted in the vaulted gunrooms we knew as casemates. Supposedly, having "never fired a shot out of anger" it nonetheless helped to establish the old three-mile-limit since that was as far as you could fire a cannon, if not accurately, at least menacingly. But it was out of date by the time it was finished for two reasons: 1) large sailing vessels were very fast and they could just sweep way out of sight and around the fort to break any blockade intended, and 2) by the end of the Civil War, rifled barrels were standard even on the largest naval cannons, and these could fire bullet-shaped projectiles (as opposed to round cannonballs) that could penetrate, and in fact even level, the stoutest brick-built forts. Fresh water was supplied by catching rainwater on the roof and venting it down to subterranean cisterns. But the fort was so big and massive, sitting on a shifting sandy island, that soon the weight of the walls began to settle, cracks developed, and the cisterns were compromised with seeping seawater. This tended to breed a strange little mosquito, the common *Aegyptus*, except here they were so weak from the saltwater intrusion that, yeah, they would swarm you for sure, and undoubtedly bite into you, but they never tried to get away. So you would be swatting and mashing these little buggers while they just did their best to drain you and slowly fly off before you got around to them. In no time at all, if you got caught outdoors at dusk without repellent, you'd have welts, and blood, and little black smashed insects all over you. (These are the same ones that caused all the recurring yellow fever epidemics at the fort, the ones where Samuel Mudd showed such medical heroism that he was finally granted a well-deserved pardon—despite having made at least two attempts to escape.) But the insects weren't the only strange animals. Cattle egrets, the beautiful white crested little heron-like birds, would come flying in from all over: some said from Africa, some from Cuba, others from the Yucatan. They would be exhausted and thirsty, hungry, and just so debilitated that they might get a small drink of water, and then just drop dead. The park staff must still pick up a hundred a month.

Then there were the tragic humans. In order to avoid the rangers from going rock-happy, back then it was a park policy that you had to go off-island at least once a month. You could go every other week if you wanted to and your duties didn't require your personal attention, but you *had* to go at least once a month, and the Park Service even provided a guest-house in Key West for that explicit purpose. And a lot of that rock-happy craziness was the result of the isolation, close quarters, and lack of privacy. One evening we witnessed a ranger and his wife having a quarrel, and even though they walked all the way to the other side of the fort, maybe five hundred feet away, before they started in on each other, it was awful and embarrassing for everyone that we could hear almost every word they said. Worse, however, was Ron, the maintenance man. Low and squat, always half-shaven and slovenly, even in a Park Service uniform, he had greasy black hair and one bad eye that looked off to the side. Ron was the only one exempt from the off-island policy. He'd gotten in too much trouble when he went to Key West, ending up in jail on every occasion, and besides, he didn't want to go; he was happy just staying on the island. He also had a bad habit of following any new women around when they came onto the island; he'd always pretend to be working on something, or checking some building component, but he'd still be follow them around noticeably. There were a few coeds on our crew, besides George's wife Nancy, who was our cook, and more than once he was put on notice to bugger off. We met Ron early on, because he really was a very good maintenance man, and he helped us set up our compressors, tuned up the boat, and was just very good to have around fixing things. Besides, he was relatively friendly. When we first got there and a couple of us younger guys were complaining about the fact that we didn't have any beer like the Team Leaders, Ron invited us over to his casemate apartment. It was the worst sort of bachelor hovel: dishes with food, bugs, dirty laundry in piles, the stench of urine and stale beer, the works. But most disconcerting of all was that along the back wall, there was a pile of broken brown glass, maybe three feet high and six feet across. Ron reached into his refrigerator, and gave the three of us a cold bottle of Budweiser. We were really thankful, as well as thirsty, but even before we could express our gratitude, he had already upended his bottle and drained it in one fell swoop. Then he took that bottle and flung it against the back wall where it shattered and the glass fell onto the top of the inclined heap already leaning against it. We finished ours, and invited to do so, we also flung ours against the back wall. Not quite the same as wine or brandy glasses into the fireplace, but the expressiveness was equally liberating.

The next day we were fishing off the dock on one of our rare days off, and here comes Ron in one of those little garden golf carts, a small John Deere tractor with a flatbed, and he loads up three empty fifty-five gallon drums with the tops cut out, and puts a big square-faced coal shovel in one, then he drives off back into the fort. He comes back a half-hour later, and all three drums are full of his broken brown beer bottle glass, right to the brim. We watch in amazement as he brings around a little sailing punt, maybe fifteen feet long if that, and maneuvers the drums off of the tractor, and deftly rolls them on the bottom rim of the drums down another incline to the floating dock next to where he has pulled up his little sailboat. He dexterously eases the three large drums full of glass onto the front of the boat, now almost pushed under water, and then gets into the back of the little vessel, the gunwale all the way around not an inch above the waterline. He leans back, pulls a beer out of his pocket, and raises the sail with his free hand, the other holding both the beer and the small tiller. In less than a minute, he is sailing smoothly, laid back, drinking the beer with the three large black drums precariously perched on the triangular flat bottom of the boat's bow right before the mast. In ten minutes we are straining to see the sail, which was just a faded green sheet, as it disappeared over the horizon. Maybe an hour later, someone points outward and we can see the little green sail tacking its way back and forth back over the horizon, and finally comes into the harbor. As he pulled up to the lower floating dock, we could see that the drums were now empty. Another underwater archaeological mystery to be solved by Park Service submerged cultural resource units of the future if and when they ever stumble across the remains of the Broken-Bottle Atlantean Culture.

Each morning we were under way by 8 o'clock and on-site and anchored by 9. First divers went in immediately and began mapping one side or the other off of a predetermined datum line that extended through the middle of the supposed longitudinal length of the wreck scatter. The visible portion of the site was marked by the presence of flat brick tiles that had once lined the walls and floors of the galleon's kitchen, or galley. These are known as *ladrillos*, and are each maybe 14 inches long by 8 inches wide and a full inch thick, made of red fired brick, and had been used to line the inside of the galley to prevent fires. On wrecking, the ship was undoubtedly shaken back and forth on top of the shallow reef, and once the structure had broken up, *teredos*, or wood-eating worms quickly devoured most, if not all, of the scattered wooden remains, whereas metal components were quickly colonized by corals and within a few years subsumed into the reef structure. One tell-tale giveaway of the underlying ship's skeleton was that wrought iron is a perfect substrate for fire coral, which was readily visible as white stalagmites with brown-and-tan edges growing up off of the ocean floor. Almost everybody wore some type of protective covering, whether wetsuits or even old pairs of jeans, to keep the fire coral at bay while we were working around the site. But for me the water was just too perfect (yes, proverbially gin-clear, and cool and refreshing), so I always just wore shorts and a t-shirt, and just tried to keep a close eye out. If you've ever rubbed up against a fire coral, especially up under your armpits or inside your thigh, you'll know instantly how it got its name (think hot end of a cigarette), and although we had desensitizing salves on board the dive vessel, it was considered quite the whiny little pussyfoot who cut his or her work dive short to swim back to the first aid kit for relief. There were other dangers present as well, some visible and some not quite so. We had the big green morays with their cold dead yellow eyes and constantly gasping mouth full of needles, some of them six or seven feet long and who were fearless once they'd reached that size and would quickly slither out from beneath a coral head and swim snakelike right between your legs. If they ever bit you, it wasn't the bite that would leave a big gaping section of muscle missing, it would be the bacteria and generally toxic mucous inside their mouth that would fester in the meat that would have to be surgically removed. Then there was one day, we were mapping and digging holes with a dredge pump, and one of the park rangers stopped by to say hello. After a quick visit, he left, and had to take his boat the long way around the reef because it was dangerously shallow and he couldn't just cut straight across. I was up and taking a break between dives and we noticed that he stopped his boat on the other side of the reef from us, maybe one hundred yards away. He just sat there for the longest time, watching something in the water with his binoculars. After maybe a half an hour he just up and drove back to the fort and headquarters. Later that evening when we came in I asked him what he was looking at. He very matter-of-factly told us that he watched as a ten or eleven-foot hammerhead devoured an eight-foot-wide manta ray one big pizza-size bite at a time while the manta struggled back and forth to try and get away. He said the monster had finished off the manta in about fifteen minutes, and all that was left was the spiked tail. One hundred yards away!

During the previous year's initial survey of the site, the crew found what was described as "a nest of swivel guns." They recovered one of them and Ken Wild did a great job of drawing it in detail, while some of the other archaeologists did a little background research. A swivel gun is a small-caliber cannon that was generally mounted by hand, slipping its gimbaled swivel into a hole along the rail. It had a small tiller on the back end so you could "swivel" it around in different directions and fire small projectiles like a solid iron ball the size of a golf ball, or more commonly, since it was for up-close anti-personnel fighting, a handful of nails or iron scrap. These were some of the earliest European guns ever made and were "built-up" guns, which meant they were built up out of strips of iron, that were then bound by several iron rings, which once heated fire-red, slipped on, and then cooled, tightened up the whole armament, creating a simple, effective and easy to construct weapon, not to mention one that could comfortably be handled by a single man. At first, there was the obvious question, "Why was there a whole pile of these small hand-cannons, all chained together, lying on the bottom in the first place?" and then of course, the followup, "What are we (the Park Service) going to do about them?" The first question was answered by the research. During the whole process of wrecking, while the galleon was trying to stay off of the reef, they would have deployed all their anchors one by one. Finally, in a desperate move, if they were short of anchors, or didn't have time to get a spare one up from below decks, they would create an improvised anchor by chaining seven or eight swivel guns together, tossing them over and hoping they would grab onto the coral bottom before the ship grounded. If it didn't hold, or the anchor line parted, well, that would explain the loss of the "nest of swivel guns." Now, what to do about it: these are very rare artifacts, and intrinsically, very valuable. They had already recovered one, and the cost of conserving the one they already had was going to cost in the tens of thousands of dollars since conservation entailed taking the whole thing apart, hooking it up to electrolysis in a chemical bath to get the salts out, then putting it back together, and finally, curating it in perpetuity. Since the other ones had sat on the seabed for over 350 years, they could sit a little while longer, but they still needed to be protected. The plan was to lay them in a small sand depression to cushion them and then to set a massive brain coral on top that no one would be able to move without a crane. This would preserve and protect them for the foreseeable future. Such a plan was not undertaken lightly, and to oversee it, they called in the Superintendent of Everglades National Park, Jack Moorehead, an avid diver and conservationist. We went in the water with Moorehead, and although George went in too as titular head of the project, he soon turned back to observe operations from the *Activa*, which had the crane on board. A nearby huge brain-coral head, nearly perfectly round and at least eight feet in diameter, had been identified nearby, and once the soft strap slings had been placed around it and the *Activa* had moved into place with its on-board crane and put a little upward pressure on it, a few of us divers went at the bottom of the coral head with hammers, chisels, and crowbars. But it didn't take much coaxing and the coral head was soon hanging suspended off the bottom. It was gingerly moved over the top of the sand-enclosed depression holding the swivel guns, and slowly eased on down. A flawless operation that many might have considered both dangerous and unnecessary, but later visits to the site showed that the coral head was thriving, and the guns were safe and sound. Known as "preservation-in-place," I imagine they are lying there to this day.

Yacht See

Since we had Moorehead with us for a day or two, and the Superintendent of Everglades being a very big honcho (or *kahuna*) in the National Park Service (actually he was the Superintendent of three South Florida parks all at once: Biscayne, Everglades and Dry Tortugas), and since we'd finished the preservation-in-place operation rather quickly, he needed to be entertained. Well, it so happened that Cliff Green, the captain of the *Activa*, had helped out the Coast Guard in intercepting a yacht used as a drug runner some three or four months earlier. Once the bad guys were apprehended, the Coast Guard had scuttled the yacht and it had settled upright on a patch of sand in about eighty-five feet of water. Would Moorehead like to go and see it? Hell yeah, he would. He needed a couple of dive partners though, and everyone else was worn out except me and Ken Wild, and we never said no to going out on a dive. The Deputy Superintendent, who was referred to as the "Park Manager," of Fort Jefferson, Kevin Kacer, also came along, since he was officially Moorhehead's host. Cliff eyeballed a couple of islands in the distance, took bearings, and said he knew exactly where it was, but it all looked like open water to me. He finally stopped the boat, putting it in neutral and letting it drift, and ran outside the cabin, looking over the rail. All of a sudden he points to me and Ken and says, "Quick, jump off the front and see if you can see it down on the bottom!" Ken and I grab our masks fins and snorkel and jump off the bow. Now the bow of the *Activa* was the equivalent of jumping off the roof of your house, maybe twelve feet off the water—not a big deal once, or even twice—but we looked around and looked around and we couldn't see anything against the sandy bottom way, way down below. He yelled down, "Okay, come on back up." We swam around to the back of the boat, climbed the ladder and settled down. By now, he'd moved the boat another hundred yards or so, threw it into neutral again, ran out the cabin, looked over the rail, and again, said, "Quick, jump off the bow and see if you can see it on the bottom!" and off we went. We swam around and couldn't see it, then swam around the back of the boat, climbed back up the aft ladder, and sat down on the deck again. This happened at least two more times, and we were getting a bit frustrated (and pissed), when finally, about the fourth time, well, damn, there's something sitting there way down on the bottom. "I knew it!" he said triumphantly (I could have strangled him). We climbed back on board one more time, and this time we all put on our tanks, nice comfortable single aluminums from the park, not our usual cumbersome ADP double steel 72s. The four of us, me and Ken, and Moorehead and Kacer, jumped off the bow one more time, and slowly descended through the blue-green darkening haze of hundred-foot visibility as the yacht came into focus from our viewpoint above. It was big! At least as big as the *Activa*, and sat upright right on the pure white sandy bottom, against whose dappled waves it gave the appearance of being afloat on the seabed. Apparently, the Coast Guard had opened the drainplugs, and then they kicked out a window, and that's why the yacht had settled so slowly and easily down onto the bottom upright. We entered the open window, letting Moorehead and Kacer go in first.

Once inside, the eeriness became palatable, and since it didn't make any sense to be swimming inside the vessel, and we all let the air out of our buoyancy compensators to make us heavier and took off our flippers, wrapping the straps around our wrists, and then gently slow-motion walked around the staterooms, bubbles bouncing off the ceiling and out the open window hatch. Other than being full of water, it was as if the vessel were still in dock: dishes in the cabinets, a television, drawers and cabinets stocked with flatware and cans of food, even a record sitting on the turntable. Ken nudged me and I turned to watch a six-foot barracuda swim slowly by one of the still-closed transparent hatch windows, his big eye peering in, and we followed watching him as he slowly circled the yacht outside. It felt a lot like we were in the movie *Thunderball*, silent except for the sound of our exhaust bubbles every few seconds. Soon Moorehead and Kacer put their flippers back on and swam out the open window. Ken and I continued exploring, looking into the bathroom, or head, and checking out the various bedrooms, clothes still hanging in the closet. We checked our gauges and it was soon going to be time to go. Ken picked up the record off the phonograph, and I was fiddling with the inside smaller steering wheel when it came off in my hand. We put on our flippers and floated out the window, where the barracuda now sat off ten or twenty yards away, slowly turning and watching us closely. Moorehead and Kacer had already gone up, so we ascended slowly and broke surface just behind the *Activa*. Immediately, Cliff yelled down to us, "What's that in your hands?" We showed him the record and the small spoked steering wheel, "Just a couple of souvenirs." "Oh no, oh, hell no," he said, "that shit is still evidence… go put it back!" We looked at our gauges. "We only got 500 pounds," we said. "I don't give a damn," yelled Cliff, "you go put that shit back!" All right, all right. Down we went, and when we got to the open window, we just tossed the crap in and turned back for the surface. As we came up, Cliff had already fired up the engines in neutral, and we had the diesel exhaust blowing in our faces as we took off our flippers and climbed up the aft ladder. It was a thrilling dive, the memory being much more valuable and longer lasting than any souvenir. The record? I had looked at it when it was still on the turntable: The Beatles' *Magical Mystery Tour*. Seemed appropriate.

The Vegan

As I had mentioned, George's wife, Nancy, had come along as part of the crew, the Cook. We all had to pitch in forty dollars each to pay for our groceries, some of which, like fresh produce, were shipped in periodically on one of Cliff's *Activa* runs each week. There had been some initial grumbling about the forty dollars, but in retrospect it was a great deal: she was very practical and inventive at the same time, and we ate very well, with everyone sharing in the domestic duties of food preparation, setting the table, cleaning up and washing dishes, etc. One of the grumblers was a guy named JC, a strict vegetarian who was a long-haired hippie (like more than a few of us), but other than having black hair instead of brown or auburn, and being rather gaunt, he was more JC-looking than the rest. He refused to pay the forty dollars and said that he would fix his own food instead, bringing along a ten-pound bag of mung beans, and two five-pound bags of rice and alfalfa. He set up a little hothouse of empty jars and started producing sprouts when he wasn't cooking up his brown rice. After ten days or so, though, it was apparent that sometimes the mung beans didn't just sprout, but rotted in place, and had to be thrown out. We were burning a lot of calories every day, and part of Nancy's strategy was to save leftovers so they could be added into later subsequent meals. One morning at breakfast Nancy announced that some of the leftovers were missing, and even some of the desserts had been gotten into. She was just putting everyone on notice that there'd be no more late-night snacking. Well, it didn't stop, so she took matters into her own hands. We'd all gone to bed one night after an especially grueling day, and we were fast asleep in our boys' dorm casemate, right next to the kitchen and dining room. Nancy had chosen that night to sit in the dark in the kitchen, just her cigarette-tip a-glowing. Around two o'clock in the morning, a dark shadowy figure came quietly to the kitchen door. She put out her cigarette, sitting in the corner in the dark by the light switch. The silent creeper walked over to the refrigerator, opened it and pulled out a small box. Softly stepping to the cutlery drawer, he slowly drew out a fork, sat down at the large dining table and began to eat. Nancy waited a minute or two, and then threw on the light switch, yelling "AHA!" both actions bright and loud enough to wake us guys sleeping next door. There, sitting at the table, with a beard full of chocolate cake crumbs and icing sat JC, wide-eyed and busted. A couple of us guys went next door to see what all the ruckus was about, but by the time we walked in, she was so busy berating him for the pilfering, the bitching about the forty dollars, the rotten fucking mung beans, et al, that we just left him to take his medicine and went back to bed. In the morning, he was once again shamed before the entire crew as Nancy recounted the results of her stakeout, with the provision that his forty dollars was coming out of his meager per diem, while at the same time making a theatrical production of pitching out his mung bean and alfalfa sprout factory, jars and all. The rice was to be donated to the general fund. After that he was invited to sit down and eat whatever portion of breakfast he wanted, whether vegetable or not. He was lucky (or maybe Nancy had changed the menu that morning out of pity): that particular morning we had pancakes, which he ate with unrepentant relish (his long black beard slathered and dripping with syrup).

The project was now finished and our last night had arrived. We'd packed all the equipment that day and it was stacked on the dock ready to load in the morning. So we decided to throw a little last-night party in the boys' dorm. We invited the Team Leaders and the girls, all four of them. The music was fired up over several radios, creating a surround-around effect. Now it was time to pull out the last of the drinks. I still had a six-pack and three from my diesel barter, and donated it to the ice chest. It was surprising how much booze and beer came magically out of the woodwork. Apparently a few people had put in liquor-and-beer shopping requests, more than amply provided for, with Nancy's fresh produce lists, once it had been established that "Alcohol's not a drug." And we were determined to drink it all up that night so we wouldn't be carrying empties home. By the time the women showed up the boys were already dancing with each other, with modified mop-wigs, and quite besotted; not unlike those penny-novel descriptions of eighteenth-century sailors crossing the equator. The girls looked in the window, saw our condition and hurried back to their own dorm; they weren't going to have anything to do with us, and no amount of pleading on our part was going to change their minds. Now that we were left to entertain ourselves, George came up with a particularly interesting trick. He went into the adjoining kitchen and brought back a handful of raw eggs. As we were all invited to watch, he tossed one up through the oscillating fan blades in the dorm's center ceiling. It went up through the whirring blades, hung for a second, and dropped back through, to be caught unscathed. Well, this *was* both interesting and entertaining. He did it again... and down it came, once again intact. In our condition we had stupidly assumed that this was a true talent, and that he knew some subtle psychic trick to time his egg going through the spinning paddles. We applauded in marvel. The third time it again passed upward, hung for a second, and then broke atop the blade on the downward trajectory, now spewing raw egg and yolk in a wide circular arc around the room. It was just pure luck that had preserved the egg on the first two attempts, that's all. But no, now some of the more drunken kids were convinced that they too, could accomplish this marvelous feat; besides, there were still a few eggs left. Before it was all over, there was egg goo in a line some six feet up and all along the casemate wall, and a big puddle of broken raw eggs and their shattered shells on the floor below the fan, right in front of some poor fellow's bunk, the fellow being the aforementioned JC, who was absent during all of this, considering himself above the lowlife social interaction of drunken revelry. George made short business of getting out of there before he was blamed as the cause of the mess, and by the time we all settled down and slunk off to our bunks we had finished all the booze and beer (and cigarettes) left at the fort. Just before drifting off we were awakened by a loud cursing groan, a light went on, and there was JC standing barefoot in a large puddle of eggshells and slime. We blamed it all on George.

13.   Coming of Age in Anthropology (1982-1985)

Grindal

Once the summer was over, graduate school and the job at SEAC beckoned, so I signed up for a class in Anthropology and Religion, taught by Bruce Grindal, the noted Humanist, maybe in his late forties back then, a handsome and affable professor who was known for his mystic views and transcendental meditative naps. When I say handsome, it was because he always reminded me of George Peppard, and the young Peppard at that, from *The Carpetbaggers* and *The Blue Max*, not the later bloated blowhard on the A-Team. I mentioned this to him once and he thought I was crazy, but it was fairly obvious how the college coeds fawned over him. Other than the fact that he was always friendly, had a great sense of humor, and a ready smile, with sad, introspective eyes, I liked him for his mysticism. He'd smoke a little pot with us students, and when we talked about tripping on LSD, he'd just smile knowingly. A serious intellectual philosopher, he introduced most of us to the concept of humanism, where human values, dignity, and interests prevail over any religious or theological overview. He was very active in the American Anthropological Association, and in fact, published one of the very few ethnographic accounts of witnessing a "miraculous" event: the temporary resurrection of an elder at some African tribe he was living with and studying early in his career. As I recall the story, he was staying with this family, sitting in their mud hut taking notes on various domestic activities, when word reached them that some guy in the neighboring village had died and they were having a ceremony that night before putting him in the ground. He followed as everyone tramped on over to the nearby locale, and sure enough, there's this body surrounded by weeping and wailing women, all stretched out, and for all practical purposes, lifeless. Midway through a long-engaged drum ceremony that lasted deep into the night, the village shaman, or witch doctor, sprays some liquor over the deceased, shakes a rattle at him, and demands that the old man arise and say one last goodbye to the locally gathered mourners. The old man opens his eyes, slowly stands up, does a little stilted walk once around the fire and lays back down, now dead for good. Bruce just reported it as he saw it, and didn't make any judgment calls regarding possible explanations or authenticity, and that's probably why it was published.

Primitive Whites

Well, the class assignment was semester-long ethnographic fieldwork and reportage on studying some religious church, group, or organization that we would not normally be associated with, preferably a church. We were expected to go to the services, note what was said and done, try to determine the core beliefs, and then report all this back to the class, with a final paper expected at the end. Sounded easy enough. It just so happened that on my travels back and forth to Woodville when I was working at DISC Village, I passed a tiny little white wooden church tucked away on a little lot with an adjacent cemetery behind a feedstore and next to a ballfield, obviously predating both, which had been later built up surrounding it. The church's sign said "White Primitive Baptist Church." I was always intrigued by what that meant: Was it for Whites only? Was it because the church itself was painted white? And what the hell did they mean by "primitive"? Hell, I thought all Baptists were pretty primitive; but these guys had established their own congregation (which had to be small from the size of the building), proudly stating that they were Primitive while the regular-style Woodville First Baptist Church, made of brick and right out on the highway, wasn't even two blocks away; obviously, there was some local dissension between the two, and I wondered what it was. So I bundled poor new-Mom Amy and little Robin in the car and Sunday we drove down to Woodville and sat in the back of the little one-room wooden church with all the gray-haired men and women turning round to give us a stare, me with my long red ponytail and beard, looking down into my hand and trying to take notes surreptitiously, and Amy keeping Robin quiet, smiling. Other than the six sets of pews and a stark wooden lectern, the place was bare except for a list of the Ten Commandments on the right-hand wall. The pastor recognized the congregation, all dozen of them, and made comment of the new participants in the back row (we smiled, I'm scribbling away). He started off with a few announcements, then they broke into a few *a cappella* hymns, the hymn books kindly handed over to us onto the open page by the people in the row in front of us. [I only learned later, and this was long after the class was finished, that Primitive Baptists are not keen on musical instruments, or accompaniment, when singing holy hymns: part of the whole "primitiveness," or getting back to their roots, aspect.] The sermon was a standard hell-fire and brimstone with the same standard warning about straying from the path, but to be honest, it was probably lost on the meager congregation of maybe 20 over-aged and already in-the-furrow flock. Eventually, the tempo rose ever so slightly to incorporate any new blood that may have wandered in. Huh? What's he sayin'? Pretty soon, he was calling out that, if ANYONE wished to come forward and declare themselves reborn in Jesus, NOW was your opportunity. I sat stone-faced as the people turned ever so slightly to see if there was any movement out of the back row—this while Amy's giving me ever so slight jabs with her elbow to go on up and get the whole experience. Not only was I chicken, but I didn't want to give them the satisfaction either. After an uncomfortable full minute of silence and no movement (the others were already "saved," so their participation was unnecessary), he finished up with a regular good old Catholic "Our Father," except for that last part where all the heretics say "for thine is the power and the kingdom and the glory for ever and ever," (that's how you can always tell the true Catholic *Lord's Prayer*, straight from the lips of the original JC himself, from the other bastardized ones). As the service ended, and we all headed outside, the dozen congregants or so swarmed us, "Hello, what's your name?" "Where are you from?" What do you do for a living?" "What's the baby's name?" "Welcome to our church…" I answered thick and fast, and made sure that Amy heard me so she could corroborate. "We live in Tallahassee." "I work as a carpenter at DISC Village." "We're just looking at different churches right now…" "Yes, the baby was born last February." "Thank you, you've all been very nice." And to Amy, once the old hens had gotten out of hearing range, "Let's get the fuck out of here!" Or maybe she said it to me, I'm not sure, but I know we were both thinking the same thing: no matter what, we didn't want to become any more "primitive" than we already were; if anything, our aspirations for our nascent family were in the opposite direction. Grindal was very happy with my initial effort, but he started right in with wanting me to get more involved. "immerse" myself in their culture, even to the point of going on up and getting "saved." Well, that's where I drew the line. I mean, I can submerge my general personality when the need arises, but as far as I was concerned, at this point I didn't need to. And Amy wasn't coming along as my cover any more. This was my own required class work and she had better things to do on Sunday mornings, like sleeping in. So, I had to go and face the primitives on my own, which I did, and once they realized I was never coming up when the call was given, they pretty much gave up on me. I did discover, while writing up my final paper, that the "White" in the White Primitive Baptist Church did stand for "whites only," because, much to my surprise, there is a whole separate set of congregants who go to Black Primitive Baptist Churches as well. Although Grindal did push for me to take the final baptismal plunge, I suppose I was still carrying around a little Catholic baggage, or maybe I didn't want to dabble with my new-found Buddhist dharma, 'cause I was damned if I was going to get "saved." Damned if you do, and damned if you don't, right? Grindal still gave me an "A" for the class.

236

Cook

So now I was in graduate school, and compared to the undergraduate classes it was like learning to swim instead of floating around in an inner tube. Graduate school was nothing like going to school at all: there were few notes to be taken, no tests, no rote memorization; yeah, sure there were papers to be written, but generally the routine was simply to read a book or set of books, and the paper you wrote was (hopefully) an intelligent expression of what you learned, or understood, or thought about the subject in question. The only way you could fail was not to read the books, not to think about what you had read, and then (this was actually the deciding factor) not to participate in the discussion. There were occasions where someone, even someone very brilliant, would do the readings, write a grand paper, and yet get a mediocre grade (which was a "B" for anything in graduate school) simply because they were too shy or introverted to speak up in class, much less defend a point of view or express an opinion. The "seminars" were actually just adult discussions, and the best of these was carried out by Ed Cook. Dr. Cook had been replaced as the Chairman of the Department, partly because of his administrative disorganization, partly because of his lack of interest in being the Chair, and partly because of his own anthropological research interests. He had been studying the Manga in Papua New Guinea for some twenty years after getting his doctorate from Yale, and he was well-known in the American Anthropological Association for his contributions, including his amazing book, *Blood and Semen: Kinship Systems of Highland New Guinea*. The title comes from the New Guinea tribal belief that when a baby is conceived, the reason the menstrual flow ceases is because the blood flow is now stopped up to build the baby, and the husband is required to have intercourse with the woman as often as he possibly can (whether he wants to or not) in order to supply the white semen that is necessary for the skeletal structure upon which the blood and meat must hang. Subsequently, if a sickly child is born, it is considered the man's fault for not providing enough of the white bone-building semen. (Kind of like Wonder Bread, "it builds strong bodies twelve ways.") At the same time, they were still practicing female infanticide, when the ratio of females to males reached a certain limit.

Freeman/Mead

It just so happened that the Australian anthropologist Derek Freeman's book badmouthing Margaret Mead (five years dead at the time) had just come out, *Margaret Mead and Samoa: The Making and Unmaking of an Anthropological Myth*, which developed into a major controversy in anthropology. Freeman put forth that Mead had been duped by women telling stories of sexual freedom that hadn't really occurred, and at the same time had misled the elders herself about her own "unmarried" status, thus allowing her access to otherwise forbidden conclaves and secret information. So Cook decided that we would try to get to the heart of the matter by reading Mead's two big books that had made her famous (*Sex and Temperament in Three Primitive Societies* and *Coming of Age in Samoa*), as well as *Blackberry Winter*, which was an autobiography of her early life. Then we'd read Freeman's book, carry out our own background study, and compare what the facts were. Again, this was before computers, so we ended up doing a lot of in-depth research, sharing notes and sources, and ended up making a timeline of Mead's actual life (which did, in part, differ from what she claimed at times). It was an incredible piece of cumulative research by the end of the semester. Our conclusion was pretty much what has been the judgment of the professional community since that time: Mead had stretched her credentials to get access to informants; Freeman was a nut, who had suffered two nervous breakdowns and had a messiah complex, but nevertheless, was a pretty good anthropologist, and had caught Mead's biases. But none of it took anything away from Margaret Mead as an excellent ethnographer, and Freeman took way too much delight in attacking Mead than in presenting his own arguments. It's still a fascinating anthropological controversy to this day, with adherents on both sides. For us, it was a learning experience we'd never forget.

A couple of interesting things occurred during and shortly after this seminar. One evening, we were waiting for Dr. Cook to show up, and he was more than his usual fashionably late. Well, someone pointed out that in the Student Handbook it said that if a professor was more than 15 minutes late, the class could be considered canceled, and the students were free to leave without being marked absent. It had been ten minutes already, so we waited another five. Then we all got up and walked out. As we were walking down the hall, here comes Dr. Cook, "Where the hell do you guys think you're going?" After explaining the Student Handbook notation, he got really mad, and started yelling, right there in the hallway, "Goddammit, I'm here now and we've got a two hour class. I'm not just going to turn around and go home; this is a bunch of bullshit, where were you going anyway?" We told him we were going over to Poor Paul's, a local beer joint next to the Pastime. He immediately brightened up, and said "Fine. We'll have class over at Poor Paul's. First pitcher is on me." We walked on over, everybody was happy, and we had one of the best informal classes I'd ever been to, concentrating on the opposing personalities of Mead and Freeman rather than the controversy itself. Two hours and four pitchers later and we all went home, glowing. The seminar on Mead had also gotten a lot of attention in the Department, since each professor had his or her own opinion after having read Freeman's new book. One of the archaeologists mentioned that she had seen Mead several times at various conferences, and once, at one of the hotels, there was an almost-full elevator going down from one of the upper floors when it stopped midway, the door opened, and there was Margaret Mead standing there with her famous forked walking stick. She stepped into the elevator, and turned her back to the rest of the riders as she faced the closed doors. Just as the car stopped at the Lobby floor where everyone was about to depart, and in that moment just before the doors opened, Mead loudly announced, "Someone in this elevator has just had sex!" The doors swished open and she walked off, leaving the riders both stunned and amused.

Rocket Men

Although I was tempted by the whole ethnographic anthropological adventure of living with some primitive tribe, studying their beliefs and culture systems, getting to know them personally, etc., etc., I still had to make a living and there was no promise in that by going the cultural route. Besides, I was already working for the Park Service as a novice archeologist which was paying the rent and groceries, and other than the fact that there was no health insurance, and I was only a "temporary" employee according to the personnel code, they were taking pretty good care of me, letting me have a free rein as far as my class schedules, and we were located right on campus, in the bottom open labs of the Bellamy Building. And we had a lot of fun. Like the bottle rocket wars. I don't know how they started (such antics only took place during Spring Break, when the place was deserted), but somebody fired a bottle rocket into our lab one day, and once we saw it coming, the fuse sparks flying and all of us ducking under our lab tables, with the resultant "POP!" the war was on. George was a notorious firecracker fiend, so it wasn't long before he'd buzzed you on the intercom to discuss some urgent matter that he needed to talk about and you'd be headed down the hall to his office, then look up to see way down the hall, his door open, and him sitting behind his desk with a cigarette poised above a multiple-load of bottle rockets aimed your way, and he would smile, light the fuse, get up, and as the rockets flew down the hallway at you and any other students who happened to be walking either with or near you, everyone was sent scurrying for cover into adjoining offices as the rockets careened off the hallway walls, popping off this way and that, then he'd calmly close his metal office door, impervious to any retaliation. Soon the wars escalated, as different factions coalesced, even to the point of sending in double-agents, and moles to scope out the defenses. We had repeater rifles fashioned out of aluminum tubes; we'd climb up into the ceiling so we could drop incendiaries into locked offices; and we started bringing in the heavy stuff, cherry bombs and M-80s. Even the venerable Dr. Dailey, Chairman of the Department, went so far as to one day load up a small Spanish culverin (an ornate brass piece of gunnery, most likely only decorative, that had graced the department for years), and let fly with a fusillade of bottle rockets that cleared the entire open foyer of the Bellamy Building and left a gunpowder haze hanging in the hall.

The Armistice

The wars ended suddenly when school got back in. It was after Spring Break, 1983, and I was in George's office probably around 3 o'clock in the afternoon discussing something about planning for the upcoming summer Biscayne investigations with him. George stands up and says "I gotta take a piss, keep talking…" So we walk on down the hall at Bellamy and I'm trundling behind, still talking, when he pushes in the door to the men's room—which at that time happens to be the infamous Men's Room at Bellamy, the one that had been advertised in the back pages of the national weekly *The Gay Advocate* as a great place to "meet," if you get my drift. So, there's me and George standing there, door half-open, and what do we see? There's three guys standing in front of the urinals (not facing the urinals, not peeing, but standing in line, facing the stalls), all smiling sheepishly at us, George and I, who are now standing there dumbfounded and silent. The stalls are all occupied, doors closed, with two pairs of feet in each, one set on their knees, and the other either standing or sitting on the toilet. [One must remember the times and the circumstances: we were not all so tolerant of gay public sexhibitionism back then, if ever, and this particular Men's Room had become a territorial point of contention between the players, the office workers, and the students ever since the advertisement in the *Gay Advocate* had been pointed out in the FSU student newspaper, the *Flambeau*. Besides, we'd come in there expecting to take a leak, since it was, in point of fact, a public restroom.] George goes "Oh shit! That's it! I've had it!" And he turns about, and says "come with me." So I follow him back down the hall to his office, and he goes behind his desk, and opens his lower right drawer and pulls out a large white tube, with a fuse on it. Now, I have to interject here, that I knew what this was. This was the grenade simulator I had gotten in the storage container auction… a big fucking firecracker, as big as a stick of dynamite, in a white cardboard tube with a dark green fuse. Well, I didn't want to keep it, and I didn't want it around the house, and I didn't want to have it anywhere near me. But I knew that, being a pyrotechnic, George loved that shit. So I had given it to him six months earlier. And now, here he was, pulling it out of his desk, with a sick grin below that wicked grey mustachio of his. "Here, you take this," he says, and hands me a lighter. "Oh shit, George, I don't know about this…" "Just follow me," says he, and back down the hall we go. We get back to the Men's Room door and we're standing in front of it, and he says, "Light it." I'm going, "Shit, George, this is dangerous." "Light it, goddamnit!" Okay, okay. I light it, and the big green fuse starts to fizz. We push into the door, George steps in, smiles at the boys lined up along the urinals, who when they see what's in his hand, lit and fizzling, scramble over each other (and us) and haul ass out the door. Then he carefully tosses it under the middle stall (of three, doors closed, all double-occupied). Then George and I turn and walk out the door. We're walking back to his office, and we can hear some scrambling sounds from the bathroom behind us, when there's a loud **PHA-BOOM**! To this day, I can recall the panels in the hallway ceiling lifting up, the lights flickered for a second, and when the panels set back down, a flurry of dust descended into the hall. No one had come out of that bathroom. We walked into his outer office and closed and locked the door, and then we went into his inner office and closed that door as well. Then we sat and waited, not saying a word. The sirens started about a full minute later. George got up, went to the outer office and shut off the lights. Then he came back into his office, closed the door, lit up a cigarette, and asked me if I wanted one. I said yeah, 'cause I was a little shaken. And then he said turn off the light, which I did. There we were, just sitting in the dark, listening, with nothing but the glowing orange of cigarette ends making little trails in the dark. Then came the knocking. The firemen were knocking on all the doors, telling people to get out and evacuate the building. We just sat there. Finished our cigarettes, and sat quietly in the dark. Maybe ten, fifteen minutes. Then we heard people start coming back in the building. You could hear the students laughing and making a racket as they came back in. The firetrucks finally pulled away, and we turned the lights back on. George had that shit-eating grin of his, and said, "Goddamn, I never did take that piss!" He got up, we slowly opened the outer door and looked down the hall— nobody there. So we walked on down the hall to the Men's Room, pushed our way in through the door, and while George was taking a leak, I could see that, under the center stall, there was a big black-ringed flashburn mark, maybe a yard across, burned into the floor. The center stall door was half unhinged, hanging awkwardly. And a few of the ceiling panels were all askew. The smell of gunpowder hung in the air, mixed with the smell of urine. All I could say was "HOLY SMOKE!" Then I had to pee. The next day, on every office door affiliated with either the Anthropology Department or the National Park Service on the first floor of Bellamy, there was posted an 8x10 sheet of paper with huge black bold and capital letters stating "**ALL HOSTILITIES WILL CEASE IMMEDIATELY!**" by order of the Chairman of the Anthropology Department, Dr. Robert C. Dailey. With the simple writ of a pen, *Peace on Earth and Good Will to All Mankind* was once again established. Ah, that it should ever be that easy.

Biscayne 1983

Now the big project was coming up: complete mapping, selective artifact recovery, and test excavations of HMS *Fowey*, a British frigate lost in 1748 at what is today Biscayne National Park. The story goes, that during the late 1970s, when everybody wanted to get into the treasure hunting business, a certain Miami restaurateur named Gerald Klein heard about a wreck out in Biscayne Bay. Having been told where to look for it, he went out there and found it, and then filed a State salvage permit to work it. [A little side note: The State of Florida had fought the treasure salvors back in the early 70s for rights to salvage (even historic) wrecks under Admiralty Law. Bottom line was that the lawyers for the State (being State-paid shills) were no match for those of the salvors, high-priced corporate shysters who were often paid in shares of 'the Company' and/or after-salvage profit (gold bars, e.g.). The State ended up with only a 20% take on the salvage permits, and the right to "observe," but not "interfere, with the archaeological data recovery. We referred to them as "The Salvor Wars," which it is more than fair to say, the State lost.] So Klein had to tell the Court where the wreck was, within a nautical mile, to get a permit. Well, the circle that he put on the map lay entirely within Biscayne National Park, which was federally-owned, as opposed to State-owned, and this threw a whole new monkey wrench into his plans, because the Feds never allow salvage on national park lands (mining, yes; even resource extraction and recreational concessions; but salvage of historic sites, including shipwrecks, no, at least not yet.) Klein sued the Feds under Admiralty Law, which allows bringing shipwrecks and their cargoes "back into commerce" and provides the salvor with a hefty (usually 75-80%) share of the profits. One of the arguments presented by Klein's lawyer, was that the National Park Service didn't even know they had the wreck inside their boundaries, so how could they be laying claim to something they didn't even know existed? The judge decided that this was a fair question and gave the Feds a 10-day window to go out and find it, using Klein's one-mile radius point of reference.

In response to the judge's order, George put together a team from FSU (Rich Johnson), Academic Diving (Gregg Stanton), and the National Park Service's Submerged Cultural Resources Unit,

240

known as SCRU (Dan Lenihan and Harry Murray). They went down to Biscayne in late June 1980 and dragged a magnetometer (and divers) all over hell and creation within the one-mile search area before they finally hit the wreck on the next-to-the-last day allowed for the survey, the 4th of July. Then they quickly photographed and filmed it, and gathered a few (of what they thought were) diagnostic artifacts. Other than Murray getting burned and starting a fire on the bow of the mag boat while trying to fill the gas tank of the generator as it was still running, the operation was a success. They had located the wrecksite, and it was undoubtedly in Federal waters. They even named it the Fourth of July Wreck, as much to put the Federal stamp on it I imagine as to celebrate the day they found it. The artifacts were carried to the Southeast Archeological Center in Tallahassee, where they were initially, and tentatively, identified as Spanish, and possibly French, from the mid-to-late 1700s. Later historical research and more in-depth analysis would reveal that the wreck was actually British, but that it had in fact captured a Spanish vessel, and spent time at the French fortress site of Louisbourg in Nova Scotia before being assigned to the Caribbean squadron, so the presence of both Spanish and French artifacts was explainable. After some legal banter back and forth, and an appeal, the judge finally ruled that Klein was out of luck and the historic shipwreck belonged fee simple to the National Park Service. Klein was so angry at the decision that he put the exact location of the wrecksite on all the paper placemats at his local restaurant, the same location which he had previously kept guarded, only divulging the one-mile approximate location under court order. His rationale for handing out the location was that if he couldn't have at it, then by God he'd let everyone know where it was so they could all go out and loot it at their leisure. Fuck the Government. Two years later, during an attempted holdup of the restaurant, Mr. Klein stepped between the shotgun-wielding robber and the cash register, and that was the end of the business, and everything else for Mr. Gerald Klein, except for the last rites, which included the depositing of his ashes on the disputed wrecksite.

Well, now in 1983, we had gotten authorization (and money) to carry out an in-depth investigation of the wreck to better identify it, determine what condition it was in, and make recommendations for protecting and preserving it. This was a National Park Service project, under George's direction, and was supported by both the Academic Diving Program at FSU and the Anthropology Department. The real brains behind the operation was Anthropology graduate student Russell Skowronek, a young historic archaeologist who had been one of Kathy Deagan's field crew for several years in St. Augustine and was quickly becoming one of the leading 18th century Spanish Colonial experts in the country. He was assisted by Richard Vernon, another of Deagan's dons, whom we amiably dubbed "Old Grog" for several disparate reasons, such as his demeanor, his love of the drink (but not too strong), and his 18th century British namesake, Admiral Sir Richard Vernon, who was the dirty scoundrel who invented grog in the first place, by cutting the ships' crews daily allotment of rum with water (which, in all fairness though, he had to do—they'd been long at sea and had he not "stretched" the ration, he'd have run out completely, and that would have ended in a much worse situation, possibly even mutiny, rather than a few floggings for the grumbling of watered-down rum). Representing the Academic Diving Program was Gregg Stanton, and then the crew chiefs were myself and Ken Wild. Various volunteers and exchange students made up the remainder of the crew, all getting some sort of summer credit through the Anthropology Department at FSU.

The whole saga can be enjoyed in the book *HMS Fowey Lost and Found: Being the Discovery, Excavation, and Identification of a British Man-of-War Lost off the Cape of Florida in 1748* (Russell K. Skowronek, and George R. Fischer, University Press of Florida, Gainesville, 2009) which I both cajoled and shamed Russell and George into writing, so I'm not going to belabor the tale of the investigation other than to simply point out many of both our behind-the-scenes heroics and misbehaviors as I recall them from that wonderful experience and life-enhancing adventure. First of all, let me begin with the cruel and unreasonable Regional Diving Officer, Richard Curry. A chain-smoking asshole and bully, survivor of only a single heart attack at that time (though there'd be others), he was forced to begrudgingly give us his sour approval when we went out for our checkout dives, since those of us who had gone through the Academic Diving Program were already consummate professionals and heavy on the safety maneuvers. Though he looked doggedly for any sort of diving safety breach that he could find and berate us for, he was frustrated in that endeavor, and then more than a little surprised when, acting as Safety Officer, I insisted on checking HIM out, and *his* equipment, and how well he'd suited up before he went in the water. Later, he took three of us and certified us for deep-water diving with checkouts at eighty and a hundred feet, though we'd been diving that deep on a regular basis for years. But he saved his real mean streak for the new student apprentice divers and anyone who showed the least bit of trepidation in or around boats and water. We weren't going to be diving below thirty feet ever (which is a general cutoff for relatively risk-free no-decompression diving), and some of the novices were a little nervous, only because they had never worked on open water ocean sites before, or for any extended period of time off of an anchored dive vessel. He was merciless in their checkouts by having them carry out exercises like treading water for fifteen minutes (which sounds easy until you have to do it), ditch-and-don their gear over and over again, swim a mile in open water, dive with their masks blacked out, and then the bastard took a sadistic delight in sneaking up and turning off their air or pulling out their regulators when they least expected it. All of this was unnecessary overkill for the job at hand, and mostly things he wouldn't have been able to cope with himself, especially considering the smoking and his myocardial infarction. And though he couldn't get around us experienced divers, he wasn't going to pass anyone for working until they met all of his demands, as opposed to simply meeting NPS or Academic Diving requirements. So we regular divers ran extra sessions at night in the hotel pool with the novice divers until they felt confident enough to face his onslaught, and once they did, he backed off. But he still continued to be an overbearing prick whenever he could put his power into play. Beside being the Regional Dive Officer, he was also the Chief Biologist for the park, and so one day he got it into his head that if we were going to carry out excavations with an airlift carrying sediments to the surface, we would have to redirect that sediment back down to the seabottom in a controlled fashion so that the silt wouldn't waft over onto other distant coral formations (forgetting conveniently that both midwinter storms and summer hurricanes routinely lifted tons of sand into the water column, often depositing it over thousands of acres of coral, which adjusted just fine). So, after once again putting on my old carpenter's belt, having already constructed the floating screens and the airlift, I devised a wraparound plastic sheet funnel-tube to channel the sediments back down into a pile on the bottom. This 30-foot-long tube came to be known as "the whale condom."

Once Skowronek and Vernon had laid out the datum line along the longest axis of visible remains on the site, it was up to Ken Wild and I to create a grid off of either side of it, consisting of three-meter squares that would become the focus of all the subsequent data collection. Since I was an old carpenter and Ken was an old bricklayer, between the two of us we knew all about levels and right angles and pulling a hypotenuse to make sure we were square. Out in the maintenance yard I had found a pile of boxes that had these T-bar metal stakes that turned out to be perfect for driving into the coral sand bottom and on top of which we could string parachute cord to create the three-meter squares across the entire site. It took us only two days, wearing the big double–steel 72s that would let us stay down for an hour and a half at a time, even working. Hell, we never broke thirty feet, so decompression wasn't an issue. More than not, it was hypothermia that threatened us, losing body heat two or three times as fast in the water, even though it was an initially comfortable 75 degrees. But after 90 minutes we'd come up blue-lipped and shaking, for a fifteen-minute break, lay in the sun, eat something, drink some coffee, and go back down for another hour and a half, sometimes knocking out three or four dives in a day. The crew then started working on photographing and mapping the site before we'd even finished gridding it off. Soon, as we prepared for test excavations, one could hear "Deploy the whale condom, sir?!," ringing out. "Aye, matey, you may attach and deploy the whale condom as you see fit. All the Captain asks is that you be gentle in so doing…" (We were practicing "talking like a pirate" long before it was generally popular or had a national day dedicated to it.)

The park headquarters at Convoy Point was a ten-minute drive south and east along those horrible South Florida canals that are always swallowing up speeding teenagers and drunks late at night. Reagan was president and had already fired all the striking air traffic controllers. Nearby Homestead Air Force base was still active and we'd watch the fighter jets taking off and landing all day and all night, what with Reagan's Contra saber-rattling. There was also some residual activity from the post-Mariel boatlift when now-desperate Cuban refugees (and spies) who hadn't made it out when they had the chance were still making their own rafts or powerboats (sometimes out of old cars) and sailing, drifting, rowing, or wet-driving onto the Upper Keys. The mini-war with Grenada hadn't yet occurred, but the Cold War was still in full microwave-ready popping mode. But we had archaeological work to do, and we both worked hard and played hard, staying at the Flamingo Inn just off of US 1 in Florida City, right before the jump off to Key Largo. At $5 a case we were swilling Schaeffers beer by the carload, and although we were also drinking cheap rum as well, the mixers were a bit dull with only coke and 7-up to cut it. That is, until I invented the Coconut Yoo-Hoo Piña Colada. This came about when the boys and girls were buying chocolate Yoo-Hoo at the local gas-station store when I noticed that it also came in a coconut flavor. Well, this was going to change things up a bit. Sure, the crew scowled and grimaced and cried "Yuck!" as I shook the little bottles and poured them over rum and ice, but once they tasted it, oh God, it was a free-for-all. Hell, soon there was a run on coconut Yoo-Hoos and the local Mini-mart stores sold out and had to double their orders.

Come Fly With Me
Things really got fired up when a couple of the guys, Ken Hoeck and Greg Toothman, came home one day from the toy store and handed out half a dozen dart pistols, the kind with the rubber suction-cups on the end. The damn things were the size of a .45 automatic, although much lighter of course, being made of plastic. But they were spring-loaded and could pack a punch, and each gun came with another half-dozen darts each, so soon there were three dozen darts flying around every corner, down from the balconies, whenever you opened a door, or when you came out of a bathroom. Sometimes you were even assaulted in your sleep. An ambush could occur at any time, anywhere. So you had to go around armed, with a loaded dart pistol in your waistband for self-defense, even when you were just going to the pool. One evening when we were enjoying a truce, several of us were in one of the larger furnished apartments sitting on the sofas just watching television and drinking. We had our dart guns by our side of course, just in case. A fly landed on the television screen, and we began plunking away at it. Finally, someone hit it, and sure enough, another one soon came flying in, then another, and we started making bets, drinking, and trying to nail it as it landed and before it flew off again. Eventually, someone would mash the little bugger on the screen, cheers would go up and bets would get settled. Then there was a knock on the hotel room door, and as we opened it, there stood the sweet and delectable dear, dear, Jenny Bjork. Jenny was a biology lab technician, working under the massive thumb and psychic brutality of "fuckin' Curry", as we now referred to him. She had

worked late and before going home thought she'd drop in on us and visit, since we had always provided a welcome respite from the day to day lab routine that had been her mainstay when Curry wasn't around and she could dive with us. I fixed her a Yoo-Hoo Piña Colada, which she enjoyed immensely, and then she sat with us to watch TV, on which there were still a few rubber-tipped darts left from our fly-killing fiesta. She wanted to see the guns, and we all let her play with them all she wanted. She was like a little kid, loading 'em up and shooting at the people on the TV. We hadn't mentioned the fly-killing, so as not to offend her sentimental biological sensitivities to various life forms, which included turtles, birds, corals, and even sea cucumbers. Before we could say a word, however, she snatched the darts off of the TV screen, came back to sit on the couch and, so as to enhance their suction I suppose, BEGAN LICKING THEM before putting them in the barrel and firing away again at the television. We were all horrified, but between spewing beer out of our noses and stifling both shock and laughter, no one could get up the nerve to tell her about the fly guts we had been splattering across the screen. She was just too happy… no one was going to ruin that wonderful giggling angel's evening of fun. So I fixed her another Yoo-Hoo Colada, and added a little more rum and a little less Yoo-Hoo—thinking "THAT should take care of any unintended ill effects."

The work progressed smoothly, when not broken up by afternoon thunderstorms that often ripped across Biscayne Bay in the summer afternoons. Depending on the severity of the lightning, we'd either sit out in the rain huddled in our wetsuits (when we weren't underwater), or if was just rain without the electricity sometimes there'd even be what we called "dancing on the Lido deck" where we'd pair up and the captain would crank up the radio and we'd cavort on the deck while waiting for those working below to come on up. I remember one particularly garrulous policewoman from Texas who had gotten her hooks into one of the handsome young interns and, never sharing him with the other girls (day or night, dancing or otherwise), she wore that poor bastard out. Other times Jenny would join us for a day, or maybe just a few hours, when Curry would be gone, and her young and slim curves under the bright red and wet National Park Service Speed-o bathing suit were a welcome distraction that allowed the boys no end of between-dive reveries. When the sun was out though, the deck could get as hot as a frying pan, and would easily blister your feet if you weren't careful. More than once we'd be pouring seawater over the tanks stacked there, cooling both them and the deck off so as to finally shut someone up (usually me) from yelling again and again after checking the pressures in a fake Scottish brogue "She's gonna blow, captain!" One day the boat captain, Corky, came aboard with an old silk parachute, and once on-site, we stretched that thing from midship to poles hoisted at the stern. From that point on, each day was simply pleasant sitting under the shade in the wafting seabreeze, and then dancing on the Lido deck became a ritualistic boredom-killing routine. As we came in to the dock afternoons, there was a bucket brigade formed to off-load the tanks, which were re-filled immediately, while all the gear was rinsed off, repairs made, and the boat washed down, fueled and oiled for the next day. We were lucky to get back to the hotel by six, washed and off to dinner by eight. Exhausted, we'd be in the sack by nine after a few Yoo-Hoo cocktails and/ or Schaeffers and a flurry of impromptu dart attacks. Days off were few and far between, and we'd have been happy to work all the time, but payroll expenses, labor laws and overall exhaustion demanded a day or two here and there. When we knew we had days off, the evenings before and during were devoted to drinking, dissolution, and debauchery.

Key Let-go

For instance, there was the time we had a weekend off and decided to visit every bar from Florida City to Key West. A bunch of us piled into the big orange project van and headed south. There was myself and Skowronek, Richard Vernon, Ken Wild, and a couple of others. Soon it became apparent that what we had planned, to visit every bar, was going to be impossible, so we pared it down and decided let's just visit every *Tiki* Bar. This also proved to be too daunting, and the Tiki Bars were notoriously overpriced and touristy, inevitably attached to some hotel or other. We finally had (only) gotten as far as Key Largo and decided to stop at the famous Key Largo limestone lodge where they had filmed a few of the scenes (mostly boat moorings) for the old 1948 Humphrey Bogart, Lauren Bacall, and Edward G. Robinson movie eponymously titled *Key Largo*. You know, the one where Edward G. as the mobster, holds Bogie and Bacall at gunpoint while a hurricane rages outside, simultaneously slapping Bacall around and making rude passes at her while Bogie challenges and insults him to the point of getting slapped around himself before eventually turning the tables. Well, now this rundown building is an open-air bar for beach bums and bikers, and we pulled in, admitting defeat at attempting to going all the way to Key West: "Let's just go in and have one last drink before turning around and heading home." It was late and crowded, but we managed to get a table near the back patio, and we settled into watching the bikers, bums, broads, and beer-sotted blues band. After a second round, there came some hollering up from the beach. We look over to see, maybe fifty or seventy-five yards away under the trees, this biker guy is holding his girlfriend by the arm with his left hand, and slapping her with his right. She's crying and yelping out loud every time he lays one across her. The other patrons in the bar look over as if it were just a coconut falling out of a tree, and go back to their drinks. Well, I couldn't sit still for this, and I got up. The boys are asking me where I'm going. "I'm going down there and stop that," I said. "You might not want to get involved," they suggested, "he looks like a biker and they sometimes carry weapons." "Shit, I'm going down there," I said, "C'mon, Kenny, you comin' with me?" Kenny goes, "I don't know…" but I insisted, "C'mon, let's go!" and he followed me out the doorway. As we walked out, another patron of the bar decided that he'd seen enough too and he was going to come with us, so the three of us walk on down to where the biker is still wailing away on this woman. We got about ten feet away, and I yelled out "Hey!" The guy and the girl both turned and saw the three of us standing there. The guy who came down with us from the bar bristled, stiffened up, and said, "You can't be doin' that, let go of her!" All of a sudden, the girl, all tousled and red-faced, straightens up, and snarls over at us "Why don't you mind your own fucking business!" The biker guy never said a word. We looked at each other. We looked back at them. They looked at us. We shrugged our shoulders, turned, and walked back up to the patio. The patrons at the door all smiled at us knowingly. The boys back at the table thought it was a funny self-sought situation, one however that I felt they hadn't properly stood up to. I was dazed and confused, and looking back down to the beach the guy and girl were now hugging, crying, and kissing. Good, bad? Right, wrong? I don't know. Just odd. Cops say that domestic altercations are the absolute worst, and I believe 'em.

Bump and Lift

The last days of the project we spent preparing for a cannon-lift. A general sample of other artifacts had already been retrieved for later analysis: some pewter plate fragments, a couple of bayonets, a few cannonballs, a boarding axe, and even a large 3-foot ingot of iron ballast. Most of these items were marked with the British "broad arrow"; an embossed arrow on the metal items signifying ownership by the Crown, sort of a government stamp of ownership. Anyone caught in possession of any item marked with the broad arrow (and they even put it hidden on the inside of barrel hoops) was automatically indictable for having stolen the King's property, and therefore subject to the maximum penalty. Now we were getting ready to lift one of the nine-pounder cannons from off of the seabed. This was a very tricky operation and not one to be undertaken lightly, no pun intended, considering that an eighteenth-century nine-pounder iron naval gun weighs in at just over 3000 pounds. We chose this one because it had already been moved, probably by Klein and his buddies, and it must have been too much for them however, because there it lay, just off-site, with an old hoisting strap still partly wrapped around it, green and yellow moss growing on the broken strap material. These things demand a hefty price tag from restaurants, bars, and tackle shops up and down the Keys, but once they're put out front as advertisements they quickly rust and flake apart as the salts in the iron recrystallize under the South Florida sun, and a generally rapid oxidation sets in. A number of them can still be seen today as large unidentifiable lumps of rusted iron out in abandoned parking lots. If they're properly desalinated at once and conserved properly however, which involves sand-blasting (with walnut shell), reverse electrolysis, and many, many coats of tannin and rust preventive chemicals and paint, all of which can take two to three years, they are then quality museum pieces that can, and should be, displayed indoors. For this process, we enlisted the assistance of Herb Bump, who worked for the State of Florida's Division of Historical Resources, in the Conservation Lab. A large gentle gargantuan, with rounded features, grey tousled hair, and a soft Southern drawl, Herb was almost-famous as the man who, for all practical purposes, single-handedly figured out how to conserve large iron cannon that had lain on the sea bottom for hundreds of years, bringing them back to very nearly what they looked like the day they went down. Somewhere I heard stories of some guns early on in the process even being fired again, using black powder and shooting out steel beer cans that had been filled with concrete. And though Herb had been known to strap on a tank or two in his youth, he was past the age where he was going down to help raise this one. So it fell to Gregg Stanton, "Iron Man" Mike Pomerantz, and Carl Sczemzak, the ad hoc "conservator," to raise the cannon. Gregg had already worked out the details under the direction of Bump, and Herb had driven down from Tallahassee with a truck carrying two empty old surplus jet fuel tanks. The idea was to fix straps to the cannon, then sink the jet fuel tanks, laying them on either side of the cannon, attach the straps to the fuel tanks, then fill the tanks slowly with air until they lifted the cannon off the bottom. Once to the surface, we'd simply tow the cannon into the park headquarters dock, where they had a large derrick winch, and we'd lift it out of the water and swing it onto the truck. Simple. I was part of the team given the mechanical task of mining one of three trenches under the cannon to slide the lifting straps through so they could be wrapped several times round the barrel, chase, and cascable (sometimes spelled cascabel, it's the round knob on the end opposite the mouth of a gun). Once the straps were attached to the gun, our job was over and Stanton, Pomerantz, and Sczemzak maneuvered the sinking jet fuel tanks into place along either side of the cannon and hooked the straps to pre-arranged welded davits on the tanks. All the boats moved off as they slowly filled them with air from scuba tanks set up on the bottom. The fuel tanks rose haphazardly, not quite in sync, and after lifting the cannon off the bottom, it all rose rather too quickly from the expanding air inside. The fuel tanks upended as they broke the surface, and the cannon came loose and rocketed back to the bottom, crashing into the marl and sending up a plume of sand and crushed coral. Herb Bump surmised that they hadn't attached the straps to the tanks correctly, and damn if he didn't strip down to just his pants and strap on a tank to go over the side and personally direct operations below. This time it was all set right and the tanks rose in unison, cradling the cannon with the straps hanging just below the surface. To be sure we wouldn't lose the location as it was towed to shore should it once again come loose, the intrepid Gregg Stanton rode the fuel tanks the entire two hours back to Convoy Point, suffering a terrible sunburn as a result.

Buh-bye Bisquayne

The final act of Biscayne 1983 was a blowout party that, like Fort Jefferson 1982, ended in drinking up all the leftover liquor and beer, with the exception that this time it was held at some of the park employees' private home, a bevy of young girl rangerettes that had come out diving with us a couple of times but had otherwise kept their distance. Most of the crew had already left for Tallahassee, but there was a contingent of the cleanup crew, all male, that had a few things to do before we could leave, so the girls thought they'd show us their South Florida hospitality on the night before we'd finish up and be gone. They liked us in general, but had no idea what devils they had invited across their threshold, and within hours we had offended them all and pretty much made a wreck of their tropical hideaway before they asked us nicely to leave. We had also been exploring the effects of mixing various concoctions of leftover liquors, so it was no surprise that the next morning, on waking up at the hotel, we were all suffering the ravages of distressed swollen brains. Worse for us though, was George, who had uncharacteristically abstained the night before, but had decided that one last pass needed to be taken over the wreck of the Fowey with the magnetometer, so as to get a final magnetic signature that we could use to monitor the site over time. "No, George, no… please," we begged, to no avail. Three of us had to go, and it fell to myself, Richard Vernon, and Ken Hoeck. The sun was already hot at 9 a.m. and it wasn't the magnetometer that was a problem—the machine is a small battery-operated data collection unit, no bigger than a makeup carrying case, that has a roll of electrically-sensitive paper for recording data—no, the problem was the scuba-tank-sized marine sensor-head and large inch-thick two-hundred-feet of coaxial cable, all packed in a large green wooden box with sharp edges that all weighed roughly two hundred pounds, and during loading and unloading was both unwieldy and dangerous, especially on a tossing sea. Oh, and the waves just had to be rough that last, hungover, and black-coffee-no-breakfast morning, with three to four-foot seas in a 25-foot runabout without a necessary Bimini-top to keep the sun and salt spray at bay. We got on site within an hour, choppy seas and all, the hull pounding in synchronicity with the throbbing pulse of our combined headaches. As George tuned and adjusted the mag data collector, we deployed the large sensor-head and slowly unwound the thick and stiff cable as George yelled at us over his shoulder, "Goddammit, be sure you don't put a kink in it!" Everything was hooked up, the data collector was tuned and running, we set out a couple of buoys so the park-ranger-boat-captain could keep us on course in the choppy surf, and Vernon, Hoeck and myself were glad that it would soon be over after a couple of passes and we could pack up the equipment and get home for food, cool water, and a quiet dark hotel room, maybe even a little hair of the dog. As we made the approach to start our first run, George suddenly stood up and said, "Keep going! I need to take a shit!" What!? What did he say?! He quickly dropped his shorts and hung his ass over the gunwale. "NO, NO, NO!" we all cried in unison… not that! Except for the ranger-captain, who stoically stayed on-course, Vernon, Hoeck and I crowded together at the aft transom to escape the visual effrontery, the sputtering bowel-sounds, and the wind-scattered stench, but it was futile. There at the taffrail, grimacing in horror, we watched the voluminous floating turds wafting their way astern in the clear blue waters of Biscayne Bay, and running along the large black coaxial cable and sensor head that we'd eventually have to haul in by hand when this questionable exercise was finally concluded. It was only then that, coupled with the tossing waves, the sour stomachs, the sight of the brown floaters, and the utter ridiculousness of the situation, the bile finally rose to the level of dry heaving. Once he'd finished, wiped himself off with toilet paper that he'd presciently stashed in a backpack, we got back on course for the first data run. George was ecstatic (despite the fact that now WE were even more miserable), and declared proudly "Well, now I've shit on Gerald Klein's grave! I'll bet no one ever counted on that happening!" We completed the mag runs, got the data, and pulled in the cable and sensor-head (without kinking the goddamn coaxial), washed our hands (twice), and made our way back home to fall into our beds, tired, sore, sick, hungover, and hungry. The sacrifices one has to make for the sake of Science…

The Widow Moore's Crick

       The 1983 school year had just started that September when George got another assignment, and this one was handed over to me to direct, my first official NPS project wherein I'd get to call the shots. Pete, the Chief at SEAC, and no fan of George's, didn't like the loose nature of these underwater adventures, but he backed off when he found out that I'd be running this one, and he really didn't have much of a choice. You see, when a park superintendent calls for archaeological assistance, in light of meeting Federal requirements, whether for construction or rehabilitation or demolition (what we call "Section 106 compliance") the Center was obligated to respond. Especially since either the park or Washington, or both, were footing the bill. So we scheduled it for the long Labor Day weekend, which didn't give me much time to prepare, but it was considered a small project anyway, so no one was much concerned about it. Except me. My first real project, finally, and I had to put a lot of time and research into the background history, the logistics of carrying it off, and cajoling my professional friends to come along *gratis* on their otherwise long weekend off. The goal was simple: the park was replacing an old wooden bridge that was on the site of a small, but significant Revolutionary War battle, The Battle of Moores Creek. We needed to explore the creek bottom in the area of the bridge and see if there were any vestiges of the engagement that took place there some two hundred and thirteen years earlier. It was a significant event in the fact that some 350 Patriots fended off and routed roughly 1,000 Loyalists, mostly Scottish Highlanders, known for their hand-to-hand fighting ferocity. The Patriots had gotten to the narrowing of this large creek first and set up camp, knowing the Loyalists would have to cross here. Initially they thought they'd defend the bridge, but once they knew the size of the force that was advancing toward them, they abandoned the camp on the foreside, and backed over to the higher ground on the far side of the bridge, while pulling up the planking behind them and greasing the remaining longitudinal "sleeper struts" with hog fat. They then dug a few earthen trenches, lit a new set of campfires, and positioned two small cannon loaded with grape shot aimed at the bridge crossing and then settled in and waited for the Loyalists to arrive. Which they eventually did with a lot of clamor, bagpipes howling and drums thumping, on February 27 (coincidentally, my oldest son's birthday), in the year 1776, thus making it one of the earliest battles of the war, and as it turned out, one of the most decisive.

The Highlanders were, for the most part, conscripts. Their fathers had fought with Bonnie Prince Charles Edward Stuart at the famous Battle of Culloden in 1746, near Inverness in Scotland, and when the bonnie prince fled and the surviving Jacobite rebels were first incarcerated, and later paroled, according to the tradition of the day they had to swear fealty to the Crown, not only for themselves, but on behalf of their entire family, or clan. This oath of loyalty carried over into generations, and when the Scots were emigrated to the Colonies to settle the Carolinas and Appalachia, they had little choice but to fight on the side of the English. As they approached the area of the crossing they saw the smoke of the abandoned campfires on their side of the bridge. Thinking they had the Patriots on the run, they charged the bridge, only to find that the planks were missing and the sleepers slippery with lard. Using the points of their mighty broadswords (the infamous Claymore, a two-handed longsword) to steady themselves as they crossed the greased timbers in the early-morning darkness, kilts a-fluttering, the Patriots waited patiently for the Highlanders to partially regroup on their side before letting loose a deadly volley of grape and musketry. Besides the twenty or so decimated immediately, many of the others still attempting to cross were blown off the bridge into the frigid black water of Moores Creek. Those on the far side saw the situation for what it was and turned to flee. The Patriots quickly laid the planking back down on the bridge and pursued the scattered Scots. There was only a single Patriot fatality, whereas some 35 to 50 Highlanders were cut down, a few dying by drowning. When they cleaned up his body, the field commander for the Highlanders, one Donald McLeod, was reported to have had twenty musketballs tossed through him. Some 850 Loyalist prisoners were later captured, now having to swear another oath, this time not to take up arms against the Colonial Army, before being disarmed and sent home.

Another Pitched Battle

Well, I figured that there had probably been at least seven bridges built over that spot since 1776, so the bridge that was being replaced, which was already at the bottom of the creek due to recent flooding, was not historic, but who was to say that there wasn't still a Claymore or Brown Bess musket or two lying in the muddy bottom? After all, it was just dark enough and deep enough to discourage any recreational swimming, and underwater archaeology in 1983 was just out of its infancy. So we headed out early on Friday afternoon in two vans full of tanks, compressor, lines, tapes, dive equipment, the magnetometer, and several dozen rounds of various fireworks. It was going to be a nine or ten-hour drive to Wilmington, North Carolina and we'd brought the fireworks along to liven up the tedious travel. That, and a couple of cases of beer (these still being the days when distance was measured in six-packs, rather than miles). The first volleys from van to van with bottle rockets didn't occur until we got off of I-10 and headed north onto Hwy 301 (at least we had sense enough not to begin firing until we were out of range of the Highway Patrol). Thus began a running skirmish that lasted through Georgia and South Carolina, at least until we got to South of the Border, where we stopped and got something to eat and renew our beer supplies, before a truce was finally called. There'd already been a couple of "incidents." One, where George was lighting M-80s in the passenger seat and dropping them out of his side vent window when we'd pull ahead of the following van, timing the burning fuse like a depth charge so it would blow beneath their vehicle, when all of a sudden he let out a loud "Uh-Oh" because he'd dropped the damn thing inside the doorwell. At least the driver, Rich Johnson, a hardened Vietnam War veteran, was alerted and drove through the ensuing internal explosion, flash, "BOOM!" and smoke filling the van; he kept an iron grip on the wheel and, other than a noticeable jerk to the left and back again, gunpowder smoke billowing out the windows, he never left his lane. Another incident occurred when at one point the road opened to two lanes on our side, and the following van pulled up on the right to pass us. Well, this would give up our superior positioning in the lead, so we had to speed up. We were both running neck-and-neck, firing bottle rockets across at each other, when they set off an incredible multiple volley. The rockets smacked against our side windows, ricocheted off the windshield, and bounced off the back of the van as we regained the upper hand and pulled ahead. Unfortunately, the volley of rockets that didn't make contact careened across the highway, and no, there weren't any oncoming cars in the other lane (thank God), but there happened across the road, unforeseen by us, to be a small, but serious revival tent in full choral amplitude, and the few errant rockets coming from across the highway stopped the singing and sent the people inside scurrying for cover. We were both ashamed of our insensitive folly as well as scared that someone might jump in their car and chase us down. Most certainly they thought we'd done this on purpose, as we were still in South Georgia at the time. The guns were silent for a good twenty miles.

We got to our hotel in Wilmington, and the next morning paid our respects to the Superintendent as protocol demanded. He was a large friendly man and glad to see us, Moores Creek being one of the smallest and least-visited national parks in the region. He told us that the only thing to really worry about was getting hung up on sunken tree snags, and oh yeah, be careful you don't stick your hand in one of those man-sized snapping turtles that lies on the bottom along the bank just waiting for something to tickle its tongue before clamping down in a death-grip. "Those things can be a hundred pounds and snap a broomstick, y'know," he encouraged us. We unpacked our gear, and started out by setting up several datum points and survey lanes, tied into a couple of

US Geological Survey monuments, from which all the measurements would be taken. Then a couple of us got on our wetsuits, strapped on the tanks, and prepared mentally to enter the murky waters, dark as Earl Gray tea. Before entering though, I wound a piece of lead wire around an M-80 left over from the previous night's running firefight, lit the fuse, and tossed it in. There was muffled "Phoom!" and a rise of bubbles. THAT ought to send any snappers scurrying, or at least close their gaping maws for awhile. We went in and found the water to be bitter cold, but only ten or twelve feet deep. The remains of the last wooden bridge were disarticulated and lying on the bottom upside-down. The pilings however, driven into the muddy bottom, were still in place, their tops broken off some four feet below the surface. We'd have to map the bridge remains, and then just probe the bottom where we could, looking for any loose tell-tale artifacts. Which is how we spent the remainder of the day: after mapping the bridge ruins, we'd just stick our arms down into the bottom muck as far as we could, repeatedly reaching for the lost ancestral broadsword we knew was just beyond our grasp.

Swear to Gawd

The next day, as the crew finished mapping and probing, George and I carried out a magnetometer survey of the creek for perhaps a half-mile or so. Rather than the cumbersome marine cable, we mounted the land-head, a coffee-can-sized sensor, to a long section of two-by-four stretching out the front of one of the park's aluminum rowboats like a bowsprit. I rowed while George fiddled with the mag recorder. There was nothing, nothing, nothing, until the recorder nearly sprang off the chart. We looked up to see a modern bridge crossing the creek at the park's furthest edges, with a large pickup truck parked on it and a bored farmer watching us from the driver's window. Turning around, we made it back to the park just as the boys were cleaning up the gear and putting it away, and a dark rumbling came in from the distance. A few large drops began to fall as we piled our equipment into the vans, and within a minute or two, a powerful drenching rain began to fall. Thunder had begun earlier, but now it was right on top of us, and the interval between flashes of lightning and the crashing blasts of the boomers was both immediate and frightening, even inside the van. And there, maybe fifty yards away, was Rich Johnson, standing on a little hillock in a cleared section of the woods, his fist raised to the sky, and yelling the most death-defying unimaginable blasphemies I'd ever heard, while thunderclaps burst and lightning seared the tops of the trees nearby. Now, this was a good ten years before we ever saw Lieutenant Dan of *Forrest Gump* fame, sitting legless at the top of the shrimp boat challenging the Almighty, and Rich was doing it right here, in reality, and an X-rated version at that. I really, really thought he'd be struck down for sure, and less for challenging the forces of Nature than for the affronts he cast upon The Old Man. Maybe, as with Lieutenant Dan, this is an old Vietnam-crazy thing, I don't know, but once the storm had vented itself and passed, Rich joined us in the van, soaked to the skin, and visibly exhausted. Our Father, who art in heaven, decided not to take up Rich's challenge (this time), but I'll tell you what, I learned a lot about cursing that day, and what a mere dilettante I'd been at it my entire life. I still can't bring myself to say out loud some of the things I heard that day, and that was thirty years ago.

Proud to be an A'merkin

Rich was also the world-weary veteran who introduced us to the concept of the mirkin. A mirkin is a wig for missing body hair, such as armpits and chest hair for men, and pubic wigs for women. Not to diverge too far afield, but mirkins were a standard piece of couture from the Renaissance through to Victorian times, very popular during the Rvolutionary War. Mostly, this was to offset the effects of bedbugs and lice, prevalent until modern plumbing and rules of hygiene. People would shave the hair from their bodies so the vermin wouldn't have a place to reside, but when a couple wanted to get familiar, or show off their physique, they might patch on a small wig over the area of intended attention. We're all familiar with the white powder wigs worn by the Founding Fathers... well, they probably had a set of mirkins somewhere in their dresser drawer to enhance their less-clothed (but still self-conscious) modesty. I've no doubt Ben Franklin had a dozen. (On a side note, it was common movie magazine gossip that when they hired Sean Connery to be James Bond, they didn't think he was manly enough in the chest-hair department, and he was helped along with a chest mirkin.) One time, much later, while having this very conversation regarding mirkins, Rich told us that, as a veteran who came back from Vietnam a peacenik liberal, when his patriotism (in not supporting the war any longer) was questioned by some other vets, he just told them "why don't we just let bygones be bygones" and that, in his opinion, he thought they were all "Great 'Mirkins," (his intent being that they hid their lack of intellect and their Christian piety behind a small pubic [and public] wig of patriotism), where the challengers stopped, smiled, and thanked him, thinking he actually said "Great Americans."

As far as the Widow Moore's Creek, wat we learned about the bridge crossing wasn't much. As I said, at least seven wooden bridges had been constructed there over the intervening two centuries. The creek bottom was both flooded out and silted in dozens, if not hundreds of times, and I'd guess that the water was much deeper then. Finally, we tend to underestimate those country boys back in the days who had no fear of snapping turtles, and could swim as good as eels. The prospect then of getting your hands on either a Claymore broadsword, or a Brown Bess, both of which would be in working order almost immediately, and would have presented the amateur treasure hunter of the day a delightful summer challenge. The investigation was considered a minor success, and I wrote up the report, with accompanying history and hand-sketches, and it was back to graduate school in FSU Anthropology.

San Pedro y San Pablo de Patale

Soon Spring arrived and all of us present-day prospective professional archaeologists had to face that formal ritual of passage, part of a time-honored and tortuous pay-for-the-privilege of indentured servitude to scientific inquiry and University enrollment fees known as Field School, before we could call ourselves properly "trained." Now normally an archaeological field school was carried out for four to six weeks during the summer hiatus from the regular nine-month school year. This was because Florida and most of the rest of the country had gone over to the semester system, as opposed to the quarter, so now there was less opportunity to devote to multiple class attendance, and a single twelve-week, or 3-month class, that would occupy a full 8-hour day, five days a week, with an accompanying lab one evening a week, without recompense, just didn't make economic sense. It was, in actuality, if not effect, a single 9-hour class where you didn't receive a grade that might help or hurt your Grade Point Average, but rather, either an "S" for satisfactory, or a "U" for unsatisfactory, which did neither . [I describe this above in somewhat political terms because I'd been elected the Graduate Student representative, to take up such issues and present them to the Chairman of the Department, and as such, I'd gotten an earful from my constituents. This began a year-long bumping of heads between the new Chairman, Dr. Anthony Paredes and myself over what the students considered rather capricious and dictatorial new "requirements." Later, I learned that, in what seemed appropriate under the circumstances, "paredes" in Spanish means "walls." Later, after I'd graduated, rather oddly, we became good friends.] Nonetheless, if we did not complete an FSU-approved archaeological field school we could not graduate with a degree in Anthropology having an emphasis in Archaeology. It was the only game in town.

The proposed site was on a hilltop some five miles east of Tallahassee, and was historically reported as an outlying mission site, sort of a satellite to the great Spanish town and fort of San Luis, then located right in modern-day Tallahassee, which is presently an interpreted historic tourist destination. The subject of this field school was the mission-site of San Pedro y San Pablo de Patale, which was probably a small rustic village of maybe a dozen houses, an outpost in the 15th and 16th century along the Kings Highway that roughly followed the present-day route of Interstate 10 and State Highway 90 from Pensacola to St. Augustine. The quandary of the time was whether it was easier and quicker to have a series of wagons take the week-long journey carrying supplies between Tallahassee and St. Augustine, or have heavier-laden ships take the longer and much more hazardous journey by sea once every couple of months. So they did both, with the land journey broken up by these small mission sites where the local natives were pacified and Christianized while producing food and goods for the garrison and townsfolk of upper-class Spanish St. Augustine. These little mission towns along the Kings Road could also signal to each other by smoke and fire in times of danger from English raids out of the north, as they were usually situated on hilltops roughly a day's travel apart.

Bilix Publeks

There was a large modern ranch-style house on top f the suspected mission site owned by Dr. Bilek, a Bavarian-American surgical oncologist who had an interest in things both American and historical. For instance, at one of his grand parties attended by a bunch of Sherriff's deputies as well as the archaeological crew (an interesting mix if ever there was one), he had one of his two restored Gatling guns set up, and we all took turns shooting up an old car wreck that he put down in a small gully out behind his house. Being one of the best cancer surgeons in the country, he had plenty of money and, besides his toys (guns) and his cars, he furnished the house with antiques and art. His wife, whom I only knew as Mrs. Bilek, was either French or Czech, or both, and shared his interest in the local history, politics, and social scene. But she didn't drive. So she would take taxis anywhere she wanted to go. Well, it happened that my brother Paul was driving a cab at the time, and once they were introduced, he became Mrs. Bilek's private driver, always on call. This was an interesting turn, since Paul drove a dark green Quickie cab, the only black-owned franchise in Tallahassee, and him being the only white driver for that company. But he was a private owner, so, unlike the other drivers, he was allowed to go anywhere, anytime he wanted to, and Mrs. Bilek liked to travel around, visit people, and shop. Money being no problem, he was often given outlandish tips, besides tallying up day-long fares. One of her mainstay forays into town was to go grocery shopping, which meant going all the way to the Northwood Mall to go to the one-and-only upscale Publix in town at the time. Well, this was a ten-mile run each way, and the distance sometimes precluded getting home with the ice cream intact. So she got her husband to begin lobbying for a Publix-based shopping mall to be built out closer to their house, and within a year the thing was under construction. We still call it the Bilek's Publix, although by now there must be ten others across town.

Real 'im In!

To the slight but noticeable consternation of my Archaeology professor, Dr. Michelle Maryann, whom I'd have other issues with later on, my brother and I, as well as my wife Amy, developed a nice social relationship with the Bileks, since the good doctor was the financial benefactor of the field school. Paul and I were making homebrew beer on a regular basis back then and we always shared a case with Dr. Bilek, who loved the stuff. He was kind enough to save the empty bottles and then trade us for some of his imported Bavarian ales, lagers, and pilsners. Meanwhile, Amy (who was a stay-at-home Mom at the time with Robin in tow at two years) was often invited over to swim in the Bilek's pool and have lunch with the Mrs., who had taken a particular fancy to having the toddler running around. Amy knew this and one day pulled the rug out from under me, stunning me to the core. It went down like this: I came home from the Park Service one day, popped a beer, sat down, and asked her how her day was. She said she had to talk to me (uh-oh, that's never good news). Mrs. Bilek had called her earlier that day and asked if she wanted to come over for lunch and a swim. Sure, she said, and then packed up Robin and went on over. Amy told me that after a nice swim and then a sumptuous lunch, Mrs. Bilek asked her if the maid could watch Robin for a few minutes while she wanted to show Amy something in her bedroom (?!? – the plot thickens). Amy described this large bedroom, four-poster bed, various furniture, and there, under the window, a large wooden chest. Meanwhile, Mrs. Bilek is talking about how wonderful it is to have a child around the house, how lucky we were to have Robin, were we expecting to have more, etc. Then she went to her nightstand, got out a set of keys, went over to the chest, and opened the padlock. Raising the hinged lid, Amy said it was full of coins, jewelry, goblets, gemstones, gold chains, the works… a typical pirate's chest like those in all the movies. After showing her the contents, Amy said Mrs. Bilek sat her down, put her hand on hers and quietly said that it was worth millions, and she (i.e., we, Amy and I) could have it all… in exchange for the child… for Robin! I was aghast, stunned, and totally dumbfounded. "You're kidding!" I choked. Amy, who until this time had been sober and serious, saw the shock and awe in my face, smiled, let out a loud laugh, and said, "Yes, I'm kidding… so, how was your day?" She had gotten me good; I fell for it hook, line, and sinker ("Reel him in!"). Like my Dad once told me, and which he practiced with a superb aplomb, you can tell anybody ANYTHING, and if you do it with a straight face, don't let your eyes or the corners of your mouth give it away, they will believe it. Alien abductions, skunk-ape sightings, death-defying acts of heroism, and my favorite, miracles… all will be believed if delivered in a proper manner and under the right circumstances. Nowadays it's much more difficult, because people can check facts instantly on their I-Pads or the Internet, but at the time, and considering Mrs. Bilek's fondness for Robin (not to mention Amy's straight-faced delivery), yes, I let the sharp-eyed Eagle of Discernment take a big crap on my head. Not that I would have considered such a bargain for even one minute, nor did I even begin to wonder how much that chest of treasure might actually be worth. Besides, the grandparents would have been appalled.

Feeled School

The field school began in January, and it was one of the most bitter and biting windy winters we'd ever seen in Tallahassee. And here we were, a dozen then-young folks, atop a bare expanse of grassy prairie, while the cold whipped across our exposed faces and hands, and the condensed frozen breath trails blown away before they'd even come all the way out of your lungs, protective snot running constantly out the nose to keep things lubricated. Though normally there would be cows in the fields, they'd been moved to adjacent tracts so we could carry out our archaeological survey. The first thing to do was to establish a grid across the rolling hillside, and this required survey stations, set up with an ancient optical transit (not much different than what George Washington used in his early surveying career), pulling tapes, constantly checking angles and distances, and driving in marked wooden stakes at the measured corners of each twenty-meter grid square. To speed things up, two transit-and-staking teams were formed on either side of the long entrance driveway that divided the property roughly in half, and these had to be checked against each other periodically so that the two great imaginary grids would jibe on paper.

Once the grid was laid out we began the laborious task of shovel testing every ten meters, roughly every thirty feet. The ground was hard clay when it wasn't wet mud, and every bit of that godforsaken dirt had to be pushed through quarter-inch shaker screens (most of it was pushed through since shaking didn't result in anything but forming round "turdballs" of clay). It was a lot of many weeks of no fun. Then the weather changed, and from being freezing, windy, cold and wet, it quickly became hot and bothersome. Now the clay hardened, and digging the brick-like chunks was carried out with picks as well as shovels, where we often had to wet the soil to soften it up enough to keep going. And all of the spoil still had to get through the screen, even when it was obvious that it was all just more of the same. After all, we were being trained in proper procedure. Any artifacts we encountered were few and far between, a pot sherd here, a glass fragment there (as a lexiconic note by the way, fragments of pottery are "sherds" whereas fragments of glass are "shards"). Nails often turned out to be modern horseshoe cleats, ubiquitous over the long-time grazing fields, or other modern machined nails and pieces of hogwire fence or barbed wire. The long-sought-after wrought nails (i.e., wrought by hand, by a blacksmith) were rare, and this made sense when you consider that iron was a precious commodity back then, and any structural hardware was probably re-used dozens of times over the centuries, if not pilfered by the local natives as ornaments.

When the shovel testing was completed, the finished maps showed some slightly higher concentrations of actual artifacts, possibly related to the mission site, and although no real structures were indicated, there were some concentrations of daub, or sun-baked clay, probably used to plaster the walls of huts, but easily broken down by wind and rain. Several larger excavation test pits were then opened up as the Spring equinox passed and the days got longer and hotter. We dug, and we dug, and we dug. In the end I couldn't tell you whether we were ever on the mission site or not. But it didn't matter. For us, the students, the object was to get trained in archaeological methods, and in that, it was a great success. We came out as weatherbeaten tight-assed record-keepers and sunburnt calloused fieldhands, intellectually stimulated and ethically-molded scientists with a capital "S". For that, Dr. Maryann deserves immense credit: she trained all her students in a rigorous manner that resulted in, for the most part, lifelong consummate professionals. Those that couldn't cut the mustard and realized being an archaeologist wasn't near as fun as it sounded usually changed either their majors or their focus after one of her field schools; in short, it weeded out the dilettantes.

Biscayne '84

Ken Wild and I however were still plugging away at becoming professional *underwater* archaeologists, having already done two summer stints with the Park Service in Dry Tortugas and Biscayne, not to mention that nasty trip to Fort Frederica, and the Moores Creek Bridge project (we even did a quick —and unsuccessful— weekend underwater survey in search of Fort Picolata, an early Spanish Period wooden outpost supposedly submerged in the tea-brown waters of the St. Johns River south of St. Augustine, where the river crossed the old King's Highway). Now we were the only two left who actively pursued working underwater. They called us the "Bubbleheads" and it would not be out of line to say that we single-handedly (that would be, double-handedly) kept Underwater Archaeology alive at FSU during the 1983-84 school year, while many other forces, both inside and outside the University, were working hard to gut it. We even put together a diorama exhibit in the large glass display in the first floor of the Bellamy Building, just outside the Anthropology Dept. offices, showing an underwater archaeological site, with pictures of boats and divers getting suited up at the top and a real sand and coral-encrusted seabottom littered with half-buried artifacts we got on loan from the Park Service. The sea-surface interface was set midway with that light blue soft plastic wrap you get your clothes back in from the dry cleaners, and it would waft gently with each bit of air that came in between the display case windows when the front door of the building was opened. It was really a very beautiful and attention-getting display, and we put up explanatory posters and flyers extolling the wonders of taking up Underwater Archaeology as a major course of study in the department.

Unfortunately, it gathered so much attention that, after only a month, the Park Service demanded their artifacts back because they were afraid that someone would crack the glass and steal them. Coincidentally however, the next Fall there were a slew of new students who wanted to make Underwater Archaeology the focus of their Anthropology major, and the Department, always struggling for students (and their discretionary tuition fees), took them in while at the same time discouraging them from doing underwater work, forcing them to run the gantlet of the field school at Patale to become "real" archaeologists.

Ken and I, both with families now, were still working for the Park Service while we were in graduate school. These were temporary appointments again (which meant no promise of benefits, permanent employment, or advancement beyond our GS-5 ratings), and we were still both working under George Fischer, who was surreptitiously trying to keep underwater archaeology alive at the Southeast Archeological Center despite resistance from the Chief, Pete Faust. But we had one more great run left in us. The powers-that-be in Atlanta were pushing for more survey work to be carried out in the parks, and they had been impressed by the Summer 1983 work we (SEAC/FSU) had carried out on the *Fowey* at Biscayne. Apparently there was some money either left over, or maybe it was just end-of-the-year money that had to be spent by September, but a survey of the park was requested, and somehow George snagged the project for the Center. Since the other guys had all graduated and there were no other qualified graduate-student underwater archaeologists at the Center, Ken and I were called in and told to put together a Research Design and Scope-of-Work for a survey of the offshore reefs at Biscayne that coming summer. Ken wrote the Research Design (i.e., "*Why* are you going to do it?" To look for wrecksites, duh), and I wrote the Scope-of-Work (or, "*How* are you going to do it?" Well, shit, that's going to be a little tricky now, isn't it?). What became really bothersome though, was that management (George and Pete) couldn't decide who should be in charge, so they made us co-project-directors—always a bad decision. But Ken and I were up to the task, and we tackled it eagerly, although later it probably caused some friction and forced rivalry that was totally unnecessary.

Another bad decision was that Gregg Stanton, the director of the Academic Diving Program, made us take along his personal boat, a beat-up 17-foot runabout with a 40-horse Evinrude and a recently-repaired cracked fiberglass hull. Despite my protests, he insisted that he was doing us a favor. ("Well, an extra boat would always come in handy," or so we rationalized it at the time. I think he tapped George for something like $40 a day.) He also insisted that we pay close attention to the ministrations of our safety officer, Mike Pomerantz, the forty-something overweight psychologist who had earned the satirical nickname "Iron Mike" the previous summer due to his predilection for seasickness, even in dead-calm waters. Little did Ken or I know then that Mike's other (secret) duty was to keep Gregg discretely informed on how well we were carrying out our mission. We set off in June, a regular convoy, with a passel of students—the project was also an underwater archaeological field school, Ken and I having been granted Assistant Instructor status—with some of us (me driving) towing that goddamn boat of Stanton's on a rusty trailer with bald tires that kept us at a nervous 60 m.p.h. for the whole 20 hours it then took us to get from Tallahassee to the hotel in Florida City (instead of the normal 12 it should have taken). Once we got established, Ken and I had to sit down and determine strategy, especially with so many people to keep busy, maybe a dozen of us in all.

Fish Hostels

There were going to be two groups working in different directions. One was the survey crew, who simply got on mark, flipped on the magnetometer, and drove north-south lanes, from one point of latitude to the next (usually a nautical mile), watching to see if there was any signal of metal in the area. If there was, we'd toss a weighted buoy with a float, usually an empty Clorox container, fixed so that it would let the line unwind on its own as the dive weight dropped to the bottom. This way we could mark the magnetic "hits," or magnetic anomalies, and circle back to refine the location. In a boat following, there would be divers, already geared up, or nearly so, who were ready to jump overboard, search the location quickly, and then report on what it might be, whether modern, historic, a shipwreck, cargo, or garbage (?). You'd be surprised what one finds on the bottom of the ocean, especially South Florida! I've seen more shopping carts than probably anything else. Okay, it's true that they're easily converted into ready-made fish and lobster traps... but shopping carts!? It's always so odd to come down from above and see an upside-down shopping cart on the bottom of the ocean, green with encrustation, with the black wheels, one or two maybe not quite stuck yet, turning in the current... an upside-down shopping cart! But even more odd to me is the vision of these guys, redneck or puertoriqueño fishermen, making off with these shopping carts out in some supermarket parking lot in the middle of the night, tucking them into each other, hoisting them up into a pickup truck, and making off with them; then getting them home to slightly re-work them into viable (i.e., inviable) death traps; and eventually loading them onto a boat and going out to sea. Then slowly dropping them one-by-one over the side and going down on scuba to place them correctly and bait them. Sometimes the ones on the bottom are marked with very small styrofoam buoys at or just below the surface so they wouldn't be seen, but many times they're not marked at all, and when they are lost eventually, they turn into fish (and lobster) killing machines, because fish go in, often chasing other fish, but they don't come out. It's a one-way trip. In any case, Winn-Dixie seems to be the favored store, by far, with Family Dollar a close second. (Yes, we would pull them up when we found them, or mark them to have the park divers do it later.) More troublesome to us during this phase of the survey was that they give off one helluva magnetic signal, like little radar domes underwater, that caused no end of "anomalous signatures" we had to investigate.

A Flash of Old

The second group in our summer field school survey and assessment investigation would pursue searching and identifying known sites within the park. There was an early treasure hunter named Marty Meylach who had bought his own magnetometer when the technology was first invented, and then had mapped many of the wrecksites all along the South Florida coast back in the 1960s, more than a few of which were within the boundaries of Biscayne National Park. Then he published their locations in his book, *Diving to a Flash of Gold* (1971), which by this time had been out 13 years and was a rarity in that all the copies had been bought up because of the detailed quality of his location information, and this was the basis for our "known or findable" historic wrecksites within the park boundaries. We tried as well to get whatever information we could squeeze out of the local old-timers, but working for the Feds, and the sad story of Gerald Klein still relatively fresh, we were generally considered *persona non grata* even when we got an introduction. Once in a while a few drinks in the afternoon might loosen up a grizzled old conch, but then all we'd get were stories of adventure, storms, violence and vengeance, but never the first piece of useful archaeological data that we might follow up on. We did have Meylach's map though, and that led us to at least a dozen known sites in the park, so the second group had their hands full with mapping, photography, some minor sampling, etc. Ken and I also had our own personal agendas: the investigation of two historic wrecks as the bases of our graduate theses. He had chosen the site of what was then known as either the *Hubbard* or the *Ledbury*, one of two ships that had been recorded as wrecking within years of each other along the South Florida keys. Both had been merchant ships carrying cargoes of English-produced chinaware, out of style in Great Britain and ready to dump on the fashionably-backward colonies. The site he looked at was certainly one of those lost ships because the bottom was scattered in heaps of broken (and burned) transfer-printed, tortoise-shell, and pearlwares, some still stacked in place. The burning reflected either the wrecking itself or later attempts to salvage the cargo by torching the upper decks.

The Popul-ah

I had chosen the site of *Nuestra Señora del Populo*, a small pinque, or flat-bottomed square-rigged cargo ship that went down as part of the Spanish Flota, or Silver Plate Fleet, of 1733. The site was well-known, and although the ship wasn't one of the "treasure" ships *per se*, the Populo carried citrus, tobacco, cochineal, indigo, and hides, as well as a few people returning to Spain. She wrecked on a coral outcropping and dropped into 30 feet of water, easily accessible to modern-day salvors. That, and the fact that the Spanish had carried out their own super-efficient salvage after the wrecking, meant there was little or no "cargo" left, much less cannon or artifacts associated with the wreck. So the shipwreck structure itself became the subject of inquiry. I commandeered a quartet of the student divers and we spent the better part of a week mapping it and putting in a couple of test excavation units. I even carried out shooting a photomosaic of the site, a series of photos all taken at the same relative height from the bottom that once put together and overlapping like a giant jigsaw puzzle would yield a complete single picture of the wrecksite as a photographic "mosaic." But by far the most excitement came from the excavation units, using the same airlift system we had developed the year before on the *Fowey*. After clearing away a good load of the ballast stones (all round, smooth river cobbles from God-knows-where, either Spain or Mexico), we began "sucking mud" out of a 1-square-meter caisson from the bottom hold of the vessel. My expectations were high (higher than they should have been), since I figured the bottom of the vessel would have been where all the detritus from multiple voyages would have congregated, washed down from above by deck scrubbings, rain and storms, and settling among the ballast stones—so I figured these would be full of wondrous stuff, giving an overall picture of life aboard ship, maybe even a lost coin or two. But after four days of underwater vacuuming all I'd come up with was one small bone and a fragment of pottery. The bone was later identified by one of my professors as a deer "cannon" bone (the proximal end of the tibia or knee-bone), which I've found out since was more likely goat; and the pottery fragment was a common Mexican redware. No great shakes. One good thing was that during the work there my old friend Bob Nolin, who was working at the Florida Sun-Sentinel out of Ft. Lauderdale, convinced his editor to let him come out and spend a couple of days with us, and we got a nice little write-up for the Sunday Travel section. It was also during this period that I learned from Amy by telephone that she was expecting again, due sometime in February. The crew all thought this was rather funny, me having been in the field for the better part of a month.

The Stan-tuna

Before we left Biscayne that summer we decided to make a nostalgic visit to the site of the Fowey, where we had spent so much time and effort the previous year. This was part of the summer field school as well, since we were in fact tasked with monitoring the site to see if there'd been any "visitors" pawing away at it in the previous twelve months, the Park having relatively ignored it. It happened to be a bad day though: blustery, dark, and choppy with three-foot seas. We had three boats on site, two of the Park's boats, 23 and 24-footers with powerful double Mercury motors on each, one of which I captained, and then that 17-foot fiberglass piece of shit of Stanton's, its sole function to operate as a dive platform for the returning divers to get their gear off and relax. Unfortunately, when the boys parked his boat over the site, none of them being watermen of any sort, they hadn't let out enough scope on the anchor, or maybe there just wasn't enough rope to begin with. In any case, when they came up after the first initial (and rough) dive to reconnoiter the wreck, as they climbed into the back of the little runabout, we could see in the other boats that there was a problem. The thing was lying too low in the water, and soon, due to the three-foot seas and the short scope on the anchor line, not to mention the weight of the three divers in full gear, water was coming over the transom. Soon it was obvious they were going to founder. Quickly, we had them get forward, and Corky, the Park captain in the 24 footer, yelled at them to untie the anchor line, cast it loose, and get under way. They tried and damn if it wouldn't start—the battery had gotten submerged and shorted. Waves were now coming over the engine and it was just a matter of seconds before the boat sank under the waves. He threw them a stern line from his boat, had them attach it to their bow, and in one or two seconds at most, he was pulling them forward, their boat now full of water to the gunwales. We yelled to them to pull the plug, but they didn't comprehend that this would let the water out as they were pulled forward. Finally they got the message, and Corky pulled that little runabout all the way back in to Convoy Point, some four miles. I had divers in the water on-site so I had to get them out before we could follow. When we finally got there the crew fell in to unloading tanks, washing gear, etc. while I got the van and trailer, and pulled Stanton's crappy little boat out of the water at the ramp. Then we discovered that the fiberglass patch on the bottom had opened up and the inside of the hull was already full of water—which is what had caused the boat to take on water so fast. I looked around for the crew chiefs and safety officer to let them know what had been the source of the problem. I got Ken and a couple of the guys, but couldn't find Pomerantz, the safety officer. Where was he? Someone said he was inside the office and was on the phone. What the heck!?!? I went in there and found him sitting with his back to me on the phone with Stanton, listening to him give a spy report on the near-mishap, when he finished by saying *the boat had sunk*. I let out a loud howl, and when he looked up and saw me he hung up. I was livid. I tore into him with a barrage of expletives, not only for his (what I considered) unauthorized communiqué, but for the fact that he couldn't let it wait, hadn't wanted to discuss it with myself and Ken Wild first (and even though we always had a requisite not-always-comfortable de-briefing to discuss every day's doings), and meanwhile the rest of the crew was working hard, still breaking down equipment and unloading (from the boat, and then reloading onto golf-cart ATVs), with air tanks to be filled, and we were all tired and sore and still working while he's here in the air-conditioned office on the phone, and oh yeah, by the fucking way, the boat had NOT SUNK! And yet he felt it was the most important thing that he had to get on the phone at once, hopefully before Ken and I noticed his absence, and report to Stanton! I couldn't contain myself. I wanted him off the project, …gone, …fired, …sent home. Other, cooler heads, including Ken, got into the fray, and throughout the evening and more than a few coconut Yoo-Hoo piña coladas later, I was prevailed upon and convinced to ease up, although I was nonetheless still pissed off at both him and Stanton.

Hookin' Up

On the way back to Tallahassee, I had the crew drop me off in Orlando. My brother Paul and I had long talked about taking Dad out deep-sea fishing, and now we were going to finally give it a shot. I called around to some of the various boats advertised in the yellow pages (again, before computers), and made arrangements for us to stay at a fishing lodge at the inlet in Ft. Pierce, since this seemed the quickest access to the Gulf Stream, and then booked us a full day out on *The Happy Hooker*, named after the recently popular book that extolled the virtues of prostitution. We headed down on a Thursday afternoon, got in that evening and had dinner and drinks before hitting the sack. In the morning Dad had us up before dawn and we got a quick breakfast with the other prospective fishermen, before making our way down to the dock. We even beat the captain and the first mate to the boat, but, who cares, it was a beautiful sunrise and we were stoked. [Jesus, I just realized that we were doing this for Dad's birthday, at the end of

August, and that he was just 58 at the time, three years younger than I am right now, and I remember thinking then how old he appeared to me.] Once the captain and mate got there we were off in no time flat. A half-hour run out to the red nun-buoy no. 2 that marked the entrance to the inlet and our lines were in the water. Drifting by, we got a barracuda or two, tossed them back, and a couple of small bonita that the captain wanted to keep for cut bait. Then we settled back for another hour run straight out into the deep blue, cracking our first beers by nine o'clock.

It was consequently both fast and slow, furious and tedious. We'd cruise for an hour and the mate looked for anything floating: a board or an ice chest, maybe just a large foam buoy, and the captain would make for it. When we got there, and it looked promising, the mate would take the first line and bait it with a shiny little shad and let it swim around, twenty or thirty feet below the flotsam, easily seen skittering down there from above. Then, out of the darkness below a bright yellow and green silver-sided dolphin (now they are all called *mahi*) would come up out of the darkness, circle the injured bait, and then quickly gobble it whole. "Leave it on! Leave it on!" the captain would yell at the mate from the upper steering platform, more for our benefit than the mate's, who knew what he was doing as he got our rigs readied. The now-hooked fish would swim round in circles, beautifully turning its silvery side every so often and showing the bright spotted green along its dorsal with the yellow tail fanning back and forth. Just as quickly, up from the darkness a wolfpack of dolphin, larger and agitated, would rise from the depths and start swimming around their snared companion. A handful of bait over the side, and as they now ate festively, it was our turn, and Dad and Paul and I tossed our lines in and one by one, hauled up their frenetic fishy forms, flapping about on the deck and losing their rainbows as they gasped their last. We got maybe a dozen in before the captain said enough, leave the rest, and once the original finner was pulled up and out of the water, the pack just as quickly disappeared into the azure gloom below. Then it'd be another hour or so, trolling, drinking beer, watching the teasers pop out of the foamy wake behind, and scanning the blue-on-blue horizon line for any other opportunity adrift.

We finished the day tired, sunburned, sodden with suds, and ecstatically exhausted. Once we hit the dock around five o'clock, the mate took a picture of us and the carnage we had wrought, then quickly filleted the mahi and packaged it for us in paper that we quickly put on ice. The captain wanted the amberjack and bonita, and we were happy to give it to him. We all shook blood and slimed hands, finishing off the beers. Even though it was supposed to be our treat to Dad for his birthday, he pulled out the credit card and paid them off (I think it was $400 back then), and topped it off with a $100 tip. Hell, we easily had $200 worth of fish, and the captain would make another $100 off the jacks. It was a very successful trip, and we drove back to Mom and Dad's in Orlando that night where we entertained Mom with our adventure. The next day, now a Saturday, we divided up the fish with Dad, and Paul drove me back to Tallahassee where Amy and Robin were waiting after my long haul down south.

Fall Back In

It just so happened that once we got settled back into school, and Ken and I were working feverishly on the Summer '84 Biscayne Report—we were being hammered every day to get it out in record time, editing and thoroughness be damned—word came down that the Southeast Archeological Center was not to engage in any further underwater activity. This was the result of several factors: the protestations to the Regional Office of the dark-hearted Richard Curry, the park biologist at Biscayne, who never liked SEAC or George Fischer, and who was pissed off that a couple of graduate students had come into his park and carried out a major survey; all of this complaining in coordination with the machinations of the so-called "elite" Submerged Cultural

Resources Unit (SCRU) out of Santa Fe, New Mexico (yes, in the middle of the desert), who felt it was an infringement upon their turf to carry out underwater archaeology in the Service, and who'd been beaten out of the summer project; and finally, the less-than-even-lip-service support given to George by the Chief of the Center (who was just as happy to have what he considered this problem-child strangled in its crib once and for all). So, George was pretty upset about this directive from Washington, as was Ken, who complained bitterly about the unfairness of it all; but I can say in all honesty, it didn't bother me a bit, as I was willing to ignore it. Oh, not right away, that's for sure, but I'd been given some good advice, which arrived in a very auspicious manner.

One day I was working at George's desk… he was out sick, and we had a standing agreement that if he was out it was okay for me to sit at his desk, in his small little office at the end of the long hall just off the southwest entrance to Bellamy. It was quiet, and he had not only an electric typewriter that I could use, but a tall-backed orthopedic chair that he had ordered from GSA for his bad neck, and finally, as times began a' changing, it was one of the few places you could still smoke, if you had a mind to, and then there was always that half-bottle of whiskey in the bottom right-hand drawer if you might need a bracer before getting called "up the hill" to get chewed out by the Chief. In any case, I'm in George's office, sitting at his desk working on the Biscayne report, when a tall and wiry white-haired older gent stuck his head in and asked where George was. I told him he was out sick, and he asked if he could come in and smoke a cigarette. Sure, I told him, glad to have a break and someone to talk to. Putting my feet up on George's desk, like a big-shot, I introduced myself as he lit up, sitting in that little fiberglass chair opposite George's desk, and he said his name was John Griffin. (John Griffin? John Griffin? Where had I heard that name before?) I was sure that we'd never met, but where the heck did I hear the name John Griffin? I finally had to ask him. He told me, "I used to be Chief of the Center." Oh my God!!! My feet came down to floor level immediately. This was the famous archaeologist John W. Griffin, who had been not only the first State Archaeologist for the State of Florida, but had hired the first Chairman of the Anthropology Department at FSU, Hale Smith, famous in his own right; and, as he had already mentioned, he'd been the Chief of the Southeast Archeological Center for the National Park Service (before Pete, our current Chief), and in fact, had been the first Regional Archaeologist for the Southeast Region. The guy was a living legend! I was sitting in the presence of what might have been considered archaeological royalty. I asked him if he wouldn't prefer to sit at the desk instead, and he said "No, no, of course not." He was in the adjacent Curation lab, working on his grand synthesis of Everglades archaeology (which he was having some problems with, between the Park Service and the State of Florida) and just wanted to take a break. He asked me what I did and I told him about the underwater program, how we'd had our ups and downs, and after this last summer's project how the Director of the Park Service had shut us down. He's the one who told me not to worry about it, these political turf wars happen every so often, and it would come back around again in just a couple of years. He'd seen it many times before. And that's why I never got upset about the whole business: he was very matter-of-fact about it in a calm and reassuring way. But then I couldn't hold back, and I begged him to tell me the story about Osceola.

The Black Drink Rises

Whenever I wanted a diversion from the regular grind, I'd go into the adjacent lab, which was the curatorial facility for the Southeast Archeological Center, holding not only the artifacts, stacked in cardboard boxes on tall shelves in a back room, but also containing the archives of past archaeological projects as well, including field notes, photos, correspondence, news articles, etc. They were fascinating reading, and as long as you never carried anything out, you could sit and go through these documents to your heart's content, not to mention that they were invaluable when you were planning a project at some park where you'd never been before. One of the accession records (as their called) caught my eye one day when I saw the word "Osceola" on it. I thought I already knew a bit about the great Seminole war chief Osceola (the name means "Black Drink," from the kick-ass highly caffeinated and thick black brew that the men used for council sessions), who had fought the U.S. Army to a standstill two decades before the Civil War. When we were kids we had visited Fort San Marcos in St. Augustine and seen the cell where he had been held (then Fort Marion) when he was captured the first time with his pal Coacoochee. We listened to the park ranger tell us how they had escaped when they discovered they could fit their heads between the bars, and so starved themselves until they could slide out their shoulders and then the rest of their bodies (my ten-year old head at the time barely made it through). The guards had not considered their medicine bags, once inspected, to be worth confiscating, since they contained nothing but some dried-up grass, leaves, and seeds. One moonless night they crawled out of their cells, went over the walls, crossed the moat, and got outside the city, where they took a healthy dose of the stimulating herbal mixture and ran continuously all night and another day and night through the swamps and marshes, easily outmaneuvering the pursuing dogs and men on horseback. Later, he was captured a second time when he met the U.S. Army general under a flag of truce to discuss ending hostilities. This time, however, he was trundled up to Fort Moultrie in South Carolina under heavy guard and died just before his family and followers were packed off onto the Trail of Tears to the Oklahoma Territory.

In reading the file marked "Osceola" though, I found a fascinating tale of intrigue, lost history, and pathos. Apparently, back in 1966 this guy named Shiver who lived in Miami had claimed in a newspaper article that he had driven up to Fort Moultrie, dug into the grave and "reclaimed the bones of Osceola," bringing them back to Florida, their rightful final resting place. Although he claimed his intentions were honorable, and this was a matter of Seminole pride, at the same time he had made plans to re-inter them at the Rainbow Springs tourist attraction, for which he'd be roundly compensated. Well, the Park Service, who owned Fort Moultrie (and therefore, the historic grave of Osceola) was not about to let a self-proclaimed Federal crime go unpunished. But first, the evidence had to be gathered. So they sent the Regional Archeologist, John Griffin (the same man sitting across from me smoking a cigarette) to Fort Moultrie to assess the damage. When he got there he found a rather small hole dug into the side of the historic gravesite of Osceoloa, out in front of the fort and alongside another gravesite marking the remains of 11 sailors who had died during the Civil War in the Northern vessel *USS Patapsco*. Once he'd opened up the gravesite (using proper archaeological techniques), Griffin found that the coffin was intact, and that the hole dug into the side of the grave had missed it entirely, and again, was just a small excavation not large enough to disinter anything really. But Shiver had claimed that he got the bones of Osceoloa!? Well, they had to know for sure, so the coffin was exhumed, taken to a nearby secured building, and opened. Inside was the skeleton of a middle-aged male, except there were two very strange anomalies: 1) the head was missing, and 2) there was the complete skeleton of a newborn baby at the feet!

Neither of these oddities had ever been discussed in the historic literature, the narrative going something like this… Osceola had been captured as stated before, under a flag of truce by one General Jasper. This not only tainted the reputation of the formerly honorable general, but showed an overall lack of trustworthiness on the part of the United States Government, and which was noted at the time throughout the country's newspapers, a black mark against the newly-elected President, Martin Van Buren. Taken to Fort Moultrie on Sullivan's Island in South Carolina and locked up under heavy guard, the Seminole war chief was met by many of the

Charleston elite as sort of an entertaining diversion. George Catlin, the famous Indian portrait painter, made plans to visit and when he got there was told that Osceola was very sick. In fact, he'd contracted tonsillitis, which had abscessed and become septic. Although he was in enormous pain (which can almost be detected in the painting, the best ever done of him), Osceola put on his best refinery, gorgets, ear bobs, turban and even an ostrich feather, and sat motionless for several hours as Catlin sketched out the proud warrior. Afterwards, the U.S. Army doctor, Frederick Weedon, had been called, but there was nothing he could do by then, and Osceola died on January 30, 1838

Here's where things get interesting. So, after Osceola dies, and while the Army makes preparations to bury him with full military honors as a defeated enemy combatant (the least they could do, considering the circumstances of his capture), Dr. Weedon asks the family for permission to make a plaster cast, or death mask, which was a very common ritual back in those days. When he finishes the death mask, Dr. Weedon takes the opportunity to secretly sever Osceola's head from the rest of the body, but hides the gruesome operation with a tightly tied scarf around the neck. The family comes in one last time, and here again, something history doesn't record, is where the infant body is placed at the corpse's feet. Osceola had two wives, one of which was known to be 8 or 9 months pregnant at the time. The Trail of Tears trek being imminent, it was not unheard of, and would have made sense, for a newborn to be suffocated and placed with the father, at his feet (this is somewhat conjectural, but fits the facts). What isn't conjectural, is that, when the family left, and before the coffin was sealed, Dr. Weedon removed Osceola's head, including his ear bobs, turban, etc. as well as his rifle and medicine bag. The coffin was then sealed, the military funeral was held, and the remaining remains were placed into the gravesite in front of the fort. This was the coffin now opened and examined by Griffin.

To be sure, there were several problems that needed to be addressed, not the least of which was "Where was Osceola's head?" Well, a set of G-men were sent to visit Shiver, the "entrepreneurial businessman" in Miami, and they returned with all the bones and other material he had collected on his rescue mission. It turned out to be handful of pig and cow bones and other stuff that would have been thrown out of the Fort kitchen. No head. Further investigation into the life of Dr. Weedon revealed that yes, he had had the head for many years, even using it to hang on the post at the foot of his children's bed when they misbehaved to frighten them into being more cooperative. Finally he tired of it and gave it to his son-in-law, who then donated it to a New York physician who added it to his phrenology collection (still a scientific question of the day) at the local Surgical and Pathology Museum, which was destroyed in a fire in 1866. The other items from the collection by Weedon were still held by the Weedon family. But the body was positively identified as Osceola's when the plaster death-mask (now at the Smithsonian) was looked at. Apparently, Dr. Weedon had put on enough plaster so that it covered Osceola's clavicles (the bones at the upper chest), one of which (either right or left, I can't remember) had obviously been broken and healed. This coincided with the skeleton, and therefore the association was made. The story pretty much ends there, except for the fact that at the unadvertised reburial, the National Park Service had a larger-than-necessary grave dug , and once the coffin was lowered down, some three to five yards of concrete were poured over it into the hole, so that no one would ever attempt to "rescue" the remains again. [It has been the argument and policy of the Park Service that historically this fort in South Carolina is the place where Osceola died and was buried, and therefore, this is where he'd stay. There have been several moves since then, especially after passage of the Native American Graves Protection and Repatriation Act in 1990, to have them returned to Florida and the Seminole tribe, but so far, these efforts have been fruitless.] Dr. Griffin stubbed out his second or third cigarette and stood up. I thanked him for the story and we shook hands. I only saw him once more before he passed away in 1993.

Opportunity Rocks

So here it is, Fall of 1984, a bunch of us graduate students are studying for, and taking, our Comprehensive Exams in Anthropology (with few if any casualties). My "study-buddy" was Steve Bryne, a thin blonde, freckled brainiac who, for some reason, the coeds were all ga-ga over. Go figure. But it was good for me: first, because he was intelligent, and second, because we'd both go ahead and read the required texts, quiz each other, and really delve into deep anthropological (and therefore, philosophical and humanistic) questions about the effects (and affects) of culture. [I might inform the reader that these were the Comprehensive Exams for a Masters degree in *General Anthropology*, not specifically *Archaeology*, which is only a single one of the four sub-disciplines in Anthropology we had to study for—unless they've invented a few more in the last thirty-five years, which wouldn't surprise me a bit.] We both did fine. So, the Summer '84 Biscayne report is finished, and comps are over, when Ken and I are called into George's office right after Thanksgiving, he wants to tell us something. He'd gotten a call from an old acquaintance, Alan Albright, one of the (other) founding fathers of underwater archaeology, who was the Chief Underwater Archaeologist for the University of South Carolina's Institute for Archaeology and Anthropology (known as SCIAA), in effect, the State Underwater Archaeologist for South Carolina. He was looking for an assistant, and it was a State job, decent pay, and benefits... did George know anybody who might be interested? George got him on the phone, and we both told him we'd be interested. Albright asked us if we couldn't come up in two week's time and interview. Well, this was going to be a little awkward, both of us vying for the same job, but what the hell; sure, we told him... we'd see him in two weeks. When the time came, we shook hands on letting the best man win, hopped in the car and got there one Thursday evening, staying at a Days Inn just outside of town. The next morning we headed to Albright's office in the basement of some dormitory/classroom building called Maxcy College, which served then as SCIAA's home base. When he asked who wanted to go first, we flipped a coin and I won, so in I went. Albright was a thin, bony old man, even then, though he was only in his early fifties, with a half-head of wispy white hair, a soft voice, big wandering eyeballs (made even bigger by the thick lenses in his black-rimmed glasses), a pencil-thin moustache with a prominent Adam's apple that bobbed up and down whether he spoke or not, and slightly sunken cheeks, as if he didn't have enough teeth to fill his jaws. And he was fidgety. Hell, he was more nervous than I was. He asked some general questions: where did I grow up, where'd I go to high school? (He was impressed that I'd gone to a Catholic high school.) Family? (Wife and one kid, one on the way.) By the time we finally got down to talking about archaeological experience I found it easier to just settle back and talk, save him the effort of thinking what questions to ask. After a half an hour I wound down and he stood up, signaling the end of the interview. Two more questions. Do you drink? Why, yes I do – moderately. Do you do drugs? No, no, of course not, I lied... that would be dangerous for a diver, now wouldn't it? We shook hands, and I walked out and Ken walked in. I sat across the hall and waited, relieved to find out that you couldn't hear a thing coming from Alan's office, behind the heavy wooden door across the hall. When Ken came out he looked a bit frazzled, but otherwise no worse for wear. Alan didn't entertain us with any small talk but just suggested that we take a look around campus, and he'd give us a call in a week or so. The campus was historically significant, having missed most of the ravages of the Civil War when the rest of the city of Columbia was torched in advance of Sherman's arrival, for which he received all the blame nevertheless. The State Capital Building, one block over, still flew the Stars and Bars below the U.S. Flag and the State Flag, which has the palmetto tree and horned moon on a flat blue background. We couldn't find a bar to have a drink (they were all private clubs!), so we headed back to the hotel, had drinks in the bar next door, and drove out the next morning. All the way home, we discussed the questions Alan asked, and our answers, and our general feeling about how it all went. Neither of us figured we'd either cinched it or blew it. A week later Albright called George and they talked briefly; then Alan called me separately and told me he was offering me the job. I reminded him that I had another baby on the way, and it wasn't due until February, so I couldn't make it until then. He said no problem. Then he called Ken and told him that, if he could, he would have hired both of us.

Fun with Forensicks

One day I'm sitting in my Park Service office that I shared with Bob and Dennis, full of file cabinets and computers; it's late afternoon and everyone's gone, when the door opens and Dr. Dailey sticks his head in. "Are you busy?" he asks. "No, not really, just finishing up a few things before heading home." "I need your help." "Sure," I tell him, always one to help the Chairman, and a good friend at that. "It'll take about an hour," he says. "Okay, what's up?" He doesn't answer, walking me silently down the hall in Bellamy; classes are done for the day and it's echo-quiet, nobody around. We go into the large empty Physical Anthropology classroom lab, with its big flat polished-black tables, chalkboards along three walls, and lectern. In the back is a smaller clean-room lab with a large wooden door, the glass in the small look-through blackened so no one could see in—the forensics lab! He pulls out his keys and opens the door. Besides the lab refrigerators in the back, and the sink and inhalation hood (for chemical reagents) on the right, there's a large stainless steel metal table in the center of the room. On it there's lying a misshapen black plastic bag, maybe five feet long and obviously with something in it. He goes, "Here, put these on," and hands me a pair of tight, thin, white rubber gloves, "and this" (a white paper apron). "Dr. Dailey," I said, "What's going on... what... what do you want me to do?" "We've got a forensic case here we have to investigate for the medical examiner. Dr. Morse and Glen Doran are going to be here in a minute. This one's pretty bad, so we need you to mop up any liquids that might spill," and he hands me a roll of that rough brown paper that you dry your hands with in the men's room—a whole roll! I set it on the table next to the body bag. "Gee, Dr. Dailey, I don't know," I start choking, "I've never done this before..." "Well, you're here now, and I don't have anyone else," he said, "get a garbage bag and line that can. Make sure everything goes in it." A big metal garbage can, a large black plastic garbage bag; I put it in. Then Glen Doran and Dr. Morse come in and start putting on aprons and gloves. Glen was a relatively young, tall, dark-haired multi-purpose anthropologist out of California, hired a couple of years earlier to replace the well-known historic archaeologist Kathy Deagan when she jumped to the University of Florida. Dr. Morse was an old professor (and I mean old, then maybe 80), who was famous in his own right as a forensic anthropologist, and he and Dr. Dailey were two of the top three guys in Florida. The other was Dr. Maples in Gainesville. So, briefly, when a body is found that is too far gone to determine anything: sex, height, weight, age, race, etc. (much less cause of death), the medical examiner usually tosses it to the forensic anthropologist to determine these basic facts as best as they can. Then he, the examiner, might look at some organs if they're in any way intact and not liquefied, and run a gamut of chemical tests (all this before DNA testing). It had been found in the swamp, and that's about anything any of us knew since the medical examiner (and the cops, usually) didn't want to give out any information that might influence the results. The anthropologists would usually get the background story later.

Dr. Dailey and Dr. Morse were getting their paperwork and tape recorder in order, discussing who'd do what, who'd record the results, and whether they had all the necessary instruments. Dr. Glen Doran, who had assisted in forensic cases elsewhere, was less preoccupied and was taking a semi-sadistic pleasure in my apparent unease before they got started. "Now, listen, Brewer," he said, "when we open the bag, and the big jumping maggots come out, they're going to be all over the place. You've got to get them as fast as you can. Do not let them get out under the door, you understand?" I gulped and nodded. "And the juice... just sop it up as quick as you can and make sure everything, and I mean everything, gets into that garbage can and doesn't get out. You okay?" I nodded again. "If you start feeling sick, or faint, you let us know, alright?" "I'll be fine," I said softly. Dr. Dailey unzipped the bag, and the smell of stale warm swampwater filled the room, followed by the stench of rotting meat. And goddamn if Glen wasn't kidding, big brown-and-grey-ringed maggots immediately started popping out of the top of the bag, landing on the table, and then falling onto the floor, inch-worm crawling along. I started tearing off handfuls of the brown paper towels and chasing the little fuckers. Jeezus Spare-me-Lord Kee-rist! There were dozens of them... going off in all directions, and I was picking them up with the paper towels and depositing them in the trashcan as fast as I could. Then Dailey and Morse started reaching in the bag and pulling out parts, and goddamn if the edge of the zippered opening didn't ease down and a pool of brown liquid drooled out onto the table and over its side and onto the floor, me trying to mop it up as fast as I can. This went on for fifteen minutes. Now I realized why Dailey had given me a whole roll and I furtively started looking to see if there'd be a spare. "David!" Glen yelled, "There's one going for the door!" I caught it with my foot before it crawled underneath, then wiped up the spot where I'd smashed it. Now they started to ease off a little, so I stood alongside the table, peering into the bag and nabbing the little parasites individually as soon as they hopped on the table, meanwhile sopping up the brown gelatinous liquid as soon as it began to spill out of the bag, dumping the soaking soiled handfuls of filth into the can behind me without even looking. Glen gave a nod toward the trashcan, and there on the edge were ten hardy nematodes climbing up the edges, their featureless heads snaking back and forth looking for a means of making their escape. I grabbed a can of Lysol that was nearby and gave them a shot, and they dropped back in. By now Dailey and Morse were making measurements on the bones, and most of the goop was out of the bag. I got another whiff of the cadaverous swamp as my adrenaline wore off, and noticed I was sweating. There was no way I could lift my hands, or my arms for that matter, anywhere near my head to wipe off my brow, as they were bespattered with brown droplets of what I could only describe as maggot mucous. I let it drip. Finally, Dr. Dailey and Dr. Morse, with Glen's help, started re-packing the body bag. By the time they'd zipped it shut, I had cleaned up most of the worst of the muck. They lifted the bag up and put it into another clean white bag on a nearby gurney, and then zipped that one shut. Once I saw them taking off their gloves and aprons, tossing them into the trashcan, I knew it was over. As they washed their hands, talking, I finished cleaning up with the Lysol spray. Then I dumped my gloves and apron in, and we zippered that little shop of horrors shut. As I washed my hands they each thanked me for my help and Dr. Dailey was especially appreciative, walking me across Tennessee Street and buying me a pitcher of beer. I didn't want to push it, but I asked for a shot of Jameson's as well, to wash away the memory as much as to disinfect my nasal passages.

Much to my dismay, I was now the go-to guy for the forensic medical exams. "But Dr. Dailey," I protested, "I'm not even a physical anthropologist wannabe, and you've got plenty of them who might want the experience." "No, I'm sorry, they either can't take it or they're not thorough enough when it comes to cleaning up; they all want to deal with nice clean bones... I need someone I can count on." Thus began a series of cases, and thankfully, none were as bad as that first one. I'd passed the trial by fire. Speaking of fire, the next one was the one we called The Crispy Critter, after the popular children's cereal of the day. Found at the bottom of a sinkhole by some recreational divers, it was in the front passenger seat of a car that had been burned before being rolled into the sink. The sheriff's department had pulled the car, removed the body, and carved the jaw out of the skull so they could make x-rays and send the dental records around, looking for a positive ID.   When we unzipped the body bag the smell was surprisingly like that of a barbecue where someone had used a little too much lighter fluid. They had suspected that it was a female and Dr. Dailey confirmed that right away, just from what was left of the skull (smaller, higher cheekbones, more graceful than a man's [what they call "gracile"]). The chest and back were completely charred, as was the top of the skull, which had a small bullet hole (which the cops had missed) in a little tuft of remaining hair just above the back of the neck. But she was wearing jeans, so Dailey took a pair of surgical shears and began cutting them off. She'd been in the sink roughly two years, so other than the skeletal material, whatever meat that was left was what we call "soapified"; this means that the fats and muscle tissue had congealed into what looks just like Ivory soap (which is supposedly 99 and 9/10s% fat-free—because the fats have been converted into glycerides with lye). Most of the soapified meat came off with the jeans, but he wanted to see if she had had any children. Incredibly, once he removed the pubic bone (the symphysis, actually two bones that separate and come back together during childbirth), he could tell that she had indeed at one time been a mother, at least once. Even though he didn't have the jaw, which would have told him right away, he could tell from the sutures on the skull that she was in her mid-twenties. The little tuft of hair left on the back of the neck indicated she was a dirty blonde, and once the bones were laid out in their proper position she turned out to be about 5 foot 6 inches tall. The jean size said she was slim. That and the height gave him a weight of about 110 – 120. The cause of death was obvious. She had once broken her arm when she was a child. Fascinating. Turned out later that it was a drug-related murder that a couple of redneck yahoos had tried to cover by pouring gasoline into the car before igniting it and then rolling it into the sinkhole. They couldn't have done a better job of preserving the evidence if they had tried.

The next one was to me the most interesting… The electric cooperative that controlled the dam at Lake Talquin, twenty miles west of Tallahassee, had decided that they needed to lower the lake either to work on the generators or clean out the silt. In any case, once the waters had gone down about five feet, someone reported seeing the top of a car along the road edge near one of the many winding curves. The sheriff's department went out there, and one of the deputies waded out and opened the driver's door of the now half-submerged vehicle. As he did, the still-sitting ivory-white corpse turned toward the opening with the outrushing water. The deputy slammed the door shut again. They got a tow truck and slowly pulled the car up onto the roadside, letting the water drain out the bottom. When they opened it again, there was now just a large lump of grey clothes and, as I said, this "soapified" pile of meat. They got it all into a body bag and shipped it to the University. This time it was just Dr. Dailey and myself, and by now I had the routine down pat. After taking all the parts out, laying them out anatomically, and giving him the once over, Dr. Dailey excused himself and made a phone call. The body was missing its left arm. Could the sheriff's deputies look for it? Maybe when the one deputy had slammed the door closed, he had accidentally knocked it off? Someone should go out and look for it. Meanwhile I'm standing over this heap of bones, clothes and white soap, all still soaking wet. I remember thinking the guy had a nice belt. When he got back, Dailey and I began gently scraping the soft grey-white soapflesh off the bones, setting aside the clothes, ring, wristwatch, and change (the cops had already taken his wallet). The wet fatty meat went into the trashcan, and the bones were laid out once again, anatomically correct. He was an older gentleman, maybe sixty-five or so, partial dentures, some missing teeth, tall, six feet, no sign of trauma to his bones, other than some wear and tear due to heavy work and his advanced age. That was it, there wasn't much to him… except for that missing left arm (the end of which Dailey examined quizzically). We bagged him up and waited for the medical examiner's office to come and get the remains. The next day, after they had come and gotten him, Dailey called me and asked me to come down to his office. They'd already put together a folder on the guy, but Dailey wanted to tell me the story himself.

There *was* no left arm! The guy had suffered an accident and it had been taken off surgically some thirty years earlier. He was an alcoholic, and the last time anyone had seen him was at an Alcoholics Anonymous meeting (now how did they know that, if it's anonymous?). Apparently the AA hadn't quite taken hold, because the passenger's side and back floor were covered with beer cans and empty pint bottles of whiskey. Also in the back seat were the remains of a dog! He'd been driving at night in the wintertime, because the car lights were pulled on and the heater switch was set, with all the windows rolled up. They don't know why he was heading *away* from Tallahassee, but apparently he just sailed straight through the curve, parting the bushes that closed behind the flying car, and landed in the lake, probably knocked unconscious and drowned. (I felt sorry for the dog.) They got his address from his wallet and went out to a trailer park off of Bicycle Road in Tallahassee (which is still there), found his trailer and forced the door. To me this is the most amazing part… a few newspapers out front, some old mail in the box, but nothing disturbed in his trailer, except for roaches, rats, and raccoon shit. It had been seven years! Seven years, and no one had missed him enough to go into his house. The electricity just went off one day (Talquin Electric!), the mail stopped, and the rats and roaches and spiders took over. You couldn't make this stuff up.

The last forensic story. I wasn't present at this one, as it had happened before I started in the Department, but it was a classic that was told repeatedly: One day a hunter had been out doing his thing somewhere out in Gadsden County and came upon a carcass out in the woods. It looked like it had been covered over with a little dirt and leaves and had been out there for some time. But the head, hands and feet were missing! The sheriff's deputies went out and tossed the remains in a body bag. Now back then in Gadsden County the medical examiner was an elected position, who didn't have to be a doctor, or trained in any way, and to be honest, nine times out of ten determining cause of death, unless it was natural, was pretty easy. Well, this medical examiner opens the bag, smells the stench and looks at the blackened skin and some tufts of red hair, and declares that it's a black man with reddish hair who'd been murdered and his head and hands and feet removed to hide the identity. It was quickly shipped over to FSU to see what more they could determine. Dr. Daily and Dr. Morse were the only ones dealing with this stuff back then. When they opened the bag, Dr. Dailey said right away, "This isn't even a human being." They took it out of the bag, laid it out on the table, and they both agreed: this is a bear. Sure the skin was black, from being exposed to the elements, if it wasn't black to begin with. The "red hair" was just some remnants of fur that had turned reddish. But it was true, the head and paws were gone. They called the Gadsdsen Sheriff's Office, who had already been canvassing the local farms and found a farmer that said yeah, he had shot a bear out that way about two years earlier, and cut off its head and paws as souvenirs. The sheriff had already told the medical examiner, who was too embarrassed to call FSU. So… what to do with the remains? The Anthropology Department at FSU, like so many others, has, for both the archaeologist and the physical anthropologist what is called a "type collection," which is actually several collections, of differing artifacts, bones and skeletons, including many animal bones, and sometimes even various plant remains. These are used for comparative purposes such as when an archaeologist finds a bone, he or she can then compare it with others in the collection to determine what type and size of animal (or human) it came from. Artifacts and plants are easy enough to deal with, but bones often present a particularly nasty aspect in that they often need to be separated from the attached skin, meat and ligaments. The first step in this process is to soften them up, usually by placing them in a large bucket or barrel of water (the universal solvent) with some loosening agent, usually a detergent. Heat speeds the process up, but since you can't really boil a large barrel of meat and bones without attracting some attention, especially when the animal is rotten, it's often left out in some remote area where the sun can get at it and the natural process of de-

267

fleshing can occur at its own pace. Small animals are often placed in a screen-sealed aquarium with flesh-eating weevils that can clean the bones in a week.

One of the students who was then handling the collections, a guy named Robert Taylor, asked if he could have the carcass and it was readily given to him. Somehow, he got the bear-body, in a barrelful of water, up onto the roof of the Bellamy Building, which is a nine-or-ten-story classroom building that used to have the Anthro Department on the first floor and other departments on the floors above. He did this on a Friday afternoon as the weekend began. Under the hot late spring sun, on the black tar asphalt of the roof, the decayed-meat bear soup began to steep in its own juices, foaming and bubbling throughout the weekend, while no one was on campus, and most of the electricity was on standby. When Monday morning arrived, the electricity kicked on, and the air conditioners fired up to cool the building for classes. Beginning at the ground floor, and rising interminably to the upper classrooms and offices, the sickly stench of decomposing bear meat saturated the building, which was quickly evacuated and the fire department called. They started at the bottom and checked every room, hoping to find the cause of what was apparently some college prank. When they finally reached the rooftop, and came out the metal door there, they found Bob, stirring his pot right next to the air intake conduit where he had unknowingly placed it. Classes were cancelled for the day. (On another note, Bob was a good friend of mine. Still is, I hope. One day he was out scalloping on snorkel gear off of the St. Mark's lighthouse and a crab boat coming back in didn't see him and ran right over him. He was lucky that the prop only knicked his shoulder and clipped an ear, and the rudder gave him a thump. Could a' been way worse. I now refer to him as "my old chum.")

I'd be remiss if I didn't mention that it was right around this time that I began seeing one of the graduate students, Ann Nightingale. She had been in most of my classes, and had serially and seriously paired up with a couple of the notable Anthropology graduate student stalwarts over the years, but it just so happened that at that time she was free, and since we had always gotten along as friends, as well as notably being the two most outspoken students in any class we were in, often initiating debates and asking tough questions of the professors, it was logical that we'd take it a step further. She was stunning in profile, smart, tough, and built. I could say she chose me, if I were looking for an excuse as an errant husband (biologically speaking, isn't it always the female's choice?), but I've got to admit I was in it for the adventure, the danger, and the rutting, and there's no excuse for that. Still, I think it would be fair to say we were good friends first and lovers second. In any case, at this point it was intermittent, short-lived, and not too serious (we were too smart for that!). Besides, I was leaving. We did hook up briefly when I came back from South Carolina, but it was again, intermittent and short-lived because she fell in love with a musician, a phenomenal guitar player, singer and songwriter (what is it with those guys?), and though they had their ups and downs, they eventually stuck it out and got married. They're still married some twenty-five years later and have two grown sons. Though she moved away, became a professional archaeologist in her own right, and we haven't talked in well over ten years, I still think about her once in a while and hope she's well.

Part II

Adultification

No man succeeds in everything he undertakes. In that sense we are all failures. The great point is not to fail in ordering and sustaining the effort of our life. In this matter vanity is what leads us astray. It hurries us into situations from which we must come out damaged; whereas pride is our safeguard, by the reserve it imposes on the choice of our endeavour as much as by the virtue of its sustaining power.

(from The Duel, by Joseph Conrad)

14. South Carolina (1985-1986)

Not Nearly Albright

Back in September, right after I'd gotten back to Tally from Biscayne, we had moved out of 214 West Brevard, behind the Governor's mansion, because Mr. Funderburk, the landlord, was making noises about selling the property there, the whole damn block, to the State as a buffer for the Governor's residence, and as a consequence had raised the rent. Not to mention (but I guess I will anyway), a couple of trees, big laurel oaks, thirty feet high or more and five feet in diameter, had come down in a storm while I was gone, and everyone in the neighborhood was still shaken about the enormity of the damage. Let me put it this way... had the wind been blowing in a different direction that night, Amy, our baby son Robin, the dog, and the house, would have all been tomato paste and splinters. It took my old buddy, Bill, a week to carve that one up for firewood for his Franklin stove. So, while I was still down in Biscayne, Amy had found a nice four bedroom place on a street named Rexwood, in a small neighborhood off of the Blountstown Highway connector between Tharpe and Tennessee Streets. When I saw it I was amazed to find that it was an exact *doppelganger* of the old house on Ballard Road, exact in every detail, except for being on a lot one-twentieth the size we boys had lived on out in the woods south of town. In the back yard there were a couple of pear trees, loaded to the gills and dropping pears all over the ground. I immediately set to making pear beer as fast as I could to keep up with the falling fruit. Meanwhile, Amy and I began a slow celebration into the holiday season. She was seven or eight months pregnant with our second child now, and our first son, Robin, almost three, was growing up strong and clever, and here I was on my way to the start of a professional career as an Underwater Archaeologist; in fact, the Assistant Underwater Archaeologist for the State of South Carolina! Mom and Dad were very proud, especially to see me finally get a real job, with benefits, even though it meant moving to Columbia, South Carolina, the heart of Dixieness. Thanksgiving came and went, soon Christmas was looming, and Amy and I went to Orlando to see all our friends and family there before we'd be moving north to South Carolina after the baby was born. Then, Albright started becoming a pain in the ass. He started calling me, first once a week, then upped it to twice a week, "When's that baby due!? I need you here as soon as possible!" "Well, I told you, Mr. Albright, the baby was due the beginning of February. You said that was okay... so we still got another month to go. But I'll head up there right after the baby's born, okay?" He still called all through January, finally pissing both me and Amy off when he suggested in mid-January "Well, can't you just have them induce labor?" Sam was born naturally on Tuesday, February 4th, and Amy's Mom came up to be with her, and a day later, I was headed up to Columbia. Then I found out why he needed me there so bad—he was going on a vacation to London and needed someone to watch his fucking house!

I spent the first night there with Alan and his wife Penny, a quiet, obviously browbeaten, congenial (but not uncomely) slender woman, then in her early forties, and, after eating a simple dinner in front of the TV, he showed me his den, the living room, the rest of the house and garage, as well as the contents of his liquor cabinet (I noticed the bottles were marked as to the level of contents), and finally his most prized possession: a Macintosh Apple personal computer (the first of its kind and the first personal computer I'd ever seen), sitting on the formal dining room table, not unlike the tabernacle on an altar, all by its lonesome. In the morning, after giving me a rundown on my house-sitting duties (feeding the cat, who was afraid of strangers and would hide), they grabbed up their luggage, or to be more accurate, he let Penny drag out the bags to the car, with me helping, and off they went for two weeks. I drove in to the office, and found it located at the end of a long hallway in the basement of the aforementioned dorm. There I met my co-worker, Alan's volunteer assistant, Mack Newsome, a big red-headed Englishman with thinning hair, thick glasses and an even thicker accent. Knowing Alan was going to be gone for awhile, he had commandeered the large desk that was supposed to be mine, and placed it at the head of the room, facing out, as if he were an elementary schoolteacher. I took a small desk along the far wall and lined up a few of the underwater archaeology books I'd carried up from Florida. He came over, looked at the books, and wanted to borrow three of them right away. Sure, I said, why not.

The Great Dane

Then I met a guy who made a very great impression on me, and whom I still consider one of my most memorable mentors ever, an example of what a solid human being should be like. In walks this tall fellow, a little disheveled, with dark brown bushy hair and a large brown walrus moustache. He says something to Mack about Alan being gone ("while the cat's away…"), and Mack introduces me. "I'm Curt, Curt Petersen," he says, and gives me a big callous-handed handshake. He asks me where I'm from and then tells me he's an old Tallahassee boy himself, having lived there about twenty years, much of which we both had spent at the same time, thus crossing many proverbial paths. Did I know Miss Kitty at the Pastime? Hell yeah, I did. He also knew most, if not all of the faculty in the Anthropology Department at FSU, including Hale Smith, the founding chair, whom I had missed by about two years. Did I know any of the folks at the R.A. Gray Building (home of the Florida Department of Historic Resources)? Sure I did! It turns out that Curt worked there for the better part of those twenty years, trading secrets of the restorative sciences with the famous Herb Bump, who'd helped us with the cannon from Biscayne a year and a half earlier. Petersen, Pyoterson, Petrosven? Irish? English? Russian? No, Danish… Viking stock! Curt was now the conservator for SCIAA, working on the problematic Brown's Ferry vessel, raised by Alan and company several years earlier and being treated with polyethylene glycol (PEG) in a large concrete tank in a warehouse several blocks away. Curt suggests that I meet the rest of the staff down the hall where they're having an impromptu reception for the new incoming Director. He and I walk on down and go into the office of the retiring Director, Bob Stephenson, another well-known archaeologist, a ram-rod straight crusty old pipe-smoking former Marine who resembled Lowell Thomas, and was now getting ready to pull the plug after thirty years. The new incoming Director was a tall baby-faced chubby and jocular fellow in a suit named Bruce Rippeteau, maybe forty, but with a PhD out of Rensselaer Polytechnic Institute (RPI) in New York, undoubtedly hand-picked by the administration at the University for his glad-handing demeanor (ergo, the suit, whereas no other archaeologist I ever knew wore one unless you were at a conference, and even then, rarely). I shook hands with them all.

Curt asks me if I'd like to meet Stan South. It takes a moment to sink in… Stan South! Over along the window (which looked up into a parking lot, since we were in the basement), sitting on the corner of a desk, slightly slumped and in a crumpled old grey V-neck sweater, there was this bum-whiskered older gentleman in glasses, slightly overweight, with tousled hair and a big wide grin across his face. Curt took me over and introduced me. I was totally awe-struck. Yeah, I had met a few famous archaeologists in my time by now, but here, here in front of me, was the one and only Stan South, whose writings I'd been studying for years as both an undergraduate and a graduate student (comps still being fresh in my mind). This is the guy who developed the Mean Ceramic Dating formula now used as a standard by all historic archaeologists; the guy who put the capital "S" in the science of archaeology while at the same time writing the (what some describe as "canonical") textbook *Method and Theory in Historical Archaeology* (1977); the guy who had found the lost Spanish settlement of Santa Elena through sheer dogged historical digging and detective work; the guy who had discovered the famous "palmetto parapets" of the Revolutionary period Fort Moultrie (the reason the palmetto is still celebrated on the State flag). Not to mention—and he'd probably agree that he'd be just as happy to be remembered for it—he was a well-respected poet. I stuck out my hand, and said, "I'm very honored to meet you, Dr. South, I've heard a lot about you and I'm a big fan." "I'm not a doctor," he said drily, still smiling. "What?" "I'm not a doctor, I never got my PhD." Though I was somewhat taken aback (How could this be? The famous Stanley South not having a doctorate?), I said, "Nonetheless, I'm still honored to meet you, *Professor* South," (which seemed to meet with his general approval). I was given a perfunctory "Nice to meet you, glad to have you aboard," greeting by him and the rest of the group, before they turned their attention to the new Director, Rippeteau. He gave a nice little talk on how glad he was to be there, what great things Stephenson had done over the years and how he'd be missed, and then mentioned that they (SCIAA) were glad to be moving out from the leaky basement under the dorm and into a specially-prepared building across the street, etc., etc., etc. Then he left. In the aftermath, I quickly picked up on the hints that apparently, Stephenson had never gotten the support he wanted from the University, and that Rippeteau was going to get not only the new building but a shitload of money as well. I had no idea about the politics behind this, and really didn't want to know, but the stink of hard feelings hung in the air just like the smoke pouring from Stephenson's pipe.

Following Curt, I headed down the hall and met most of the rest of the staff, those who either weren't invited nor overly compelled to meet the new Director. Me, I was going to have to break the ice on my own. There was Tommy Charles, another volunteer, an amateur archaeologist who nevertheless was probably the most knowledgeable man in South Carolina about not just prehistoric projectile points (arrowheads, spearpoints, et al), but the rest of the prehistoric stone tool kit as well (hammerstones, flensing tools, hand-knives, awls, etc.). He was short, tough, clean-shaven, and not only well-respected in his field, but a bit of a roughneck as well, which made him welcome back in the woods where he dealt with most of his "informants" (collectors and active Indian grave-diggers, as well as black market artifact dealers). A good portion of my job was going to be just like his, dealing with cracker collectors, but on the underwater side, so I paid him the gravitas due, even though he was "only a volunteer" (i.e., subsidized with grants, but not really *paid* by the Institute). An interesting note about Tommy… when I left the Institute a year and a half later and went to say good-bye, even though we had both crossed the State multiple times (him way more than me), often crossing paths seeing each other on the road, and often staying at the same hotels (but never drinking together), he was still the tough low-country cowboy that I met that day. I liked him, but I was never sure if he liked me, even though he was always polite, respectful, and friendly. Anyway, the day I left, I went to his office and said so-long, adding "I'll bet you guys are gonna miss me around here" (by then I was a known as a bit of a rabble-rouser, on the side of the working stiffs). He sat back in his chair, and looked at me, neither mean, nor kind, or for that matter, uncaring, but just said, "David, you know that hole you see in a bucket of water, just for a second, when you drop a stone into it? And then it's gone?" "Yeah?" "That's about how much you're gonna be missed around here." I was totally deflated. "Tommy!" I yelped, "How can you say such a thing! That's about the meanest thing I ever heard. And I thought we were friends!" "Hey," he said, "I'm just being honest with ya." I left quite shocked; it was only later I realized he was probably not only the *most* honest, he was probably the only one. He'd already seen my kind come and go a dozen times, and the world goes on. That little pearl of wisdom, as far as professional attachments, has served me well over my lifetime.

Then there was Dr. Al Goodyear, a good-looking bright-eyed and always smiling prehistoric archaeologist out of the University of South Florida. Al's become famous in his own right by finding and working one of the earliest human occupation sites in North America, the Topper site, pushing back the earliest habitation dates there to at least 14,000 years B.P. (before the present), and possibly as old as 18,000. The story as related to me was that Al was somewhat of a wild guy in his youth when he first got to Columbia, tooling around town in a small sport convertible with his pal Bill Marquardt, another well-known prehistoric Southeast archaeologist who was Assistant Director of SCIAA at the time. Apparently, their skirt-chasing and other bad habits got Marquardt an invitation to go back to Florida, and when Al was left alone he got a new wife who converted him, turned over a new leaf, found religion and sobriety, and settled down to pursuing the Pleistocene. When I left SCIAA in June of '86 and went to say good bye to Al, he suggested that we both get down on our knees next to his desk and say a prayer (shades of Nixon and Kissinger! Did we even know about that then in 1986?). "Thanks, Al, but no, I'm not getting down on my knees and praying here in your office. Tell you what though, I appreciate the offer, and if you'd be kind enough to say a prayer for me by yourself later, I think that would be just fine." One thing we never talked about was how a born-again, right-wing, fundamentalist Christian could be a top-notch logistician in the anthropological sciences. Some people would say that there's no conflict here, but trust me, there is, and it's as deep as any artifact-laden alluvial deposit you can imagine.

More Tigers

There were a few others: Keith Derting, a friendly but wily hobbit-like Star Wars/Star Trek geeky sort of guy, before geeks were cool; Kenn Pinson, the long-haired hippie editor for all the Institute publications; some old guy who was the grouchy and complaining photographer for the Institute; and one last archaeologist, a fellow named Jim Michie. Michie specialized in the Waccamaw River lowlands area, both prehistoric and historic. He was a relatively young slim tall guy with fair and fine thinning blonde hair, but he had an outstanding feature that you couldn't miss. He couldn't have been two years past forty then, but he didn't have a tooth in his head, and apparently he didn't care. It did make him look much older, like fifty-something, but like I said, he didn't care, and he didn't miss 'em either, 'cause I eventually saw him eat just about anything, hamburgers, hot dogs, even an apple once. Don't ask me how... he just chomped it all down. He made enough money working for the Institute, and had dental benefits (hell, I think he even got some sort of lawsuit settlement while I was there, which would have paid for them handily), but he just wouldn't get those teeth replaced. I'd heard the rumor, never confirmed, that he'd lost his teeth as the result of a month-long affair with some tainted moonshine. Despite this minor (for him) handicap, Jim was famous for something else—he once held the record for the largest tiger shark caught in South Carolina. It didn't take much prodding, and soon he told me the story that went something like this: He and a friend used to go shark fishing for sport (though, as you'll see, how you could call it sport was beyond me). They would go down to Sullivan's Island, or James Island sometimes, and they would row a small boat out a couple of hundred yards and drop a large pile of fishbacks and chicken carcasses with a big hook in them, attached to a ten-foot length of chain. This chain leader was tied to a nylon line that wound through an inner tube, with a loop of slack, round the other side of the inner tube, and it was all unwound as they rowed back to the beach. Then they would sit around a fire drinking and telling stories until that inner tube out there started stretching back and forth, and they knew something was going at it. When it finally went taut, they would get in the pickup truck to which the end of the rope was tied, and drive up the broad flat face of the windswept beach, and pull whatever monster was on the other end up onto the sand, where they would admire it and then either shoot it, or let it gasp out its last breath before stripping the side flanks to sell to local restaurants as "whitefish." This one night something was playing with it, and the inner tube was stretched again and again, the line finally went taut, and stayed taut, the inner tube stretched to its length, and this time it took the four –wheel drive to get the truck moving. When they finally did pull it in, it really was a monster this time, with the familiar striping that identified it as a tiger. I think it came in at just under a half-ton, 900 and some pounds, at the time the State record, which has subsequently been broken again and again over the years.

The odd thing about tiger sharks is that they're not like other sharks. They're the ones that hang around harbors and river entrances (bull sharks actually go up the rivers, sometimes hundreds of miles). Tigers have poor eyesight (which isn't so bad when you're swimming around in muddy dark water) and therefore eat first and digest later. They're the ones you always hear about that have shoes, tires, license plates, *et al*, in their stomachs when they're opened up. See, whatever they can't digest they'll just regurgitate, but sometimes, the stuff gets stuck 'cause of its odd shape, or material, and then the beast can't shake it and it just stays. So they cruise back and forth along the harbor bottom gobbling down whatever comes their way whenever they get hungry. I always kept this (and Michie's story) in the back of my head when I was diving in the dirty dark waters of Charleston Harbor. But my first dive in Charleston Harbor was more worrisome for other reasons.

Tally-go!

Meanwhile, I was staying at Alan's house until he got back, and spent the later afternoons looking for a house to rent for myself, Amy, and our two young sons. I finally found a small two-bedroom brick house across the river, in a little redneck suburb of Columbia called Cayce. When Alan and Penny got back, and I had gotten tired of staying at that obviously unhappy home, Curt had offered to let me stay at his house until I got settled, and he was very tolerant as I went out in the evenings, exploring the local watering holes. I tried to pay him back by installing a couple of door locks, drawing upon my latent carpentry skills, of which I was only partially successful. I told Alan I had to get back to Florida to pick up the wife, furniture, the babies, etc. He grudgingly let me go, to be back in a week. Even though I was driving a Toyota pickup I had bought from my old friend Dennis (his reliable red paper-hanging truck), I had to take a train back to Tallahassee this time because I needed to drive the moving van with all our furniture back to South Carolina. Amy would follow with Robin, our almost three-year-old and the new baby, Sam, in our second car, an old Gremlin we'd bought from her sister Sally. Toby, the dog, an Eskimo Spitz, would ride with me in the rental van. When I got back to Tallahassee, after a day or two of relaxing and finally bonding with the baby, as well as the family, my Mom came up to visit from Orlando. To get the household goods loaded into the van, I negotiated a quick going-away party at the Ballard-twin house on Rexwood, and then made all the party-goers help carry furniture up the rental van ramp after they got loaded, but before they got too loaded. By midnight the house was empty, there were bottles, food scraps, and garbage bags everywhere, the van was full, and Amy and I slept in a hotel, courtesy of Mom. The next day I cleaned out the house, we kissed Mom good-bye, and we headed north. Amy had been in the hospital giving birth exactly three weeks earlier.

Toby, or Not Toby?

It was a grueling 11-hour trip that should have taken nine, and other than multiple stops along the way, it was long, slow, and uneventful. Except for the one time when we stopped at a highway rest stop somewhere along I-95 in Georgia to stretch our legs, change diapers, and pee. I let Toby out to do his business, and when I got back in the cab of the van I just assumed that Amy had taken him into the Gremlin to keep Robin company. We had pulled out of the rest area almost a mile or so, just getting back up to speed, when Amy pulled up next to me, horn blaring, and pointed to the side of the road. There was Toby, trying to pace us on the grassy shoulder. I pulled over, Amy pulled in front, and, feeling like a bad Dad, I got Toby back in the cab, and on we went. It would have been horrible to have lost him like that. Try explaining it to 3-year-old Robin.

Me haul? No, U-Haul!

We got there late that Friday night, pulled out a mattress and all four of us slept on the floor. The next morning, while Amy was making the long-deserted place clean, i.e., clean enough for a month–old baby, I tried to wriggle a few pieces of furniture out of the back of the U-Haul and get them into the house. I quickly discovered that it just wasn't going to happen. Daunted, but not defeated, I put the old melon-brain to work. I drove up to the local Swifty-Mart and looked in the Yellow Pages (again, we only had pay phones back then), called a couple of moving companies, and found out that they were either too busy or too expensive. By now it was after noon. I went in and got a beer. As I sat in the goddamn Gremlin watching traffic go by, a flash of insight lit up in the old brainpan. Now I could relax. It was just a matter of time. The boys rolled up within about a half an hour—three burly South Carolina rednecks, obviously half-way there, tumbled out of their car looking for more… it was Saturday afternoon after all. I beat them to the door. "Excuse me, gentlemen… you're not going in there to buy beer are you?" "Yes, we are," the big one puffed up, "what's it to you?" "Can we talk a minute?" Within five, I'd convinced them that I'd buy a case of beer, ice, etc., AND give them $20 bucks each if they'd unload the U-Haul van for me. No problem… except they wanted their buddy in on this too. No problem. I got the beer, ice, etc. and then followed them to pick up their pal. In ten minutes we were at the house. In less than an hour the van was empty, and everything was exactly where we told them to put it down. Best $100 I ever spent.

Institutionalized

Now it was time to get to work in earnest. While I was gone they had all moved into the new building, Bob Stephenson was gone, Rippeteau was decorating his new office, and I came back to find Mack formally ensconced in a new three-sided desk just outside Alan's office door. I again picked a desk along a wall. Alan called a meeting with myself, Mack, and our new technician, Joe Beatty, whom he'd hired out of the Transportation Division of the University. Joe was a robust Carolinian, maybe five years younger than me, but strong and friendly and more important, he knew not only everyone on the University of South Carolina Campus, he knew where all the skeletons were buried; that is, he knew all the dark secrets of who was who, how they had gotten where they were, and what things, good or bad, were going to happen before they actually did. At the meeting Alan laid it out that there was an important contract coming up that the South Carolina Department of Transportation had signed with the University, part of Federal Highway compliance regulations. Our job was to survey the underwater section where the new highway bridge was going to cross the Ashley River down in Charleston. I was going to be in charge of the planning and logistics; he was going to be in charge of Administration, whatever the hell that meant (I assumed, correctly, it meant managing the money and taking all the credit). Joe would lend me all the muscle and assistance needed for boats, materials, diving equipment, etc. Mack would assist Alan in, well… assisting Alan. After we went down to Charleston to reconnoiter the situation, I quickly wrote up a combined Research Design and Scope-of-Work.

First Dive

But I didn't come back to Columbia right away with the rest of the crew. Alan wanted me to meet some Civil War nut who had found the remains of the *USS Patapsco*, an iron-hulled steamship that had been shelled and sunk in the harbor during the North's blockade. This was the very same *Patapsco* which yielded the corpses now interred next to Osceola at Fort Moultrie on Sullivan's Island. So I meet this guy named Howard Tower and he wants me to go diving with him and check it out. Apparently he was angling for the rights to dive on it and do some relic-hunting. It was still late February, early March, when I met up with him and some friends of his. I was piloting the 23-foot Institute boat with my dive gear from Florida, and I followed him and his buddies out of the marina across the harbor to the south side where he had marked the *Patapsco* with some buoys. We dropped anchor and tied up side-by-side, and then we got on our dive gear, just me and him, and prepared to go over the stern. The story on the *Patapsco* was that it was part of the Union blockade of Charleston during the Civil War, but on one of its forays into the harbor to fling a few shells into town and frighten the populace, it came under fire from the Southern batteries, and turning to get back out, ran aground. Then it was just a matter of the Southern guns taking target practice and blowing it to smithereens. I think eleven men died, the guys buried at Ft. Moultrie, while the rest made off in a large lifeboat. The ship was an iron-clad steamship; in effect a regular wooden steamboat covered in iron plates where practical, and fitted with naval Dhalgren cannons. After the war, the hulk, with some parts still protruding above water, was deemed a navigational hazard, and it was further blown to bits again by demolition charges intending to level it to the seabottom. This didn't happen, and it was still on the navigational charts as an obstruction, although its identity had been forgotten until Tower had resurrected its historical interest. The tide had just changed and it was ebbing out slowly, but picking up speed. He dropped over the side first and immediately got tangled in his "safety" line—not a good sign. I stood on my deck in my thin Florida wetsuit, and noticed that although it was sunny, the wind was cold and coming hard across the harbor from the north. He called up to me and asked if I didn't want to wear a hood, it was gonna be cold. I figured we were only going to be down a half-hour at best, so I said no, as I've always found hoods to be too restrictive, and I'd never worn one in Florida. I eased over the side and let out a Whoosh! as the water came into the wetsuit and I felt it with my hands and head. Jeezuz Keerist! It was cold. "Let's go," I told him and we slid below the surface. We quickly grabbed onto each other's arm, since the visibility was less than two feet and if we didn't maintain close contact we'd lose each other for sure. We settled on the dark grey and swirling mud bottom in about twenty-five or thirty feet, got settled, checked our gauges, and then I followed his flippers as he signaled the direction, and headed away. Finally, rising onto a shoal, we bump into this large misshapen metal girder sticking out of the bottom. I know it's metal because I take out my dive knife and give it a few raps. Tower ties off the end of his line to it and starts heading into the darkness. The next thing I know, we're crawling up, over, under and through a twisted sharp and rusty metal labyrinth covered in barnacles, sea urchins, oysters, hard sponges, and god knows what else. Sure, there's fish, but they're all small and quickly feeding off the broken shells we create in our path. Then I feel the first tug. My progress is stopped. I slide my hand down my leg and feel some tight fishing line caught on the dive knife sheath strapped to my calf. I unfasten the line and continue on, but now the cold is starting to sink in deep and I can feel the first shivers coming on and my face is getting numb. We've been down maybe ten-fifteen minutes. We get through most of it and come out the other side. I signal to him to head back, and he leads on, taking a different trajectory, since he wanted me to see as much as possible while we're down, even though "seeing" anything beyond the length of my arm is problematic at best, and back we go into the very thing that we've always been warned about not to dive into (besides caves): torn-up wreckage. Down into what could only have once been the hold, it was dark black, cold, and scary. Did I say cold? We'd made our half-hour now and the shakes started coming on in waves, which meant they weren't dangerous yet, but would be soon if we stayed in much longer. Then I got another tug, this time in the shoulder. I reach up and it's a goddamn rusty old fishhook, on the end of a metal leader, embedded into the neoprene of my wetsuit, luckily in reach. I couldn't cut the wire leader, so I slowly and methodically backed that fucker out and stuck it into a soft sponge nearby. That's it! I'd seen enough. I tapped Tower and signaled to him it was time to surface, and from the look in his eyes as we glared into each other's mask across nine inches of dirty swirling water, he was ready too. As we got out of the wreckage and began ascending it became clear that the tide had picked up considerably, maybe running as fast as two knots. We surfaced thirty yards downstream from the boats, inflated our b.c's (buoyancy compensators, or air vests), rolled over onto our backs and just kicked and kicked until one of his buddies spotted us and let out a buoyed line we could grab. If no one had been watching we'd have been swept out to sea within the hour. I got out, numb and shaking, stripped down and dried off quickly, putting on warm clothes. Told him it was an interesting site (to die in!) and I'd get back to him in a week. After driving the boat back to the marina and loading it onto the trailer, I drove back to Columbia. The next day I told the office secretary, Azalee, that whatever I had signed up for as far as life insurance, cancel that and put me down for the maximum, whatever it was and whatever it cost.

I told Alan about the dive, emphasizing the cold. Oh yeah, he agreed, WE NEVER go diving from October through March… (didn't he realize that he'd just sent me to go diving with Tower and it was early March?). Well, if you want to carry out this bridge crossing survey project in the next month, we're going to need better suits, I told him. He put Mack on it, and lo and behold, within a week, we were all going down to Charleston to get fitted for dry suits. They were being ordered out of a dive shop in Charleston now run by the same guy Alan had fired before he hired me, a guy named Ralph Wilbanks. He had been Alan's right-hand man for something like ten years, helping to excavate and raise the Brown's Ferry Vessel, Alan's crowning achievement, during that time. When he asked for a raise and permanent status though, Alan told him to piss up a rope, whereon Ralph walked, and in his shoes quickly stepped the Englishman, Mack Newsome, who had been a volunteer diver on various projects, always pouring poison in Alan's ears about Ralph's ambitions, hoping to get the Assistant position himself. But Alan didn't see any irony in any of this at all, and was maybe trying to throw some business Ralph's way to sort of make up for things. It didn't work. Yeah, Ralph was happy to take the orders for the dry suits; hell, he'd make an easy grand off of it. But the minute we walked in the door of the dive shop the hatred between Ralph and Alan and Ralph and Mack, and the resentment of me, the new Assistant Underwater Archaeologist, was, as they say, thick enough to cut with a knife, even a dull dive knife. The only one Ralph was happy to see was Joe.

The Dashing Chamber Made
Now a dry suit is a one-piece underwater suit you crawl in feet-first, pull up around your waist, stick your hands out the rubberized wrist holes, and push your head through the topmost neck ring; then there's a zipper with a short lanyard that you grab and pull to seal up the back. The rubberized wrist holes and neck opening are very tight to keep out water, and everything inside the suit stays dry, hence, a *dry* suit. There's an optional set of long fuzzy underwear for insulation in extreme cold water, and with this AND an insulated hood, you can stay down for an hour or better in the coldest water, even under ice. They take some getting used to, and you have to practice with them, like scrunching down in a ball and letting all the air out of your neck hole before getting in the water, or you might get in and turn upside-down with all the air now in your feet, and unless you have something to grab onto, it's extremely difficult to right yourself. Generally, you end up wearing extra weights to keep your waist the center of gravity. But the cool thing is, you can wear your regular clothes underneath: zip in, go diving, come out, unzip, comb your hair and walk into a restaurant. One time though, I did it in style.

278

I'd been invited to give a talk to the Charleston Chamber of Commerce, who were having one of their monthly meetings at the Yacht Club. I'd been on one of my Hobby Diver Licensing rounds, so I had the boat in the water already, and decided to make a special entrance to the Chamber meeting. I pulled up a hundred yards or so offshore, and even though I was wearing tennis shoes (you couldn't wear hard shoes in the dry suit), I had on khakis, a nice white long-sleeve shirt, a tie, and I even slipped on an old sportcoat. Then I put on the dry suit over all, strapped on my weights, tanks, flippers and mask and went over the side. I'd timed it so that I'd arrive just on time, that way I knew everyone would be there, but the emcee would be wondering if I was going to show. The Yacht Club meeting room had a nice broad plate-glass window that looked over the boats in the marina to the left, with the broad beach view of the harbor out front. I swam the hundred yards or so along the bottom and then rose up out of the water like Captain Nemo in *Mysterious Island*. That got their attention from inside the dining room. I took off my flippers and then just walked up the wooden steps of the outside deck, and standing just outside the plate glass window, unhooked my tanks, belt, etc. and unzipping the dry suit, stepped out of it like James Bond, already dressed in coat and tie. A quick stop in front of one of those beer-advertising mirrors to comb my hair and I walked in to the meeting, ready to go. They loved it. The talk was less exciting, like a good Chamber meeting talk should be, concentrating on the importance of South Carolina's underwater cultural heritage, the hard work the Underwater Division at the Institute was doing, the ethics of not collecting artifacts, blah, blah, blah. But I got a very good appreciative round of applause at the end, and after a quick fish and crab luncheon, I said good bye and went back out, donned my dry suit and gear, and walked back out to the water, put on my flippers and, after taking a quick bearing on the boat, sunk below the water.

Two questions (maybe more) might bother the reader at this point. First, what actually was my job? And second, why was I always diving alone? My job, other than the overall duties of the Assistant Underwater Archaeologist, was specifically to manage the Hobby Diver Licensing Program, a strange sort of hybrid that Alan had put together a few years earlier and had gotten passed by the South Carolina State legislature as part of an underwater antiquities protection law. When it was realized at some point that there was a large fraternity of divers throughout South Carolina (and North Carolina as well, for that matter) who made a rather tidy addendum to their paychecks by diving on the weekends, collecting bottles and other colonial-era knickknacks and then selling them out of storefronts in downtown Charleston, well, Alan decided that some sort of regulation was in order. Basically, after stating unequivocally that material found on the bottom of the rivers (and offshore submerged lands) was State property, the law said that a diver who purchased a $5 annual license could collect what he wished off the bottom, and once reported, the State had an opportunity to look at the material and determine if it had any archaeological value. If not, the diver could keep his finds. If it *did* have archaeological value, well... that question was never really answered clearly. It put me in a hell of a quandary. I tried explaining to Alan that "an artifact does not an archaeological site make," and that the real goal should be information on where real archaeological sites were located, so we ought to be compiling the information on maps, looking for patterns. His response to this was to send me out a week at a time, traveling all over the State, talking to dive clubs, dive shops, collectors, individuals, groups, etc. to gather information and promote the sale of the licenses, which he used as his discretionary Division slush–fund. Since I was the single-handed manager of the program, it was only fitting, according to him, that I go out alone, towing the Division's 23-foot center-console runabout, investigating promising leads on the rivers and in the harbors when I wasn't either lecturing groups or visiting divers. Then I'd come back to the office, write up my trip report, do followup calls, and get ready for the next trip. After the first couple of trips though I stated rather emphatically that I'd been trained by some of the best scientific divers in the country, and the one rule we never broke, was that you don't dive alone. He gave me the ultimate bitch-slap, "What's the matter, are you scared?" That lasted until I suggested to the Director (who was also an amateur diver) that we create a Diving Safety Control Board like all the other scientific diving universities had, and then we could join the American Academy of Underwater Sciences (AAUS) as an Institutional member. What a great idea! Albright raised hell and tried to stifle it quickly, since he saw that he wouldn't be able to control the Control Board and he'd just be another voice, but I won out, and ended up writing the new SCIAA Board's first set of safety procedures, emphasizing buddy-diving, as well as the usual stuff. It didn't matter much in the long run though, Alan just ignored them and refused to pay the dues to join the AAUS. So I kept hauling that boat all over South Carolina, putting it in the water off the trailer by myself (no mean trick), cruising the rivers and Intracoastal, and yes, diving by myself, more often than not in what is known as "black-water diving." I became pretty good at it, too; but it's one of those things that will eventually kill you. Or, to put it more accurately, the odds in your favor diminish considerably by the number of times you do it, especially alone.

Down on Ashley

The Ashley River survey was pending so we had to get a move on it. I'd devised a plan where we'd lay lines running parallel to the flow of the river across the stretch where the new bridge was going to be constructed. The lines had to be straight and they had to stick to the bottom. I got them to stick to the bottom by using simple sportfishing technology, building a couple of dozen triangular weights out of concrete, maybe twenty pounds each and to which the lines would be attached every fifty yards or so. I was going to keep them straight by shooting in the parallel lines from the sidewalk of the existing Ashley River Bridge using a transit. Since I was the only one who knew how to use a transit, that meant I was on the bridge and would guide them in from the downstream side, signaling right-left by walkie-talkie, and they would lay the lines with the weights until they were strung out. Alan ran the boat (as always), so the heavy lifting of the weights fell on Joe and deploying of line to Mack, and that meant Joe was the muscle (I could always hear the constant grousing of Mack over the radios). When enough lines were deployed for a day's worth of diving, they would pick me up at the base of the bridge, and once we'd gotten our dry suits and dive gear on, Joe, Mack and I would start at the downstream end of a line segment and pull ourselves hand-over-hand upstream along the bottom in three-diver-wide lanes while scouring the bottom for any identifiable cultural resources. Whereas we were really looking for something significant, like a shipwreck, whether it was a sailing ship, a ferryboat, or a small fishing boat, or whatever, we also looked for any evidence of the Colonial era habitants of Charleston as well. The water was so dark and muddy, stirred silt constantly swirling before your mask that it was just easier to close your eyes and reach around by feel, since you couldn't see past your forearm's length anyway. More frightening though, were the sounds. There was the sound of the boat engine as Alan hovered over us, the sharp prop a-turning (he insisted on this, following our bubbles, though I pled with him not to—if he'd just park the boat at the downstream end we could surface and just float back down to him, but nooooo—as it was, whenever we surfaced we'd use our left hand upraised to break the water, since you can always do without a left hand if needs be); but worse, besides an incessant clicking, which was tolerable, periodically there was a loud, and particularly unnerving "SKRRNCH" that you would hear, often close by. I had visions of Michie's tigers swimming around us waiting for a chance to tear off a leg or an arm, and only found out later that this was the sound of large black and red drum fish chewing up clams, oysters, and crabs on the bottom as they foraged.

When it was all said and done, we knocked the survey out in about a week. It was dangerous and hard, but it was done. All we'd found was a single intact Colonial-era liquor bottle, what they call an "onion" bottle, made of black glass, which is really dark green glass, the natural color of glass for most period blown bottles of the 18th century. Since we had apparently been given $20,000 to carry out the survey, I referred to it as our "$20,000 bottle," which pissed off Alan no end. Later I heard that he didn't like this because, although we had received $20K up front, we later got another $20K upon completion, which he never told me about, and he was worried that I'd start calling it our "$40,000 bottle." When it came time to write the report, although I wrote it, Alan insisted that, as the boss (a.k.a. Administrator), his name would go on as principal author. Fine, that's standard practice, although still poor form. But then, he wanted Mack to get second author by virtue of "editing," as well as his "administrative assistance." More shit, but I didn't care, I'd take the anchor position, it wasn't worth fighting over. They needed the recognition more than I did.

Sad Santa Monica

Soon it was back on the road for me, which I rather enjoyed, since I was out of the office, traveled all over the State of South Carolina (you can't beat Charleston, or Low Country seafood), and was relatively independent for at least a week every month. Inside the office it was generally unpleasant. Alan and I were always arguing about how to carry out proper archaeological investigations, what was important and what was not, and Mack was always backing him up, chiming in how we didn't need all these "scientific controls." They loved making fun of me when I'd get all "professional" on them; it really didn't bother me though, I recognized it was out of insecurity as much as ignorance. You see, although Alan was one of the recognized "fathers of underwater archaeology," as was my old boss, George Fischer, Alan really had no formal training whatsoever. Most of his learning curve was seat-of-the-pants stuff like a lot of the old-timers, but Alan had sat at the foot of one of the truly big names, Mendel Peterson, Director of Historic Archaeology and American Military History at the Smithsonian Institution. Mendel had written the seminal work on underwater archaeology, *History Under the Sea*, and at some point Alan was hired by the Smithsonian to work as a technician in their lab, where Mendel managed the conservation of various items having been brought up from underwater, usually seawater. So this is where Alan's bug for underwater archaeology began, and he soaked up whatever information Mendel let slip. Before Mendel retired in 1973, somehow Alan ended up at the College of the Virgin Islands, where he took up with Ed Towle of the Island Resources Foundation, a well-respected scientific clearing house for environmental studies in the islands at the time. I'd heard that Mendel didn't like Alan much so he actually wrote a glowing recommendation for him in order to get him out of the Smithsonian. I think Mendel pulled one over on his old buddy Towle, and when I later met Dr. Towle and asked him about those early years working with Alan, all he could do was growl.

Through the Smithsonian and Mendel, Alan had become an acquaintance of Bob Marx, the famous underwater archaeology "consultant" and contributor to *Argosy* magazine, who had dug into the submerged seventeenth-century pirate town of Port Royal, Jamaica, and had gained fame and fortune as a result [I remember reading these stories out of my Dad's copies of *Argosy* and *True* as a kid, and was just as enamored with the adventure as anybody—but it was so extraordinary I never considered making a living off of it at the time]. So Alan was infatuated with the idea of doing the same thing in and around the Virgin Islands. Having gotten a position with Island Resources and by default becoming a faculty member at the college, he somehow finagled it into doing what he considered "underwater archaeology" by getting some grant money. But other than carrying out a half-assed magnetometer survey, and partnering up with

Marx for authorship on a List of Virgin Island Shipwrecks, Albright had nothing much to show for his precarious position, and so put forth his efforts on punching holes in the wreck of *HMS Santa Monica*, a well-known British wreck off the east end of St. John. Since he was already by that time a cocker-spaniel-frenzied Anglophile, this was just the ticket to put him on a par with Marx and the other "professional" underwater archaeologists. Unfortunately, after a year or so of intermittently tearing into the shipwreck with a dredge and airlift, he'd recovered all the bottles, pewter plates, mugs, and cutlery that the wreck would yield, and the result was a fifteen-page report that recounted the history of the wreck, and had a brief description of some of the stuff. Methodologically, it was an archaeological travesty, even for being recognized as an early effort. When the site was visited by professional archaeologists from the National Park Service's Southeast Archaeological Center a couple of years afterwards, they described it as "reminiscent of a World War I battlefield." Alan threatened to sue them for defamation, and the management of the Center buckled and took the reference out of their final report. The artifacts he'd recovered had been stored at the College of the Virgin Islands where Alan was reportedly "conserving" them in the lab there on Brewers Bay. They all eventually disappeared. Many years later I was told by a dive shop operator that he remembered that, for awhile back then, if you bought a copy of the report for something like $40 you would get a free old bottle with it. Not that Alan had anything to do with it… but somebody did.

In any case, while we were living in South Carolina it was always rather difficult. I found out that the many "private clubs" surrounding the University in downtown Columbia were actually regular bars, with the windows shaded and the doors closed. I could have gone into them anytime I wanted, paid the dollar, or five-dollar, membership fee and had my fill. They were "private clubs" to keep out any blacks. No, I stuck to the open clubs, my favorite of which was Group Therapy down at Five Points, a tiny little bar that couldn't hold more than twenty people at a time. Then Curt turned me on to the Faculty House. Since we were *de facto* faculty members (I was even faculty advisor to the University's Dive Club), we could go to the Faculty House after work and drink 25 cent beers and eat free appetizers. At first, we started taking the Limey, Mack, as our guest, but once it became apparent what a pompous ass he was, Curt and I just waited until he left for home before going there by ourselves, where we could enjoy a plain old North Florida thematic conversation and get toasted for under a fin. Mack had become problematic at work, always trying to undercut me and sucking up to Alan. As already mentioned, Alan was an unabashed Anglophile; he loved everything English: tea sets, pith helmets, the BBC, et al, to the point where he even decided he disliked the Irish, had nothing but disdain for East Indians, and well, I don't know how he felt about blacks, I never saw him speak to one. But the British, oh God, they were just peachy, hence, his nearly yearly trips to England, and the delight he took in having Oing-lish Mack as his right-hand co-conspirator. Curt, however, once put it succinctly, "Why is it that people automatically give someone ten or twenty IQ points just because they speak with an English accent?" But Mack was working constantly behind the scenes to bolster his standing with Alan in order to become a regular paid "professional" archaeologist. On one of the few occasions when Alan and I were getting along and cracking jokes back and forth, Mack got all upset and took me aside later and said, "Don't try to get up Alan's asshole, because I'm already up there, and there isn't room enough for two of us!" Truth is, I never ever tried to usurp his most exclusive and unenviable position.

Silver Lake

After a year it looked like we were going to be there in South Carolina for awhile, so Amy and I decided to get out of the suburbs of West Columbia and get a place out in the country. We found a nice little ranch house on 4 acres of land on a hillside out near a little town called

Lexington and put a down payment on it. It was on a stretch of road called Silver Lake, and sure enough, it had maybe a 2-acre lake down the road that would swell to three or more acres after the rains, and it was a great hangout on the weekends for those approaching hot and dusty days of summer. Since it was early spring when we got the place, I decided to become a gentleman farmer, and after asking around found out that peanuts were the big thing around there, considering the sandy soil and the sketchy rainfall. So I went ahead and plowed up a quarter-acre out back and planted twenty rows of goobers, and they sprouted right up. Robin was four now and we started calling him Rib-bone because one evening I barbecued a slab and with his face, chest, and stomach slathered in barbecue sauce he fell asleep in his high chair, gorged, with a big old bone still grasped in his greasy little paw. Somewhere there's a picture of him like that. He was very curious and I would take him for walks in the woods behind the house. One day we came upon a freshly dead dog, and over several weeks he watched it decompose, wanting to go out and take another look every couple of days. Sam was just over a year and had started walking and I can still picture him running naked and laughing through the peanut field with the sprinklers on, his arms up straight up and akimbo on either side of his head, like a little gibbon. Toby was also with us and because of the large forest behind us, he could run to his heart's content... but he avoided the dead dog remains like the plague and, rather than follow the trail that ran by it, he would tiptoe a long sniffing semicircle around it in the brush when I'd take Robin out for our walks.

Kluxin'

Amy and I were sitting on our back deck one late afternoon, facing north for a beautiful fifty-mile view of unbroken rolling hills and forest, sipping our White Zinfandel coolers, and relaxing from a Saturday of tending low peanut bushes and swimming with the kids down at Silver Lake, when we heard an intercom loudspeaker, far off, but not that far. The flow of words was indistinct, but the echo resounded with the unmistakable staccato of "n***ers this, and n***ers that." We sat up straight and tried to discern the direction. We also sat up because we had a new set of black neighbors just west of us whom we waved to as we went to work. The direction was definitely coming from the northwest. Since the boys were napping, I told Amy to sit tight and I'd go check it out. Hopping in the little red pickup, I headed west on Silver Lake Road, past the neighbors, past the lake, and came upon a dirt road that cut north, the loudspeaker clearer now. Not a mile up the road it cleared to a broad sandy lot behind low-strung sagging barbed wire, several acres in size with a large (what I call) redemption tent, a couple of scattered trailers out behind it, and maybe three dozen pickup trucks parked haphazardly around the perimeter, with people milling around drinking beer. In the center of all the hubbub was a tall, maybe twenty-foot high, pine tree cross. The noise was audible now, and the speaker, a loud and energetic woman, was pouring forth a mouthful of venom mixed with patriotic vitriol that rang out across the adjoining countryside. I drove by slowly, watching the beer-swilling rednecks and their broad-beamed and short-shorted wives watching me. I went past, and way down the road turned around, then hustled back to the house. I told Amy what I'd seen and after trying to listen to what was being said... well, we had to go back in the house (oh, it wasn't just about the blacks, the catholics and the kikes were getting it too, not to mention liberals and queers and especially liberal queers; but other than the labels it was hard to make out what they were going to do about it), Just as well, the no-see-ums and mosquitoes were starting to come out as the sun went down. That evening, although the loudspeaker had been quelled somewhat, there was a distinct orange-and-yellow glow in the northwest, maybe two miles distant. Late the next morning, which was a Sunday, I drove Amy and the boys by the scene, and the broad sandy lot was empty, the tent was gone, and other than the scattered trailers, no sign of the people. The pine tree cross was just a smoldering heap of charcoal and ash surrounding the remains of a solitary smoking stake. Welcome to South Carolina!

South Carolina had its other quirks too, and the blue laws were still in effect back then. For instance, you couldn't buy beer or wine on Sunday. Fair enough… but it made for hell shopping for groceries on Saturday afternoon, with all the idiots loading up shopping carts with beer they'd forgotten to buy either Friday or Saturday morning, and couldn't make it to Monday without. If you did buy liquor on Friday or Saturday, or any other time, you had to buy it from a State-sponsored liquor store, marked with a large red ball painted on the side of the building that had no other advertising or even identification. When you ordered a drink from a bar, they had to pour it out in front of you, and it came out of one of those tiny little airline bottles. The reason? So you could see the bartender wasn't cheating you, you got your full ounce, and more important, taxes were paid by the bottle. Now grocery stores and dollar stores were open for business on Sunday, but they had a long posted list of what you could and couldn't buy on the Sabbath. You could buy a white shirt because you might need it for church (but you couldn't buy a short sleeve colored sport shirt). You couldn't buy a mop or a broom, because that meant work. You could buy oil for your car: you might need it to put in your car so you could make it to church; but you couldn't buy an oil filter, or an oil filter wrench, because, again, that meant work. So, between the beer hoarders on Saturday, and the blue-law list on Sunday, it was just best to go shopping during the week. They also had a penchant for that yellowish mustard-based barbecue sauce, apparently developed right there in Columbia by some Bible-thumping restaurateur. It's a developed taste, but once you get used to it, you can see the fascination. Supposedly, when you buy the original brand, and not some knockoff, a portion of the proceeds goes to support whatever wild-eyed fundamentalism the inventor subscribes to. Ah, but Charleston, also known as "The Holy City" because of the number of churches, now that's a town that will warm anyone's heart. Nestled between the Cooper River to the east and the Ashley River to the west, it comes to a point at the harbor at Battery Point. The food, the ambience, the history… well, one could go on and on about Charleston, and this is probably not the place to do so. [Little known fact: in 1718, the dastardly pirate Edward Teach, commonly known as "Blackbeard," once blockaded the harbor at Charlestown for the better part of a week, having captured the mayor's daughter and other town notables on an outgoing ship as hostages. Did he demand gold? Or silver? No. He asked for a box of medicinal supplies to treat the syphilis his men had acquired celebrating their earlier plunders. Once delivered, he let loose the hostages and sailed off peacefully.]

Well, I guess it's time to tell how I finally stepped in the shit. Let me preface it by saying that I'd already known Mack was out to get me. He was always asking prying personal questions: had I messed around on my wife? did I smoke pot or do cocaine? had I ever been arrested? I was pretty good about dodging these, but he'd bait me by telling me his own misadventures, without details: how he'd gotten a blowjob from one of his wife's friends in a closet at a party; how he had met the Beatles when he was a concierge at some hotel in the Bahamas, and had subsequently gotten so drugged up that he walked off a cliff in the darkness and they found him with a broken back on the ledge below in the morning; how he had to leave the Bahamas when the mob was after him for not properly doing whatever a "bagman" supposedly does, and which is why he chose South Carolina as a backwater where they'd never think to look for him. He'd changed his appearance, and for all I knew, he'd changed his name as well. Now, some ten years later, he felt the heat was cooling off and he was trying to legitimize himself as Alan's "Administrative Assistant." I was still in the way though, and outranked him as the Assistant Underwater Archaeologist. We often had to travel together, staying in the same room at some hotel to save the Division money, and one time after a particularly grueling day diving, we had a few drinks in the hotel bar, and when we got back to the room he asked if I had any pot, 'cause he'd really like some to relax. Yes, I had some, and to be honest I never considered it a major deal. I rolled up a joint and we smoked it and he was very grateful. Then he wanted me to buy some for him and that's where I said no, sorry. Two weeks later, he and Joe and I had a long day diving and were headed back to Columbia when I suggested we smoke a bowlful. Both of them knew my feelings about it, but I hadn't counted on the fact that Joe knew Mack was going to use this against me. They both said no, thanks, so I just had a toke or two to myself, but I could see it in Joe's eyes that I'd fucked up.

He gone

Another week went by and I headed out by my lonesome again to interview divers and check out spots up and down the rivers. I remember stopping by a trailer out in the woods and meeting two cousins, simple-minded country boys, who showed me the sharks' teeth they had found: quite a collection, more than a few of which were as big as your hand and from *Megaladon megaladon*, the greatest carnivore that ever swam the seven seas (a million years ago). What they did with these teeth is they would mount them on polished wooden blocks, and there were a couple of the local redneck girls who would trade blow jobs for these mounted monster maulers. I had to laugh when I heard this and they thought I was laughing at the whole premise (which I was, but only on the insanity of it) and told me that if I would hang around and drink a few beers with them they'd prove it was true. I just wanted to hold the camera and record the whole transaction. Besides, I wasn't interested in shark's teeth; that's paleontological, not archaeological... I'd seen enough sharks' teeth to pave a parking lot. I had the beers, but the girls couldn't make it that day, since they already had a surfeit of giant prehistoric dogfish dentine and didn't need any more (God only knows what *they* did with them... sold 'em?). Next stop was a park up near Georgetown, at Georgetown Landing, where I stopped to take a break and interview a couple of the old-timers. I'm sitting on a park bench talking with this little old man, 75 or 80 years, and he's telling me the history of the place as he knew it and how he remembered it growing up. I've got my camera out for a couple of location shots, and I'm taking notes. A couple of black kids walk by, soaking wet, and one of them, in a lackadaisical manner, says to the others, "That boy dead. He gone." I perked up and said, "What did you say!?" They turned to me and the old man sitting there and said, "That boy drowned." I said, "What boy?!" They pointed behind me and down the dock where a small crowd of black teenagers were standing on the dockside, looking into the water. "He went in and he sunk. He ain't come back up." "How long?!" I said. "Coupl'a minutes." "Oh shit!," I yelled, "Somebody call the fire department!" Then I turned to the old man and said, "Will you watch my stuff?" as I emptied my pockets of money, keys, wallet, shoes, the works. He nodded, and I ran down to the dock, some ten feet off the water, where maybe ten or fifteen teenagers were looking down into the brown swirling river. "Where?," I yelled, and they all pointed in a general 10-meter circle at the water. I dove in, wearing just my khakis, and made it to the bottom, but it was deep, probably twenty feet. I looked around, visibility was low, maybe five, six feet, and swam around, but couldn't find him. When I got to the surface I figured the current must have taken him downstream some, so I tried again. But swimming down from the surface was harder than diving from the dock, and it was hard to get to the bottom, with not much time to look around. I dove again and again, maybe three or four times more before someone said the fire department was on the way, and I had to give up,

I have to admit that local rescue team had made pretty good time. They were there in ten minutes, with a small flat-bottom boat coming up the waterway and divers already decked out in wetsuits and tanks. That ten minutes, and maybe five earlier, meant the kid had been down now

285

about fifteen. As the flatboat got on site, the divers went over the deep channel side, and then I was shocked to see the chubby rednecks still in the boat haul out a couple of grappling hooks and gingerly toss them out into the shore side. They brought them up again and again, with tires, and other junk from the bottom, yanked out of the mud. Oh God, I thought, they hook that boy and this is going to be ugly. Finally, after another ten minutes, one of the divers came up twenty yards down the river and said they'd found him. When they brought him to the surface, we only saw him for a second or two as they hauled him into the boat and covered him, but in those few seconds, with his eyes wide open and the water pouring out his nose and mouth, it was clear that he was dead and no attempt at resuscitation was going to be attempted. The family women who had been called down to the river's edge began to wail, and an ambulance came wobbling down a dirt road I hadn't even noticed, parking on the dock's concrete apron and opening the back doors. The rescue team came along carrying the body on a board covered in an old green and wet blanket, and set him on the ambulance gurney. The family got one look at him before they covered him up once more and put him in the van, which pulled away slowly, no hurry. When I walked back to the park bench, the old man was gone. In his place, and sitting there guarding my wallet, camera, shoes, etc. was a middle-aged black man. He said he watched the whole incident from start to finish, but the old white guy had to leave, and so he watched my stuff for me. He thanked me for my efforts, and told me that he knew the boy was going to be dead; apparently, not only was he a poor swimmer, but the boys had all been drinking too, even though it was now just getting on two or three o'clock in the afternoon. I put on my shirt and shoes, thanking him, and when I got back into the Division station wagon, with the big old boat trailered behind me, I had to stop before pulling out of the parking lot and onto the main road: even though I felt fine, out of nowhere I got a set of the shakes, even some teeth chattering, and they took a minute or two to wear off. It was Sunday, June 8th, 1986, my 34th birthday.

That afternoon, early evening, when I got to my hotel room I poured myself a stiff one, then called Amy to tell her my day's adventure and let her know I'd be coming back the next day. As soon as she got on the phone she said, "Joe called and he wants you to call him right away. He said it's important that you call him no matter how late." Okay, I said, and then told her about the drowned boy. "I'm glad you're coming back tomorrow," she said, "don't forget to call Joe." What could this be? I thought. Joe and I were pals, but why would he want me to call him on a Sunday? What could be so urgent? When I got him on the phone finally, he told me that he'd been called in to Alan's office on Thursday right after I'd left for my trip. Newsome was in there too, and Alan began to give him the third degree about me smoking pot. Joe was evasive and told Alan he didn't feel good having Mack in the room. Alan sent Mack outside but continued to harangue Joe, who just shut down. Frustrated, Alan forbade him to talk to me under any circumstances, and the next day, Friday, this was all repeated in the Director's office. The Director, Rippeteau, who we all jokingly referred to as "Triple-toes," or sometimes "Tippy-toe," actually liked me as opposed to either Alan or Newsome, and he was young and hip enough not to think that this was a serious issue; he thought that it could be handled easily enough with a letter of reprimand. But Alan wanted a firing. When Rippeteau wouldn't go for it, Alan got threatening and demanded that as my supervisor he had the right and if the Director overstepped him, well, that was going to be another fight. Soon they decided that this had to go legal with the University and they'd wait for that outcome before dealing with me. Joe had gotten all of this from the Director's secretary who sat just outside his office and heard it all. He'd waited until Sunday because Alan had threatened him with reprisals if I found out, and I promised Joe it would go no further (than Amy). Shit! Shit! And double-shit! And the worst thing was, I had to go in the next day and pretend I'd never heard a thing and be nice to both Alan and that slimy limey Newsome! Oh well, I'd just have to tough it out, that's all there was to it. I thanked Joe and then called Amy back and told her all the sordid details. Happy Birthday to Me!

I drove back the next day, put the boat and trailer away, and made my way into the office, just after lunch. I said hi to Joe and then a nice "How ya doin'?" to Mack. Alan was still out to lunch, so I sat back in my chair, and coolly asked if anything had happened while I was away, keeping my eyes on Newsome. Other than him stiffening, then casting a quick glance over at Joe, he turned his back and pretended to be typing something important. "Well, I've got some news," I said, and then both Joe and Mack sat up straight, turned toward me and all of a sudden I had their rapt attention. Then I told them about the young black kid who had drowned at Georgetown. You could see the relief draining into Joe's face as he understood what I was doing and from him the story of the unsuccessful rescue only elicited a slight smile. Mack was completely at sea and didn't know what to think, finally saying "That was unfortunate" before turning back to his typing. When Alan came in I didn't wait and told him I wanted to talk to him. He was beyond his usual nervous self, as jittery and fidgety as ever (possibly due to the handfuls of Sudafed he was consuming daily, buying them by the thousands, but just as likely he was worried about me confronting him). I briefed him on the trip, as I usually did, and told him about the encounter with the drowned black kid, but he had no interest in anything I was saying and kept his eyes averted any way he could. "That's it," I told him, "anything you want to discuss?" No, he said, he'd get back to me. I settled down to my desk and began typing up my trip report on the computer. Alan called Mack in, and they closed the door. After Mack came out maybe fifteen minutes later, the afternoon turned in an odd direction. Alan never came out of his office, and the door stayed closed, although this was unusual. Mack however, turned on the charm, asked me if I wanted to have beers after work. No, after being out of town I was looking forward to going home. Well, it just so happened he said, that he was going back to his own home in Edgefield, on the Georgia border and he'd be driving west by Silver Lake Road (although it was out of his usual way), could he stop in and say hi to Amy and the boys? This caught me off-guard, but since I was still supposedly unwary of him and Alan's maneuverings, well, what could I say? Sure you can stop by. He got the jump on me that afternoon after work and left early without saying good-bye. I hopped in my own car and rushed home, getting there luckily just after he had arrived, making small talk with Amy, and cooing up to the boys. I offered him a beer (an Irishman always offers a guest libations, even the very evil he invites into his home), and quickly running out of anything pertinent to say, he asked if I'd show him around the property, since he'd never seen it. Even though it was getting near dusk, I said sure, and we went out back. Not waiting, he bee-lined it for the back stretch of woods (?!). I followed and he walked around nosing about, looking here and there. Finally I got him to come back up by the house, where the peanuts had withered from the hot sun and drought that year. I pulled some out of the ground and showed him that they were as good as roasted nuts you'd buy in the store and ate a handful. He wasn't interested. I didn't offer him another beer and he knew it was time to leave, which he did. "What was that all about?" asked Amy. I really didn't know. It only dawned on me later that night lying in bed — he was looking to see if I had been growing any pot on the land out back! Probably figured that since I wouldn't sell him any, I must be growing it. I got up right then and there, in the middle of the night and gathered up my pot, pipes, and paraphernalia and drove down to Silver Lake and threw them in behind the dam at the spring that created the lake. A sunuvabitch like that would call the cops just to have the house searched, Amy and the kids be damned.

The next day it all came home to roost. Alan and I were both called into the Director's office and Alan officially accused me of smoking pot. For the first time ever, his argument was that safety

287

was the issue, not our personal animosities. I asked where had he heard this. He hemmed and hawed and said that wasn't important. Well, I denied it, and Rippeteau asked why anyone would accuse me of such a thing. Professional jealousy, I answered, and left it at that. Alan said he wanted me fired; Rippeteau said it was only hearsay. I didn't say anything. Very soon it was the three of us sitting there in silence. So I pulled out my ace in the sleeve. "What about the Davis Quadrant?" I asked to no one in particular. "What about it?" asked Alan. Now the Davis Quadrant is a small wooden device, simple in nature, but absolutely necessary for determining latitude for ocean-going vessels from the early 17th to the mid 18th century, until the development of the sextant. One had been found by a guy named Hampton Shouping, the same guy who found the Browns Ferry Wreck. Maybe a year earlier I asked Alan if I could see it, and he blew me off and told me it was somewhere in the Institute collections and he didn't know where it was right then. Some other time. When they moved the collections into a warehouse and thus had to inventory them as they moved everything, I asked the Collections Manager to keep an eye out for it, giving him a description of what it looked like. After a month or two he called me up and said it wasn't in the collections. I told Alan that it wasn't in the collections, and asked him if he knew where it was. "It's in my attic," he said. "What's it doing there?" I queried, and he said, "It's mine, I traded a bottle for it." (Shades of the Santa Monica!) Well, how can that be, I pursued, and he told me that he had given Hampton Shouping a bottle for the (only existing North American) Davis Quadrant. "Where'd you get the bottle?" I asked. "I bought it with my own money, and since I traded it for the quadrant, the quadrant is mine," he looked up at me, challenging, but he knew I'd caught him up in it. One thing a professional archaeologist never does, under any circumstances, is buy, sell, or trade artifacts. I let it go at the time, but on one of my trips I made it a point to visit Mr. Shouping, and he told me quite a different story, several different stories in fact. He said Alan came to his house upon the reporting of the Browns Ferry Wreck and saw the quadrant over his mantel. Alan got very excited about it (probably knowing what it was from his time under Mendel Peterson at the Smithsonian) and wanted to buy it, explaining that in any case it was such an important piece of American history that it had to come back to the Institute with him. Shouping said no, he wanted to keep it, but Alan got rather belligerent and told him he had the legal backing to take it outright (since everything recovered from the river bottoms was State property, and he being the State Archaeologist). Shouping agreed to let him take it to the Institute if Alan would replace the mantelpiece with something colonial, and in the meantime, he wrote a short letter explaining that this was a long-term loan, and *not a gift*, to the Institute (and thus, the people of South Carolina) and he wanted any display of it to reflect his (Shouping's) endowment of same. Alan agreed, gave him a bottle, and then stashed the quadrant in his attic. Shouping gave me a copy of the letter. He also said that the quadrant wasn't found on the Browns Ferry Wreck, as Alan had told everyone, even the author of an article on the wreck in *Early Man* magazine (Winter 1981) that had a little inset on the "The Davis Quadrant Puzzle." Shouping said he found it almost a hundred yards away. Then he asked me if I knew about the Model T (or was it A?) axle that was found *under* the Brown's Ferry Wreck? Now wait a minute. That boat, as old as it was, had several thousand bricks on it when it was found (probably the reason it sank). But if there were the remains of a Model T (or A) underneath it, then it had to have sunk **after** 1920 (what we archaeologists refer to as the *terminus post quem*, or date after which something had to occur). This was getting weirder by the minute. Then Shouping, with a little grin, said, "By the way, ask Alan what happened to the bricks." I never got the chance (although I found out what happened to them later on my own). So here I am, sitting in the hot seat, knowing this was the end of the line for me at the Institute, and therefore, South Carolina, no matter what. Even if I beat the pot smoking, Alan and I were going to be mortal enemies forever. He was not to be trusted, and his sycophant, Mack Newsome, was even worse. As I was dismissed, and headed back to the office, I could hear Rippeteau over my shoulder ask, "So, Alan, what's all this about the Davis Quadrant?"

But it did not all end gracefully. It was decided that I should undergo purgatory in the local archival museum, attached to the University. My temporary assignment was to research ferry crossings everywhere in South Carolina. Throw Me in the Briar Patch! Finally... some research. The very thing I'd been originally hired for, or so I'd been told. I loved it. Yes, I know I was under duress duty (K.P.), but I actually always wanted to do this, had mentioned to Alan several times that this is what we needed to do (and been rebuffed), and now here I was doing it. My last mission. After four or five working days, I'd gotten maybe 80% of the way through all the literature, and damn if they didn't call me in (I really hoped to have had it done before they did, and to this day somewhere at the Institute, there's *Brewer's List of Colonial Ferry Crossings for the State of South Carolina*). I think it was a Tuesday, the 17th when I was called back in to the Director's office. Alan sat there stone-faced, staring silently forward and Rippeteau took the lead. He explained that Alan wanted to fire me, but he wasn't going to allow that to happen. However, he was sorry to say, any chance of continuing to carry on at the Institute under or with Alan was simply unworkable, since I was hired as the Assistant Underwater Archaeologist. Therefore, although it was my decision, he recommended that I resign. I asked him if I'd get a good recommendation from him, as Director, and he assured me I would. Well, that was that. I asked if he wanted it typewritten, and he said handwritten would be fine, addressed to him. I asked for pen and paper and sat down at a nearby table. He sat at this desk, shuffling papers, Alan continued to stare at the wall or out the window (I got the feeling that he'd been roundly chewed out for letting this rather small incident get out of hand... but he felt justified, so be it). After fifteen minutes I handed the signed two-page letter to Rippeteau, and asked for a copy. He called in his secretary, and I got the copy, shook his hand (but not Alan's, who never got up) and thanked him for being so good about the whole business. Then I went downstairs and cleaned out my desk, smiled and winked to Joe, while Newsome hunched over his computer monitor in the corner. Then I made the rounds described earlier and said good-bye to everyone. I heard later that Rippeteau made Alan bring the Davis Quadrant back in and put it with the State collections (which was another reason Alan was so angry—that thing was easily worth 20 grand on the open market, maybe more—I'll bet he thinks about it every time he watches *Antiques Roadshow*).

Things didn't stop when I left. If anything they picked up speed. In quick succession, Newsome hoodwinked my replacement by playing up to him as he had to me and got him fired too, this time for cocaine. Then the young underwater archaeologist who replaced that guy, a young Canadian I got to know real well, named Gary Brewer (no foolin', Alan must have choked on that) accused Alan of plagiarism when Alan blatantly stole something he had written—Alan never could write worth a damn, and thought that anything anyone produced while working for him by rights belonged to him—and Alan ended up writing a formal apology. Then Rippeteau got sued by Alan when, digging for dirt to try to get him fired, he made the mistake of asking around the Institute if Alan was gay, and Alan found out (he was an effete misogynist, but he wasn't gay). Alan made 500,000 off of that, a matter of public record, and then resigned. Rippeteau then got in further trouble with a couple of sexual harassment accusations, well-founded, and then he resigned. And finally, Newsome got canned after claiming in the newspaper that he had found the *Hunley*, the Confederate submarine that sunk the Union frigate the *Housatonic* in Charleston Harbor, when in fact, Clive Cussler (yes, that Clive Cussler) had bankrolled the expedition and his divers, including Ralph Wilbanks, had put their hands on it first. When Cussler read the article it was reported that he was so mad that he made a late-night phone call to the Governor, waking him up, to demand Newsome's head in the morning, ...and got it. All this occurred within two years of my departing. I'd gotten out just in time. Good-bye and good riddance! What a mess.

15.   The Southeast Archeological Center (SEAC) (1986-1990)

So it was time to leave South Carolina, and just as well, because neither Amy nor I had been happy there, it was a bad atmosphere to raise kids, and the job would have killed me, either through accident or stress or subterfuge. But it was a good experience. I'd learned the pitfalls of professionalism, and the first bitter taste of bad management (not the last time I'd see that particularly sad and ugly mutant). We put the house up on the market, and it wasn't long before we got a buyer (who even got a backyard full of roasted peanuts). The trip back to Tallahassee was actually pleasant, and between my retirement money and what we made off the house, we were able to find a nice little place to rent on Yancey St. with lots of kids in the neighborhood and an elementary school within walking distance. It was good to be back home, among friends and closer to family, and Robin was even accepted into a forward-thinking experimental Pre-Kindergarten sponsored by FSU. A week or two later I called up my old boss George Fischer and told him I'd made plans to go back to graduate school, any chance I could get back on with the Park Service? Within the month I was hired to help Bob Wilson in the newly created Database Section at SEAC, this time as a GS-7, Temporary, what they called Intermittent, still no benefits or any chance of either a permanent government position or promotion. But it was a job, on campus, and in the same building as the Anthropology Department, and they were willing to work around my school schedule. By Christmas, Amy and I discovered that she was pregnant once again with our third, expected in August.

Brake on Through

Living at Yancey was really very nice, with a Christian family of five next door, the Publix grocery store a block away, and a City-managed baseball-soccer-swimming complex at the end of the block, attached to both Ruediger Elementary and Raa Middle Schools. In February, Sam was two; Robin turned five and Grandma and Grampa Brewer had given him a bike. I took him out onto our short street and we practiced with me pushing him ever so slightly, running alongside until he seemed to be sitting upright, and letting go. Sure there were a couple of spills, but nothing serious. I told him if he thought he was going to fall, aim for one of the open front yards on either side so he'd fall onto the grass. Well, he started getting the hang of it, little by little, but he didn't get a feel for the brakes (all kids have this problem, it's a matter of finesse, to ease on down backward on the pedals rather than just press them as you do when going forward). No matter, he started to coast. Now the street had a slight incline down to the south end, about six houses down, and then dead-ended at the cross street, 8th Avenue. Even though this was a slow neighborhood, and it was early mid-morning, I'd seen cars wheel down that cross street both ways, either trying to catch the light at the bottom of the hill or gunning it as they came up. Robin started gaining speed down the street. "The brakes!" I yelled. He was staying up marvelously, but going faster. Then he started screaming as he gained momentum and just hung on, forgetting about the brakes. He was way out of reach now, picking up speed and screaming, heading straight past the Stop sign. I said a quick prayer, "Please God, don't let a car be coming," and he went straight across, crashing into a wooden fence at the crossway house, knocking the gate open, and flying head over butt into their flower garden. He was crying and bruised, but I just hugged him and laughed with relief when I got to him. We got the brake part down in no time flat.

1517 Jackson

Summer came and our third son, Dennis, was born on August 13th. He was named Dennis partly after my old friend, Dennis LeFils, but also because it was a solid Irish familial, and we gave him the middle name of O'Brien, after Mom's maiden name. For nicknames, Robin had become Robinowitz, Sam was called Samborino (couldn't really call him Sambo, now could we?), and Dennis became Denbo (sometimes referred to as "Denbo Magnifico!"). When summer ended we started looking for a bigger place, since there on Yancey the boys were in one bedroom, and Amy and I were in the other, and the baby was in a crib in our room. Amy had a friend named Julie, a thin redhead with freckles, married to a consulting engineer named Robert, and they were renting a nice place, a double-barreled shotgun house on two lots only a couple of blocks away, even closer to the schools and playground. They had two kids, a young boy the same age as Robin, and a two-year-old daughter who suffered from a type of autism called something like "Pixie Syndrome." I say suffered but that was not true. This little girl was amazing in that she was always smiling, giggling, and happy, part of the makeup of symptoms for this particular handicap. It was a handicap though because she couldn't talk, or walk, or concentrate on any particular thing for long, and her arms and legs were usually waving about as if she were a little marionette. But she really was a delightful little girl, and she took particular interest in running her fingers through my beard, long and red back then. (Julie was a saint the way she doted on that child, and for years she did everything in her power to see to it that the little girl was given the opportunity to be exposed to the company of regular kids.) They were planning on moving out and were having a new house built for themselves up in Killearn, the high-class neighborhood north of town, so we asked them to talk to their landlord and see if we couldn't move in right behind them after moving out, and soon it was all arranged. Julie and Robert didn't like the place because, I've got to admit, it was pretty ramshackle, being one of those houses we'd now call "vernacular" even though it was built according to a standard 1930's North Florida structural formula, the double-barreled shotgun. It had been built by the landlord himself some fifty years earlier (he was now in his eighties), where his family lived on one side, while the other side was rented out. Both families then shared a single kitchen and bathroom at the rear. Now however, it was a single-family residence with only one front door and a broad porch, and as you entered, on the right a living room, dining room and then a kitchen. Off the dining room to the left was a small hall with bathroom and two bedrooms, one facing the street and the other having two side windows. In the back, off the kitchen was another bedroom, the master bedroom, with its own bathroom. Then there was a small utility room also in the back of the kitchen and a side door that led to the back yard. The house was on two lots, which were dominated by laurel oaks, pecan trees, a couple of large camphors, and along the property line and toward the front, maybe thirty-five, large and blooming red, white, and pink camellias. We couldn't move in right away, while Julie and Robert's house was being finished, and once they'd left, as we finished up our lease at Yancey I had a couple of weeks to get in there and do some work on it, painting a room or two, and sanding down the oaken flooring. Crawling up under the house and then up into the attic, I could see that when the guy built it he had used a lot of "found" material, and the house actually rested in places on rocks, broken bricks, and fragments of cinder blocks. The roof was one of the last tin roofs in downtown Tallahassee, and the wiring was frightening. But I loved it.

Back Off

It was just getting to Christmas when the house was ready, and we made plans to move in after the first of the year. Amy and I were going to Orlando to see our families and spend the holidays, where we'd have built-in babysitters and the grandparents on both sides would spoil the kids rotten. But first, Amy wanted me to do something special for the kids before we left

Tallahassee. Since I was going over to the new house on Jackson Street all the time working on it to get it ready, and I had all my tools over there, why not build them a little playhouse as a Christmas present from us? "A playhouse? I don't want to build a playhouse... besides..." Besides nothing. She insisted that I build them a playhouse before we go to Orlando. Fine, fine, fine. I went down to the lumber store and found out that my old sub-contractor's line of credit was still active, so I grabbed a few things not only to build the playhouse, but to fix the big one as well. I was all set and the little Dodge Colt van was loaded when I remembered I needed some shingles for the playhouse roof. Usually there'd be a broken bundle laying around and I could make off with an armful for a buck or two, but this time, there weren't any broken bundles, or squares as they called them. But the yard clerk said, "Tell you what, there's a squashed roll of roll-roofing, which is equivalent to a whole square... I'll let you have it for ten dollars." Well, this was a great deal, and there it was sitting on a ledge up a ten-stair climb. "I'll get someone to help you bring it down." "Naw, don't worry," I said, "I got it," and went up the stairs, hoisted the 85-pound roll up onto my left shoulder, turned, and walked heavily down the wooden stairway. When I got to the van, I dropped the roll-roofing, opened the back, then picked it up again and put it in, closing the gate. Oooh, something didn't feel right. Ah well. I got back to the house on Jackson Street, and went right to work on the playhouse. By now it was afternoon, and I remember it was dark when I finished, finally topping it off with a couple of stretches of that roll-roofing before dragging it out to the back yard so it would be a surprise. I got back to Yancey after nine, told Amy that I'd finished it, had some dinner and a beer, and hit the sack so we could get an early start to Orlando the next morning. When I awoke, I couldn't move. My back was locked up as if in a vise. If I tried to turn, or roll over, or even lift my arm, there were shooting pain-spasms from the middle of my back, down the backside of my legs, all the way to the big toes. It hurt so bad that just lying there beads of sweat popped out of my forehead. Amy said she'd go to the store and get some deep-heating rub for the ride to Orlando. When she left, I realized I had to pee. It took the whole twenty minutes she was gone for me to ease off the bed, crawl hand-over-hand the ten feet to the toilet, hoist myself up, and let it go (the whole time stopping intermittently, crying out in pain, and looking like a parapalegic without his wheelchair). When she got back I was lying on my back next to the bed on the hardwood floor, which seemed to ameliorate the pain somewhat. It was a long, stiff, and excruciating ride to Orlando with Amy driving and managing the kids, and then I spent the entire time there lying prone on my back on my parents' carpeted living room floor while the kids ran around playing with their new toys all about me. Only a few stiff drinks could loosen it up enough for me to sit upright in a chair.

George Dis-engages

When we got back to Tallahassee I went straight to the Health Center on campus. A very good-looking young lady doctor checked me out, took a couple of x-rays, and let me know that I had squished one of the cartilage discs in my lower back, undoubtedly when I was manhandling that goddamn roll-roofing. It hadn't hurt immediately because your back muscles on either side clench up and act as a temporary brace. When you go to sleep, and the muscles eventually relax, well, that's when you get the full effect. This would hurt for a long time. What else can I do, I asked her. You can have back surgery, but that's not recommended in your case, the solution often being worse than the problem. Besides, you're still young (I was 35), and it'll heal itself with time. She gave me a temporary removable plastic-and-Velcro back brace, a bottle of pain pills, and sent me on my way. Well, call it coincidence or sympathy, but just at this time my old boss, George Fischer, got word that his long-awaited request for a disability retirement finally came through. Maybe twenty years previously he was putting on a tank to go diving, in the old-fashioned macho manner of lifting it up and over your head, when the tank slipped out of its sleeve, fell on the back of his neck, and cracked one of his major vertebrae. The crack never

293

healed correctly and began a degenerative decline down his spine. Eventually, he had to have surgery to fuse the bones together since the cartilage discs between them were deteriorating, and between the pain and general discomfort he'd been advised that since it had happened while on duty, he could apply for, and probably get disability. Pete had been fighting it for years, but now, things had soured between them to the degree that Pete said sure, let it go. So now George was going to leave. It was sad and short and not a big deal, other than a get-together at Poor Paul's, the local pub, with promises of let's do this again. He was only 50 or 51, and I owed him a lot for the jump-start on my career, especially with the Park Service, but he didn't leave campus entirely, and continued to teach up at the Academic Diving Program. Then ADP asked me to come in and cover some classes, and I began teaching as a guest lecturer on certain subjects such as Survey Techniques, Project Logistics, Scientific Writing, and Research Design. I got a little extra pay for that from the University, which helped out considerably. But I had to concentrate most of my effort on my new job with the Park Service, now that I was working under Bob Wilson.

Chick-Chat

Bob Wilson was one of the best bosses I ever had. He was calm, professional, and kind. At the time there were only three of us in the Database Section, me, Bob, and Dennis Finch. Bob, average in stature, bald with sideburns and a back brown-haired half-circle tonsure, wore glasses and was soft-spoken. As the manager, he was the titular head of our little group. Dennis was always intense, full head of black hair, tall and slim, and was the computer whiz, the brains behind what constituted the various databases, whether they were artifact collections, site descriptions and locations, project reports, maps, photos, etc., and an expert at extracting the information out of them whenever management needed it. Me? I didn't know a database from diddly-squat. But I could write like a motherfucker. So, it soon fell on me to produce the latest flavor-of-the–day manifesto demanded by the powers that be in Washington in the National Park Service, which at that time was the Archaeological Overview and Assessment. This was a document for each and every park in your particular Region (ours being the Southeast), that described the cultural resources in that park, inventoried them, and spoke as to why each was important, and just how important from a standpoint of significance on the national level, and then described their condition, finally making recommendations for how they might best be managed. The first one, sent down to me from Pete, the Chief, through Bob, was for Chickamauga and Chattahoochee National Battlefield Park, the scene of the great two-month-long running conflagration of the Civil War, September –November, 1863, often referred to as the Death Knell of the Confederacy, wherein after fighting up and down Lookout Mountain and Missionary Ridge the rail lines at Chattanooga were finally seized by the Union and provided the eventual supply route for Sherman's March to the Sea. Bob and I went up there to test the location of an expansion of the Visitor Center, so I got to nose around the park's archives, but hell, we had more information about the archaeology back at SEAC.

To be honest, not very much archaeology had occurred at these two parks (or rather, this one large consolidated park crossing the Georgia-Tennessee border) since all the major issues had been settled by the surviving generals and the legions of historians who followed them. Why dig anything up? From my perspective, it was a simple task, and I pounded away on an old IBM Selectric typewriter, the ones with the ball that swiveled around at lightning speed to hammer the letters home, no more getting keys stuck; one that had been assigned to me rather than having been "surveyed," which is what they call it when they either ship something back to the General Services Administration, or more often than not, just throw it away. I knocked the O&A out in about six weeks, and because the park was happy with the product, Pete, the Chief at SEAC, was happy, and my boss, Bob, was happy. I was just happy to have it done. So they tossed another one my way immediately, for Shiloh. I was quickly becoming a Civil War veteran. Little did I know that SEAC was getting paid by each park around 20 grand for each of these documents, while at the time I wasn't making that in a year.

Shiloh

I should have done Shiloh first, since the two-day extremely fierce battle had preceded Chickamauga-Chattanooga by almost a year. So now I had to step back in time and figure out what had led up to Shiloh, and then how that turned into Chick-Chat, as we referred to both the park and the subsequent battle. Well, the secret here was Corinth, Mississippi which was another main nexus of the Confederate States' railroad system. Maj. Gens. Ulysses S. Grant and Don Carlos Buell were sent by Maj. Gen. Henry W. Halleck, commanding U.S. forces in the West, southward to sever the Southern railroads. Grant took his troops down the Tennessee River by steamboats and offloaded them at Pittsburgh Landing, having the men camp up and around a little log church called Shiloh. Buell was moving his troops by land from Nashville and Grant was ordered to wait for him, so he took his time unloading. Meanwhile, at Corinth, Gen. Albert Sidney Johnston, supreme Confederate commander in the West, heard of the plans and decided to attack Grant before Buell would arrive, then push him back into the river (which he very nearly did). In two days, Johnston moved his men (roughly 44,000) from Corinth and was ready to attack Sunday morning, April 6th, 1862 (I wonder how services went at the little log church that morning). Just after dawn, the Confederates came swooping down and out of the woods surrounding the field and down the road the church was on, then down the road to the landing area and caught Grant's 40,000-man army relatively by surprise, much of their gear and artillery and ammunition still being unloaded down at the river. The Federals quickly rallied and, despite extremely fierce fighting around the little church, the Confederates gained ground throughout the day. Grant was forced to fight a defensive military battle with his back against the river. The day's fighting included the Hornet's Nest, where troops on either side fought in a blindingly tight oak thicket where they couldn't see more than ten feet and the sound of hundreds of bullets zipping through the brush was like that of a swarm of hornets. The Peach Orchard, was another site of rapid-fire retaliation, but here, between standing lines of men, it was notable because the bullets knocking the pink and white petals off the blooms made it appear to be snowing in April. The Confederate assault began to lose cohesion, and in an afternoon attack on the Union left, Confederate General Johnston got hit by a bullet behind the knee, knicking his femoral artery, and as he leaned on his horse up against a large tree, he bled out and died (to this day he is the highest ranking American officer, albeit and arguably, Confederate, to die in combat). I remember seeing the limbless dead trunk of that tree still at Shiloh in 1987 and wonder if it's still there; nearby is a marker showing the location of a mass pit burial of unknown Confederate soldiers. With Johnston dead, the command of the Confederate Army fell to Gen. P.G.T. Beauregard, he of launching the initial firing on Ft. Sumter fame. By the time darkness fell, Grant had set up a defensive line of artillery, and the fighting stopped. Overnight, Buell's army arrived to support Grant, and in the morning the Federals launched a massive counterattack, pushing Beauregard back to Shiloh Church, and then retreating back to Corinth. Grant and Buell did not pursue them, and were later criticized by Lincoln for not doing so. At the end of two days, almost 24,000 men on both sides were casualties, either killed, wounded, or missing. Grant and Buell's commander, General Halleck, advanced south from the west and by May had surrounded Confederate fortifications at Corinth with artillery, and Beauregard, after having his men rip up the train tracks, withdrew to Tupelo.

Now all of this was fascinating, and undoubtedly of national historic significance, but archaeologically, what were the ramifications, or possibilities, inherent in a mere two-day event?

Or, to put it more bluntly, what questions concerning the physical, mental, or cultural evolution of mankind might be addressed that were not already answered in the history books? The entire battlefield had been walked over by the opposing generals and other officers in the days after the war, and now monuments marked every encounter, every line of fire, every heroic stand. As I said, even the old tree trunk where Sidney Johnston had bled to death for lack of a tourniquet was preserved. But none of these presented any archaeological potential. There was, however, the mass burial of some 125 Sons of Dixie who gave up the ghost that awful day, now resting in a well-marked grave, no larger or deeper than a backyard pool. Now, that would be interesting. The whole reason they were put there and not laid to rest individually with honors in the National Cemetery now located at Shiloh was because they were rebels to the Government that created that cemetery. By the time the Daughters of the Confederacy were formed and considered individual re-interment in their own sacred grounds, the difficulties were apparent: removing the remains would just create a worse jumble of bones; sorting individuals, much less identifying them would be impossible; not to mention, the Federal government was adamant that this is where they were placed historically, and this is where they would stay (the old Osceola argument); and finally, even that small of an effort (at the time) would probably have been cost prohibitive, even for the DAC. But today, what with the country united (although presently divided by blue and red states, as opposed to blue and grey), and with the resources now enjoyed by the Confederacy's great-granddaughters and great-grandsons and their burgeoning wealthy descendants, ever-proud to be Southern (whether by heritage, music, land, or investment), the money issue has evaporated. Analysis by both forensic anthropologists and DNA extraction would identify the number, age, sex (prob. male), any osteological and genetic deformities and/or injuries, nutritional adequacy, etc. and answer a range of other as yet unspecified questions. Family associations and heritage, including race, could be ascertained. In effect, if not in fact, every individual would have his own post-mortem "biological biography." Identification of the individual's specific identity might be a matter of process by elimination. So here was an idea for archaeological examination that might yield some positive results.

Another was the site of Bloody Pond, which I think was originally known as Water Oak Pond. This is where the combatants of both sides, injured and decimated, lay down their arms to partake of the shallow, fetid waters to quench their thirst and dress their wounds, the runoff of which was soon turned bloody red and muddied with gore and ordure. Well, no one had ever investigated the pond, and sometime in 1994 or 1995 I was invited by the park to come and do an underwater survey there. I arrived with one of my technical assistants and we did some shovel tests around the perimeter and then put on our diving gear and got in, only to discover we could walk across it waist-deep and the bottom was asphalt, the same as we had discovered in the surrounding shovel tests. Apparently the Park Service, or maybe it was the Civil Conservation Corps, had dug the entire area up and laid down asphalt, which is perhaps why the pond holds water still. The archaeological potential however, or what little of it that had probably ever existed, had been destroyed.

But the real archaeological potential of Shiloh had practically nothing to do with the battle. It lay in the fact that the naturally-contoured Pittsburgh Landing was composed of, and surrounded by, one of the last remaining intact prehistoric Native American mound-and-village sites left on the Tennessee River. Occupied from ca. 0 AD (that's JC time, as opposed to 2,000 B.P., or before the present) until it was abandoned around 12-1300, these were some of the ancestors of the Choctaw, Chickasaw, and Creek, as they were known in historic times. Whoever they were, they lived along the Tennessee River and carried out trade and raiding using the waterway as their predominant means of travel. The numerous house mounds can still be seen on the ground, with the large burial mound "C" located on a path downstream and probably was not within the village proper, which would have been palisaded for protection. Most notable, however, is the monumentally large Mound A, right on the edge of the river bluff, and threatened with erosion as the river undercuts the ground below as it has for a thousand years. This was a ceremonial mound, built for the various chiefs through time, with new layers added so each new chief could lord it over his inferiors from a slightly higher perspective than the previous. Up in the fields around where Shiloh church is found, they grew corn ("We call it maize"), beans, squash, sunflowers, etc. and the woods abounded with deer, turkey, squirrel, raccoon, rabbit, possum, and the like. And of course, the river provided plenty of large fish, easily caught in weirs, nets, and with bow and arrow.

As stated above, Mound A, unlike Mound C, is not a burial mound, but rather, a chief's mound, and undoubtedly the great chief Ulysses S. Grant stood atop it often in April 1862 (he was there for a month after the battle). It was reportedly dug into later by amateur archaeologists, during the 1890s when the Shiloh Park Commission was looking to commemorate the great battle there, and further digging into Mound C, the burial mound, yielded grave goods showing trade with areas as far away as Illinois. It was rumored that there was a "cathouse" or ramshackle brothel built on top of Mound A sometime in the 1920s or 30s and vehicles could pull right up to the mound so that clients could climb a set of wooden stairs and enjoy themselves while overlooking the river. Then sometime in the 1970s, archaeologist John Hardinger of SEAC led an investigation that dug a telephone-booth-sized excavation right down into the center of the mound to the bottom, but it only revealed the successive layering resulting from its construction. Other than that, no archaeological work had been carried out before I wrote the O&A.

Pete Pops a Top

Again, like the others, this one was written long-hand first, then edited, and finally typed on the old IBM Selectric. Just about this time (1988), computers were just coming onto the FSU campus and there were some half-assed attempts to teach a few of us how to access them. The disks were huge, about 8 inches square, and could only hold 40 pages of text at a time. The Park Service bought one (and only one) machine, with the brand new smaller 5 ¼ inch floppy disks that would hold eighty pages. They put it in the very back of the archaeology lab under the guardianship of Guy Prentice, who had some familiarity with computers, having just come on board from the University of Florida with a PhD, and he and Dennis Finch in my Division were the only ones authorized to touch the damn thing, the data to be shared by the Division heads. The Chief of the Center, Pete Faust, who was gruff and stern (and kinda scary) gave strict orders that no one was to use this computer except Guy and Dennis. It just so happened that the only other people in the huge Park Service lab at that time were myself and Ken Wild. After a month or two, well, Guy was an amiable fellow and he wanted to be friends with everyone, being new to SEAC, plus, he really did know how to do things like word processing and database management and was happy to share the knowledge. At the same time Ken and I were curious about this new technology, so after awhile Guy would give impromptu lessons as we stood there looking over his shoulder while he typed documents or carried out some other computer magic. One day he said "I'm going off to lunch, why don't you guys practice a little… don't worry, there's nothing you could do to mess it up," and he took out the disk he was working on and left. Well, Ken and I were a little nervous, but what the hell, this thing could really simplify our lives as far as typing and editing reports, compiling data, etc., all the things we were doing on typewriters and tabular sheets, using pens, pencils, white-out, and scotch-tape. So we sat down side-by-side in front of it, got out a new floppy disk, and then Ken said, "Where does it go again?" I looked at it, and you could see there were two drives, one on top of the other, apparently for copying disks. "I don't know," I said, and I took the disk and slipped it into what looked like a proper slot between the drives. It slid right in, no resistance whatsoever. Nothing happened. We at least knew that something was supposed to come up on the screen, but nothing changed. In walked one of the young smart-ass interns from the Anthropology Department and I called him over. "Hey, do you know how this thing works? We put the disk in here and nothing's coming up." He looked at the machine, then looked back at us, and said "You idiots. You slipped the disk in the space between the two drives… that's not good, it gets hot in there and it might melt," and he started laughing. "Well, how do we get it out?" I asked, now very scared. "The only way is to take the computer out of its case, then you can get at the disk, and once you got it, slide the computer back in… you'll need a couple of screwdrivers, see?" and he pointed to the screws on the sides and back of the computer. "Will you help us?" I begged. "Fuck no," he said, knowing the Chief's admonition about anyone touching THE computer, and he walked out still laughing. "Oh, shit," we both knew we'd be in a heap of trouble if anyone found out. "Let's do it," I said and in two minutes we had the screws out, the computer lying there with its guts exposed, and extricated the floppy from between the drives with a flat knife. Another two minutes and we had it all back together. I was shaking I was so nervous. Ken then slipped the disk into the right slot and the thing started humming, a black-and-white screen came up and said something like C: A/, which meant it was up and running. I said, "I'm sorry, Ken, that scared me so bad that I don't want to have anything to do with it. I'm going back to my typewriter," and I crossed the lab and sat down at my old Selectric and started rat-a-tat-tatting away. Ken hadn't been playing on that thing for two full minutes when the lab door opens, and the grey cloud of his pipesmoke preceding him like Mephistopheles himself, in walks Pete, the Chief. He looked at me and said, "Where's Guy?" "He's at lunch." Then he looks down at the end of the lab, and there, unsuccessfully trying to hunker down and hide behind the monitor that sat atop THE computer, was Ken. Now, just like in the cartoons, the smoke started coming out of Pete's ears as he turned red, took a deep breath, and amid a whalespout of obscenities told Ken to get away from that machine, didn't he know that no one was supposed to touch that thing except Guy and Dennis, if I EVER see you near that machine again…da-da, da-da, da-da…As he ranted and raved at Ken, I just sat there, hands on my lap, staring at my old IBM and the white concrete wall behind it, thanking sweet Mother of Outrageous Fortune that Pete hadn't walked in eight minutes earlier when Ken and I had that goddamned thing spread out in pieces on the lab table.

Poor Ken. I don't think he was ever treated nice by Pete, who eventually warmed up to me, although it was a long haul. I think I took him by surprise one day when he asked me, out of the blue, "What's the last book you've read?" and I told him "*The Satyricon* by Petronius," and his eyebrow shot up as he gripped his pipe and took a puff. Part of Ken's problem might have been his own fault. As I may or may not have said before, Pete kind of reminded me of my Dad, so I had an idea how to deal with him, and it worked. When Pete would call me in to his office, and I'd sit there across from his huge, always spotlessly clean, and therefore intimidating desk (Christ, you could roller skate on it!), and he'd tell me what my new assignment was… for instance, "I need you to write the Overview and Assessment for Virgin Islands National Park. How long is that gonna take?" I'd sit for a minute, think about it, and say, "Six months." Then he'd say, "You got four." Then I'd get up and say, "okay," and leave. If I found out in three months that I wasn't going to make it, I'd ask to see him, and I'd tell him, "I need another two." Then he'd say, "okay," and by God, I'd have at least a draft to give him at the end of those last two months (which might even get me one more, that last, sixth month, to put the finishing touches on it; but at least he had something in his hand in the meantime). When he called Ken in and told him, "I need you to do so-and-so… how long is that gonna take?" Ken would think about it, and then say, "Well, that depends, Pete, on how many people I've got helping me, and whether

I can get this or that information, and well, how much we've got to work with, and I'm gonna need..." and Pete would lose all patience and tell him to get out and come back when he could tell him how long. And if Ken didn't have it done when he finally said he would, he'd be worried to tell Pete, and then wait until the last minute, and Pete would give him hell.

Cumberland Falling

Well, it so happened that the next Overview and Assessment WAS going to be for Virgin Islands National Park, and I got all excited because for both Chick-Chat and Shiloh I had gotten to visit the parks so that I'd know what I was writing about. When I asked Bob if Pete was going to send me to the Virgin Islands he said, "Nope, too expensive; you'll have to wing it from here." But they did assign me an assistant, a cute short-haired and sharp-featured redhead undergrad named Susan Hammersten. She turned out to be both smart and tough—tough enough to earn the nickname "Hammerstone." She was really very good at doing research, which I would then fold into the written format of the document. Sometimes I would let her run for a week or two gathering information while I did something else. Bob was in the same situation, since he didn't really have to "manage" either Dennis or myself, so he came up with a little research project to address a problem that had been (ironically) eating away at the Regional Office in Atlanta: the serious erosion occurring at the barrier island that composed Cumberland Island National Seashore. The southernmost sea island on the Georgia coast, Cumberland became a national park after the Andrew Carnegie family got tired of living in their mansions out there and donated the whole island to the Federal Government. The mansions, particularly Dungeness (before it caught fire and was gutted) and Plum Orchard, slowly fell into disrepair, and the whole Carnegie-properties aspect of the island was always considered a white elephant by the Park Service, which didn't have the money or manpower to maintain them. [Historical note: In ancient India a white elephant would be given as a present to a rival maharajah, who would then end up going bankrupt just maintaining the majestic and beastly gift.] But the island was otherwise well-suited for a national park since it had a long history from prehistoric Indians to Spanish conquistadors, Franciscan and Jesuit missionaries, English adventurers and colonists, Revolutionary War heroes, sea-island cotton plantations with slave owners and villages, a free black town, and then, of course, the Carnegie family's winter playground. As part of the transfer from the Carnegies, there's still a large gated vacation compound on the north end, with its own private airstrip, owned by the successors to the Coca-Cola empire, the Candlers. It also has a nice three-par practice golf hole there, its flag planted atop a low Indian sand burial mound. Even the Park Service, despite being the Federal Government's leaseholder, doesn't go in there uninvited.

The west side of the island had been eroding for decades, if not hundreds of years, but it had been slow and gradual. This was the side that faced the mainland and which was separated from it by the Intracoastal Waterway. Directly across from Cumberland is the Kings Bay Naval Submarine Support Base, and when that section of the Intracoastal was dredged so that the subs could get in and out unimpeded, the increased water flow also increased the rate of erosion on Cumberland. Then when the Park Service started regular twice-daily ferry service, the wake from the large ferry boat exacerbated an already troublesome situation. It was on the protected western shore you see, away from the dynamic and sandy seashore, that most of the historic and archaeological sites were located, prehistoric shell middens, Spanish mission locations, the Carnegie's carriage road, even the great Guale Indian village of Tacatacuru, not to mention many of the great large oaks and loblolly pines, and now they were all just dropping into the water on a constant and continual basis. But how fast? Well, no one really knew. There were lots of estimates and some comparisons with historic maps and nautical charts, so we knew it was serious; but how much could be ascribed to man-made influences and how much was just natural? So Bob Wilson came up with this research design to find out. A simple, yet clever plan, he decided to set up some seven survey stations along the western edge of the island, two on the southern end, three at various points northward, and as a sort of control, another two on the eastern side. He and I would go and measure the profile of the eroding bluffs and sand dunes, wait a month, or two, or three, and do it again. Within a year we had distinct proof of the erosion and a fair idea of its rate. We could knock out the survey in a matter of two or three days, and since we were driving over from Tallahassee and the park put us up in visitor housing, it cost nearly nothing. It was really a brilliant piece of science and the data did nothing to ease the mind of the powers in Region; in fact, it made perfectly clear that the erosion was increasing, and thus, threatening all those irreplaceable archaeological features along the western side of the island. Although alarms went off, and the Park Service saw the problem clearly now, financial considerations prevailed. I was sent out with John Hardinger, then working out of the Regional Office, to carry out an experiment at Brickhill Bluff, where we filled burlap "croaker" sacks full of oyster shells and arranged them three-deep in a semicircle around a section of the bluff that was threatened. The idea was that as the tide rose it would carry silt in over the top of the bags, then as it receded, the silt would be captured behind the seine of the burlap and shells, thus accreting sand to counteract the erosion. Though it was touted as a success in the beginning, two years later there wasn't a rag of bags or a shadow of shells, and the erosion was as bad as ever. Later, there was even a move to get the Seabees at Kings Bay to come over and carve up the large trees that had fallen down off the bluff and use them as a natural breakwater, but that fell through. Finally, the Park Service threw in the towel and said, "It's a natural process, and therefore, let Nature take its course." At the time, we young and hungry archaeologists at the Southeast Archeological Center thought this might be a good thing: if the Government threw up its hands, and decided to let Nature take its course, then according to the Secretary of the Interior's Standards, some effort was required to "mitigate" the potential damage to the cultural resources, which meant money ought to be appropriated to go out and "save" the sites, or at least the information contained in them, by archaeological excavation before they fell into the water. We'd be busy for years. Washington, and therefore the Regional Office, didn't see it that way, and decided to "save" the money instead and avoid the headaches instead by allowing the sites to tumble into the Intracoastal by "attrition," or rather, natural cause. Same thing as letting the termites eat your house because you're too cheap to get it treated. (No, I take that back, it's more like using the books out of your private library in the fireplace to stay warm because you don't want to go outside and chop wood.)

But all of this was years in the making and breaking. Meanwhile, when I wasn't working on the Virgin Islands Overview and Assessment, I was exploring Cumberland Island with Bob. And Bob was a great teacher. He'd been to the island many times before, apparently even a couple of times with Pete, back in the early 70s, when the driving distance from Tallahassee to St. Mary's on the South Georgia coast was measured in bottles of beer, not minutes or miles. And Bob knew the other things besides the history: the natural stuff, the plants, the tides, the animals. He'd point out deer, snakes, armadillos, and feral hogs long before I'd spot them. Funny thing though, he told me there were more rattlesnakes per square mile on Cumberland, especially the southern end, than anywhere else in the South; but we never saw a single one when we were together, except one day when we got out of the truck, and he stepped on a baby rattler that couldn't have been six inches long; stepped on it accidentally and killed it. I'm the one who said, "What's that?" He hadn't even noticed. Later, when I was on a project there in 1999, a friend of mine, Rolando, with two of the girls, was on the beach on their day off, just soaking up sun and swimming, and while they were lying on the beach, up over the dunes came a huge rattlesnake, maybe six feet long, thick as your arm. It came down over the dunes, and they all jumped up as it slithered down the sand, right between their blankets and, ignoring them completely, headed out into the ocean! They couldn't believe it and watched it as it swam straight east, out to sea and out of sight. I didn't believe it either, until Rolando showed me the series of pictures from the camera he was quick enough to grab. Being an old Florida boy, I'd seen rattlesnakes swimming plenty of times, but always in fresh water. I'd had no idea that they would even go near salt water, and then, straight out to sea? That's just strange… the obvious question being "Why?"

Back at SEAC, Hammersten and I were plugging away at getting the Virgin Islands O&A written, but even Pete knew it was going to be a long one (it took the whole six months and then some—near the end, whenever Pete saw me in the halls he'd take a puff off his pipe, look over his glasses at me, and say "Give it birth, Brewer, give it birth."). What I didn't know, and only found out years later was that numerous plantations and even particular areas (known in the Virgin Islands as "estates") had the same name between the islands of St. Thomas, St. John, and St. Croix, so even though I tried to straighten it out as it went down on paper, some minor confusion settled in, especially since I'd never been there, and no one ever told me otherwise. But when we finished, it was a monumental work (if the slightest bit sloppy), incorporating a number of primary and secondary resources. It was, in fact, the last major report ever produced on a typewriter out of the Southeast Archeological Center. From then on, everything was done on a computer, since by mid '88 the Government was mandating the use thereof. Meanwhile, one of the reasons that the VI O&A was taking so long was that Bob and I began to be recognized as a sort of "archaeological firefighting" team, getting assigned small jobs that had to be done for the various parks on a quick schedule and with short notice. Besides our periodic jaunts to Cumberland Island, in a year's time we went to the large Indian mound at Seminole Rest in Canaveral (with Dennis Finch) to test for a possible parking lot, to Fort Moultrie back on Sullivan's Island in South Carolina to test for a drain to alleviate the flooding inside the fort, to a dry lake off the Blue Ridge Parkway that had suspected prehistoric and historic components. We were very popular with Pete because (unbeknownst to me at the time) we were making money for SEAC when the parks transferred a shitload of Federal funds to the Center to get these jobs done, and then Bob and I would whip them out in half the expected time using just our two-man team, instead of the standard four to six (or more), and we were willing to rough it. We bought more than a few computers for the rest of the Center that year.

When I had the time, I was also working on my Master's thesis, though rather haphazardly. It was going to be a write-up and description of the Spanish shipwreck, the *Nuestra Señora del Populo* of the 1733 Flota, the one I had investigated at Biscayne back in the Summer of 1984. But it soon dawned on me that I was getting nowhere fast. There had been very few artifacts recovered, the structural components were sparse, and I had only dug two test excavation units which bottomed out at the ceiling planks (the bottom of the vessel), without any substantive revelations. As far as the history of the ship itself, although I became pretty good at reading (and even translating) Old Castillian, which looks like Moorish wallpaper, there was nothing in the microfilm collections at the University library that shed any light on that particular vessel, even though they supposedly had a complete set of *legajos* (or bundles) of historic documentation from Seville. I explained the difficulties I was having to my major professor, Dr. Michelle Maryann, but she just told me to keep digging. I eventually realized I wasn't going to get anything more unless I went to the Casa de Contracíon in Seville, which housed all the pertinent documents relating to the ill-fated fleet of 1733, and even that would be a crapshoot as to whether I'd find anything I could use. Well, this was not going to happen on my salary, not in my wildest dreams. So for now I was stuck.

Then Pete tossed me another Overview and Assessment, this time, for Canaveral National Seashore. Well, this was right up my alley. I'd grown up in Orlando, and New Smyrna Beach was in my backyard, the favorite beach of my teen and young adult years, swimming and surfing, where I'd gone out fishing and where I'd spent the summer with Nolin and Celia. I already knew it like the back of my hand, and now, I was given free rein (and government money) to learn all I wanted. And I went at it with a vengeance, piling up the data on a daily basis, and getting immersed in it deeper and deeper. The park ran twenty-four miles south from New Smyrna and encompassed the whole of Mosquito Lagoon and a thin stretch of the mainland all the way down to Canaveral and Kennedy Space Center. South of the site of the old Eldora Hotel and nearby Statehouse, which were dropping-off points for smugglers during Prohibition, the bulk of the barrier island was the same as when the Spanish, and before them, the Indians, wandered through and/or lived there. It had only been preserved in its pristine state because of Kennedy Space Center and the need to set aside a large area of "no development" to the north—no development for anyone but Kennedy Space Center that is, which still has the rights, and plans, to build at least two more launch pads up into more than half the National Seashore. As part of doing research, I got to visit the park often, almost as often as I liked, and I became friends with the Resource Manager, John Stiner. At the time John was a young Amish-looking ranger out of Gettysburg, tall, thin, soft-spoken, with a light red beard, and a high dedication to the ideals of the National Park Service, as well as a driven work ethic, the quintessential Park Ranger in his pressed grey pants and shirt, with the gold badge, broad leather belt, and Smokey Bear hat. He introduced me to the Superintendent, an affable old round sort of pleasant redneck named Sib (short for Sibbald) Smith, and after maybe fifteen minutes I told them both more about the cultural resources in their park than they knew themselves. Quickly I was given *carte blanche* to rifle their files and go anywhere in the park I wanted. They also had plans to build a set of wooden stairs to the top of Turtle Mound, one of the largest remaining shell mounds in the country, to alleviate the effects of foot traffic, and I took samples at the bottom and the top for radiocarbon dating. The dates came back ass-backwards, with the older one, roughly 700 AD at the top and the younger one, roughly 1300 at the bottom. At first, I figured I must have gotten them switched, but after checking I found out, no, they were right. A simple explanation dawned on me: when you're building a pile of shells like that, once it get so high, you have to broaden the base before you can keep going up. So the base was broadened at a later period, thus yielding a more recent date. I really didn't have a beginning date, but from what we know it's fair to assume that the Indians were eating clams and oysters there for over a thousand years, before the Europeans came and wiped them all out by the mid 1700s.

The Canaveral O&A was another long one, but it was a labor of love. The more I discovered the more interesting it became, and what was essentially a strip of sand between Mosquito Lagoon and the ocean began to yield even more incredible secrets. For instance, when Juan Ponce de Leon first set foot on a remote beach somewhere between Daytona and St. Augustine in 1513, it was an inconsequential affair. We'll never know the spot, there were no witnesses, not even the Native Americans, and after a hurriedly-read proclamation on the bare sandy beach, he went back to his ship. Ah, but his *second* landing, now there was an encounter to remember. Heading south along the coast, his three ships, all simple square-rigged and therefore hard to sail against the wind, couldn't make it around Cape Canaveral because of the Gulf Stream and so they anchored, waiting for a favorable wind out of the north to help them out. One of the ships, a barkentine, "twisted its cables," which means the anchor wasn't grabbing, and it had to veer offshore so as not to run aground. While waiting for the ship to return, Ponce took a small boat into a nearby inlet to search for water and firewood. This inlet was at 29 degrees latitude, and though called Mosquito Inlet through history, it is now rightfully named Ponce Inlet. [One point to remember is that these guys were very good at determining latitude accurately, really a very simple affair, especially at night when you can see Polaris, the North Star. Longitude however, was tricky business right up until the late 1700s.] He was met by a small group of Florida Indians and a fight broke out when one of Ponce's men got clubbed on the head while keeping the Indians away from the landing boat. A couple of Spaniards got skewered with the native shark's tooth or stingray-spine-tipped arrows before the Indians ran off into the bush. The next day he had his men bring ashore a large stone cross, carved with attributes to the King of Spain, and set it up as a formal designation of his rights as discoverer, like staking a claim out West by sticking a "stake" in the ground. Still looking for fresh water they headed up what must have been present-day Spruce Creek, and were now accosted this time by some sixty natives, who sent the Spaniards packing ("Run Away! Run Away!"). About a week later, they finally got the wind they needed and rounded the cape, which they called Cabo de Corrientes, or Cape of the Currents, now Cape Canaveral. The first recorded encounter, and beginning of the end for Native Americans, on mainland America (although there had been tales of slave raiders coming up from Hispaniola, capturing Indians to work in the mines there after the native island population had been decimated; which is why Ponce probably got such a warm welcome). That large inscribed stone cross has never been found.

So, Ponce Inlet was at the north end of my study area, even though it was actually outside of the boundaries of the park, and for all practical purposes, Canaveral, or actually the cape itself, would be a natural southern limit, all surrounding the natural tidal estuary known as Mosquito Lagoon. I worked on that Overview and Assessment as hard as I could and eventually became known as one of a handful of experts on the area since I kept digging out more and more little-before-known details and became friendly with a number of the locals. My deadline was approaching though and I had to hand in a draft of the report soon. I was also still stuck with the writing project on the *Populo*, and time was catching up on any attempt to move along toward getting that Masters degree until I came to grips with the thesis. I wasn't getting any encouragement or good advice, and I wasn't going to get any more data. I sat and worried and fretted over the situation. How could I move things forward? Then I decided to practice one of my tried and true problem-solving methods that I'd picked up years earlier in reading *The Crack in the Cosmic Egg* by Joseph Chilton Pierce. I forget what he called it, but I called it Saturation-Incubation-Inspiration. What you do when faced with what appears to be an insurmountable problem is, you concentrate on all the parameters, give it your best shot at looking at all the facts and figuring out what the options are. Study the issue until you are saturated. Once you've strained it to the limit, and still decided you can't solve the dilemma or problem, then… you get away from it, you forget it, get as far away as possible, do something else, … let it go. Meanwhile, once you truly do let it go, your sub-conscious takes over and continues to mull over the enigma, whatever it is. This is the incubation period. Might be a day, may be a month, but eventually (and here's the tricky part) an answer, a solution, or an alternative will suddenly pop into your head. The reason it's tricky is because you have to be ready for it. When that flash bulb goes off, that moment of inspiration, you've got to grab it quick and write it down, or otherwise implant it into your waking consciousness in some deliberate fashion, because if you let it go ("Oh, I'll remember it in the morning," or worse, "Of course, it was so simple after all, I won't forget that."), you'll either lose it entirely, or lose the critical portions that actually pulled the answer together. Now I know that this isn't new. The technique has been used by sages, philosophers, scientists, and poets for centuries; I'd just never heard the methodology put so analytical and clear-cut before. This is the reason Samuel Taylor Coleridge never finished *Kubla Khan*: …after a drug-induced dream laid out the poem in its entirety, he woke and began writing it down, but only got as far as he did when he was interrupted by the arrival at his door of "a man from Porlock" who wanted to talk some silly piece of business. The break caused him to lose his train of thought, and that's why the subtitle is, "*A Vision in a Dream. A Fragment.*" [It had also been suggested at the time that the man from Porlock was actually an angel, perhaps his own guardian angel, sent to disrupt the writing of it on purpose, since it very nearly walked the edge of necromancy: "As holy and enchanted as e'er beneath a waning moon was haunted by woman wailing for her demon-lover!"]

In any case, I had my own moment of inspiration while lying in bed thinking one night, in those moments of thoughtful recollection of the day one has before falling into unconscious repose. Amy was next to me reading when I suddenly sat up, and instead of shouting "Eureka!" (wherever the hell that came from… Archimedes?), I yelled "AHA!" and there it was… To hell with the *Populo*! Sure, I had always wanted my thesis to be related to underwater archaeology, but damn, now I'd found plenty of inspiration in the Canaveral research, and an overview and assessment of archaeological (and ethnohistorical) data for a defined geographic area was a more than acceptable topic for a thesis, since what you were positing in fact was why that particular area was significant in human history. Jumping out of bed, I quickly wrote down what needed to be done. I'd need to talk to Pete first, and make sure that he'd let me use the research I'd already garnered at taxpayer's expense to turn to my advantage. Then I'd have to figure out how to approach Maryann about switching thesis topics. It's still meant a lot of hard work, but at least it was do-able, whereas the *Populo* shipwreck thesis was (dare I say it?) dead in the water. I was energized and couldn't wait for morning to come. When it did I made a beeline for Pete's office.

He sat there puffing his pipe, listened to my argument, and was surprisingly supportive. He told me that I'd have to re-work the Overview and Assessment, which was primarily a management document for the Park Service, to whatever form the Anthropology Department, and Maryann specifically, required. But he also reassured me that this is why SEAC had been established at Florida State in the first place: to take advantage of the University in furthering higher education as well as to utilize its resources. Also, a large number of Masters theses had once been generated over the years as a result of this cooperative arrangement with the Park Service, although the number had fallen off critically in the past decade, so he was glad to see the opportunity of it being realized once again. I asked if he'd sit on my Committee and he said he'd be happy to. He also suggested that I talk to the Chair of the Anthropology Department, Dr. Dailey, before talking to Michelle. Which I did. I got the impression that Pete had already talked with him before I got there, because Dailey was neither surprised nor enthusiastic, but that may just have been his demeanor, since he always maintained an attitude of detached attentiveness. What's one more graduate student changing his thesis topic? Other than listening and agreeing to sit on my Committee, he only warned me that I might have trouble dealing with Dr. Maryann. When I went to her, however, it went rather smoothly. I explained what I wanted to do: drop the *Populo*, and that I wanted to use the Overview and Assessment that I'd been working on for Canaveral, but that I'd take out all the management crap, beef it up with more of the ethnohistorical background material, and continue to concentrate on the archaeological aspects. She told me to write a new prospectus, and that she had no objections. Congratulating myself on this stroke of ingenuity, I thought, that went well; this is now going to be a smooth ride. I couldn't have been more wrong.

About this time a couple of very interesting things occurred. First of all, there was the rumor of George's replacement. Who was going to replace him at SEAC? After a month or so, we found out that the Chief Archaeologist for the National Park Service, the top dog in our profession (in the country), Buddy Kale, who had once lived in Tallahassee, had gotten in some hot water in Washington D.C. between his drinking and philandering. Apparently, he made the wrong pass at a very high-ranking (and no doubt, good-looking) professional woman who had very strong feminist tendencies, and she wouldn't (couldn't) be talked out of pursuing justice. He eventually had to resign that singular post, but was given the choice of where would he like to go. Home, he said, to Tallahassee, where he could still be a big fish in a little pond. He also got to keep the base salary and benefits he'd had in Washington, but now SEAC had to foot the bill. Buddy was a ramrod-straight and deep-throated sun-wrinkled old Marine, who, even though he wasn't big, had been an MP at one time. Tough but brilliant, he'd earned his archaeological creds by writing a book on Cherokee prehistory, and directing some of the largest river and reservoir projects ever undertaken in the United States on the Big Tombigbee River. He was down to earth, friendly, and knew his stuff. At first, we became fairly familiar friends. Later, it changed rather drastically.

St. Croix Calling

Then we got a visit from John Hardinger, who had once been the go-to guy for big projects here at SEAC, but had been promoted to the Regional Office in Atlanta as the head of the "External Program," coincidentally (?), the position held by Buddy before he had gone to Washington. The external program was in charge of handling anything in the Region that involved coordinating archaeological projects between the National Park Service and any outside agency, such as Departments of Defense, Army, Navy, etc. or various State programs, or any other Government-agency contractual (that is, "money-making") agreements. It was pretty powerful, because of the money it brought in to the Region, which was then generally divided up rather preferentially by the suits in the offices in Atlanta. So John, who had previously worked for Pete, was now at his same level. I was called in to Pete's office and there was John, whom I had known from his working at SEAC before, and who I always liked. Apparently they had already talked this over, and now it was just a matter of letting me know. How would I like to go to the Virgin Islands? (What? Now that I've *finished* the Overview and Assessment, you want me to go!?) There was a new park that had been created on St. Croix, and it was one of a handful of co-managed parks in the entire system, to be managed in coordination with the local Virgin Islands Government, which is why the external program was called in. This was at Salt River Bay, the only place in U.S. territory where it was recorded that Columbus had ever landed, on his second voyage in 1493. Everybody was gearing up for the celebration of the 500-year Quincentennial in 1992, and so money had been appropriated by Congress to go look at the "Columbus Landing Site." Well, Columbus himself never stepped off the ship; but he had sent his men ashore presumably to look for fresh water at the source of this obvious riverine estuary. His men had a fracas with the local Indian population with a few casualties on both sides, and thus began the Spanish hegemony of the Americas that resulted in the decimation of the Native Americans. (But we're not going there.) Among other things, the money was going to pay for an underwater survey of the natural harbor and part of the offshore submerged lands, to see whether there was anything that might be tied to Columbus's visit. Since I was now the Virgin Islands guy by virtue of the Overview and Assessment that Hammersten and I had finally finished, AND I was one of the only two NPS-certified ("blue card") divers at SEAC, they needed me to lend a hand. The Park Service's Submerged Cultural Resources Unit (SCRU), based out of Santa Fe, New Mexico—go figure, only the Government would put the underwater specialists in the middle of the desert— was going to carry out the work, but since the money was being funneled through the Southeast Regional Office, they wanted someone of their own to keep an eye on the operations. John was going to go down for a couple of days as they set up and started operations, but since he didn't dive, they wanted me to go and act as the Southeast Regional representative when he left.

I flew down one long day from Tallahassee, to Miami, to Puerto Rico, to St. Croix, and arrived in the evening at the very small Alexander Hamilton Airport, as it was known then. There was a tall black man with one of those hand-drawn signs saying "Brewer" on it and I found out it was the rental car company driver, who would drive me to the Farleigh Dickinson University Marine Lab housing at Salt River Bay on the other side of the island. He grabbed my bag, tossed it in the back of the car, and I was fascinated by the speed at which he drove that night, unerringly twisting and turning down unmarked and unlit byways, all on the left-hand (and therefore, to me, the wrong) side of the road. We got there in about twenty or thirty minutes. When he got out of the car, he handed me the keys and said, "Doan fogget, mon, you gotto get de boss in two hours." I said "What!?" "De boss-man, Hahrd-Ringer, you got to gettim." "I can't drive to the airport," I choked, "I don't even know how we got here… and it's dark… and driving on the left…" He smiled and said, "You be fine. Stay on de left," and walked over, got in a car already parked there, and drove off. I knocked on a door with a light on, and some student pointed up a set of wooden stairs and said that was where we were staying. So I went on up, turned on the lights, and threw down my bags. I was the first one to arrive. Well, if I got to get Hardinger at the airport, I better leave now, since I'm going to have to learn to drive on the left-hand side, and find the airport on the other side of the island …in the dark. And it took me all of an hour and a half, horns beeping at me, lights flashing, stopping and asking for directions, and then tenuously negotiating each and every intersection to get there. When I did I was a nervous wreck. Hardinger came down jauntily off the plane ramp, and when he got to me I handed him the keys and said "You're driving." We got back to the dorm in good time, and John pulled out a bottle of rum he'd gotten in Puerto Rico. This led to a discussion of the merits of various Caribbean liquors, all rum. Since we had the next day off, and the SCRU crew wasn't expected in until the day after, there was only one way to settle it. In the morning we went shopping, and besides foodstuffs, we each bought three bottles of our favorite rums, being sure not to duplicate the same. That afternoon we carried out a blind taste-test of the different island varieties. To my own surprise, my favorite was Brugal *Añejo*, out of the Dominican Republic, even though I'd always claimed that *Mount Gay Eclipse Rum* from the Barbados was the most superior. But for standard drinking rum, you still can't beat *Cruzan* from St. Croix. I don't remember which one John insisted was the best; in fact, after our several different trials, I don't remember much of that afternoon.

The next day SCRU arrived: Harry Murray, Toni Carrell, and Jim Sinclair, maybe some other guy, with all their equipment packed in heavy waterproof cases. I knew Harry but had not met Toni before, a strong, beautiful and hard-headed woman. Jim was just a big galoot to me, nice and calm. After they had gotten settled I walked into the dorm room to find all my stuff tossed up on the upper bunk, even though I'd already slept in the lower one two nights in a row, Harry's stuff on the bottom. I asked him what was going on, and he said he was too big to crawl up onto the upper bunk every night, so he'd moved my stuff. Well, that was true; he was a big man, bordering on heavy-set, with long brown hair and a beard, whereas I was still fairly small, average, and nimble back then, and it didn't make any sense for him to try to climb up there. Still, it would have been nice to ask, or at least talk about it, but then Harry was always a bit of a bully (if you let him get away with it, which I did that time in the spirit of cooperation). Any spirit of cooperation, however, was on my side only. Oh, they were extremely pleasant while John was there, explicitly explaining to him their research design, plan of operations, and expectations, but then they also knew John was exiting the scene soon. And the next day as I took him to the airport, John impressed upon me again that I was the Regional Representative for the Southeast, and that I had all the authority that he did, and don't let them get away with any shit. At the same time, it was important to get the work done, and in a timely manner, under budget. If there were any problems, I should call him. Then, just before he got on the plane, John goes, "Oh shit!" "What?" "I forgot something," he says, "I need you to do me favor." Then he goes on, "You know that little reggae music store in Christiansted?" "Yeah," I told him "of course, everyone knows where it is, it's the only one." "Well, I promised a friend that I'd get a record for him there. It's a comedy record put out by some Jamaican band… it's called *Chop Up De White Man, and Put 'Im in Da Stew*." "WHAT!?" I sputtered. And he said it again… "It's a joke record, very popular, but you can only get it down here." Then I pushed him… "You're kidding." He looked at me with some regret, "No, I just forgot to do it while we were in town— Look, I can give you some money—would you get it and send it to me?" "Well, yeah, I suppose… what was the name of it again?" *"Chop Up De White Man, and Put 'Im in Da Stew."* "All right…" I whispered, "No, I don't need any money… who's the band who did it again?" "I forget…," he said, "just send it to the office. Thanks, I appreciate it…" and off he walked onto the tarmac.

The next morning it was time to start the survey. The crew of SCRU began plotting lines on a large map where they were going to set up their transits so they could track a boat dragging the magnetometer. Once they got some magnetic anomaly hits, then later they'd dive and discover what they were. I thought this was a little odd, since anything doing with Columbus would be outside the bay, his ships never having come in. There was no record of him having to cut his anchor cables, so what did they expect to find? Salt River Bay had been a marina and a hurricane hole for twenty years or more, so yeah, there'd be plenty of junk and modern wrecks on the bottom. Maybe you'd find an historic wreck from the English/French/Spanish/Danish occupation of the island, but it was a relatively shallow bay, and with the relatively clear water any wreck would have been salvaged immediately back in the day. I suppose it didn't matter, the place had to be surveyed eventually. I tried talking to Harry and Toni about what role they wanted me to play in the survey, expecting to be one of the anomaly investigators, since they were obviously in charge of the mag survey. But they didn't have any plan, or not one they were going to tell me. I was going to have to fend for myself. Okay, I figured, I can handle this. I took out one of the small outboards and explored the bay (actually Salt River Bay is composed of the waters from two smaller bays to the south, Triton Bay on the east, and Sugar Bay on the west). I was particularly fascinated by Sugar Bay, where Columbus's men in a longboat presumably went looking for fresh water. It had mangroves that were forty feet high (before Hurricanes Hugo and Marilyn), something I'd never seen in Florida. I became convinced that if there was something to discover, it would be found along the shoreline. Since they were preoccupied with the mag survey, which couldn't go into the shallow shore waters anyway, and they'd made it clear there was no place for my participating with them, I put together a small crew and told them that we'd be surveying the shoreline and shallow shore waters surrounding the bays. Good, that'll keep me busy and out of their hair they figured, even giving me one of their extra divers. The next day though, out of nowhere (probably Harry), Toni tells me that I need to pass their (SCRU) swim and diving standards test. Now, wait a minute, I protested, I'm already a National Park Service blue-card diver, trained under the Academic Diving Program at FSU and been diving for years, I don't need no stinkin' swim test. Oh, these aren't the regular NPS standards, these are SCRU's standards. Okay, now my Irish was up, fine, you dish it out, and I'll eat it up. There was a large pool at the house next door, owned by some rich dentist who was absent six months out of the year but allowed the Marine Lab students to use it when he wasn't there. We went over there and after having me swim a hundred laps, then tread water for fifteen minutes, then five more without using my hands, then diving and retrieving a cinder block (that I had to first gently set on the bottom so as not to scratch the pool), and doing some ditch-and-don with the scuba equipment, it became obvious to Toni that I could swim as well as she could, probably better. When she couldn't make up anything else for me to do, she called it, and then (like I said, she was a looker) I asked her to come on in and enjoy the water for some recreational swimming. She left me there treading water.

Lend a Hand
A day later, the Chief of SCRU, Dan Lenihan, flew in from Santa Fe. Dan is a small, thin, almost gaunt individual, with ex-hippie frizzy hair, an intent stare and a quick mind. I thought he was brilliant, but when I once expressed this to my bosses at SEAC later that year they looked at me like I was nuts. Nonetheless, I liked Dan; he was down-to-earth and enjoyed cutting through the bureaucracy and getting to the root of a problem. For instance, he was not happy to hear about my having been put through the paces by Toni, knowing from my reputation it was totally unnecessary, and insulting to boot. Then we all had to go through a quick physical examination by the doctor at the Farleigh Dickinson Marine Lab, the renowned Dr. William Fife, so that we could use their dive equipment; everyone passed easily except Dan. He had some sort of inverted sternum, which looked like his chest had caved in, and apparently it was congenital, he'd had it his entire life. The doctor was, if not shocked, then seriously concerned, because it meant he had a considerably reduced lung capacity. As a result, he refused to sign off on him. But Dan had been diving his entire adult life and here he was, the Chief of the Underwater Cultural Resources Section of the United States National Park Service! Apparently, he'd either convinced or cajoled doctors in the States that it wasn't a serious condition (although it looked horrible), and in fact, he was actually the guy who authorized other NPS divers by issuing blue cards out West; but here, under the purview of a by-the-book University diving officer, he was not going to be cleared to dive. They argued and there was a lot of yelling and cursing, but in the end the doctor only allowed him to dive after Dan signed a waiver that he was doing so without the doctor's okay and he wouldn't hold either the doctor or Farleigh Dickinson University responsible for any incidents. I remember that day very well because we had then-Senator Lowell Weicker of Senate Watergate Committee-fame visiting, who went out diving with the Farleigh Dickinson crew after we all got to say hi and shake his hand. But Dan was a cool customer as they say and nothing ever really seemed to upset him for very long. He immediately wanted to go out diving and visit the abandoned site of the world-famous HydroLab, which was sitting in the underwater canyon just outside the bay. He needed a dive partner and I volunteered right away. There was at least one other guy with us, the Park Ranger boat captain. Before leaving, Toni suggested to Dan that he give me one final open-water dive checkout when we got out there (she was pushing it to the limit, looking for a way to keep me from diving). When we dropped over the side and got down about twenty feet, Dan told me (in sign language) to take off my mask and put it back on, a standard move. I did it and cleared it, he gave me the "okay" sign and that was the end of my final checkout. We headed over to the HydroLab.

HydroLab (sometimes written Hydrolab or Hydro-Lab) was an underwater research habitat, one of those Popular Science future experiments, funded in part by NOAA that was constructed in 1966 and then moved from the Bahamas to St. Croix in 1977. It could house four people, had a lab and bunks, and was slightly pressurized to keep out the water. It wasn't very big, the size of a small recreational vehicle, but had a large glass portal at one end that looked out into the underwater canyon. I'm thinking it was in water something like 45 feet deep, and you entered from the open water-hatch below. There were some 80 missions carried out while it was in St. Croix from 1977 until it was decommissioned in 1985. Here we were in 1988 and the thing had been empty for almost four years. Me, Dan, and the ranger took off our flippers underwater and slipped them by their straps over our wrists, then climbed up the ladder from below and came up inside the dark metal-walled rusty enclosure. We lifted our masks and cautiously took the regulators out of our mouths in case it was saturated with carbon dioxide. But it was only musty and wet and cool. Plenty of light came in the large round window at one end, which looked out over the flat sandy bottom out into the deep blue beyond. As our eyes got adjusted to the dark interior, at the other end we could see that it had been stripped clean, nothing that wasn't bolted to the walls remained. It was hard to imagine living in there for days, weeks, or even a month at a time, but I'll bet in its heyday it was comfortable with lights, a refrigerator, bunks, etc. with all kinds of fish hanging around looking for food from lab specimen scraps. At night there'd be phosphorescent shadows of larger fish cruising in and out of the dark, and blinking shrimp and plankton floating by instead of stars. Just imagine how very romantic it must have been at times for those few coed crews that ever stayed there. Just imagine.

I suppose we were some of the last people to ever go inside while it was still under water—the thing was hauled out and taken to the Smithsonian for conservation shortly thereafter, and now it's on display at NOAA headquarters in Silver Springs, Maryland. Well, we couldn't stay long and we headed back up to the boat, anchored nearby. Then Dan (like I said, smart) grabbed the opportunity, and had the ranger hook up the anchor line to one of the stern davits with maybe 80 feet of line. It was a regular Danforth anchor, the kind with a couple of triangular "wings" on either side of the stock, and he asked me if I'd ever used one for visual survey. Yes, I had, which took me back to my very first offshore dive with Academic Diving off of Ochlocknee Shoals almost ten years earlier. Well, we're going to drag you around the opening of the bay, he told me, and in a minute I was over the side and at the end of my rope, so to speak, gliding about fifteen feet below the surface over waves of bright white and yellow sand forty feet below, a view of a hundred feet of the bottom easily on either side, ringed in a dark blue horizon. A small lone fish here and there, a manta ray lying just under the sand thinking he couldn't be seen, once in awhile a couple of blue runners pacing me on either side, while the ranger captain made long broad S-shaped sweeps back and forth. I lasted about forty-five minutes before my air ran out, but it was marvelous. Only one shopping cart.

Law 'n Forcement

Dan got on the hook for about twenty minutes before his arms gave out. We had finally come up to the entrance of the bay, where I'd seen some suspicious rocks. The captain ran the boat up onto the beach and Dan and I went out in snorkel gear to check them out. Sure enough, although there were some other natural rock formations, out in the sand was a pile of round-rock rubble. It was a ballast drop, where sailing vessels would have a load of rock, usually round manhandable-sized river cobbles, as ballast, but before taking on a cargo that would replace the weight of the ballast, they would come in close to shore, and drop the stones overboard (sometimes ending up in two piles on either side of the ship) into shallow water, where they could easily reload them later on some other trip. We agreed that in and of themselves the stone piles were not archaeologically significant, other than their location, although once in awhile you could trace the stones to some particular river, say in Europe or Central South America. But I liked what Dan said about them, "It's like when paleontologists find petrified dinosaur shit; that means there are dinosaur bones around somewhere." We didn't find anything else, and it was getting late, so we headed back; but it was still a good day diving. In the morning, Dan took the others out to show them the ballast drop, they rinsed off in the dentist's pool, and then a few of us decided to go into Christiansted. Me, Dan, Harry, and some other SCRU technician piled into the back of a small pickup truck and headed into town. They were all in their NPS uniforms: grey shirts, green denim pants, badges, name tags, etc.—they loved wearing the Park Service stuff, whereas any other Service archaeologist I knew, myself included, were thankful we weren't required to wear them and could get by on jeans, boots, and a workshirt (although I must admit I always wanted one of those Smokey the Bear hats). We were coming down Company Street (which allowed two-way traffic back then), just getting to where the old market was, when we heard a commotion up ahead. Out of a side street to our left came running this young Rastafarian guy, dreadlocks bouncing and him yelling, "Help! Help! Dey tryin' to kill me!" and right behind him, maybe fifty feet, were a couple of the local police in their blue uniforms and hats, with a billy club each, running after him. We had to stop as they ran past, and Harry, Dan and the other guy started scrambling out the pickup. "Where are you going?" I asked. "We're going to help the cops," said Harry, "We're authorized to assist local law enforcement if they need us." Dan still had on his swimming trunks for the ride in, even though he had his grey uniform shirt on, and he jumped out the back of the truck with his pants in his left hand. "Aren't you coming?" they said. "Nope, sorry, I don't know what's going on here," I said, "and it looks like the cops already got a couple of bats in on the guy." They ran off down the street, and I can still see Dan trying to pull his pants on as they ran down and through the market area. By the time they got there, the cops had cornered the guy and beaten him senseless. When they got back to the truck and climbed in, we started down the street again and as we came abreast of the cops, they were just lifting the guy to his feet, blood streaming down his face and chest. I wonder what he did to deserve that (and they never asked).

Da Stewpid White Man

Once we got into town and parked, we split up. I didn't want to see those guys any more than they wanted to see me. I met an old friend who happened to be stationed at the fort there and he agreed to show me around. As we were walking around and he's filling me in on the history of the place, we came around a corner and there was the Reggae Record store! I told him I needed to go in there for a minute. We walked in, a little bell ringing over the door as we entered, reggae music blasting, incense burning, and maybe four or five customers inside flipping through the record stacks, the place festooned with Bob Marley flags and posters, not to mention Ras Tafari, the Lion of Judah, King Haile Selassie himself, more often than not with a crown and cape. I looked through the records for a little while, and while my friend was wandering about, I eased on up to the counter. There was a big, dark-skinned Rasta man in a plain white T-shirt by the register, plaited dreds hanging to his chest and beyond. He looked down at me, and nodded politely. I leaned over the counter and whispered, "Excuse me, I'm looking for a record, I hear it's very popular, it's called *Chop Up De White Man, Put Him in the Stew*, do you have a copy of that?" His eyes got very large, and he said "What you say?" I whispered again, "I hear it's a joke record, you know, a comedy song, called *Chop Up De White Man and Put Him in the Stew*, have you heard of it?" And then he reached under the counter and turned off the loud music. Everybody in the store looked up. "CHOP UP DE WHITE MAN AND PUT HIM IN DE STEW!!" he yelled, "ARE YOU CRAZY? I NEVER HEARD OF SUCH A 'TING!" Now everybody was looking at me. My friend moved over to me quickly, grabbed my arm, and said "What's the matter with you?" Now the guy behind the counter was coming around, his fist raised in the air, "CHOP UP DE WHITE MAN?! PUT 'IM IN DA STEW?! WHA' DE FUCK DASS'POSED T'MEAN?!!" My buddy said, "We gotta go," and pulled me out the door. When we were on the street, and no one came out behind us, he turned me around, looked me in the face, and said again, "What is the matter with you? Why did you do that?" I told him about Hardinger and him asking me to get this record for him, that he said it was a joke record, and you could only get it there… how he wanted me to send it to him… He looked at me shocked and stunned for a few seconds, then smiled, and then started laughing, "Well, looks like the joke's on you."

SCRU-ey

Just before we finished the survey, one evening we drove out to Frederiksted on the west end of the island, 'cause Harry and one of the other guys wanted to do a recreational night dive under the pier there, a huge monstrosity of concrete a quarter-mile long, built for nuclear subs that rarely ever came there. They had their gear all packed: tanks, weight belts, BCs, wetsuits, and lights. It must have been a beautiful dive, but Dan and I opted out, preferring to sit in a bar nearby and wait for them for a couple of hours. This was good for me, because I never got to talk much with Dan, especially under the influence, and there was something I wanted to ask him (or as the West Indians would say, something I wanted to "ax" him). There'd been bad blood between SEAC and SCRU for years, and there was definite tension between my boss Hardinger and the SCRU crew, not to mention their overt dissing of me. For the life of me though, I couldn't figure out why. Dan and Harry had both lived in Tallahassee and gone to FSU at one time or another, and I knew they had worked with George on the *Fowey* discovery back in 1980. Why was it so difficult to work together? When I asked George about it years before, all he could do was turn it into an *ad hominem*, and said, "because they're assholes, that's why." So I figured I'd wait until Dan had a few and then put it to him. Frederiksted, then and now, always reminds me of a town like you might find in a Clint Eastwood spaghetti western, except on the ocean. It's small and hot, with a dusty Main Street, no buildings over 2-stories, mostly wooden and cut coral-rock, lots of bars, and always a passel of surly ne'er-do-wells standing either under the awnings or in a doorway, smoking cigarettes and eyeballing you as you come into town. And if you walk a block or two off of Main Street, day or night, you're looking for trouble, and sure as hell, you'll find it. We picked a little saloon a block away, but in sight of the pier. Damn if it didn't have swinging saloon doors too. There might have been one other guy in there except the bartender. After a half –hour and a couple of drinks I had to ask, "So, Dan, what's the problem between SEAC and SCRU? I know there's something gone wrong, but to be honest, I don't know what it is. Will you tell me?" Immediately I knew I'd put him on the spot. He stiffened up, suddenly sober, and just stared at the bar. He must have thought I was sent to dig. After a short uncomfortable silence, he eased back down, realizing that I was serious, but he still wasn't going to play his cards. "Did it have anything to do with the Fowey business?" I asked, giving him his out. "Yeah, that's a big part of it," he said, "George never really gave us the credit due on that… and then shut us out of the 1983 work. I don't really want to talk about it." And that was that. Now slightly ill-at-ease, I tried to make some upbeat small talk, but I'd ruined whatever headway I'd made. It was time to go pick up the boys at the pier. Much later I found out that it really all had to do with the establishment of SCRU in the first place. Dan had first been a loyal follower of George's at SEAC and was assigned by Washington to carry out reservoir inundation studies to study the effects of creating dams and flooding at archaeological sites. This is where he recruited Harry (the macho muscle-diver; Dan being the brains), and the two of them used the opportunity of working with Washington to lobby successfully for a national underwater archaeological team. Apparently the counter-lobbying involved a lot of bad-mouthing and back-stabbing by both SEAC and FSU in general and George in particular (who had few if any friends left at the NPS in D.C.) that very nearly squelched the whole deal. This explained a lot.

In-TOXIC-ants

The survey was done, it was time to go home. The SCRU team hadn't quite finished their mag survey, and they didn't check all the anomalies, but my part was finished and I told them I'd write it up and send it to them to incorporate into the report. I called Hardinger to let him know how things had gone, that we were finished, and we were heading out. He felt that the reason they had not finished was on purpose and they were hoping to get more funding to go

311

back, but that this wasn't going to happen. And he said not to send my part of the report to them, but to send it to him directly, because he was putting the final report together himself out of his office. Then I told him I couldn't send the record about chopping up da white man because it didn't exist. "You didn't really go in there and ask them, did you?!" he laughed. "Well, yes, I did," I said, "You seemed so serious…" He still thinks it's the funniest thing he ever heard. (Again, if you tell anyone anything with a straight enough face…) The SCRU team left and I had an extra day so I went into Christiansted one more time. I visited all the usual hangouts, including the Club Comanche, which had a bar down by the water and the water mill (more on the Comanche later). Finally, I bought my six bottles of liquor that you're entitled to duty-free (and tax-free I might add), but they didn't have a box to put them in so I carried them back to the dorm at Salt River in a bag. You have to put them in a box for the flight home though, so I rooted around until I found a box that would do the trick. I packed it up and taped it, and then put my name and address on a big sticker on the top. The next day I was all packed, went to the airport and dropped off my rental car, checked my luggage and got on the plane, a nice window seat just ahead of the right wing. As we sat, I watched the luggage handlers loading the plane's belly. There went my luggage, up with the rest. But my liquor box didn't go up the ramp like everybody else's. Damn. Nope, that was it, no more luggage was coming out. Oh shit, I thought, it must have gotten swiped by some handler just like I'd heard happen a hundred times. Then, two minutes later, out from the terminal, a small tractor came pulling a flat car behind it, nothing on it but a single small cardboard box sitting square in the middle. It was my liquor box! I watched as the handlers talked to each other, pointing to the plane, talking, pointing… and then one of them strapped on a large pair of black rubber gloves, walked over to the box, and gingerly lifted it off the cart and walked slowly up the luggage ramp. As he did so, I was close enough to read on the side of the box "HAZARDOUS" in large white letters on a black background. As he turned I saw the old skull and crossbones on the other side over the word "POISON." I hadn't noticed when I found the box, I just wanted it to fit all six bottles of booze. So my liquor got very special handling, obviously stored in a special section in the hold. And yes, it arrived perfectly safe and sound. It was a box for some kitchen-floor cleaning fluid. Remember, this was thirteen years before September 11. Thinking back on the ensuing party upon returning home, and its aftereffects, maybe that cardboard box wasn't mismarked after all.

Back at SEAC, the Canaveral Overview and Assessment was finally in draft, so I quickly wrote up my part of the Salt River survey and sent it to Hardinger, who was very happy with it. Then hurricane Hugo hit that September and devastated St. Croix. It not only tore down all the telephone poles and tore palms right out of the ground, but what trees it didn't knock over, like the stately mahoganies that had been there hundreds of years, it denuded completely, not a leaf left. In some places along the hillsides, it ripped the grass right out of the ground. On the television, watching the news of it back in the safety of Tallahassee, I saw students I knew from the Farleigh Dickinson Marine Lab, following the reporters' boats, begging to be taken off the island. On the rooftops of grocery stores were the owners, with rifles, determined to keep their places from being looted. Soon they just gave up and let the people take what they could. Electricity was out for months. The roads were impassable. Windows were gone. Then the mosquitoes and biting black flies descended. People went mad. Enclaves of neighbors would gather in the evening to barbecue and smoke any food left in the freezers before it went bad, then they shared the canned goods. Clean water was a scarcity and large pots were constantly boiling. They bathed in the sea, and defecated in the woods. Years later, while sitting at a bar one day in Christiansted, I asked an older gentleman, a tough old guy, what it had been like the night and day of the storm. Within ten minutes, with tears streaming down his cheeks, he choked up and couldn't continue. I wish I hadn't asked.

So the Park Service sent out a couple of teams to assess the damage that Hugo may have wrought on any historic ruins or other park holdings. I was with one team that went to St. John, the smallest yet most beautiful and least developed of the U.S. Virgin Islands, with Beth Horvath, who was in charge, and my assistant, Susan Hammersten. We stayed at the condos out on Gallows Point, where pirates, recalcitrant slaves, and other ne'er-do-wells would be strung up in the old days at the entrance to the harbor as a warning to others, sort of a Public Service Announcement billboard for its time. The condos were great: when they made your bed they didn't put a chocolate on your pillow, they put a half-pint of Cruzan there instead. The work was pretty humdrum, except for one interesting occurrence. The Park Service was considering building some new hurricane-resistant housing down the side of a hill and wanted us to test the area ahead of time and make sure there weren't any historic features in the way. Well, there were, but they were terraced fields from back in the 1700s when St. John was the big sugar-producing center of the then-Danish West Indies. All overgrown now with brush, and a particularly nasty thorn bush called catch-and-keep (for obvious reasons), these terraced fields had been built by hand by the enslaved black workers, many of whom had come directly from Africa. Although the terraces were historic in and of themselves, with dry-laid rock walls and dirt piled up behind them, that wasn't going to save them when it came to building Park housing. We have a standard survey method of digging a shovel test every 20 meters, roughly 60 feet, so we went along these terraces and dug a hole every 60 feet along the hillside before dropping down to the next terrace level. A day or two into it and Beth lets out a hoot and we all gathered to see what she had found. On these agricultural terraces you usually only found one of three things: a hoe-head, a cane knife, or a machete blade; but this time Beth had found a pile, and I mean a pile, of prehistoric pottery: bowls, pots, cups, griddles. We tested to one side, then the other, nope, there wasn't any more. Well, it was strange enough to find prehistoric pottery on a hillside, much less in a terraced field that had probably been hoed, furrowed, and planted probably a hundred times. She gathered them all up in a dirty old bag and took them back to the condo. The real surprise came that evening when she started cleaning them. They had numbers on them! Uh oh… something's not right. Making a less than long story even less so, we came to figure out that the Park's previous curator lived just up the hill from where Beth fortuitously found these ceramics and he had tried to hide this pile of prehistoric ceramics that he didn't know what to do with, having lost the information as to where they came from. So, at some point, he crawled down the side of the hill and dug a small pit and buried them, only for Beth to put her shovel in the exact same spot some ten years later— I mean really, what are the odds that when digging a hole only once every 60 feet, that you would come down on top of this "hidden" cache? The tell-tale giveaway was the individual numbers written on each of the pieces, which corresponded to "provenience unknown" in the Park's catalog book. The guy was another Vietnam-crazy vet (with a steel plate in his head) who was transferred out West somewhere, and ended up shooting and killing a drunken Indian just off the reservation who had attacked him with a knife. Other than that, he was really a nice fellow. Strange, but true.

Black Ops

A couple of weeks later, once we were back in Tallahassee, I was told to go to Charleston, South Carolina, to assess Hugo's damage there as it had rolled up the Carolina coast. At SEAC they had just bought a new Government Jeep, all black, tinted windows, and all it said on the side was U.S. Government, with a red, white and blue shield. It was intimidating as hell, and I loved it. When I got to Charleston, the place was a disaster: plywood over windows, no traffic lights, trees cut up and piled on the roads, abandoned cars everywhere from having been submerged by storm waters. I found a grocery store that was open, even though it didn't have any electricity and bought some canned goods and water. As I was pulling out to get back on the road, I cut through a bank parking lot, but at the roadside, they had constructed a huge plywood sign right up to the road edge that said "Bank Open" with a big spray-painted red arrow pointing back at the bank. The trouble was, the makeshift sign completely blocked mine and anyone else's view to get out onto the road. It was dangerous as hell. After five full minutes and nearly getting clipped two or three times, and I mean really close calls, I lost all patience, threw the Jeep into reverse, and backed into the drive-in teller. "Get the manager!" I told the surprised teller. In a minute a tall sweaty balding bureaucrat came to the window. "How can I help you?" he said. I was hot too, and yelled at him, "You see this vehicle," pointing at the Gov't symbol on the side. He looked and nodded. "I'm with the Federal Government," I said, "and that goddamn sign out there is dangerous. Somebody's going to get killed. You get your people out there this afternoon, and move that sign back ten feet so people can see oncoming traffic. Do you understand?!" "Yes,sir," he said, assuming I was with FEMA, or worse, the FBI, in that black Jeep, "We'll take care of it right away." "See to it," I said and peeled out. A day later when I was coming back that way, I saw that the sign had been moved. Hey, I didn't lie; I *was* with the Federal Government. I just forgot to mention that I was just an archaeologist.

Spirits of Sumter

Fort Moultrie had held up pretty well other than being flooded, so other than a few photographs, there wasn't much to do there (Osceola and the *Patapsco* boys' tombs were fine). The park then asked me to go out and look at Fort Sumter. This was going to be exciting, because I'd never been out to Fort Sumter, the lonely historic sentinel out in the middle of Charleston harbor, of which I'd heard so much. Apparently the storm surge had forced the two huge metal doors at the entrance and then when the waters receded they'd scoured out a large hole from the interior parade ground. Everybody was busy with cleanup work on the mainland, so a boat was scheduled to just take me out and drop me off, to return a couple of hours later and pick me up. Which is what they did. I was dropped off at the dock at Ft. Sumter, and as the boat pulled off, I walked quietly up to the fort's main doors, huge, iron, and knocked askew off their hinges. I walked in, and there was a large washed-out hole in the middle of the fort, maybe forty feet long by twenty feet wide and seven or eight feet deep. And here I was, alone at Ft. Sumter, a still and hot October day—hot in the sun and cold in the shade—so I set to work right away, and pulling out my pack and trowel, and a small spade and my camera, tape, and notebook, just started taking pictures, taking measurements, cutting some profiles, and picking up whatever artifacts were laying out in the hole. There really wasn't much to deal with; it was obvious that when they'd put the fort back together post-Civil War, and especially after the Park Service had gotten hold of it, there was some major restorative work, including bringing in fill. Other than a few pieces of chinaware, all broken, and some bottle glass and a few nails, the only thing of interest was some colored wire, and lots of it, all modern. After awhile I figured out what the wire was. It was blasting wire. There must have been sections of the damaged fort that had to be taken down by blasting at some point before the restoration work. I took all the artifacts, laid them down on the concrete with a ruler, and took a picture of them before throwing them back in the hole. A few more notes and I was done. I spent the next hour crawling around the ruins, staring over at where the pummeling Confederate batteries of Charleston would have been, and communing with the ghosts of Sumter, both Union and Confederate, before they came to get me. When I got back to SEAC, and showed my draft report to Pete to review before we finalized it for the Regional office and Washington, after looking at the photos, he asked me, "What did you do with the artifacts?" "I threw them back in the hole," I said. He looked up at me from behind his desk and said, "Good Man!" They had no primary context, and thus no archaeological value and we both knew that every piece of junk you pick up ends up costing the Service hundreds if not thousands of dollars after analysis, conservation, cataloguing, and then storage in perpetuity. If you bring the stuff home, you got to deal with it. That FEMA money was now safely in SEAC's discretionary account.

Strongarm? No.

Then we got a rather odd call, from the State no less. They were coming over to have a meeting and Pete asked me to attend. The Director of the State's Department of Historical Resources, Jim Miller, and their chief conservator, Jamie Levy, came over to SEAC and at first we were going to meet in Pete's office, but it was too small, so we walked on down to the Curation Lab, where we could sit quietly at a large table and talk. Bob was there too. They had been approached by a middle-aged engineer out of the St. Johns Water Management District, who had an interesting story to tell. He and some friends had gotten it into their head to go treasure-hunting back in the early 70s. Everyone knew about coins being found periodically on the broad beaches both north and south of Canaveral, and metal detectors were just coming out that were sophisticated enough to actually produce results on small discrete objects and not nearly as cumbersome as those WWII surplus jobs. So this guy, Doug Armstrong, and a few of his friends decided to use their spare weekends and go out searching. Although this was the period of the "salvor wars" with the State, where offshore boaters with money and magnetometers and prop washes were making claims and signing leases for long stretches along the coast, little guys with metal detectors had no restrictions at the time. So they went up and down the coast wherever they could, covering miles of beaches and ducking into the hammocks wherever it was possible. They even took out small boats and hit the islands in Mosquito Lagoon and the Indian River. At one point they found some spikes, ships' spikes. Then they found a couple of coins. They returned to the spot again and again, spread out, and found more. Eventually the site petered out and they continued their hunt down the coast. Finally, after a year or so, they split up the loot and gave up the chase. Except for Doug. He knew there was something special about this one particular place where they had found most of their stuff. Being an engineer, he was somewhat knowledgeable about conservation of metals, and he taught himself even more. Also being naturally inquisitive and intelligent, he started delving into the history of the area. Some of the coins weren't Spanish; they were French, and they had dates on them, unlike the Spanish ones that were simply marked with the name of the reigning sovereign at the time they were struck. The French coins dated to 1550, 1552, 1554, etc., and unlike the Spanish coins which were practically pure silver, they were composed of an alloy of silver mixed with tin and bronze, which made them less valuable intrinsically, but nevertheless preserved them dramatically over the centuries. This alloy was called *billon*.

Armstrong realized that the French coins probably had some relationship with the short-lived attempts by the French to settle Florida in the 1560s. He knew that the area had come under the authority of the State as a state park in the 1960s, but didn't realize that it had been authorized as a national seashore by the Park Service in the mid 70s. So he had approached the State when he finally realized how important a find this had been. No other solid evidence of the French had been found anywhere else in Florida. The Department of State realized that they no longer had any authority in this matter, since it was now Federal lands, and that is why they had come to us. Well, at first there were questions of legality. Could we prosecute him? *Should* we prosecute him? If anything, the taking of material from then-State lands had occurred almost twenty years prior, surely beyond any statute of limitation. I had to jump in. Any talk of prosecution would make him shut up, when what we needed was information: who, what, when, where, why. He had come forward of his own volition, so he was already willing to cooperate; what we needed to do was to encourage his further cooperation, and to do so we had to guarantee him immunity. It was a simple enough thing to do. The State was actually out of the picture, and if there was no evidence that he had been in there metal–detecting and pilfering since the time it became a national park, then again there was no crime. I advised strongly that we nurture this relationship, catching more flies with sugar, if you will. The State was more than willing to hand the whole thing over to us... less headaches for them, and they were even willing to put it in writing that they had no interest in pursuing any former illegalities, if any ever existed. We all shook hands, Miller and Jamie left, and Bob, Pete and I reconvened in Pete's office. After asking Bob if he could spare me, since I was the Canaveral go-to guy for now, and finding out I was between assignments anyway, "All right, Brewer, it's all yours," Pete said, "You know what to do. Keep us posted." I told Pete that we should keep the Canaveral Overview and Assessment document in draft for now, until we knew how this thing was going to develop, and he agreed.

It's funny how things work out. My motive for keeping the Overview and Assessment on ice wasn't totally pure, but then chance, or in this case, serendipity, stepped in. I'd been working on my Canaveral/Mosquito Lagoon thesis pretty hard of late, and was closing in on a final draft that I could defend. Nine-tenths of it relied on the work I'd done on the Overview and Assessment, and my major professor, Maryann, had let it slip during one of our conferences that once the O&A was published... well, then I couldn't really usurp major portions of it (even though I'd written it), whereas if the thesis were accepted first, in that case I'd be free to then publish the O&A. It was a matter of the cart before the horse. I was going to have a hard time convincing Pete to sit on the Overview for my own selfish reasons, but here, with the Armstrong business breaking forth, it made perfect sense. I called the park first and let them know the situation and in a broad sense, the implications. Then I called Doug Armstrong. He was a very affable fellow on the phone, glad to hear from me, and offered his complete assistance. Then I called Dale Durham, the Regional Curator, who was an old friend and a great guy. A long, tall Texan who always wore cowboy boots, he'd worked with us on the artifacts recovered from the Fort Jeff and Biscayne shipwreck surveys of '82, '83, and '84. When I filled him in on the details, he was as excited as anyone, realizing that this was a serious opening to a long-smoldering historic mystery.

De François en La Floride
In a nutshell, in 1562 Jean Ribault (pron. Ri-bō) was sent by the child-King of France, Charles IX, to scope out and claim any territories in the New World that Spain wasn't particularly making good use of. The mainland of North America seemed ripe for the picking, Spain being preoccupied with the Caribbean and Mexico (Nueva España). When he got here, Ribault coasted up and down the shore, naming any rivers he encountered after those in France. He reconnoitered from Canaveral to the Carolinas, meeting the local Native Americans with good will, friendship, and lots of trade trinkets. He leaves two large stone columns bearing the royal arms of France, sort of a territorial marker, like Juan Ponce had done fifty years earlier: one at the St. Johns River (which he called the River May) and one at Port Royal (named by him) at present-day Parris Island in South Carolina. At Port Royal he also built a small earthwork fort, named it Charlesfort, after the kid-king, and left around two dozen men before sailing back to France, promising to return in a year with supplies and colonists. On that first voyage, he had as his lieutenant a young and able sailor, René Laudonnière. When they got back to France, Ribault got caught up in the religious civil wars between the Huguenots and Catholics, and being on the Protestant side ended up fleeing to England. There, he tried to persuade Queen Elizabeth to send ships (with him in charge) to supply the poor bastards left at Charlesfort. Somehow he pissed her off (probably just by being a snooty Frenchman) and she threw him into the Tower of London. By 1564, the Admiral of France, Coligny, convinced the young King Charles to send three relief ships to what they were now calling New France. They put Laudonnière in charge since he knew the waters

and Ribault was still locked up in England. Before Laudonnière gets to Florida, however, Spain has heard about the French and sends out a punitive expedition from Havana, headed by one Manrique de Rojas. Rojas doesn't find the stone column at the St. Johns, but does find the one at the now-abandoned fort at Port Royal (the Frenchmen there all took off in a small boat, except one young boy who decided to stay with the Indians). Rojas burns Charlesfort and swipes the stone column, figuring that's that. Laudonnière shows up less than a month later, finds Charlesfort burned, the men gone, and sets up at the St. Johns where the Indians had been particularly friendly in 1562, even to the point of having hidden the large stone column there so the Spanish wouldn't find it. He builds a new, bigger fort, and calls it Fort Caroline, again after the boy-King of France. Laudonnière unloads the supplies and sends the ships back to France, determined to make a foothold. He's there with roughly 130 men, 1 woman (his handservant) and a few boys. They generally get along with the natives, other than a few misunderstandings and a skirmish or two, but after a year, with food dwindling, mutinies afoot, and no indication of resupply, he decides to build a boat and make for France. They're just about to launch when word comes that Jean Ribault, freed from prison and now commanding seven ships to re-supply Laudonnière, has been spotted ambling up the coast. (Ribault had actually landed at Canaveral two weeks earlier and slowly meandered up the coast, taking two weeks lackadaisically "exploring" to get to the St. Johns—a trip that could have been made in a day or two. Apparently he wasn't all that worried about his countrymen.) Laudonnière and his men are ecstatic, although sickly and at the end of their rope, and Ribault tells him that he has been directed to "take command," much to the dismay of Laudonnière, who had done all the real work so far. Ribault hadn't even started unloading the supplies when another fleet appears over the horizon, that of Pedro Menéndez de Avilés, a particularly ruthless Spanish captain, now commissioned as the *Adelantado*, or royal governor of Spanish Florida. King Phillip II of Spain ordered Menéndez to head off Ribault's relief fleet and remove the heretic French Lutheran (i.e., Huguenot) interlopers. A few shots are fired between the fleets, when Menéndez, applying the better part of valor, discretion, decides to put in at the next major port south, that of St. Augustine, and build his own palisaded fort and get his supplies and arms off the ships. This is the founding of St. Augustine and the reason it is the oldest continually-inhabited city in the present United States.

Meanwhile back at Ft. Caroline, less than forty miles away, Ribault, having assumed command, and against all good advice, decides to up-anchor with four large ships and go after Menéndez before he can get too well-established. He loads what able soldiers remain of Laudonnière's and heads south, leaving sick Laudonnière in charge of maybe two dozen old men, a few boys, and the sick and wounded. Immediately a storm comes up, and not just any storm, since it is mid-September. Just as Ribault gets to the mouth of the river at St. Augustine, a violent hurricane strikes and over the next day and a half sends his ships down the coast, scattering and wrecking them on the long sandy beaches from Daytona to Canaveral. Menéndez, pursuing the advantage immediately after the storm subsided, marches his men through the swamps north of St. Augustine and attacks Fort Caroline. Laudonnière and a few others clamber over the fort's walls and escape by dropping into the St. Johns and hiding in the reeds along its edge. They finally make their way to one of the ships that had been left behind, in safe harbor, and commanded by Ribault's son, Jacques. With the fort lost, and the fleet obviously wrecked, they head back to France. Menéndez kills everyone he can get his hands on except one or two as prisoner-witnesses, cleans the place up a little, renames it San Mateo, and leaves a skeleton crew to "hold down the fort"; then he returns to St. Augustine.

A week later, some friendly Indians come and tell Menéndez that there's a bunch of straggling French shipwreck survivors at the inlet south of St. Augustine looking for a way to get across. He marches down with an armed company to check it out, and sure enough, on the other side of the waterway, several dozen French soldiers and some noblemen are encamped. A flag of truce, and he sends for a boat to bring a few of the captains over so they can parlay. Give us free access past St. Augustine, maybe a little food, so we can get back to Ft. Caroline, and we'll see to it that you get a big ransom, they offer. Ft. Caroline's been conquered, Menéndez tells them, it is now Ft. San Mateo. They don't believe him, so he brings out one of the prisoner-witnesses to corroborate the story. "Oh Shit!" I imagine the Frenchmen think at this point (only I guess in their case it would be "Oh Mierde!") Menéndez counteroffers, I will bring you all over to this side, but you are my prisoners and only God can tell me what to do with you then. The French captains went back and convinced their men that they had no choice. They were ferried over to Menéndez, who had their hands bound, "since there are so many of you and so few of us." Once they'd all been brought across, he gave them an ultimatum: renounce your Lutheran hereticism, convert to Catholicism, and your lives will be spared. They refused, and after being led across the dunes in groups of tens, they were slaughtered by sword, lance, and crossbow. He spared a couple of musicians, being less concerned about their spiritual leanings than their talent to entertain his troops. Two weeks later, the entire scene was repeated: an Indian tells him of straggling survivors at the inlet, flag of truce, send over a boat, parlays, and slaughter. This time, however, more than half the Frenchmen, figuring out what was going on, said the hell with this, we're going back south. Of those murdered on this occasion, Menéndez happened to nab the famous Captain Jean Ribault himself, and to prove it, had his singular and notably well-trimmed red beard scalped from his chinny-chin-chin. When it was finished, over two hundred and twenty men, hands tied, outside the bounds of war, had been killed under a flag of truce, in the name of the True Faith, to preserve the hegemony of Spain, and with the blessing of the Holy Roman Emperor. Thus, the place has been called "Matanzas" (Massacres) ever since.

While the corpses of those unfortunate Frenchmen were being picked clean by the crabs and crows, another month passes and Menéndez once again hears from the Indians, some of whom are now friendly spies by promise of reward. There are almost 200 Frenchmen still afoot, down near Canaveral near the wreck of the flagship, the *Trinité*, behind a makeshift breastwork of sand and cannon, building a boat from the wreckage. Enough already, Menéndez decides to mount one last punitive expedition to wipe out the remaining French. He wasted no time and with his main contingent of foot-soldiers, accompanied offshore by three armed vessels, he marched down the beaches from St. Augustine to Canaveral, covering the distance in less than four days. When he was spotted coming over the dunes as he approached the earthen fort, the French all ran in, prepared to fight, knowing what had happened to their countrymen. Menéndez had his trumpets sounded and sent in a flag of truce with the sworn oath that he would not murder those who surrendered but would do all in his power to see to their return to France. By now, hunger-stricken, thirsty, demoralized and desperate, 150 Frenchmen decided to surrender. One of the captains, and twenty-two of his men, said no, they did not trust the lying Spaniard, and they would "rather be devoured by the Indians." After destroying the fort, burning the wreck and the boat being built, and rolling the large brass cannons into a nearby creek, the Spaniards marched the 150 who surrendered south to present-day Hobe Sound where they were placed under the watchful eye of a local Indian chief, again, friendly to the Spanish by way of reward. Menéndez, then taking to his ships, went south to Havana, planning to get supplies and return to St. Augustine. Once in Cuba though, he was ordered back to Spain to help command the Armada that was being built for the invasion of England. It was two years before he could return. *Of the French captain north of Canaveral, and his twenty-two men who took to the swamps and decided to take their chances with the Indians, nothing more was ever heard* (emphasis supplied).

Helluva story. It'll make a great mini-series someday, once they can work in the love interest (there *is* the maidservant to Laudonniére, whom he was accused of diddling, and in the expanded history, there's more than one beautiful Indian princess, but in all the extensive eyewitness accounts no real romance to speak of). In any case, this is what we were faced with: it looked more than likely that from the items described as being found by Armstrong and his buddies, there was a good chance that we were very near some historic dead Frenchmen; at least there was more than the hint of it, which is closer than anyone had ever gotten before. Yeah, the Park Service had spent hundreds of thousands, maybe a million or two, up in Jacksonville, on the banks of the St. Johns, building a one-third size replica of what they thought Ft. Caroline looked like, near where they thought it had existed. They'd even built a replacement stone column for the one that had been lost, setting it up on top of the landmark St. Johns Bluff. Why, they'd even sponsored an archaeological survey by the famous Charles Fairbanks out of the University of Florida when they were planning all this. But nowhere in Florida had the first piece of French material ever been uncovered. (Some guy once found a ring on the banks of the St. Johns that he claimed was from the French encounter, but there was no proof of that, and it's still considered a questionable find.) But here was material undoubtedly from the shipwreck (or shipwrecks), the location of which was an even larger mystery, since no evidence of them had ever been seen, even though there'd been Spanish coins and wrecksites identified all up and down the Florida "treasure" coast for generations (all dating to the 1700s, however). Somewhere else along that stretch north of Canaveral in 1565 the four ships of Jean Ribault had wrecked when caught in a hurricane, after he had hastily gone after Pedro Menéndez de Avílés at St. Augustine. But where?

Dale and I made arrangements to go down to Canaveral and then visit Doug Armstrong at his home. I called Doug to arrange the meeting and asked if he'd mind if I videotaped it while Dale inventoried and looked at the collection. He said no problem. A week or so later, we arrived and finally met Doug face-to-face; he was a thin, graying, and wiry middle-aged man with short hair, large glasses, a plastic pocket protector, and a friendly handshake. It was obvious that he was glad that someone was finally taking notice of his collection. As he pulled out the pieces one by one, Dale and I were astonished at not only what they represented, but the shape they were in as well; it was evident that Doug was an extremely accomplished (if self-taught) conservator. He tenderly brought out each piece, explaining what he thought it meant, handing them each to Dale, who wore his curatorial white linen gloves, all while I videotaped the proceedings. After we'd looked at everything, and while it was all spread out on the table in front of us, I took a chance. I asked Doug if he'd be willing to loan the collection to the National Park Service on a short-term basis, so we could take it back to Tallahassee and do a detailed analysis. To both mine and Dale's surprise he said sure. Dale transferred the inventory to a pair of Park Service loan forms and Dale and Doug then both signed them. Then he gently packed it up for us and soon we were on our way. It was incredible really, since these were unique historical items, their value being (as the commercial goes) "priceless."

When we got back to Tallahassee, Dale and I had a quick showing for the staff before the collection was locked up in the Curatorial Lab inside its huge and heavy fireproof safe. I spent the next few weeks sitting at a lab table with a notebook and magnifying lens, and running back and forth to the University Library. I quickly learned what a *douzain* was (the small French coins, the size of a quarter, that bore the name and emblem, the *ecu*, of Henry II of France, 1547-1559), what *billon* was composed of (silver and base metals), and how the ships' spikes had been re-worked (hot-forge fired with charcoal and a bellows, made cherry-red, and then cut with a cold chisel and hammer—think of Charlie Allnut and Rose on the *African Queen* when they had to fix the shaft and propeller). Other than Armstrong (and of course, Durham), the last person to touch these things before me was most likely a shipwrecked Frenchman hiding from the Spanish with the Indians 425 years earlier. As I sat in the quiet back lab alone and handled the items, learned their history, and felt the "vibes," I was transported through time to a shady hammock on the edge of Mosquito Lagoon, campfires smoldering, meat and fish being smoked in long strips over a *barbacoa*, birds flying overhead, mullet jumping, the sound of the pounding seashore faint in the distance while women sat in a circle stretching and scraping deer hide, children running through chasing each other or lying in hammocks slung between the palms, while tall tawny men in loincloths leaning on the bows as tall as themselves, black hair knotted atop their heads, stood watching intently as I sweated and cursed a blazing fire, encouraging the bellows-pumper to keep pressing, and tried to work a small piece of red-hot iron for their pleasure (and my keep). My fantasy continues when one of the young Indian maidens watching from the women's group smiles as I look up, wink, and say to her, in the only French I know, "Voulez-vous coucher avec moi?" and her smile broadens though she doesn't understand. (Hey, it was cold and lonely under the fluorescent lights in that old windowless concrete lab!) Once I was finished we made plans to return the collection, which meant I got to go right back to Canaveral, and this time the park and I would be taking Doug out on the Lagoon to show us where the site was. Meanwhile, copies of the collection report and videotape were requested by the NPS suits in the Regional office in Atlanta and soon there was a lot of buzz, which Dale had already gotten started when he got back to his office there. Before long, the money for a serious investigation of the Oyster Bay (Armstrong) Site was provided from Region. This was to be an in-depth survey, testing, and evaluation study and it was a big damn deal. Too big to leave to me. The investigation was to be headed by Beth Horvath, my very dear friend of the female gay persuasion, who was an ace archaeologist, a cute, tough, intelligent tomboy. I'd be her crew chief. This was all good, even though I'd done all the preliminary footwork, because, even though I was now 38 years old I still had not managed to snag my Master's degree. It was an acknowledged fact that, until you had your Masters, you had not yet met the National Park Director's standards for a "professional" archaeologist qualified to direct a Service-level large-scale investigation (even though I'd been doing it for years), especially one that would probably hit the news. I understood completely.

So, while Beth was preparing the project and its participants by boning up on the history, the artifacts, the park geography, etc., I turned my attention to finishing up the thesis I'd drafted, and turned it in to my committee. Then I pressed Maryann for a defense date. After some hemming and hawing and her dealing with that damn field school out at Patale, we settled on July 11, 1990. It was a Wednesday. As I recall, it was a cloudy overcast day, a harbinger of what was to come. I was in relatively good spirits, since I knew the subject better than anyone, if not a little nervous at the prospect of sitting across a table from your professors, all ready to quiz you and look for chinks in your argumentative armor. They'd each had a copy of the thesis for almost a month so I was sure they'd all read it. I'd been given back a draft that I had left with Dr. Maryann, and it had a few markups here and there: typos spotted, a question or comment or two, but nothing serious that couldn't be fixed rather quickly. No major issues or problems. One thing struck me as odd however; although it was over two hundred pages, she'd not made a single mark after page 85. Even I found some typos and a grammatical error or two after that. Had she just read right through them? Had she just stopped reading after that? I didn't know. They had me wait in the front office of the Anthropology Department while they got together in the small conference room in the back. Besides Maryann, whose office was right across from the conference room, there was Dr. Dailey, the chairman of the Department at the time and a good friend, if a bit too formal sometimes, especially in matters like these; then there was Pete, the Chief of SEAC, who had sat in on many graduate theses defenses in the past, but not in the past five years or so; and finally, there was Dr. Glen Doran, whom I had asked at the last minute a month or two earlier to sit on the Committee, since he was yet another archaeologist, and this was primarily an archaeological thesis. Only three committee members were required, but I thought it would be good to have a fourth. Some of the other students thought I was crazy by possibly upping the odds against myself. No matter, I felt good.

Remember the Alamo?

After ten minutes or so, they called me in. They had a seat waiting for me, at the head of the table, with the three men down on the right, and Dr. Maryann alone on my left. I would have set it up differently, but that's the way it was. Dr. Dailey, as chairman, took control of the proceedings and stated bluntly that they were convened at the behest of Dr. Maryann to hear the defense of the thesis presented by Mr. David Brewer, entitled *An Archeological and Ethnohistorical Overview and Assessment of Mosquito Lagoon at Canaveral National Seashore, Florida* (like I said, sometimes a little too formal, for my taste anyway). Then he opened up the questioning himself by asking "So, what is an overview and assessment?" I won't belabor the reader with the details of the questions asked and the answers given; let's just say it was standard stuff, until… About half an hour into it, the men are still intermittently asking questions but quickly coming up dry. Maryann has only asked one or two, and there are long pauses between, when, all of a sudden, she says, "I can't go on with this. I'm sorry, but this is a blatant piece of plagiarism!" "WHAT?!" I said. The men on the right stiffened in their chairs. "What do you mean, it's a blatant piece of plagiarism?" I asked again. Finally, she directed her attention to me instead of down at the table. "There are huge sections that have been taken verbatim out of the Canaveral Overview and Assessment that you've been writing for the Park Service," she said, "and that's work that you're being paid for!" "That's right," I said, "and I told you that I was going to use the O&A as the basis for the thesis, and I was going to remove the management stuff, and beef up the rest with the ethnohistorical information. You said that would be fine." "But I didn't say that you could take large sections out of it, word for word," she countered. "But I WROTE IT," I said. "Then it's blatant self-plagiarism," she countered again. Silence. I was dumbfounded, taken completely by surprise. Dr. Dailey finally broke in, "First of all, I've never heard of self-plagiarism; second, people use work here at the University all the time as the basis for their graduate work, and finally, Michelle, as the major professor, you're the one who called for this defense. If you had any reservations regarding this thesis, they should have been addressed long before coming here." More silence. "Now wait a minute," I said, talking directly to her now, "I did talk with you about this, and you told me that if the thesis were done first, I wouldn't have any problem. The Overview and Assessment for the Park Service is in draft, and it looks like it's going to stay that way for awhile. Am I correct, Mr. Faust?," now addressing Pete. "That's the situation at present," he said. More silence. Michelle cut the quiet with "and another thing, I don't believe that Pete Faust is qualified to sit on this committee." "What?!" Dr. Dailey was getting hot now, "Pete's been sitting on committees since before you came to the University. The Southeast Archeological Center is a recognized partner in the Anthropology Department, and he's got graduate faculty status as you are well aware." "But he's David's boss," she began to waver. "All the more reason to have him on the committee," said Dailey, "if there were an objection from SEAC, he'd be the best one to express it." Now, a long delay, at least a full minute of silence, with Glen setting his head on the table on top of his folded hands, the rest of us just staring forward, looking at nothing in particular. Finally, I said, "Well, if there are no further questions, then I think I'll wait outside for your decision," and I stood up, pushing back my chair. "Wait a minute," Dr. Dailey interjected, then turning to Michelle, said "Dr. Maryann, it appears that you were not prepared to carry out this defense today. As far as Pete Faust being qualified to sit on the committee is concerned, I think that is nothing but a red herring. In fact, considering how this has gone today, I think you owe Mr. Brewer an apology." Now *she* was shocked.

"NO," I cut in, "no apology is necessary. These are issues that are out of my hands. You guys need to resolve them. Like I said, I'll be outside, waiting on your decision," and I picked up my stuff, turned and walked out, closing the door gently behind me. Then I went out into the hall in Bellamy outside the Department office and sat on a little black and backless settee they had there and thought about it all, stunned and amazed.

I was there for more than half an hour, but that was good. It gave me time to calm down and relax. I also figured that, considering the way things had ended, the longer they took the better it was for me—apparently there was a lot to talk about. Finally, the Department door opened up and out came Michelle, who came over and sat next to me. "Well, David, you know I want to help you get this done, so you can get your degree…" (What?! Now she was being sweet as sugar, after having just tried to cut my balls off. Well, okay then.) "There's just a few problems we have to work on, but if you're willing to make a few changes here and there, I think we'll be able to put this thing to bed. We've decided to reconvene tomorrow morning, if that's all right, and then I'll help you to make the changes necessary. Now, tonight I want you to write up what you think needs to be done to finish this, and I will too, and tomorrow we can compare lists with the committee and make this happen. I'll see you tomorrow at 9." After she left, I got up, walked across Tennessee Street to my favorite watering hole, Poor Paul's, and got a snootful. When I got home, I told Amy the whole story, and did the list in the morning.

The next morning I was there first, so I went right in to the conference room, and each of them came in one at a time. Dr. Dailey was first, and when he sat down, after the usual morning salutations, he said, "You know, in thirty years of teaching, I've never seen a thesis defense go like yesterday's, and this is only the second one that I ever remember that lasted more than one day." It was a somber affair, nobody smiling. He opened the proceedings formally once again, and took the lead, although it wasn't addressed to me. "I got a call from the Dean this morning, Michelle. He told me about your phone call to him yesterday afternoon, after we had left here. He suggested that this was an internal Department matter, and that we'd settle things here." Well, that was interesting. She had tried to go over the Chairman's head and take whatever case she had to the Dean, who said he didn't want any part of it. Then Dailey pulled out a piece of paper and said, "Here is a letter authorizing Richard Faust [Pete] to sit on graduate committees here in the Department, I got it out of the files. You can keep this copy. As far as the charge of self-plagiarism, I consider that a non-issue, and in fact, I think that Mr. Brewer's thesis is one of the better written pieces of work that has come through here in a long time. Now, please tell us what you and Mr. Brewer have resolved to do about getting this thing done." Whoo! I certainly had not expected that. Now *she* was on the hot seat, but calmly stated that we had talked and I had agreed to make whatever changes she required. I said this was true. Then Dailey said something to the effect that I might want to consider changing my committee and putting someone else in as my major professor. I said no, and stated that I was not going to go around Dr. Maryann, I was going to go through her. I looked over and Pete was looking at the ceiling, and Doran was looking into his lap. "Then we're finished here," said Dailey, and when he did I got up and thanked them all, picked up my stuff and walked out. When I got to my office, I took the copy of the thesis that Maryann had marked up to page 85 and threw it into the wastebasket.

Hurry Up and Wait

The next day I had to drive down to Florida City, Florida. There'd been a report of vandalism at the 1733 *Populo* shipwreck site and I was tagged to go down and evaluate it and make a report. I got to the hotel that night, went out to the park the next morning, and was taken to the wreck. A ranger and I dove on it and photographed it, and I documented a couple of places where the ballast stones had been moved around, but it was obvious that very little damage had been done. One more night and a drink or two at the White Horse bar in Homestead, and I headed back to Tallahassee the following day. Within a week I made an appointment to see Dr. Maryann and get started on the revisions. I figured if I hurried, I could graduate in August. She made me wait a week, and when I got to her office, she wanted me to fix any typos and grammatical errors (duh), and suggested that I should put back in some of the management issues that I had taken out (contrary to our original agreement). Then bring it back and we'd take a look. Well, that told me that she hadn't looked at it since, or even in the week before. Okay, I said, and went straight to work on it. A week later I tried to make another appointment, and this time she put me off for two weeks. Then when I got in, she didn't like the changes regarding the management issues (too technical). I could see where this was going. There was no way to make an August graduation now, so when I finally got another appointment (after the end of the semester hiatus and now into Fall), I took another tack. This time I took explicit notes, as verbatim as I could when we met. Then I marched back to my office and typed them up and e-mailed them to her, saying something to the effect, "As per our meeting today, [date], these are the changes that you have either recommended or required. If they are not correct or there are additional changes, please respond to this memo and let me know, otherwise I will proceed as directed." And I cc:'ed the email to the committee. Now I started to make progress. At least now I was no longer playing the Penelope to her academic odyssey, tying and untying the same old knots.

At the Southeast Archeological Center we were preparing for the Armstrong site testing project at Canaveral, which was to take place in November. In the Anthropology Department they'd given Dr. Grindal the chairmanship, since Dailey was sick of the headaches and wouldn't take it again. For the Fall semester I had to take more graduate thesis hours, which cost an arm and a leg, but I didn't care, I was moving forward. After a couple more meetings on the thesis, and the changes getting less and less substantive and more and more capricious, I decided that's it. I printed out the three copies for the Committee, and another for the University Library, as the Registrar required, 90 bucks worth, and the day we left for the field I put the copies in Maryann's mailbox with a memo saying that I'd finished making changes, and I was done. The crew from SEAC drove south and set up shop in a condo that Beth had rented for us in New Smyrna Beach. I followed in my own van later that day. The next morning we left a couple of the girls behind to set up house and go shopping, and the rest of us went out to the site, set up our datum point and grid, hacking our way through and clearing the undergrowth with our machetes. It was cold out on the edge of the Lagoon and thus, an exhilarating first day. When we got home the girls told me that Grindal had called and wanted me to call him back right away. When I did, he told me that Maryann had come into his office and raised hell, the argument being that she'd decide when the thesis was finished, not me, and I had a lot of nerve to just leave the copies to be signed. I explained my side, to which Grindal was sympathetic, but he wanted me to call Maryann at home and talk things out... he really didn't want to get in the middle of it, even though he understood my frustration, etc., etc. (They didn't call him the Prince of Peace for nothing.) So he gave me Michelle's home phone number (which I really didn't want to call, but he insisted). When I called she was curt and dismissive, and when I tried to talk she got loud and hung up on me. I expected all of that, except the hangup. That really torqued me. I was half-tempted to call her back and give her some shit, and then thought better of it. Hell, there was nothing I could do until we got back to Tallahassee anyway. It was just as well to let it go for now and concentrate on the project at hand. But I was still steamed. At the time, my buddy Nolin was then separated from his wife and living in a small upstairs apartment in New Smyrna, so I thought I'd go pay him a visit and cool off.

Rum and Just the Lash

I got in my van and headed across the large South Bridge from the beachside to the mainland across the Intracoastal, took a right and parked, since he was only a block away from the waterway. He wasn't home from work yet, but he had told me where the key was, and the liquor, so I went in and fixed myself a drink. When he finally got home, I'd already had a couple, and after a brief mutual commiseration, he of his separation and me of my major professor, we got down to drinking seriously. This was the night he introduced me to the Pogues, from an old second-hand tape that a friend had given him. I've been a Pogues fan ever since. The album was "Rum, Sodomy, and the Lash," reportedly the answer to the question once put to Winston Churchill, "What do you consider the greatest accomplishments of the Royal Navy?" (You've got to remember, Churchill was with the British *Army*.) Once we'd gotten properly soused, we stumbled up the large bridge nearby over the Intracoastal singing "Dat Ol' Man River," and "Molly Malone" at the top of our lungs and neither in tune nor in tandem. When we got back to his place, all my troubles had dissipated. Or so I'd thought. After resting awhile and drinking some water, although I thought I'd sleep on the couch until daylight, I stupidly felt good enough to drive the two miles to the condo, so I could be up with the rest of the crew in the morning. When I left, I went up over that same bridge and headed east down toward the beach. Then I saw a cop car pull out slowly from behind some shrubbery. I was the only vehicle on the road. He followed from a distance, and I watched in my rearview. I'd gotten a mile down the road and was just turning south onto A1A when he turned on his lights. I immediately pulled over into a real estate office parking lot, and had my papers ready when he got up to the window. "Do you know why I pulled you over?" he said. "Nope." "You were going 40 in a thirty-five mile an hour zone. And your tire touched the center line." (Where had I heard that before?) "Would you step out of the car, please," which I did. "Have you been drinking?" We'd been drinking cheap dark rum and he had to have been able to smell it on me. "Yessir, three drinks in the past three hours," I said, as if I'd been counting. (It was now almost midnight.) I took the initiative, "Look, officer, I'm an archaeologist with the National Park Service, and I'm working with the Park here, and I'm only a mile down the road at the Sea Woods…," hoping to nip this thing in the bud. But nooooo… "Tell you what," he said, "you pass a roadside test, I'll let you go on home." Well, he had me there, what was I going to say, "no?" "Okay," I said, "Let's go." He pulled a little worn pamphlet out of his back pocket, checked it with his flashlight, and then had me do dog tricks. The first one was arms out, eyes closed, touch your nose with the index finger on your right hand, then your left, returning your arms straight out. Okay, done. Then I had to walk a straight line heel-to-toe, ten steps out and back, again with arms out. Y'know, it's amazing what a powerful hormone adrenaline can be… I did it perfectly. Then, "Okay, just one more…" he said, obviously getting a little frustrated with me, "recite the alphabet." "Recite the alphabet?" I asked incredulously. (Hell, I'd just walked a straight line heel-to-toe, arms out, ten steps out and ten back. Try doing that completely sober sometime.) "Yes, recite the alphabet." Okay, this ought to be easy enough. I started, "A,B,C,D," etc. and, just as I'd been taught in school, "Q,R,S, and T,U,V… W, X, Y, and Z." (At least I had sense enough not to be a smart-ass and say, "now I've said my ABC's, tell me, aren't you proud of me," which, all by itself should have indicated I was sober enough to get home.) "Sorry," he said, "that's not correct." (!?!?!?) "What do you mean, that's not correct?" I said, offended. "You put an "N" between S and T, and another one between Y and Z." "No, I didn't" I said loudly now, "I put an "and" between them just like you just did." "Sorry," he said, "I didn't tell you to put an "and" in there." I looked at him and said, "Oh… now I see what's happening…" but he couldn't keep eye contact. "You want to move your car over to the side of the building?" he said, and when I got back, he already had the back door of the cop car opened for me.

First he took me to the New Smyrna police station, and asked me there if I'd submit to a breathalyzer test. "No," I said, "I've learned my lesson and I'm no longer cooperating with you in any way." After an hour or so, he said they were taking me up to Daytona and the Volusia County jail. Fine, I told them. By two o'clock I was able to lie down on a steel slab and catch some shuteye. In the morning I got out about 9 o'clock, and by 11 a couple of the crew members had driven up from New Smyrna to get me. They didn't ask, and I didn't offer any explanation. On the way home, I was happy to see that my van was still parked where I'd left it, and hadn't been towed away. Later, I called Nolin, who was slightly amused by my misadventure, and gave me the name of a great lawyer friend of his who specialized in this sort of stuff, and was considered by many to be one of the best. Luckily, the coming Monday was Veterans Day for us Fed workers and I made an appointment to see him then. His name was something like Smock, and he was jolly, friendly, and upbeat, with a wry sense of humor. After I told him what had happened and how I was working at Canaveral on the archaeological project, he said not to worry, he'd take care of everything. He wanted $200 up front, which I gave him, and another $200 when it was done. When I left, even I felt good about it. Coulda been worse. Three weeks later, the project is almost done, so I called Smock and he said meet him at the Magistrate's office (?) the next morning at 10. (I didn't even know they had magistrates any more, but apparently their like minor judges.) I show up and there's Smock, and he takes me into a small office with a pudgy little bald guy in a white short-sleeved shirt. After some small talk about archaeology, Canaveral National Seashore, and New Smyrna in general, the pudgy little man says, "Well, you're lucky to have Mr. Smock as your attorney, Mr. Brewer, he just happens to be a friend of mine," and he opened his desk drawer and pulled out my license, sliding it across the desk. "You're still going to be charged with the speeding ticket, and you'll have to pay that at the New Smyrna station. Like I said, you're very lucky." With that, Smock signaled me it was time to go, and we walked outside together. "I'll send you a check as soon as I get back to Tallahassee," I said. We shook hands, and that was the end of it. I was almost giddy at being very lucky indeed... until later that evening. I was lying in bed, just going to sleep around 11, when the phone rang. I knew it was Amy, because she would call late sometimes. I was sleeping on a cot in the loft, and as I ran down to answer the phone downstairs before it woke everyone up, someone had left a sweatshirt on the stairs, and I got my feet got caught up in it, fell down the (luckily) carpeted spiral staircase, head over ass, and upon landing at the bottom, slammed my big toe into the iron railing. There I was cradling the phone in my neck, and my foot in my lap, sobbing from the pain, when the lights all went on and the wakened crew all stood around me, laughing. The next day I had to go to the hospital and found out I'd cracked it good. "Sorry, there's nothing we can do except tape it to the next toe; it'll take about three weeks or a month to heal, depending on how much you stay off of it. Still, you're lucky you didn't break your neck falling down those stairs." Lucky indeed: lucky that even though karma may be a harsh master, at least it's not totally unforgiving.

Buddy and the Jest

Back in Tallahassee, it was time to get back to hammering out the thesis with Michelle. First of all, I had to let her cool down a bit, but then I started pressing for more conferences, more direction, and more finality, all of which was given begrudgingly in a passive-aggressive tug-of-war. Dr. Dailey was telling me again and again, "Drop her, get a new major professor, and you'll be out of here this semester." His advice was solid, and well-intentioned, and he was right. But by now, having gone this far, I stubbornly stuck to my guns, even as another semester passed with little or no basic changes to the thesis from a year prior. Meanwhile, Buddy Kale, the former Chief Archaeologist of the whole Park Service, had come on board, tucked away in a little office adjacent to where George had been. In those days he was still drinking sporadically, but had cut back considerably, and still smoking, and because he was friendly and well-known I was happy to act as his assistant on a couple of projects. One was the search for the site of the Battle of Thom's Creek, an early 18th century British-Spanish confrontation just north of Jacksonville, where the British tried a sneak attack from the north, hoping to get a shot at St. Augustine. Unfortunately, the actual location was never accurately mapped, and it was a running skirmish on horseback for the most part. The best guess was that it was on some land now owned by Ron Rico distilling, and we got permission to drive around their land looking for likely places where they might have fought. I was the metal-detector specialist back then, so when we'd find an empty field, Buddy would send me out and I'd wander around swinging the detector for the better part of an hour while he sat in the truck. We never found shit. To be honest, I don't know what they were expecting anyway, it was just a couple of dozen men on either side, mostly on horseback, and from the historic accounts, through the swamps. What would we hope to find: a bullet, a horseshoe? It was historically significant because the Spanish pushed the British back up into Georgia, which was now recognized as English territory, and preserved the status of St. Augustine as being America's longest continually occupied city. The English would have burned it to the ground. When we got back to the Ron Rico headquarters to check in the badges that let us roam freely on their property, the director offered us a few shots of the newest varieties they were getting ready to promote. I was more than happy to give them my unqualified opinion, but Buddy begged off, his AA training kicking in, scowling at my enjoyment.

At SEAC in Tallahassee it became apparent that Buddy was not going to be just one of the regular archaeologists. Even though he and Pete got along pretty well, being old-timers, Buddy had been the alpha-dog in Washington too long, and he was just going to work on what he wanted to work on, and go out in the field when he wanted to go out. Besides, even though he'd been demoted, that didn't mean he lost anything except the title; he was still a GS-15, with all the pay and benefits. So they ended up advertising to hire another guy to replace George Fischer and supervise the regular working archaeologists. The job announcement went out and they got more than a few really good prospects. Pete was relying on my boss, Bob Wilson to help him make the decision, but after all their work searching and then evaluating the candidates, Bob came into the office one day, obviously distressed and frustrated. He and Pete had decided on what they considered the best applicant, a guy named Marvin Smith, a preeminent Southeast archaeologist, and they were ready to offer him the position, but Buddy pulled some strings and had one of his yes-men from Washington, a certain Gordon Schmidt, hired instead. Buddy described him as a good soldier, and they all knew what that meant: he'd be Buddy's boy. We found out that he'd been Buddy's go-fer back in Washington, and this was his way of getting out of the expensive rat race there and settling down in laid-back Tallahassee. Apparently he'd been a Floridian before graduating from the University of South Florida and putting in a stretch in Alaska and then going on to the Park Service in D.C. So he followed Buddy down to FSU. This was the beginning of a major breach in the sanity of SEAC. Up until now the place had operated as a family, and cooperation was the keyword. We worked together on common goals, knew what the job was, and helped each other out whenever we could, even when we disagreed. But now factions developed as Pete and Bob, representing the old SEAC, tried to maintain stability, and Buddy and Gordon Schmidt now began to pursue their own agendas. Gordon was a nice enough guy, average in height, average in weight, clean-shaven with black hair cut in the regular style, Clark-Kent glasses, a regular guy. I took the initiative to show him around and introduce him to all the worker bees, and tried to explain how things operated. He was very friendly and polite, almost too polite, and used 1970s exclamations like "Cool," "Neat-o," "Nifty" and the like. (Think of the guy who's the manager in the TV show *The Office*, played by Steve Carrell.) Pete and Bob took an immediate dislike to him, partly based on the fact I'm sure, of his being hired over their

326

hard-sought choice, but for the most part because of his D.C. manners (which is to say cocky). Then there was the book. Gordon had come with a little baggage: he was working on a book (with John Hardinger, who undoubtedly helped swing his hiring as well), and he told Pete that he was almost finished with it, so, before he could handle his duties as hired in any full capacity, he needed to finish it first. Pete, under duress from above, grudgingly agreed. This meant that Gordon's duties were taken up by his right-hand (wo)man, Beth, who had just run the initial Armstrong site survey and testing. He dumped everything on her while he "worked on the book," which included her doing the planning, scheduling, keeping track of time, and generally supervising the handful of regular working archeologists in his division. Luckily, I still worked for Bob. The book turned out to be one of those edited varieties, where you call up your friends (or professional people you want to be your friends) and ask them to write a chapter for a book, say on "Public Archeology", which is what this one was; then you "edit" them by putting the chapters in some sort of order, write a brief introduction, put your name on the cover, and voila, you're now an author in the archaeological sciences. [Man, I want to do one of those "edited by" books someday, maybe *Tales from the Dark Side of Public Archaeology*. Now there's a catchy title! And it'd be easy enough to get contributors.]

Finishing the book took the better part of a year, partly because Gordon couldn't edit worth a shit; even his inter-office memos were filled with misspellings and incomplete sentences. Meanwhile, poor Beth was working double-duty, and both she and Pete, from below and above, were getting tired of hearing about it, much less covering for him. I loved Beth because she was really down-to-earth. She'd get so frustrated with Gordon's lack of leadership that she'd cuss him out right in front of everybody, and he'd just go "Now, now, Beth, that's enough," then give her a private "talking to" later. No matter, she got a promotion anyway, and rightfully so. But then he started to tick off Bob, who was the most patient man I'd ever met, by requesting my services. There were plenty of archaeological technicians at the Center, you see, mostly student interns, but not a lot of full-fledged archaeologists who could carry out projects in a timely, professional, and most important, economical manner, much less write them up. Well, Beth and I were two, and Ken was the third, but he was down in Puerto Rico helping them out down there, and now that Beth was overloaded, a couple of projects came in that needed to be done ASAP, when Gordon asked Pete to ask Bob if he could spare me. One was a stupid little treefall evaluation up in Ocmulgee that anyone could have done in a day, even Gordon. What's a treefall evaluation? Well, when a storm rolls through a park that hasn't had any tree-cutting in many, many years, and the winds come through, they tend to knock down a lot of the larger trees, and when the trees are torn from the ground, the archaeologist gets a chance to look in the holes and see if there are any artifacts or features exposed. Basically you walk through the woods in the storm path, look for toppled trees, look in the hole and scrape around with your trowel a little bit, collect anything interesting you find and map and photograph any that yield anything. Basically it's equivalent to random shovel-testing, except that nature has done the grunt work. I call it stupid because they rarely yield anything interesting, and if they did, since it's a random pattern, and the tree roots, having already grown deep into the ground and then, being ripped up suddenly, disturb any context, so even any information you might luck onto is next to useless. In short, it flies in the face of the scientific method. [Not that the scientific method is always all it's cracked up to be. Back in April of '84, I had presented a handwritten paper to the Florida Academy of Sciences as part of a student paper competition. The paper was titled "A Defense of the Inductive Approach in Archaeological Theory-Building," and the gist of it was that when the facts don't always conveniently line up, sometimes it's best just to go with your intuition. It won first prize in the Anthropological Science division! Historical note: the Academy competition that year was held at Saint Leo's College in Tampa/Sarasota, the aforementioned alma mater of actor Lee Marvin.]

The other project Gordon needed me for was a bit more interesting. Once again I was sent down to Canaveral, since I was now the Canaveral guy for the most part. Fish and Wildlife was cleaning off some mosquito-control dikes that had been built back in the 60s, and because a few archaeological sites (mostly shell scatters) had been recorded way back when, they wanted me to evaluate if this clearing would impact (i.e., harm) any known or potential sites in the area. Well, I knew the answer before I left Tallahassee, but I wasn't going to pass up an all-expenses-paid trip to New Smyrna again. You see, the dikes were created by draglines that scooped up mud out of the bottom of the lagoon, laid out ahead of the earth-mover in these meandering dikes some thirty feet across and a mile or two long each. The idea was that it created deeper water adjacent to the dikes so that more fish could get in and eat the mosquito larvae, as opposed to the shallow swamps at the south end of "Mosquito" Lagoon that had existed there previously. These dikes also allowed access for fisherman and especially, duck hunters, and this is why they were being cleared of vegetation now, after some twenty-five years. They were covered for the most part in Brazilian pepper, a particularly fast-growing and hearty exotic from South America. So Fish and Wildlife was going in with bulldozers and pushing the bush down, crushing it, and when it died they would have a controlled burn (where could the fire go except down the dike?) and the dikes would be good for at least another ten years or so. The reason I already knew there wouldn't be any impact was because these dikes were man-made, and only twenty-five years old at that… so, how could there be any damage to any historic or prehistoric sites? But I surprised myself. I hadn't counted on *finding new sites*. And this is what happened… driving on the newly-cleared dikes I came across a few shell scatters maybe fifty to a hundred feet long. Checking the maps of known sites, I could see that these had been recorded by some conscientious State archaeologist when the dikes were first built, and they were created from the dragline depositing material out of the adjacent now-deepened slough onto the dike as it was constructed. But back then, the dikes had only been built so far. They proved to be so effective and popular with the sportsmen however, that later, several more miles were added on. Once I got on to these new sections I was recording new sites. There weren't many, but the ones I found were exciting. They were first noted as shell scatters, just like the rest, but here, out near the deeper portions of Mosquito Lagoon, they had a few ceramics mixed in here and there. And not just the run-of-the-mill dime-a-dozen St. John "chalky" wares that are found everywhere from Canaveral north into Georgia, the ones we knew dated from the time of Christ to the mid-1700s when the local Indians were wiped out. No, these were older. In fact, they were some of the *oldest* ceramics found in Florida. Rarer than hen's teeth, I was picking them up by the handful! Over two thousand years before Christ, or as we prefer, 4500 B.P (before the present), natives here in Florida were experimenting with making pottery with the local clay, when they could find it. They added vegetal material, probably grass, maybe some Spanish moss, as a tempering agent in the clay so that after they dried it in the sun and then put it in a fire, it wouldn't crack as it expanded and then cooled. Not too much, and not too little, and the grass or moss would burn off, and if the mix was right, there wouldn't be any holes in the pot, or the cup, or the plate, or the bowl. So that's how you identify it: it's usually pretty thick, and both reddish (from the clay) and black (from the fire), with these impressions of grass or moss burned out. It's called fiber-tempered pottery, and like I said, it's some of the earliest ever made, at least here in the Western Hemisphere. What had happened was that the dragline, as it dug the slough and deposited the muck bucket by bucket, while building the dike, was creating a reverse stratigraphy; that is, the older material from the bucket digging into the bottom of the Lagoon was put on top of the dike, and the oldest, from the deeper part of the Lagoon was now on top. So adjacent to the dike, at the bottom of the slough, was where this material was coming from, when it had once been dry land (obviously). Well, as a scientific exercise, I wondered how much the sea level had risen in those 4500 years. I estimated that the slough was roughly 15 feet deep. The material was 4500 years old. If it had happened regularly and continuously, the water had risen 15 feet over the site in 4500 years; that's 1 foot every 300 years, or 1/3 of a foot (4 inches) every 100 years. It just so happens that 4 inches is almost exactly 10 centimeters. So the water rose 1 centimeter every 10 years, or roughly 1 millimeter a year. Yes, there was the muck, and yes, the dragline had created the slough; my argument is about the water level rise in the Lagoon, which, having no real tide down at this end, reflected nearly true sea level. Now that increase seemed a bit excessive then, even to me, until I remember now that, when we stayed at the beach as kids, we had to trek down a path through the dunes and then run fifty yards to get to the ocean. Now, the hotels, without exception, have built seawalls along the ocean side for those times that the unusual high tide or storm surge laps at their foundations; all this occurring in the past 50 years (5 centimeters?) of my life. I tried explaining the significance of finding the fiber-tempered site to Gordon, and even though the other archaeologists at the Center, even the interns, were impressed, he just didn't get it (just like he didn't get the importance of the Armstrong site at Oyster Bay, because he didn't understand the implications of the whole French-Spanish colonial rivalry and the effect of the Ribault disaster.) But his book was coming along, and that's what was important. Besides, it now being 1991, the Park Service was shifting into high gear to celebrate the "Quincentennial," the 500th anniversary of Columbus' discovery of the New World.

The Big 'Ol Fish

Around this time, my brother Paul and I noticed that Dad had slowed down considerably. Always a hard drinker and two-pack a day smoker (Kools, menthol), he wasn't moving around much, and having retired finally from Martin Marietta a couple of years previously, he'd put on a lot of weight and was showing all the signs of serious diabetes. We decided to try and re-create the deep-sea adventure of seven years earlier, and made plans without his knowledge, but still at Mom's urging, sort of a surprise 65th birthday present. He was a little wary of the whole thing when we showed up, but Mom was footing the bill and he knew this would probably be his last chance, so he went along with it, trying to muster up the necessary excitement. We headed down the turnpike again to Ft. Pierce to the same fishing lodge at the inlet we had gone to before, when damn if Dad's big wide and yellow old-man LTD didn't just quit on us along the highway. One minute we were doing seventy-five, cruising along and talking, when it gave a sputter, then a shudder, and the next thing we know we're easing over onto the shoulder. Luckily, cell-phones had just come in by then, and I had mine so we called Mom, who called a wrecker, and since we were only an hour out of Orlando, she said she'd come get us and take us the rest of the way down to Ft. Pierce. Dad was all for letting the whole thing go, but she insisted. We also had Mom and Dad's video camera with us, and I began recording as Mom arrived and the tow truck driver pulled the useless luxury car up onto his flatbed. It was not an auspicious beginning, but we were on the road again, undaunted. So Mom drove us the remaining hour or two down to the lodge, dropped us off, and said to give her a call when we got off the boat. Then she drove back to Orlando.

We checked into the lodge, which seemed a little more rundown than we remembered, and had dinner, which was a little more expensive and not quite as good as we remembered. But hell, that had been seven years earlier, and nothing was as good as it used to be. Dad bought a bottle of rum from the adjacent liquor store and we had a few before hitting the sack. Again, Dad was up before dawn, and got us up. A quick light breakfast, coffee and English muffins, and we were at the dock just as the sun was peeking over the horizon on a cool and hazy morning, all videotaped. And again, we'd beaten the captain and first mate. But not by much. The captain, a thin, intense, ball-capped guy in T-shirt and shorts, about thirty-two, met us on the dock, introduced himself and started puttering around the boat, a bit nervously. This was *The Happy Hooker II*, but other than the name, nothing was the same; it was a little smaller, only one fighting seat instead of two, and just a little cramped. After twenty minutes or so, it was obvious the captain was just killing time waiting for the first mate, who was late. He walked off the boat onto the end of the dock and made a phone call. When he got back you could tell he was a little miffed, apologized for the delay, and we all cracked a beer. Must have been 7:30 or so. In fifteen minutes the mate showed up. He was a stocky kid of twenty, dark-hair and tanned, bleary-eyed and still smelling of booze from the night before. The captain gave him the look and he set to his duties immediately. Finally we were off but it must have been 8:00 by now. Then the captain says he has to get ice. We pull up to another dock, he goes in and negotiates, and then they hand the mate a large hose and he directs the outpouring of shaved ice into a hold below a hatch on the deck. This takes another twenty minutes and finally we're really off, heading out the inlet. The captain then takes a right turn, running offshore, instead of heading straight out, like we had done last time. He eases off on the power and the mate hands Dad and Paul and I each a tiny little rig with three or four small gold hooks each. What the heck? "We gotta catch some fresh bait," the mate says, and he dangles his little gold hook into the water and it's immediately pounced on by a tiny shad. I dip mine in, and get another one, Paul dips his and we're pulling them in as the mate throws them into a live well at the back of the boat, the air pump bubbling. Dad says "The hell with this, I didn't come out here to catch bait," and leans his rig into the corner of the boat, then cracks a beer while Paul and I try to hurry this up so we can get on with business. In ten minutes we have all the bait we'll need, and finally the captain turns toward the open ocean. It's now nearly nine o'clock, and the sun has burned off the haze and is starting to heat up the deck. Dad's not happy. But once the engines open up, and we're catching the wind, the ocean gets darker, and the shoreline drops behind us, the mood gets brighter. Near a lighted bell-buoy the captain eases down on the throttle and we drift back and forth by it. We've made a pact that, unless we hit a pack of dolphin (mahi), only one of us at a time would fish, until he caught something, and then the next guy. Paul went first and hooked a nice three-foot barracuda that put up a jumping fight, but was nonetheless subdued in ten minutes, precariously taken off the hook by the mate, and let go to fight another day. Dad went next, and as we circled this big red buoy that let out a loud "bong" every so often, he finally hooked a bonita, and we brought it in, but only if we'd need cut bait later. I put my line down, and after awhile I got a hit, but whatever it was, it got off the line before we could even see it. So it was still my turn. The captain revved the engines and headed out toward The Stream.

Once we got out there, the mate began rigging up the teasers and two stern lines for trolling, using a couple of frozen ballyhoo that had been professionally wired, and a couple of side strips off the bonita Dad had caught. It was now nearly noon, and we settled back with our beers, knowing that this was a matter of patience as much as pursuit. If we caught a trophy fish, like a swordfish, a sailfish, or God help us, a marlin, we were going to just videotape it, take a few pictures, and let it go. If it was a wahoo or kingfish however, it would be sacrificed as steaks. Hell, even the big bull dolphins were known to occasionally hit a trolling lure. With the droning hum of the engines, the hours ticked by. Once or twice, the line would snap out of the pin, the pole end would dip, but nothing got hooked; the mate would reel in the bait, usually mauled, throw it off and put on another, reset the line, and one more hour would go by. I got up by the captain and helped him scan the horizon for any floating crap that might attract a pack of mahi, but other than individual foam cups and a broken ice chest, or other trash that we recovered, there was nothing. It was soon getting time to head for home. Suddenly, the pin snapped, the starboard stern pole dipped and the drag started to whine. The mate grabbed the pole out of the transom socket, set the hook and looked at me. I settled into the fighting chair, while he reeled in the other stern line, swung the teasers back into position, and the captain eased back on the throttle, still going forward. It hit hard and it was big. The captain's yelling at me to keep it taught, keep the pressure on, while Paul and Dad are standing, looking astern to see what it might be. I kept the pressure on, but I couldn't get any gain, and the drag just buzzed and whined as it was pulled back off the spool. Finally it stopped and I started reeling in, but it was easy to tell that I wasn't pulling on the fish, just bringing in slack that had bowed out into the water. He was heading toward us. I reeled in as fast as I could and in seconds, he was running again, pulling out the line against the drag. Then he jumped. It was a sailfish! He did the little tail dance on top of the water, fell back in and again peeled off another twenty, thirty yards of line, everything I'd gained. I put the pressure back on, given plenty of encouragement from Dad and Paul, as well as the captain yelling "Pull! Pull!" The mate talked to me and got me to try and relax, deep breaths, and pull slow and hard, gain some, and reel it in; then do it again. It was hard but exhilarating at the same time. Sometimes I'd gain ten or twenty yards, only to lose it, pull slow and get it back. Eventually, I was gaining a little more than losing. This is when the captain reversed the engines and slowly backed down. Every so often the fish would dive, as I could see the line pointing straight down, and then it would go slack and I'd reel in as much as I could. He'd only jumped once or twice when we'd first hooked him, but now he was careening back and forth behind the boat, the sail, and sometimes the bill, breaking the surface. It'd been almost forty-five minutes; seemed like ten. As I pulled up the exhausted fish, my arms cramped, I had to literally lift it with each pull of the rod. As it came up alongside, the mate grabbed a gaff hook, leaned over the side and hooked it under the gills. It was dead by the time he pulled it over the gunwale, quickly turning from blue and silver to a dull grey. Congratulations, smiles, beers and photos followed. But what was I going to do with this large dead fish? The captain said "You have a choice, you can either eat it or mount it." I can't do both? Nope. "We'll put it on ice for now, and when we get back to the dock, you can decide." More beers, smiles, and congratulations. Dad and Paul were sincerely happy for me.

Unfortunately, the battery in the video camera had died before the fish struck, so the memory of the fight is all that's left. It was time to head back, and any regret over the death of such a royal animal was overshadowed by the experience itself. They put it on ice and we turned for shore. When we got to the dock I'd made up my mind that I was going to have it mounted, since I'd likely never get another one in my life. A couple more pictures on the dock, and Dad paid the captain, this time something like $500, but only a $75 tip to let him know how ticked off he'd been at the late start, and the general unpreparedness. The captain gave me the name of a good taxidermist, one of the best in Florida, out of Yeehaw Junction. I signed a quick contract for $500 and he said he'd take care of the details. Only much later did I find out that yes, you *can* have the meat and the trophy too. At that time, all they needed was the head and the tail, all connected by the backbone, to mount a fish. The rest was fiberglass, painted to detail. Hell, that captain probably had the thing filleted before we were out of town (and probably made another $200 off it as well). No matter, it had been a relatively successful trip just in the bonding aspect alone. Plus, I'd get a good mount out of it. After we called her and went to the restaurant bar, Mom showed up a couple of hours later, and we headed back north on the Turnpike, regaling Ma with the adventure. On the way we charged the battery for the video camera in the cigarette lighter and damn if we didn't get stuck up somewhere just south of Kissimmee by a huge traffic jam that closed our side going north and slowed down the southern lanes considerably. Soon we crawled up enough to see three or four cars turned over, some upside down, and others resting on their sides, with bodies, blankets, stretchers and rescue teams scattered all about. Above, a helicopter circled. We were moving so slow, that I grabbed the camera, got out, and easily outdistanced the car. Creeping up between the other onlookers and rescue personnel, I did my best to document the disaster, figuring hell, the closest any news agency was going to get was the helicopter. The worst of it would be cleaned up in a half-hour anyway. I hopped back in with my prize footage. When we got back home in Orlando, I was convinced that the accident footage was worth some money if I could get it to the television station in time. Dad and Paul thought I was nuts, but Mom said she wanted to go with me, and off we went. The people at WFTV were very nice and grateful, but they wanted to see what I had first. We downloaded it onto their big recorder, and they thought it was interesting, but no, they weren't going to give me any money for it. Could they keep the copy for their file footage? Yeah, sure. I was disappointed, hoping to offset some of Mom and Dad's money for the fishing trip, maybe even a hundred bucks, but oh well… That night on the evening local news: Exclusive WFTV footage of the major accident on the Turnpike! Both from the air and on the ground! (Maybe ten seconds' worth, and no, no credits. Oh well.) A week later, Mom calls me in Tallahassee: I was on TV! What?! After she had gotten the photos from our trip developed, she sent them in to (who?) WFTV for their sports channel segment, *Big Ol' Fish*, that showcased local anglers and their catches. She wrote up a little bio and the sports guy, Pat-something, showed a photo of me and my sailfish on the air. They saw it at six o'clock and then Dad videotaped it off of the TV at eleven. The headline below the photo says the fish was 94 lbs, when in actuality it was 54 lbs. I guess Mom embellished it a little.

Rescue at Sea

Back in Tallahassee, besides working at SEAC I was teaching at the Academic Diving Program as a teaching assistant for some extra money, and we were associated with the FSU Marine Lab down at Turkey Point. One of the Geology professors, Joe Donaghue, was carrying out research on the offshore springs, fresh-water founts that burbled up from the seabottom ten miles or so offshore in the Gulf. These things would have been gathering places for mastodons and men in the Pleistocene when the water level in Florida was some 100 feet lower. Well, we archaeologists had an interest in these offshore springs as well, and since I was already an FSU Marine Lab diver via the Academic Diving Program I was invited to go along one weekend. I'd also had experience using the undersea dredge, an airlift, so I had that going for me as well. Now this had nothing to do with my job at the Park Service, but there was another Service underwater archeologist along as well, Rik Anuskiwiecz, whom we called "The Polish Prince," and we agreed that this would make a great paper if we found anything related to any human use: tools, bones, flakes, anything. Sites like this were a rarity. Well, Donaghue had a spring located, and we set off in two large boats one early Friday afternoon. We worked until sundown, when one boat went back in for the night. I stayed out with Steve Wilson, the Marine Lab captain, Anuskiwiecz, and a couple of others on the R.V. (Research Vessel) *Lady Seminole*, the Marine Lab boat, and we made ready to go to sleep. I decided to sleep up front on the foredeck rather than inside, and after we'd eaten, and everyone was down, I crawled out there and made up some bedding while Steve sat inside watching a small television. Ten minutes later, he calls out to me through the front windshield hatch, "Hey David! Off the bow, one o'clock, keep an eye out, tell me if you see something!" Two minutes later, there's a small red flash on the horizon. "Oh shit," he yells, "Get the anchor up!" He fires up the engines, wakes everyone up, and sends someone up onto the bow to help me lift the large heavy anchor over the rail and batten it down. "Keep an eye out!" he yells, and we're under way in a minute. Almost thirty-five minutes later, all the time on the radio with the Coast Guard and the Marine Lab advising them of the situation, Steve begins to slow down, he tells me to get back up on the bow and use the hand-held searchlight to scan the top of the water, now night-black and choppy, as he slowly advanced. "There!" he yelled, pointing, and I got the light up to see, maybe fifty yards away, some "things" floating in the water. Then we could hear yelling over the boat engines, and I kept the light on three men and a cooler rising and falling in the waves. Steve maneuvered theboat maybe twenty feet away and yelled out, "Swim over here!" at the same time telling Anuskiwiecz and the other crew members to get a line and the boat hook ready, get some blankets. One of the guys let go of the others and swam to the boat; they snatched him up over the side and he fell to the deck, which Steve had lighted up from overhead. Then a second one came on over, and he too was yanked over the gunwale. "Gct those wetsuits off of them!" Steve yelled, "and get some blankets!" Then he called over to the last man, whom I had kept the searchlight on, and who was floating with an ice chest, obviously tied to something below the surface. "C'mon!" Steve yelled. "There's a boat down here," the guy yelled, "the line's attached to a boat!" "Goddamnit!" Steve yelled back, "I've got the position! Let go of that line and get over here!" The guy obediently swam over and, pulled up over the stern, was quickly stripped of his wetsuit to join his buddies wrapped in blankets in the cabin up front, where Steve had made room for them along the sleeping bench behind the captain's chair. They were shaking uncontrollably and Steve cranked up the heat. I came down off the bow and climbed in the window hatch, sitting opposite the guys as hot coffee was brought up for them. Their teeth were chattering like castanets, as Steve got on the radio, calling in to the Coast Guard and the Marine Lab to let them know we got 'em. "Was there anyone else?" he turned and asked them, but they just shook their heads no.

As they warmed up, amid the effusion of teary thanks for being saved, the story as it came out went like this: These three spoiled rich macho frat boys decided to go spearfishing. They borrowed a friend's boat, loaded up their dive gear, beer, and spears and drove out some thirteen miles offshore to a place called "The Ledges," which were limestone outcroppings running in ridges anywhere from twenty-eight to thirty-five feet deep. The weather was marginal, especially for a small boat like they had (less so for the larger *Lady Seminole*), but hey, they were invincible, and all beered up. So the three went down with their spearguns and prowled the seabottom, apparently without luck, until they were close to running out of air, and when they got to the surface, hard adrift downstream from the boat, they could see it bobbing dangerously up and down as they swam for it. They had not let out enough anchor line, so the scope, as it is referred to, was very sharp (that is, not having let out a lot of line the boat didn't rise gently on the waves and advancing tide, but was tied down rather tight to the bottom, thus jerking hard up and down—they were lucky as hell that it hadn't come loose). When they got to the boat, now nearly exhausted, they clambered over the transom and the water was coming in behind them. As the boat began to founder, and as they moved forward, water also came up over the bow with their extra weight (they still hadn't thought to loosen the anchor line). Standing in knee-deep water in the boat, they knew they were in trouble. Their "leader" tried to start the engines but the water had shorted out the battery. He said he had the microphone to the radio in his hand when the boat went down underneath them. Now they inflated their BCs (buoyancy compensators) and held onto an ice chest that came bobbing to the surface. They still hadn't taken off their tanks, weight belts, or flippers, their masks sitting atop their heads. The "leader" at least has the sense to quickly dive down to the boat, now loosen the line from the boat (but still attached to the anchor) and retrieve the flare gun kit. They tie the ice chest to the line and hang on for dear life, now at 3 or 4 o'clock in the afternoon. Finally having sense enough to drop their weight belts and tanks, they fire off one of the flares. Since it's still midday, it goes unnoticed. As the sun begins to set, and we were getting comfortable to bed down for the night, they fired off their second flare, which is the one Steve thought he saw. When the sun went down and they began to panic, they fired off the last one, and that's the one I saw, and which Steve used to get a bearing on them. Had Steve not seen them, we would have been reading about their floating bloated corpses in the *Tallahassee Democrat* two days later.

All the way back to the dock, they went on and on about how they were going to buy Steve and the rest of us a steak dinner, bottles of booze, take us out on the town. Steve got a radio call in to their girlfriends in Tallahassee to come and get them at the Marine Lab, and by the time we got there an hour later, they were warmed up and talking normally. When we tied off the boat, their girls were there at the pier with a large SUV; they hugged and kissed and started to pile into the car. I couldn't help it, Steve and the others were securing the boat, putting away gear, including the wet blankets. I walked over to the car and before they could pull out, got them to put the window down, and leaned in and said, "You know, boys, you really ought to go over there and shake Steve's hand and give him a real thank-you before you drive off. You owe him your lives." The girls looked at them, they looked at each other, and got out of the car. They shyly walked over to the boat, and I watched them each thank Steve and shake his hand. They gave me a glance, standing there with my arms folded, scowling, before getting into the car and driving off. There never were any steak dinners. But six weeks later I get a message over the intercom that Pete wants an impromptu meeting with the staff in ten minutes. We meet in a small conference room and he makes a to-do about giving Bob Taylor his ten-year pin, although Bob was still a temporary employee, subject to getting furloughed at any time. We all thought it was rather ironic: ten years a temp. Then, Pete pulls out this large green padded folder, opens it and starts reading, "In recognition of actions above and beyond the call of duty, this commendation is hereby presented to David M. Brewer…" (!?!?) and it went on to detail the rescue of the month earlier. "But, Pete," I said, "this didn't have anything to do with the Park Service. It was an FSU thing, on the weekend, and by the way, I had very little to do with it… Steve Wilson, the captain, is the real hero." Pete explained that, "apparently Anuskiwiecz, who works for Mineral Management, put himself in for it and got one and so the Park Service decided you had to get one too." Later that day, I called the Director of the Marine Lab and told him Steve deserved some sort of recognition, especially if we were getting some. He said he'd see what he could do. I ran into Steve at the oyster bar some two or three months later, and he said, nope, never even got an "Attaboy." But he wasn't bothered by it; he saw it as part of the job. Me, however, when Pete handed me the commendation, shook my hand, and said "Congratulations." Well, smart-ass that I was, I had to ask, "So, where's the check?"

16. Entering the Fourth Dimension: The Degree, Death, Disaster, and Divorce (1991 - 1994)

The Degree

I was still battling with Dr. Maryann over the goddamn thesis and she'd put me off for over a year now since the defense with minor rewrites and missed appointments, when one day I walked into the SEAC Curatorial Lab and she was sitting there working with another professor on cataloguing some collections. Out of the blue she asked me if I had the cover page of the thesis, the one that had to be signed by all the committee members for it to be "certified" as passing. I said sure (hell, I'd had it ready for over a year, and all the other committee members said they'd sign it as soon as she did, since the major professor had to sign it first). She said to bring it in and she'd sign it. I went to my office, got four copies (for four original signatures, one for each thesis copy) and brought them back, and she signed them without a comment. I thanked her and went to each of the committee members and got them signed. Only later did it occur to me that someone must have taken her aside and told her to put an end to it, and it being summer, the Department was always notoriously short of graduates and needed to beef up the numbers for the School of Arts and Sciences. It was probably Dailey, whom she respected and who was once again Chairman, and as tired of the delays as I was. I quickly signed up for graduation in August, and went to the bookstore and got fitted for a cap and gown. It may have been a triumph, but it sure didn't feel like one. Nonetheless, the ordeal was over.

We had a big blowout after the graduation ceremony. Mom and Dad came up from Orlando, and we had a bunch of friends from work and school, and even Amy's Mom and Dad came up too; it was an eclectic makeup of old-timers and young hipsters, but I left all the professors off the invitation list, as well as the bosses, except for Bob Wilson and his wife, and my old boss George Fischer and his. This was truly a time to celebrate and I didn't want any awkward moments to dampen the spirit. Later that week, back at the University, I took in my cap and gown, and before I handed them back I asked the professors on my committee to come outside and take a photo, it being sort of a tradition. While we're standing outside, this clean-cut white-haired gent in a suit stopped to watch us. He was the new University President! I can't remember his name right now, and he only lasted a year, but he was wandering around campus getting himself familiarized since he was taking over in the Fall. The outgoing President, Bernie Sliger, was a great big round man with a moustache, a big bright smile, and an extrovert personality whom everyone at FSU had loved for over ten years. But then he had a stroke and it really put him out of business, so they had to get this new guy. I asked him if he'd take a photo shot with us and he was happy to, since no one else had even recognized him. On the flip side, I was in the last graduating class to have their diplomas signed by Bernie, a real memento. That was it… I finally had my Master of Science degree in Anthropology. When someone would ask if I was going to go on for a PhD I always said, hell no, "I'm not going to read another thing the rest of my life that I don't want to read," and besides, a PhD actually *over-qualifies* you for a lot of jobs ("Hey, if you got a PhD, *Doctor* So-and-so, what are you doing out here in the dirt?!"), and most of the people with one end up teaching, instead of doing. I could do both with my Master's.

Death

Thanksgiving that year was at our house on Jackson Street. Mom and Dad came up from Orlando, and Paul and his wife Celeste and their daughter Stephanie came over as well. After dinner and dessert we had a bunch of other people over too, Ed Quinby and his girlfriend Rhonda,

Celeste's mother and father, and our good friend Greg Halfide. We had all been hitting the bottle pretty hard, and Dad, Paul, Greg and myself were smoking, sitting around the large kitchen table, telling stories and joking around. I got up from the table to check on the women in the living room. I'd just gotten to the dining room when Amy put her arms around my neck and gave me a big wet kiss. Over my shoulder I heard a voice say "Barney, are you all right?" Then again, "Barney, are you all right?" I disengaged from Amy and turned into the kitchen to see Dad slumped over in his chair with Ed and Paul propping him up, but it was obvious he was unconscious. "Lay him on the floor," said Paul's father-in-law, Dan, but I said, "NO, help me get him into the bedroom!" which was just adjacent to the kitchen. Ed, Paul, and I got under his arms and lifted him, dragging his feet, into the bedroom and laid him on the bed. "Call 9-1-1!" I yelled, as we took off his shoes and loosened his shirt collar. His breathing was shallow, but it was constant. The medics were there in no time flat, and we led them into the bedroom, where they started the routine: stethoscope, blood pressure, looking into his eyes. He started coming around groggily, and they asked point-blank "Have you all been drinking?" even though the answer was evident. "He'll be all right, it was just too much today. Let him rest." He slept for about an hour before getting up and insisting that Mom take him back to their hotel.

In the morning they showed up bright and early before nine, and although Dad seemed fresh as can be and in good spirits, I was still a little shaken from the event of the night before. I'd been thinking of getting him on videotape for some time, maybe get a reminiscence or two, and the night before made it even more pressing that morning. He balked a little, but once I assured him it would be a good thing and got him settled out on the front porch with the camera looking over my shoulder, he was quite compliant. I asked about his earliest memories, growing up in the Depression, etc. and I learned a lot in that first go-round (that first go-round that we never got to finish, nor see a second…, though I still have the tape). This is where I learned about the Italian rag-picker that lived above them in a wooden tenement who would walk his horse up and down the steps each day. How the toilets would freeze in the bitter-cold Detroit winter and they would have to take an icepick to them to get the water moving, and how he'd pay his little sisters a nickel to go sit on the toilet seat and warm it up in the morning. About the time they were crawling between the train cars when the train gave that lurch when it gets started again and somehow one of his buddies got his leg lopped off just above the knee. Things like that.

It was less than a month later, on Saturday, December 7th (yes, I know, Day of Infamy and all that), when the phone rings and Amy hands it to me, upset. Mom's on the other end, nearly hysterical, saying "Daddy's passed out! We were watching TV and he lifted his head and said, 'Call a priest, I'm dying' and then he passed out and I can't get him to come to. Shall I call a priest!?" "Hell, no, Mom," I said, "Call 911! Call them right now! I'll call Paul and then call you back, or you call me back. G'bye." Then I called Paul and he was out, but I told his wife Celeste to have him call me as soon as he came in. Mom called back in a half an hour and said they had just taken Dad to the hospital, and he never came to. She was going down there right away. I told her that Paul and I would get on the road just as soon as I heard from him. He called in 15 minutes and I told him what I knew, and we made plans to get on the road as soon as possible. I don't remember who drove that first trip, probably Paul, but I know we made it in four hours (which isn't bad: my all–time record being 3 ½ at 80 miles per hour and not stopping for gas or to take a pee). We got to the hospital, parked and ran up the stairs to where they said he was. When we walked in, he was sitting up, cheerful and talking with Mom. What the hell? Well, it turned out that he had passed out from low blood sugar, hypoglycemia, the opposite of diabetes. His doctor, a young boyish redhead, Mark Williams, had told him the previous week that he needed to lose weight, and lose it fast, or he would be in serious trouble. And that was it:

no proscribed diet, no regimen, no guidelines. Dad's solution? He stopped eating. So, being diabetic anyway, the lack of any carbohydrates, or anything else for that matter, put him into hypoglycemic shock and he passed out. He wasn't far wrong when he said "Get a priest, I'm dying," because given another hour or so, he would have died. Once they had him in the hospital, they stabilized him rather quickly, and now he felt fine. But they weren't going to let him go. No, now that they had him in there, and taking note of both his general condition and the generous insurance package Martin Marietta had left him, they weren't about to let him get away just yet.

Dr. Mark Williams was unsure of himself, and it showed; he couldn't make a decision, he was nervous, and he was rightfully embarrassed that Dad had ended up in the hospital despite his frequent consultations. The next guy that came in though, was older, tough, a straight-arrow, and clinically cold; but goddamn if he wasn't good at what he did. His name was Snyder, and I'm not sure we ever knew his first name because everyone called him "Doctor" Snyder, even Williams. And we all noticed that when he addressed Dr. Williams he always called him "Mark." Snyder said a lot, if not most, of Dad's problems were the result of smoking, and that once the lungs were operating efficiently again, the rest would follow. He was emphatic about this and started Dad on an inhalation-therapy regimen. At first it went well and Dad seemed to respond, but Snyder wasn't convinced: "The worst hasn't happened yet. His lungs are going to take a week to clear out and that time is critical." Early on, Dad even played a trick on Williams, who showed up one morning with the usual, "How are you feeling today?" Dad said, "I feel much better after having had a cigarette…" Williams looked up from the chart, all the tubes in Dad, the monitors, etc. and said "What do you mean you had a cigarette? How did you get out of here to go downstairs and have a cigarette?" Dad said, "I didn't leave. I had a cigarette in here." Williams said, "Where?" and Dad pointed over to a small linen closet in the corner, "I just went in there and smoked a cigarette." Williams got up, walked over to the linen closet and opened it, and stuck his head in, smelling the air. The thing couldn't have held two brooms. "You went in there?" Williams asked. "That's right," Dad said. Only then did Williams realize that Dad was yanking him around. But Snyder was right. Within three days, Dad's breathing got more rapid, and somewhat labored, even though he was breathing oxygen-enriched air. We didn't know what was going on, but Snyder said it was COPD, chronic obstructive pulmonary disease, and Dad had to beat it or he was going to die anyway. Now things began to appear serious. Dad's breathing got faster. I remember one evening we're sitting by his bed and he's huffing and puffing away, open-mouth breathing and his tongue turning bluish, and the nurse took us aside and said, if this keeps up, his heart will fail soon, and we'll lose him. "Dr. Snyder wants to do a tracheotomy and put him on a ventilator. You need to talk to him about this because it means surgery." We asked her what she thought. "It'll make a difference right away, he'll be able to breathe and calm down, and even sleep. But he won't be able to talk. And he can't come off the respirator until he can breathe easily on his own." Oh shit. Now we knew he wasn't coming home anytime soon. We talked to him about it, and he said no, he wasn't going to go on any goddamn machine. Paul and I left Mom with him, and I went out in the hall and called Uncle Tom, Dad's favorite brother, out in California. At first I just wanted to let him know the situation, but soon I was crying and told him about Dad not wanting to go on the ventilator and what the nurse said about his heart failing if he didn't. I told him it was bad, and if he wanted to see Dad, he ought to come out right away. He told me he'd call me back. Apparently though he called the hospital and talked to both Mom and Dad, and between Tom and Mom they convinced Dad to have the tracheotomy done. In two hours Dad was back in the hospital room, his color was back, but he was out cold, and his breathing was a mechanical, but fairly benign, "whish-woof" from the machine attached to the light blue plastic hose now taped into his neck.

Tom arrived the next day from California. Since Paul and I were staying at Mom's there wasn't much room at the house so we made arrangements with the next–door neighbor Pauline Gaskins, an 80-year- old Florida-grown widow who lived alone, to let Tom use a bedroom at her house. She loved it. She was always a big fan of Dad's and here was his younger brother now sharing her big empty house. And Tom was a hilarious flirt, kidding her (and us) about having to lock his door at night so she wouldn't sneak in on him and "take advantage." Pauline's husband was Herb, the old grove manager with a bad ticker, who had died in his sleep some ten years earlier. She had two grown sons, one who was a colonel in the Air Force, retired and living in North Georgia. The other, Jerry, who was closer to my age, maybe ten years older, had taken up after his father and bought a lot of orange grove acreage way back when it was cheap. He was now a millionaire many times over and had just invented a machine that would shake the oranges down out of the tree when ripe, catch them as they fell and load them into a truck. Then he dropped dead: bad ticker, just like his dad.

We were already making regular pilgrimages to the hospital, sometimes twice a day, and Dad had responded well to the ventilator, so he was as good as could be expected, being confined to the bed. He couldn't talk, but he was writing notes back and forth, and he was really glad to see his brother. Tom had brought Dad a gift to cheer him up: it was a small black-face doll, with big red lips and a wide toothy grin, big white eyes, raggedy clothes and a torn straw hat, holding a big slice of watermelon with a bite taken out of it. Mom and Paul and I were horrified, but Dad got a big chuckle out of it and Tom put it on the window sill. When no one was looking I snatched it up and hid it in Mom's purse before any of Dad's nurses, most of whom were black, could see it. The Brewer boys were never known for their political correctness.

After a week or so, Dad was stable, and Tom had to go back to California. After Tom left, Dad's other brother Bob flew down from Detroit. It was a complicated family dynamic: Dad and Tom had always been close, although four years apart. Bob was right between them, and although not the intellectual, like Dad, or the wise guy like Tom, Bob was the good-looking, tall, athletic one. He was a submariner in the Navy after the war, and apparently while he was off on duty, Tom had taken up with his girlfriend Pauline, whom he later married, but the bad blood carried on forever and they never spoke again. Dad had sided with Tom and told me that once he had tried to broach a rapprochement with Bob after they'd had a couple of drinks in a hotel room, and Bob just stood up and cold-cocked Dad unconscious before walking out. That took a few years to settle down. But Bob was there to see Dad, and we were glad to see Bob. He was an affable fellow, the spitting image of Dad, and had been a long-suffering attentive and generous single-father to a set of challenged children. The night he showed up we sat on the back patio having drinks, and even though it was December, he wanted to go for a swim in the pool. So I gave him a pair of Dad's swim trunks (a few sizes too large) and when he jumped in we all laughed to see the trunks sitting on the bottom of the pool while he swam around unaware.

It was now getting near Christmas when Bob headed home. Paul also headed home to be with his family. Dad was stable and improving, and I made plans to have Amy and the kids come down to Orlando; maybe Dad could be out of the hospital by Christmas Day. When they got here, Mom and I decided it would be a little too traumatic for the boys, who were still very young, to see Dad with all the tubes and bags, and equipment, so we didn't take them in to see Granpa. The nurses then let us know that he wouldn't be out by Christmas. So I took Amy in with Robin, who was almost ten by then, to see him on Christmas Eve, and he was smiling and comfortable. We went home to sleep that night hoping to have a half-ass Christmas the next day for the boys. Then they called us from the hospital at 4 a.m. and said we should get down there right away. Mom and I went there as fast as we could. Dad was in real distress, writhing back and forth on the bed and rubbing and pointing to his lower abdomen. They took him in for X-rays and within the hour we had some doctor, one we'd never seen before, taking us aside to talk. "He's developed a large bleeding ulcer—these things are very common when someone has been in intensive care... we even call them intensive care ulcers... from the stress of being in the hospital. We've got to operate right away; but I wouldn't worry, we've done thousands of these and they're relatively straightforward. You're also very lucky since it's Christmas. The best internal surgeon is on duty. He's Jewish and covers for the other doctors over the holidays; I'll be assisting him." Ths guy was very confident so we felt pretty good about it. "Will we be able to talk to him before he goes in for surgery?" we asked. "Oh, sure," he said. We were waiting outside the room as they prepped Dad, and the next thing we knew, they were wheeling him off to the operating room. "What about talking to him?" "No time!"

We did see the Jewish surgeon, Dr. Simon, who stopped briefly and said he'd do his best. Mom and I were both stunned—he was a short guy who could have passed for Paul Simon's twin! Two hours later it was early morning when the 'confident' assistant doctor came out in his bloody scrubs to talk with us. Now he wasn't so confident, and was stuttering and stammering. "Oh, it was awful, we had a hard time finding it... and it was difficult to work on... Doctor Simon had to stand on a large box to get up over him... there was a lot of blood loss... we'll have to keep an eye on him... you may as well go home, he'll be sedated for a couple of days..." All this from the guy who said don't worry, we've done thousands of them... We left and were quite shaken by the turnaround from just a day earlier. Needless to say, it was a somber Yuletide.

Well, everything went to hell after that. Dad was constantly drugged, and when he did come to he was confused and delusional (he thought the nurses, who were the only ones we really did trust and rely on, as opposed to the doctors, were torturing him). It got so bad that they had to tie his hands to the bed rails so he wouldn't tear out his IV tubes. That really affected us; it was just heartbreaking. Then we saw them cleaning out his open incision from the operation. Apparently, since it had to heal from the inside out, they had left it open, and it had to be cleaned continuously. All this was just more and more horrifying. There were only brief periods when Dad was comfortable, and they seemed to be getting fewer as the days wore on, which meant they just sedated him more. Days turned to weeks, and now the respirator was doing all the work. Then he began to swell up, retaining fluids, with liquids coming right out of his pores to be mopped up. Again, the nurses told us what was going on when the doctors weren't around: his kidneys were shutting down, not a good sign. The doctors started prescribing stuff to make his kidneys work overtime, but this was just a stop-gap measure. Then there was the "blue food" that dripped straight into his stomach to provide nutrition. It was stop-and-go and that meant that his body was rejecting food. One of Mom's acquaintances, some old lady whose husband had passed away a year or so previously, suggested that we remove the feeding tube altogether and just let him go quietly, like she had done with her husband. Mom was very upset over this and it fell on me to call up the old bitch and tell her off. In retrospect, her intentions were probably not as cold as we considered them at the time. It didn't matter. A month after Christmas, Dad was in a semi-conscious coma of sorts and responded very little to outside stimulation. Then they hit us with the worst of it: his operation incision had gotten infected and he was in danger of a systemic blood infection. I went to sit next to him the night of the Super Bowl that year, and as I getting ready to leave the hospital and say good-bye, I noticed a little dribble of black bile out of the side of his mouth. I called the nurse, who didn't seem very upset, and cleaned it up telling me to go home, they'd let us know if there were any changes. Sure enough, I hadn't been home an hour, telling Mom that it didn't look good, when they called and said come down right away. It was maybe one in the morning. When we got there they told us that the blood poisoning had kicked in, and he was going to go into septic shock, and that now it was just a matter of time. I called Paul, who had been up watching the Super Bowl at home in Tallahassee with friends (having a few drinks), and told him he'd better come on down to Orlando. He was there in four hours.

I remember while waiting for Paul to arrive, Mom and I had been up for twenty-four hours straight already (and hadn't gotten much sleep in the week prior), and along with the hypnotic "wshh-foof" of the respirator resonating with the "dip-beep" of the heart monitor, there seemed to be another presence in the room, over by the window. Although dark outside I could see it peripherally, slightly huddled over by the curtain. In aspect, it was featureless, but dark, almost a black-green shadow. Patient and unthreatening, it calmly waited. When I'd widen my eyes, and looked hard enough though, it wasn't there. But it *was* there, waiting... Paul arrived right as the sun was coming up, but once he walked in and we all hugged, it wasn't but a matter of minutes, and then he too, was simply standing there, waiting. The nurses started coming in at the shift change, which must have been about seven. They looked at us piteously, and said that if he hadn't passed just before sunup, the odds were that he would last another day. "Are you sure?" we asked. "It's just the way it seems to go," they said. Oddly, less than an hour later, we heard monitor alarms go off down the hall, a quick bustle by the nurses and some resident in scrubs, and when the nurse came back in a half an hour later to check on Dad, she told us that a little old lady down the hall had cashed in.

The sun was up now and we took turns going down to the cafeteria for coffee. At lunchtime, they brought a tray for Dad, even though they knew he wasn't eating, and we picked it apart. But the rest of the day passed in mostly silent vigil. Then the dark came on again, and we settled on the fact that this was it. A few prayers: Our Fathers and Hail Marys; but for my part, they were just time-killers. If Dad heard them (which he probably did), it couldn't have inspired much hope. The presence in the corner waited calmly. After midnight, and as the morning approached, there was some minor activity. Dad's heart monitor began fluctuating somewhat, and the nurses would come in periodically from their station down the hall where they could see the monitor on their own screens. They checked his pulse, adjusted things ever so slightly, and would squeeze Mom's hand as they went back to their station. Finally, Mom went over to Dad, leaned over him and said, "It's okay, honey, you can let go. Don't worry about us, we'll be fine." I guess it was about four or five by then, and within fifteen minutes, Dad gave a whole shake of his body and the monitor alarm went off. Mom and I were standing next to the bed and Paul was at the foot. All of a sudden there was rush of nurses, a young doctor, and someone pushing a cart into the room. Mom and I grabbed each other and just watched in shock. Paul straightened up, and said, "NO!" and the doctor, nurses, and orderly stopped cold in their tracks. They looked at Mom, whom I was holding, and she shook her head. Then they calmly filed out. We looked at each other, looked at Dad, Mom kissed him on the forehead, and we did another Our Father. The respirator was still pumping slowly, "fwish-voof." After a few minutes, a nurse came in and turned it off, turned the lights down, and left us. We stood there for about ten or fifteen minutes before they came back and told us they had to clean and wrap the body, were we ready? Yes, we'd go down to the cafeteria and get some coffee, which we did. When we came back up, he was swaddled in a sheet with a wrap around his head and his face exposed, and he finally looked at peace. The left hand of dawn was just beginning to show, and the presence was gone. When we got home we all went right to bed, Paul on the sofa in the living room, Ma in her room and me in mine. After a few minutes Mom came into my room and crawled into bed with me and I held her as she cried, sobbed, and bawled like a baby. After ten minutes, she got up and went back into her room.

Even though she could turn on the waterworks whenever it seemed necessary as we were growing up, I'd never seen or felt her cry like that before or since.

The next day we made the rounds to the funeral home and cemetery. Ma wasn't much help at first, and didn't want to look at caskets or talk with the funeral directors. But she was right at home in the city cemetery, picking out the plots and throwing in a couple of extra on either side so her and Dad wouldn't be "crowded." Finally we got her to sit down with the funeral directors at Carey Hand, which was the preferred mortuary for upper middle-class Orlandoans. We settled on a coffin and she put some money down. Then we stopped at St. James and made arrangements for the funeral at the Cathedral. Dad hadn't been to church since the early 70s. He stuck it out when they went to English; he kept going when they turned the altar around; he even kept going when they had the guitars come in for the "hootenanny' and "kumbaya" masses. But he said that when he went in and saw a woman in slacks handing out communion, well, that was it: he didn't leave the Church, the Church left him. The Church was agreeable, however (and though I don't know it for sure, I suspect Ma slipped them a nice donation). It was a rather sedate affair with well over a hundred people attending. The viewing the day before at the funeral home had a few of Dad's work friends attending and more than a few of them spoke. Most notable to me was Dad's old boss, Bob Ammerman, a real man's man, boar hunter and handsome *bon vivant*, who talked about how he had worked for Dad for years (?) and how well they got along. After he spoke, Mom went up to him and said, "But Bob, you didn't work for Barney, he worked for you…," and he replied with a smile, "That's what everyone else thought…" Another example of Dad's winning ways.

The viewing was a little traumatic, seeing Dad laid out like that. Since retiring from Martin Marietta three years earlier, he only had two suits left, one dark for funerals and one light blue seersucker for summer, whereas when he was working he probably had ten. So he was buried in the dark suit. And he had given all of his ties to Goodwill, swearing never to tie one of those "goddamn nooses" on again as long as he lived. Well, now that that no longer applied, rummaging around in the closets I found one last tie, one that his workmates had given him when he retired. It was dark blue and had a single line of small text repeated diagonally down it in white and yellow a dozen times: "Illegitimi non Carborundum," a bastardized Latin motto for "Don't Let the Bastards Wear You Down." The sentiments were perfect, but the tie was all wrinkled and dirty from age. I took it to a dry cleaner and told the owner why I needed it back quickly. He said come back in an hour, and when I did, he told me "no charge." So Paul and I had to go to the funeral home early before the viewing to check on everything, that they had done him up right. Ma was going to come later, in the company of a bunch of her widow friends. I brought the music, which was a compilation of maudlin Irish drinking songs, many by the Pogues, some Patsy Cline, and of course, Dad's favorite, Roger Whitaker. When we were looking into the casket, it seemed a little odd that Dad still had his glasses on, even though his eyes were closed, but I suppose he would have looked a lot stranger without them. Paul said, "Something's not right," even though everything looked okay to me. "I'll be right back," he said and left. In the meantime, Dad's longtime best friend, Jerry, the retired mounted policemen from Detroit, came in early with his wife, my godmother Mary, Mom's longtime childhood best friend. Jerry was really hit hard; he and Dad had shared many a laugh, many a drink, and many an adventure together over the years. They're dedicated Catholics, and so, soon started in on a low-rumble rosary. When Paul got back, he pulled out a pack of Kools and a little book of matches and put them in Dad's upper breast pocket. "There," he said, "now he looks natural," and it was true. The wake at the house after the funeral and the trip to the cemetery was raucous, a typical Irish celebration of life and the liberation of death. It even got to the point where Mom and the priest who officiated were dancing Irish jigs in the kitchen. Dad would have loved it. We were all drinking rather heavily, and at one point Paul went into the kitchen to console Jerry, who was still a bit distraught after losing his old friend. Paul mentioned that he had went out and bought the pack of Kools and put them in Dad's pocket, so that he looked natural and would be able to enjoy a smoke on the other side. Jerry smiled and said, "Yeah, I know... I saw you." Jerry had always given Dad a hard time about smoking, as he was a reformist, having given it up cold turkey some twenty years earlier. Jerry reached into his own breast pocket and when he pulled his hand out, he had a small pack of matches in between his fingers. "If he wouldn't quit now," he laughed, "he's going to have to quit over there." We all laughed at the thought of Dad checking his pockets for eternity to find a light. Later, after many more drinks, Paul and I whispered furtively that we hoped that was the case and that Dad wouldn't find a light all too readily available.

Before passing on to other matters, one last intriguing item must be addressed. Maybe a week after the burial and wake, Paul and I had gone back to Tallahassee, and Mom made a visit to the funeral home, Carey Hand, to make the final payment on the whole deal. While she was there, the mortician, the guy who does the real down and dirty, not like the pseudo-serious "consoling agents" who lurk in the foyer and hallways, asked if he could talk with her in his office. Ma told me he was very nice, a pleasant sort of guy, old and grey, but he wanted to tell her something. He remembered Dad from the previous week or so, for a specific reason, and he felt he needed to tell Mom. He told her that first of all he was amazed at the open incision wound from the ulcer surgery of a month previous, as this was very unusual, and also mentioned all the wartime scars. But even more so, he had to tell Mom that Dad had had the most infected blood he had ever seen in his career, and that in his estimation it was a miracle that Dad had lived as long as he had, that he must have had a very strong constitution. He just thought it was important to tell her, and she told me that if he hadn't been so kind and concerned about it, she otherwise would have been put off by the whole conversation. As if to convince her that he was serious, he pulled out a notebook with a sheaf of newspaper clippings. There it was... amazingly, he had been the mortician for Elvis! Yup, Memphis, what, twelve years earlier? The clippings were just interviews, none of that National Enquirer pictures-of-dead-Elvis stuff, but were evidence that apparently he'd been quite sought after by the news media when the King had died. He'd moved to Central Florida to semi-retire, and he was now working at Carey Hand part-time; he just felt it was important to let Ma know about the infection. The fact that he had been Elvis's final makeup artist (as well as Dad's) wasn't a brash claim to fame on his part at all, he just wanted her to know and showed her the clippings just so she'd believe his sincerity; they were his credentials, if you will. (The King is Dead! Long live the King!)

Disaster
It was a quiet summer as I passed into my 40th year (although I had to take a quick trip that took me on my 40th birthday to Cape Hatteras, working on recovering some Spanish armor that had washed out on the beach after a storm). The boys were happy and healthy, all enjoying the summer with baseball and swimming before going back to school, and now that I'd finished my long and gradual graduate program, we decided it was Amy's turn to go back to the University and pick up where she'd left off. I had to go off again though when, at the beginning of the Fall semester Hurricane Andrew struck South Florida, and the Park Service, just like much of the rest of the Government, went into emergency mode. You'd be surprised at how, when FEMA is activated at such times, it sends ripples throughout the other Federal agencies as well. Not to be too cynical about it, but a good portion of that concern is driven by the knowledge that certain government emergency-only coffers are sure to be opened quickly and generously. For

such disasters there is created a Case Incident Command System, with some high muckety-muck in each agency forming his own emergency response teams, and then he and the other high muckety-mucks consult on how they're going to carry out and coordinate their resulting damage assessments and then make recommendations up the line on how to proceed. So the Southeast Archeological Center (SEAC) was tapped to carry out an assessment of what damage may have taken place to the cultural resources, or archaeological sites, in the parks of South Florida, most notably in the path affected by Andrew, those being Biscayne National Park and the Everglades. A team of guys was put together from the Center: myself, Ken Wild, John Cranston, Guy Prentice, and then we had our mediocre manager Gordon Schmidt as our team leader. Since I was the only NPS blue-card diver at SEAC at the time, and was already familiar with the underwater stuff at Biscayne, I was designated to team up with Harry Murray of the Submerged Cultural Resources Unit (SCRU) to handle the assessment of any damages to the shipwrecks out there. Although Harry and I had had our moments over the years, we knew we were both lucky to be going out onto the islands offshore, in the company of one of the Park rangers, to go diving every day, barbecuing and drinking every night. The other crewmen were going out on daily treks into the Everglades, nasty with the ungodly heat, mosquitoes, snakes, thorns, and lots of machete-work, to look at Indian mounds, shell middens, and maybe an old Seminole camp or two.

They issued us these little white paper government credit cards for our expenses, so we went shopping at one of the few grocery stores (and one of the even fewer liquor stores) still operating out of Homestead. Then we booked on over to the Incident Command supply center near the park headquarters at Everglades. These were two or three large concrete buildings left over from a Cold War arsenal out in the swamp, now packed with all kinds of survival gear: mosquito netting, firefighter shirts and camouflage pants, bug spray, cans of water and orange and grape soda pop, machetes, shovels, tape measures, gloves, boots, notebooks, pens, even large all-terrain vehicles, gas cans, etc. We had our pick of whatever we wanted or needed. I went for clothing and the cases of canned water; Harry occupied himself with the more exotic electronic stuff; and the Ranger, Rick, well, curiously enough, he wanted a couple of cases of the cheap, sugary drinks, and grabbed himself some ammo for his sidearm and a couple of bags of charcoal. Then we quickly made our way to the Convoy Point Park headquarters at Biscayne, where Ranger Rick commandeered a nice boat (one of the few operational ones that hadn't been tossed up on land or otherwise wrecked) and several sets of dive gear with maybe a dozen tanks; we loaded it all up and we were off to the park housing at Elliott Key, about three miles offshore. For the next four days we went diving all day, every day, documenting any storm-damage scouring of sand or loss of turtle grass, or broken stands of elkhorn coral that were on any of the wrecksites that Ken and I had documented back in '84. As far as the wrecksites themselves, there was really very little damage. This was surprising at first, because a lot of them were in shallow water, less than 30 feet, and we expected the storm surge to have been horrendous, like it presented itself on land. Soon we figured out that the outer deepwater reef shelf, at maybe 80 to 100 feet, had taken most of the fight out of the surge, except for the rising water. The wind was extremely dangerous and powerful above the water, but not so fierce below. In fact, when you think about it, those wrecksites had been down there for hundreds of years, and considering the number of hurricanes that had rolled over the top of them in those ensuing decades, if not centuries, well, no wonder they (and every other archaeological site) looked pretty much the same. Nonetheless, much later we were given a demonstration of the true power of Hurricane Andrew.

Popcoon Fun

One night, after a long day of diving, and after we all had enjoyed a dinner of grilled steaks and more than a few rum and whiskeys with wild lime juice, I laid down in my cot to read. Harry was watching television (we had a small generator, and there were still a few local stations on-air). Rick the Ranger sat down at the kitchen table with a lit candle and opened a box of 38 caliber bullets, spilling them out onto the table. Then he got a small pair of needle-nosed pliers and slowly twisted the bullet out of the brass shell casing. Glancing over at him, both Harry and I got curious, and asked him what he was doing. "You'll see," he said. Then, after lining up maybe a dozen of these bullet-less cartridges, he took the candle and filled each one to the top with drips of liquid wax (?!). After letting them cool and harden, he loaded his pistol with six of the paraffin pellets and pocketed the rest, grabbed a couple of sixpacks of the orange and grape generic sodas and went out the back door. Harry followed him. I went back and lay down on my cot. After ten minutes or so, a shot rang out. Soon another followed. Then lots of laughter. Every two or three minutes there'd be a shot, and then peals of raucous laughter. Well, I knew they were target shooting, but it was pitch-dark outside! Finally, my curiosity got the better of me, and I looked out the back door. There they were, sitting on the back steps, and Rick was tossing a can of orange soda out into the blackness. Harry had the gun held out, but he was wearing some kind of headgear or binoculars. Then he fired, and I heard a loud "YIP!" and they both laughed and laughed. "What are you doin'?" I asked. "Shooting raccoons…" said Rick. WHHHAAATT? "Here, you try it…" and he took off the headgear from Harry and put it onto my head, "Sit down." As I looked into the darkness it was now lit up like a nice luminescent green day—they were night-vision goggles! Rick tossed a couple of cans out there maybe ten yards, which I could plainly see, with a bunch of other ones all torn up. He handed me the gun and I thought he wanted me to shoot the can. "No… wait a minute," he said, and sure enough, out from the bushes a couple of raccoons, their eyes glowing brightly, slowly and cautiously crept out. They went right over to the cans and started biting the thin aluminum until it sprayed out all over their little faces, chests, and opposable forelimbs. They were really ripping into them and then lifting them up and guzzling the soda like drunken sailors. "Okay, whenever you're ready," he said. Feeling guilty now as I write this, at the time we'd had a few drinks ourselves, and it just seemed the right thing to do, so I let one off and hit that coon right in the ass. "YIPE!" He jumped a foot or two in the air, dropped the can, and ran back off into the bushes. And yes, we laughed and laughed. Rick assured me that the melted wax just gave them a little sting, and that, uh huh, as we watched and he threw out another can (my eyes now getting adjusted to the darkness out there), here comes the little bugger, uninjured, either him or his little brother, creeping out to get some more of that goody-good joy juice. One was enough for me, and I left the boys to carry out their harmlessly sadistic sport. It really was kind of funny. Even more funny, odd, and even a little frightening, was the next day when we were riding a little electric golf-kart down a dirt trail on the island, and there in broad daylight, we come upon a whole family of raccoons out in the island palmetto bush, some with bright orange day-glo faces and paws, and others with deep blue-purple hair and ears, some with both, looking like a wild-eyed pack of demented clowns, or Joker-faced miniature hunchbacked harlequins escaped from the circus, all wearing little black burglar masks.

Money for Foowey

Coming back off of the island, we joined the rest of the crew who were housed at the Holiday Inn in Key Largo. I was amazed to see that the hotel had somehow come into possession of the original *African Queen*, used in the movie, either the one from Africa or the one filmed in the studio in England. They were using it to give tours of the Upper Keys. They also had the wrecked version of the boat used in *On Golden Pond*, where, in his last movie, Henry Fonda hits a rock and gets thrown overboard. So I quickly had one of our guys take pictures of me both standing in the Queen and sitting on the wrecked Golden Pond boat. But then we had to settle down to business and write up our results from the assessment of the offshore wrecks in Biscayne National Park. Again, as I said earlier, there weren't really any great effects on most of the wrecksites. One however, *was* affected: the remains of the old British frigate, *HMS Fowey*, which we at SEAC and FSU had worked on back in '83, almost ten years earlier. The storm surge, even underwater, had scoured out a lot of the loose sand and even tore out some of the turtle grass, and exposed a moderate section of the wooden structure, frames and planking, as well as a few artifacts. Not only did we document the effects of the storm, but we were pressed to come up with some sort of plan to mitigate those effects. So, the solution was pretty simple: as long as parts were exposed, let's document them as well as we can, collect what artifacts are laying around (after mapping them in place), and develop a long-term stabilization plan. Easy enough for an assessment report. The trick was, putting a figure on it. We didn't want to look greedy, but we also wanted enough to do the job right. After a quick determination of time and personnel, Harry and I agreed on roughly $30,000. Then I piped up and said, "Put down $40,000." No, that was too much, Harry said, it would make us look like we were padding the figures. "That's exactly right," I said, "ask for $40K, and maybe we'll get the 30." He couldn't argue with that, so, $40,000 was our estimate. The team leader, Gordon Schmidt, whistled at this, since the most the other teams had come up with was less than $10,000 for all the land sites they had visited combined. Harry and I stood by the number and it was submitted as part of the overall report.

Swamp Stomp

Before leaving South Florida I had to take on one of the land assignments, well, really a swamp assignment. There was a large Indian mound called Bear Mound out in the middle of a large saltwater swamp that hadn't been visited in over ten years, so they wanted somebody to go out and look at it. They picked me and John Cranston, as we were the two toughest sons-a-bitches they had. John's a big man, three-hundred and something pounds, rotund, balding and with a large brown beard. We had known each other from the Canaveral excavation and we were getting along pretty well back then. They put us in a boat with Harry and a ranger to take us out to the very tip of the peninsula of the state, and from looking at the USGS map, we plotted where they could put us in, and then, following a trajectory with the compass, we should come upon the mound in a couple of miles, and then, after we did our "assessment," beeline it east out of the swamp and into Florida Bay, where they could pick us up in a couple of hours. While getting the map out of my backpack, I inadvertently took out the bug spray and set in on the boat seat, where it rolled down behind the cushion. We found the point of entrance, and also found that it was solid mangrove at least thirty or forty feet thick. Easing off the boat into waist-high water, fully clothed, with T-shirts and backpacks, we clambered over the mangrove roots, slimy and slippery, and finally came through to a large expanse of turgid, brown, bubbling, and algae-matted open swampwater. As we sat on a log before attempting the crossing we could hear the hum of the boat as it pulled away, which was quickly replaced by the droning hum of the mosquitoes. Already exhausted by the scramble over the mangrove roots, now I rooted through my backpack frantically for the bug spray (NOT!). Oh God – the boat was gone, and we had miles of knee-high, waist-high, and chest-high stink and (what can only be best compared to) baby poop to wade through. The quicker we got done, the quicker we'd get out. We eased into the fetid mire, took a bearing, and began slogging through. It was slow and hot (even the water was hot), and grueling… I held the backpack over my head to keep it dry, and John generally led the way, me following in his lumbering wake. After about a mile, he turned to me and asked, "You know that thing you see in cartoons and Tarzan movies, where a guy gets swallowed up in a swamp by quicksand? Is that only in the movies, or is that real?" I told him I think it's real, but quicksand isn't what they make of it; it doesn't swallow you up, it's just really wet mud or very watery sand, and if you don't lose your cool, apparently you can swim right out of it. It's when you panic that you drown in it. We walked on another half-mile. I couldn't help it, but I had to say it, "I'm not as worried about quicksand as much as the fact that there's only one place left in the United States that has free-roaming oversized saltwater crocodiles... and that place is right here." He turned to me with eyes as big as saucers, but didn't say a thing. We plodded on for another mile, now scanning right and left constantly. Out in this broad open shallow lake of scum there were no trees, either the water was too warm or too salty, so when we saw a single dead trunk poking up some twenty feet above the stink, we decided to stop, drink some of our bottled water, and rest. As we leaned against it, the thing began to vibrate, as if a radio signal were passing through it. Then we heard a loud thrumming like a small plane flying over, far away. As we looked up, we could see that the top of the trunk was alive with thousands of bees coming out of various holes up there and swarming, apparently alerted by our presence. "Oh shit, we better get out of here," I said, "they might be Africanized." On we went, looking over our shoulders to see if we'd be followed by the bees, and still scanning the periphery for any large man-eating reptiles (we hadn't even considered escaped feral pythons back then, although they were probably there as well). Eventually, we came back upon the mangroves on the other side of what had surrounded this oversized shallow bowl of a rotten vegetable-broth death trap. Never once did we see anything that could have been remotely considered an Indian mound, not even a hump of ground that might have served as an alligator nest. As we got into the mangroves, the mosquitoes again lit upon us with a vengeance. Besides biting us viciously, they were thick enough to get into your nose and mouth as you breathed, so we were coughing and swatting and slipping as we again clambered over the slimy tangled mangrove roots to get to the open water of Florida Bay. When we finally got out, we sat down to our chins in the cooler clear seawater and waited for the boat. When it came, as we handed up the backpack and started to climb in the boat, both Harry and the park ranger/boat captain began laughing, and we asked what was so funny. Well, they said that besides smelling and looking like we'd been dipped in diarrhea, our faces, lips, ears, and arms were all swollen horribly from mosquito bites like we'd just gone twelve rounds, and we were red as beets from sunburn. Ha, ha, very funny. That evening I applied my paper credit card generously to the hotel bar, even to the point of uncharacteristically buying other people drinks, glad to be alive, only to find out weeks later when my expense report was kicked back that liquor wasn't covered, unlike everything else.

Flying Frog Lips

Just before I left Biscayne on that trip, the park personnel threw a large picnic party at Convoy Point one afternoon, just outside the devastated headquarters building to sort of celebrate the work they'd done over the last month since the hurricane had shattered their lives. There were still a few boats sitting in the middle of the road from the nearby marina we had to drive around on our way in, but this was supposed to be some sort of a triumphant get-together of all the park personnel and us others who had come in from elsewhere to assist. It was fun, the food was good, and the liquor and beer were flowing. Everybody was in their work clothes, lots of ragged t-shirts and cutoff jeans, and more than a couple of people were sporting casts and bandages from either the effects of the storm or subsequent accidents while doing the cleanup. Despite the minor injuries, the inconvenience of working long days with sporadic paychecks, and the fact that there was a lot more work ahead, spirits were high. At some point someone got the idea for a group picture, and slowly everybody started to get in line. All of a sudden out of nowhere, this small two-seater helicopter, the kind with the big bubble up front, comes hovering on in, finds a spot and sets down nearby. Out of the chopper hops a small guy in a spic-and-span

346

National Park Service uniform, Smokey Bear hat and all. It was the Superintendent of the park! The same one who disappeared even before the hurricane hit and hadn't been seen for the past month (rather than tell you his name, I'll just tell you that we used to call him Frog Lips). Now he had shown up just in time for the party and picture. There was an ugly undercurrent of grumbling. People refused to shake his hand, and most just turned their backs to him. The photographer was still trying to get people to line up for a group photo, and when he'd almost had them ready, the Superintendent moved up into the forefront. Now the grumbling got louder. A few people even yelling out, "Hey where you been?" and "Who are you?" Some of the others in the front of the line just turned their back to the photographer, who was now getting impatient. Then somebody tossed a paper cup at the Super, which was quickly followed by a flurry of cups, some still having liquid in them. The yelling picked up and it was soon evident there wasn't going to be a picture with him in it, and in fact, he needed to go. And go he did. The chopper fired up, he climbed in, and off they went. I really thought it might get physically dangerous for him, but once he was gone, and the picture was taken, everybody just went back to enjoying themselves. I heard he was soon transferred to the northernmost small and secluded (and cold) park in the continental United States, where frog lips freeze nine months out of the year.

Divorce: The Beginning

Before beginning this string of emotionally tumultuous tales, let me first acknowledge that I still see Amy, my first (and only) wife, that we are still partners though living apart, are in constant communication, and I continue to love and respect her dearly. Having said that, over both 1992 and 1993, I was still being called out to the field a lot. Besides the stint in Homestead after Hurricane Andrew, I'd been sent to Canaveral again to do more clearance on the dikes, as well as to witness and document the destruction of the once-famous Eldora Hotel, and when SCRU sent SEAC $20,000 for me to draft a *Submerged Cultural Resource Overview and Assessment for the Virgin Islands National Park*, this time I insisted on going there personally for at least a week to do the requisite research (since now I knew they had the money to do so). It was on this trip that I met Dr. Edwin Towle of the Island Resources Foundation, who had once been Alan Albright's boss, and who filled me in on the sources of a lot of Alan's personality quirks and his checkered history. When I was back in the office, I was working hard (and often overtime) writing not only my field reports, but some large "planning" documents, like the *Research Design for Archeological Investigations on 16th Century Contact Period Sites in the National Parks of Northeast Florida* with Buddy Kale (as absentee principal author), and the *Regionwide Archeological Survey Plan for the Southeast Region (SER): A Part of the Systemwide Archeological Inventory Program (SAIP) of the National Park Service's National Archeological Survey Initiative* with Buddy (this time more as disinterested editor than as absentee principal author) and John Cranston. These planning documents were Washington-based assignments not to be taken lightly, and we borrowed heavily, but judiciously, from other government-produced publications (a well-known and accepted practice in the Service) to meet the critical deadlines, when not putting our own spin on what we thought was important and would require further future funding. Nonetheless, we were working long days, the stress factor was high, and often (maybe too often) I would decompress for a couple of hours down at Poor Paul's before going home. All this is to say that, other than the weekends when I was in town and at the house, I was in all likelihood not giving my domestic duties their compensatory due. Meanwhile, Amy had gone back to the University and was pursuing a Masters in Communication. The boys were in school all day, so she was usually home when they got there, or shortly thereafter, and on those nights that she had a night class, well, I just made it a point to be home. Needless to say, we didn't see much of each other during this time.

When we were home together and talked about work and school, I learned that she was taking a couple of classes that she enjoyed from a professor named Topher Mulligan, a tall guy with receding hair, medium build, and a slight limp. Apparently he was both knowledgeable and entertaining, and certainly supportive of her being a somewhat older, but conscientious student (and one who asked questions). After hearing about what a great class it was, one evening I cut across campus after getting off work, and snuck into the back of her classroom just to observe. He spotted me right away, not knowing who I was, but no one else, including Amy, noticed me. It was a pretty average class, and when they took a break Amy finally turned around and saw me, and she wasn't all that happy that I was there. What the hell, I was just checking out this class she'd gone on and on about. I told her I'd see her at home, left, and walked back to my car. When she got home she still wasn't happy about me going in there without telling her. No big deal, I said, it wasn't all that interesting to me, and I promised I wouldn't do it again. I got to meet him again later at some faculty mixer, and he was interested in the fact that I made beer, so I told Amy to take him a couple of bottles from out of the cupboard. I'd just started going to the local brew-club meetings for a couple of months, when I was in town, taking my brother sometimes, and damn if I wasn't surprised now to see Topher show up a month or two later. He'd suddenly decided to become a home brewer! And not just a regular run-of-the-mill one either, he'd gone ahead and studied up on it and knew the detailed chemical lingo in no time... better than me, who'd been making beer for over fifteen years by then: a quick study being one of the benefits of a degree in Communications, no doubt.

Sure enough, he started getting friendlier. First, we were invited over to parties at their house, mingling with faculty and graduate students, and no matter what department they were in, it was always fun. Then it was "Why not bring the boys over for dinner and go swimming?" where he and his wife, Lena, would make home-made pizzas, and while we adults would all share bottles of wine, his two older boys and younger daughter played in the pool with our kids. It was all rather idyllic: a very nice family, with a nice two-story house (nicer than ours) and a big yard in an upper-class neighborhood. And the homebrew meetings became so regular that when he campaigned for, and was elected president, and I became vice-president, the after-tasting tabulations and awards soon melted into hours-long finishing of various beer samples that had been brought in and left behind, with attendant discussions of philosophy and opinion. Little did I realize it at the time that he was also probing me for weak spots. If I had noticed, it wouldn't have much mattered anyway, I had plenty to keep me busy, and I didn't think much about him one way or the other when I wasn't around him. But I did notice that Amy was getting rather cold and feisty at home. She also developed what I considered a bad habit of moving the furniture in the living room around when I went out of town. When I came home, I simply moved everything back. Obviously, our sense of *feng shui* was out of whack. I have to admit though, that she carried on pretty well when I was gone, balancing school, the kids, and the house. Slowly and surely however, I began to notice that things were not quite what they seemed.

Permanency?

Meanwhile, things were still jumping at work. When I wasn't in the field, or at work at the Park Service, I was teaching evening classes at the Academic Diving Program, specializing in archaeological ethics and legislation, survey methodology, report writing, and underwater excavation techniques. At the Center, because of my efforts on the write-ups of the 16th century research design, further trips to Cumberland Island, and work on the newly-formed Regionwide Archeological Survey Program (a.k.a. RASP, which was another Washington-based, *and funded*, initiative to push the Park Service to inventory their cultural resources and make determinations of how to manage them), I was placed as head (or Team Leader) of that program at SEAC, the survey team. That and the Masters degree meant I finally got permanent status in the government after 13 years as a temporary. It also meant we finally had health insurance and I could begin accruing retirement benefits. It was long overdue, and the managers at SEAC said they couldn't justify not making it right any longer. John Cranston also got a promotion and permanent status at the same time (besides his work at SEAC, he'd been a helicopter mechanic in the Army for eight years, so there was that veteran status to consider as well). I remember Gordon Schmidt calling me in to tell me about the promotion. Even though I was now working for Buddy Kale, who never gave a damn what we did, just as long as we did what we were told, Gordon called me in to congratulate me, and tried to make the case that it was all his doing, that he'd been pulling for this for some time. "We wanted you to head up the Survey and Evaluation team. Cranston is going to head up the Compliance section" (*compliance* being the business of going to parks when the installation of waterlines, or toilets and septic tanks, or any other ground-disturbing construction was going to take place, to check out whether some archaeological site that might have been missed was going to be affected). Survey and evaluation meant you went out looking for new sites "where no man has gone before," or looked at previously recorded but relatively uninvestigated sites, and then evaluate their size, depth, and condition. It was definitely the plum of the two. Gordon winked at me and said, "You know, we don't really consider that compliance work real archaeology." When he saw the shock on my face that he'd even said such a thing, he surprised me even more when he continued, "and if you ever repeat that, I'll swear I never said it." Fuck him… I went to Buddy's office next door and thanked him for the promotion and permanent status. He was disarmingly honest. "We didn't have a choice. Personnel at the Regional Office said we had to do it… congratulations." This reminds me of what my old boss George Fischer, whom I always liked (and still do) said to me about a month after he "retired" with a disability three years earlier, "I just wanted to say I'm sorry. You know how all those years I kept telling you that we couldn't put you on permanent status? Well, that was bullshit. We could have done it at any time. It was just cheaper not to." Thanks for your candor, I told him.

The Retirement Party

It was right about this time that Pete retired. He'd been Chief at the Center for over twenty years, and now the new regime was moving in. Much to Buddy's dismay (and Gordon Schmidt's delight) they put John Hardinger from the Regional Office in Atlanta up as the "Acting" Director—the Park Service was retiring the term "Chief" since it was now considered politically incorrect vis-à-vis the Native American aspect (though they'd never complained). When I heard John was going to be the new director, I was overjoyed. I'd always liked John: he had great sense of humor, and he knew how to play hard when the work was done. Others at the Center didn't quite see it the same way, and they warned me: "Watch out what you wish for…" The non-competitive appointment was made by the Associate Regional Director for Cultural Resources, Paul Hartwig, whom I always referred to as "Earwig," a big lumbering bureaucrat from Atlanta whose main attributes were that he didn't make waves and he managed money well. He came on down to Tallahassee for John's installation, and Pete's retirement party, which Pete didn't want to celebrate, but they insisted. So we all went out to the favorite local Chinese restaurant where they had set aside a banquet room for all the staff. After the usual pleasantries about his long service, and what a great job he'd done over the years, where Pete listened painfully ill-at-ease, Hardinger and Hartwig presented him with a nice card and a large glass vase with layered colors of sand in it. Hardinger went on to say that these were samples of soil taken from each of the 64 parks in the Southeast Region, and how it had taken him months to get them sent to him in Atlanta from all the parks so he could put together this retirement "award." Now Pete was really feeling awkward, and just gave a short thanks. Everyone headed back to the

Center on campus, and Hardinger and Hartwig went back to Atlanta until Pete vacated his office a few days later. When Hardinger finally came back down and got set up in a week or so, I happened to be "up the hill," where the Administrative offices were, and overheard John and Gordon Schmidt laughing over how funny it was that Pete had been honored with "a jar of dirt." I realized then that Pete knew exactly what it meant when they gave it to him. I wonder if Hardinger really did get the samples from the Southeast parks, or whether he just scooped them up in handfuls out of a parking lot somewhere.

Fe-Fi-Fowey Again

Amy was knee-deep in schoolwork, and I was up to my neck dealing with the new survey program, RASP, when we got notice at the Center that money had come out of FEMA as a result of the Hurricane Andrew cultural resource assessments. One hundred thousand dollars had been set aside for, of all things, further studies and development of a stabilization plan for the *Fowey*. This was the result of the work Harry Murray and I had done, and for which I had talked him into bumping the estimate up to forty thousand, hoping to maybe get thirty. Trouble was, FEMA had given it directly to the park, Biscayne, which in turn handed it over to SCRU, the Submerged Cultural Resources Unit, headed by Dan Lenihan and Harry Murray. In effect, it was a blank check. I'd been called up to Hardinger's office and apprised of all of this, since I'd had a direct hand in it. When I heard all this I sorely chided Gordon Schmidt, who had been the manager for the cultural resource studies, why he had let this happen. Since he was the Head of Cultural Resources for the Hurricane Andrew Case Incident Command System, he should have had a say in how the money was to be distributed and used. But he just lamented that it was a done deal. So I told Hardinger, yeah, it may be a done deal as far as the money goes, but they still have to come into the Southeast Region. We had the Regional Archeologist, Buddy Kale, here at the Center; and the Regional Archeologist is the guy who signs off and says how it's going to be done. Lenihan and Murray were coming to Florida in the next week to discuss the project with Biscayne, so Hardinger insisted that they stop by SEAC on their way. When they showed up, we all crowded into Hardinger's office, and not only did they *not* want to discuss the money, insisting that that was Biscayne's business, but then they only glossed over lightly what they planned to do on the site. When they went out to lunch, I told Hardinger, "Ask them to show you the research design," which he did when they came back. Boy, did that piss them off. It wasn't quite "We don't need no stinkin' research design!" but more like, "We've never been required to produce a research design before." Well, you're gonna need one this time. They later produced a three page summary of what they wanted to do. Hardinger and Buddy reluctantly accepted it.

The next thing we hear is that they're going to shut out SEAC altogether and bring in a bunch of amateur "avocational" underwater archaeologists from out of Maryland, under the direction of Dr. John Seidel, then teaching history at the University of Maryland. They were a club of well-to-do divers, lawyers and such, who wanted to do underwater archaeology in their spare time as adventure. It was called the Maritime Archaeological and Historic Society, and I already knew about it because I had written them a year earlier, as a Park Service underwater archaeologist, congratulating them on the good work they were doing and especially for bringing archaeology to the public in a specialized, ethical forum. As a result, they contacted me back and asked if I'd be on their Board of Advisers, which I was for a couple of years. Seidel was planning to stop by SEAC before going to Biscayne, so he could look at the collection of artifacts that we'd recovered from the *Fowey* in '83. When he showed up, I gave him the grand tour, and explained what we had seen and done almost ten years earlier. Then I was surprised to find out that he didn't know a damn thing about it. Murray had never told him about our work down there, and

350

he hadn't seen the report by Skowronek and Fischer, so I gave him a copy. As he looked at the report, and the artifacts all laid out on the lab table, another problem asserted itself.

You see, it's an unwritten (yet commonly understood) rule that when an archaeologist has begun research on a site, unless he boggles it completely, or is divested of it from some higher authority, or either declares it open again, or dies, then that site is considered his personal research prerogative for at least ten years, especially if he continues to publish articles or carries out further studies on the site, whether or not he ever puts foot on it again. All this has to do with the amount of time it takes for analysis, conservation, following research leads, and publication of research reports, not to mention getting the requisite feedback from peer review, often either supported or challenged in its own right. Well, it hadn't been quite ten years since we (SEAC) had been on the site, and both Russell Skowronek and George Fischer had continued their research and publishing on the *Fowey* in the interim. Seidel didn't even realize that Skowronck (whom he knew by reputation) had been the principal investigator who worked the site and, with Fischer, was considering writing a book on it at the time. He just hadn't been provided this information by Murray when SCRU invited them to come work the site with the Hurricane Andrew FEMA money. So I filled him in, especially since I'd been with Murray the summer before and put together the assessment that was now going to pay for his summer adventure with his amateurs. Seidel was uncomfortable with sidling in on Skowronek's research, but I told him it was easily resolved: just invite Skowronek along (and oh yeah, offer to pay his way). Seidel said he'd run it by Murray, who was really directing the whole operation. That invitation to Skowronek never came, much less a courtesy call, and when they were finally gearing up for the project, Hardinger called me in and told me he was sending me south to Biscayne as the Regional representative (again), to keep an eye on the doings. Yes, he'd contacted Murray and company, including the Park Superintendent, and let them know. When I arrived at the hotel in Florida City, I rang up Murray and told him I'd arrived. Sounded like he'd been drinking but he said okay, he'd see me the next day at the park. Ten minutes later, he calls me back. Now he's in a rage and starts to give me shit about having talked to Seidel and telling him about our working the site back in 1983. He's cussing and mad because Seidel had pinned him down on it, asking why he (Seidel) hadn't been told about the previous (and ongoing) work. I knew I was on solid ground, so, even though I hadn't been drinking (yet), I worked up a little rage of my own and fired back, "So, *how come* you didn't tell him about the previous work? Seems like he's figured out you're not being totally honest with him, muscling in on someone else's turf, now doesn't it?" He hung up on me. Well, this is going to be a lot of fun, I thought.

In the morning I met everyone in the park, and although Murray tried to ignore me and pretend I wasn't there, I already knew Seidel and a lot of the park personnel so I just made my own introduction to the rest. I knew the drill better than all of them, and after a quick welcome speech from the new Superintendent soon we were loading tanks and equipment. Once on the site we all made an introductory dive to familiarize ourselves with the layout, before Murray and Seidel began laying down a baseline to work from. They found one of our 1983 datum points, a piece of rebar halfway driven into the sand on the north end of the site, but couldn't find the other, and tied it off at what I knew was a lopsided angle. If they didn't lay it down exactly on top of our 1983 axis line, then it would be just like a new investigation, rather than building on what had been learned before (*not* the scientific method, but rather a duplication of effort). I explained this to Murray and Seidel, and Murray was perfectly happy with the idea that this was not a continuation of 1983. Soon I found the old 1983 datum point at the south end of the site, but Murray refused to use it. So be it. I was surprised to see how much the wrecksite had regenerated its sandy cover since we'd seen it the year previously; obviously it was covering back

351

over nicely after the hurricane. By the second day however, they had pulled out the Venturi dredge, powered from the surface, with hoses extending down, and the exhaust hose lying on the bottom with a mesh bag around the end to catch any haphazard artifacts. Unlike our expedition in 1983, where the park resource guy, Curry, made us construct the whale condom to divert any sucked-up sand to a central location, Murray and company were given the okay to just shoot it around out of the way. Then they started sucking. It became apparent that they just wanted to suck the sand off the exposed timbers, map them, and move on: everything we'd done in 1983. And now the site was more covered up, and thus, protected, than it had been even the year before. But no... they were gonna suck some sand, and sand they sucked. I stayed out of the way, took a few pictures, and simply observed (I wasn't invited to participate anyway, and I sure didn't need the "practice.") At the end of a week they'd uncovered maybe half of what we'd mapped in 1983, but they sure had cleaned it up good. They only had a few days left on the project, so before they had to cover it back up, Murray came up with a plan for "preserving" all the exposed and loose ship parts and other artifacts, like iron fasteners, wooden deadeyes, copper barrel hoops, pewter plates, cannonballs, etc. He was going to dig a big hole in the bottom of the sea, pick these things up (hopefully, after mapping them in place), place them in the hole and cover them with sand. Needless to say, he never told me, or anyone else for that matter, that this was the plan. He just went ahead and did it, with the help of all these amateur archaeologist wannabes.

Now this is a serious piece of business. Anyone who knows the least bit about maritime archaeology knows about how things stabilize over time, about electrolysis (the passage of electrons between metals), and how any act of disrupting this balance-over-time causes renewed, even exacerbated, deterioration. That's just by moving things around. Putting a lot of different metallic items into a single repository, even a hole in the sand, is in fact creating an electrolytic "stew" that may take decades to stabilize at the cost of major sacrifice of the more energetically ionized (and usually the smaller and more delicate) artifacts to the larger more "accepting" artifacts (cannonballs, ship's hardware, barrel hoops, e.g.). The result? Smaller artifacts of the one-of-a-kind variety are lost to the larger, denser, dime-a-dozen types. The lesson? If you're not going to lift the stuff and commit yourself to a many-years-long program of careful and exponentially expensive conservation, don't fuck with it. This however, was a major fucking–with. They did their best to cover the site back up with sand, reversing the dredge and blowing sand from the surrounding seabottom to deposit onto the wrecksite, essentially putting the thing to bed.

It was on this trip that one of the rangers decided that they needed to go look at a modern wreck just outside the Park boundaries, lying upright in maybe 130 feet of water. It was a steel cargo ship, a couple of hundred feet long, sunk in the 60s and a spectacular dive (the name escapes me right now). I had gone on it maybe four or five years earlier, and that time, like this, I didn't plan to go below the superstructure at 100 feet, just to be safe; besides, you can see the bottom from there and get the feel of the whole ship. I remember that it was in pretty good condition the last time I saw it. The ranger got us on the GPS coordinates, but something was wrong. According to the depth sounder, the wreck wasn't there! He must have got the location wrong. Everything else seemed right, the depth, the general location, the way the islands to the west lined up. We drove around some, looking, but it was useless: the damn thing wasn't there! This was a huge steel ship, thousands of tons in weight, and had been sitting on the bottom for decades, covered with a light crust of coral encrustations. We looked around and finally had to give up. Six months later I heard from the park that they'd found it, only it was a mile and half closer to shore and now rested within the park in 85 feet. The only explanation was that the deep underwater waves of Hurricane Andrew had picked it up off the sandy bottom from 130 feet and moved it shoreward. Such a thing had never been documented before, the power of deep submerged storm waves. It's still one for the books.

Beach-Face Magging

Part of the Regionwide Survey Program centered on getting previously unsurveyed acreage in the parks covered, one way or another. The more acreage we got done the better we looked. But digging shovel tests at a 20-meter interval takes lots of time, lots of people, and therefore, lots of money. So I came up with this idea of using electronic remote-sensing; specifically, a magnetometer (in effect, a super metal-detector), dragged behind an all-terrain-vehicle, to survey the entire beach-face of Canaveral National Seashore. Shit, we'd knock out a couple of thousand acres in a week or two. Twenty-four miles of beach north to south, and I figured three good runs, one at low tide, one mid-beach, and one up along the dunes ought to cover the roughly 90-yard-wide (30 meters-wide) beach face. Laid side-by-side, these three runs would give a great picture of any metal under the sand. What I was really looking for were the remnants of any iron-fittings that would indicate a historic shipwreck site under the beach. We'd dragged the mag many times behind a boat, and we'd even used it on land several times, even on beaches, but then it was always point-by-point. I didn't know of anyone who had dragged one down the beach continuously recording, so I turned to Dennis Finch, our computer guru, who quickly established a setup program on one of our laptops that, once set in motion, would automatically record the magnetic signature and time once every three seconds. Thus, if I ran at a steady pace, not too fast, say 10 miles per hour, I could make each run in a little over 2 and a half hours, and collect roughly 4500 data points.

The problem was in figuring out how to correctly position the data points. How would I determine exactly where a "hit" occurred on the open beach? This is where Cranston came in. He liked that technical stuff, and SEAC had only recently come into purchasing a Global Positioning System, now made available to the non-military government as a result of the first 1990-91 war in Iraq, the one known as "Desert Storm." The trouble was that the hand-held units could only collect 999 points at a time, while at the same time at least 180 points were necessary to get a proper position because they had to be "processed" to phase out the military-coded scatter factor. And those 180 points had to be recorded at a standstill, then later downloaded into the processing program on a computer. Luckily the park had put up numbered wooden posts every quarter mile, and even though they weren't *exactly* at every quarter-mile mark, they broke the stretch of beach into ninety-six discrete sections. At 10 miles per hour and a reading every three seconds, it would be easy enough to interpolate any hits, or anomalies, within a couple of yards between the posts. We still needed the exact positioning of the posts however, so Cranston would get the 180 readings necessary at each post (5 posts at a time), then rush back to the Maintenance Area, where we had set up a field lab, download the data, recharge the batteries, and then head out to collect the positions on another 5 more posts. Most of the time we didn't see each other, and although we had radios, we tried not to use them (at least I tried not to) because they would interfere with the magnetometer. The mag head was pulled by ½ inch nylon rope, wrapping the recorder cable and taking the strain off of it, affixed with duct tape, to a length of 125 feet so that the effect of the ATV would be minimal outside the 30-meter range of the instrument. The head, or sensor, was encased in one of those five-gallon clear plastic water bottles you find upside-down at the office cooler, packed with rags. The initial test run didn't work as planned and the plastic bottle would spin itself and the rope into a twisted mess; this was solved by adding a couple of PVC runners or small outriggers to the container. This gave it the distinct appearance of the old *USS Enterprise* (the one captained by James Tiberius Kirk, not the aircraft carrier) so I got out a big felt tip pen and put the letters NCC-1701 on both sides. It all worked together exceedingly well. As long as I didn't go above Warp 10 (m.p.h.) there was little or no chance that she was gonna blow.

Magnificent! It's the word that comes to mind when I remember riding that ATV alone slowly up the beach, sand and dunes and scrub to the left, and the ocean to the right: twenty-four miles of beach without a soul on it, just the way the natives and the Spaniards saw it. Every so often a "thing" would present itself on the horizon, getting larger as I approached, only to reveal its true character upon closing in on it. Let's see, there was a large barge, washed into the shallows sometime after WWII. There were several refrigerators, sometimes even standing alone on the open expanse of deserted beach (an incongruous sight if ever there was one), a couple of television sets, a broken up boat or two, hundreds of foam buoys, and thousands of plastic bottles, plastic containers, coolers, fishnets, pieces of lumber, etc. But for the most part the view was that of steady roiling waves, dune faces topped with scrub and the saltwater mist in the distance merging the two.

We found lots and lots of "anomalies" (magnetic signatures) that weren't so obvious, buried deep beneath the sand. There were only two known shipwreck sites that we could run alongside of and obtain what a comparative shipwreck signature would look like. One was "The Ghost Wreck" which was actually a turn of the century large wooden fishing boat, possibly a shrimper that had washed ashore and although once buried beneath the dunes, would become exposed time and again after serious storm episodes. That is why it was called the Ghost Wreck, because it would appear and disappear over the intervening decades. The other was The Saurwalt Wreck, named after the first guy to seriously try to salvage it back in the 60s. He and his buddies had found coins dating to the early 1800s on the beach back in the day when families had first camped up in the dunes on holiday. Using a metal-detector, he found some more and soon pinpointed the obvious location, although the wreck itself was offshore. He tried and tried to work that wreck, but it just so happened to be exactly in the surf zone, so stationing a boat over the top of the site was nigh on to impossible. On those few and silent sun-hanging summer days when the water would lie down to a gentle roll for a couple of hours, they were chased off the site by large sharks patrolling the coastline for any edible activity. He finally gave up and once the State and then the Feds acquired the land, any salvage permits were curtailed. But since we knew the general area within a hundred yards or so, I'd watch the mag carefully, and sure enough, it was easy to pick up the 'bell-shaped" signature that identifies a historic shipwreck site. More often than not however, what I detected were "spikes" in the data: large jumps but quickly gone. These tend to indicate a large individual item, a dipole in the language, which sure, could be a cannon, but without any other adjacent signatures was more than likely a car. A car you say!? Yes, for years and years cars were allowed on the beach. Usually they were either beach-cars, barely running, or beach buggies later on, modified to drive on the sand, or sometimes even stolen or "borrowed" cars, any one of which might end up stuck or out of gas, or just abandoned, to be slowly undercut by the tides and eventually buried by the storms. (Ten years later, long after I'd gone, the Center, SEAC, finally sent an expeditionary team to go out and evaluate some of our anomalies by digging down to them. Unfortunately, the team picked spikes as opposed to the bell-jars I had recommended. And what did they find? Cars.)

One day Cranston and I got a call over the radio. The Park Superintendent wanted us to come in to the Office in downtown Titusville as soon as we could. We quickly finished up where we were at, packed up and put away all the equipment. Then we drove down into Titusville and went into the Park Headquarters and were told that the Center wanted us to call the office in

Tallahassee right away. We called, and asked for the Director, John Hardinger, and I put it on speakerphone so John and I could both talk and listen. John told us that Buddy had had a heart attack. Apparently this wasn't his first either and it was pretty serious. He was in the hospital and was going to be out for quite awhile. Wow. We were both a bit stunned, but at least we were glad to hear he was still alive. Hardinger said not to worry, that it didn't affect our field operation, and we could continue as before. "But…" he said, "from now on you'll be reporting to Gordon Schmidt as your new supervisor." We looked at each other, knew this was bad news (certainly as bad as Buddy's heart attack), and then we both simultaneously let out a loud groan. Unbeknownst to us, Hardinger had also put his phone on speaker, and he said, "and Gordon is right here and wants to speak with you." The loud groan from us was probably still reverberating in the room when Gordon got on, "Hey guys! I know it's a bad situation with Buddy, but we'll be able to do some really cool things together. We'll talk about it when you get back. Meanwhile, call me if you have any problems." We said goodbye, hung up, and had to start laughing. They both must have heard that instinctual gut-moan when we were told we'd be reporting to Gordon now. Ah well, that's the way it goes. We went back out, but not so hurriedly this time, less inclined to get back to the office.

Time Tunnel

There were several other trips in quick succession over the next year including more to Biscayne and Cumberland Island, even a Washington-office sponsored trip as the Southeast Regional representative to the Denver Service Center to report on the progress of the Regionwide Archeological Survey Program (RASP, as it came to be called) in the Southeast. After seeing an advertisement, I darted off one afternoon after a meeting and caught a bus to one of the semi-deserted wooden Western mining tourist towns, Telluride, to do some erstwhile gambling. Then we got a project request from Moores Creek, North Carolina, where I'd started so many years earlier. It was a small survey and testing project at the reconstructed earthworks, presumably where Colonial forces in 1776 had lain in wait for the Loyalist Scottish militia to approach the creek bridge from the other side. Our job was to determine if the reconstruction of the earthen fireline, done by an early Park superintendent with a backhoe thirty years earlier, was reflected in any way by historic below-ground remains. I went there with Cranston, whom I'd worked with at the Canaveral Armstrong site, and who had inherited the Compliance section, and since ostensibly this was a compliance project, therefore it was his; so I went along for the survey end of it at the earthworks, and because I'd been there before. We were still getting along pretty good back then, and we had two girls working with us named Carroll and Wendy. Carroll was a lively slender sport chick who ran marathons and biked ten or twenty miles at a time. She was from North Carolina so she was right at home. I always liked her because she was generally upbeat, easy on the eyes, had a long slow Southern drawl, and a crop of peach fuzz on her neck and face that I found particularly appealing. Wendy was a tall blond, but she had made plans for her boyfriend to visit and they spent all their time together so we didn't get to see much of her when we weren't working. We all worked well together during the survey, where we laid out lines of flags for shovel testing, and we had a set of walkie-talkies to keep us in contact over long distances. While Cranston and Wendy were cutting transects with machetes through the tough blackberry brambles, without the communication sets, I'd be working the transit laying out lines and directing Carroll on staying on-track with the stadia rod. When she'd turn to pace out another 20 meters with the tape I'd talk dirty to her over the headset telling her how nice her ass looked in the scope, and what I'd like to do with it. She wiggled and never complained. When it came time to dig the test units along the reconstructed earthworks, I found out that Cranston didn't know much about proper excavation techniques and I tried to gently direct him on what was necessary to carefully dig it, things like not to sit on the edges of the unit, and why we needed to keep going even when he thought we'd gone far enough. He wasn't very patient about it, but we muddled through, and sure enough, at the very bottom we hit the remains of an old firepit. Well it just so happened that, according to the historic accounts, the Patriot defenders of the bridge had spent the last night before being assaulted sitting around their warm but dampened fires beside their hastily constructed foxholes along the earthworks, waiting for the approaching Scottish Highlanders. Gently carving into the ash-encrusted soil, recovering an unspent musket ball, here was another instance in my life of going back in time, sitting on the edge of an old ashen firepit, with the spirits of the long-gone musketmen, waiting that otherwise quiet and bitter cold February night a little over two hundred years earlier, listening for the approach of tramping feet, a few lolling drums, and maybe a pipe or two coming up the road in prelude for a pre-dawn battle.

Dumbing While Intoxicated

On one of our days off, Cranston and I went to see *Forrest Gump*, which had just come out and was getting great reviews. It really touched me and I lauded it to anyone who'd listen, telling them "You've got to see it!" (It was also on this trip that I sat at a the hotel café counter having breakfast one morning, and on the TV above the grill O.J. Simpson was riding in that white SUV threatening to kill himself while his buddy drove, people standing over and along the freeway in Los Angeles holding posters and shouting "Run, O.J., Run!" just like dear Jenny had encouraged Forrest.) When I got back to Tallahassee (and put the furniture in the living room back in place), I told Amy that I wanted to take her to see the movie since she hadn't seen it yet, and it was oh, so really, really good. We could make it a "date." A babysitter was procured and we headed out. But as soon as we got in the car, Amy said no, she didn't want to see the movie, she just wanted to go to Bullwinkle's, the premier Friday night after-work-week hangout. I put up a little fuss, but what the hell, I could go for a few beers. The beers turned into pitchers, and Amy switched to gin and tonics. It was probably during this night out that I realized that there was serious trouble in Paradise. Amy got pretty cantankerous, and was itching for a fight; she didn't want to see the movie; she didn't want to stay at Bullwinkle's; she didn't want to go home; she just wanted to drink, and complain. We left Bullwinkle's to go explore the rest of the Strip on Tennessee Street, and I took her to a little hole-in-the-wall place I liked, but since it only served beer and wine, we had to go somewhere else. It just wasn't working out; no matter where we went, she didn't like it, the drinks were lousy, and my company was boring. Eventually we got into an argument and she stormed out. I'd just ordered a beer, so I wasn't leaving till I'd finished—the heck with her. When I did go out looking for her it took fifteen minutes and halfway around the block for me to finally find her sitting at the top of the stairs of a defunct business smoking a cigarette. Obviously there was something on her mind. I made nice and talked her down, but she just wanted to go have another drink.

We went to another haunt and soon got into another pointless argument. Again she stormed off. That was it; I'd had enough and I wasn't gonna play along. Yes, I was getting polluted, but I still thought I had my wits about me. Unfortunately, when I went out back to the parking lot, a watchful Tallahassee PD lady spotted me right off (it was a very busy Friday night and she was walking the parking lots behind the string of bars). She told me, "Don't even think about getting in your car and heading out of this parking lot, 'cause I'm checking everybody out, and now you're on my list too." Jesus Christ! I knew I'd had a lot to drink but (yes, I know, stupidly) I only had six blocks to go to get home, and all of those were away from the main roads and down dark and quiet midnight residential streets. I spent the better part of the next hour looking for Amy, but she was nowhere to be found—I later found out that she had called a cab, and apparently had her own adventure when the cab driver made a pass at her on the way home. After not finding Amy, and now feeling a bit more sober, I decided to head home. Looking around, I didn't see the lady cop, but I hadn't moved fifty feet before she pulled me over in an unmarked car (unmarked except for that fear-installing intermittent blue flash of foregone fate). To the station I go, distracted, dejected, and disgraced. Since it was Friday night, I didn't even call home, but just stretched out on the steel slab to sleep soundly onto Saturday. The next day, Amy let me stew for a while until she finally managed bail later that afternoon. She also made it a point to let the boys see Dad walking out of the County Jail. The upshot of it all was that I got a lawyer who had the charges reduced to reckless driving (which I thought was interesting, since I hadn't even driven out of the parking lot), and who ameliorated the sting of a huge fine by a light sentence of twelve days in jail, which I was allowed to do on three consecutive weekends, with credit for time served. The first day I went in I got my bunk assigned, rummaged around in a cardboard box of old paperbacks, and settled down to finally read *Crime and Punishment* (how appropriate!), and that kept me busy for the three weekend stretches that Dostoevsky and I became old pals.

Divorce: Revelation

But there was still an emerging cold war now developing with Amy. I couldn't put my finger on it; yeah, I'd been out of town a lot, and she had to handle the kids, the bills, the groceries, the housework, etc., but had I not been a good provider? Then again, maybe that was it: she was getting along pretty good on her own when I wasn't around. All that and balancing school as well (and her grades were reflecting that she was doing very well). But I couldn't turn my back on my finally-blossoming career at the Park Service; hell, they were leaning on me more than ever. About this time, Ken Wild was going down to Puerto Rico a lot on a couple of big projects at the fort there. He was staying for weeks and months at a time, and when he'd come back he was telling me that the Superintendent liked him and they were trying to create a position for him as the Park Archeologist. He and they were negotiating behind the scenes, and this was all hush-hush, mostly because SEAC was making a shitload of money by him travelling down there and back, with the attendant contracting fees, and if the park hired him and he left SEAC all that would end. Meanwhile I was carrying the load as far as dealing with any underwater archeology, along with a renewed interest in Canaveral, and managing the Regionwide Survey Program. After the stint in the hoosegow, which I had kept quiet from my fellow workers, I began riding my bike (a Christmas present, and no, not a motorcycle) to work every day, expounding a healthy lifestyle, but in actuality hiding the fact that my license had been suspended for six months. Fortunately, I'd been issued a U.S. Government driver's license a year earlier so I could drive Government vehicles with impunity while in the field (as long as I never admitted to, or they never found out about, the State charges). It was a low time, what with the stress at work, Amy's cold shoulder, and riding a bike back and forth to work no matter the weather, and then things just got lower. I had to go on another Biscayne trip, a short one this time, four days, and all land stuff. I went with Gordon Schmidt, who didn't really need to go, but just wanted a trip down south. In fact, we'd agreed to switch off digging a line of shovel tests on Siesta Key for a proposed telephone line, but after the first one, he conveniently went missing to discuss the project with someone who had nothing to do with it. After work, I took him to The White Horse bar and strip club up in Homestead, and he went fucking nuts. This is one of those lower-class B-girl all-nude strip joints, but it had cheap beer and once the girls knew you weren't going to tip them more than once, they'd leave you alone. But he was like a kid in a candy shop and started throwing money around, and the girls, smelling a sucker, flocked around him. He even started buying girls for me, but I told them to just take the money and leave me alone to drink my beer. I wasn't interested, something was gnawing at me. It was the business at home.

357

On the way back, flying home, I thought about it and thought about it, and then it hit me. It all fell into place, like a set of dominoes. She was carrying on with Topher Mulligan! It was so obvious I couldn't believe it. Oh, he was so smart, such a great teacher, another Irishman, her professor, all those dinner invitations, his kid baby-sitting ours (for what? for WHY?). Of course. I remember sitting on the plane looking out over Florida and actually feeling relieved. I wasn't going crazy; and though I'd never been a saint, I hadn't been a total shit either. I still loved Amy and I'd do what I could to fight for her. When I landed I called the house for her to come and get me at the airport, as we'd arranged earlier, but she said there were people over and I should take a cab. When I got home, there was her brother Charlie and a few other friends out back and they'd all had a couple of drinks. It was early Friday afternoon, so I had one or two myself after telling everybody about my trip down south, and then waited for everybody to leave. When they finally left, I sat her down and told her I needed to talk to her. I told her what I'd figured out and asked her how long it had been going on; she broke out crying uncontrollably and told me it had been about six months. I don't know why, but I was very cool about it: I wasn't angry or adrenalized at all; again I was more relieved and maybe because of her crying and carrying on about how sorry she was, I didn't even raise my voice. But then I told her to call him, "Call him and tell him to meet me at Finale's," which was the site of the old Lucky Horseshoe Bar, re-designed and under new management. She stopped crying immediately and asked me what I was going to do. I said I just wanted to talk. She went into the kitchen and called him while I went out back and smoked a cigarette. She came out and said, "He's not going to meet you. He's at the University and doesn't want to talk to you." I told her "Go back in there, call him again, and tell him that if he doesn't meet me at Finale's at four o'clock, I'll be at his house at five." She came back out and said. "He'll meet you at Finale's." Since it was already after three, and I didn't want to talk with her any more right now, I headed down there, found a nice table off to the side, ordered a beer and waited. He showed up slightly after four, obviously unhappy and nervous.

At first, he wanted to appear confident, (dare I say it?) cocky, and ready to fight. I ordered a beer for him, which took him by surprise. Then I think I disarmed him completely by calmly saying, "Well, these things happen…" and let him know that Amy had told me it had been going on for six months. He claimed only four. By now that first flush of adrenaline had left him, he took a long slip off his beer, and asked me what I was gonna do. I let the question sit. He got very frightened, stiffened, and said, "You're not going to tell my wife, are you?" His wife was a very temperamental, fiery and intelligent middle-aged woman whose scorn would undoubtedly ignite a firestorm of proverbial hell-fury. To look at the realization on his face that it was now inevitably coming, I actually felt sorry for him. "No, I'm not going to tell your wife," I said, "I promise." I let it sit for a few moments while he tried to hide his relief. "*You're* going to tell her," I told him. "What!?!?" "Look," I said, "if she's half as bright as I am—and I'm sure she is, and in fact, she's probably smarter than all of us, you, me, *and* Amy—then she already knows something is up. No, I'm not going to say anything to her. But now that it's out, it's just a matter of time. So *you're* going to tell her… and believe me, the sooner the better… she finds out on her own, it'll be worse." He couldn't have been more deflated, desperate, and depressed had I hit him with a baseball bat. For being such a smart professor, the fact that this hadn't occurred to him in any sort of real-life scenario appeared to be a jolt. While he sat there absorbing his newly-fractured future, I began my offensive: "Now, as I said, these things happen… people get attracted to each other… they take it to a certain level… men and women, well, inevitably this occurs… but now that it's out, I'm going to have to tell you, it's over. And you can drop the whole charade about being my buddy at the beer-making meetings… to be honest, I never really liked you. I thought you were a bit of a pompous ass and a fraud, and I guess I was right. In any case, I've got a lot to

358

deal with myself, with Amy, and you've got stuff to deal with too. Since you've finished your beer, and I'm not going to buy you another one, I guess we're done here." He got up, still shaken by his eventual impending evisceration, straightened himself up, and left. I ordered another beer for myself and sat digesting the long day's development.

The situation at home did not look promising. After the crying had stopped, and the realization of any continued connubial bliss was foregone, within the week began the recriminations: I was not a good husband (not true); I was an absentee husband (true); I was neglectful (somewhat true); I was lazy (when I could be); I drank too much (true, but so did she); I was a lousy lover (that was a lie, but one I couldn't argue against, now could I?); and the worst, that I was not a good father (well, this was not just a lie, but a damnable lie, and she knew it, but it was meant to strike a reaction, which it did). But the basic gist of it was that, after twelve years married, I had not been the shining knight I started out as, and she was once again being appreciated for herself, and goddamnit, she was going to make the most of it. It probably didn't help things that money was tight, and I'd been pushing my out-of-town trips further afield so as to make extra money on per diem and sometimes, even mileage. And now I'd laid down the patriarchal law of the land: it was to stop, immediately. Silly me. Of course they were going to talk, which they did, and it soon presented itself that he was putting off telling his wife, Lena. Another beer-makers' meeting was soon approaching, and hell, I'd have to go, being the vice-president and in charge of tabulating the tasting results. The night it arrived I asked Amy if he'd gotten around to telling the head of the household yet about his amorous indiscretions. No, she told me, and they were both thankful that I'd stuck by my word not to divulge. I remember getting dressed to go out, and telling Amy how much I enjoyed pulling on my new steel-toed boots, chuckling wickedly. It took her a minute, but finally she said, dead serious, "You know, those can be considered as concealed weapons." I didn't think that was true, but I let the matter lie. I left a little early so I could get a beer or two in before the meeting started. When he arrived it was obvious that Amy had called him after I'd left; he paid particular attention to my feet. But the meeting went well. Interestingly enough, although this wasn't the usual situation, that evening there was a surfeit of home brew samples, and even though we could set aside and save the bottled stuff, there were a couple of small kegs (in fact, small CO_2-fed soda-canisters), and it would have been a crime to let them go to waste, so a few of us stayed late to finish them off, including both Mulligan and myself. After a couple of pitchers, the others started drifting off homeward and soon it was just the two of us. I told him what a sneaky sleazy bastard I thought he was, and he countered with me being a closet redneck (which didn't bother me a bit, I was proud of my Florida frontier connections). I did strike a chord when I accused him of cowardice in the face of his wife, as it had now been two weeks since the initial unveiling and he still hadn't gotten around to a declaration. He couldn't stammer out an excuse, and it was suddenly time to go. We cleaned up the place as best we could and left together. He had a sheaf of papers, probably schoolwork that needed correcting, and when we got to the bottom of the stairs and were standing face-to-face laying out our parting insults, he accidentally dropped them. I stood there as he tried picking them up in some orderly fashion, then decided to help. He stood there as I picked up the last of them (we'd both had quite a few beers), and I remember thinking "Now would be the perfect time. One great sweep of my leg, undercutting his, and I could easily bring him down, and then it would be easy enough to kick the shit out of him. He could later plausibly claim he fell down the stairs." Then I realized that it would only make him a more pitiful creature than he already was, and by taking him down like an old dead tree I would only elevate him to the higher ground. So I just handed him the papers, told him to go fuck himself, and went on home, three blocks away. Amy was still up when I got there; she had sensed that something might go down, but when she saw my still new and unscuffed boots she was relieved. I imagine in another universe, in a different time, things went differently, as I suppose everything else did as well.

Divorce: Denouement

Understanding that it's already too late to make a long story short, I'll condense the following year and months into a Reader's Digest sequence of events, so as to move along the dialogue. He did tell his wife soon thereafter, and she went after Amy with a vengeance, threatening to "cut off her tits and stuff them in her mouth" (whew, harsh stuff!). He was put on a short leash for the foreseeable future, but that didn't stop him and Amy from talking in the meantime during the day. I wasn't happy with Amy's demeanor, or rather, lack of it, and at some time between arguments she decided that she wanted to move out and live alone. I thought this wasn't a bad idea, since she'd become a real pain in the ass, moping around and complaining. Her brother Jimmy had bought a trailer out on some land in Greensboro, a small former tobacco-growing town a half-hour drive from Tallahassee, initially an investment, with a small creek running through it, and though he'd tried living out there with his wife and three kids, the commute and confines of a small trailer soon drove him and his family back to Tallahassee. But he needed someone to live out there and maintain the place, so Amy packed up some of her stuff and went out there to commune with nature and I'd take the boys out there to be with her on the weekends. This lasted maybe three or four months, before the solitude, the commute, and finally, the cold, got her back into Tallahassee. She was home maybe two months, still communicating with Topher and probably sharing sick days with him as well (by this time I didn't care much anymore; I knew that if Lena caught him now he'd be singing castrato; so, living in constant fear while at the same time feigning renewed fidelity and affection, and then trying to balance Amy as well, would rather quickly put him over the edge). Then Amy announced that she wanted another separation, and got herself a chalet-style apartment about two miles from the house off of Ocala on the appropriately-designated Rumba Lane. This was going to be her private in-town love nest where she could control the situation, but part of the rather lame rationale was that when the boys stayed with her "it was only a two mile ride on their bikes [along busy Tharpe Street] to go to school and back." Hell, I wasn't going to have this, when they could walk back and forth from (now) my house on Jackson Street. So they would come to my house after school and then I'd drive them over to Amy's when I felt like it. My Mom had become aware of the situation, and (saint that she was) tried to maintain a judgment-free stance between Amy and me (even loaning Amy the deposit for the apartment), hoping for an eventual reconciliation. But Ma was hot over the fact that the professor, Mulligan, had overstepped his boundaries ("and an Irishman at that!"). Ma was so angry that she once proposed to me that if I would make the arrangements, she'd gladly bankroll a couple of thugs to cut him out one day and knee-cap him. I thought she was kidding, but from the look on her face I spotted some deep historic O'Brien-family Irish Republican recklessness. "No, thanks for the offer, but I'll handle it my own [Buddhist-Christian] way." Slow and steady wins the race.

We were now into the whole sordid mess over a year, when Amy finally realized that despite his promises, pronouncements, and proposals, and even though she had made moves toward independence herself, Topher was not going to leave his wife. The worst, venal reason? "I don't want to lose my house." Thus, despite the declarations of undying love, the fires of passion were beginning to wane. I imagine after she'd had a couple of drinks he'd also gotten a dose of Amy's own brand of ferocity, which I had witnessed periodically over the years (Yipes!). She couldn't keep up the rent at Rumba, so she moved back in once again, and we decided to go for marriage counseling (what the hell, it couldn't hurt). The first counselor was a heavy-set woman who was all New Age touchy-feely and in my mind didn't address the underlying problems at all. After two sessions with her I'd had it and requested another therapist. This time we got a middle-aged stocky guy named Mark Lyons. We both liked him as he got right down to business (in a Dr. Phil sort of way) but had a sense of humor and immediately set us at ease by telling us about a few of his other clients' problems and therefore assuring us that ours were at least "treatable." I also liked how he would let each of us rant and rave and then sum up the session in general psychological terms. He even asked us to come in separately once or twice for some one-on-one. After a while, Amy didn't want to see him anymore. She was still sneaking around with Topher when they could, and I was getting less and less patient about it; not to mention, I still had to go out of town once in a bit for work, and this didn't help my temperament imagining what was going on while I was gone. One day we were scheduled to visit Dr. Lyons together for a regular session, and Amy just refused to go. "I don't like him and I don't want to talk to him anymore," she said. Well, I like him, I told her, and since we had an appointment that we'd have to pay for anyway, I decided to go alone. When I got there, and walked into his office, he said, "Where's Amy?" I told him that she didn't want to come, so I figured I'd just come alone. "Well, I don't want to see you," he said, "there's nothing wrong with you. I only want to see you with Amy, so next time, tell her she has to come." I was a bit surprised and said "But I've got some issues I want to deal with, and since I'm paying for it anyway…" "Too bad," he said, "You'll be fine." "But what if this all ends in a divorce?" I stammered, still rather shaken by his abruptness. "Then you'll be divorced," he said, "but you'll be fine. You'll adjust and you'll move on. Now, go on home, and next time, make sure Amy comes with you." When we did go back to see him, we'd been fighting pretty hard and steady and she was still convinced that Topher was going to cut his wife loose eventually, and by now I had lost all patience with her. At that session Dr. Lyons was more of a referee than anything, and when Amy loudly and defiantly announced that she no longer needed me, something clicked inside, and we left in hot angry silence. Two days later, after perusing the yellow pages, I made an appointment to see a lawyer.

When I told Amy that I wanted a divorce and I was hiring a lawyer to make it happen, I was surprised at how complacent and cool she was. She didn't hire a lawyer herself, but after talking with some of her feminist girlfriends decided she wanted to go the way of the Mediator. This was fine with me, the less I had my lawyer to do, the better (and cheaper). We hammered out the deal over two days with a lot of yelling, wailing, and gnashing of teeth, and more than a few time-outs to cool off. Afterwards, I showed it to my lawyer, who asked me more than once "Are you sure about this?" but after I convinced him that it was all what I had agreed to, he said he'd process it. The whole deal was still going to take awhile, but my mind was made up. It was now a one-way trip.

17.   Parks, Partings, Parts, and Partnerships (1995 -1996)

Meanwhile, I had let the folks at work know what was going on at home, and I was surprised at the reactions. Buddy, back from his period of recuperation and with the taste of mortality still fresh on his lips, had the most empathetic view, having gone through a troublesome divorce years earlier (and then ended up re-marrying the same wife later on). He was very good about sharing advice and really helped guide me through the process. Gordon Schmidt was another matter; try as he might, any sympathy he evinced seemed a put-on. I know he liked Amy, they always seemed to get along at cocktail parties, but I couldn't help but feel that he took a little sadistic pleasure at my own underlying distress. Cranston began to show his true colors. He was totally unsympathetic, which was *de rigeur* for his macho big-man persona, and reflected the way he dealt with his own dysfunctional family situation with a former wife and troublesome teenage daughter back in Mississippi. That really didn't bother me, since I had to toughen up about it anyway, but what did bother me was I found out later that when I'd go outside to work at one of the picnic tables on the University Green (a common practice for all of us, to get out of the stuffy cramped [and to my mind, cruel] cubicles Gordon Schmidt had built within the once wide-open Lab), and even though I'd tell him where I was going, when anyone came around and asked where I was, Cranston would say he didn't know where I was, that I'd been gone a long time, maybe I was over in the Student Union (whereas I was actually just outside the door), giving the impression that I was fucking off. Him running the Compliance section and me running the Survey section, we were now in competition I suppose, and when he smelled blood he was going to take advantage of the situation any way he could. In any case, we were both now working under Gordon, who didn't really understand what we did, just as long as we were seen to be moving forward. Therefore, we had a lot of freedom to design projects and propose them, and if there was money to cover them, all the better.

Pulaski's Immortal 600

At one point we got a call from the superintendent at Fort Pulaski National Monument. He wanted us to try and find the burial plots of Confederate soldiers who had died there while imprisoned, part of the contingent known as "The Immortal Six Hundred." The story goes that, after the fall of Ft. Sumter, during the Union bombardment of Charleston in 1864 from nearby Morris Island, the defenders of Charleston decided to scatter some 600 Union prisoners, mostly officers, throughout the city to try to deter the Union cannon fire. To offset this blackmail, Major General John G. Foster, who directed the Union batteries on Morris Island, which were receiving return fire from both Confederate-held Forts Sumter out in the harbor, and Fort Moultrie on Sullivans Island, encamped 600 Confederate soldiers in tents just in front of, and surrounding his gun emplacements. Although none of the prisoners were killed by gunfire, the conditions were deplorable, and more than a few died from wounds, starvation, and exposure, all this while sitting under the constant bombardment. It might be noted that there were no military targets in the city of Charleston, whereas Foster was obviously protecting his guns with these sick, wounded, and certainly nerve-wracked Confederates now christened "The Immortal Six Hundred." When yellow fever broke out in Charleston the Union troops held there were removed from the city, and Foster could no longer defend the use of human shields out on Morris Island, so the remaining 550 or so were moved to Fort Pulaski at the mouth of the Savannah River, now a prison and in solid Union control.

That in itself is an interesting story, since the fort, just like Fort Sumter in Charleston, and others, formed a part of a series of "invincible" defensive brick forts along the eastern coast (of which Fort Jefferson, down in Dry Tortugas was the largest), conceived under Jefferson, but finally put into place by James Madison after the War of 1812. This particular fort, Pulaski, was the last on the site of a string of earlier forts that had been built at the mouth of the Savannah River since the time of Oglethorpe. The new "invincible" brick design wasn't begun until 1828, and when the original U.S. Army Major in charge of construction fell ill, he turned over the construction to his assistant, a young engineer named Robert. E. Lee. Once it was finished it was named after the Revolutionary war hero, Count Pulaski, who was mortally wounded at the Battle of Savannah. After the fall of Ft. Sumter, and during the opening forays of the Civil War, the Fort was quickly overrun by Confederate forces who once again, under the guidance of Robert E. Lee, strengthened it and manned it as a deterrent to the Union gaining entrance to the Savannah River. In 1862, the Union had begun experimenting with, and then deploying, rifled cannon shells (as opposed to the former smooth-bore), and these proved to be not only more accurate, since they spun like having an internal gyroscope, but devastating in the fact that they could deeply penetrate brick and concrete walls instead of just battering against them or bouncing off. To show the effectiveness of their new weaponry, the Union decided to use Fort Pulaski as a demonstration, no doubt because of the tactical need to get up the Savannah River, but also probably because everyone knew that it had been constructed and fortified under the direction of Robert E. Lee himself. The fort was quickly turned to rubble. Abandoned by the Confederates, the Union troops again re-fortified it with hard reinforced concrete, but left the brick wall facing the sea (although reinforced from within) pockmarked with holes from the rifled shelling to show the effect. Besides protecting the entrance to the Savannah, the fort became a prison for the remainder of the war. And it was here that the 550 men left of "The Immortal Six Hundred" were taken. Conditions were bad, food was scarce, and Savannah can get pretty damn cold in the winter. Because of their notoriety in the Southern press, they were treated especially bad, and by the war's end in 1865, although they'd only been there a little over a year, roughly 24 more had died. The bodies were placed in the same cemetery which sat just outside the fort's western wall that contained the Union war casualties and those who died from sickness; their section however was marked apart, as the "Rebel" area. After the war, the Union soldiers were disinterred and moved to more suitable "Federal" cemeteries, whereas the Confederates were left to lie. This was more than faintly reminiscent of the mass Confederate burial I'd noted earlier at Shiloh.

So Cranston and I were sent to try to find the remaining Confederate graves with the idea that they could eventually be memorialized, at the very least with a park interpretive sign. We used what was called a ground conductivity instrument, which measured how well the ground conducted electricity. It actually shot an electromagnetic pulse down into the ground to a depth that was equal to the length of the instrument itself, which was a meter long, and then that returning pulse was recorded as a digital readout on a recorder hooked to the machine. This was the opposite of a resistivity survey, which had been used by archaeologists for decades (we even used it at San Pedro de Patale during field school back in '83). The resistivity meter's copper probes, however, were ungainly and tiresome since they had to be stuck into the ground, and two or three people had to bend over each time and push them into the surface, then hold them there while the reading was taken, measuring the soil's *resistance* to electro-conductivity. This ground conductivity instrument we used however, allowed us to take a reading at a meter's length and depth every two or three seconds, and we could cover a lot of ground rather quickly. We'd been able to determine the location of the cemetery pretty accurately from old maps, but unfortunately it looked like the bulk of the graveyard, if not all of it, was under the present parking lot. The data seemed to verify this, so now it was a matter of if and when the park wanted to pull up the asphalt, and then subsidize a major archaeological excavation, not to mention what might occur as a result of Confederate skeletons being unearthed. As a matter of fact, we hadn't verified that the Confederate dead were actually there, we'd only confirmed that there was *something*, or some group of things there. While we were at the park and after we'd finished the remote-sensing, the park historian came out and showed us a picture of a cannon that had once marked the site of the cemetery (in fact, placed there while the cemetery was being used). It had been buried muzzle down, the standard symbol for peace and the end of hostilities, and was only removed by the former park superintendent back in 1974. Well, hell, we just took the photograph, placed ourselves in the same position from which it had been taken, and quickly triangulated in on where it had once stood. It was dead-on (pun unintended), and was just south and west of where we had predicted the Confederate graves lay, just as an old map of the cemetery had shown. This threw the question back on whether the park wanted to dig up the parking lot or not, as well as dealing with the Daughters of the Confederacy, not to mention the major expense of a hundreds-of-thousands-of-dollars excavation (as well as forensic analysis and reburial). To this day, having never heard anything otherwise, I believe the decision, the dead, and the dilemma all still lie quietly, economically, and ironically below the parking lot macadam. *Requiescat en pace*.

Fowey Three Times

Once again I was sent down to Biscayne as the Southeast Regional representative when the final shoe was supposed to drop on the *Fowey*: a seminar to be held in Key Largo on site stabilization, or "what do you do with a British shipwreck [sung to the tune of *What Do You Do With a Drunken Sailor*]?" This was a means of disposing of the last of the $100K that had been set aside as a result of the 1992 Hurricane Andrew assessment, and which Murray and SCRU had only burned through maybe 50K in the 1993 investigation with Seidel and company. So they had hired some consulting company out of California, Ocean Sciences Research Institute, to set up this seminar with a number of invited guests, all experts in their fields, to meet at the Hilton in Key Largo and spend several days deciding how best to put the *Fowey* to bed. I had not specifically been invited, since Richard Curry at the park and SCRU didn't want to hear anything I had to say, but Hardinger (who *had* been invited as the Chief of the Center) let them know that I would be showing up in his stead, seeing as how I probably knew more about the Fowey than anyone on the list, and the Regional Office was damned if they were going to be shut out. It was an interesting group, mostly scientists and faculty from the University of Miami, a few rangers and managers from Biscayne (including Curry), and three or four maritime archaeologists, including myself, Jim Tuck of Parks Canada, John Seidel of the Maritime Archaeological and Historical Society, John Gifford, University of Miami, and of course, Harry Murray of SCRU, who presided over the entire meeting. That first morning, after coffee and donuts, I took a seat all the way at the far end of the long conference table, and Murray began by asking everyone to introduce themselves, starting from his left. I found it interesting that right after the guy on my right introduced himself, Murray decided to have the other half of the table then introduce themselves, starting from his right. When the guy on my left finished his introduction, all of a sudden Murray decided that now we should begin with the agenda. Not only was I aware that he had cut this off before I introduced myself, but there were several of my colleagues whom I'd known for years that noticed the omission as well. I raised my hand and coughed. "Yes?" he queried incredulously, taken aback by my nerve. I took the opportunity to just jump right in and not only introduced myself, but let everyone know that I had worked on the original Fowey investigation by FSU/ADP back in 1983, that I'd been there for the assessment with Murray after Hurricane Andrew in 1992, was present for the 1993 SCRU/MAHS investigation, and that I was there as the National Park Service's Southeast Regional representative. When I was finished, you could have heard a pin drop. Murray was hopping mad, and it was obvious to everyone in the room that his attempt at overlooking me had been done on purpose.

After a brief promo of the Ocean Sciences Research Institute (I never really figured out what they did other than send out the invites, book the hotel and conference room, and provide snacks), the agenda again began around the table as each specialist presented his or her take on what was best for the resource. It was pretty predictable stuff: The ecologists wanted to plant sea grass over the top of it, the engineers wanted to build blocks over it or encase it in gravel, and the archaeologists wanted to do more work on it to document and recover what they could. The one or two voices of disagreement were the materials specialists, the conservators and chemists. They had recognized from the briefing papers that there was a serious problem that needed to be addressed before dealing with any type of site stabilization. This was the infamous electrolytic stew that Murray had created when he dug his big hole and deposited all the loose items of artifacts therein: rigging, armaments, pottery, glass, wood, copper barrel hoops, and ship's fittings. The chemists jumped on it immediately and dubbed it "The Pit Problem." What was to be done with all this material? Murray tried to downplay the whole thing, claiming it was "off-site" and therefore not pertinent to the stabilization of the site of the wreck structure itself. This was quickly negated and became a recurring theme throughout the day: if the material in the pit were not dealt with, and considered part and parcel of the site, then why were we here? It became a separate issue that everyone realized was going to be difficult to reconcile with the question of site stabilization, and even the preliminary discussion, which Murray tried unsuccessfully to quash, came to the conclusion that dealing with this "Pit Problem" was going to be a long, time-consuming, and exorbitantly expensive operation.

Going round the table counter-clockwise, it finally fell to me to recommend a solution for site stabilization on the wrecksite of *HMS Fowey*. Putting aside "The Pit Problem" which I acknowledged, but didn't dwell on, I put forth the proposition that in my opinion, and after having studied this from various angles, the best way to encapsulate the site, so as to protect it from weather, anchors, looters, vandals, and overly enthusiastic amateur treasure hunters was to cover the site with sandbags. Not just any sandbags, but those made from the newest plastics, nylon or nalgene. I'd seen these large sandbags used as breakwaters up in Hatteras, and if they could take the battering of a mid-Atlantic storm, they sure as hell could take sitting on the bottom of Biscayne Bay—besides, they were cheap and could be made to various sizes, laid in different patterns, and embossed or printed with numbers and/or Federal warnings. Once dropped off of a barge just off-site, the already-filled bags could be placed strategically over the ship timbers gently and methodically using airlift bags by experienced divers, all mapped in. Should the day come when someone wanted to do some further investigation, it would be a simple matter to lift just those bags that covered the section needed for testing and put them back afterwards. In the meantime, and between time, they would provide an immovable substrate to collect sand and you could even plant seagrass in the crevices between the pillowed bags. (My old boss and mentor, George Fischer, had once facetiously suggested that, after cleaning it off, we should pour a large glob of clear acrylic over the site, so the public could see what a shipwreck looked like from glass-bottom boats overhead, and the looters and vandals would be kept at bay. I chose not to mention this audacious and humorous solution, not even as a joke, or I'd have surely been accused of promoting it.)

Although there was a lot of quiet consideration and nodding in assent round the table, well, Murray didn't want to even talk about it, and dismissed sandbags out of hand. "These have been considered already and determined to be inadequate," then moving on to the next participant. Two members down, he came to the well-known and respected Jim Tuck of Parks Canada, the maritime archaeologist in charge of the Red Bay investigations. At Red Bay, Labrador, they had found the site of a 15th century whale-processing site, assumed to have been used by Basque whalers out of North Spain and Portugal, whalers who had ventured overtime westward to the New World, where they had struck and boiled down the leviathans before later abandoning these probably secret hunting grounds. (Mind you, this was the late 1400s, while Cristobal Colon was still whining to Ferdinand and Isabella to finance an expedition westward to the Indies.) Offshore, in the frigid waters, the Parks Canada divers had discovered one of the wrecked vessels, probably the oldest historic shipwreck in North America; and Tuck, the chief archaeologist, led investigations every summer when the ice thawed, for well over a decade. Surprisingly, he took up my cause, telling everyone that they had used large plastic sandbags every year when they'd put the site to rest: they were easy enough to put in place and remove the following year. Why, they even protected the exposed site from being gouged by ice floes over the winter, which simply rode up and over the large protective sandbags. He seconded my suggestion, and Murray and company shut the fuck up.

In the end, after two or three days, no decisions were made. Murray and Seidel unwrapped a large site drawing made from the 1993 investigation which had uncovered a good portion of the wreck and showed some new features, such as the canvas-covered gunports, but nothing that either differed or improved on the 1983 work. Ocean Sciences, the so-called sponsor of the symposium, was supposed to produce a synthesis of the discussions, and come up with a final report to lay out the best options to the Park Service. It's been over twenty years since the 1993 post-Andrew investigations and almost as long since the 1995 stabilization symposium and to this day not even a summary, much less a report, on either one has surfaced. So much for the $100K Hurricane Andrew Case Incident Command assessment money (but still, it was a very nice couple of days at the Hilton in Key Largo).

Swift Running Brook
Amy and my "mediation" was finalized on February 27, 1995, sadly on our son Robin's 13th birthday. Now it was just a matter of time before the divorce was final. A source for adolescent teen-angst trauma? I don't think so (although he did end up joining the Marines). I'm of the school that it's better for parents to live apart than to openly disagree or fight at home. Amy and I had been going at it for two years now, and even though she was still occasionally seeing Topher on the sly, he was getting scarcer and scarcer as he got more and more frightened of being found out by the scary wife Lena. Meanwhile, Amy and I had come to a truce and she had moved finally into an apartment near both my house on Jackson St. and the boys' schools. I threw myself once again into work, and it so happened that things were heating up at Canaveral again, this time back at the Oyster Bay site. As a result of our 1990 testing, which pretty much proved that French survivors from the Ribault fleet had lived among the natives, at least for awhile, a lot of attention was now being centered on the site as the only physical expression of the 1565 French presence ever verified in Florida. Since Beth had pretty much had enough of Gordon Schmidt by then and left the Park Service to work for a private consulting firm in Tampa, and I now had the Masters in hand and knew more about the Canaveral connection than anyone else, I was asked to put together a team to go down and do more testing and evaluation at the Oyster Bay archeological site. I used the clout to form a small team of my own, all women, who I knew would work hard and with whom it would be fun to be around whenever we relaxed. I was tired of dealing with Cranston by then since it was obvious that he was undercutting me at every opportunity, and though I had a few male interns to choose from, I'd found from experience that when you had a mixed crew, problems inevitably occurred. I felt the girls got along well, and they were sharp, easy-going, and also easy on the eyes; we were a good team, and this proved to be the case as soon as we arrived in New Smyrna, just north of the Canaveral National Seashore North District ranger station. I'd gotten us a large apartment with three bedrooms at the

old San Marino, a Mom-and-Pop motel on the beach just off the AIA-Causeway intersection, which had a tiki bar and restaurant out back overlooking the beach. We had just gotten settled when the Park asked us to do them a special favor, before we settled down to work on Oyster Bay.

A park visitor, who just happened to be a retired detective, was walking down the beach one day and noticed a bone sticking out of the dune-face. He pulled it out and recognized it as human, a femur at that. Being a good citizen he took it to the ranger station and handed it in. The park sent it to the medical examiner's office (since it was not unknown to find recently deceased crime victims and/or their parts in the park), who determined that it was "ancient" and forwarded it to the Human Identification Lab up at the University of Florida. Since we were in the area, everyone thought it would be a good idea for us to carry out an archaeological investigation to see if there was any more to it. Before we got to work though, we had to deal with the Seminole tribe, since they represented all Native American human remains discovered throughout the State, and this being on Federal lands, we were obliged to comply with the recently passed Native American Graves and Repatriation Act of 1990 (known as NAGPRA). Up in Tallahassee at the Center, they told me to deal with it, so I got in touch with Bobbie Billie, the shaman down in Homestead (no, *not witch doctor*, the shaman is a holy man of power who helps to guide the spirits home, and it's serious stuff, not to mention that consultation was now Federal Law), and he told me that they had no objections to an archaeological excavation since the remains were in danger of eroding out of the dune-face anyway, but that after we had done the work, call him back and he would try to drive up for any reburial. We set to work immediately and in a single day uncovered the rest of the skeleton.

The girls were really good at exposing it and photographing it. Being the manly boss, some park rangers and I helped with shoveling a lot of the overburden, which luckily was nothing but sand, but once the thing was coming to light they took over with the plastic spoons, paint brushes, wooden cuticle sticks, and gentle maneuvering. Watching them, I wanted to show my fine-tuned excavation skills as well, and asked them to let me have a go at it. I wasn't in the hole a minute when my clumsiness dislodged a small fragment and they told me to get the hell out of there ("Okay, okay, already!"), so I took up my position watching from above, arms folded, pretending to be "supervising." Once open to the light of day, we had to put a tarp over the hole to keep out the sun so she wouldn't dry out too fast. And it was a she (even I could tell that). We documented it as well as possible in place, before any attempt was made to remove the bones. It was a remarkable burial. The reason? It was a rather tall female (wide hips, graceful cheeks, jaw, and forehead), roughly 27 or so (teeth and skull suture closures), Native American (shovel-shaped incisors), and she was buried as a Christian, but not necessarily Catholic (!?!). How would we know such a thing? First of all, barring any secular cemetery rules, Christians are usually buried with their feet to the East, their heads to the West, and here she was with her feat pointing to the Atlantic, which is why the femur was eroding out of the dune-face in the first place. Now, one may ask, why do Christians do this (so religiously)? The answer lies in the question. A Christian, on the day of Resurrection (when Jesus comes back to judge the living and the dead), upon hearing Gabriel's trumpet blow and quickly reconstituting the elemental form, then sits up in the grave to witness the rising sun (ergo, head to the West, then to sit up facing East). And the reason it may not have been Catholic? Her hands were to her sides, whereas Catholics (again, generally speaking) usually fold the hands over the chest (heart). Native Americans, it is fair to say, *never* bury their dead supine, but prefer a bundled, flexed, or fetal position, sometimes even head down, rebirthing back into Mother Earth. This also requires less digging than a European rectangular grave. Well, it just so happened that the French of 1565, whom we thought had lived with the local Timucuan Indians, were Protestants of the Huguenot persuasion, and if one recalls their history, were being prosecuted for their heresy rather drastically off and on in France at this time. The beginning of a story was quickly unfolding: a young Indian woman died and was buried, probably by a European, near the beach… It got way more interesting as time went on.

The burial was gently removed, bone by bone. Later, after each one was gingerly cleaned, they were laid in correct anatomical position out on a long table at the North District Ranger Station in a small garage room they let us have as a working lab. Here the girls really went to work, measuring everything, photographing each bone, taking notes. Since the left leg was missing, the femur in Gainesville, we had to go looking for any other bones that might have fallen out, foot and ankle bones and such. No luck. Once the preliminaries were done I put my own foot down as the boss, "We're going to take the skull down to the hospital and get it X-rayed!" The girls looked at each other, consulted, and then decided they would allow me to have my way. So Margo and I boxed up the skull, which was full of sand, and after I'd called ahead and made the arrangements, we headed into New Smyrna and Fish Memorial Hospital. They were expecting us and led us into the X-ray waiting room telling us that the tech would be out in a minute. I still had the box with the skull in my hands and stood up when the technician came out, saying that he was excited to do this, that they didn't get this kind of job very often. Before I handed it over to him though, I had to ask how we were supposed to pay for this, since it was a bit out of the ordinary, and how much it was going to be. He said not to worry about it, this one was on the house as a favor to the park. We sat down to wait and Margo, a fiery and brilliant redhead whom I'd worked with for several years now, let go of her usual professional demeanor and said, "You know, we should give her a name. It doesn't seem right to just call her 1184-1 (which was the field specimen, or FS number)." "Yeah, you're right," I said, "what do you suggest?" "How about 'She Who Sleeps in the Sand'?" she offered, recalling that this was right after *Dances With Wolves* came out, and the main female character was the cantankerous white-woman hostage who lived with the Indians called She Who Stands with a Fist. "No, that's too long," I said, "let's just think about it." The technician came out in a few minutes, handed the box back to me, and handed the large envelope with the X-rays to Margo. "Anything interesting?" I asked, but he seemed disappointed that no, other than it being full of sand, it was just another skull. Thanks, I told him, thanks for everything, and we turned to leave.

"Oh, Jesus" I said, and we both stared in disbelief. I'm holding the box with the skull, Margo's holding the envelope with the x-rays of the head, and as we turned to go, there, up on the wall which had been over our own heads the whole time we had been sitting there waiting, was a life-size portrait in watercolor of a young Indian maiden in half-profile looking out at us, her two braids hanging below her headband, and the shoulders draped in fringed buckskin. I leaned forward to read the penciled-in title below, and it said "Swift Running Brook." Margo and I looked at each other and kind of shuddered, and speaking for myself, the hairs on the back of my neck gave a tingling rise, and the proverbial chill ran down my spine (and still does, when I think about it). I said it out loud, "Swift Running Brook," and Margo said, "Well, that's it then," and we walked out of the back door of the hospital in a bit of a daze.

The other girls, Carroll and Heather, were pleased by the decision to name her and eerily puzzled by the process. Nonetheless, we'd finished with the analyses and I called the Seminole shaman Bobbie Billie to ask him what to do now. He said he couldn't drive up from Homestead right then to carry out the necessary reburial rituals, but asked if we would rebury the bones in a shallow grave in the same alignment as we had found them in a secret location near to where they were originally found, and that would suffice for the present. He'd come up later for the requisite ceremony. Working with our good friend, John Stiner, the park resource manager, we picked a nice quiet spot near the beach, but far enough that she wouldn't erode out again anytime soon, and placed Swift Running Brook back in the ground. Just to close the deal, and figuring it couldn't hurt, we said an Our Father and I read a good-bye sonnet from Shakespeare. We had gotten rather attached to the Indian maid in just a few days. All this was reported to the managers at the Center in Tallahassee, Buddy and Gordon, and we were told that we'd done an exemplary job. Well, you'd think that was the end of the story, and we could get down to the original work at hand, the project over at Oyster Bay, which we did, but two other incidents occurred with Swift Running Brook: one, again bordering on the Twilight Zone, and one that would cost me years of conflict.

Chainsaw Archaeology

Meanwhile, we got to work at Oyster Bay, also known as the Armstrong site, after the discoverer. Unlike the initial work carried out under Beth Horvath in 1990, a survey which determined the general size and depth and age of the prehistoric site, this was a testing and evaluation of the *historic* period features that had been detected at that time, an opportunity to better define the suspected French and Indian relationship of the mid-16th century, based on the archaeological context. The girls were eager to get started, and once we had procured a boat from the park, and made a couple of trips carrying all our equipment, we got started cutting into the ground. We knew exactly where to start: there were several concentrations where European materials, coins, ships' spikes, and small tools had been noted in 1990, so these were the areas we wanted to open up. I was convinced that the best approach was to open large horizontal, but shallow test units. Even though we were on top of hard-packed oyster and clam shell middens, we'd dug these before, and we weren't intimidated by that, and it was easy enough to clear out a work area with our machetes, but we were then immediately stymied by the dense root mass of the palm, myrtle, and other bushy undergrowth, all of which only extended maybe 4 inches (10 cm) below the surface. Cutting through this shit was going to kill us, and eat up a lot of time and therefore, money, all this before getting into the excavations proper. While the girls struggled with the root mass, I thought about it and thought about it, and suddenly the little light bulb went on. "I'll be right back," I told them, hopped in the boat and was at the North District maintenance shed in fifteen minutes. I'd worked closely with the maintenance guys before, when Cranston and I had done the beach mag survey, and we'd even shared a few beers after work, so they were friendly and cooperative when I told them what I needed. When I got back to the site, I clambered out of the boat and proudly showed the girls my inspiration. Gassed and oiled, I fired up the small brand-new chain saw and deftly cut through the wiry roots along the test unit edges. Then I cut out sections roughly a foot square, and we lifted them up, shook them gently and tossed them to the side. In ten minutes I'd eliminated all the encumbering mats, cut the clean edges of our test units as laid out, and invented the new pseudo-science of chainsaw archaeology! Yeah, it was a little rough on the new hardware, cutting through dirt, shell, and roots, but we'd probably saved the taxpayers enough money in time and wages to easily pay for another one. As it happened, we used it throughout the project.

The investigations went smoothly and we enjoyed the work, right on the eastern shore of Mosquito Lagoon and the western side of the beach barrier island. It was cool in the mornings, when the wildlife, especially the flocks of white pelicans, were active, and even though it was early summer and could still get hot in the afternoon, we were under the shade and it was generally pleasant with a steady breeze off the water. Sometimes for lunch I'd pile the girls into the boat and we'd drive right up to the dock at JB's Fish Camp, have shrimp and oysters, and a couple of beers before going back to work. In the evenings, back at the San Marino, we could

370

swim in the pool and eat or drink at the tiki bar to relax before the next day's work. At one point a team of reptile specialists from one of the nearby universities vacated one of the park houses, and we moved in behind them to save money and thus extend the project. It was pretty rustic, but the girls made it homey in no time flat. One night after we'd just moved in a raging thunderstorm came in at night from the northwest over the marshes up near Daytona. It was a wondrous show of environmental fireworks that lit up the sky with Tesla-coil electric finger-lightning that illuminated briefly the rolling cumulonimbi as they advanced quickly across the horizon. I had gotten stoned and was admiring the show, even though it was the middle of the night when the girls came out and finally shared the view. One of the most amazing storms I'd ever witnessed in my entire life.

Cruel Buggery

It was right about this time, a couple of days later, that Gordon Schmidt decided he was going to come down and check our progress. This was unusual, especially for him, and I found out later that there was another reason. There was always another reason. And I have to confess, I carried out one of the meanest acts of my life. Although I stated that the working conditions were pleasant under the palms along the shore, they don't call it Mosquito Lagoon for nothing. As long as we had plenty of poison spray to marinate ourselves in, we were fine; but if we forgot, or the sweat rolled it off of us, there was hell to pay. That's not to say that there's some sort of acclimatization that occurs as well. I used to wonder how the early pioneers of Florida, especially here along the lagoons and rivers, were able to survive the onslaught of the blood-sucking bastards. Having talked with some of the old timers though, they would tell me that if you just go ahead and let them bite the fuck out of you, you'll quickly find that they lose interest. Their theory was that something built up in the blood that made the insects no longer attracted to you. It certainly worked for them, most of whom would never touch any damned repellent. They pointed out that the mosquitoes were always worse for newcomers, but anyone who spent enough time in the woods were much more wary of chiggers, or redbugs, as they were called, than mosquitoes; those redbugs would dig in around your "privates" and would keep on chewing until you dealt with them by washing down in kerosene. When Gordon arrived, I got the phone call out at the site via radio from the ranger station, so I told the girls I was going to pick him up in the boat. Before I left, I had them all spray down, and then I hid the cans in an old bucket with a top. I got to the station and after getting his stuff stowed at the field house, I put him in the boat and off we went. It was a beautiful day on the water, porpoises rolling, fisherman waving as we passed them by, and me skimming over the still waters between the now-familiar channel markers. I slowed down, cut the engine and coasted onto our landing, the bottom scrunching into the shell sand. "Quick, Gordon, I want to give you a tour of the site, and then we can sit down with the crew and talk about it, okay?" "Yeah, sure, whatever you want," he said. I led him down the short trail to the girls working in the test unit and manning the shaker screen. "Hello ladies," he said, and then slapped his neck (the first one had landed), "good to see you," slapping again. "We'll talk in a few minutes," I said, "but first, let me show you the rest of the site," as I led the way back into the bush. He began slapping his face, and followed me. As I looked back, the girls were shaking their heads at me—they knew exactly what I was doing. As we walked down the trail, away from the water (and thus away from the breeze) a light cloud of humming vampires began to descend. "Damn," he said, as he was slapping the air, "do you have any bug spray?" "Yeah, sure," I said, leading him further into the darkening hammock, "but it's back at the landing, we'll get it in a minute, I just want to show you something…" By now he was getting, as they say, 'swarmed' and he couldn't keep them at bay. I started to feel bad about it and said, "okay, let's go back and get you some spray." I led him back the way we had come, and as we passed the girls, they were shaking their heads, trying to keep from laughing, and then followed us to the landing where I finally got out a can of bug spray, which he damn near emptied onto himself. Too late, the welts were rising all over his face and neck, "Jesus Christ," he said, "how can you guys stand it?" "You get used to it," I said and the girls' looks made me ashamed of my meanness. I just wanted him to know what conditions we were operating under and in some slight way, outside of his office, to better appreciate our efforts. I overdid it, I admit.

Accept This?

He did get to see the site and the work we were doing, and he was somewhat impressed, but I was surprised that he didn't show more enthusiasm, bug bites or no, because we really were doing a helluva job. That night, back at the field house, we showed him the artifacts, and then we all went to dinner at JB's. Afterwards, when we got back to the house, we had a couple of beers and after showing him a site map on the computer, he asked me if I'd ever played Solitaire on it (?!). Yeah sure, I told him, why? Well, would I show him how to play. This was strange, but okay, and in ten minutes, he was totally engrossed. We had to work the next day, so the girls hit the sack, and after sitting up reading for an hour or so, I told him I was going down too. He was still playing avidly when I went. In the morning when we all got up and we drank our coffee, ate our bagels, and got ready to go, he said he didn't want to go back to the site, he'd seen enough, and he wanted to talk to me alone, then he was going to head back to Tallahassee. I told the girls to go on ahead and I'd join them later that afternoon. After the girls had left, I got him in the truck and gave him an impromptu tour of the park, which I knew like the back of my hand, and after an hour or two of driving around, showing him various archaeological sites, and mounds and trails, he asked if there was somewhere we could go have an early lunch and talk. Sure, I told him, my favorite place was the tiki bar on the beach at the San Marino, and it was just a couple of miles up the beach. We drove up there, and sitting by the ocean, ordered a couple of grouper sandwiches and beers. It was probably eleven o'clock. "What's up?" I asked.

What had happened was that Ken Wild's approaches to the superintendent in Puerto Rico had gained footing enough that a position for a full-time park archeologist had been finally advertised. I knew this (but only found out after we had left the Center for this project in Canaveral) and it looked to me as a result like the advertisement had been hidden from me. Well, after we got to New Smyrna a friend called me from the Center and told me about it, so I put together a quick application and sent it in some two weeks earlier… I just wanted to let them all know that I knew about the job and that I felt I was as eligible as anybody. I really had no intention of going to Puerto Rico. Well, the job advertisement had been reviewed in Atlanta, and Kenny and I had both made the short list. Since he had threatened Ken not to talk with the superintendent down there, Gordon was really pissed off that he had done so and wanted to punish him somehow. I was a dark horse that no one had counted on (because everyone had tried to keep me from finding out about the advertisement, even timing it until I'd left Tallahassee), and when my name came up, well, Gordon figured he'd use me to squelch Kenny's ambitions. Anyway, that's how I saw it as the following conversation unfolded: "So I understand you applied for the position being advertised down in Puerto Rico…" "That's right," I said, "I didn't hear about it until I was already down here, but I put one in anyhow; I'm sure Kenny put one in too." "Well," said Gordon, ignoring the comments about me not hearing about it and Kenny, "what if I were to offer it to you? Would you take it?" Even though I knew that the job wasn't his to offer (it was the superintendent's down in Puerto Rico), he was playing a game to see if I was willing to help him fuck over Kenny. "Are you offering me the job?" I said. He repeated himself, "I said *if* I offered you the job, would you take it?" I countered with "Well, offer me the job, and then I'll tell you." He smiled, knowing I knew what he was up to, and said, "Good answer." He also knew that I wasn't going to play along. "You know, as your boss, I could just send you down there," now

372

pretending to be a tough guy. "Well, you could try," I said, knowing that he really didn't want to raise that sort of stink with me, Kenny, and the Puerto Rican superintendent. And that pretty much ended the conversation which then turned to how beautiful the ocean was, what a great project we had going, how well the girls were working, blah, blah, blah… "I've got to get back to Tallahassee," he said. I think the highlight of his trip was learning how to play Solitaire.

Running Swift Brook

We finished up the project at Oyster Bay in about three weeks, and it was very successful. Although the girls did most of the actual muscle-work, as well as the faunal analysis and schematic drawings, it was up to me to pull it all together, make some sense out of it and present the findings in a final report. Since Beth had left the Park Service I also had to integrate the 1990 findings as well. It took me almost five years to get the final report out, but I still consider it probably the finest work I ever did, and one of the best archaeological reports ever put out by the Southeast Archeological Center. No brag, just fact. But just before we were about to leave Canaveral to go back to Tallahassee, the park asked us to come into the office. They told us that the other bone had arrived. Other bone!? What other bone?! Why the bone from the Human Identification Lab up in Gainesville, that bone, the femur. Oh shit! We'd forgotten all about that one. Where was it? It was at the county medical examiner's office, which was the proper return as far as the chain of evidence: from the park to the medical examiner to the Human Identification Lab and back again. Would I go pick it up? Yeah, sure, but the girls could go back home if they wanted, I could handle this myself. So they left, and I called Bobbie Billie first to ask him what I should do ("Dig a little slot trench next to the right side of the reburial, and put it in there."), then I called the Center in Tallahassee to let them know what was going on. When I got to the medical examiner's office, I was shocked that he walked out and just handed me this long leg bone, no wrapper, no box, no cloth, just the bone… and an envelope. It was a hot, sultry summer afternoon and I set the large bone on the car seat next to me, and opened the envelope. There was a short white sheet of paper with the letterhead of the Human Identification Lab (actually the C.A.Pound Human Identification Lab), and a short description by Dr. William Maples, the chief forensic anthropologist. It said that the bone was from a female, approximately 27 years of age, tall, roughly 5 foot 8 in height, and it was hundreds of years old, all of which we had determined on our own. Then he went on to describe "a pathology." *It said that this femur exhibited indications of an individual who suffered from severe hip dysplasia, probably congenital, and that she had probably walked with a pronounced limp throughout her life, and was probably never able to run.* Oh God, I thought, looking over at the large bone lying on the seat next to me as the heat built up inside the car, and a wave of disorientation quickly rose and passed as a drop of sweat fell off my nose. Swift. Running. Brook. [The Twilight Zone theme begins playing in the background, softly as first, getting louder, until the crescendo… and then, "Imagine if you will…"]

But she still hadn't let go of me. When I got back to the park, I showed the bone and the strange note to my buddy, the park resource manager John Stiner, who asked me to tell the superintendent about the whole thing, the project, the bone, the works. I said sure. Superintendent Wendell Simpson was a large serious black man with a military bearing. We had become friendly when he first took over the park a couple of years earlier, because I went in to his office then while on another trip and said that if he would give me a half an hour of his undivided attention, I would tell him everything he needed to know about the cultural resources in his park. The half-hour turned into an hour and a half, but in the end he was just very glad that someone was brash enough to fill him in on all the stuff he needed to know without his having to slowly worm the information out. I knew it was going to be hard for him as a black professional in mid-Florida coastal Volusia and Brevard counties, still some of the most backward in the State, but he was tough and he realized that knowledge was power. I liked him because he was a no-nonsense square-shooter. The one thing that disturbed me was that he didn't wait. If he had a question or concern that needed answering or addressing, he would have his secretary call whomever on the phone immediately and then would deal with whatever the problem was. Personally, I'm more cautious and like to let things stew for awhile before grabbing the bull by the horns, usually trying to figure out ahead of time how those horns should be most carefully grabbed. After I'd briefed Superintendent Simpson on the project at Oyster Bay, and the strange case of Swift Running Brook, all with John Stiner sitting there as well, he asked me if we could date the bones. I thought about it a minute, and told him, yeah, we could date them; but according to Bobbie Billie, the big femur had to go back in the ground as soon as possible, so we couldn't send it off, and the only stuff left was a small, not even a handful, bit of bone dust we'd swept up off of the lab table. That little bit of dust would be enough but it would require some advanced processing, not the regular old radiocarbon dating. That advanced processing could run as high as $650. What kind of date could we get off of it, he asked. I told him, we could probably get within 50 years or so of when she was buried. He asked Stiner if they had the money, and Stiner said that, yes, they did; in fact we had come in under budget for our project and there was more than enough left over to cover it. Let's do it then, said Simpson. Well, wait a minute, I said, I have to get authorization from SEAC first. Go call 'em, he said. So I went into Stiner's office and called Gordon Schmidt, filled him in on what the Superintendent wanted, and he said he'd call me right back. I waited and five minutes later he called back, said that he had talked to Buddy (the Regional Archeologist), and Buddy had said no, we're not going to radiocarbon date the bone dust. Okay. I went in and told Simpson that Buddy had said no, we weren't going to do it. Why not, he said. I didn't ask, I told him. He immediately buzzed his secretary and told her to get Buddy on the phone. Uh oh, I knew this wasn't going to go well. I sat there and could only hear Simpson's side of the conversation. He was telling Buddy that he wanted the radiocarbon dating, he had the money, and (damn!) that I said it was do-able. The voice raised ever so slightly but in the end I suppose Buddy pulled out the card that as Regional Archaeologist only he could authorize the dating (which would not have been true). In any case, Simpson gave up, and somewhat frustrated, hung up and said forget it. Personally, I thought that was the end of it, and didn't think any more of it. Since it was Friday and the girls were gone, and the project was over, I went back to the field house, put on my shorts, grabbed a bucket and went out into the lagoon and decided to go clamming. Never having done it before, I figured how hard could it be? Well, I'd find about one clam every minute, lying prone in the shallows and using both my feet and hands to scoop through the muddy bottom. A minute's a long time when you're looking for something, and I almost quit several times, but in the end, after an hour, the bucket was full. I took them inside, rinsed them off, put them in a pot and steamed them. I must have had three dozen large chewy clams, with nothing but butter, but my God, it was one of the best meals I ever ate. Now I knew how the Indians lived so bountifully, and how the great shell mounds rose so high so fast. ("Hey, you kids! Run on down to the store [the lagoon] and pick me up a couple a dozen clams for dinner tonight… grab a fish or two if you see one.")

Divestiture

So I get back to Tallahassee, and I'm in my cubicle typing up my trip report (you always write up a quick trip report on returning from the field: what you did, where you went, any problems, etc., mostly for the managers to get a quick summary of how it went), and I get buzzed to come on down to Gordon Schmidt's office. I saunter on down and he asks me to close the door. "Buddy's pretty upset over getting that phone call from the superintendent on Friday," he says. "Yeah, well, it wasn't my idea to have him call, I was just trying to explain about the radiocarbon dating, and he really wanted it, even though it was going to be expensive," I told him. "Yeah, but Buddy had already told you no." "That's right," I said, "and I passed that on to Simpson, but he wanted to know why and I couldn't tell him, so he decided to call himself." "Yeah, but Buddy said no, and that's all you had to tell him." Now I could see that something wasn't right; this didn't make a lick of sense. I said "And he talked to Buddy and that's apparently what Buddy told him." "But he shouldn't have had to call Buddy," he said, "Buddy had already told you to tell him no." "Which is what I did!" I said, now getting a little hot, since we were now engaged in a circular argument. "Hey, you don't want to get in a pissing contest over this!" he threatened, and then I knew it was getting serious. He never used language like that, and had obviously picked that up from Buddy, who *always* used language like that. Buddy must have told him to straighten me out. The trouble was, I hadn't done anything wrong. They were just pissed off that the superintendent had called them out. Exasperated, I said, calmly "No, Gordon, I don't want to get in a pissing contest over this." "Well, Buddy's going to want to talk to you later about it," he said. I told him "Fine," and walked out. I went back to my cubicle and finished typing up my trip report, but now, though I hadn't planned on it, I wrote down everything that happened with Simpson, figuring I should get it down on paper exactly as it occurred, just in case. And no, I didn't refer to my discussion with Gordon. I handed in the draft to Gordon, so that he could look at it before giving it to Buddy and the Chief of the Center for final. That afternoon I get a buzz on the intercom that Buddy wants to talk to me, but not in his office, outside at one of the picnic tables out on the Green. Not a good sign. I go out there and Buddy's sitting there with the trip report in his hand, and I sit down across from him. For an old Marine ex-M.P. it's easy to tell when he's angry, and damn, he's angry. No sense in repeating the expletives flung at me, but the gist of the message was: dare to challenge me and I'll chew you up; I've seen this sort of thing back in Washington, and I've destroyed way bigger fish than you; when I tell you to do something, you don't ask why, you just do it, and so on. He finished by telling me to edit the trip report and take out any references to the burial (Swift Running Brook! …again back to haunt me), and the radiocarbon dating. Fine, I said, no problem. I took the trip report, went back to my cubicle and took the references out. After lunch, I carried it back to Buddy's office, next door to Gordon's and handed it to him. Gordon came in and Buddy handed it to him, and they both seemed satisfied. "That's all" Buddy said, expecting me to leave. But I had to push it. "So, I've got to ask you, why didn't you want to have Simpson get the radiocarbon date; he had the money, and he really wanted to know how old it was. For that matter, so did I." They looked at each other, and Buddy said, "Because I didn't want to fuck with those goddamn Indians any more, that's why." I stood there, amazed at what a great waste of time and energy and goodwill had been expended over nothing at all. "But I was the NAGPRA representative, and I'd been getting along just fine with Bobbie Billie… so, what you're saying is you guys were yellow, you were scared and just didn't want to deal with, with what?... the inconvenience of it…" "Get out of my fucking office," he said.

Now the above story, other than the recurring haunting of Swift Running Brook, would not be that interesting, a small intra-office disagreement over a radiocarbon date, except that it was a turning point in my professional career. The next day (I remember it was a Tuesday), Gordon called me in and told me that they had decided to put Guy Prentice in charge of the Regionwide Survey Program and I wouldn't be running it any more. He had a PhD and I would still be the Team Leader, running field projects. They just wanted Guy, who admittedly had a great reputation, as the project manager. Other than that, there'd be no other changes, and I was still a valuable member of the team. And, by the way, said Gordon (with a straight-face), "This has nothing to do with that Canaveral business; we had been discussing it for some time." "Bullshit," I said. From that day on, as far as Gordon and Buddy were concerned, I couldn't do a thing right, even though I continued to receive kudos from park staff throughout the Region, and luckily, John Hardinger, the Director, stayed out of the fray. At one point, Buddy even started "grading" my reports (never above a "C," even though he knew I was one of the best writers at the Center) with snide little comments written in the margins, that is, until I started sending *his* back to him the same way. Then he didn't comment at all. Gordon still needed me and only came after me some four years later.

Mo Bones

I hadn't been back in Tallahassee two months when we got a call from Canaveral again. Some guy had heard about the work we had been doing there (it was in the paper) and came forward to one of the rangers, telling him that he also had some Indian bones, would they like to see them? Sure, they said, and he brought them in: a skull top, two jawbones and a smattering of various other parts. I was sent down to look at them. When I got there and was shown the bones two things struck me: they had numbers written on them (indicating that the guy was a "collector" and marked his finds), and, from the number and types of bones, more than one individual was represented, so this stuff was from a burial ground, or multiple-burial mound. I told the superintendent that from the looks of it this guy had been pilfering bones from inside the park for awhile, and probably considered himself an amateur archaeologist. Although he had done the right thing by bringing them in, he probably wouldn't have done so, except he thought he'd get a little glory, maybe make the newspaper as a "good citizen." But he'd been breaking the law for some time, stealing human remains and God knows what else, and we should make an example of him instead, gently enough to put out a warning to anyone else who considered doing the same. This is what we'd been instructed to do, according to the Archaeological Resources and Protection Act of 1979, and for which we'd been undergoing training by the Federal Law Enforcement Training Center out of Glynco, Georgia at SEAC every other year. Several of us had carried out numerous investigations with various levels of success. Somewhat unfortunately, it now put us archaeologists in the law enforcement business. I suggested to Superintendent Simpson that we pursue a civil case rather than a criminal one. This way we could just slap him with a fine (which would drop right into the park's coffers), get some information on what else he knew, and send a message out there not to mess with the stuff in the park, especially any Indian bones. This also allowed the Superintendent to be the arbiter, and would keep the whole thing out of the courts. He agreed that this was the way to go. So we called the guy in (I can't remember his name, but later he had a television show called "Weird Florida"), and he had a real chip on his shoulder: How dare we accuse him of stealing bones, when he had "innocently" recovered them and brought them in for us? "So, what's with the numbers," I asked, "we archaeologists only do that after we've made a decision to keep something." "Uh, I was just keeping track of where they came from," he said. "Well, good," I told him, "then we can start with that," and we pulled out a map of the park, "show me where you found them." He was still pissed off and wanted to start negotiating, "What'll I get if I show you?" "I'll tell you what you'll get if you don't," I countered, all this under the watchful eye of Superintendent Simpson, behind his large and shiny oaken desk, "we'll call the sheriff and hand him these bones, and let him take it from there. As it is, the worst you're facing is maybe a $200 fine and no one will ever know, but if you want to argue, the newspapers are always interested in grave robbers." That shut him up and he placed his finger on the map. It was a tiny island out along the edge of Mosquito Lagoon. I knew exactly where it was. We called Bobbie Billie and he said he'd come right up from Homestead since this was an active case and he still hadn't dealt with Swift Running Brook. Could we meet him at the North District Ranger Station in the morning, 5 a.m., before sunrise? Yeah, sure, Stiner and I said we'd be there.

We got to the station around 4, so we could get both the boat and bones ready. Bobbie Billie showed up around quarter to five and we met under the light at the Ranger Station. I hadn't met Bobbie face-to-face before and he was immediately impressive. Short, stocky, and typically dark, quiet, and long-haired, he definitely had an aura, if not mysterious, strangely awe-inspiring, where time and space take on an eerie uneasiness, like when you're tripping. He didn't look at you, he looked *through* you, and I was quickly reminded of the Carlos Castaneda books, even though I hadn't read them in years. My first impression was one of kindness, at least toward me so far, but dangerous at the same time: you wouldn't want to fuck with this guy. Maybe it was the early hour, the odd circumstances, the Lagoon in darkness, the reburial mission at hand, I don't know, but everything quickly took on a surreal glow. He had a large medicine bag slung over his shoulder, and I had a cardboard box with the bones and asked him if he wanted to look at them. He said no, for me to keep them close, and he'd tell me what to do. Stiner got the boat started and off we went. Maybe twenty minutes later we pulled up to the small myrtle and willow-covered island, and the sky began to barely glow in the east as the birds started chattering. It was just light enough that we could see each other in silhouette. Stiner tied the bow off to a large limb hanging low over the water and stayed with the boat. Bobbie stepped off the boat, as if he had been on this little islet a dozen times, and followed a little sandy trail I hadn't even noticed in the dark. He was all business, and after maybe ten or twenty yards he stopped in a little clearing and set down his medicine bag. As he started unpacking stuff, laying it out, he pointed to a space on the ground and said, "Dig there, not too deep, but big enough to hold all the bones." I hadn't even brought my trowel, so I dug the hole out with my hands, the box of bones lying to the side. Once I thought it was big enough, he told me to place the bones in, somewhat in their proper placement, with the head to the north, legs to the south. Once they were laid out he told me to cover them lightly, and to use plenty of leaves and grass as well. By the time I'd finished he had gotten a small flame lit in the bottom of a coffee can with holes punched through the lower half. It had strings attached and I recognized it as a censer, or incense burner, then he put on what I can only describe as a scarf, or stole, over his head and down his shoulders. He told me I had to leave now, to go back to the boat, but don't get back in, just wait for him, and leave the box. I started down the short trail, and as I did, he began some ritualized chanting and I could smell the smoke wafting out of the Folger's coffee can. By now the sun was just ready to come up and the blue-black glow in the sky was ambient all around. When he came out he told me to stand with my arms out, as he had to "cleanse" me from the handling of the bones, and he first shook the can about me, the acrid smoke billowing about my clothes and arms, then he took out a large feather (owl, eagle?) and brushed me off from head to toe. I was done. Clean as a whistle, and feeling as good as the result of any adolescent confession I'd ever made. He extinguished the can, packed up his medicine bag, and when we got back to the Station we took him out to Swift Running Brook's burial spot where he carried out a shorter version of the reburial ceremony, this time without the cleansing. When he left from there, we shook hands again, and he cracked the smallest of smiles. I felt truly blessed by his presence, and when he drove off it only dawned on me then that he probably hadn't said twenty words the whole time we'd been with him, though in my mind a whole long conversation had been going on the entire time.

Dem Restless Bones

You'd think that would be the end of the bones for awhile, wouldn't you? And it was, for some six months or so. Then we get *another* call from Canaveral. A sheriff's car had pulled over some speeder one night in Port Orange on U.S. 1 heading up to Daytona. The guy was acting suspicious, had empty beer bottles in his car, and his girlfriend was extra nervous, so the cop searched his car. Baggies, with a roach in the ashtray and a pipe under the front seat got him bent over the hood, but when the cop searched the trunk, what did he find? A box of bones! A skull fragment, a couple of jawbones, etc., but the funny thing was, they had numbers on them. "Oh those?" he admitted, "those are just some old Indian bones from down in Canaveral." (!?!?... Need I say more?) Oh, sheee-it! I was dispatched to the park, where the bones had been sent after his declaration, and yes, they had the same numbers as those we had buried with Bobbie Billie six months earlier. What had happened? Well, the story (from the girlfriend) was that this redneck fisherman, Goodrich, had been out on the lagoon the night and morning that we had buried the bones, either fishing, or netting, or emptying crab pots (whatever, he didn't have a light). He was far away, but had seen our boat (and light) come in and he just eyeballed the little island where we had stopped. After we left, he had gone in there, and now, the sun being up, he found the cardboard box (I knew we shouldn't have left it!), and the scattered ground cover. Thinking treasure, he dug the hole up but only found the bones, put them in the box, and carried them home. At some point he carried them over to his girlfriend's house, probably showing them off, and they ended up under her bed for most of the intervening six months. She didn't like this one bit, and eventually he made some deal with a guy in Daytona to trade them for some cocaine. The dumbass didn't maintain a safe speed on the way and here we are.

Well, we had gone the soft route with the prior Weird Florida guy, and that didn't turn out so good, so this time, especially since Goodrich was a bad egg anyway, and was well-known for being one as well, and was also trying to use these relics to further another crime, we decided to play hard ball. We were gonna charge him with a criminal Federal case, under ARPA, and we had the goods, his admission, and the (now ex-) girlfriend to make it easy. Or so I thought. The trouble started when we made an appointment, the chief law enforcement ranger at the park, Mike Chambers and I, to meet with the Assistant District Attorney in Orlando. Very formal, not at all like the stuff on TV where they sit around bullshitting. We had to wait in an outer office (these guys *really are* very busy), and when we finally got in we had a half-hour to make our case. I was the lead, but before I could discuss the bones, I had to brief the ADA on what the Federal law, ARPA, even said. Well, hell, that took fifteen minutes. Then I told him about the case. He said he'd have to review the law (I gave him a copy), and then decide if it was worth prosecuting or not (something we hadn't counted on), letting us know at the same time that in Central Florida, rife with murders, drug deals, and tax evasion, stealing a few Indian bones wasn't considered high crimes, much less misdemeanors. He told us to come back in a month. When we came back a month later, he had boned up on the law (both figuratively and literally), and decided that he wasn't going to decide to prosecute it; he was going to let a grand jury decide. He also let us know that he was pursuing it more as a novelty, since this was an odd one, rather than what anyone would consider a serious crime, and therefore when the grand jury was convened, it was going to be more up to us than him to convince them that it was worth dragging someone into court over. He'd let us know when the next grand jury would be convened. Back at the office in Tallahassee I was catching hell for pursuing this "minor" incident, while at the same time others were getting kudos for chasing ARPA cases where they didn't know who it was, when it occurred, or what was taken (if anything). Like I said, I couldn't do anything right any more, or as we used to put it to each other humorously when Pete was still the Chief, "it was just my turn in the barrel," the allusion being that stuffed in a barrel, with the bunghole appropriately positioned, everyone else (males, of course) got their turn at plugging away at it. But when the certified letter arrived requesting my attendance at the grand jury hearing in Orlando as an expert witness, Gordon and Buddy pretty much put a lid on their grousing.

Once again, I went down to Orlando, stayed at Mom's house to save the Government money, and me and Chambers, the law enforcement ranger, dressed in a suit and uniform respectively, waited to be called in to the grand jury hearing. They called us in one at a time, Chambers first, to

378

discuss Park Service rules, regulations, and enforcement of Federal laws within the county and State. I was called in and took the stand. The ADA asked me some simple questions about the bones, a little bit about archaeology, the previous burial with Bobbie Billie, and the Archeological Resources Protection Act. Then he opened it up to the jurists themselves to ask questions, and I began a quick set of mini-lectures on who the Timucua were, how long they had lived in Florida, especially before the appearance of the Europeans, what they were like, what we thought their beliefs were, etc. I always find it compelling to answer people's truly inquiring curiosity about the people and things that got us to where we are; it's amazing how ignorant the general populace is of a history that really wasn't that long ago. In any case, the ADA had to cut me short as the questions and answers got further and further from the matter at hand.

Well, much to the surprise of the ADA, who'd seen many cases more heinous than this go by the wayside, apparently Chambers and I had convinced the jury that this was a serious breach, an insult to Native Americans, and that a lesson needed to be made: they chose to prosecute. So now the bulk of the job lay with the ADA, since we had already given him all the evidence. I was notified of the trial, a bench trial to be held in front of a judge some three or four months later. I drove down to Orlando, sat in the back of the courtroom alone (Chambers couldn't make it), and much like The People's Court, or Judge Judy, the formalities began. Unlike the television courts, the judge didn't agree with the grand jury, and, being a good old boy himself, thought that the ADA was making a mountain out of a molehill regarding some old Indian bones, and charged Goodrich a mere $50, with time served. I was appalled (and would have welcomed an opportunity to address the court: "Objection, Your Honor!"), especially to think of all the time that Chambers and I had spent working together on the case, our travel, our trips to the ADA's office, not to mention *his* time, and the grand jury hearing, etc., all of which had to have topped $10 grand easily. The only, and I mean only, silver lining to this cloud was the fact that it went down in the books as a successful prosecution under ARPA, they being few and far between in any case. And yes, once I was back at the office in Tallahassee, the big boys took a special pleasure in rolling out the barrel once again to celebrate my rather insubstantial, if not pyrrhic, victory.

CPR RSQ

Another very interesting thing happened that spring in New Smyrna. The combined families, kids and all, had a grand get-together during Spring Break. This was all the Gears, Jimmy and Nancy and their kids, Molly and her kids, Amy and I with our three, and God only knows how many others. We all got separate rooms and would pal around with each other intermittently, depending on who was drinking, who was swimming, who was napping, who was eating, etc. Amy and the boys and I hot gotten there a day or two early, so we all shared our favorite room up on the second floor of the old San Marino (gone now somewhere under the footprint of a large condominium). It used to be just north of and adjacent to the Sea Vista, which had the outdoor tiki bar and café, and still does. But both places each had their own pools, and our room had a large wooden deck that overlooked the pool down below and the ocean out on the beach. One evening we had cooked some snapper, since we had a kitchenette in our place, and after dinner, once the kids left to play, Amy's sister Molly and I stepped out onto the deck to smoke and have a drink, watch the sun go down over the ocean, while Amy cleaned up inside. I had just fired up a cigar, and as we stepped to the deck rail, I looked down and noticed a frumpy woman, middle-aged, in a single-piece striped suit with a plastic bathing cap on, just lazily floating in the pool. Thing was, she was floating face down, arms and legs spread wide. She didn't move, and I said to Molly, "See that woman down there? You think she's just floating and meditating, or do you think she's unconscious?" Before Molly could answer, a young girl maybe fourteen, was approaching the pool gate, and as she let herself in, I yelled down to her, "Hey, you, little girl!" She looked up and I said, "See that lady there? Go check on her and see if she's alright." The little girl said, "I don't want to…" and I yelled even louder now, "You go over there and check her!" The girl walked over to where the woman was floating near the edge of the pool in the deep end, and surprising to me, instead of reaching down and tapping her, the girl kicks her with her foot! The woman just floated away from the edge. "Oh Shit!" I yelled. I set my cigar down on the flat deck rail, turned and ran down the balcony, taking my wallet and money and change and keys out of my pocket as I ran, throwing them to the ground and racing down the stairs. When I got to the pool, I ran in to the enclosure and reaching out, with that adrenaline-induced superman strength that you always hear about, I lifted her right out of the pool, and turning her on her back as I pulled her out, dropped her onto the pebble-encrusted concrete deck. I immediately felt bad for two reasons: when I dropped her onto the deck her head gave a sickening "clunk" as it fell heavily down; and then I was staring at her wide-open fisheyes, fixed and as colorless as her grey pallid skin. Water was drooling out of her half-open mouth. I listened to her chest and there was no heartbeat. Then the CPR training that I got every year because I was a diver kicked in. I yelled as loud as I could, so they could hear me at the tiki bar next door, "Call 9-1-1!! Somebody call 9-1-1!!" Then I started on her, tilting back her head, pinching her nose, getting in a couple of quick breaths. There was a lot of unconscious gurgling, but she was unresponsive. I turned her head to the side and let a lot of the water drain out, and then I went back to the CPR and gave a few good quick chest pumps, then back to breathing. Quickly, I was joined by some lifeguard type who had heard me yelling, so I told him to do the chest pumps and I'd do the breathing, and soon we were in sync. A couple of more breaths, more water coming up and out; she spasmed and jerked, her eyes blinked, and "goosh," I got a mouthful of poolwater and all the salad fixings that she had eaten for lunch that day. I coughed, gagged, and rinsed my mouth out with a handful of nearby poolwater, and got her breathing on her own as I heard the sirens pulling up. When the EMTs came in they told us to back off, and I was as happy as I could be to do so. I slowly walked back up the stairs, went out to the deck where Molly and now Amy were both watching, took a slug off my drink, and as I watched the EMTs lifting the woman onto a gurney and give her oxygen as they wheeled her off, I was amazed to find that, after a couple of good puffs, the cigar was still lit!

One last minor incident occurred that weekend. It was Sunday, and we were all checking out, so the kids were treated to a last going-home meal at the tiki bar café. As they were finishing their French fries and drinks I decided to take one last dip in the ocean before we hit the road. I walked on down to the beach, and there was a guy and girl lying on a towel all alone, kind of snuggling. I took off my shoes and shirt, and stuffed my wallet into one of the shoes. "Would you mind watching my stuff?" I asked, and the guy said "No problem." I waded out into the cool surf and dipped into the waves. Aah, how refreshing! I swim out some more, lay on my back, look at the sky, and let the waves roll over me. Then I touch down on the hard sandy bottom and look to the shore. Where's the guy and girl? Where are my shoes and shirt? I look toward the Sea Vista, and there they are, heading to the stairs leading to the tiki bar, WITH MY SHOES AND SHIRT! I run out of the water as fast as I can. I run up the sand toward the Sea Vista. I start yelling, "Hey! Hey! Hey! Hold up there!" The guy turns, the girl turns, and they start moving up the stairs faster. By now I'm at the bottom of the stairs, still yelling, "Hey! Those are my shoes and stuff!" I run up the wooden stairs, past people watching me and drinking, get to the top and the guy throws my shoes and shirt down by a garbage can. I'm hot now, and he keeps walking, a big biker type with tattoos and muscles, ignoring me. I go after him and clap a hand on his shoulder, "Hey, motherfucker, you were stealing my shit!" We're now in the middle of the crowded tiki bar. He turns and grabs me with one large hand by the throat, lifting me to my toes, and says "Don't you call me a thief, you son of a bitch!" "You're a goddamn motherfuckin' thief!" I squawk as I'm swinging desperately around his arm, trying to reach his head. He reaches back with his other hand, making a fist to pummel me, when the crowd moves in and pulls us apart. Now my brother-in-law Charlie is between us, and he's as tall as this other guy, and the bar manager is yelling at both of us, "Get OUT! Get OUT! You both have to leave, or I'll call the police!" "But, but," I protested, "He was stealing my stuff." "I don't care," the manager said, "You've got to leave." Well, we were heading out anyway, so it was no great loss. I got my stuff and gathered the tribe together. As we were getting into our car I saw the guy, and his now-embarrassed girlfriend getting into their van, and shot him a bird. The kids however, were mightily impressed with the whole fracas.

18.   Moving: Off, On, In, Out, and Along (1996 -2000)

At the end of 1995 the Southeast Archeological Center moved off of campus at Florida State University to the Robert Johnson Building out on the southwest of town at the University's technology center, Innovation Park. When I was heading up the Regionwide Survey Program, I had been scheduled to have an office near the front of the building (Schmidt was always aware of ranking and if you were closer to the front, you were physically closer to the Chief, now "Director," like *he* wanted to be). When in the good graces thereof, Gordon had even originally put my office right next to his (which I never wanted, knowing he'd be both watching me and "popping in" repeatedly). But now that I'd been slightly demoted, slapped down so-to-speak, I was given an office in the hinterlands, around the back. It was perfect. I couldn't have chosen a better office. It was slightly larger than most, nearer to the kitchenette and thus, the coffee, as well as the back door to the building, which opened out onto the building's central garden atrium. My windows looked out over the quiet landscaping, very zen-like and both quiet, shaded and cool. Those either facing or near "the front" often had the afternoon sun blasting into their offices and all of them ended up putting in dark plastic liners behind their curtains to obscure the glare. (When the Director, Hardinger, ordered a set of ostentatious red-velvet light-obscuring drapes, and had them hung on the sprawling front windows facing the University golf-course, I couldn't help myself and put an anonymous post-it note on his door, "Did Scarlett need a new dress again?" Took him a week to find out who left it.)   But I was happy as a tick on a dog ball, and since I was partly in charge of bringing in the various furniture and setting them up for the offices, I scarfed a few extra bookcases and file cabinets into my own office and before anyone could say anything (and since the big boys had all ordered new furniture for themselves) I commandeered Pete's old desk, the one that had intimidated so many of us over the years. It was all set up with lamp and computer and in-box before anyone could say anything. Only after all the dust had settled from the move did the aristocrats discover that they had thrown this bre'r rabbit right into his favorite kind of shadowy briar patch, while their own gilded cages shone brightly in the hot afternoon's solar brilliance.

The work at Canaveral that had definitively shown the early French presence in mid-16th century Florida had gotten the attention of former Congressman Charles Bennett, who had represented northeast Florida in the House of Representatives for decades before retiring. He was an extraordinary man, tall, thin, white-haired and impeccably dressed, and a well-respected historian in his own right, concentrating on the early colonial history of the Jacksonville area, especially the French encounter. He was instrumental in the establishment of Fort Caroline National Memorial, a reconstruction of the French fort of the period. It is a "memorial," as opposed to a park because no one had ever been able to find any remnants, or even any evidence, of the actual fort or its inhabitants. Not even the renowned Charles Fairbanks, probably the most famous Florida archaeologist of them all, had been able to establish its exact location back in 1952, although there had been many historic accounts written at the time, even a drawing or two, and from the descriptions we all knew approximately where it should be. When even Fairbanks couldn't find it, everyone assumed (and still does) that it had eroded into the St. Johns River. Well, after a trip up to St. Augustine where I was to brief Bennett on our work at Canaveral, the former Congressman somehow got some money thrown our way to take another look at searching for Ft. Caroline, or at least anything that might have been related to it. I put together my team of girls again, and off we went to Jacksonville to see if we couldn't find the real Fort Caroline. I got us some rooms at a hotel on Atlantic Beach, which wasn't a long way off and also allowed us to get relaxed after work. Since I was still somewhat *non grata* as far as Buddy and Gordon were concerned, they sent my new boss Guy to set the project up. After two days spent simply establishing a datum, or reference point, from which to take all our measures, Guy headed back to Tallahassee to deal with administrative stuff, and now I was back in charge. That weekend though, while we're plotting Guy's datum point, a small team of students from the University of North Florida had come out to lend a hand. One of them struck me as intriguing: a short, dark-haired, slightly older woman, a smoker, but rather serious, good-looking, and well-shaped. I guessed her to be about 28, probably a graduate student. She had that dark black hair and I recall it had a slight red, almost purple, sheen to it. I found out later that it had been dyed and a little too much red had been mixed in. She stood about five-two and had a very determined look to her face. That first day she was wearing a red, white, and black plaid shirt, open, but tied at the waist, over a white long john top. Small breasts. Jeans, boots, and a backpack. It was February and the wind was cold off the river. Her name was Pam and I immediately forgot it. Her features though, were very sharp, and as I said before, determined. I was working the surveyor's transit. "Want to see how it works?" I asked, and gave a quick lesson on how to set it up, level it, and take a bearing. Later I put my girls on the job of quizzing her on the particulars, so I could find out more about her without asking directly. Since she only worked part-time and went to school part-time, she would have plenty of free time to come out and help us on and off for the rest of the project. As it was Sunday I let the volunteers go early and my crew and I went back to the hotel, celebrated a successful beginning to the project, and sipped champagne in the outdoor hot tub.

There's three types of archaeological survey that you can carry out: systematic, random, and selective. Systematic is the best, because that means you're x-ing out areas one by one, completely testing them systematically, and moving on. Random is probably the worst, because as any gambler knows, there is no pattern and your chances of finding something are hit and miss, often with large areas left unsurveyed, or rather, untested. Selective means you rely on both common sense and intuition, pick your areas according to landforms, geology, water resources, et al, and then usually test those areas systematically. And when I'm talking about testing, I mean shovel-testing: just digging a hole as deep as you can, or as deep as you need, and screening the dirt looking for man-made artifacts. You can mix these types up, and I decided to proceed with a selective-systematic approach, and the survey proceeded well once Guy had left.

Moving On

In the next couple of days, Pam showed up periodically and was a very hard worker. She was enthusiastic and inquisitive, and I began to take an interest in her. Once she began talking, it was apparent she was a Southern girl. No twang or "y'alls," just plain vernacular, and particularly deep-voiced for such a small girl (must have been the smoking). She was married, had kids, was going to school, still working on her Bachelor's. Since I had asked the girls in my crew to find out her story, they were all too happy to do so (and would have done so anyway, but now it was more fun for them because they could see I had an interest as well). She was married to an engineer, who worked at the electrical plant that we could see across the river. We all thought it was a nuclear plant, because of the large cooling towers, but no, apparently it ran on coal or oil. She made no bones about the fact that he was an asshole. In fact it was not long before she let on about her 6-year plan to leave him. Six years: once the kids were grown. I liked her. She was very forthright about things. And she really wanted to learn about archaeology. So I took the opportunity to share as much as I could about the instruments, the methodology, the rationale etc. And I got to tell stories: stories about the history of the area, what we were looking for, why it was important. Here we were looking for Fort Caroline, the early sixteenth century outpost that the French had built in 1564 to solidify their claim to La Florida, as it was called. The Spanish were none too happy about this and took the opportunity to wipe them out the following year, after a hurricane had destroyed the French fleet. It's a great story (told above, regarding the Oyster Bay site at Canaveral), full of intrigue and adventure and bloodletting, and I used it to full advantage to dazzle and amaze all the volunteers, but especially Pam. I still think it'd make a great mini-series.

I think I really made an impression on her though the day I spoke in front of Buzz's class. Buzz Thunen is the professor of archeology at the University of North Florida in Jacksonville, and it was his class that provided the volunteers. "Buzz" comes from his days on helicopters in Vietnam. He asked if I would come talk to the class one day and I was happy to do so, having a slide show already in the can. So I talked to the class, doing one of our "magic lantern shows" and telling all the gory details of the events that led up to why we were there, doing archaeology on the river. She sat right up front, soaking it all in, and didn't hesitate to butt in and ask questions. In fact I think she was the only one who asked anything. Anyway, I ran a little over and Buzz gave me the wink, so I shut it down rather quickly. The bell rang and they all left. Buzz and I went to lunch at a little barbecue place nearby and I dropped him back off at campus. But I didn't leave. I asked him where the library was and he pointed it out, but he was late for another class. So I sauntered on over and walked in. I wasn't looking for any books. I thought I might luck into Pam. But I walked all over, even upstairs, and didn't see her. Then I walked outside. Something however, made me want to go back in. And even though I'd looked everywhere, I went back in. And there, behind a large brick pillar, was Pam, quietly studying. I walked up and sat down. She had a bit of a quizzical look on her face, like "what are you doing here?" and I guess I was rather taken aback and didn't know what to say, something brilliant like "Studying?" Yeah, she had to use the time as best she could while on campus and away from the house. Things were too hectic at home. So what *was* I doing there? Oh just checking out the research facility. It was awkward, but I didn't care. "Maybe we could have lunch sometime?" Maybe. I left, rather embarrassed.

The project along the river went on. We cut transects with machetes and weed-whackers. We did shovel tests. We opened up test units. We water-screened. We worked hard. And Pam worked harder than anyone. One day when we were shovel-testing, I was standing over her and behind her, and I thought I smelled something. We were all pretty ripe from working all day, but this was a distinct odor. I bent down and smelled her shirt, and yes, I smelled her, even through the sweat. From then on I was struck (pheromones!). The project was ending that last week, and we were finishing up some test excavations. I allowed Pam to assist us, the real archaeologists, while the other volunteers finished up the shovel tests. So, working in close quarters together, we all got to talk, and it was the usual banter, mostly about men and women. I was starting to fall.

It was a Friday, before we were going to finish the project the following week, and Amy called and said she wanted to come over. I had a great room at the beach, a large suite, and I thought that would be fine. She had a lot of studying to do, and I had to work over the weekend so that would work out pretty good. She showed up Friday evening about 7. I'd had a few drinks after work with some of the park residents, and I was in a jovial mood despite the previous two years, the result of the affair with her Communications professor, which to this point hadn't really ever ended. Still, I was glad to see her. I fixed her a drink and we sat and talked, deciding where to go for dinner. She wanted to go to Riverwalk, a big posh eatery in downtown Jax on the river, hence the name. I said no, that was a long drive and it was expensive, and I had to work early in the morning. There was a nice Irish pub that served good food just down the street, and we had the ocean, and like I said, I had to work in the morning. She wanted to go to Riverwalk, and in fact, had been counting on it all day, and besides, so what if it was expensive, I was on per diem, wasn't I? Well, I'm not going to Riverwalk says I, so if you want to have dinner, I'd like to take you to the Irish pub, and besides, I repeated, I've got to work tomorrow, early. Well, as you can see, things degenerated from there and very soon the "fuck yous" were flying. She declares, "That's it! I'm going back to Tallahassee" (a three hour drive), and I'm telling her good riddance and don't let the door hit her in the ass on her way out. Good-bye, and she left.

Well, once I cooled off in just a couple of minutes, I thought, oh shit, this isn't right. She shouldn't drive all the way back to Tallahassee, we shouldn't have been fighting over something so silly, maybe I could still catch her. When I got to the lobby, there she was, talking to the receptionist, trying to get another room. I walked up and started to apologize, when the receptionist said, "Did you want me to call security ma'am?" I turned to her and dumbstruck said "what?" Then Amy said no, I think he'll be o.k. Then I got really hot really fast, with these two women scowling at me, and said "What the hell have you been telling this woman, Amy?" "Just that you physically threw me out of your room." "That's it!" I said "You go back to Tallahassee, get another room, whatever, just don't bother me again, I've had it." And I went back to my room and didn't look back.

During the next week, my marital dilemma was a hot topic with the crew, including Pam. They wanted to know if I was going to call home on Wednesday, Valentine's Day. "No". When we were finishing up on Wednesday for the day, and Pam was having a cigarette while the crew was packing up, I asked if I could have one too, and she said I didn't think you smoked. Once in a while, I said. As we sat there smoking, I asked her if she'd have lunch with me tomorrow. She thought about it, cocked her head and smiled, and said alright. So the next day we finished up early, at lunchtime, and I took her to the Sun Dog Diner, which I really liked, all silver and glass, on the beach. We talked for two hours. On the way back I made a crude attempt at "Want to see my hotel room?" which of course, fell flat.

Well that was going to be it. She wasn't going to be out the next day, which was the project's last, because she had to work out at the Nature Preserve at the power plant, where she had a part-time job as a nature education specialist. So we said good bye on Thursday afternoon, shaking hands, me telling her how nice it was to have met her and worked with her, and I cut the crew loose to return to Tallahassee, because I had to stay another day to show the Superintendent the results of our several-week project. The next day, while I'm showing the Superintendent and a couple of rangers what we'd done and what I thought it meant, I got a message delivered to me that said "Call Pam" and a number. So when I could, I called, and Pam said "I was thinking you might want to see where I worked. If you want, come on over this afternoon when you're done and I'll show you around." She gave me directions. When I got there the security guard let me in and told me which building she was in. I walked in and saw her at her desk, looking into a microscope. I stood and watched her and when she looked up she was startled, not having heard me. I looked around at the stuff in her office, animal parts, nests, plants, stuff. She'd been looking at a gall, one of those nodules you see on an oak leaf. I always thought they were some sort of seed, but they're actually like a wasp larvae laid onto, or into, the leaf. She was looking at the larvae and showed it to me. Cool. She got the park vehicle keys and we headed out onto the trails, her pointing out various features, including her favorite bridge over the tidal creek, an old Indian mound, osprey nests, the kids education center, etc. Then she wanted to show me a shell midden where potsherds had come out by tidal action. It was a large flat midden at the end of a long trail that stopped at the water's edge. An old building was nearby that once was a hangout for old-time illicit cockfights – inside you could still see the old broken benches and the small arena. We parked and got out. It was bitterly cold, so much so that it hurt any exposed skin. We walked along the water, picked up a sherd or two, and soon I'd seen enough. To me Indian shell middens are a dime a dozen. It was just too cold. When we got back to the truck however, it was locked… and she couldn't find the keys. I looked around on the ground and in the windows of the truck, thinking she might have locked them inside; she headed back down along the water, retracing her steps. The sun was getting ready to set soon and it was gonna get serious if we were stuck out there. I had visions of huddling to keep warm, but more than likely we would have just tried to hoof our way out. After a few more fretful minutes, she found the keys (in her pocket!).

We drove back with the heater full blast, then stopped on the little wooden bridge that spans either Clapboard Creek or Sisters Creek, I'm not sure which. It was her favorite spot. We smoked a cigarette and watched the sun going down, the water running out with the tide, the cooling towers on the horizon. It was very romantic, so I asked her if I could kiss her. She said no, not a good idea. I asked again. She said it wasn't a good idea. Finally I just leaned over and yes, she kissed me back, hard. Both of us had the breath taken out of us. What to do? She suggested, or maybe I suggested, we go somewhere, like a bar. She knew about a little fishbait beer bar, Dunns River Fish Camp. So we got back to our cars and I followed her out there. It was still cold, even inside the place, so we got a couple of beers and sat down by the little space heater. We talked briefly about country music. She said two beers were her limit. So after the first, we played some darts. As I recall she was pretty good and beat me even though I was playing for another kiss. By now we were hungry so I suggested we get something to eat, which meant driving a couple of miles over some bridge. We went to a generic Chili's, went in and ordered. It was crowded, being Friday night, and when she went to the bathroom, then came out, she walked past the table, and I called out to her "Pam!" I remember thinking this was the first time I'd called her to me. She ate a little bit and didn't finish it, whatever it was, and she had to go. I walked her to her car, saying goodbye because I was heading back to Tallahassee the next day and might not ever see her again. We kissed long and hard and I squeezed her ass. Later she would tell me she thought I was trying to find out what kind of underwear she was wearing, but all I cared about was the ass. We drove away, and the next day I drove back to Tallahassee. When I got there, I checked on the progress of the divorce. The lawyer said maybe by the first of September; he'd let me know the court date.

I'd had the number to Pam's job and I began calling her in the afternoons. We talked about lots of stuff and I started sending e-mail as well. At first it was semi-official. She and her boss had given me some material they wanted conserved. Turned out to be junk, but it gave me an excuse. Then I asked if I could see her. When? Whenever. Maybe we could meet somewhere? Finally she agreed and said she was going to the beach on Wednesday next. This was early March. We could go together, if I drove over and met her at the Country Buffet restaurant parking lot. I took off work, hopped into my little Toyota bomb and drove to Jacksonville. When we got to the beach we found a remote stretch, laid out the blanket and she took off the T shirt and shorts. First time I ever saw most of her. She was wearing a dark blue knit swimsuit, one-piece, and what struck me was her proportions. Yeah she's short, but so am I. Very small breasts. Nice ass. And although she thought her thighs were too big, they looked more healthy than big. Her arms were slender and her shoulders broad. Her hair was shoulder length then and as I said, dark with a reddish tint. Her features were rather sharp: a dimpled chin, rather high cheekbones (some Native American ancestry), full lips, and a high forehead, small ears, a long neck, and her eyes, if not overly large, very expressive. She was beautiful. Lying on the blanket I kissed her, leaned over her, and kissed her again. She said to stop, that it was against the law and we'd get arrested. I laughed – there wasn't a soul as far as the eye could see, and I was sure it was not against the law to neck on the beach. We talked and swam and laid around, and I kissed her whenever she closed her eyes. At one point in the early afternoon she said something about if we don't play it cool we'll either have to leave or climb in the backseat in the car. I wanted in the car. When she had to pee, she got up and ran to the water. And as I watched her I was amazed and thrilled at the way she ran. Very sporty and efficient, with a swing to her hips. But when she walked, walking back, she put her head down and walked very deliberately, shoulders back, then head up. Again, beauty incarnate. On the drive home we ate pimento cheese cracker sandwiches that I made for her as she drove. We talked about what was happening between us, and I told her that I wanted to see her, she warned me fairly straight "You don't know what you're getting into. I use men up and spit them out. I'm only good for about four months, tops." I said I'd take my chances, and that I didn't see that happening. In retrospect, it may have been an honestly auspicious warning.

The next time I planned to meet her, two weeks later, I figured this was going to be it – The Big Enchilada! So I made reservations at a small, rather cheap, motel on the beach, the Atlantis. I took two days off of work, told Amy that I was going to Orlando to visit my mom, but told the two girls who worked for me that I was going to meet Pam. I drove like a bat out of hell because I'd made plans to meet her at the Sun Dog Diner at 11 and I got a late start getting out of Tallahassee. Once I got to Jacksonville, I saw a sign that looked familiar, like a short cut, so I took it. Blanding. Little did I know that this was the worst thing I could have done, leading me God knows where, but not to the beach. And since I'd been running late, I hadn't stopped to pee and my bladder was about to bust. I'm lost on a busy highway and I have to pee and it's about 10:45 a.m. I knew I wasn't going to make it. So, first things first, I stopped at an Amoco that had restrooms detached from the building. I parked and ran into the john. When I came out, feeling better, I went to the store and found a set of pay phones (back when they had them) on the other side. Then I tried calling the Sun Dog to let Pam know I'd be late. She wasn't there yet so I left a message for the waitress to let her know I'd be late. While I'm on the phone with the Sun Dog, the guy on the other phone next to me has a friend of his come up who says "Hey man, you better come out here, there's been an accident with your truck." I remember looking at him and saying "That's too bad, man." Then I was finishing up my message when a policeman came walking up asking people something, one at a time. He came up to me and asked "Do you own a little grey-blue Toyota?" "Yes, I do" I said. "You'd better come with me, there's been an accident." When I saw my car backed up across the street, smashed into a pickup, I cried "Oh no, God no," almost weeping with the fear of what had happened and the frustration that now I wouldn't be seeing her at all. Apparently, when I went to the bathroom, I was in such a hurry that I left the car in neutral and didn't put on the parking brake. Since the ground was relatively flat, it hadn't moved when I first came out, but while I was on the phone it began to roll ever-so-slowly backwards, picking up speed, and rolled backwards across four lanes of moving traffic, cars screeching and veering to avert it, then bumped up the curb on the other side of the road, where it banged ass-end into the driver's door of the pickup truck belonging to the guy who had been on the other phone next to me. I apologized to the pickup guy and sat down to fill out the paperwork with the policeman. He said he had to check on some stuff, so I asked if I could make another phone call. I called Pam at the Sun Dog, told her what had happened and asked her to please wait. She said she would. Turned out to be a $35 ticket, let your insurance know within 48 hours, on your way.

It was about 1 o'clock when I got to the Sun Dog. May as well have been the Hang Dog the way I looked. Pam told me later that she had already made up her mind that she was not going to sleep with me yet, hotel or not, but when she saw my face she felt so sorry for me that she changed her mind. "Bad day?" she said. "It was until now," I said, trying to muster up a smile. We ate a little lunch and went to the Atlantis. Shitty little dark room off the parking lot. She went to the bathroom, I sat on the bed, then got up, adjusted the drapes closed. When she came out, we put our arms around each other, began kissing, and the rest is history. We screwed until about 7 and then went to the Irish pub for dinner. When we got back we did it again and she had to leave, it was almost nine. We hugged and kissed and she left. I went and bought a couple of beers, thought about the day and went to sleep.

The next morning, at the hotel, I get a phone call about 8:30. It's Pam. "You're in trouble. Some woman phoned Amy and wants to know why you haven't reported the accident. She's threatening all kinds of stuff." Wait a minute. How come you're calling me? "Margo and Carroll got a call from Amy this morning wondering if they knew where you were at, because you didn't show up at your Mom's in Orlando. They said no, they didn't know, then they called me, and I'm calling you." "Oh shit." "You're going to have to call Amy," she said. "Yeah, I guess so." So I stopped at a pay phone on the way back and called Amy. "You bastard, you lying bastard. Where are you? And who are you with?" "Look, Amy, I'll talk to you when I get back. Is there someone I need to call about this insurance thing?" I'd lost all semblance of sympathy or patience over the ensuing years because of the Professor affair. Now though, she knew there was someone else for me.

In April, Pam came to Tallahassee with her boss, Kelley, to attend an environmental conference. I got them a room at the Executive Inn and got myself one as well. I gave them a brief tour of Tallahassee, and even drove them by my house, which looked like hell because I had torn up the porch, fixing rotten wood, and hadn't yet put down the new floorboards. We went out to dinner at Lake Jackson, driving down Old Bainbridge with the brights on because my low beams didn't work at all. We had a small shrimp dinner and got back to the hotel by about 9:30 and there was an old movie on in my room. Kelley really got into it and Pam and I waited for her to leave, making goo-goo eyes the whole time. Finally Kelley got tired and went to her room. Pam and I were going to go out for drinks across the street. But we didn't. We went back to my room and made love. Then we went out to the Silver Slipper, had a few beers, and danced. And we found out we danced pretty well together. When the bar closed we went back to my room and made love again. This time it was serious though, and I told her that I was falling in love with her. She put her fingers to my lips and said "Shhh, don't do that." But it didn't matter. I was already done. Had been.

Pam had to go back to "their" room so that Kelley wouldn't be suspicious, since she also knew Pam' husband pretty well. And the next morning as we got ready to go for a drive, Kelley said "What happened to the rear bumper on your car? Looks like someone hit you there." Pam and I looked at each other and laughed. Kelley wondered what was so funny and I said it's a long story and I'd tell her sometime. We went down to the coast to the old Spanish fort at St. Marks and then had lunch at Posey's. When Kelley would wander off to either get a beer or go to the bathroom, Pam and I would exchange quick passionate oyster hot-sauce and smoked-mullet kisses. But then we drove back to town and they got into their van and I didn't even get to kiss Pam goodbye, but just waved as they drove off. A couple of weeks later, however, I got a different room at the old Atlantis in Jax Beach (second-floor, beachfront) and we met for a long afternoon of lovemaking, not even going for the obligatory walk on the beach. This was the time when the maid just walked right in without knocking and we were (almost) too distracted to notice.

Cumberland Island Beach Bongo

At the end of April we went to Cumberland Island. I got her to volunteer to assist me on an archeological survey, another remote-sensing magnetometer survey of the beach-face. I had been slightly underhanded in not letting anyone at work know about the assistance. She however, was primed for it. Both of us knew it was an excellent opportunity to be alone together for four or five days. And since it was archeology, even her husband was accepting, if not enthusiastic, of the opportunity. I considered it a honeymoon.

I'd arrived a couple of days earlier with Carroll, my assistant, and we'd arranged to have her boyfriend be a volunteer as well, so we could both enjoy the company of our significant others. Rough, gruff Cranston came over and helped set up the operation, coordinating the global positioning system with the magnetometer and the computer data collection and then he left. I was worried about him finding out about Pam as I knew he'd squeal at work, causing no end of trouble down the line. But apparently they passed each other on the ferry over to the island–he leaving as she boarded, without recognizing who the other might be.

The night before she arrived I was extremely agitated in anticipation. Couldn't sleep, so I went for a walk. The walk on the island took me down the main road to Dungeness, the Carnegie ruins that had been a Scott Fitzgerald-type mansion from the 1890s through the 40s, but had burned up in 1968 as a result of cigarette-smoking juvenile delinquents. As I walked the deserted quiet road in pitch black, the fireflies started to come out, and they became so numerous it was like a faerie dream, almost disorienting in the discontinuous dancing and day-glow green wafting of the flying insects. This was magic, and I knew I had to show it to Pam the next night. I slept fitfully in anticipation.

When she came I was waiting for her at the dock. God, she was better-looking than I remembered. Maybe it was because she too was happy to see me. We packed her up and I took her to the dorm room. She immediately took control and pushed the two twin beds together , rolling a towel or two together to shove down and close the gap between the mattresses, to make it one big double bed. We pushed it up against the east window so as to be able to catch the morning light. I gave her a quick tour of the south end of the island and we ate dinner with Carroll and the other volunteer staying in the dorm and then went for the firefly walk. It was just as amazing the second night and I remember we were even surprised by one of the feral horses on the island, just standing silently in the middle of the road, huffing and then trotting off just as we approached. I can't remember if it was that first night or later that we drove up to the field at Stafford and watched the full moon rise and listened as the whole herd of island horses went into a gallop, where we could barely see them all running across the field but could feel the earth tremble below our feet. Each day was like a dream. We woke in the morning, early, before the sun came up, made love, and watched from our upstairs bedroom window as the wild turkeys and feral horses slowly grazed in the gathering dawn. Again, a certain magic like nothing else ever experienced except by a favored few. By now I think we were both deeply in love.

The trip to Cumberland was a turning point. We walked out onto the beach at night, laid there and looked at the Milky Way and dreamed of a future together, letting the sand lightly blow over us. During the day we continued the pulling of the magnetometer, 10 miles per hour. Smoked cigarettes and talked for hours. We told each other the secrets of our lives. All the secrets. Some of which hurt. But it brought us closer. We began to know each other, really, and truly. And we listened to country music on the radio, which up until then I had always hated. But I developed a real appreciation for it there, a genre, if one can apply that term to it, that touches the human condition. And as I looked at her I recognized the person she really was. Or so I thought. We had a lot of fun. We got up to our asses in mud, clamming on the North End with Carroll and her then-boyfriend, Rodney (he later turned out to be an abusive asshole–I never saw it firsthand, but all the girls who ever met him said they saw the signs right off the bat. Go figure.) Later, we went for our own private clamming excursion on the south end (where I was sure we'd find 'em) but ne'er a clam was to be found, so we ended up exploring the tidal pools, which was seriously interesting. We made love in the surf, in midday on a deserted beach, not a human in sight (this after being so cautious about just making out on St. Augustine Beach!) By now we were a pair, adventurers, although I still didn't countenance the term "soul mate" since I was so familiar with the popular touchy-feely literary bastardization of the term. I'd rather be her unequal equal. And I knew that soon she was going back home to her husband, Coop. Damn!

When she had to go, it was bitterly sad. We sat at a picnic table and waited for the ferry to take her back to the mainland. My heart was breaking for the loss of her that hadn't even happened yet. She pulled out of her pocket two (almost) identical cowrie shells that she had picked up on our last clamming venture. She gave me one and said something to the effect that "These will be our tokens. One for you and one for me—a reminder of this trip together." The ferry came and we said goodbye. I watched her leave, waving and watching til she was out of sight. Then, sitting alone at the picnic table at the ferry dock, I sat quietly thinking of the cruel vicissitudes of love, what I knew as an anthropologist (and we jokingly referred to) as "the biological imperative." I both laughed and wept.

She never said please, and hardly ever said thank you, and she never apologized, ever. Didn't matter, she always thought she was right, and truthfully, she often was. But her decisions were impulsive and not thought out; not enough forethought given to the eventual consequences. This too became a problem.

I couldn't bear to be away from her for long, nor (did I believe) her from me. So it wasn't long before I got a room for us at the Wakulla Lodge, a famous honeymoon retreat at the "World's Largest Spring," south of Tallahassee. It had a tiny hard bed that suited us just fine, in an old Spanish-stucco tiled room. I don't think there was even a TV and if there was, we didn't watch it. This was when I introduced her to dinner at Spring Creek, and she always ordered the bacon-wrapped shrimp. We got back to the lodge late and tried to go for a walk, but it was dangerously dark, the mosquitoes were out, and we wanted to be in the room anyway, as much as possible. The next day we had breakfast there on the veranda out back, made love once more before checking out, and laid out by the Springs, heating up and cold-water swimming intermittently. It was Sunday and she had to go. God, it hurt each and every time. We got a little better at it though, and I'd like to think it was because by now we were talking about, if not planning, a future together, so we had something, somewhere, even if it was just seeing each other again soon, to look forward to. Back at my house in town we kissed and she left. I had to pick up my boys from Amy's now that we were divorced, and wouldn't you know it, since it was hot out, they insisted on going to Wakulla Springs! So there I was, later that afternoon, on the same patch of ground where I'd been lying next to Pam that morning. An old friend from the Anthropology Department ("Dawn, Go Away I'm No Good for You!") spotted me and came over. She was a short-haired brunette, very intriguing and attractive (and scary because of it), who had recently broken up with her entymologist boyfriend, and we had always shared a tenuous interest in each other. Just above the bottom portion of her bikini bottom there were the rainbow-colored wings of a hummingbird tattoo (I'd been told that the long, thin tongue of that iconic bird dipped right into the knob at the top of the "honey-pot"; now *that* I would have liked to have seen for myself.)

She sat down with a friend and wouldn't leave. Any other time I might have pushed it, but right then I was (literally and sexually) exhausted, and I was deeply in love with Pam, so all this dear girl could get out of me were a few "uh-huhs" and a "good to see ya". She left rather unhappily. The boys knew I'd been seeing someone else other than their mother, but they had yet to meet Pam, so Sam, always the inquisitive one, asked if that was my new girlfriend. No, I laughed. "You'll meet her soon enough."

Weeks later I made plans to go to New Smyrna Beach for my birthday—one of my favorite places—take the boys, invite Mom over from Orlando, and see if Pam would come down for a day from Jacksonville. She said she would, since Kelley and her wanted to see the archaeological sites at Canaveral that I was familiar with. I think they were coming back from a conference somewhere, so I offered them a tour when they came. We were still having to invent reasons; when she came to Tallahassee, it was to check out the university, or visit her cousins. All this for Coop's sake, although by now I was sure he must have had some idea. Mom came over and then Pam and Kelley arrived. Pam brought her daughter and although the little girl was a little put off by the boys at first, before long they were playing in the sand together while Mom, Pam, Kelley, and I talked and got acquainted. I don't remember it being awkward, Kelley by now in the know, or what we even talked about. I just remember eating and staring into Pam's eyes whenever Mom wasn't talking at her, and playing footsie under the table. The boys were almost totally unaware that there were any of us adults around.

Well, we couldn't very well sleep together, so I had gotten another room for Kelley, Pam and her daughter and the next morning I was surprised to see Pam up at dawn, out on the balcony, having a cigarette. I got up, even though it was rough, having had more than a few beers the night before, and joined her. It was a beautiful dawn rising, cloud-filled and brightly-colored with the sun playing off of approaching morning storm clouds. Another auspicious omen that I thought at the time was just very pretty. After breakfast, Mom left for Orlando and I took Pam, Kelley, and the kids on a quick tour of Canaveral National Seashore and shared some of my archeological insights on Turtle Mound, Castle Windy, Eldora, and a few other sights. The kids were unimpressed. Since it was my birthday, Ma had slipped me some money so we could enjoy ourselves, so I took everyone to J.B.'s, the famous outdoor seafood grill south of New Smyrna. Then, when we got back to the motel, Kelley left that afternoon, as I had offered to drive Pam back to Jax on the way back to Tallahassee. She whispered to me to take care of Pam, as it was going to be rough with Coop, and she didn't want anything to happen, but she was happy for us. I told her I'd do whatever it took. The kids played well together on the beach all day, and Pam thought her daughter had a crush on Sam. Finally it settled out with Pam and I laying on the beach talking, smoking cigarettes, watching Dennis and her daughter playing together, while Rob and Sam went off adventuring. We were happy.

That evening we ate pizza and played putt-putt, which was disastrous due to my inability to (attempt to) control the situation, a sign of things to come. Although we didn't get to do the dirty deed, it wasn't necessary. We got a walk on the beach, we talked, and we were together. The first meeting of the family had gone well. The next day as we drove to Jacksonville, all the kids were tired and slept most of the way, while I held hands with Pam and rubbed the inside of her thigh. When she got home, she finally told Coop about us, and, as can be expected, it wasn't good. He figured it was just a fling and quickly "forgave" her, figuring it would fizzle. He was wrong. It was just about this time that a day or so later Pam, while giving one of her nature lectures at the Preserve, got bit by a rabid raccoon. She thought he was a bit too friendly and while getting him away from the kids by enticing him with food, he had bitten her thumb, and in subsequently subduing it, it had also scratched Kelley. Within a week they had the test results: positive, begin the shots immediately. My girl was rabid!

Pam and Coop had long beforehand made vacation plans to go to Belize at the end of June, now two weeks away, and although I had known this, it only now sunk in on me. We had talked about it, and of course, I wanted her to go; the plans had been made a long time ago, and she really wanted to go to see the country. I had been in Belize and the Yucatan way back in '74 so I knew she'd enjoy it. I just didn't like the idea of her enjoying it with Coop. There was nothing I could do (except either beg or insist that she not go, both of which were unacceptable). But she negotiated. I think it was then that I wrote him the letter. A nice long handwritten letter explaining how I really felt about her, that this was a very serious matter, and although I understood his feelings about me, I was not going away. She said he read it alone, put it away, and never commented on it at all. Now he knew. As the new school year went on, and I agreed to let them take their best shot at fixing their marriage, he softened somewhat and said that as long as we were just friends, platonic, he'd allow us to communicate (as if). So we picked back up on our phone calls, and we wrote long passionate letters. Pam sent them to work, and since they were usually scented (I thought it was just Pam's natural scent, but found out no, she was dosing them), I had the office secretary look for them and pull them out, so they wouldn't get mixed in with the regular official government mail, and they made me high for days. At the same time however, I could see from the misspellings that her early education had obviously been sporadic; nonetheless, though slightly distressing, I've never been one to equate knowledge with intelligence: it's all a matter of exposure. And so, we passed a year like this.

Water Island Nuts

During this year I carried out a hiking survey at the Blue Ridge Parkway's Mountain-to-the-Sea Trail and saw the remarkable devastation of the Chestnut Blight of the early 1900s. Though I'd seen a handful of chestnuts growing up, and knew what they looked like, I don't think I'd ever eaten one or ever seen a chestnut tree, and here I walked along a ridge top that had thousands of dead trees all fallen by the wayside. More than fifty years later and the wood was still hard as nails; I wondered that no one had ever taken the logs out for furniture or some other use, until I remembered that this was a national park. I'm sure that any wood outside the park boundary had been recovered and utilized. Apparently this all happened around 1900, when some Japanese chestnuts infected the American variety, and by 1940 they were all gone. [By the way, what do you call a titty-sucking maniac? A chest-nut.] Then I was chosen for two special assignments. The first was a quick excursion to St. Thomas, U.S. Virgin Islands, with David Anderson, a well-known top-rated archaeologist who had just been hired by the Park Service's external program out of Atlanta who was heading up a major land-transfer project for the Bureau of Land Management. The large harbor-isle of Water Island was to be transferred from BLM to the Territorial Government of the Virgin Islands, but before that could happen the island had to be surveyed for its cultural resources. Since I had been to the Virgin Islands before, and was comfortable working boats, which was going to be necessary, they sent me along with Dave to reconnoiter the island before any serious undertakings would be planned. We flew down together and met up with a young architect from the Regional Office, then we checked into Blackbeard's Castle, a friendly inn on a hilltop overlooking the main town of Charlotte Amalie. We soon discovered that Blackbeard's was a notoriously gay hotel at the time, our first indication being the movie shown that first night, Woody Allen's "Mighty Aphrodite," and the dozen moviegoers or so were all "sensitive" guys who laughed and cried throughout the film. No matter, we had a good time and after the movie a lot of the boys bought us drinks to welcome us.

It was a pretty straightforward recon. We looked at the already-recorded sites, which included a few World War II 15-inch gun emplacements with a three-story underground silo that the residents of the island now used as a hurricane shelter, and an old ammo bunker that they had converted into a handball court. Our guide was a British expatriate named Randy Bastid, and he made us laugh at how he'd be at an airport and over the intercom would come "Randy Bastid! Randy Bastid! Has anyone seen a Randy Bastid? If anyone knows a Randy Bastid, please have him report to the checkout desk!" Other than that we were on our own and most of the time, it was just me and Anderson walking around looking at some of the pre-Columbian sites, and checking out likely areas where there might be more. At one point though, he and I were crawling among some large boulders that were perched high over the mooring bay, and Dave quickly backed out from a large crevice between two huge rocks. He had a strange look on his face and I asked him what was the matter. He said, "Go inside there and tell me what you see." I crawled in to this small dark cave-space and as my eyes adjusted to the dark, I went, "Oh Shit!" and backed out twice as fast as he had. "Did you see what I saw?" he asked, "What does it look like to you?" I told him that it looked like about two or three pounds of plastic explosives taped together and wired for detonation. "That's what it looks like to me too," he said. I scuttered back in and took a couple of quick pictures to document it. Dave had been videotaping the whole reconnaissance and he had me on tape yelling "Oh Shit!" with our subsequent conversation, which is now part of the field notes for the project, to be curated in perpetuity by the U. S. Government. Later we talked about what we should do, and Dave decided to call agents for Alcohol, Tobacco, and Firearms, but not until we were getting on the plane on our way out; otherwise they would have kept us to show them where it was and further useless questioning. We later found out that the agents had located it just fine, and apparently it had been set back in the post-World War II era when the Navy and Marines ran the islands, the idea being to blow these precariously-perched boulders so in the case of an earthquake they wouldn't naturally fall down on the small-boat anchorage a hundred feet below. This just happened to be one of the charges that hadn't blown and therefore had been sitting quietly in the small cavern for over fifty years.

Fixing the Trace

When I got back to Tallahassee, my next special assignment was already waiting for me. The archaeologist for the Natchez Trace Parkway, a notoriously troublesome redneck and bad drinker, had been finally put out to pasture. During his tenure of some twenty years or so he had not only alienated both the Tennessee and Mississippi Departments of Transportation (and their staff archaeologists), but had somehow set them at odds against each other as well. Since the Parkway cuts across both states, and is a major (scenic) highway in its own right, with numerous historic and Native American archaeological sites along its breadth, the park was in a bit of a quandary on how to repair the situation. It just so happened that the new superintendent was my old pal, Wendell Simpson, the stiff-backed no-nonsense large black superintendent from Canaveral, who was obviously being promoted up the ranks with the Natchez Trace appointment. He requested my assistance. The big boys at SEAC, Buddy and Gordon, tried to talk him out of it, offering several other candidates. Nope, he wanted me, and by God, he was going to get me. Seeing they couldn't sway him, I was called in and told that I was getting a temporary assignment for the next four months to assist the Natchez Trace Parkway and see if I couldn't help them get their cultural resources program back on-track, especially as it might concern the Mississippi and Tennessee DOTs. It was pretty open-ended. But what really pissed them off was that, since I was replacing the former twenty-year veteran, I had to receive a temporary promotion for the four-month stint. No way around it, they had to give it to me. So for four months I'd travel back and forth between Tallahassee and Jackson, sometimes staying overnight in Tupelo for a day or two (visiting Elvis's birthplace and plotting how I might steal the meteor that sat on a pedestal outside the local hardware store). In no time at all I had the DOT archaeologists from both states sharing beers and laughs and working together. At the end of the four months, Superintendent Simpson offered me the job full-time. I asked him if I could live either in Nashville, at the northern terminus of the Trace, or Natchez, at the southern end, but he said no, I'd have to live in Tupelo, near the headquarters. Though I thanked him profusely, and told him that I would otherwise be honored to work for him, I begged off and went back to SEAC, content with the job I'd done; there was just no way I was cut out for the Deep, (and t'was ne'er so as t'were there) Deep South. I got some sort of commendation for the work (maybe it was just a letter from Superintendent Simpson), but I never got the first nod or "attaboy" from the SEAC sophists. The better I did, the more they were gunning for me.

Caroline Carries On

Well, the next June finally came, and I had another project scheduled for Fort Caroline, this time for some serious testing and evaluation, and my two-woman crew and I drove over to Jacksonville on Sunday. It was June 8, my forty-fifth birthday. I was hoping I'd see Pam that evening, but there was no way she could get away, so I celebrated alone with a Mexican dinner and margaritas. The next morning we got to the park, and Pam was waiting. It was so good to see her again. But we were pretty circumspect. Maybe a hug, but that was about it, and we all got to work. We set up the transit, laid out transects, and started cutting lines again, on a smaller interval than the previous year. We worked up a killer sweat, blisters and all. I called it about 4 that afternoon, hoping to have a little time to talk with Pam before she had to go home. Surprisingly, she said she had time to go back to the hotel for a beer. Well, when we got to the hotel, I asked if she wanted to see my room, which was one of the unused larger suites they gave to government employees, because the general public usually can't afford them. The door hadn't closed when we were all over each other. We didn't even take off our boots.

It was a good if not great project, although we never found Ft. Caroline, which was a terrible disappointment. It has to be out there somewhere! We did find a ditch, which angled off in the right directions, and I was convinced it had to be the moat for the old fort, but as much as we dug, and shovel-tested the vicinity, not the first piece of sixteenth-century evidence availed itself. At one point I convinced both the powers-that-be in Tallahassee as well as the park to let me rent a large mechanical ditch-witch and I plowed a couple of meter-wide swaths through the potential site. Nothing. I've since modified my views and question whether the reconstructed "memorial" fort was put in the right location when it was first considered, back in the 30s.

Moving In

We were out there for over a month, and Pam and I had plenty of opportunities to renew our romance. But every night she still had to go home, only spending a single night when Coop had to go out of town. By mid-July, when the project was winding down, we knew we'd be separating again, with no reconnecting in sight. It was another hard parting. Then, on the evening of Monday August 12th, 1997, I received a very strange phone call. It was about 6 o'clock when the phone rang. I answered it and it was Coop, Pam's husband. He said he was calling because Pam wasn't doing well (?!?). "What's wrong?" I asked, fearing the worst, that maybe he'd finally lost his temper with her. "She's been drinking for three days… she says she's not happy," he continued, "I think maybe you should come over and see her" (once again, I'm stunned, thinking, "What the fuck?!?"). "Okay," I told him, "I'll be over in three hours." "Let me tell you how to get here," he said. "It's okay, I know where it is." Now it's his turn to wonder (?!?). Amy and I had reached an impasse, but we were still friendly, and both of us now had our hands full with our not-yet-significant others, so I called her up, and knowing that my little Toyota probably wouldn't make the trip, I asked her if I could use our mutual Dodge Colt Vista wagon, and told her why. She said sure, and I then asked if I could borrow $25 for gas. Yep, that too. She reminded me however that the next day was our son Dennis's 10th birthday and I promised to take the boys out for chicken wings. Okay, I'll be back by then I told her. I went over, got the car and the money, leaving her my Toyota and headed to Jacksonville, a three-hour drive. When I got there, he answered the door and invited me in. It was the first time we'd met face-to-face. He was a couple of inches taller than me, well-built, head full of blondish-brown hair, sharp features (a soccer player!). As he led me through the living room, he pointed over to Pam who was sprawled on the couch in the adjacent Florida room, asleep, "She hasn't moved in two days." We walked past her and he pointed to a chair across from his easy chair, so I sat down. But before he sat down himself, he went into the kitchen, slightly behind me, and fixed himself a drink. Then he came in and sat down. Personally, I don't think he realized it, but this was a major breach of Irish etiquette, even under these circumstances. You never fix yourself a drink without offering one to whomever you've allowed to cross your threshold, even if it were the Devil himself. But I hadn't come there to socialize, and his ignorance of this basic courtesy showed me what an asshole he really was. He started in giving me shit about ever seeing Pam in the first place, although he knew it had been going on for well over a year now. I cut him to the quick however, when I told him that we'd fallen in love, that we hadn't planned it, and I was sorry for how it had affected him, but it was just one of those things that happens that no one ever expects, and so, here we are. He didn't know what to say. And to my surprise he didn't argue, or even claim the primacy of his own affections for her. He just got up and fixed another drink. This time I got up and followed him into the kitchen. As he got out the ice and made a short scotch and water, he said "All right, here's what I'm gonna do. In the morning you guys talk about it, decide what you're going to do, and have Pam give me a call at work." "Well, I guess I'm going to go and get a hotel room nearby then," I said, knowing that I didn't have the money on me to cover it, and I'd end up sleeping in the van by the side of the road. It was now almost midnight, and he surprised me by saying, "No, you can sleep on the couch in the living room… I'll get some sheets," and he walked past me and came back with an armful of sheets and tossed them onto the couch in the front living room. Then he threw back the drink, gave me a scowl, and said, "Have her call me." I went into the living room and lay down as he walked on down the hall to where I imagined the bedrooms to be. Needless to say, I didn't sleep a wink all night. Maybe he wanted to murder me… maybe Pam too… he was just waiting for me to go to sleep… a guy like that surely had a gun or two or three in the house… he'd been steeling himself with those stiff scotches… how to explain my presence in the house? Jesus Christ! You read about this stuff in the papers every day: "Domestic Violence Takes Two in Orange Park, Husband Held for Questioning." And there, not ten feet away, was Pam, softly snoring away on the couch in the next room. I lay awake for five hours until I heard his alarm go off. In a few minutes, he came down the hall, went into the kitchen, and started fixing coffee. I waited to get up until he'd had a cup and had gotten dressed for work. This time he invited me to fix my own cup. Then he reiterated what he'd said the night before, emphasizing that Pam should call him, and left. I sat down drinking my coffee, looking at Pam, and she slowly stretched awake, but I had a feeling that she'd been awake, listening throughout the night, just as I had. She wasn't surprised to see me, but she was glad. Probably glad to see that I was still alive.

Well, what are we gonna do? Now it was my time to step up, and I knew it. "You're gonna pack up whatever you need. We'll put it all in both vans, and you're going to follow me to Tallahassee. This is our time, and Coop's pretty much opened the door." I was surprised to find out that her teenage son was also in the house, asleep. "Wake him up, tell him what's happening, have him gather his stuff." She didn't hesitate, and in an hour we had packed up the vans. Then we had to stop at a friend's house and pick up her six-year old daughter, who had been spending the night there. The friend's name was Dixie and she was a typical blonde country girl in jeans; she knew all about me and wasn't surprised that we were taking off. Apparently her feelings were mixed about Coop, even though her own husband was supposedly Coop's best friend, and she took an approving appraisal of myself, romantically running off with Pam and the kids. Later I was to learn that Coop's "best friend," and Dixie's husband, Caleb, had been carrying on with Pam off and on for years, when he wasn't using Dixie's backside as a beer-stand while watching TV and fucking her from behind (aah, rednecks!). But that was to come later.

Off we went, heading out of Jax. But first, stopping for gas, I told Pam to call Coop. She said "I'll call him when we get to Tallahassee," but I said no, you'll call him now, before we leave town. She came back from the pay phone a bit shaken. "He took it pretty hard... he said he didn't expect me to leave..." she said quietly. "Ready?" I asked. "Yes... let's go," and she piled into her own van with her daughter, and her son and I followed in mine. When we got to Tallahassee, I brought the boys over to the house and they finally met Pam's son. We all went out for chicken wings on Dennis's birthday and it proved to be an auspicious beginning. It was going to be tough though in the long run. That first night, with the boys staying over, we found out how crowded that little house of mine was going to be, now with Pam and her kids too.

Amy seemed to get along with Pam alright, even though on their first meeting they spent an inordinate amount of time out back at the picnic table talking about me and wouldn't let me sit and listen in. Later that week, I went to the elementary and high schools with Pam and we got her kids enrolled. There were still a few angry phone calls coming in from Coop periodically, but for the most part we had settled in. I filled out an application for Pam at Florida State, and when she balked at whether or not to send it in, I went ahead and forged her signature and mailed it in before the deadline. She got accepted. In the meantime she started painting the kids' rooms furiously, and I had to admit, I couldn't keep up. When she was done, we moved the boys into the front room and her daughter got the middle room to herself. We settled into the master bedroom comfortably, and I began reading *The Egyptian* to her aloud at night as she went to sleep. It's one of my favorite books, written in 1949, and an amazing piece of historical fiction. It tells the story of a struggling young physician, Sinuhe [pron. Sin-u-way], who comes of age during the transition from Pharaohs Amenhotep III to his son, Akhenaton, the misshapen monotheist, around 1350 BC. The story is full of detail concerning what life was probably really like in ancient Egypt and is a first rate romance as well, the poor Sinuhe pining away for and being rebuffed constantly by the beautiful Nefer-Nefer-Nefer. As an historical note, Akhenaton was the father of Tutankhamen, who replaced the monotheism of his father with the return of the many gods again, and re-established the new Dynasty just in time for Ramses the Great, Moses' apparent nemesis. In any case, Pam didn't want to read it herself, but enjoyed my reading it to her instead as she drifted off at night.

There was a captivating fear that gripped her and wouldn't allow her to be really happy. It couldn't let her be alone either. It was probably the result of emotional trauma and sexual abuse that she had suffered as a child and had learned to cope with by a mask of cold demeanor, sometimes broken by a manic fierceness, especially when it came to real and perceived slights or protecting her children. But I knew her like no one else.

Once the school year started I showed her around campus and introduced her to the faculty in the Anthropology Department, and they were somewhat pleasantly surprised by her enthusiasm. My

397

former major professor, Michelle, quickly signed her up for the mandatory Spring semester field school at the Spanish mission site of Patale, at the old Bilek's ranch. I thought this was a good thing; it would keep her busy during the day while I worked, and with a few night classes, her graduation would be imminent, especially with the hours she had already gathered at the University of North Florida. I didn't think it was so great when I found out from her that the field school discipline had slackened over the past decade and now the students were sneaking off into the woods, smoking dope, and fucking off. But she was having fun with these younger students, having missed a good part of high school and her early twenties raising her kids.

Loggerhead

Other than a short rough spot over Christmas when she and my Mom seemed to bristle slightly, we were relatively happy and the kids all got along. In the meantime back at SEAC I had come up with a survey plan for Loggerhead Key in the Dry Tortugas that made everyone jealous. You see, Everglades National Park, who controls Dry Tortugas for the Park Service, was planning to remove the exotic Australian pines that had festooned the sandy spit for seventy-five years. (Originally introduced in the 1880s as a wind-break and soil stabilizer, in the 1930s some idiot came up with the idea that dropping imported seeds from an airplane all over hell and creation in South Florida would dry up the Everglades [cf. also, melaleuca, or "paper tree"], and then they could be utilized for cattle and a new phenomenon called "suburbs."). Since this was an island, and a relatively small one at that, the whole thing could be cleared by the Service and then easily monitored over time. Well, before they could do any serious eradication, the place had to be archaeologically surveyed to determine if any significant cultural resources would be affected. At the north end of the island is a monument to Alfred Goldsborough Mayer, a world-renowned corals and jellyfish zoologist, and the remains of the old marine research laboratory he founded there for the Carnegie Institute. It was the first tropical marine laboratory in the Western Hemisphere and some of the first color photographs ever taken underwater were made there and published in National Geographic. Mayor, who was known as "The Seafaring Scientist" worked there for 18 years and died on the island in 1922. So, avoiding this already significant site, I planned to shovel-test the remaining seven-eighths of the island, and then we could claim it as "done" for the Regionwide Archaeological Survey Program. We also knew from previous research that in 1622, when one of the ships of the Spanish Treasure Fleet, the *Nuestra Señora del Rosario,* went aground on the reef to the south, the survivors clawed their way ashore here onto Loggerhead and camped out for some three to four weeks while a rescue party was put together in Havana. I figured there ought to be even some minor remnant of their stay, not to mention the resulting salvage camp that the Spanish would have subsequently established while recovering the cargo. Besides myself, I put together a crew of six, three guys and three girls, and off we went, driving down to Key West, going shopping for food, beer, and liquor, and then loading all our equipment onto the park's supply boat, the *Activa*, still captained by the renowned Cliff Greene, for the six-hour ride to Fort Jefferson. After a tumultuous ride in three-to-four-foot seas, the magnificent brick fortress finally appeared as a bump on the horizon some twelve miles out, and by the time we landed at the park dock on Garden Key, the monumental fort encompassed the view of at least half of the immediate horizon. After checking in with the superintendent, we were carried over to Loggerhead where we were allowed to set up in the park housing unit for visiting scientists that was rebuilt after the hurricanes of the 1930s. There was Cranston, since this was a partial "compliance" project as well, a young graduate student, Tom Hodgson, our good friend Rolando Garza (Park Service, out of Texas), and the three girls were Lou Groh, an older blond biker chick archeologist, an intern named Rowena (who was once reported to have been caught bent over her boss's desk taking it from behind), and a sharp ex-Navy graduate student, as well as a looker, who later became a very good friend of mine, Rhonda Brewer (no kidding, same last name). We got established and all took a swim in the crystal azure waters that spread out to the west of the island exhibiting the imperfect architecture of the elkhorn reefs festooned with their brightly-colored yellow-and-black-striped sergeant-majors and rainbow-hued parrotfish.

The next day we started work, and the first piece of business was to set out the survey lines, transects along which we'd dig a shovel test as far as we could in the soft pliable sand, checkerboarded every 20 meters. We marked each potential spot with a red pin-flag, and although we'd always done this before by pulling tapes guided by an optical transit, this time we had gotten proficient enough with the new Global Positioning System technology, and carrying a backpack antenna that gave us precise location (down to a tenth of a meter), we could wander in and out of the large cacti and around the huge agave and place our flags exactly where they needed to be. A day or two later, when we were allowed a quick visit up to the top of the Loggerhead Lighthouse in the middle of the island we could see our flags, hundreds of them, lined up and stretched out below as if drawn with a ruler on the island by the hand of some aerial alien. Then we set down to the digging part. It was hot, even though it was only mid-March, but the digging was easy, nothing but beach sand, and we knocked it out in less than a month, without finding any of the 1622 Spanish stuff. We did find some Civil War bottles and pipe stems, but that was it, and no surprise there: the North had occupied the Tortugas all through the Civil War without provocation. At one point I noticed that volunteers who came out to the island had been collecting dropped coconuts and were piling them up in an old above-ground cistern. Dozens had sprouted, so I got the crew to start carrying them out when we got to digging and plant them in our shovel-test holes. If you ever go out there and see coconut trees lined up one every 60 feet, those are the ones we planted. There wasn't any television, even the radio was sketchy, and I'd forgotten to bring a book along, but luckily someone had collected a bunch of old paperbacks for visitors, so Raymond Chandler and I became old acquaintances again. I did bring my fishing pole, and one day caught a nice three or four pound barracuda. Although you're not supposed to eat them because of the potential for fish-poisoning (*ciguatera*, a toxin build-up from them eating lots of smaller less-poisonous reef fish), I knew there was little to worry about with a small one, so I grilled it one evening and ate half of it, sharing the rest with the more adventurous crew members. It was delicious. Speaking of adventurous, Tom Hodgson was my snorkeling pal and the two of us would go all over the outside reef, exploring. One day there were three tourist girls sitting on the beach, while we were quite a ways off, and I spotted a large turtle heading their way and called out to let them know. They jumped in the water, and when Tom and I caught up to them while they were intercepting the turtle, he and I were both surprised to see that one of the "babes" was swimming with her top on, but no bottom (!?). They waved and swam off, laughing. Strange.

Moving Out

When I got back from Loggerhead there was somewhat of a weather change. I'd only been gone a month, albeit incommunicado. I couldn't put my finger on it. Pam was not happy (evinced by her colloquial complaint one day "When Momma's not happy, no one is going to be happy!"). Maybe it was that she had seen how much fun I'd had on Loggerhead without her; maybe it was that she was having too much fun with the young graduate students in her field school; maybe she realized that we were at different levels in our careers, and ne'er the twain would meet. In any case, she started complaining: bugs, the house, the kids, the schoolwork, my goings away. I didn't take it well, since it was a surprise to me, and I ended up speaking rather harshly to her on occasion as a result (daresay, she was bitchy at times, bossy, and didn't take criticism well—constructive or otherwise). This was sometimes provoked by her, as she knew how to press my buttons, and we began to argue. Only later did I find out that her own divorce had (quickly) come through while I was gone, and Coop had given her some $30,000 to settle. So she was now free to do as she pleased and, compared to her schoolmates, I was no longer the young studly that had wooed her away from the hubby, and in fact, I had more in common with her professors than her peers. I didn't know about the money, or the divorce for that matter, and later wondered why she hadn't told me (did she think I'd try to weasel her out of some of it?), but I did know that things were changing, rapidly. Then one Sunday (it was April 26th, 1998, I'll never forget it) she had a term paper that she was doing for her field school on certain seeds that they had recovered; she needed some high-resolution photographs of these small, and sometimes charred seeds. I offered to go to my office and use the SEAC digital camera (a new concept back then), which I had become familiar with. There were dozens of these things, and they were very tiny, so, between getting the resolution needed, with a comparative scale, and the proper lighting, on a mounted camera, and then transferring those files to my computer and then burning them all to a disk, it took me some eight hours. I got home around 6 and was getting ready to barbecue out back, our usual Sunday-dinner routine. We started gathering the kids but her son and mine were missing. They often went out around the neighborhood together, so we weren't worried, and I said I'd go out looking for them. I drove around the block, then several blocks, and as I widened my circle, I went past the nearby middle school, and there, in the parking lot, was a police car, and next to it was a policeman with my son Sam. I pulled in, got out, and there, in the back of the police car was Pam's son. My heart sank! I knew this was the end. Apparently the boys had been going down the hallways trying combination locks, and had sprung a few, not taking anything, but just rooting around. The principal was putting in some overtime and heard them down the hall. She called the police and there we were. I went to her, got the story, and talked to the police. They said it was up to her as to press charges or not, but she was a crusty old bitch and wouldn't hear of anything but the two of them going down to juvenile hall. I tried to reason with her; I begged her; I promised the worst kind of punishments if she would just let me take them home. Nope, if she let this one go, then, the next time… The police had no choice. We could pick them up at juvie in an hour or so. The boys in the back of the police car were the saddest thing I'd ever seen. Now I had to go home and face Pam. But I knew, in my heart of hearts, that this was the end.

When I got to the house, I sat her down and told her. Her face went steely cold, her eyes like a couple of ball bearings. "Let's go," she said, and though I might have talked the whole way driving to juvenile hall on the other side of town, I don't recall her saying a word. We got there, signed the papers, and retrieved the boys. When they tried explaining, along with some complaining and apologizing, she cut them off, said she didn't want to hear a word. When we got home, they were sent to their room and the other boys and her daughter went in to hear the details. She retreated to our room, and closed the door. By now it was almost nine o'clock. After an hour I went in, and she said, "We're moving out." I told her that I wasn't surprised, we could talk more about it tomorrow, I'd go sleep on the couch in the living room. We didn't talk about it the next day, or the next after that, but by Wednesday, she told me that she had gotten an apartment and they were moving out Friday, May 1st. I asked her how she could afford it and that's when she told me about the divorce and the settlement (though she didn't tell me how much). I didn't help with the move, and don't know how she did it, but my boys and I went over on Saturday, the day after, brought some pizza, and saw that she had bought a bunch of new furniture to fill the place. We all got along fine that day, but I didn't set eyes on her or hear from her for nearly another six weeks.

Summer of Lust

Tuesday, June 9th, the day after my 46th, I get a call in the early evening. She asks if I'll come over. Well, I didn't have the kids, so sure, and maybe she just missed my birthday by a day, thinking it was the ninth instead of the eighth. I went on over and brought a six-pack, and we sat at her dining room table. A bit at a loss for words, while she smoked a cigarette, I began to tell her how much I'd missed her. Soon I was declaiming how things had all gone amiss, how this wasn't what I'd planned, how great it had once been between us, maybe it could all be reconciled? She didn't mention the birthday: it wasn't an issue. She didn't mention us at all. She finally did complain that she hadn't been laid in the five weeks we'd been apart, and that in her recollection this had been the longest dry spell she'd ever had. All the emotional heart-rendering and blubbering I had made was for naught; she just wanted to get screwed! Well, a man's got to do what a man's got to do. By the end of the evening we made a pact that when she needed servicing, she'd give me a call. Thus began the summer of lust. And it really wasn't too bad, as I'd get a call every three or four days to come on over, bring some beer and a pack of cigarettes. There wasn't much talking, there wasn't much need. Sometimes she'd show up at my house, and more than once we spent the night together. But she wanted it kept on the q.t. I suppose since it was common knowledge that we had "broken up" and she wanted to keep her options open. But all her schoolmates were a decade younger and generally had girlfriends of their own. For my part, although I enjoyed it and had a lot of freedom otherwise, I knew I was being used, and sometimes resented the cold calculated nature of the whole affair. On more than one occasion I told her to leave my house before we'd done the dirty deed, just to salvage my own self-respect. But I was never that stubborn and a day or two later, I was ready, willing, and available. Funny, but I learned a lot about "the feminine mystique" that summer by being on the receiving end of the sexual cycle. Nonetheless, she was getting certain phone calls that kept her in the living room for a half-hour at a time; phone calls she didn't want me asking questions about while I lay in her bed sipping a beer, watching TV and waiting for her to get back in the sack.

One time way back in the previous spring when we were still living together, we had been laying in bed talking one evening and she was telling me about the various students in her field school. She mentioned one, a certain Grady, who would talk to her about his personal life. He was a goofy kid, slightly overweight, but tall and stocky, very mild-mannered and polite. He always called me Mr. Brewer even when I told him not to. He had friends, including a so-called "girlfriend," but apparently there was very little action going on, since she was more of a pal than a paramour. Pam felt a little sorry for this kid, not only because he was a quiet gentle giant, the teacher's pet, but because he often lamented loudly "why aren't girls attracted to me?" I told her not to worry, his time would come, it was just a matter of growing up a little more, that's all. Well, that summer, after she had moved out, a large crew from SEAC went to the Virgin Islands to do the testing and evaluation studies on Water Island that I had set up with Dave Anderson. Although I was one of, if not the most experienced person regarding the Virgin Islands, from my previous excursions, Schmidt wasn't going to give me an assignment they all considered a vacation. So even though I wanted to go, it worked out fine, because it was hard, hot, grueling, and tough (as I knew it would be), and in the meantime I was happy to be in Tallahassee, banging Pam at least twice a week. But Grady had gone on the project, and I learned that it was him that was calling Pam almost every night. He had gotten it into his head that, since we had broken up and she had moved out, he would call her and "talk." Things got a little squirrelly though when he'd call and, laying there in her bed, she'd put her hand over the mouthpiece and ask me not to sneeze or cough, 'cause she'd told him she was alone; then I'd make faces at her and try to get her to laugh while she was talking to him, sometimes licking the inside of her thigh. It didn't bother me since it gave me the requisite time to regain my rigidity. Besides, I didn't take him as a serious rival.

At the end of the summer, early-August, she complained that we never did anything outside the bedroom (which wasn't true, we'd shoot pool, go out to dinner often, and I'd even attempted a go at seeing *Hamlet*, which she couldn't handle), so I made plans to rent a canoe, got two sets of scuba gear, and took her out to Blue Hole, a large spring on the Wacissa River. We had a wonderful day, it was hot in the sun and the water was cold and clear. We'd never scuba-dived together before, but after I checked her out and we got in, I was surprised to find her comfortable under the water. We paddled back at the end of the day, and when we got back to her apartment and she decided to take a shower, I uncharacteristically and regretfully demurred from joining in and sat on her deck smoking a cigarette, thinking over what a great day it had been. Later I took her down to the coast and we had dinner at Spring Creek. We got to my house that night and she asked to stay over. Now she told me that she was going to the beach with some friends the next day (the Water Island crew had returned). She seemed happy and satisfied, and we kissed goodbye, and I told her I'd call her at the end of the week, since I was driving down to Orlando with the boys. It was Dennis's birthday again (a year from the phone call and abduction of the previous summer) and Mom had agreed to take us all out to Medieval Times in Orlando: a dinner theatre that featured a tournament, with jousting, a heroic back-play of quarrelling kingdoms, a hawk swooping over the diners' heads, and finally a magnificent staged swordfight between the protagonists. It was a lot of fun, even though the "dinner" was just a chicken quarter and a small cob of corn—the beer served by the 'wenches' was $7 a (small) tankard, but the iced tea was free. Nonetheless we had a great time, even though the good guy was eventually "slain" by the Black Knight, which I thought was a little inconvenient for the younger audience. Afterwards, everyone was allowed to mingle with the cast and take pictures, get autographs, etc. and I couldn't help but sidle up to the White Knight when he wasn't busy and ask how come it was that he had lost the otherwise really good swordfight. In his best prizefighter's Bronx accent he stoically admitted "It just wasn't my night." That was Thursday, Dennis's birthday, the 13th of August. We drove back on Saturday. On Sunday evening, the 16th, I got a call from Pam. Must have been about 10 o'clock. "Uh, David, I uh, just wanted to let you know, that Grady and I are going to do the boyfriend-girlfriend thing, and I thought I should call you and tell you, before you found out somewhere else. I want to thank you for everything, you've been a wonderful guy and taught me a lot, and I won't forget all you've done for me." "Well, okay," I said (what else could I?), "Good luck; it's been fun," and I hung up.

Pamalot

The next morning I saw her van at the end of the street where her daughter went to school with my son Dennis, and I walked on down. When she came back out and saw me, surprised, I had only one question, "Have you sealed the deal?" Yes, she told me, although Grady wouldn't acquiesce until she had made the phone call and cut me off officially. "Well, that's that," I said, "I'm gonna miss you." The next day at work Grady showed up (he was an intern at SEAC now). He was wary and tried to avoid me, but I caught up with him and said let's talk, much to his distress. I took him outside and sat him down at a picnic table nearby. "It's all okay," I told him, "you got nothing to worry about from me," and I reminded him, "Remember, it's always up to the woman." He mentioned that yes, that's right, she had pushed him to have sex right away, but he insisted on the phone call first, and she was a little pissed at being put off a day or so til I got back from Orlando. I had to laugh and told him no hard feelings, "She can be a pistol, and I hope you're up to it." Did I mention that she was 11 years his senior (37 vs. 26)? She was bound and determined to recapture that lost youth, whereas I was already an old man of 46. Ah well.

Exactly three weeks later I had a sense there's problems in paradise and asked if she'd like to go out after work and have a beer. Coincidentally, we met at the Paradise Grill, and she said she could only have a couple since she had Grady watching her kids at home. I asked her did he know where she was, and with whom? Yup, and he wasn't too happy about it. Anyway, she and I talked and after a few she was complaining that it wasn't all she thought it was gonna be: the kid was totally inexperienced, so she was giving him "lessons," and he was shy, totally wrapped up in his peers and cautious of what they thought of his excursion into serious adulthood with a full-grown woman, while also afraid of what would happen when his former long-term gal-pal found out, since he'd forgotten to mention his new arrangement to her yet. Pam wasn't too impressed with his "manliness." He was *too* damn polite. Well, that's rough, I told her as I walked her out to her van. But before she got in I grabbed her gently, turned her around, pressed her up against the side panel, and laid a big wet one on her. She didn't resist. Climbing into the van, she gave me a sly smile, and said, "I'll see you later."

She didn't know that I had filled out an application for her that summer to try and get her a job at the Park Service. She had just graduated and needed a job, bad. Somehow I had talked her into signing a blank one when we still lived together (that was one signature, on a federal application, that I wasn't going to forge), and early on in the summer, when we were grooving along, I submitted it. Now a week later I had Cranston sitting in my office, "I've got two applications for an internship in my division, Pam's and another one. I'll let you make the call," he said. He knew we'd broken up. He knew it would hurt me to see her in the office every day. He should have made the choice based on points, merit, and experience, like he was supposed to. "She needs the job," I said.

She got hired and two more weeks passed when Columbus Day fell, and the feds all got the Monday off. I get a phone call about 11 a.m. and she asks me if I'd come look at a house she was thinking of buying, give her my opinion on it. Sure, no problem. We drove out to a rundown house in a nice neighborhood not far from Lake Jackson. Although rundown, it was made of brick, didn't leak, and had a big back yard. The place had lots of potential including a large derelict in-ground pool, with a deck and a greenhouse out back. In the far corner was a ramshackle storage shed full of old furniture and various household goods, all dusty and dry-rotted. The place had been abandoned for a couple of years and though it was locked, I found an old cat-or-dog-door that I could just squeeze through and I got in and opened the front door from inside. It was a nice place but would take a lot of work, even just to get it livable; still, you could see a lot of potential, given enough time and money and sweat equity. We then went to lunch at a nearby seafood restaurant and she sprung another wild one on me, "Do you think it's big enough?" "Big enough for what?" I asked. "Big enough for both our families..." "What?" I wasn't sure I'd heard her right. "Big enough for all of us if we moved in together." Well, now I was as they say, totally flummoxed. "Yeah, it'd be big enough," I said, "but we'd have to agree on a few things first... by the way, where's the money coming from?" "I've still got about $5,000 left from Steve for a down payment," she said, "If we can get the owner to sell it owner-financed, and you sell your house, we can probably cover the payments pretty easy." Well, I had to admit, she'd been thinking on it alright. My turn. "Let me think about it," I said. Then I took her to my house for the rest of the afternoon, and even though we didn't do the mattress-dance (since she had promised Grady she wouldn't, especially with me), we did everything else.

This began the fall and winter of me as a malcontent, with a running rut of off and on semi-frequent fornication. The house-business quickly went by the wayside, even though I had quickly contacted the owner in rural Ocala, and had by twist and turns convinced him to come down from his original price of $60,000 to 35. We came within a hairsbreadth of driving down to sign the papers and give him the $5000 deposit. But there were problems. I didn't want to sell my house; she didn't want to co-sign a loan; the kids would all be in a new school district; it was still gonna be a lot of work; and putting two and two (and two more) together, in the final analysis, I didn't trust her. She broke up with Grady, wanted to get back together (that was November), by Christmas she had gone back with him; New Year's Day she called me that morning (Amy and I were reconciling slowly and she had spent the night; the phone call rousting me out of bed, her upset that I answered it), "Could you come over? We need to talk." Sure, what the fuck. I get over to her apartment, she's cooking the obligatory New Year's good-luck black-eyed peas and ham hocks, and she offered me a beer (it's not even ten o'clock in the morning!). She's just chatting, "How was Christmas? How are the boys? What did you do last night for New Year's?" I finally had to cut to the chase, "What's up? What do we need to talk about?" "Well, it's a new year (1999) and I'm getting tired of Grady constantly doing schoolwork, I sort of miss you, yadda, yadda…" Yeah, well, ain't nuthin' gonna happen til you give the kid the heave-ho, straighten up, and fly right, I told her. "By the way, where is he?" I asked, "Did he spend the night last night? And if so, what did *you* guys do?" "He's down at the University," she grumbled, "working on his goddamn THESIS—Jesus, if I hear that word one more time I think I'm going to lose it… We didn't do anything last night, we just stayed home." I looked at her in her tattered sweatpant cutoff shorts and t-shirt, and felt the old familiar tumescence. The sunlight was shining in from the east through the living room window and played a bright-paned light-shadow on the floor. I thought of inviting her to lay in the warm brightness on the carpeted living room floor, then thought again, and regained my composure. The phone rang. It was Grady calling from school. He hadn't been gone two hours, but even then he was checking the henhouse. She told him I was there (though she forgot to mention that she had invited me over), so we both knew he was now on his way. She asked me if I'd like a bowl of peas and another beer. It was a setup, and I knew it (which are the best kind, the ones you realize). Sure, I told her, what the hell.

He showed up within 10 minutes, just as I was finishing the bowl of peas, halfway down the second beer of the morning. He was hot, flushed, angry, and inflated, huffing and puffing when she let him in the door. He came right over and sat down across from me, glaring. "What are you doing here?" he demanded. Although I was sorely tempted to tell him that she had asked me to come over, which is why I was there, I just said, "We were just talking." "What were you talking about?" he again demanded. Just things. Pam stayed in the kitchen, keeping her back to us for the moment. "Yeah, well, I don't want you coming over here," he said, "she broke up with you and you need to get over the fact that I took your girl." "First of all," I said calmly, "I don't care what you want. Second, although she broke up with me she's changed her mind at least twice in the past six months, and finally, before you think you 'took my girl' you might consider that maybe *she picked you up* as a diversion, and one that's getting less and less entertaining all the time." He mulled that over for the better part of a minute, and then (surprisingly to me) said, "You don't care about my feelings at all, do you?" and I had to admit, "No, Grady, I'm sorry, I really don't. All I care about is her." Now she was out of the kitchen, standing between us. I finished my beer and stood up, and, when he couldn't see, she winked at me and said, "Maybe it's time to go." I said "Maybe you're right. Thanks for the black-eyed peas, they were delicious," and I left.

The "Pompetous" of Love
Now I must beg the reader's indulgence. The above episodes, from the time I met Pam on the banks of the St. Johns River until this New Years had spanned nearly three years. They do

little or no credit to her, me, Coop, or Grady, or anyone else for that matter. It's confusing, and ultimately illogical, as Spock might put it. But these are matters of the heart, both biological and psychological, enmeshed in a social structure that also changes over time. In putting them down on paper, as honestly as I can remember, at the same time, I'm also trying to figure out what happened. Worse, I'm trying to figure out why. I might mention that throughout the time she moved out and was with Grady (and god-only-knows-who-else), and for another year afterwards, we were seeing each other on an unplanned, impromptu basis, or so I thought. At some point around this time, as strange as everything appeared, and my life beginning to unravel somewhat, what with the other shit going on at work, and not knowing what was going to happen next, I went and visited the old marriage counselor-therapist, Dr. Lyons. As I'd said before, I always liked him, and he was not only professional, but cut right through the shit and told you what was going on. I told him about Pam, the whole mess: me taking her away from her husband, her moving in with the kids, her moving out when the kids got in trouble, her divorce, the Grady business, the almost-bought house near Lake Jackson, and finally, the intermittent trysts. I'd even started plotting the times when these occurred on an Excel spreadsheet, since I was doing other things with Excel while writing reports. I found that the call for duty from Pam would happen every 11 days *on average*, but that it might be as short as 3, or as long as 20. Nonetheless, if 11 days passed and I hadn't gotten a call, I knew I'd get one in a day or so. Lyons listened quietly and I'd eaten up maybe 40 minutes of a 50-minute session, when he put up his hand to hush me, and said "You ever hear of Basic Personality Disorder?" I said no, and he told me to look it up. "What you've described is a classic case. She's been playing you like a finely-tuned violin… probably ever since you met her. And now… well, let me put it this way, you know how when you put a quarter in the coke machine, and you don't get a coke? Then, you shake the machine, and sometimes a coke comes out, and sometimes it doesn't? Or better still, you put *another* quarter in the machine, and then you get the coke? That's what she's doing to you. It's called *delayed gratification* and it's a very powerful training device… developed by B.F. Skinner, the behaviorist. Let me ask you this… when you do finally have sex, I'll bet it's almost always very good." Well, yes, I had to admit, it was. "Then it's up to you to decide what you want to do, and how far you want to go with this, but right now you're responding exactly how she wants you to. Time's up, nice seeing you again." Told ya I liked that guy. Now THAT was $80 well spent!

Back to the Grinder

Once I had a method I could put to the madness, I was better able to control my own responses, and soon I quit answering the "dinner bell," so to speak. Amy and I were getting along better, which was better for the kids, and now I had a more serious situation to deal with. My titular boss Schmidt, being goaded by Cranston, who was now in full-rivalry mode, had decided to go for my jugular, and had sent me a memo that I was behind in four reports and if I didn't get them out in two months he was going to initiate a PIP, or Performance Improvement Plan, which I recognized immediately as the first move to try to get me fired. Well, it was a funny coincidence that Cranston, who was pushing his own agenda in order to attempt to become a "manager" (something I would never ever want to be called), initiated what he called a "charrette." This was a misnomer, because a charrette is usually convened to solve a certain design or system problem, bringing the best minds to bear, whereas, Cranston's "charrette" was simply an ad hoc staff meeting, which management refused to attend, and was a result of them never having staff meetings no matter what, because they couldn't control the discussion (and there were plenty of issues to talk about). I was all for it, because it gave us senior staff members, maybe a dozen now, the ones who ran projects, a chance to compare notes. Things started off slow, no one wanted to take the lead, and even Cranston knew that around the table there were bigger fish swimming in the pond, so he sort of let it wander. Then I piped up and suggested we just go around the table, no introductions necessary, and tell the rest of the table the projects we were working on, their status, and any problems we were having. Everyone liked this idea and I started taking notes out of habit, listening intently. Soon it became evident (to me, especially), that almost every archaeologist at the table had *at least* four backlog reports hanging over them, and some had six or seven. Hell, when Ken Wild had left for his promotion in Puerto Rico, he had eight. After everybody gave their summaries, there wasn't anything left to talk about (no one was going to complain about management, not with Cranston's ear at the table), so we all went back to our offices. I immediately drafted a fire-back memo to Schmidt telling him about the fact that most of the other investigators were in the same position I was as far as backlog reports, and some were even worse, so what the hell? A day later, he called me into his office and gave me the old, "This isn't about other people; this is about you" line. Well, now my alarms were going off. I'd been sent to supervisory training myself, so I knew that this was a standard ploy for homing in on someone you wanted to get rid of, truth, fairness, and justice be damned. I reminded him of my special assignment to Natchez Trace, how that had taken four months out of my previous year. He conceded that I'd done a good job and gave me an extra month on my reports. Well, I knew there was no arguing. There was no arguing because, as my dear old Dad told me (when he wasn't telling me not to put anything in writing that may come back and haunt you), "If it ain't in writing, it never happened." So I knew there was no talking to Schmidt. At the same time, I knew I could write rings around him, and that now *we really were in a pissing contest*, so from then on, and starting with his original missive, every time I got a half-page, half-assed memo, I answered it with a two-page formal response, cc'ed to the Chief. Meanwhile, I started cranking on those backlog reports, since they had to be done anyway.

By sheer strength of will, I stayed away from Pam the rest of that winter and spring, making up somewhat with Amy and concentrating on the boys and work. In February I had a nice assignment where I was sent to St. Marys, Georgia to participate in a Wilderness Development Planning team for Cumberland Island. By this time, I was the *de facto* expert on Cumberland Island, second only to the Chief, and he asked me to represent the Center on how to develop the northern half of Cumberland Island into an official "Wilderness Area." This is a tricky piece of business because, when you create a Wilderness Area, that means no vehicles, no power tools, and even hiking and camping are strongly regulated. That also means that even any research scientists, like archaeologists for instance, would have to carry in all their equipment on their backs. Plus, there are people living on the northern half of Cumberland who owned cars and ATVs, not to mention the necessary vehicles and equipment needed in the attempts at removing feral hogs, and overabundant armadillos. So there were a lot of issues that needed to be addressed, and though Schmidt wanted to go instead, it became apparent in a prior planning meeting he didn't even know who the Superintendent was, much less the issues.

Seagle's

I drove out on a Tuesday for a meeting that day and the next. On the way I stopped by the fort of San Marcos in St. Augustine, where Cranston and his crew were working on some wall-settling issues. Pam was there working with them, and I said hi, told her about going to St. Marys and Cumberland Island. She said she wished she were going with me. When I got to St. Marys, I checked into the Riverview Hotel, a small antiquated little place on the corner across from the river. It's got a small bar café called Seagle's attached, and as the lady was checking me in to the hotel, she sighed and looked up at me, "Say, you wouldn't know how to tend bar would you?" "Yeah, sure, I've done that," I said, omitting that it was only in a beer and wine venue. "Well, my regular bartender can't come in tonight until midnight, and I need someone to run the bar from five until then, are you interested?" "Sure," I told her, "I'd be happy to." She said she couldn't pay me, but I could keep all my tips and she'd even let me have an extra night at the hotel for free. Great, I said, I'll see you at five. When I got to my room I made it a point to put on a long-sleeve white shirt with my jeans, a la Jackie Gleason's Joe the Bartender. Then I went down the block and introduced myself to the Wilderness participants. We broke up about 4:30 and I told them to come on down to Seagle's and I'd wait on them. I went into the bar, met the lady owner, who showed me where everything was, and how to work the cash register. We counted the cash in the register together, I rolled up my sleeves, put on an apron, and was ready to go. People started coming in immediately, including my Wilderness crew, and in no time flat, the bar was full; I was even running beers and drinks out to the tables. It finally fell into a manageable steady crowd about eight o'clock, and from then on it was relatively smooth sailing. The patrons were particularly fond of me because I was giving generous pours, and the only drink that stumped me was a Manhattan, so I just told the guy who ordered it to tell me exactly how he wanted it made. I followed his directions with a flourish and he loved it. The regular barmaid came in at 11:30, congratulated me on a job well-done (I tried to keep everything clean, especially glasses, as I went along), and counted me out $83 in tips. Whoo-hoo! Then I sat on the other side of the bar, and the remaining grateful patrons wouldn't let me pay for a single drink until I stumbled up to my bed around 2. I guess I always got that to fall back on.

Summer w/ Zabette

Two months later, I had avoided Pam by degrees, although seeing her every day at work, sadly doing clerical work for the large and lumbersome Jack Cranston, and still dinking her boy, Grady; but hell, at least she was getting a paycheck. Then we received a priority assignment from the Regional Office in Atlanta: they want a team from SEAC to go to Cumberland Island for the summer and carry out investigations on the remains of the dozen or so Stafford slave cabins in the middle of the island that were still marked by the presence of chimneys, some toppled over, some leaning and propped up, others still standing up straight. Stafford, the plantation homesteader was one of those wild-eyed slave-owning entrepreneurs just before the Civil War who sought to make his fortune off of both sea-island cotton and indigo, with some tobacco and fruit trees tossed in as well. (I always thought it interesting that the whole indigo industry in the South somehow supplied most of the blue dye for the uniforms of the North.) Then there was the whole growing, breeding, and selling of slaves as a sort of cottage industry as well. Stafford was neither good nor bad for his time and place, but he wasn't averse to some good old whipping and dog-baiting when he needed to make a point. He was thought to be less of a concerned caretaker though, when he abandoned the island during the Civil War, while the North occupied it and freed his slaves, and after the war, when he came back and tried to get them to go back to work and they wouldn't, he burned their houses down. Not a nice person, by any day's standards. Well, the whole push behind the project was that our Chief, John Hardinger, had been part and parcel of the production of a modern opera called *Zabette*, based on the reminiscences of one of the female slaves who had lived on Cumberland during that period. (Apparently, Stafford had bought Zabette, and then, after giving her her freedom, had six children by her who were eventually educated in England. She was one of those few freed black women who also owned slaves for awhile, and then, the War set them free, but some continued to work for her after Stafford died.) The opera had opened to good reviews in Atlanta, and so the Park Service had decided to spend a little money on discovering what life in these former cabins had really been like. Unfortunately, they made me, the Cumberland Island-guy, and Cranston, co-directors again, as I've said before, never a good idea. Two bosses are one too many, and the fact that we were in rival divisions (which I never recognized as such, but which Cranston relished) meant there was going to be some competing for both resources and recognition. To be honest, I wasn't up for the competition; I just wanted to do a good job with the archaeology, and if the crew got along, there weren't any fights, and working conditions were tolerable, we'd be successful. So I threw my efforts in that direction by taking on the one thing that usually led to dissension, logistics: this meant handling housing, transportation, catering, and putting in a large stock of beer.

The ladies I hired to cater for us were island residents, actually living in the pre-Civil War-era Stafford servants quarters, a couple of big-boned old-maid spinster sisters, who were both sweet and gruff at the same time; probably as a result of island-living, where they had to be tough and resourceful when alone, yet happy now to have some outside company for a change. (More than once I felt they were sizing me up for a romp, but who would take priority, or in what order, or whether they were plotting together I never found out, thank God.) They were wonderful cooks and when we got up before dawn, and stumbled in to the large industrial kitchen once used by the Carnegie servants (now maintained by the park for just the likes of us, visiting scientists), the scrambled eggs and sausage and pancakes were already steaming in large colanders from which we'd shovel out large spoon and forkfuls. After eating, we each made our own bagged lunches from the previous night's leftovers with sides of fruit and canned drinks. Then we were off to the site, which was in the middle of the island, north of the large grassy meadow that served as pasture for both the deer and the feral horses, and which had served over the years as both a three-par golf course and private landing strip for small planes. The weather was beautiful when we started: cool mornings, seabreezes wafting through the trees, the smell of myrtle and camphor as we cut the vines and shrubbery away from the tabby-brick chimneys. Though the days started off softly, as the sun rose, the breeze lessened, the weather got still, and the dirt and sweat commingled. By the end of the day we were all exhausted and had to pace the showers so as not to use up all the hot water at once before dinner at six sharp. While waiting a turn to shower, this provided time for a couple of beers, and maybe even a quick dip in the ocean. Did I mention that Pam was part of the crew? But not her boy-toy, Grady.

Snakes Alive!
It was a large crew too, at least a dozen student-interns and three of us as staff members. Besides Cranston and myself, we had Rolando, the Tex-Mex roustabout, as our Crew Chief. He was perfect for maintaining the quality–control of the artifacts as they came out of the ground and while they were processed in the field lab. Pam was his right-hand (wo)man. Cranston and I controlled where the digging took place, as well as supervising the crews and switching people around as the situations dictated. There were also a lot of public relations to deal with, which usually fell to me; but I was pretty good at keeping Cranston informed, which was not always reciprocated. We had a lot of visitors coming and going as well. For the first week or so, I kept my distance from Pam and treated her as just another field hand. But because I was one of the head guys and had been to Cumberland many, many times before and knew the island like the back of my hand, I commandeered a set of keys for one of the park's island jeeps, and made friends with the guys who controlled the gas pump. As it was, I was going for rides all over the island after work, and it wasn't long before Pam asked if she could go with me. Our first "encounter" happened one weekend when the crew was off (we weren't allowed to work anybody more than 40 hours a week) and had taken the ferry into St. Marys for some R&R. She and I decided to stay on the island and go exploring. We found ourselves in the small walled cemetery just south of Stafford Plantation and directly across from the large wild horse pasture. It was a quiet sun-dappled afternoon and she was taking photographs, various art and nature shots, when I pointed out a large multi-colored corn snake, maybe four feet long, laying up on the gray stone slab of Mr. Stafford himself. It was a really interesting shot, one that you couldn't have planned in a thousand years. She eased up and got it just before the snake noticed her and quickly slithered off. It was a little exciting, being as big as it was, and how close she had been able to

get to it. Me? I was in a playful mood, so I began to talk to her about the symbolic mystical qualities of the snake, and what it signified mythologically. How Freud was fascinated by the phallic symbolism of life when it would show up in his women patients' dreams. And how now, here we were *in a cemetery*, with this large snake sunning itself, gathering solar life-energy on top of the slab of a grave of the very man whose life was built by the suffering of the slaves whom we were studying. Why, just the whole universal concept of it all, and her and I just leaning against the cemetery wall, made my pecker just stand straight up. She realized what I was up to then, and mad as she was, she was also excited, her breath coming in short gasps and her eyes wide. I took a chance and unzipped my shorts. She told me she had promised Grady that she wouldn't do it with me while on this project. Who said anything about doing "it" I asked. Maybe just a hand job. Between old friends. She reached over, telling me what a rotten bastard I was, and let me just say that had she gotten her hands around that corn snake's neck, he wouldn't have stood a chance of coming out of the confrontation alive. I rubbed her on the outside of her jeans, but once I was done, she turned, wiped off her hand, and left me there leaning on the wall. We got back in the jeep. I fired it up, and as we pulled onto the dirt road heading back to the dorms, we looked at each other and laughed. We were back on track. Suffice it to say that over the next six weeks we did "it" in the woods, in the jeep, in our rooms, in the shower, in the ocean.

Floor Flushing

The work went well, and we dug a shitload of test units across the whole "Chimneys" village area. What was puzzling though, was the dearth of artifacts from inside the footprints of the houses. We found more artifacts, considerably more, outside in the common yard. This was strange, since we knew they had hard-packed dirt floors, and even though they would be swept out once in a while a dirt floor usually captures items as they are inadvertently trod underfoot. And, knowing where each chimney was, we knew that a lot of time was spent directly in front of the fireplace not only while cooking, but especially during the cold winter months when not much growing was going on, and the occupants would spend a lot of time on tools and handicrafts sitting by the light and warmth of the hearth. The answer came from an unexpected source late in the project when we had gathered a lot of attention in the local papers and had unexpected visitors, curious old-timers and amateur archaeologists and historians, coming over on the ferry to see what we were doing. And we were happy to give impromptu tours to these groups of usually older folks, though sometimes it was a small school group of kids as well. I was the usual designated tour-guide and in fact, when the star of the *Zabette* opera came to the island, the Chief asked me to personally give her a one-on-one and show her all the things we'd recovered and explain their significance. We had handmade fishing weights and hooks and woven line from one structure, so we knew he was a fisherman. We had flint and molded bullets out of another, so we knew he was a hunter (surprising to some, slaves were not only allowed to have guns, they were sometimes encouraged to, in order to be able to supplement their diet themselves and take some of the responsibility off of the owner, caretaker, or overseer). There were harmonica parts and flutes, so we knew they enjoyed some music once in awhile; and there were plenty of animal bones (pig, cow, raccoon, squirrel, turkey and other birds, deer, etc.) which indicated that they ate well on occasion, obviously enhanced with a lot of the local plants and herbs (mallow, fennel, poke salad, palm hearts, corn, and nuts). And of course, there were ceramics and glass: teacups, goblets, china plates, etc, more than a few items of cutlery, and enough buttons and thimbles that one young intern got a Master's thesis out of them. Now none of this was surprising, we all knew generally how slaves had lived, but to have these items in front of you, and to handle them knowing their place in space and time, well, as I've said before, this is the closest thing to time-travel we've got. In any case, the diva from *Zabette* was extremely impressed.

Occam Rocks 'em

To get back to the question of why these items were in the yard and not in the house floors, one day we had another visitor. He was an old man of eighty-some years, a white guy, just an old redneck who said that he had grown up on the island when he was a kid. Well, *that* was interesting. He remembered when people still lived in the Chimney houses, rebuilt from old barn-wood and lumber retrieved from the beach off of storm-tossed ships. He remembered playing with the black kids who lived in the houses, sometimes even spending the night. This would have been in the 1920s, but he said people lived the same as they had from the previous century. Then he answered our question without even being asked. He said that each house had a large palm-frond woven mat that covered the floor from wall to wall and when Momma got fed up with the accumulation of stuff on the floor, the few pieces of furniture they had were taken outside, the mat was rolled up, taken out in the yard and shaken. Then everything was returned. This was easier and quicker than sweeping, and in the meantime the easily-replaced mat kept them off the dirt. When it wore out, it was easy enough to replace. And there it was: not necessarily an example of Occam's Razor, that the simplest explanation is usually the best (that would have been our initial 'sweeping' hypothesis), it nonetheless simply and succinctly explained why the crap was found out in the yard and not in the house. A better example of Occam is the hypothesis I came up with to explain why, on almost every chimney, at the outside corners, there was a worn-away indentation in the tabby-bricks and mortar at about the height of roughly two and a half feet. I noticed this from the drawings made, and then saw that they were readily visible in damn near every chimney. It was if at two and a half feet, on the corners, the bricks had been eroded, some badly, sometimes to the point that they actually threatened the integrity of the chimney. No one else really noticed this, nor did they care. I would point it out and they'd all say, "So what?" I thought it was a strange "thing" and one day I was leaning on one of the chimneys, looking down at it when it struck me. I had to pee. And if I were going to piss, I had by nature to look for a place to do it. I walked off the site, away from the staff, and into the adjacent woods, and picked out a nice tree to pee up against. Looking back through the brush at the chimneys, then looking down at the tree I was pissing on, it was all so suddenly clear. If I were sleeping in the cabin, and woke up in the middle of the night, slave or no, having to pee, I would walk outside, and well, there'd be no sense in walking down to the outhouse in the dark, which was probably outside the village bounds anyway, and pee there. That was for taking a dump. Why I'll just walk around to the back of the chimney here and pee. If I pee'd up against the chimney brickwork, well, again, over time, I imagine that the uric acid in my urine would eat into the calcium carbonate of the tabby brick and erode it just a tad each time, like concentrated acid rain. Three hundred and sixty-five nights a year, over the two hundred years the chimneys had stood there, at least a hundred and fifty years occupied, yup, that would have done it. I thought I'd made a great cultural finding: *Archaeological Evidence of Multi-Generational Mid-Night Micturation on Tabby-Brick Tumuli and Its Social Significance Among Enslaved African-Americans, as shown from 19th Century Stafford Plantation, Cumberland Island, Georgia.* No one wanted to hear it.

One afternoon, Pam and I decided to take a walk out in the woods between the Carnegie ruins at Dungeness and the beach. It was really a beautiful shadowy undercover with meandering animal trails below the majestic live oaks, some over two hundred years old. We had followed the branching trails this way and that, avoiding a small pond or two, when we found ourselves in tall sawgrass and lost. Not quite totally lost, because we knew the direction of the setting sun, we knew the ocean was to the east, we knew we had come from the north. But as we tried to follow the trails back in the direction we had come, they twisted this way and that, often turning back upon themselves. At one point we just cut through the sawgrass to the east, toward the ocean and

410

the beach, but the grass was tall and sharp, and we were both in shorts. I took the lead so that she wouldn't get her legs all cut up. Meanwhile I'm keeping an eye and an ear out for rattlesnakes, some of the largest on the East Coast having been spotted here (this was the project wherein Rolando had seen the big one come over the dunes and swim out to sea). The sun was beginning to set and we started getting a little nervous. At one point we found ourselves in a small clearing in the grass trampled down by either deer or feral hogs. It was already getting dark, and she suggested that we carve out a double-bed in the sand, curl up and try to sleep, then get up at dawn and make our way out. Much as I liked the idea of it I said no, we had to make one more push for the ocean, it just couldn't be that far. I put her on my shoulders so she could see out over the grass and had her point to the setting sunlight. That was west. We headed in the opposite direction and in ten minutes of pushing our way through, we could hear the waves. Another five minutes and we came upon the backside of the dunes. Over the dunes and we were on the beach. We stripped and got into the cool dark shallows and just held onto each other. Now, that was nice.

The project was generally successful, and the last night we were there we celebrated the time-honored tradition of drinking up all the leftover beer and liquor so we wouldn't have to carry any back on the ferry. This made for a poundingly painful last day, which we had saved to backfill the last of our great excavations. It was going to be a solid day of slinging dirt for a few of the short-straw chosen men. One of the young bucks, a twenty-something kid named Tyler was so hungover that he refused to get out of the rack. We tossed a bucket of water on him, but once he'd gotten dressed, we found him again asleep, so we slipped his boots on and carried him out to the jeep. When we got to the site, we let him sleep for about a half-hour before we rousted him out for his turn on the shovel. Poor kid; it's a sad state of affairs to watch a young man throwing up and then burying the bile, all the while on his knees, and then falling face-down into the dirt pile, to be lifted out moaning and snot-smeared, begging for death. As painful as the throbbing was for the rest of us, the whole scenario lent a bit of humor to an otherwise generally painful ordeal. Pam pulled up in the jeep and we had her take Tyler back to clean up and pack to get off-island with everybody else on the first ferry trip out. She and I had had our last rendezvous the evening before, driving down to the south end of the island, where we could see Ft. Clinch across the St. Marys at Fernandina Beach on Amelia Island. After engaging in our own furtive clinch, while smoking cigarettes and watching the sun go down, she told me what a wonderful summer it had been, but that now she had to go back to "reality." "Shit-fire," I said, "*This* is reality! The rest, the business at work, the paying of bills, grocery-shopping… *that's not reality*! If we learned anything from these excavations, it's what reality was really like living on an island." She stuck by her guns. Apparently the kid was picking her up the next day when we hit the mainland. Other than seeing her at work, which was slightly distracting, we didn't see each other, or talk again for that matter, for six months.

Belly-achin'

I was working hard on those backlog reports, while Schmidt was trying to bust my balls. But I put two of them to bed right away, so he had to shut up for awhile. Meantime, I took my case to the Chief, Hardinger, whom I'd always considered a friend. I let him know that I knew this was a hatchet job, and you know, he didn't disagree. But he also let me know that he wasn't going to undercut his manager (although he said he'd talk to him). I was unimpressed and more than pissed, considering all the times I'd represented him and the Region over the years. I'd even defended his directorship, which a lot of people around the Service, both inside and outside SEAC, had considered a "gimme" gift from his boss in Atlanta, Ear-wig. Nonetheless, I'd beaten back Gordon Schmidt for a little while. Everyone at SEAC knew what was happening, but the only people I had pulling for me were the ones who worked for me. As far as management was concerned I was anathema, as we had become at odds over the years as SEAC became more and more of a corporate enterprise and less and less of a family of archaeologists. One example that had set me off years before was how Schmidt, for instance, would ask me to put together a budget for a particular project in a particular park. Now I was pretty good at this, and to be honest, it's pretty easy. It's just a matter of how many people, including their salaries and benefits, and how much time (which would include housing and per diem, and of course, lab analysis). Things like logistics (mileage, gas, e.g.) and equipment were pretty much minimal and set at something like 5% of the total. The trouble was, unbeknownst to me, the park had usually already committed the money to SEAC by telling him something to the effect, "We have $50,000 to do this job." I might write a budget that came to $35 or $40K. Then I'd be asked, "Could you bump it up?" until I reached the $50K allotted for the job. That's all fine, and part of the game. But then Schmidt would fuck up by assigning *me* to do the job... for $35K! Even this would have been alright, until the pressure was on to hurry up, get out of the field, get back and analyze the results and write up the damn thing, all within the $35K budget, and then find out that in the next month or so, Schmidt is going to a cross-cultural glad-handing meeting in Switzerland and taking his wife for a week or so. Cost? Around $15,000! If I ever said anything or complained, well, I really wasn't a team player now was I? No, not on that team. Worse, as far as I was concerned, was the favoritism. Call it what you will: ass-kissing, dick-sucking, brown-nosing, et al, when Pete was the Chief there weren't any "factions" per se, they just weren't allowed to develop. Oh sure, there were individuals who hated others, there were oddballs, and even slackers, but there weren't competitive "teams" and when the Center had to pull together, well, by God, we pulled in tandem (like the old 40-mule team Borax commercials). After Buddy and Gordon divided the place into divisions, which was allowed to continue, if not encouraged by Hardinger, and then supported one or another, against each other, either by funding or personnel or again, favors, the whole place became a hotbed of intrigue: who was getting what, how much, and my favorite question, why?

One of the worst at this was Cranston, who was a consummate gossip and instigator of trouble. He had the office next to Schmidt's so, first of all, he could hear Gordon on the phone (which was right next to the open door) setting up deals, or bitching to the Chief about this or that or whomever (often, me); then he would place little poisonous nuggets of discontent in Schmidt's ear, especially any complaints that he might have heard while wandering the halls and "dropping by." I knew this first–hand because I wasn't afraid to complain, even to Schmidt personally, and I'd often plant a spurious seed with Cranston to see how it would sprout later. So Cranston became Schmidt's informant, and sure as hell, was rewarded amply for his efforts. One of the rewards took the form of an in-house talking-to (rather than a formal write-up) when Cranston would have one of his famous meltdowns and either berate or fire some intern for questioning one of his (dumb) field decisions. These meltdowns were often either insulting or derogatory to the extent that they bordered on abuse (sometimes crossing that border as well), and more than once the question in point was fully justified considering the job at hand, whether dealing with safety, efficiency, or fairness. In my own case, I always deferred to the crew on matters of safety or efficiency (unless I knew better and could successfully argue the case), but as far as fairness, well, when one of the girls (generally speaking) would come to me and complain about their perceived unfairness of a decision, I would give each of them the same advice, "If you seek fairness in this life, and especially in this line of work, you are setting yourself up for a lot of disappointment and heartache; it would be better to step beyond that perception and just be the best at whatever you're given"; then I would try to adjust accordingly. It sure sounded good at the time, and usually did the trick for the moment. Cranston however, was a graduate of the old "my way, or the highway" school of mismanagement, and although he'd been called out on it several times, he seemed always to get away, even in the most egregious instances, with ne'er the first reprimand. That was one of the rewards. Another occurred yearly during our performance reviews. He'd get a glowing one, no matter what, despite the talkings-to, or any run-ins with outside park personnel, much less in-house confrontations or complaints. I always had to justify every accomplishment I'd made over the year, often with an attached detailed memo explaining what I'd done and why it was important to the overall operations of the Center, which Schmidt would conveniently overlook, and often only got what I wanted when I'd refuse to sign the damn thing until it was changed in my favor. It was just getting harder and harder to carry out my day-to-day duties, much less (as they say in corporate-speak) "accomplish my goals." I used to refer to it as running a race (the rat-race?), except I was expected to carry a bowling ball along.

More Bitchin'

One day I was outside sitting at a picnic table, weighing my options, when Pam came out, sat down and lit a cigarette. We hadn't talked in awhile and she asked me how it was going. She knew, just like everybody else, what I'd been up against, but she didn't know the details. So I took a few minutes and filled her in on what was really going on. After a little while, and without the least amount of sarcasm, she said, "Well, why don't you just kiss his ass? That would solve all your problems." I looked up, across the table, and tried to discern the joke. It wasn't there. She was serious. I was immediately reminded of the story of Michael Collins, the famous Irish national hero. He was quite the man's man and although he never married, already being married to The Cause, he always had some woman that he was either carrying on with or wooing. Well, there was a certain woman he had become exceedingly attracted to (I can't remember her name), and was considering asking her to marry him, and they were sitting on a park bench one day in Dublin, talking. He was already deep into the Nationalist agenda, and had already participated in the Easter uprising, etc, and the civil war between the Nationalists and the anti-Treaty contingent was going on, so he was always in danger. At some point in the discussion, and before he had mustered the will, or more likely, mastered the timing, to ask her hand in matrimony, she blurted out something to the effect, "You know, I don't know what I'd do if I were married to one of those poor men who might have his legs or arms shot off. I don't think I could handle it." He was so stunned and shocked and appalled at what she had said, that he simply got up, and without a word, walked off, never to speak to her again. Me? No, I didn't get up and walk away, but I was reminded of Michael Collins, and I told her, "I can't believe you said that," and I'm afraid my opinion of her, after four years, changed that very moment.

2000

Though still living apart and now divorced, the Millenium was arriving and Amy and I made plans as a family to go to St. George's Island and rent a couple of adjacent hotel rooms. Mom was only seventy-five then and still spry and sharp. She put up the bulk of the dough, and Amy and I sprang for the food and refreshments, including a dozen bottles of champagne. Paul and his wife and daughter came as well, and the weather was picture-perfect, cool and sunny, warm enough to wear shorts, and bright enough to warm the sand. We went fishing, swimming, exploring, and had a great time, and it was very important to be together at that supposedly significant event, lots of champagne and fireworks. Amy and I had reconciled as best we could, the boys were happy, and when I got Mom alone and told her that I was finished with the Pam-business, she seemed relieved, never having given me any grief about it, despite her (and Amy's) constant misgivings, and said, "You know what happened, don't you?" I didn't quite understand what she was getting at, and said, "No, what happened?" "You missed a bullet." And she was right. Nobody could ever tell me a damn thing; good friends had tried to talk sense to me—I'd been convinced I knew what was best for me; even after the well-intentioned yet dire warning from Dr. Lyons. It just had to run its course… and thank God it had. She would have taken me for everything: house, car, retirement and everything else she could have laid her hands on, before she would have finally cut me loose. Mom was right, and it's not many times in your life that you can say you missed a bullet. Reminds me of what the Romans used to say. They thought of being in love as actually being physically sick, or somewhat mentally deranged. "You need to conduct business with Davidicus today? I wouldn't if I were you… he's in love right now. Better that you wait until it's passed somewhat and he's back in his right mind so that you both can get a fair deal. Shouldn't be long… give it a couple of months or so."

Final Blow

The phone in the kitchen rings one Saturday mid-morning in April. "He's left me," she said. I didn't even ask why. It was the day of the Anthropology Department fish-fry, but a few of us had decided to go downtown instead and carouse with the faux-Cajuns at a big crawfish boil that was going on down there; it sounded like a lot more fun. "How would you like to come along with us?" I said. She goes, "Yeah, anything to get out of the house." I picked her up around noon and we met a bunch of the older graduate students downtown at Po' Boys Creole Café, staked out a table, and started swilling beer and popping crawdads. There was music and singing, the weather was warm with clouds skipping by and a small sprinkle or two, but we were under a canopy so it was fine. We were all having a good time, but Pam was mopey. Eventually, with enough beers she opened up and began enjoying herself. Around five we'd all had enough, and I drove her home. I was going to a stage show that evening, political and humorous skits put on by the Mickee Faust Revue and asked her if she wanted to go, it'd cheer her up. No, she didn't want to go, but would I come by afterwards? Well, I'm an idiot (and I'd had a few beers), so I said sure, not knowing where that might lead. I went to the show with my good friend Rolando, who'd never been before, and we both had a few laughs and a couple more beers. Then I headed back to her apartment. Now it's around ten. When I get there her kids were still up watching television, so we went out on the porch to talk and smoke a cigarette. After a little while she mumbled something. I didn't quite get it. "What did you say?" I asked. "I think I'm in love with him," she said. That was it. I stood up, flicked my cigarette butt off her balcony and said, "You are one self-centered, narcisstic, white-trash, mental, fucked-up bitch, you know that…" I said, rather vehemently, and walked out. In the morning I made it a point to call her around nine. "You know what I said last night? I want to apologize for calling you white-trash. That was unfair, because it reflects on your family, who I happen to like. As far as the rest of it though, I want you to know I meant it." While she was sputtering an attempted comeback, I hung up. We never spoke again. It had been almost exactly four years to the day I saw her on the banks of the St. Johns. I could hear the "zzzppp" of the bullet as it sped by.

Buh-bye

As I finished up the summer of 2000, I was pretty much fed up with SEAC. It wasn't much fun anymore, and it didn't look like it was going to get much better. My last two projects included one under Lou Groh, the older blonde biker chick (who later died tragically from a brain tumor), where we went to Manteo, North Carolina and made an unsuccessful attempt to find any remnants of the lost colony of Roanoke. The highlight of that trip was while we were sitting in a small bar in town late one night, a fully bedecked Blackbeard impersonator, in a red velour suit, tricorner hat, knee-high black boots, and having long flowing dreadlocked beard tassels with burnt-out candles interwoven, stumbled in loaded to the gills after one of his "gigs" and drew his cutlass, threatening to "gull somebody" if he didn't get a drink pronto. The barmaids were less impressed than we were, and told him to shut up and sit down, they'd get to him when they could.

The second and probably my last project with SEAC was as a crew chief with Margo. Whereas once she worked under me, she was now leading her own projects, and doing a great job of it too. This was a survey of a large section of land that was going to be added to the Big Cypress National Preserve, a portion of south-central Florida that few white men had ever been in, and even modern-day Seminoles only used for seasonal hunting camps. We knew from other places that the small island hillocks that dotted the landscape were often sites of prehistoric shell middens and burial mounds, usually found on the higher, north ends. The Preserve floods during the wet season so we had to go in during late spring before the summer rains began, and the area we were investigating was so remote that we had to go in by helicopter, which meant we had to train briefly on proper procedures and wearing flight suits and helmets. Somewhere I have a picture of me standing next to the chopper, generously filling out a flight suit with helmet in hand. From the air, the brown and green tear-drop-shaped hammocks were scattered from horizon to horizon, some of the most desolate yet beautiful scenery in Florida. Once we were set down, we hoofed it from hammock to hammock, often wading single-file through wet troughs between the islands, through what are called "gator-holes" for the obvious reason that this was where the reptiles hunker down until the rains come back (first person goes down, I promised I'd go for help). We didn't consider the possibility of pythons back then, although they had already been reported as an "oddity." But there were plenty of water moccasins and rattlesnakes to keep us on our toes.

Every now and then we found that one of these hammocks housed an open shack in the sheltering sun-speckled shade under a spreading live oak, and we'd go in to explore. These were hunting shacks, made of scrap materials and more than likely visited by Seminoles moving between them by canoe when the waters flowed. There'd be cans of food, and half-bottles of cheap booze, maybe a stretched animal skin or two on the wall, but we never disturbed anything, only taking photos. In any case we documented many new archaeological sites, and even got to the point where we could predict where more would be found in the future. One of the participants with us was a young Louisiana Cajun named Bill Andrus, who went by the nickname "Clutch." He had been on the Roanoke trip as well and he and I became good pals. He was an avid fisherman and knew how to tie flies like an expert, which he'd then practice casting with considerable accuracy. A couple of years later I was saddened to hear that he had gone back to New Orleans, and gotten married. He and his wife had a domestic argument and the police were called; when he came out of the house brandishing a machete, they didn't waste even a minute arguing with him and gunned him down in his front yard. Sad, because he really was a gentle guy (when he wasn't drinking). I passed another birthday, and so the summer ended, and I was back in the office finishing up my reports, which now I'd whittled down to one or two. But it didn't matter much, since Buddy and Schmidt were pushing from above, and their lapdog Cranston was now working on me from the side. He stopped sharing the data from the Stafford chimneys project, so I couldn't make any headway on that write-up, much less fulfill my role as co-principal investigator—it was the typical passive-aggressive ploy he'd practiced for years: the data was still coming in; he couldn't find the stuff; he'd get back to me; the lab analysis wasn't complete yet... In effect, he was sabotaging me, but by this time I didn't care: let him have it. The handwriting was on the wall. Then the most interesting thing occurred.

Porn Again

We had all heard that the Virgin Islands was looking for a new head archaeologist, and the Chief, John Hardinger, had asked Buddy and Gordon who they thought might be interested. Buddy chose one of his favorites, a young kid named Mike who had recently married the renowned Rowena of bent-over-the-desk fame, and offered him the job *gratis*, no competition.

415

Mike and Rowena were happy as clams for the unadvertised (and therefore, uncontested) opportunity to move to Paradise, and Buddy wrote him a glowing recommendation. Mike went down and interviewed and it looked like it was all a go. They made plans to move. Then, it just so happened that the guy in charge of the entire SEAC computer network, Dennis Finch, was checking the Center's hard drive storage and noticed that we were running a little low on memory, which was odd, because there had been plenty of space some six months earlier and not that much work had occurred in the meantime. He checked a little closer and found that there was a huge partition that was full of nothing but images. Having the necessary permissions as the computer administrator, he opened up a couple to find that they were all large-scale high-definition pornography. He looked up the owner and lo and behold, it was Mike. Well, Finch had no choice in the matter and took it to the Chief. The Chief got Buddy to have a talk with Mike, and even though Finch cleaned off the hard drive, and (maybe *because* he cleaned it) management tried to keep it hush-hush, but word got out that someone had loaded the hard drive with porn. Soon everyone knew who it was, except the nosy Rowena, whom everyone wanted to shield, her being newly married to Mike and all. But she wouldn't let it go, and kept prying, pestering, and bothering people until one of her friends (not!) finally got fed up with her and blurted out "It's your husband, you stupid bitch!" She was devastated, and Mike was officially shamed. But the worst of it was, some two weeks later, checking the hard drive again, Finch found that Mike had continued to pursue his prurience and just tried to hide it a little better. Well, now it was certain that the boy had a problem, and if he was going to keep his job (which anyone else would have been relieved of forthwith on the first offense), he had to undergo some sort of rehabilitation. This quashed his (and management's) ambitions as to handing him the Virgin Islands archaeologist position. By the back door I let it be known to the Government of the VI that I'd consider it if offered, and when they called and talked to me, they wondered why I hadn't been suggested in the first place, having had some experience there, and being an all-around cultural resource management guy, even having done underwater work. They asked me to come and interview, so I took a couple of days off and secretly flew down to St. Thomas.

Down Island

Heading down in late October, I took a cab to Blackbeard's Castle, where Dave Anderson and I had stayed a couple of years earlier. I was met at the check-in by a young black girl, cute as a button, with a slow sexy smile, and a deep dangerous voice. Her name was Monica. She checked me in right away, took me to the room, and pointed out where the bar was, which had moved since Dave and I had been there. I went down and only had a single drink, since I wanted to keep my wits about me for the next morning's appointment at nine o'clock. When I woke at seven I had plenty of time to clean up, walk downtown, have breakfast, and still be at the office on Government Hill by 8:45. Silly me, I'd forgotten all about island-time. The receptionist told me to wait downstairs, and that Ms. Lewis and Mr. Jackson would be there shortly. Claudette Lewis was the *de facto* head of cultural resource management in the Virgin Islands. Slightly older and slightly big-boned, she was a no-nonsense black woman bureaucrat who ran things with an iron hand. No one said "no" to Ms. Lewis, not even the Governor. Mr. Jackson (Myron) was more of an enigma to me. I'd heard that he too was no-nonsense, but that he was also a good guy. Tough and good, what the hell did that mean? I entertained myself by reading some of the general literature downstairs at the big conference table, and at 9:30, the buzzer to the front door went off, and I got up to let in Claudette and Myron. I had met Ms. Lewis before, and we'd even talked on the phone, but I'd never met Myron, so as I let them in the door, I introduced myself to him, and tried a little humor, telling him I'd heard a lot about him, and that most of it was good. He didn't crack a smile and just walked past me, repeating what I'd said, saying "*most* of it was good?" Uh oh, I thought, no sense of humor, this guy's going to be a tough nut to crack.

Even though I'd followed them up the stairs into the main office drawing room, I was again told to have a seat and they'd be with me in a few minutes, while they retired into the Director's office. Soon they called me in and, with Myron sitting behind the desk and Ms. Lewis sitting next to me, we began a friendly conversation. Apparently Claudette had already called the Chief of SEAC, Hardinger, whom she knew, and asked about me. He must have spoken highly of me because they were talking as if I already had the job. Figuring honesty is the best policy, and even though it was risky, I had to set them straight. "You know," I said, "if I come to work for you I'll be switching my loyalty from the Park Service to the Virgin Islands." They didn't know what that meant. Ms. Lewis said, "Why would you be switching loyalty? You wouldn't be doing that... we all work for each other toward the same goals." Myron just listened. "Well, our goals may not always be the same," I said, "as you may know, the Park Service, or more accurately, the Feds, can sometimes be a little aggressive. I just want you to know that if I come here to work, I will be working for you and not for the Park Service, and in that regard I will defend your interests..." Myron was smiling now; he knew what I was talking about. Whereas Ms. Lewis dealt with the Feds to get money to run the programs, and the Government of the Virgin Islands was glad to receive those funds, Myron was a strong supporter of the man-on-the-street, and the history of colonialism was fresh on his plate; he wanted someone who would be tough when he needed him to be. This little tete-a-tete I believe got me the job as far as Myron was concerned, and Ms. Lewis' conversation with the Chief at SEAC had already convinced her I was more than qualified. The rest of the dialogue was more mundane: when could I start, would I ship my car over, where would I live, things like that. We were done before an hour had passed. Leaving the building, I walked downtown, got a paper and had lunch at a little café overlooking the harbor, sailboats plying back and forth, the seaplane coming in and landing, then taking off again every half an hour, the water a shimmering deep blue surrounding the offshore islands, and a large cruise ship maneuvering in slowly to dock itself. It still hadn't sunk in, so I walked back up Government Hill again, and this time took "The 99 Steps" (there's really 103) up to Blackbeard's, where I was staying. Stepping out onto my balcony with a nice stiff rum and tonic and watching the harbor again, I took a deep breath of flowery esters and looked to my left to see a bright iridescent blue-green hummingbird flitting from blossom to blossom, close enough I could have reached out and grabbed him. Then I felt the eyes of someone staring at me, and turned abruptly to my right, where a large grey-green iguana was sitting on the balcony banister a mere three feet away, watching me intently, cocking his head to get a better view. Looking down there was a young woman oiled-up and floating face-up on a blowup mat in the back hotel pool (the more private one of two they had); she had removed her bikini top and drifted slowly 'neath the noonday sun. I can live with this, I thought, I can live with this.

Back in Florida, the jig was up, and they all knew I'd been down to the islands. What they didn't know was whether I'd taken the job or not. So I let that one stew for awhile. Schmidt came into my office and said, "You know if you need a letter from me, I'll be happy to write one." "Thanks, but no thanks," I said (and at the same time thought, "The last thing I need is a letter from you"). The Chief, Hardinger, came in one day that week, and for the first time in a long time, we had a nice long talk, and he said he would be sorry to see me go. He seemed sincere—I realized of course that, at the same time, my leaving would make life so much simpler for him since he'd been having a lot of trouble walking the line between his managers and myself. After talking things over with Amy and the boys, we all decided that it would be a great opportunity, it was certainly more money, and it would give all of us the chance to travel and discover the Caribbean. I called Ms. Lewis in St. Thomas and told her I could start in March, since I wanted to spend the holidays with the family and I had to get my retirement money from the Park Service to cover the move. She said that would be fine. So I drafted my resignation letter, effective

Friday, December 15, and handed it in. No bridge burnings, just a simple thanks: it's been real, and it's been fun, but lately, however, it hasn't been real fun. Later that afternoon, right after lunch, Big John Cranston came into my office wearing his I-got-you-now shit-eating grin, and said, "Well today's the best day of Gordon's [Schmidt's] life! First, he finds out that you're leaving, and then he finds out he's been given a doctorate!" What the hell? Well, me going was no surprise to anybody, but him getting a doctorate was like finding out that Mr. Ed really could talk! How in God's name did Gordon, who could barely write his name without a dictionary, much less think systematically, get a doctorate? Sure, he was good with numbers, and loved to balance the books every week in his paper ledger with a pencil and a calculator, but they sure as hell didn't give out PhDs for that, not even honorary ones. And that's what it was. He'd been secretly canvassing old acquaintances and guys he'd worked for to write letters of praise to the University of South Florida on his behalf to get him an honorary degree. He had to do it in secret because if the word had gotten out, there'd have been twice as many letters against it. No matter. It was just an honorary one, they give those things out a dime a dozen; although a nice contribution doesn't hurt either. No, the trouble started within the last two weeks I was at the Center, when he started signing things "Doctor Gordon Schmidt, PhD." Then he asked if the staff would call him Doctor Schmidt. Well, that was never going to happen, and when he'd sign something "Gordon Schmidt, PhD," any and everyone who got their hands on it either typed or wrote in "(Honorary)" after it. I didn't much care. I was facing my last two weeks at somewhere I'd worked at, had many happy memories with, and fed the family on for over twenty years. I started cleaning out my office, little by little. First of all, I had to get rid of all the golf balls.

Balls

As I've said, our new offices at Innovation Park (now 4 years in) were on the University golf course. When we first moved in, a few of us who were golfers would join up in the afternoons and play the reduced after-work twilight green fees. It was a lot of fun, but just like anything else at SEAC it began to develop into factions and soon wasn't so much fun anymore, and pretty much died off. That last year, since I wasn't going out to lunch with Pam, or really anyone else for that matter, I started going for long walks at lunchtime along the edges of the course, picking up loose golf balls that had been knocked out of bounds. My pockets would be full in no time, and as I walked along a certain stretch I would almost daily come up on Bobby Bowden, the famous FSU football coach, hitting balls on the private driving range the University set aside for him. As I walked along the short chain-link fence, we'd be only twenty or thirty feet apart, so I'd always wave and say hi. "Hey, Buddy!" he'd call back, raising whatever iron he was hitting, and one day asked me what I was doing. "I'm just taking a walk and collecting balls that I find outside the fenceline," I told him. "You got any good ones you can spare?" he asked. Sure, I told him, and picking out a couple of newer ones, I tossed three or four over the fence. "Thanks, Buddy!" he yelled back and from then on whenever I saw him out there it was a standard thing for me to toss him a few. The rest ended up in a box in the corner of my office; and it was big box too, maybe two cubic feet. Soon it was almost full, with two hundred and some-odd balls in there. One day my immediate supervisor, Guy, brought his two young children into the office, a young boy and a young girl, both under three or four. They were running up and down the halls, squealing and having a great time. As they passed by my office I called them in and told them they could have all the golf balls they wanted. Soon there were golf balls clacking down the halls in all directions. After Guy gathered them up, he tried to give them back to me, but the kids got upset and I insisted that they keep them (I was trying to get rid of them by this time anyway). Later that night I got a phone call at home from their mother, "Goddamn it, Dave, the kids are throwing them all over the house and just took out a china cabinet... I'm scared the TV is going to be next." That's a shame, I told her.

Heads Up

One day I was walking inside the fence, along a fairway but still out of bounds, underneath a grove of large pine trees. As I was walking I heard a quick "swish-swish" and turned, looking up to see a small golf ball coming through the pine needles above. Just like in the cartoons, the ball quickly magnified in size until it took up my whole line of vision and "BAP!" hit me on the forehead. I stumbled back a step, but didn't fall, and then heard a plaintive distant cry of "Fore!" I reached up and touched my forehead, and there was just the smallest drop of blood. Soon, a foursome came walking up and one of the guys said, "It didn't hit you did it?" obviously worried. "Yeah, popped me right in the forehead," I said, "but it was my own fault, being in the fenceline." "Don't worry about it," I reassured him. By the time I got back to my office though, I was feeling a little woozy, and after everyone came in one-by-one to make fun of me, I was even feeling a little nauseous, which I knew was a symptom of a concussion. So I had one of my interns drive me to the hospital, just in case, and after an hour in the emergency waiting room, when I saw the doctor and he looked me over, he just said, "I could put one stitch in your forehead, but I'm not going to... take an aspirin, you'll be fine." Later, since it was coming up on Christmas, and I was a little short on cash, as usual, I took the rest of the golfballs in my office in bags to the FSU driving range. It was a cold dark night and there were only one or two other brave souls out, but I had a mission. The driving range had a large flat billboard-like advertisement, sponsored by some car dealership, out approximately 180 yards. In the center was a light, and if you could hit that light, well, the reward went up $10 a night and it had been over three months since someone had hit it. Something like $1200 riding on it. I'd worked myself up mentally, and after a couple of practice shots, I rationalized that this was not luck at all, but rather, a matter of skill. And you know, there's something to that, and I suppose that's why the pros are so good. By concentrating and being careful, I got closer and closer, and even once or twice heard the "clunk!" as the ball bounced off the plywood. But two hundred balls later, each ball being a lotto ticket that I controlled to some immoderate degree, I was as impoverished and even colder than when I had started. Another lesson learned: you can have luck without skill, but you can't really have skill without some bit of luck.

A Going-Away Party

My last real day at SEAC was on Friday, December 15, 2000. That morning it was announced that there would be a staff meeting at 11. Well, this was exceedingly unusual; in fact, we hadn't had a single staff meeting in the previous four years we'd moved out to the new building. What could generate such interest as to warrant a gathering? There were even going to be donuts and soft drinks! Again, stupid me... well, this *was* my last day, and I had been with SEAC since 1980, except for my brief respite in South Carolina. In fact, I had spent more time at SEAC than any other person on the payroll. They said good-bye to Pete, they said good-bye to Kenny; here I was, going off to become the State Archaeologist for the U.S. Virgin Islands, a really big-damn deal. I suppose it was just a nice gesture that they'd be having donuts and saying bye to me. I'll try to keep it upbeat. Just thank everyone for the good times... tell a funny story or two... try not to cry. At 11, everyone gathered in the main lab, the largest room at the Center. I got my donuts and a cup of coffee and sat up front so I wouldn't have to walk so far when they called me up. Maybe they'd even be giving me a 20-year pin. The Chief came in, welcomed everybody, then went on to say he had an announcement. At some gathering in Washington, where they were handing out awards to various divisions in the Department of the Interior, SEAC was recognized for its exemplary work. It was a small glass award with some inscription on it. "Well, that's it... that was my announcement, please have some donuts and soda, and enjoy the rest of your afternoon." And that was my going-away party from the National Park Service. They knew enough not to let me speak; I was too much of a wild card and they didn't know what

I'd say. Could'a been worse; could'a gotten a jar of dirt. I came in the next day, on Saturday, to pack up my office, mostly books and files, and left my keys on the desk.

Les Be Friends

We all had a nice family Christmas, and I remember Mom giving me a copy of 'Tis, Frank McCourt's dour memoir of his childhood growing up in Ireland. I read it in one sitting, alone, the day after Christmas, when Mom and Amy and the boys were out with my brother Paul and his family. It was a cold dark day in Tallahassee, and I felt the deep dank cold of McCourt's Ireland all day, not eating on purpose, and drinking hot tea intermittently throughout to throw off the chill. After New Years there was nothing for me to do but wait for the retirement check from the NPS so I could plan my move to the islands. It finally arrived on March 1st and I threw a going-away party to say good-bye to all my friends in Tally. As far as I knew, it might be the last time I ever saw them (you never know). The one thing I wanted to do before I left town was to hook up with Mindy, my old lesbian friend. I'd run across her in town and it just so happened that she was between lovers. We'd kidded for years that it would be a lot of fun to get together, 'cause we really did like each other. But now here we were almost 30 years older than when we'd first met. (I did confess to her about the spying on her and her girlfriend in the shower from the owl's perch on the roof way back at East Call Street back in the 70s. She was very forgiving, didn't really care, and suggested that had she known, they might have given us a show.) Our running joke over the years was "Well, we're not dead yet, so there's still a chance." Well, now was our chance; we were both single and I was leaving for the indeterminate future. She told me she'd be over on Tuesday, 11 a.m.

We sat at the kitchen table, her in her jeans and t-shirt, and had a cup of coffee, talking. Since we hadn't really sat and talked in years, there was a lot of catching up to do. After a half-hour or so, I started getting antsy. She laughed at me, and told me not to worry, we'd do it, even though she hadn't done it with a man in some twenty-odd years. Well, let's go, I said. Then she did the typical woman thing and went to the bathroom. I was waiting under the covers when she came out, wearing just her panties. Jeez, I hadn't realized how boyish she'd look… but once the panties came off, there was no question: and she seemed as curious about me as I did about her. She looked at my cock as though she'd never seen one before (even though many years earlier I had been riding in her truck and curiously opened the glove compartment, there to find an oversized double-ended black rubber dildo—emergency road equipment, I suppose). Then she commented on the fact that I "didn't smell like a woman." But once we got going she was enjoying herself, and although it didn't last long, I think we both found it entertaining enough. I'm sure we would have had an encore performance, except that while we were sitting there talking, there comes a bang, bang, bang on the front door. What the hell!? I get up and go out into the living room, and who's out on the porch? Amy! "Daviiid… are you home?" Oh, shit! Not that I was upset about her finding me with Mindy, since I was single now, as much as that it was going to put the kibosh [note: from the Irish, caip bháis - pronounced as kibosh - for a candle-snuffer] on any further fun for the day. I went back and told Mindy, and we laid low, but Amy started walking around the house, calling me, since she saw my car out front and figured I was home. It was obvious she wasn't leaving. We didn't have any excuse, so we quickly got dressed and I met Amy at the front door, and invited her in. She and Mindy had been acquaintances for years, so they exchanged pleasantries while I fidgeted around, fixing more coffee. No, Mindy didn't want any more, and decided to leave. Amy stayed and gave me some friendly shit, since she knew Mindy's lesbian leanings, and it was obvious what we were up to. I was less than amused, having had my candle snuffed.

19.   Seven Years on St. Thomas: Virgin Islands (2001-2008)

Well, now it was getting time to get serious about leaving for the islands. I called my brother and some friends and told them to come and take whatever books of the five hundred or so I had on the wall they might want. I made arrangements with my oldest, Robin, who was now eighteen and in college to take over the house, get some roommates, and we'd do what we could to keep making the house payments. We had the going-away party, and even though it rained we had a large canopy up, we cooked out, had oysters, and my brother-in-law Charlie played his violin alongside the rock 'n roll. I said good-bye to a lot of old friends, and after packing two large suitcases with clothes and tools and such, I made plans to eventually fly out of Orlando, after seeing Mom. I left Tallahassee one evening late by train, with Amy and the boys taking me to the station. While we were waiting, the boys and I put a lot of change on the track so when the train arrived it would leave some flattened souvenirs. We waited in the station and as we did, Amy began to cry. I wasn't so glad to be leaving all of a sudden, and started thinking of all the things that could have been. When the train arrived, the boys manned up and each shook hands with me. Amy gave me a long hard hug and a kiss, and I climbed on board. The train had some delays with freight trains switching tracks in Jacksonville before turning south towards Orlando, and by the time I'd gotten there it was 4 a.m., although it had been scheduled to arrive around 2. Poor Mom had waited at the station since arriving early at midnight, and entertained herself by talking with other folks waiting. We drove to the house at Tradewinds, and after catching a few hours sleep, we went out for a late breakfast and it was time for me to go to the airport. Ma drove me again, and it was another heart-wrenching good-bye as I headed off to St. Thomas.

Down to the Islands

It was March 14th and I told them I'd start on Monday, the 18th, the day after St. Patrick's. This gave me a few days to get settled and look for a place of my own. When the cab took me to Blackbeard's early that evening there was Monica, sweet as can be, ready with my room key. I asked her if she'd come down and have a drink with me at the bar, and she said sure, but she had another hour of work ahead of her first. While I sat at the bar waiting, talking with the bartender, I asked him if she had a boyfriend. He said that yes, she did, although there may be some contention as to how serious it was. Well, well, well, I said, commenting on how cute she was. "You know, you're right," he said, "she does remind me of someone." Yeah, who? He couldn't put his finger on it, and then suggested, "Who's that little cartoon girlfriend of Underdog?" Oh, wow, I knew this one, "Why, that's Sweet Polly Purebred!" And he said, yeah, that's who she reminded him of. I had to agree… there was a certain similarity. The next morning, I saw a car out in the parking lot with a "For Sale" sign on it. It looked clean and in pretty good shape, and I asked a young girl who worked in the gift shop at the hotel if she knew who was selling it. "Yeah, I am," she said. So I asked what do you want for it? Well, she was going to have to talk to her dad, since he was the one who really owned the car, but she'd call him and find out. She called him right then and he said he'd come right over and talk to me. It was a little blue Mitsubishi Mirage two-door sedan, and when he showed up, he told me he wanted $3000 for it. I offered 2, and we settled on $2500. Her dad was a large round man with thinning hair and a loud chortling laugh that ended with a little bit of a wheeze. His name was Ray, and little did I know it at the time, but was soon to find out, he was well-known around the Virgin Islands. In fact, this was the famous Glass Ray, who owned one of the few, and certainly the largest and best-known glass stores on St. Thomas. He sold to hotels that were habitually denuded of their windows by hurricanes, not to mention the Government with all its buildings, and then finally, the millionaires up on the hillsides. He didn't have to deal too much with the little guys, and between the big interests always building shit and insurance companies paying out for hurricanes and earthquakes, he was making money hand-over-fist. Luckily for me, we hit it right off, and not only did I write him a check for the car, but he spent the rest of the day taking me around and, using his secret knowledge on how to cut bureaucratic corners (which was easily worth the $500 we dickered about on the car), by the end of the day I had transferred the title and registration and purchased insurance as well, a feat unheard of on St. Thomas in a single day, even up to the present time. We were sitting in the Offshore having drinks by 3 o'clock that afternoon, his usual quitting time. Other than a bump or two here and there, we've been pals ever since. He's a character in his own right and I'll try to do him justice.

Back at Blackbeard's by dark I asked Monica if she'd let me take her out to dinner in my new car, and she said sure. When I came to get her at the check-in desk though, there was her Bahamian boyfriend sitting there glaring at me. I just ignored him, figuring this was her problem, not mine, and we headed out to the East End to get a bite. On the way, even though I was now quite familiar (and comfortable) with driving on the left side, she began teaching me things that later became invaluable; things like, "drive in the middle of the road, not on the edge, then go to your lane when you see an oncoming car," and "use your horn… all the time, …think of it as carrying on a conversation." The first is because of the precipitous incline on one side of the road or the other, St. Thomas being a volcanic mount jutting out of the sea with winding roads all along the steep sides; and the second is a customary pattern of communication that includes letting someone know to go ahead, saying hi to a friend or acquaintance, maybe just announcing "be careful," or actually complimenting someone in another car for yielding (an island "thank you"); all of these horn beeps distinctively different in number, tone, and length, depending on the message . Hardly ever is it used to admonish someone, other than someone sitting inattentively at a red light. Even then, it's just a reminder to get moving, never a blaring "WHAT THE FUCK?!" like you experience in the States. But the one thing you *never* do in the VI is honk at someone blocking the road, conversing with a friend standing alongside the car. In that case, you just sit and wait. It was even written into the Department of Motor Vehicle handbook, "How long should you wait for someone stopped in the road talking?" The correct answer wasn't a) 10 seconds, b) 30 seconds, or c) a minute, but rather, I kid you not, d) "A little while." Yep, the Virgin Islands were going to take a little getting used to, culturally. Not just because the general population is black (probably 80%, so now I was a member of a minority), but because they were black Afro-Caribbeans, descendants of slaves, and that of the Danish West Indies. A little background history is probably in order here. So let's go, starting from the beginning, as far as we know it. Therefore, for your educative enjoyment I present: A Short History of the U.S. Virgin Islands.

In the Beginning

I suppose I could go the James Michener route and start with "As the Earth began to cool, the dinosaurs roamed the earth…," but let's keep this manageable. The islands were created, as most islands are, by volcanic upwellings as the tectonic plates separated. That's why they're so steep and the flat areas so few. Because of the tradewinds that happen to run east to west, the eastern ends of the islands are generally arid and desert-like, whereas the western heights, which actually block clouds passing over, often bunch them up long enough to allow rain to fall, and thus, the western ends of most islands in the Caribbean are usually where the rainforests occur. The first visitors to the islands were what we call Archaic (no duh), also referred to as the Ciboney, who arrived around 3000 BC or roughly 5000 years ago BP (Before the Present, which is a more logical method of recording the past than measuring from the martyred carpenter's birthday). They were pre-ceramic in that they had not yet mastered the technology where they could create pottery. [On a side note, there is an archaeological theory that women were actually the innovators of ceramic technology, possibly worldwide: gathering clay, processing it, casting or molding it into various shapes, and then firing it after it had dried in the sun. All this occurred as a result of their association with gathering, playing with and teaching children, and then of course, cooking. This theory is called *Women as Vectors of Technology*, and when you consider the additional technological advances of weaving basketry and fibers and developing cloth, well, making a spear point to stab a fish, to which men were so adept, doesn't seem so remarkable in comparison, now does it? This is to suggest, ultimately, that women were the first true alchemists.] The original "archaic" island inhabitants were pretty sad individuals, who used any stone or shells they could find as tools, and were so generally bad at fishing (as shown by the few small fish bones found in their middens, or garbage piles) that they relied to a great degree on eating land crabs. So many, in fact, that for many years they were referred to as "the Crab People." It appears that eventually they died out, to be replaced around 4000 BP by the first great sea rovers of the Caribbean, the Taino. The Taino are recognized as Arawak-language descendants, and probably came from South and Central America up the chain of Windward Islands from the Orinoco basin, as well as sailing across from the Yucatan, to inhabit the larger islands of the Greater Antilles for over three thousand years. Other than inter-tribal raiding between themselves for territory and women, the Taino were relatively peaceful agriculturalists and fishermen. The early pottery styles, called Saladoid, indicated that they had a lot of time on their hands and exhibit very fine detailed work with coloring and intricate designs; later, by 1400 BP, probably because of increased population pressures, the detailed work got fewer and farther apart, mostly for ritual use only, and the day-to-day cooking-and-eating earthenwares became, like today's plastic cups and paper plates, plain and utilitarian. This period is the Taino Ostionoid, when they were at the crest of having populated the big islands of Cuba, Jamaica, Hispaniola, and Puerto Rico, and then started moving down into the scrubbier Lesser Antilles, of which the U.S. Virgin Islands are part and parcel. Around 800 AD, or roughly 1200 years BP, a new group began to emerge out of the Amazon, a fierce hunting group of quickly-accomplished sea rovers, the Caribs. One by one, they worked their way up the smaller Windward Islands of the Eastern Caribbean, fighting, killing (and eating) the local inhabitants, until, by the time Columbus had made his second voyage, they had gotten as far as St. Croix, where they settled a foothold, but had not yet conquered the local Taino (think of the Taino as Athenians and the Caribs as invading Spartans and you get the rough picture, Native American style).

Columbo

When he landed at Salt River Bay, St. Croix, on his second voyage in 1493, Columbus sat outside the Bay and sent a longboat in to search for fresh water, check out a small Indian village they could see on the shore, and hopefully grab a native or two to act as interpreters and guides later on. The men checked out the small village which the natives had run away from, and in one hut made note of a pot on a fire containing a human neck boiling away. Then they got back in their boat and went up the bay searching for the freshwater source, if there was one. When they couldn't find it, they turned back and while they were heading back to the ships they noticed a couple of canoes with some "Indians" who were dumbfoundedly staring at these large wooden islands with funny-looking bearded men in strange clothes on them that hadn't been there that morning. Columbus signaled to the longboat to intercept the canoe, which they tried to do, but the natives outdistanced them, and upon reaching the shore with the Spanish in hot pursuit, they jumped out of the canoe in waist-high water and started firing arrows back at the longboat. Out of the seagrape bushes a dozen more natives ran out and let loose a flurry of arrows as well. The Spanish, a few them severely wounded by the nasty stingray-spine and sharktooth-tipped arrows, beat as hasty a retreat as they could manage. (To this day the place is called "The Cape of the Arrows" or Cabo de las Flechas.) Just as they're pulling away from the beach and heading back to the ships, another canoe came around the headland of the bay, with two men paddling and a woman and a boy apparently captive. This time the Spanish in the longboat pull hard and rammed them, knocking them all into the water. Dragging the captives into the longboat, one of the natives puts up such a fight that they subdued him by slashing him open with a sword, and tossed him into the bottom of the boat. Once back at the ship the captives are brought up on deck, the one cut open lying there with his entrails spilling out. As they're interrogating the other man, while admiring the relatively naked woman, and examining the boy, who had been castrated some time before, the wounded Indian leaps up and bounds over the side, swimming toward the beach, his intestines flowing out behind him. They wing him with an arquebus shot, and then get a couple of grappling hooks into him and haul him back up on deck again, finishing him off by grabbing a boarding axe and lopping off his head. The captain of the ship (remember, Columbus was no longer just a captain, but now the "Admiral of the Oceans Seas" and thus, the fleet) took a fancy to the woman and asked Columbus if he could have her, request granted. The captain immediately pulled her down into his cabin to have his way, but she put up such a clawing, scratching, howling resistance that he finally took a knotted rope-end to her and beat her into submission. Once he exposed himself and she realized that his intentions were more lustful than violent, and that he wasn't going to lop off *her* head, she took to it "like the most formidable whore in Seville" and subsequently became his devoted companion and paramour. (Obviously, these were different times. Remember *Brandy, You're a Fine Girl*? "She could feel the ocean fall and rise *when she saw his raging glory…*" Must have been something like that.)

It's well-documented that Columbus never realized that he'd bumped into a new continent or two, based on his miscalculation of the actual size of the planet, believing to his dying day that he really had gotten to the islands of Cipangu (Japan) and the East Indies (ergo, "Indians"). All of this took place at the only location in present-day U.S. Territory that Columbus is reported to have ever visited. We know that he must have went north from there and went through the Virgin Islands, naming them after the legendary St. Ursula and her martyred eleven thousand virgins (originally there were only 11, but what the hell, over time the number got a little inflated…) because there were so many rocky islets, with St. Thomas named after the Apostle to the Indies, our own doubting Thomas, the twin. Christobal himself probably went ashore at some point in the Virgins, and certainly somewhere in Puerto Rico, before going on to Hispaniola [Haiti and the Dominican Republic] where he had established a small colony with the crew of the first voyage, to which he was bringing supplies. But it's a sad fact that, although Columbus was pretty good about documenting his travels, all the notes and chronicles from the second voyage (out of four) are missing and the above incident only recounted in a subsequent letter from the ship's doctor.

Slaving

In any case, the Spanish, having laid claim to these islands soon lost them to the English, then the French, who loaned them (esp. St. Croix) for a decade to the Knights of Malta, then back to the French who then gave them up to the English again during the Napoleonic Wars, then abandoned them back to the Spanish, who finally let the Danish West India Company have them without a fight. The Danes held on for over 200 years and carved the islands up into "estates" (read "plantations") for various entrepreneurs to take advantage of the sugar craze that had swept across Europe—not only was sugar the oil that drove the industry and trade of its day (actually, sugar was more valuable by far, comparatively), but besides sweetening tea and making cinnamon-sugar croissants, it had the added benefit of producing rum, another valuable commodity, from it's by-product, molasses. Unfortunately, making sugar from cane on these hard-scrabble islands had another by-product, one needed for construction and agriculture: slavery. The Danes had gotten into the slave-trading game rather late, certainly much later than the Portuguese and the Spanish and the English, and so by the time they hit Africa they had to go into the interior and/or rely on raiding parties that did. By that time, all of continental Africa was aware of slave-raiding, and many of those interior tribes were both prepared and resistant. As a result, the slaves that the Danes took were less peaceful than the original coastal-trading natives and the efforts by the slave traders who took them and transported them were harsher, and the treatment they received on getting to the Danish West Indies was thus, more rigid and severe as well. Because these Africans were more astute, lived in established kingdoms (the Akwamu, e.g.), and were familiar with modern weapons, they were much more "dangerous" and less likely to adapt to the role of servility. The Danes, more autocratic than the Germans, ran a tight ship and punishments were severe. As a result, following a drought which led to famine, and then a devastating hurricane in 1733, there was an uprising on St. John that held sway on the island for six months until French forces from Martinique came with dogs and horses (and ironically, slave-hunting slaves) and forced the rebels to one end of the island. There many of them took their own lives and jumped off cliffs into the sea rather than submit. It was one of the first (relatively) successful slave rebellions in the New World.

The Great Emanci-Peter

Slavery was abolished in the Danish West Indies on July 3, 1848 when a general uprising took place in St. Croix (then the seat of government), and the plantation slaves surrounded the fort at Frederiksted, demanding immediate emancipation as opposed to the 11-year phased-in plan of the Danish government. Peter von Scholten, the Governor-General, had been under the influence of his maroon mistress, Anna Heegard, to build schools for the children of slaves, which he had done starting in 1844. The next step was Emancipation, but the people couldn't wait and the sound of conch shells blowing signaled the movement to surround the fort. As the crowd waited for von Scholten to make his way from Christiansted by carriage, one of the white merchants from town who had taken refuge in the fort, urged the soldiers to "Shoot 'em down! Shoot 'em down like the dogs they are!" The soldiers held their fire and the crowd marched down the street and burned down the merchant's store, making sure not to ignite the adjacent buildings.

When von Scholten arrived, he had already drafted the articles of Emancipation and they were read to the crowd and officially sanctioned by his signature. The day is still celebrated as a Virgin Islands holiday, joined with the 4th, and commemorates one of the earliest peaceful (except for the storeowner's place) ends to slavery in the Western Hemisphere (a full seventeen years before the United States, which again, Civil War and all, wasn't quite so peaceful). Poor Peter von Scholten was called back to Denmark, and even though the King agreed with him that the time was right and the circumstances made his decision unavoidable, he was censured and demoted because he had acted *before* asking the permission of the King, a minor bureaucratic detail. Anna Heegard continued to live in Christiansted as a free woman of mixed heritage, and she is considered to be one of the islands' greatest heroines. Alas and alack, it just so happened that the year 1848 is also when the potential of the sugar beet was realized, and now that you could grow sugar beets just about anywhere (even in Russia!), the tropical zone that made sugar cane valuable was no longer geographically necessary. This was the beginning of the end for sugar cane production in the Virgin Islands, and slave or not, it meant a long period of economic decline.

Alex and der Flag

I forgot to mention young Alexander Hamilton, raised in Christiansted. In short, his Scottish father took up with his (possibly maroonish, but definitely not prudish) mother in Nevis where he was born. Whether Mom and Dad were legally betrothed was always a matter of question (and she had been somewhat married before, which also raised the issue of bigamy). They moved to St. Croix, but Dad couldn't hack it, and he bailed, leaving Alexander, his brother James, and his mother to fend for themselves. The Mom, Rachel, had a small dry-goods store where Alexander learned basic accounting, but after spending some time in a jail cell within the nearby Fort Christiansvarn for indebtedness, she took sick and died when Alexander was only 11. He was then employed at an import-export firm that traded with the American colonies, and became so good at it that he was put in charge of the firm for several months while the owner was away. He was only 14 or 15 at the time. Then he wrote an essay describing the effects of a powerful and devastating hurricane that had passed over the island, and the description was so overwhelming (to this day it will raise the hairs on the back of your neck) that it was published in the Danish paper, then somehow as a result, papers in Philadelphia. People were so impressed they took up a collection to have the young man educated in New England. The rest is as so often said, history. What impresses me is that the building he worked in is still standing, and the jail cell his Mom was in is still there, and some of the many paving stones that line the galleries of Christiansted are the same ones that he walked on as a young man. John Adams once referred to him as "the bastard brat of a Scottish peddler," and it all really started in Christiansted on St. Croix. Amazing. On another little-known fact regarding the island of St. Croix and the founding of the United States, there are the remains of a plantation great house and outbuildings that can be seen from the highway near the airport. They are referred to as "Spanish Town." Apparently the plantation owner there, who prospered growing sea-island cotton and sugar cane, decided that once he'd made his money, he no longer was keen on living on St. Croix. He wanted to go to Philadelphia, then the cosmopolitan center of the American colonies, and now declaring to become an independent nation. Well, according to the story, he becomes friends with Washington, Franklin, and that whole group, when one night in 1777 after some serious drinking, the idea is put forth that they ought to have a flag. This guy, and you'll forgive me, I don't remember his name, goes home that evening and draws up a design. When he shows it to the rest of the boys, they like it and ask a certain Ms. Betsy Ross to sew up a model based on the design. That is supposedly the original "Betsy Ross flag." True? I don't know; but it is certainly part of island history.

War and Peace

So by the mid 1800s the Danes are stuck with this pile of rocks and an economically downtrodden populace, when who shows up interested in buying the whole lot? The United States of America. After the Civil War, the U.S. realizes that St. Thomas has one of the best natural harbors in the world (it's probably a large ancient caldera, or volcanic crater, blown out from the south side), and would make a great base of operations for blockading. So the Government sends a delegation to discuss a high-pressured sale in 1867. While they're ashore negotiating, a huge earthquake hits and for all practical purposes, drains the harbor; then, while people are out on the harbor floor picking up fish and marveling at exposed wrecks, the resulting tsunami, or tidal wave, comes rushing back in, lifting the delegation's ships and crashes them onto the shore, way up onto the shore. Needless to say, the deal was off. Then, as we let a few decades roll by, the deal is re-considered in 1917 while the U.S. is in the throes of World War I and the Danes are viewed askew as somewhat sympathetic to the Nordic cause of the Huns. This time the strong-arm deal goes through for $17 million in gold, and the U.S. acquired the three islands that now are contained in the U.S. Territory of the Virgin Islands. They then put the military (Navy and the Marines) in charge of the whole place to construct a sub-base, dredge the harbor, build ammo bunkers and large gun emplacements, and even conduct mustard gas experiments with goats and pigs on Water Island. The military, unused to dealing with a civilian population, and an Afro-Caribbean one at that, generally pushes everybody around and bullies the people into accepting the changes, selling land, etc. When it all goes back to civilian control (roughly 1954) the U.S. Virgin Islands begins to stand on its own, and only when the former military guys come back to visit, bringing their families, does the all-important burgeoning tourist trade finally provide some economic relief (as well as comic—see Herman Wouk's *Don't Stop the Carnival*, which I've heard the locals describe as "not very complimentary," but it's very funny nevertheless). That, and of course the rum tax, where $10 per gallon of raw rum sold to the mainland is set aside to be returned to the government of the Virgin Islands to help subsidize the general fund. Since sugar cane was no longer being commercially produced (after 1961), but the rum subsidy was still needed, molasses are now bought elsewhere and brought in to be processed, with the resultant leftover second-run molasses shit-stain "slurry" piped off the south side of St. Croix down into the large 13,000 foot deep-sea trench there.

Dorothea

Now they are threatened by over-development, as the billionaires buy out the millionaires, and being a U.S. Territory, and "America's Paradise," they are targeted as a getaway, which doesn't always jibe with the view of the locals. Prices are high enough, because most goods have to be shipped in, but also because those "mainland" vacationers and part-time residents want the comforts of home and are not only willing to pay for them, but have the expendable cash to do so. This was the situation I was headed into. I had a car now, so I took to driving around looking for a place to rent, and I found a large upstairs apartment on the side of a hill up on the North Side near Hull Bay that was going to cost around $1000 a month. It was a lot of money, but hell, I was making good money too. I figured I could use the extra room for visitors. So I was driving the winding shoreline road and made a wrong turn; down, down, down the pot-holed and partly dirt road I went, looking for a place to turn around and get back on track. As I got to the bottom however, it opened up into a large, beautiful, flat piece of ground with horses running around, towering mango trees dropping fruit, and bright flowery trees known by their neon-orange-and-red foliage as "flamboyants." There were also maybe nine or ten sets of condominium-type apartments, four to a set (two up and two down), scattered under a grove of 80-ft-tall coconut palms. Most important however, was that the whole setup lay at the base of a cove, really a small bay, facing north into the the Atlantic, and which was embraced to the east and west by surrounding arms of brown boulderous escarpments. Finally, it had a large, almost-olympic-sized freshwater pool. This *truly was paradise*, under the shade of the swaying palms, fruit dropping with a thud all around, and the bright blue sea endlessly cascading over the horizon. I found the manager and asked if they had any openings. Mike, the manager, was a very friendly and mellow middle-aged guy, like me, but he walked with a severe leg-swinging limp. Well, it just so happened that there was one apartment available, but he couldn't show it to me unless the "owners" approved, so he took me to meet them first. They were a French-Canadian couple who had put a down payment on the whole place, called Dorothea Condos, and had made plans for it to be a sort of meditative spiritual artist's retreat, having gotten caught up in the "ambience" of it all. They were leaving in a week to go back to Toronto to secure the rest of the financing, after having dickered for months to settle on a final price with the Palestinian-Arab gentleman who really owned the place. They were very sweet New-Agers, if a bit naïve, and they loved the idea of an archaeologist moving in, although the wife warned me that the previous apartment occupant was a terrible "al-colic" who had drank herself to death there. "You mean an 'al-co-*hol*'-ic'?" I asked. "That's what I said," she repeated, "an al-colic."

Having gotten their blessing to be allowed to rent the apartment, Mike showed it to me and it was perfect. A single bedroom, living room, kitchenette, storage closet, and large bathroom with a shower, it also had a nice back porch overlooking the horse stables and corral, with the bright flowery flamboyants right out my window. Out the front triple-pane picture window that could slide open on the ends to let the breeze through, you could see the ocean waves lapping into the bay some fifty yards away (or less). After walking me through the place, Mike asked if I wanted it. Sure, I said, how much? He hemmed and hawed, as if he were just then figuring it out, "How about $750 a month?" he said. I decided that he had played his hand by thinking it over. "Well, you know," I said, "the place needs re-painting, and I think that that's a standard clause when renting an apartment, especially since the woman died in here." "Yeah, I guess you're right…" he muttered. "I'll tell you what," I said, "if you'll rent it to me for $600 a month, I'll give you first and last month's rent, and *I'll paint the place* top to bottom. Whaddya say?" He thought about it for a moment and said okay, and we shook hands on it. I went out and bought furniture, had it delivered and set up the next day, hung up some decorations, and not once in seven years did a paint brush ever touch those walls (although I had to sweep out the corners of the ceilings with a broom once a month to get rid of the spiders). And I had the alcolic's death-couch reupholstered by a middle-aged high-strung seamstress named Penny (who kept a running diary of her UFO-abductions and insisted that I read them, since, after all, I was an archaeologist [?!]).

Mike and I became pretty good friends, and we yammered on about philosophy and religion, but after he had told me he'd been to Vietnam, I just couldn't bring up the subject of his leg and that debilitating limp, so I never asked. The poor French-Canadian couple, after going to Quebec and setting up the financing to buy the whole condo complex, got shafted when they came back and the Arab guy once again raised the price on them. They ended up leaving in frustration, never to return. But I settled in and was very happy with the outcome. The place was a veritable village of characters. There was Nelson, the short macho Puerto Rican hairdresser, who was an avid and accomplished spear-fisherman and lobster wrangler. He had (and the word seems apt here for some reason) a plethora of babes he'd met through his hair salon, and he went through them like a pelican diving into schools of smelt. Nelson told me that he had gotten fed up with life in the Virgin Islands and moved back to South Florida in the States *four times*! He said he'd get frustrated with island life, sell everything, go back to the mainland, set up a new hairdressing business, and in six months there he'd say to himself "what the hell have I done?" Then it would take him a year or two to set aside enough money to make his way back to St. Thomas. Another four or five years would pass and he'd say, the hell with this, this place is crazy, I miss the States. Then he'd sell everything, go back, and sure enough, six months later, "how could I?…, the islands are so beautiful, the water so bountiful, the women so dark and delicious!" and another year later he'd be back. But we all admired him, he was fit and youthful and full of energy (and he gave us free haircuts, …usually by announcing on a Saturday morning, "You all look like hell, come over here and I'll cut your hair," then put us each in turn on a chair in the yard and let fly with the scissors and clippers while the others waited, beers in hand).

Then there was Larry, a stocky Frenchie (the Frenchies were descendants of emigrants from St. Bart's who settled on St. Thomas in the late1800s, when economic depression had hit all of the Caribbean, but wasn't quite as bad here as elsewhere—the ones who settled on the North Side were farmers, while the ones who settled on the South Side, the site of "Frenchtown" were mostly fishermen). Larry was referred to as "the Mayor" because he was well known all over the islands, as was his identical twin Tommy. Born and raised on the island ("I bahn heah") both had been former Army Rangers in their youth, then Virgin Islands policemen (Tommy was still a ranking detective), and had both served stints as DEA agents. Larry was now the head of the Department of Motor Vehicles, and it was he who had written the vehicle-testing handbook that suggested strongly that you "wait a little while" if you came upon someone blocking the street talking. It was a cultural thing. They spent all their time at The Pony Bar, a little dive in

Frenchtown that specialized in perky puertoriqueña barmaids and off-track betting, and if they didn't own a portion of the interest there, they managed it by their attentive presence, everyone deferring to their "hot tips" as they came up. During their law officer days they saw (and probably carried out) a number of grisly takedowns of Caribbean drug runners. Larry once explained to me how the bad guys told him once how they would take an informant or debtor out on a boat at night, all tied up, and on the way out gently explain to him why what needed to happen needed to happen. Once out in the open water over the 13,000-foot trench that separates the islands, the doomed one would be dispatched, and then carved up into quarters, each weighted down with its own cinder block, so as not to ever surface again. Then the deck would be washed, and as the sun came up the fishing poles came out and any fish caught were gutted and bled sloppily over the deck, gunwales, and transom, and once they got back in to the dock, the boat would be washed once again, this time with detergent, ready for another run. The car of the unfortunate would be torched in a remote, but not hidden location, since it needed to be found and identified as belonging to the missing person in order to leave a public message in the papers regarding the consequences of loose lips or non-payment of goods.

My best friend and favorite neighbor however, was Rick. Rick was a tall, slightly younger gangly blond Pollock out of Detroit, my birth-town, who had come to the islands with his buddy John. John and Rick had already made a passel of dough in the Motor City by running a couple of strip clubs, so they decided to make a stab at living on St. Thomas in America's Paradise. They started a fuel-delivery business with some extra backing from their big-city brethren, and in no time flat were making money hand-over-fist. Rick got tired of the daily grind and grease, however, and struck off on his own. In a matter of months he became known as the Best Bartender on the island, rattling off a set of one-liners amid a repertoire of filthy dirty jokes that he used to shock and awe the tourists with, especially the wives and girlfriends (and I mean blood-curdling "I can't believe you use that mouth to eat with!" dirty jokes—and he would have had a comeback for that one too). Besides running Caribbean Petroleum, John became the manager at Dorothea when Mike decided to sell all he had and take up spiritual training at an ashram in India. [Funny (?) note—before he left I had Mom and the boys come down for a visit, and one evening while we were all eating a potlatch dinner with the other folks from the condo, Mom told Mike that she was sorry about him getting his leg shot up in Vietnam. "I didn't get it shot up in Vietnam," he said, "When I got out of the service I got a job on a barge on the Mississippi, and one day the large steel cable to the tugboat snapped and broke my hip. Where'd you get the idea that I'd gotten shot up in Vietnam?" Mom and the boys all looked over at me and I just shrugged. Guess I should have asked him.]

It was on that first visit of theirs one morning, when Mom and I had gotten up early, and the boys were sleeping, that she and I had our first geophysical reckoning. Me and the boys had been drinking beer the night before and the terrazzo floor was festooned with dead soldiers, all lined up next to whatever chair we'd each been sitting in. It was a beautiful sunny morning, cool and breezy, and Mom and I were having coffee and talking when I sat up and said "Shh." I thought I heard a train coming down from up the road at the top of the mountain. But there are no trains in the Virgin Islands. No, it wasn't a train, it …it sounded like a truck, a big semi that must have lost its brakes and was barreling free-fall down the hillside. Mom and I looked at each other, and then we could hear the empty beer bottles clinking as they began to vibrate. Soon they started shaking loudly, and then they started walking across the floor! As they started falling over, I yelled "EARTHQUAKE!" and pulled Mom outside. Standing there out in the yard, we could hear the thunder-rumble just as it passed, from east to west, and then you could feel it rolling through the meat and the fluids and the bones inside you. It was a good one, a big one. And then it passed, and everything was quiet once again, except for the birds chattering in the trees. Mom and I were both a little shaken, never having experienced such a thing before (such a frightening power!). The boys? The boys slept right through it.

On Government Hill

So I began working in the office, which was located on Government Hill, two buildings down from Government House, and right next to the Lieutenant Governor's office. We were located in the Knud Hansen house, a two-floor Danish design that once housed Hansen, the island's only doctor during the late 1800s and early 1900s. It was white and wooden, shaded by several large lignum vitae trees out front and was built around a large stone-and-mortar cistern that actually sat right below my office upstairs (the access opening was a large covered square in the floor that my desk corner sat on, and every so often we'd have to open it up to add a little chlorine or check for cracks). Dr. Hansen apparently had his waiting and examining rooms downstairs, and then lived with his family on the upper story. The downstairs was now converted into a conference room with a broad mahogany table, and all our offices were upstairs. There was a large gallery porch where we could sit and eat lunch while overlooking the park across the street downstairs, and if you craned your neck you could get a glimpse of the blue-water harbor and hear the large cruise ships' horns as they glided in and prepared to dock. Absolutely annoying however, was the Disney ship horn that once a week insanely blasted the opening strains (no pun intended) of *When You Wish Upon a Star*, "Buh, buh, buh ya, Buh Buh WAAH!"

My director, Myron, and I warily checked each other out, dancing around the big decisions, until he realized that all I really wanted to do was to give him the best advice I could, and then, whatever he decided was what we lived with. I was not there as the white male Mainlander who was going to challenge his authority. Once we'd worked out this scenario and he saw that I *really was* looking out for not just his and the office's interests, but those of the people in general, and ultimately, the cultural resources, we got along quite well. It wasn't long before he was actually soliciting my opinion before crafting a response, and ultimately, after we'd talk it through, I ended up crafting those responses single-handed (for his signature). Later on, years later, I remember he once said to me after reading one of these crafted memos ready to go to the higher powers (the Commissioners, the Governor, or the Feds), "David, you're going to go to jail over this one." I told him, "No, Mister Jackson, *you're* the one going to jail, not me; I just wrote it, you're the one who signed it." I always called him Mister Jackson, and although some of my white mainland acquaintances couldn't understand why (I *never* called anyone "mister" in the States), I knew this was, again, a part of the Caribbean cultural milieu, and it stood me well throughout my tenure there. Just like the "Good morning" and "Good afternoon" which necessarily precedes every conversation, whether a phone call or a bank transaction; if it wasn't initiated, you weren't getting the deal done; better still if you ask how their day was going, or if you knew them at all, how the family was getting along. These little formalities had been adopted by the Danes during slavery, where the white overseers threateningly insisted on being addressed politely before any other thing was discussed, and even though I don't think the current Afro-Carib population realizes any more that this was the origin (and now they adhere to it so strictly that at 11:59 a.m. it's "Good morning" and at 12 noon it suddenly converts to "Good afternoon," make no mistake about it), it's still a nice civilized way to carry out your day-to-day business.

Also in the office were Fern, the pleasantly angelic caramel-colored administrative assistant who handled the meetings with the Historic Preservation Committee, a group of local preservationist patrons who decided what, if any, changes were to be made to the local Danish-period

430

architecture by the ever-persistent diamond merchants, perfumeries, and other tourist-tempting merchandisers; and the affable and energetic Anthony, who handled all our purchases, including travel (his father had been President of the University of the Virgin Islands, and though the position Anthony held at this time was a rather mid-level bureaucratic interlude, eventually, his intelligence and family renown got him a proper Government position). Then there was Sean, a wiry young historic architect who was both smart and politically astute. He knew where the tripwires were located when we'd maneuver the jungle of the Government bureaucracy, often warning both Myron and myself when we were in dangerous territory as well as offering an alternative route. Finally, there was the formidable Ms. Gooden (not Mrs. and not Miss, but "Mizz"), who ran the office like a master sergeant—she didn't take any crap off of anybody, not even Mister Jackson, and got in trouble more than once by cussing someone out and slamming down the phone. And she made no bones about the fact that she didn't like white folks. It took me a solid year before she warmed up to me, chewing me out for my cross-cultural infractions, and even worse for improper formatting on a Government memo. Jeez-lou-eez, she could be a pistol (Joyce was her first name, though I don't think I ever addressed her as such), but I liked her because she was unflinching in her correctness and it got me going in the right direction in record time; eventually we became pals, and got to the point that we could even argue vehemently without any residual rancor. It was years later when she retired that she told us that she was half-white (apparently unhappy with the absentee pale-faced Dad, which explained a lot—sort of like the Bob Marley syndrome). The only white person I ever saw her take to immediately was my Mother when I brought her into the office; maybe it was because Mom was from Detroit (Motown), but in any event she and "Flora" hit it off with a quick discussion on Thurgood Marshall, civil rights, Lena Horne, Nat King Cole, Adam Clayton Powell, et al, before I could drag Mom in to meet Mr. Jackson. Mom was also enamored with him, pleasantly embarrassing him by stroking his face and kissing his cheek ("Okay, Ma, that's enough," I told her.) Ma had some kind of special relationship with black folks.

Holy Cross!

So, soon I was regularly flying back and forth to St. Croix from St. Thomas on the seaplane, since a good deal of the fieldwork by necessity occurred on "the big island." Here I'd be met by Terry Vanterpool, my assistant per se, and we'd drive all over the island looking at various pre-project development areas. Terry is a wonderful person, dark-skinned with a broad bright smile and speaking the thick island patois that always kept me asking "What? What?" to be reminded, as Fern would tell me, that, in the islands, it was impolite to ask "What?" but rather, one should say "Excuse me?" But Terry was very tolerant of my brash mainland ways, like the time we were visiting Bethlehem, the old historic sugar factory created by the U.S. Government to subsidize unemployment (and continue producing rum) right after the Depression, and I spotted a bulldozer skirting some of the old worker-house ruins. I had her stop the car, jumped out and flagged down the operator, telling him that this was unacceptable, these were historic ruins, and he needed to stop. He climbed on down and asked us to wait a little, he'd be right back. Within fifteen minutes we were surrounded by a number of uniformed soldiers, including a General! Apparently the land had been transferred to the VI National Guard and one of the first orders from the General had been to go out there and "clear the bush." Now the General was staring down at the white-boy archaeologist, and asking me, "How long you been on de island, son?" "Four months," I stammered, then gathering my nerve, "but it doesn't matter how long I've been here… these ruins are important to the people of the Virgin Islands and this dozer was getting too close. My job is to protect them and I'm gonna do that." He laughed, the soldiers laughed, even Terry laughed. "Okay, son," he said (even though I was almost fifty and probably as old as he was), "but next time you come and see me first. That's what we call protocol." And

431

then he introduced me to his "Resource Manager," Captain Crooke, before turning on his heels and walking away. Captain Crooke liked the way I'd (sort of) stood up to the General, and he and I became very good friends after that. The General? Not so much. Terry just thought I was crazy.

I almost always let Terry drive. She knew all the locations, estates, and short cuts and besides, she drove like a true Crucian (a "Crucian" is a person from St. Croix, whereas "Cruzan" is the rum), which is to say she drove fast. One day we were going back to Bethlehem again, but this time by the back road, and she was barreling down this long dusty dirt road, tall guinea grass on both sides, with maybe a tamarind tree or two along the edge. Way up ahead I could see a horse on the side of the road munching away. She's going maybe 45 or 50, kicking up rocks and gravel and dust, and I notice there's a tree on the opposite side of the road from the horse. We're coming down pretty fast, when I spot a line laying in the road. "Slow Down, Terry!" I yelped. She doesn't want to, but she puts the brakes on anyway just as we get near the grazing animal. He's startled by the car's sudden appearance, and yanks back. As he does, the line raises up off the road, and we come to a sliding stop just as we get to it. The horse calms down, goes back to eating, watching us warily, and the line, tied to the tree opposite, settles back down onto the road. We creep across it. I shudder to think what might have happened if we had hit that raised rope at 50 miles per hour—I'm sure we would have ripped that horse's head right off.

St. Croix is an incredible place, and because it is the largest island, it has a history of overt land-use, from agriculture in the days of sugar cane and sea-island cotton, to cattle production (this was the birthplace of the Senepol breed, large red cows that are heat-tolerant and give good meat and milk, now naturally polled, i.e., hornless), then the sugar factory described above, and finally, industrial uses such as aluminum extraction and an oil refinery. The sugar factory went belly-up in 1961, while the aluminum extraction business started with Alcoa, who brought in bauxite ore from South America, then transferred the business to Martin Marietta (my Dad worked for Martin Marietta, in the missiles and finance divisions in Orlando, but told me that they made *way* more money in the aggregate sector—stone and sand and cement, and obviously aluminum—than they ever did in weaponry and gadgets), who then transferred it to a Virgin Islands semi-autonomous enterprise, each time the company down the line getting less and less aluminum out of the ore and the red-mud residual heavy-metal mounds getting higher and higher and running off into the ocean out of the "holding" ponds. The oil refinery, Hovensa (**H**ess-**O**il-**VEN**ezuela-**S**outh **A**merica), is the second-largest oil refinery in the Western Hemisphere, and no matter what anybody says, or how bad they want to bad-mouth Hugo Chavez, Venezuela has always been ready, willing, and able to sell oil to the United States; it's liquid money, for God's sake... The place has been shut down since 2012, citing weak demand (I don't think so) and high operating costs (what, at $100+ a barrel, producing a half-million barrels a day?), but all this may have more to do with a year-earlier 2011 EPA fine of $5.3 million, and a forced promise of $700 million to install clean-air pollution controls (or maybe it's just a coincidence in timing, eh?). So, "America's Paradise" is a bit of a misnomer when you see the abandoned refinery and red-mud refuse of the old aluminum plant. There is however, still hope, with the Cruzan rum distillery still kicking and now, Captain Morgan as well, having been wooed away from the P.R. with promises of rich booty going both ways (to the distillery owners and the VI Government that is; the hell with Puerto Rico).

Speaking of "America's Paradise," there's the apocryphal story about when Jimmy Buffet was driving around the island and he spotted the local bar (one of my favorites) called "Cheeseburger in Paradise." He pulled in, went inside and confronted the manager/owner and said that he was

432

Jimmy Buffet, and he had the copyright on that name, and they'd better change it, or else. Now it's called "Cheeseburger in *America's Paradise*." Take that, Parrot-beak! My new buddy, Glass Ray, told me that he and his family used to live on Islamorada back in the early 70s when Buffet was just an itinerant strummer in the neighborhood. While he was trying to make a living busking on the dock in Key West, often they would feed him on the weekends out of compassion. Ray said that his daughter, whom I'd gotten the car from, used to sit on Buffet's lap as a baby while he composed songs and drank Ray's beer. As a result of these early kindnesses, Ray got a Christmas card every year until about 2002 when they suddenly stopped. One day Ray spotted Buffet in an airport and, despite the intimidating entourage, went up and gave him some shit about not being able to afford an extra Christmas card, and apparently Jimmy apologized (but Ray still got no more Christmas cards). In all fairness, it's also a part of island lore that Buffet sailed his windjammer into Christiansted Harbor, and then sailed it out again a week later, all under sail and no motors. Anyone who's familiar with that narrow, twisting, and reef-wracking entrance can appreciate that this is a feat that only an accomplished mariner could or would attempt (*if* he didn't have a hired pilot who did it for him). However, after reading the disappointing *A Pirate Looks at Forty* and then again …*Fifty*, I think the Coral Reaver should stick to writing music, and not tell us all what a cool rich bastard he is and how much he dislikes the common folk, the same ones (Parrot-nerds, e.g.) who lap up his stuff and support the grand lifestyle he now espouses. Just an opinion.

Bone Again

Even though I was now a year or two in the harness, living on St. Thomas, where all the administrative and Government offices were centered, it was clear that I was really going to have to pay attention to development initiatives on St. Croix. For instance, one day I got a call from Captain Crooke at the VI National Guard that they had a situation. There were plans on the books to build a new National Guard headquarters across from the abandoned sugar factory at Estate Bethlehem (which is why I had come up against the General in the first place), and while one of the guys was "clearing bush" again, this time with a front-end loader, he kicked up some bones. Turns out they were human bones. I flew on over on the seaplane and quickly assessed the situation. It was a shallow grave that had been exposed by the scraping of the ground. Shit! If there was one grave, there were probably more. Captain Crooke and I discussed our options, and lo and behold, after talking to his handlers in the National Guard on the mainland, he asked me for an estimate to carry out a survey and testing of the area. Whoo-hoo! We had been strapped in the office for upgrading our computers, as well as a lot of griping every time we asked for some travel money to go to St. Croix, so this was an opportunity to establish a little slush fund of our own, just like every department head in the Virgin Islands Government had already done with, shall we say, "creative financing." I even found a small provision in the Antiquities and Cultural Resources Act that had stated there was an Archaeological Preservation Fund where monies could be donated or otherwise stashed (when I called our finance department and asked how much money was in it, they said nothing, not a cent, and they didn't even know it existed; I sent a $10 check to them right away and told them it was a donation to get the thing rolling). Then I called a couple of grad students I knew, Steve Lenik and his girlfriend, and Tyler Cremeens, who had worked with me on Cumberland Island, and got them to sign on.

The Tod Mann

Having written budgets for the Southeast Archeological Center for years, this was going to be a pleasure; now I'm going to write one for myself. With a little prodding and poking, and a disguised game of twenty-questions, I found out that I couldn't go over $25,000. At the end of three days, a few phone calls, juggling the numbers, and convincing Mr. Jackson (Myron) that it was all okay (legal even), I submitted a budget to Captain Crooke for $24,800. Told them (the National Guard) to make the check out to the Archaeological Preservation Fund, DPNR, Gov't of the Virgin Islands. Sure enough, this freaked everyone out in the Government, and I'm sad to say it was probably because it was done in a way that didn't allow for any "administrative costs" to be siphoned off. Well, this was corrected as soon as the check arrived, and the funds were immediately transferred to the Government Employees Retirement System (GERS). The argument being (which I railed against unsuccessfully) that only a certified government budget officer could write checks, not even Myron, who was only a division Director. This was all bogus, but allowed GERS to charge the fucking 40% administrative fee, and put it wherever they (i.e., the Governor) wanted; it also meant that whenever I needed some money for this project I had to call Tod Mann, the Budget Director of GERS, who would then write a paper check, and send it over on the seaplane from St. Thomas to St. Croix, where I would pick it up, and then it would be up to me to find a bank that was both open and would cash it, after *they* called the said GERS Budget Director on the phone and got his authorization to cash it. Half the time they didn't even want to see *my* identification. It was crazy, but typical island bureaucracy. What really threw me for a loop though, was that Tod Mann was never in his office. I would call all hours of the workday, every day of the workweek. The secretary would take a message, but they never got delivered. I ran up a lot of I.O.U.'s on St. Croix waiting on those checks, and more than once Mr. Mann left me standing in the dark at the seaplane dock after the last plane for the afternoon had arrived without the goddamn check, sometimes even after telling me on the phone that it was on the very next plane. I later learned that Tod was preoccupied with some new woman, other than his wife, and the only time he could get away to visit her was during working hours, which is why he was generally unavailable and never got the messages ("Please don't call me at my home on the weekends… I can't write a check from home anyway. Call me Monday." I'd get so mad, that at one point I considered asking him if I could talk to his wife for a minute). Mr. Mann eventually ended up going to Federal prison for egregiously mismanaging the government employees' investment fund by taking kickbacks from semi-reputable bad investment companies to buy their stocks with the employees' pension funds. Sad but true, and he was a nice guy; and other than the fact that he was unreliable, a philanderer, and mismanaged the government employees money (all things for which you could not seriously hold a Virgin Islands government official responsible), I liked him.

The Comanche

Now I must speak of The Comanche. It is a long and arduous tale, full of mystery, mirth, mayhem, and movie stars. I will do my best to keep it short and to-the-point…, ergo: There once was an entity known as The Comanche Club, which was some Pennsylvanian university social club for young well-to-do men of promise, and one of their ilk was a young man named Ted Dale, born around 1920. I don't know a lot about Ted Dale, his upbringing, what promise he had, what he did for a living (although I had heard talk of him being a Navy fighter jet pilot during the war), etc. But what I do know about him makes me want to write a book about him, a book about him that needs to be written. He traveled south by sailboat from New Jersey to St. Croix in 1948 and fell in love with the place. Returning with a plan in 1949, he purchased an old Danish manor-house built out of wood and coral block on the Christiansted waterfront (purported to have actually housed young Alexander Hamilton and his mother for a while), and built a real hostel-type hotel/bar/restaurant with the first pool on St. Croix. It's a large saltwater pool with an adjacent "sugar mill" which isn't a mill at all (he had it built to resemble the old historic sugar mills that dot the island), except that it did have a windmill on top that pumped water into the pool from the harbor and back out again, and at one time the top floor apartment in it was rented out to newly-married couples as a honeymoon suite. Ted was a man's man, a real Hemingway-esque fellow, hard drinking, boxer and wrestler, troublesome to women (who apparently had no trouble with him), and an avid sailor. He named his new hotel The Comanche, after both the young men's club and the 27-foot sloop that he kept in the slip he dredged in the harbor adjacent to the hotel. This slip was later used as a welcome ramp for the old Grey Goose seaplane that flew between St. Thomas and St. Croix on a semi-regular basis (for $25 round-trip). The real and (to me) most notable *Comanche* however, was a 20-foot pirogue he had made by natives in Surinam, and which he sailed back and forth many times across the Caribbean, often single-handed. It now rests upside-down among the rafters of the famous Club Comanche restaurant. One day I met an old gentleman sitting on a bench in the shade on the Christiansted boardwalk and we struck up a conversation. He was a very old white guy with wispy hair, and a terrible stutter… one of those that's so bad you want finish the thought for them, but you know you shouldn't, so you wait, and wait, patiently, 'til he gets it out. Nonetheless we talked for over an hour, because, once he found out that I was interested in the Ted Dale story, he brightened up, lost most of his debilitating stutter, and told me that he was Ted Dale's best friend for over thirty years, and had made several of the voyages with him in the narrow dugout sailing canoe, to Dominica, Trinidad, and Venezuela. He said that Ted would just get a wild hair up his ass when it was time for a trip, and with nothing more than a five gallon tub of peanut butter, ten gallons of water, and a hand-line fishing rig, they would head out, sailing by dead reckoning and the stars, and meet their wives (who would fly) somewhere in South America or whatever island they hit a couple of weeks later. If Ted couldn't make arrangements for the return delivery of the canoe, he'd sail it back to St. Croix by himself.

I'd heard a story that among Ted Dale's friends who stayed at his Club Comanche during the 60s was a young Hugh Hefner who was getting his Playboy Enterprises started and took an interest in the small island in the harbor, Protestant Key. This little island is called Protestant Key because heretic Huguenots were buried there in the early 1700s to keep them out of the town's Catholic cemetery. Because of Ted's connections, Hef saw the place as a potential Playboy getaway for the rich and famous. Whether or not it's true, I was told that he built the stylish Hotel on the Cay (still there) as a result, but soon found out that there really weren't enough high rollers wanting to go to St. Croix, which was still pretty rough and rugged back then, and if they did go, they'd rather stay with Ted, so soon after it was built he quickly unloaded it and it never did join the Playboy empire. Other famous friends who visited Ted at the Comanche were Gary Cooper, Ava Gardner, Maureen O'Hara (who moved to St. Croix later, and ran the seaplane business with her husband), John Wayne, and others. But the most prominent (to me) was J. Robert Oppenheimer. After Oppie had been blackballed and thrown out of government service as a result of the McCarthy hearings (although not a Communist himself, he brashly admitted that some of their ideas weren't all that bad) and pissing Truman off with his open opposition to the H-bomb (the "Super Bomb"), his good friend Ted Dale invited him and his family down to St. Croix to relax and get away from it all. Oppenheimer liked it so much he decided to permanently move to the Virgin Islands, but wanted to distance himself from Ted so Ted wouldn't get "smeared" by his friendship. So he moved to St. John, bought a couple of acres on the beach, and built a bungalow house with all the vernacular island amenities (most of it done with his own two hands). The Defense Department pulled an old CIA agent out of retirement and constructed a large house for him on the adjacent hilltop where he could keep an eye on Oppie (just in case he might go rogue and begin entertaining Russkies). The two of them became good friends, drinking buddies, and fishing partners. The sad rejoinder to all this is that once Oppie passed on, and the wife too, the place fell to his daughter, who had serious issues with depression, and once you add in the isolation, drinking, and family history, it's probably not a surprise that one day she was found hanging from the rafters. The place was then gifted specifically to "the people of the Virgin

Islands" as opposed to the Government of the Virgin Islands (although the argument can be made that the Government *is* the people, and the elite in the government have thus considered this the case and have used it as their private party house and romantic rendezvous ever since). The large wrought-iron gate at the entrance there still reads "Oppenheimer Beach," even though most of the native residents have no idea who Oppie was or what he had accomplished.

Back to Ted Dale in St. Croix… Besides being an avid and accomplished sailor, as I said, Ted was also a boxer and wrestler, and he would stand on his pool deck behind the knee-high balustrade and challenge large men walking with their wives or girlfriends on the then-makeshift harborside boardwalk below, willing to take on all comers and offering either free drinks or a room for the night to any man who could either knock him down or pin him. Not content with these infrequent episodes, he created the Virgin Islands Wrestling Association and began teaching the large black high school kids the manly arts as a way to keep them off the streets. At one point a challenge was made to Ted by an off-island group, and an exhibition match was set. It was so popularly advertised that the venue had to be moved to the ballpark. Tickets were sold to support the wrestling team, and bets were run up into the thousands (after all, it was better than the standard cockfight, or even an illegal, but all too prevalent—even in recent times— dogfight). Unfortunately, the opponent was a huge Mexican streetfighter, who was known to fight dirty and was easily ten years younger and fifty pounds heavier than Ted. Rather than go round by round, let's just say that both boxing and wrestling were involved, and both men were bloodied. The Mexican had bitten Ted's ears, kicked him in the groin, and head-butted him, but Ted stuck to the rules and eventually prevailed; nonetheless, at the end they shook hands and retired to the Comanche to have more than a few stiff painkillers (not to be confused with The Painkiller, which is a fruity pineapple-coconut-rum concoction topped with nutmeg, invented on Jost van Dyke in the British Virgin Islands, and now endemic throughout the Caribbean).

Then came Richard and Mary Boehm. Richard was an old friend of Ted's and a helluva top-rate chef. Since Ted's restaurant was now catering to the high and mighty, he brought Richard in to spruce up the menu and even made him a partner. Richard in turn brought his wife Mary, a short feisty well-educated Brit, who walked with a terrible lopsided limp, the result of a bad accident when she was racing motorcycles professionally shortly after the war. In the 70s, when the tourist trade dropped off and the old Hollywood stars quit coming (and Ted's age and lifestyle started catching up to him) Ted cut a deal for Richard and his wife to take over the hotel and restaurant. Once Ted left and they had gained controlling interest in the business however, they began to fight with each other: loud yelling matches on how the place ought to be run, disagreements on how to handle the money, even what ought to go on the menu. It got so bad that eventually they resorted to a legal separation, with the judge giving temporary management of the hotel to Mary and that of the restaurant and bar to Richard. He also made it mandatory that if and when they absolutely needed to speak to each other they had to meet halfway on the wooden bridge walkway that straddles Strand Street and connects the old part of the hotel (the Danish manor section where Mary had set up house) to the newer restaurant/bar and modern section (the part built by Ted Dale, where Richard lived). This arrangement seemed to work for several years; they remained civil and the business carried on. Then one evening while they were talking on the walkway, Mary suggested that, hell, since they were getting along, the business was doing well, and Richard was working too hard in the bar and restaurant, doing most of the cooking… "What do you say I fix you dinner for a change," she suggested. That would be nice, he agreed. The next evening she took over the kitchen in the restaurant, and they had a nice quiet candlelit fish dinner overlooking the pool with the mill and the harbor in the background, and glasses of wine under a clear starlit evening moon. The next day Richard wasn't feeling too good. He got worse throughout the day. By that evening he was in the hospital. By the following morning he was dead. Must have been something he ate.

So now Mary owned the Club Comanche outright; and let there be no doubt that Mary was, and still is, a strong-willed, smart, and savvy woman. She and Richard had one son (Darren? Daniel? Dick? Maybe he's Richard Jr., I forget) who is an expert lobster catcher and spearfisherman. But the hotel and restaurant had fallen on hard times, especially after Hugo in 1989, and the place began to deteriorate. By the time I got to know Mary in 2001-2, the place had taken on a distinct Bates Motel sort of feel, especially when she'd be yelling at her son in the evenings, and you could see their shadows behind the back-lit window shades, and he'd return with "MOTHER! Please!" In the daytime you might feel a pair of eyes looking down on you and glance up to see her standing in the upper room, peering out of the dark from behind the drapery, watching. But I loved the place, and she and I generally got along. So it was here I got a couple of rooms for the duration of the National Guard cemetery project, and placed my graduate student assistant and his girlfriend in one (in the older hotel section down the hall from Mary and her son's apartment), and then I put Tyler, my other hireling, in with me in the newer larger loft room that overlooked the harbor. One night while we were working on the cemetery site, we all came home and tied one on at Styxx, the ($2, 16 oz, 3/4 rum drinks) bar down on the waterfront. The place was a real local hangout for all the "boaties" and other dockside derelicts, and it looked like a large jail cell because of the iron cage and doors that were used to lock it up at night from the predators that stalked Christiansted after hours. Around 2 a.m., they would lock you in and stop serving drinks, keeping out the riff-raff while they tried to close by 4. It was always a little unnerving to be locked in there with all these raging drunks of disreputable character clamoring for "just one more." There was a kitchen upstairs at the time and I always wondered what might happen if a fire broke out and they couldn't find the keys. Wouldn't have surprised anyone to see it in the papers the next morning. Well, this one night I went to bed early, around midnight, and Tyler came stumbling in around 2. I heard him come in and get in the bed next to mine, and after a few minutes I heard a loud gulp; then 30 seconds later another. "Oh Jesus!" I thought… and I yelled out to him, "Tyler, goddammit, don't you dare!" I turned on the nightside lamp, and he sat up, looked over at me with a blank stupid stare, then turned away to his left and let fly. "ROOOWWWLLLFFF!" Again and again. "ROWLF!" "Rowwullf!" "Damn you, Damn you, Damn you!" I shouted, jumping up, turning on the lights, and throwing some wet towels over the despoliation. I cursed and yelled and even threw one of the wet towels on Tyler, but he just groaned and rolled over. "Sunavabitch! You're gonna clean this up in the morning!" I threatened as I got back in my own bed after opening the window to let in fresh air. I might mention at this point that Tyler was the same young man who had suffered so on the last day at Cumberland Island—the boy could drink, he just couldn't keep it down, and his hangovers were crippling.

So I fall back asleep, the room stinking of rum-punch vomit, and damn if the phone doesn't ring around 4:30! I figure it's going to be Mary, bitching me out for making a lot of noise, but no, it's some guy calling me from the States, and he's bitching me out because his daughter called him crying and upset, and apparently it's all my fault! First of all, I ask him, who are you, and second, who is your daughter? Ahh, it quickly fell into place… My graduate student and his girlfriend (a young tall, leggy looker) had been down at Styxx getting shit-faced after I'd left. All the bad young dudes had been buying them drinks, probably with the intent of separating the two, and when 2 o'clock rolled around and the bartender locked them in to "the jailhouse" she flipped out, figuring that this was how she was to be captured and ultimately molested, raped, and sodomized while Steve, her boyfriend, would be murdered before her very eyes. When she quit screaming, they pushed her and Steve out the door and told them not to ever come back (the boys were bad, but they weren't that bad—they were just drawn that way, rather "piratey"). Still shaking when she made it back to their room, she called her Dad, crying and upset (and drunk), who then called me. I told him I'd get to the bottom of it and I'd call him back. Now it's around 5 and the left hand of God started to glow in the east as I trundled down the hall, not quite sober myself. I had to bang and bang, because they had both fallen drunkenly asleep, and when I finally got them to open the door, I verbally laid into her without mercy (and him too, for not having controlled the situation). Then I told her to call her Dad back and tell him she was okay, she'd had too much to drink, she'd overreacted, I was a good guy, etc. She did so, and the next morning all of them were sheepishly apologetic, especially Tyler, who I wouldn't let out of the room until it was clean and smelled of lavender. Mary, however, was pissed over the loud goings-on all night long, the dirty towels, and having to transfer the phone call to me at 4:30 a.m. Later however, she got me back good.

The Lost Cemetery

Well, out at the National Guard we began work on what came to be known as "The Lost Cemetery" site. I got the original front-end tractor driver to scrape the top 1-2 inches off of the first exposed grave and keep on going. The ground was covered with a light layer of brush and guinea grass, but immediately below was a bright white layer of calcium carbonate, what we called "caliche." In the caliche you could easily see the outline of the individual graves, since whomever had dug through the ground cover, interred the remains, and then filled it back in, leaving a darkened stain in the otherwise pure white limestone soil. After three days we had exposed the outlines of some forty-two graves, everything from tiny baby-sized holes to large ones that overlapped each other. They all surrounded a large tamarind tree in the middle that must have been two hundred years old, and obviously marked the location. Later, I had the opportunity to interview some of the older residents of the surrounding estates, a couple of them eighty-plus in years, and none could recall ever having known there was a graveyard there; so the thing was old, certainly historic, and probably pre-Emancipation.

We didn't open any of the graves, but simply documented the outlines, giving each a field specimen number. If you open them up you're committed to documenting the remains, identifying the individual bones, assessing the age, sex, etc. and noting any deformities or skeletal injuries. We didn't have the time, the wherewithal, or the money to do that, and we had no intention of moving them. We were just there to define the limits and then advise the National Guard on what to do. There were, however, some very distinct features outside the limits of the graveyard, and a few of these *were* excavated. They were large round holes, obvious firepits, with not only blackened soil, ash, and charcoal, but items embedded therein: pipe bowls and pipestems, bottle fragments, ceramic bowl fragments, and a number of animal bones (cooked, cut, and gnawed upon). I called these features "wake circles" because it appeared that this is where the friends, family, and gravediggers sat around cooling their heels by smoking, drinking, and eating after taking care of the essentials. The same holes had been used time and again over several generations, judging by the stratigraphic layering of the residue: a very significant cultural marker, essentially Afro-Caribbean, and one which brought home the empathetic humanity of the otherwise coldly scientific investigation (even though it was hotter than hell out there on the reflective white caliche, even in April). Steve, the graduate student, who had already done archaeological work all over the Caribbean, took such an interest in it that he used it as the basis for a dissertation.

Across the road was the old abandoned Bethlehem Sugar Factory, with its monumental smokestack, and the ruins of the workers houses (that I had raised hell with the General about), and it just so happened that the VI Legislature had recently given a lease on that property to the St. Croix Farmers Association, to let them begin growing fruits, vegetables and coconuts in order to supplement the school day lunches. The president and vice-president, a couple of middle-aged dreadlocked Rastafarians, Percival Edwards and Kendall Peterson, saw us working out in the sun and came across the road to check us out. They weren't allowed on the National Guard property however, tightly guarded after 9/11 so they just stood outside the fence. I went over and after introductions I arranged for them and their workers to come onto the property and I'd give them an impromptu archaeological tour, which I did. They were amazed at the features and artifacts, and thankful that we had left the graves intact, as well as the interpretation of the "wake circles," which they supported. So grateful were they that they bestowed on me the Rasta sobriquet "King David," and though I tried to shake it off, they insisted, and to this day that's how they refer to me. They are good men and friends in Jah spirit.

No Sexo sin Protección

I might mention that, while we were working on the Lost Cemetery, we became acquainted familiarly with the St. Croix centipede. These 6 to 9-inch monsters are a half-inch thick and have pincers that grab hold to the death, leaving a large poisoned welt that takes weeks to heal (that is, after you've cut off the head and pried them loose). As the front-end loader scraped the ground these devil's spawn were released from their burrows by the hundreds, and the white cattle egrets would pounce on them relentlessly. But the damned creatures gave as good as they got and I'd say the egrets ended up consuming only half. Meanwhile, the other half scurried about looking for cover and got into all our tools, boxes, bags, knapsacks, buckets, and would have gotten into our shoes and clothes had we held still long enough. Like roaches, removing the head is only a minor insult until hunger, heat, or an egret finishes the job. We were very lucky and none of us got bit, but we had to keep a constant vigil and shake things out constantly. Several years later, when I'd gotten less afraid of the buggers, I was in a safety meeting being held for one of our consulting jobs; the meeting was being handled by a Mainlander who had never been to the Virgin Islands before, but had now been conducting these safety briefings for about two weeks. A bunch of us "natives" were sitting around the table when he began to discuss insect bites. He told us to watch out for the centipedes because they were really wicked (which we already knew), and that we had to keep an eye out because these things could get up to two feet long and as big around as your arm (!?!?). Well, they'll get up to maybe 9 inches and as big around as your thumb, but we all had to laugh when he said they'd get two feet long. "No, I mean it, I'm not kidding" he insisted, "I've actually seen them that big with my own eyes!" We laughed some more and he got really upset, "Are you calling me a liar!?" We suggested he visit the dive shop down on the waterfront that sponsored a "largest centipede" contest every year and kept the winners in pickle jars over the cash register; the biggest might have been 10 inches. That afternoon when we left the job site we were still chuckling over the two-foot long centipede sighting. Where the hell had he gotten that idea?! As we waited at the light, across the road on the corner was a public health billboard that, with typical VI overkill, had a beautiful dark-skinned woman lustily caressing a photo-shopped two-to-three-foot-long centipede as thick as her arm with the warning (in both Spanish and English) "No Sex Without Protection!" THAT's where he had seen it! With his own eyes.

Along Comes Mary

As we were finishing up the Lost Cemetery site, soon it would be time to go back to St. Thomas. It was a Saturday and Steve and his girlfriend took the day off, laying around the pool when not canoodling in their hotel room (they both swore that Mary had a secret peephole to spy on them because she would warn them about "no lighting any candles" the day after they would do so the romantic night before—in this regard, and not the spying, Mary was right, because the place was a tinderbox). I'd sent Tyler back to St. Thomas early because he was starting to get insubordinate (which I usually tolerated, but after the puking incident I didn't cut him any more slack). I decided to use the morning to do some laundry, packing up my dirty shirts and jeans and walking down the two blocks to the laundromat. I'd just put my stuff in the washer when in comes Mary, asking me to help her carry in the hotel's dirty laundry from her car, which I was happy to do. After it was all put in four large front-loading machines, she asked me if I'd do her a favor (the alarms should have gone off then, but they didn't). She handed me a small jar of quarters and said, since I was doing my own laundry anyway, would I please put the stuff in dryers when they were finished washing, if she wasn't back by then. Sure, I said, no problem. My stuff finished and I dried it quickly and folded it. By then the old black women were coming in and eying the four large washers full of clothes, but soon these were done and I transferred everything to six large dryers, all they had, and began feeding them quarters. I finally had them all going, but now I was getting short on quarters. These were towels, sheets, bedspreads, the standard hotel fare, and there were lots of them. The old black women began finishing their loads of wash and stood staring at the tumbling dryers, trying to will them into completing their cycles. When one stopped I ran over and, reaching in, discovered they weren't dry yet, and so dished out another handful of quarters. In no time I was feeding my own dollars into the change machine and taking out those items that were almost dry, consolidating them so I could free up at least one of the dryers. Now the old black women were eye-balling me, shaking their heads, and sucking their teeth (another slave-era insult that just might pass under the awareness of the overseer). One by one I liberated the dryers, but now I had a huge pile of laundry, the entire hotel's, two tables of laundry damn near to the ceiling, but I was god-damned if I was going to fold 'em. The clock ticked away, I had nothing to do, and as the black ladies' laundry came out dry, they were going to want a table. I couldn't just walk out and leave all the hotel laundry piled there, someone would steal it for sure. Fuck me, I thought, as I slowly began to fold the shit. Another hour-and-a-half passed, as I was just finishing, when along comes Mary. "Thank you, oh thank you so much," she said. My whole day off shot to hell. She knew. And I knew. And she knew I knew. She got me good.

The Battling Brewer Boys

One last Comanche Mary story… I'd invited Robin and Dennis down to the islands to visit and decided to take them over to St. Croix since they'd never seen it and I had a small drainfield monitoring project to do over there for the National Park Service at Fort Christiansvaern. Sam was living with me on St. Thomas and was still working at the Shipwreck Tavern but couldn't get off of work, so he couldn't come. [Short little side story here… just take a minute: Sam had invited his cousin Nick down to live in St. Thomas for awhile, and the two of them were staying at my little apartment on the beach at Dorothea. Sam got Nick a job helping at the Tavern's kitchen and one day they're driving down the mountain in to work when the car ahead of them hits a large iguana. The mortally wounded reptile is flopping around on the pavement, so they get out of their car to check it out. They decide to put it out of its misery with a chunk of cinderblock to the head. Then they look at each other and have an idea. Tossing it on the back seat floor, they take it in to work, skin it, clean it, and carve out a couple of dozen bite-size chunks. Dipped and rolled and deep-fried, they hand out samples round the restaurant. I came in on the tail end (so to speak) of the tasting and it wasn't bad. Chicken? I don't think so. More like alligator and not at all like frog legs. How did they get here? Trussed up and laid in the bottom of Taino canoes like cordwood, to be fattened up and released later (not to mention, they're marvelous swimmers between islands). Now they are as common on St. Thomas as snakes are in Florida.] So I've got Robin and Dennis visiting and we fly over on the seaplane to

St. Croix and I get the same old loft room at the Comanche that sits above the dockside dive bar of Styxx. That evening we go down and have more than a few drinks—hell, Dennis couldn't have been sixteen—and by the time we're headed back to the room after midnight, we're hanging on to each other, singing, and staggering up the steps. Robin knocks over a large ceramic flower pot outside the room and breaks it. We get inside and we're up in the loft, the large double-wide window open to the sea breeze. We start tussling and drunken me challenges Robin, "Okay, Mister Tough-Guy Marine, think you can still take your old man!?" Before I know it, he has me in a headlock, arms behind my back and face-down on the bed, when... out the open second-story window goes Dennis! "Oh my God!" yells Robin, letting me go and dashing to the window. We look down, and there's Dennis hanging by his fingers from the sill, dangling over a dead tree with spiked-branches reaching up and surrounded by a thick stand of large-spined cactus. If he fell he would certainly have been severely impaled, if not killed. I reached over quickly and grabbed an arm, yelling "Help me, Robin!," who grabbed the other and we slowly lift him up over the sill and into the room. I was adrenaline-charged, upset, frightened, and still intoxicated and laid into Dennis, slapping him repeatedly, "God-damn! god-damn!, god-damn!... What's the matter with you!? You coulda been killed! Jesus-fuckin- riiist!" I forgot, however, that Dennis knew karate... and after the third smack on my part, he shot out one of those piston-fast knuckle-fists the karate guys like to use so much and it caught me right over the right eye. BAM! The blood flowed fast down the side of my face as I shut the fuck up and grabbed a sheet and began blotting it from out my eye. Apparently you can't just go messing around with your boys any more when they're full-grown, inebriated, and either in the Marines or exhibiting their prowess in the martial arts. It was stupidly funny, and once we all realized how dumb we'd all been, and that the night's festivities had obviously climaxed, we all hugged, laughed, and lay down to sleep.

In the morning I woke up late and got dressed quickly. Splashing water onto my face I saw a large blue mouse over my eye with a long slit in it, still oozing (probably should have gone and gotten stitches). I grabbed a handful of tissues, combed my wet hair and made my way down the stairs and along the boardwalk toward the fort. It was already hot by 9:30 or so, and as I met the workmen, who had already started the trenching, I could see from the look on their faces that I must have appeared something like Anthony Quinn in *Requiem for a Heavyweight*. I was also surprised that these burly black men, who had already raised a sweat that morning, smelled rather pleasant compared to my own alcohol-laced perspiration now soaking my jeans and shirt from the day before. When the resource manager for the park, a good friend named Zandy, saw me dabbing away at my eyebrow while I'm trying to write notes and take photographs, she seemed rather shocked and asked me what happened and I told her I had fallen and cracked my head on the corner of a table, but she kept saying "Are you all right?" and "Are you sure you're okay?" Luckily, the whole job didn't take more than an hour and soon I was making my way back to the Comanche. Since we had to check out by 11 or so, I got the boys up and had them start packing. I wadded up the sheet and found out that we had also broken a chair the night before during our little melee. I went down to the office and knew that I had to face Mary. Clutching the bundled bloody sheet (my own shroud of tourneying), I rang the checkout desk bell, dabbed my forehead once more and stiffened my spine to face the Anglish harpy as she came hobbling out of her apartment. But, surprise of surprises, she didn't seem to care. In her thick British accent she says "Yes, I heard you boys coming in late last night, sounds like you had a good time." A bloody sheet? "Don't worry about it, I have to deal with them all the time." Broken flower pot? "That's okay, I've got plenty of them." Broken chair? "I'll just move one in from another room." I offered to give her $100 extra, but she refused, saying "You've always been a good tenant, and I'm glad to have your business. And I know that you've given recommendations of the place to others, and I appreciate that. Have a nice flight back to St. Thomas." And that was that… or so I thought.

Contrary Mary

Robin and Dennis went back to the States, and I settled back in to work at the office. Three weeks later I got a letter from Mary. "Please be advised that the total for damages incurred on your recent stay come to a total of $450. To avoid further litigation on this matter please remit the amount owed in the form of a cashier's check within the week." Goddammit. I called her on the phone, "Jeez, Mary, you said it was no big deal. I understand you might want some money, and I did offer you $100, remember, but hell, $450 is a bit much, don't ya think?" Then there was that long English drawl, "I had to replace the sheet and a pillowcase, and that flowerpot was almost an antique. The chair could not be fixed and was a very expensive piece…" "Aww, Mary, that stuff was just a bunch of common hotel fixtures… I'll tell you what, I'll come over and replace it all; even that'd be cheaper than $450." "No," she said, "You'll send me the $450 or I'll see you in court." Knowing Mary and having been a keen observer of Judge Judy over the years, I knew she had me by the balls. "Okay, Mary, you win… give me a month," and within the month she had her $450. I've stayed at the Caravelle, a Danish tourist hotel, ever since. It's cleaner, nicer, and sits over the well-known Rum Runners bar and restaurant, where you can get lobster with your Eggs Benedict in the morning for about $10. (Rum Runners is also the place that started the whole "The Liver Must Be Punished!" T-shirt craze.) And they love me there. Mary eventually lost control of the Comanche when she reluctantly took on partners. Once they wrested it out of her iron-maiden grip, they put a cool million in it and had the place renovated (*not restored*, mind you, probably to its detriment since it no longer qualifies for a nomination to the National Register of Historic Places as a result). It's now called something like the St. Croix Hotel, very pricey, and the guy who manages it, yet still struggling to keep it afloat, is named Pickle. [Reminds me of the local joke: How do you leave the Virgin Islands with a million dollars? Come here with five million.] That was my penultimate run-in with Mary. The last time I saw her, about a year ago, she was standing on a corner in Frederiksted in a rather dangerous neighborhood (when I saw her I thought, Jesus, she must be pushing eighty by now), and so I pulled over. She was waiting for a cab to take her to Christiansted (a twenty-minute drive and a $25 fare). I told her to get in and I'd take her. She talked the whole way about how she was going to get the Comanche back and (her words, not mine) "put the bastards out on the street." She had a sheaf of legal papers in her hand and was headed back to Christiansted to see her lawyer. I reminded her about the million of their own money the new owners had already put in it, but she was undeterred: she was going to get it back. You know, if it was anybody else, I'd think they were full of shit. But Mary…?

The Arthurian Legend

Back on St. Thomas life had settled into a tropical routine. On my days off, I'm eating my mangoes in the clear (yes, gin-clear) waters off Dorothea Beach, sipping rum and 'wah-tuh' from green coconuts twisted off the stem of low-hanging pods that I could just reach by standing on top of my truck (my neighbor busted out laughing one day when one of the clunkers fell out of my hand and shattered the truck's back window). Small hand-picked limes by the dozen, and even a few yard-bird eggs from the wild chickens that laid them in nests under the condo stairs. With my mask, fins, and snorkel I'd come in from an hour-long swim with my pockets full of fist-sized whelks that I could steam out of their shells and gobble down dipped in melted butter. Nearby, within walking distance (although we never walked, since you can drink and drive with impunity in the VI) was the lesser known, but locally infamous, Larry's Hideaway at Hull Bay. Drinks that would curl your toes ("No, we don't serve any fuckin' frozen drinks here!"), and even grilled bar food cooked by the famous (no stretch there) Arthur. Arthur is a large black man, now graying, generally quiet, but when he does speak, unless you are a local with a fine-tuned ear for the island Creole patois you wouldn't understand anyway (a lot of island communication is also done non-verbally: pursing the lips to point, for instance). He is a legend. And the legend is that thirty years ago, Arthur started coming in to this very quiet and rather locally-exclusive ramshackle hand-built beach bar under the palms. It was considered exclusive by the rough white fishermen Frenchies, that is. He would sit by himself in a corner and drink his drink, silently. After a while, Larry got curious and started fucking with him one day, "What you doon heah, (n-word)?" "Lemme be," says Arthur. "Dis he-yah ma place," pushes Larry, "I axe you a ques-ty-on…" "Lemme be, says Arthur again. "Or you gonn do wha?" say Larry. "Or I knock you down," says Arthur. Larry was a big man, tough as nails: a hand-line, net, and trap fisherman when he wasn't tending the bar, and those Frenchies are mean to boot; even the old ones don't age gracefully and will pick a fight over even the smallest perceived reproach. "Oh, I gots to see dis!" says Larry, undoing his bar apron and throwing it to the floor as he rounded the bar. Arthur's on his feet as Larry comes up to him, and before Larry can say a word, Arthur hits him up under his chin, lifting him off the floor, onto which he then drops like the proverbial sack of potatoes, out cold. Arthur sits back down to his drink. As Larry comes to, he slowly gets up, rubbing his jaw, looks at Arthur sitting there and says, "You need a job?" Arthur's been there ever since. I met Larry once, and after confirming the story above, I asked him if I could interview him at length, since there were many other colorful tales to be told as well, but he said no, they were all his and he was keeping them for himself. He sold the place and the surrounding five acres for a million (seems to be the standard price for things in the islands) and it's been the Hull Bay Hideaway since, although the owners keep changing. Arthur, however, is still there. I was recently informed that after the million ran out on drink, gambling, and bad investments, Larry dispatched himself with the .38 that he normally kept under the bar.

Jesse Girl

I loved going to the Hideaway on Sundays, early afternoon. It was quiet, cool, and generally unoccupied, just a few of the locals. One day I'm sitting there quietly enjoying my dark rum and tonic, slice of lime (my standard fare; it's very refreshing, and having gone eight years in the VI without ever once contracting dengue fever, unlike everyone I knew, black or white, I credit the quinine in the tonic). In walks this tall, tanned, short-haired brunette, broad shoulders, long legs, and a big toothy smile. She's wearing tight short shorts, and a cutoff t-shirt that enhances her mango-sized breasts and her six-pack abs. She sits down about three stools down from me and orders a drink. Of course I noticed her walking in and sitting down, but when I look over at her it seems to me I've seen her before: a long time ago, in a place far, far away. It really starts to bother me. After ten minutes or so, it suddenly kicks in: Jesus Christ! This is the long-legged girl who was roller-skating so many years ago at the opening of The Lucky Horseshoe Bar! I can't believe it! I'm staring at her now, with a big smile on my face, when she looks over and says, "What are you looking at?" I'm still smiling, as sure as I can be, and I said "I know you." She chuckles, and says, "You don't know me… and that's a lousy line." She's kinda mad now, and turns her back to me, looking down at the other end of the empty bar. "Yes, yes I do know you," I said, rather strongly. She turns back and says, "Oh yeah? Where do you know me from?" I go: "Twenty-eight years ago, Tallahassee, Florida, the opening of The Lucky Horseshoe Bar; you were wearing roller skates and doing pirouettes and stuff, you had a boyfriend who played the blues named Julian; he played with Pat Ramsey and Crosscut Saw…" Her mouth dropped open, and she said "You really do know me!" She got up, carried her drink over and planted her ass next to mine at the bar. And I said, "…but I never got to know your name…" Jesse, she said.

We talked for two hours, while I plied her with drinks. I told her about building the Horseshoe for Jimmy and Charlie, and how the grand opening was so memorable, especially with the underage leggy girl in skates. She asked me what I was doing in the Virgin Islands and was visibly impressed that I was the State Archaeologist. I asked her what she was doing and she told me that she was working off a series of grants in fisheries management. She was tagging large pelagic fish: marlin, swordfish, sharks, things like that. "Oh really?" I asked, "that must be fun, going out on a boat and catching them and releasing them like that." "Oh no," she said thickly as the liquor started kicking in, "I go diving. I'll be down 80, 90 feet, down in the dark blue and I just hang there, waiting. These large fish, when they come by, they're curious, and they'll swim around you, looking at you with their big eyes... and when they get close enough, I stick them with a tag, and they swim off." "WHAAA?" I hiccupped. I'd been diving for over thirty years, in all sorts of waters, but the scariest, by far, is the deep blue, as we call it. Out there, deep like that, it is frighteningly dark, without any references other than the slightly lighter hue from the surface, and the black below. And when something comes out of the distance, you never know right away what it is, or what's its intent might be. I get disturbed just thinking about it. "Aren't you afraid?" I asked, telling her "I just don't like that deep blue, it's scary." "Well, you get sort of used to it after awhile," she said, now obviously drunk and slightly weaving in the telling of it, "but there is one thing I'm worried about..." "What's that?" I was really, seriously interested... and she slowly said "I get really worried that some big shark, like a tiger, or a great white, or hammerhead, might come out behind me before I see it... and I'm scared that it might... just... bite my leg off... and then... no one... would want... to... fuck me." I couldn't believe what she said, and I busted out laughing. The tension had built up and then she said *that* (she did *not* say "no one would want to make love to me"). She straightened up and said, "What's so funny?" I couldn't help it, it was just so... so... unexpected! I tried to gather my composure, and lighten up the conversation, but still chuckling, I said, "Well... you know... there might be some guys who would find that to be attractive..." She was really mad now. "It's not funny," she said, "and you're being an asshole..." and she got up in a huff, and walked out, slightly staggering.

Maybe a month goes by and I'm in Betsy's down in Frenchtown on the other side of the island. It's early evening and I'm having a beer, when in comes Jesse, and sits down beside me in the only bar stool available. She looks over, sees me and smiles. "Hi Jesse," I say to her, and even though she recognizes me, she says, "I'm sorry, I forgot your name." David, I tell her. I buy her a beer and we make some small talk; I ask her how the fish-tagging is coming along. "Well, I'm working on getting another grant right now," she tells me. After a while, although I really should have known better, I couldn't help it, and said, "Do you remember the last time we met?" And she says, "No, not really." "We were down at Hull Bay Hideaway. Remember I told you about remembering you from Tallahassee." "Oh, yeah," she says. This is where I needed to put a lid on it, but no, I've got to push it over the top. "Remember what you said about that deep diving stuff?" I push. "No, what?" "You said that you were really worried out there in the deep blue that a shark might get you..." "Yeah," she said, "I really do worry about that." And then I stuck my foot all the way in and said, "... because then no one would want to fuck you." She sat up abruptly, and said, "I never said that!" "You sure as hell did," I told her gently, "that's why I couldn't forget it. You got mad 'cause I started laughing..." "I would never say such a thing!" she insisted. "Well, that's exactly what you said... but don't worry, we'd both been drinking, and..." "I never said that!" she said again, loudly now. "Okay, okay," I tried to calm her down, "it's no big deal..." "You're a sunuvabitch!" she yelled for the whole bar to hear, and up from her stool and out she went. Betsy comes over and asks me if everything's all right. "Miscommunication," I tell her.

"Bones"

Betsy's was a great bar (and now I'm talking about the old Betsy's, not the new one). Hell, the bar couldn't have seated ten people, but it was either empty or packed, maybe a dozen more standing as well late in the evening: lots of comraderie, serious talk, flirting and laughing. Betsy is a short-haired Irish Wisconsin gal, always with a smile, and remembers your name even if you haven't gone in in ten years. She's sweet and tough, but fair. I guess I'd been going in for about a year when I noticed someone saying "put it on my tab" before he left. I asked Betsy, "Hey, Bets, can I run a tab?" and she says, sure, "You've been coming in for awhile and you're always good for it, besides, you work for the government so I know where to find you." (Even the Governor would stop in periodically to have a beer or two, and then shake hands all around as he left.) "Just a minute," she said, then came back with a little notepad in her hand on which she kept her tallies. She leans over the bar and tells me, "You know, David, I have a lot of other Davids in here as well, so, to keep you apart, from now on we're goingto call you 'Bones' and you just tell whoever's behind the bar to put it on 'Bones' tab, okay?" She knew I was an archaeologist and well, it just so happened that that day I had made the front page of The Daily News with a big picture of me and my assistant standing in a grave that we were digging inside of Ft. Christian. The article went on to talk about the bones we had found and what they meant (the remains of probably the first pastor of the first Lutheran Church, which happened to be located inside the fort at the time, ca. 1700). I'm always a little wary of nicknames, and I told her I wasn't sure I'd want to be stuck with that one. She said, "no problem... I'll just put you down as Asshole, then, how's that?" I told her Bones would be fine. To this day, when I walk in, even after a year or two hiatus, the locals who know me yell out in Cheers fashion "Hey, Bones!" and Betsy plants a kiss on my cheek welcoming me home. I've not only gotten used to it, but relish it as well: one of my favorite characters on Star Trek was always "Bones" McCoy ("Dammit, Jim, I'm a doctor, not an archaeologist!") Like I always say, coulda been worse.

Gov't Inaction

So things had also settled into a Virgin Islands bureaucratic routine at work too. I was reviewing development plans and archaeological surveys, making recommendations, and advising the local divisions when called upon: Coastal Zone Management, Environmental Protection, Building Permits, and Public Works. All of this work was above and beyond what we were given money by the Feds to do: the Feds just wanted us to review anything that had any federal funding behind it, and to dish out around $40,000 in local historic preservation grants (as well as monitor and follow up on those grants as well so the money didn't "fall through the cracks" like every other federally-funded initiative in the history of the U.S. Virgin Islands had). So, by default, since I was the only one to take the time to read and understand the Federal Grant Manual, I also became the Grants Manager, which meant I sent out the notices, helped rank the various project proposals, and then issue the awards. Later, we'd assess whether the applicant performed as promised. It's a funny thing with Territories, as opposed to States. In the States, the various Historic Preservation Offices are given one large grant to operate, based on their population, but to get it, they have to match it, thus showing that they have an investment in their historic and archaeological programs. In the Territories however, whether the Virgin Islands, Puerto Rico, Guam or American Samoa, they get the grants without having to match it. Most of them (all of them?), except the Virgin Islands, match it just to show their seriousness regarding preserving their cultural resources. The Virgin Islands legislature, in its consolidated wisdom, has repeatedly decided that, since they don't have to match it, they're not going to. So the Virgin Islands State Historic Preservation Office (commonly known as the VISHPO) operates at a distinct disadvantage than all the rest in the country, and for all the crying and chest-pounding about how important the local prehistoric and Afro-Caribbean history and culture and artifacts are, it's a sad state of affairs compared to how much government money is handed over for the week-long Carnival and other local holidays each and every year, not to mention horse-tracks and drag strips and casinos. And for all the other subsidies, the rum tax for instance, it sure as hell ain't going to education, public safety, filling pot holes, etc. [As far as potholes, one gentleman on St. Croix got so tired of hitting the giant tire-popping and rim-bending pavement paucities that he carried a can of bright red spray paint in his car and painted large bright red target circles around each and every one he came upon in order to embarrass the Public Works department into patching them. When that didn't work, he went out in the middle of the night and planted small coconut trees in them so that in the morning drivers had to veer around these palms that had suddenly sprouted in the road overnight.] Enough belly-achin' about the VI Government… I don't have the time or the pulp or the inclination to cover it. I apologize for the rant; it's an island thing. One of the many things that will drive you, as they say, "rock-happy."

Ship-Wrecked!

Here's another island thing that *is* worth discussing however. One night I was in the Shipwreck watching football after having a large burger and beer. It was Monday Night Football and I was expecting some old friends from the Park Service to fly in the next day to do some NPS background work on various sites around the island. It was about 10 at night and I decided to go on home, but when I went out back to the alley behind the restaurant, where my rusted-out Isuzu Trooper was parked, I saw that I had left my lights on. Damn! Ruhrr, ruhrr, ruhrrr… nope, it wasn't going to start. But you know, sometimes when you turn the lights off and wait a little while, there'll be enough juice to turn it over, so I went back in the bar and ordered another beer, while also looking for a friendly face to maybe give me a jump if I needed one. In about ten minutes a good friend of mine, Mike Potter, comes in and sits next to me. Mike was a photographer and sometimes reporter, for the VI Daily News, and he happened to live in one of the apartments down in Dorothea. I asked him if he might give me a jump if I couldn't get my car started, and he said sure, no problem, and if we couldn't start it, he'd give me a ride home; he'd just come in and wanted to have a beer and watch the end of the game. Now I could relax and we talked as the game wound down. It was over in another half-hour and we headed out. He pulled his car up next to mine, left it running with the lights on, and we popped both hoods and hooked up the jumper cables. I climbed into my driver's seat with the door open and turned the switch… Ruhrr, ruhrr, ruhrr… but quicker now. "I think it's gonna catch!" I yelled. He was fiddling with the connections. The next thing I know, I have this hard object pressed up against my ribs, slightly from behind. I turn to my left and there's this large roundish black guy with a dark ski mask and two holes cut out for the eyes pushing this gun into my ribs, "You got a wallet?" "Yeah…, yeah I do," I stutter. I look out the front window and in the headlights see Mike with his hands in the air, another lanky black guy with a ski mask pointing a gun at him from behind. "Well, hand it over," says my black guy. "Sure, sure," I say, and start fumbling for my wallet out my back pocket. ["Fumbling." Always wondered about guys "fumbling" for their wallet, but you know, it's the perfect word for the situation.] I hand it over to him, and take a quick glance out the front window to see Mike, now facing his guy and arguing with him, his hands still in the air, the two of them standing in the glare of the headlights. I look back over my shoulder at my guy, who is literally "fumbling" with my wallet, holding it over his head upside down with both hands, money and cards falling out on the ground, his gun pointing up in the air, while he's trying to straighten the ski mask eye-holes so he can see better. I say, "Hey, can I help, man? If it's just the money you want…" and as I step out of the car, he goes "Get back in the car!" and points the gun back at me. "Okay, okay… easy, man!" and I get back in the driver's seat, now watching Mike and his guy out the front windshield. Mike's been arguing, "No, no I don't have any money!" The guy's telling him he's lying, asking where's he hiding it. Mike says he's not lying, he used his debit card, but he won't hand over his wallet. He's about six to eight feet from the guy, and then he does something that shocks the shit out of me—he steps TOWARD the guy! The guy immediately takes one step back and BLAM! He shoots Mike. Oh shit! Oh shit! Oh shit! Time stopped and I remember that moment as it was being burned into my brain. I looked down at my hands on the steering wheel and thought, "Damn... now they're going to have to shoot me too," and as I looked at my hands I said to myself, "You know, even if they just shoot off the tip of my little finger, and nothing else, it's going to hurt like a motherfucker." Maybe two seconds had passed. I turned to look over my shoulder, expecting my guy to be lining up to plug me—but— he's gone! I look back out the windshield and in the halo of the headlights (now a scene of stage-drama surrealism) the two of them are standing over Mike, who's starting to squirm, lying on the cement. As they stood over him, guns drawn, I thought the worst, Oh God no, they're going to finish him off. THEN they'll *have* to come over and do me. But instead, they stepped over Mike, turned, and ran up the hill to another parking lot behind the shops.

I jumped out and ran over to Mike who was gripping his left thigh, "I've been shot! I've been shot!" he yelled. I said, "I know man, you'll be alright... I've got to get some help, I'll be right back." As I stood up I saw a black Jeep back out up the hill and peel off. Too dark to see the plate. I run into the Shipwreck and yell "Call 911! My buddy's been shot! Call an ambulance!" One of the bartenders jumps the bar, grabbing a roll of paper towels, and follows me out back, where Mike is lying still in a large pool of blood oozing thick and slow out of his left thigh, soaking his khakis. The bartender, who knows Mike, pulls off a handful of paper towels and clamps them onto the wound, which initiates a howl. We're kneeling in the light of the headlights from Mike's car, which is still running, both car hoods up and the jumper cables still attached. Now some other people are coming out of the bar and walking round back. "Let's get him into the car!" I yell, knowing how long an ambulance can take and that the hospital is less than a mile away. They open the back door, and slide him in the backseat, while I disconnect the cables, slam the hoods down and then jump into the driver's seat of Mike's car. The bartender jumps in the passenger seat, and we hot-dog it to the hospital, ignoring lights and what little traffic there was, and I pull into the emergency entrance in less than two full minutes (never did see an ambulance). We rush in and get the attention of the attendants and they take over, wheeling Mike in on a gurney between slamming swinging doors. The bartender and I, covered in blood, sit down in the waiting room. The bartender gets up and moves Mike's car to the parking lot, while I have a mild case of the shakes.

In about fifteen minutes, a black car pulls up outside and a tall thin handsome young black man in a grey sportcoat and black pants comes in and sits down with us. He's a detective. He asks the usual questions, takes my phone number, gives me his card: Det. Joel Dowdy, and then gets ready to leave, telling us that he's going back to the Shipwreck where the Case Incident team is looking over the crime scene. The bartender and I ask him if we can get a ride back with him, since we both have cars there and it's now closing on midnight (and I'm the only witness). No, he says, he can't do that, we'll have to call a cab. "But I don't have any money," I said, "...remember, the bad guys took my wallet." Sorry, he says, can't do it... regulations... (which I think is a bunch of hooey.) We're getting ready to call a cab when the hospital swinging doors open, and out comes a very nice young East Indian doctor, "would you like to see Mike?" Yeah sure, we say. He leads us into the back and inside a curtained bed where Mike is lying, his pants cut off, his leg slathered in mercurochrome, a big patch of gauze covering his wound, and a sheet wrapped around his privates (six inches further to the left and his balls would have been shot off). He's kind of smiling in a painful sort of way, and he looks weak. "Lost a lot of blood," the doctor volunteers. "Geez, Mike, I'm so sorry," I said. "Don't be," he tells me, "it wasn't your fault." "Well, yeah, it was," I said, "you wouldn't have been out back there except that you were helpin' me." "No, don't worry about it, he shot me because I wouldn't give him my money," he said, "What about you?" "They got my wallet and $200," I said, "I'd just taken it out to finish out my rent. The stuff in the wallet's the worst part... you know that." Then the doctor said, "Hey, you want to see the x-ray?" "Yeah!" we all clamored, Mike too. He pulls out the x-ray negative from a large envelope and puts it up on one of those viewing screens at the end of the bed where we can all see it. "You're very lucky, Mike," he says, pointing to the image, "it came in here, and went out there... missed both the artery and your femur; just went through the muscle. If it had hit the artery, you wouldn't have made it to the hospital; if it hit the bone, you might have lost your leg." "Jesus," I whispered. Then, Mike starts shivering, like he's real cold, then he's shuddering... soon he's shaking hard, almost like he's having a seizure... and his smile's gone, eyes rolling back. "What's happening?" I ask the doctor. "Oh, that's just shock," he says nonchalantly, "it's nothing, he'll come out of it." Then, to a nurse, "Nurse, please put a blanket on him, and when he comes around, give him a coke if he wants." As he calmed down and got his color back I patted Mike on the shoulder, told him we'd check on him, and me and the bartender walked on out and called a cab. When we got back to the Shipwreck the cops were all out back, but when I tried to tell them what happened they told me to back off, they had it all under control. Luckily, my Trooper fired right up.

The next day I picked up my Park Service pals at the airport, took them to their first site visit, and then, since it was lunchtime, decided to take them to the Shipwreck for burgers. I hadn't mentioned the goings-on of the night before, and as we drove into the parking lot I drove around back and suggested they look out their window at the pavement below. "That looks like blood!" one of the girls exclaimed on viewing the thick dried brown puddle outside. "It is," I told them, "let's go inside, and I'll tell you what happened to me last night. By the way, Welcome to St. Thomas."

A couple of weeks later, I'm going downtown, with Sean, my office mate, and we're headed to the Post Office to check our mail (I'd just about forgotten about the shooting, except when I'd see Mike hobbling around on his crutches and I always picked up his tab whenever and wherever I saw him). As we cross the street in front of the Post Office, and the cars are all backed up because of the tourists, I notice that one of the cars stuck at a standstill in traffic is a black Jeep. Now why does that get my attention? Black Jeeps are a dime a dozen on St. Thomas. This one has a thin, lanky black guy driving and a rather roundish black guy in the passenger seat. I walk up the steps at the P.O. and suddenly stop, turn around, and stare at them. Holy shit! It dawns on me: I think it's the gunmen. Am I sure? No. That's why I'm staring... trying to fit the car and the men into what I saw that night. But now it's daytime, overcast, dark clouds billowing. The driver catches me staring at them, maybe thirty feet away, on the steps. "Wha yoo lookin'a?!" he yells. I just stand there. He yells again, "Goddamn you, muhfugga! I said, wha you lookin' a?!" Now he's talking to the other guy and both of them are staring me down. He looks at me watching them from beside a large pillar at the P.O. and spits out his window. He's spitting at me! People are walking all around, but nobody notices the interaction between us. He's still stuck in traffic and can't move. "Oh shit," I think, "I need to get the license number!" So I walk down the steps toward their Jeep and they get visibly nervous that I'm approaching, when I just turn and then step behind the car, quickly memorizing the plate number. He looks in the rear view, while his buddy is turned in the passenger seat, checking me out. Then the driver goes berserk, slamming the steering wheel and dashboard, yelling and cursing. As I go back up the Post Office steps, he hangs out the window and starts screaming at me, "You muthuscunt! I gonna get you!" My buddy Sean comes out and says "What's going on?" And I tell him, "I think those guys are the ones who robbed me and Mike." "Oh, no" says Sean, rather sadly. I turned to him and said "What? What's the matter?" and he says, "Oh my God, now they've seen *me*, and they've seen me talking to you!" The traffic starts to ease up and when it does the driver sticks out his hand and shoots me a bird, then he peels out, makes a sharp right-hand turn and barrels up the hillside. Sean and I turn to go back to work as thunder rumbles and a torrent of rain starts to fall. We're a block up from the Post Office, across from the Lutheran Church, and the rain's really coming down. "Let's duck into the church," I suggest and Sean deftly jumps across puddles in the street and up the church stairs. Me, being a little older and more cautious, I wait and watch for the traffic before stepping out. As I step into the road, a black Jeep cuts me off and the two bad guys are sitting in the front seat looking out at me, windows down. I back up, maybe twenty feet away. "Come heah," they say, motioning for me. I'm standing on the sidewalk in the pouring rain, and say, "Nope, ain't gonna happen." They go "We jus wanna talk…, what's your name?" I'm thinking they can't really get a good shot off at 20-30 feet, out the car window, in the rain… but if I walk up to that window… "My name? Well, my name is… FUCK YOU!" I yell, "I ain't getting anywhere near you!" Now traffic is starting to back up behind them and people start laying on the horns. "We jus wanna talk at ya!" they yell, but I just turned and started walking in the direction opposite the one they're heading, knowing they couldn't turn around right away. When they started moving and went over the hill out of sight, I ran across the road, back up the street, and up the church stairs. Sean had seen the whole thing from inside the doorway. "Oh my God," he said, "We have to get back to the office and you need to call the police!" We went out the back door of the church, up the alley stairs, and made our way back to the office up on Government Hill. We were both soaked by the time we got there, and both of us shivering from the drenching as well as the close call. I phoned my detective, Dowdy, and told him what happened. I also gave him the license plate number. He said he'd get back to me. He calls a couple of days later and tells me the car is registered to some girl. She lent it to her boyfriend. "Yeah… so?" I ask. She didn't know where the boyfriend and the car were. Thanks, Dowdy. You'd think that would be the end of it, but there was another (even stranger) twist.

Another week goes by and I get a call. It's from the Virgin Islands Police Department. "Is this David Brewer?" "Yes, how may I help you?" "Do you know Detective Joel Dowdy?" "Why, yes, …yes, I do." "Have you talked to him lately?" "Yeah, I just talked to him last week." Now they got me going, "What's this all about?" "Well, we were just wondering why your number was on his cell phone." I explained the robbery and the shooting at the Shipwreck, then the followup with the black Jeep guys, and said "So, did you get 'em? Did you get the robbers, the guys who shot my buddy?" "We'll get back to you," they said and hang up. That afternoon the news comes over the radio (everybody in the VI listens to the radio all day long, mostly local talk radio): Two hours earlier Joel Dowdy had pulled his black cop car up outside the Bunker Hill Hotel (a small ratty little downtown flophouse), got out and went inside. He flashed his badge and asked the guy behind the desk what room a certain guy and girl were in. He walked up the stairs and knocked on the door, and when the guy opened the door a crack to see who it was, Dowdy, gun in hand, shot him in the face. Dowdy goes in the room where the girl is in the bed, naked and screaming. He grabs a pillow, pushes it over her face and pins her down, then fires three shots into her pillow-muffled screaming mouth. He walks out of the room, down the stairs, gets back into his black cop car, drives back to the Police Station, puts his gun in his desk and starts filling out routine paperwork, as if nothing had ever happened. After the phone calls, 911 and an ambulance, then a quick survey of the situation (the girl was a "former ex-girlfriend," despite Dowdy having a pregnant wife, and the guy was her new disc-jockey boyfriend, just over on the seaplane from St. Croix for the tryst), the cops go back to the Police Station and confront

Dowdy, who calmly admits that, yeah, he shot them both. He was disappointed however, to find out that the guy survived, and had just played dead after getting shot in the head. They took him into custody, and while going through his things, they came across my number in his cell phone, thus the phone call. Later, he claimed he was insane due to emotional distress and threatened suicide, but when a video showed up on the local television news with him playing basketball with the other prisoners, and handily at that, high-fives and all, that line of defense was abandoned. As they say in the islands, "He be gone now," serving twenty-five years somewhere in the States. As for Mike, he recovered completely, and I bought him a round every time I saw him, until he finally left island. I did ask him once, why he had taken that step toward the gunman, and he told me that he was a black belt in karate, and he knew that if he could just get close enough, he would have been able to disarm the guy. But that's NOT what happened now, is it? I think there's a lesson in there somewhere. Me? I was out $200, and had to buy a new wallet, and replace my driver's license, debit card, and other papers… but at least my little finger was still intact. All three little fingers.

Michigandering

It was late 2007 by now, summer was passing, and Mom told me that she wanted to go to Michigan in September to help celebrate the 60th wedding anniversary of her best friend (and my godmother); would I escort her? Sure. I took some vacation time, flew back to Orlando, and then we flew up to Detroit, rented a car, and drove up to Dryden, a sleepy little one-stoplight town in rural mid-Michigan where "Aunt Mary" and "Uncle Jerry" lived (he of the Detroit Mounted Police fame; the same one who disarmed the unruly teenage Uncle Allen—Mom's brother— from atop the baby-grand piano way-back-when), and where they held sway with their large Catholic-bred brood, including grandchildren and great-grandchildren. My brother and I had noticed that Mom had been getting a little "wiggy" recently, forgetting things and binge-buying (magazine subscriptions and Beanie Babies, e.g.), not to mention repeating herself, and we thought this would be a good pick-me-up for her to get away from the house in Orlando and see some other part of the country, a part she knew very well. Mary and Jerry owned half of a large farmstead called Valley View, shared with Mary's brother and his wife, Mom's other best friend, Marilyn. The three girls had all gone to grade school together at St. Theresa's (where Mom's uncle had been a priest) and grew up in downtown Detroit at a time when you could still ride the electric trolleys or your bicycles around safely. Valley View was bought by Mary's dad, Mr. Rheume, who had run a string of working-class restaurants in Detroit, when he decided to retire to the country in the 40s and become a gentleman farmer, raising sheep and starting a cherry orchard. He bought it from Wally Cox, the well-known 1950s TV star of "Mr. Peepers" (and who was later the voice for the cartoon character, Underdog). I remember visiting the farm in the 50s when I was a kid and seeing a dead lamb in the bottom of a gully, and the adults warning me not to fall into the hog pen "'cause they'll eat ya." It was also the first time my Dad put a rifle to my shoulder and the kickback of the recoil was so bad I thought I'd broken my shoulder. (I may have cried; what the hell, I was only five or six).

She and J.C?

Okay, I was hesitant to ever bring this up, but Ma insisted it was true, and after doing some research, maybe she was right, so here goes: Ma told me many times about the working-man's restaurants that Mr. Rheume ran throughout Detroit in the 40s and 50s. (Heck, we went to one several times with "Mudder" when I was a very little child: chrome, and glass, and green tiles; mmm, waffles!). One evening in 1950 he tells his daughter, Mary (Mom's BFF, above), that he was so busy he needed some help waiting tables during lunchtime in the restaurant, and Mary tells Mom (they're both 15-16) and asks if she wants to earn some extra money. Well,

Mom's family never really needed money, but she felt she had to help her best friend's family, and it was also a chance to get out of the house for a 15-year-old girl, not to mention earning her own unaccountable spending money. With her parent's permission, she starts working at the restaurant, and her and Mary are soon the most popular waitresses, the short teenage redhead and the blonde. Back in those days, the automotive plants were working three 24-hour shifts, even after the war, and the restaurant, within walking distance of the plant in Pontiac, was bustling constantly. There were also a large number of Southerners, both black and white, who made their way to Detroit, looking to get on at the auto plants when they could, picking up odd jobs elsewhere in the interim. So happens (according to Ma) that the restaurant hired a young lanky (what they thought was a) Tennessean to work in the kitchen as a prep cook, slicing carrots, onions, potatoes, etc. He was thin and lean and had slick black hair; couldn't have been eighteen. He asks Mom out for a cup of coffee one evening after work. She said okay, just coffee, at a nearby drugstore, and she said he was the nicest, most gentlemanly young man; talked about his life in Arkansas, and other things; lonely and homesick, just wanted someone to talk to. She said he told her his name was "Jack Cash." Later, after marrying Dad, she saw him on television one evening and told him the same story, saying that's the guy. Dad's reply? "Yeah, right."

Well, Ma told me this whole story one day out of the blue (and this was years earlier when she was still *compos mentis*), and my response was similar, but I wondered seriously why she'd make up such a thing. Then, after he became famous, I heard the story about "Jack" Cash, Johnny's older brother, who was killed in a sawmill accident when John was roughly 14, cut by the blade across his chest (took him days to die), and the profound effect this had on young "J.R.," as Johnny was known then. Still, Ma might have read this in some biography of the now-blossoming country singer. I looked in all the biographies… but no, no mention of him going north to Detroit, ever. She must have been mistaken. And why would she insist that he said his name was "Jack" Cash, not "Johnny"? Well, if you think about it, he was 18, the draft was on for the Korean War, and he could use his brother's name to circumvent that, while at the same time using the Social Security Number as well to get work. Finally, I find an obscure biography that mentions him going to Pontiac, Michigan where he got work sweeping the floor in an auto plant briefly before joining the Air Force. Well, I'll be god-damned, he *was* there! And, like I said, this was years before Ma started getting nutty; when she was still the sharpest knife in the drawer. Believe it or don't!

As I was saying before taking that swerve of deviating detours, Ma and I made it to Valley View in September of 2007 and met up with the extended families. It was a wonderful celebration of a 60-year marriage and friendship and all the "cousins" were extremely hospitable, friendly, and loving to both Ma and myself. Yeah, there was a lot of Irish drinking and dancing and carousing, even some dope-smoking, but never the first bit of trouble. (Ma would want to stay up later than me, and although she never drank, she'd drag me out to meet them at the local watering holes at all hours of the night and was always the last to leave. It was kind of embarrassing when I'm yawning and looking at my watch and Ma's still putting money in the jukebox. Remember, she's now 81.) At the end of a week of celebration we headed back to Orlando, where after a day or two there recuperating, I ended up (at Ma's insistence), a full-grown man, cataloguing Beanie Babies (hey, I said Ma was getting wiggy). Then I had to get on the plane back to St. Thomas. When I got there, we all had a surprise waiting.

SHiPO-ing Out

There was to be an unannounced meeting, quickly scheduled in the conference room downstairs, and they said the Commissioner was coming too. (Since I was somewhat of a player by then, both by opinion and influence, I think they must have been holding off for me to get back before springing the news.) The Commissioner is a high muckety-muck (the highest) in the Department of Planning and Natural Resources and sits on the Governor's cabinet. In State politics the closest thing would probably be the Secretary of State. This particular guy was an affable, tall and big white guy named Bob Matthews. He'd been a pal of the Governor in the old days, and when the Governor won election, he chose Matthews to be his designated Commissioner of DPNR. Matthews ran Public Works some twenty years earlier (with mixed success), and how well-advised he was on the current situation, I have no idea, but I can tell you that from his confirmation hearings before the (almost) all-black Legislature, he sure pulled out a lot of I-don't-knows and I'm-not-sures. Usually this would sink someone immediately (especially a white guy), but in this instance the Governor had called in his political chits and the guy was confirmed unanimously. Matthews was a nice guy, if a bit full of himself—a typical professional bureaucrat. We're all nervous while he kept us waiting, showing up a half-hour late (the usual "letting you know who's boss" ploy for the VI), and Myron wouldn't tell us what was going on, although it was obvious that he knew. The guy finally shows up and he's got a short, hot-looking (if a little chunky) black chick with him. We all sit around the conference table, the Commissioner at the head, and he cuts right to the chase: the Governor is re-arranging a number of divisions, and Myron has been designated to head the Virgin Islands Cultural Heritage Council (a glorified arts-and-pageantry put-on). This new girl, Lorraine Thomson, will be our new Director. She has a degree in History from Princeton University and has been involved in VI Government affairs for a number of years. They'd like us all to help her get settled and offer whatever assistance we can provide. Meanwhile, Myron will be getting his papers in order and cleaning out his office to move to the new Cultural Heritage headquarters up the street. Thank you for your time, and let's make this as easy a transition as we can manage. And that was it. We all go back to our desks, rather stunned.

We all loved Myron. Yes, he could be exasperating, but usually to the point of perfection, which is a good thing, getting everything just right before handing it in. Nonetheless, we all knew where his heart lay, and as such, there was probably a never more-determined guardian of the Virgin Island's cultural resources. Way back in 1984 when I worked at the Park Service at SEAC and had only been there a year or two, in the flush of being a "professional archaeologist," I remember one day when I'd gone on a rant about how we needed to spend some money and time and effort and fight the good fight to save the threatened resources at a particular park... and the Chief telling me, "Look, David, we can't save everything!" Now it was more than once I had to tell Myron the same thing. We'd become not just friends but a formidable deterrent to undisciplined development in the islands, the kind that destroys not just history, but artifacts, landscapes, architecture, and even hard-earned scientific evidence, for the sake of "progress." We finally had CZM and the rest of the Department of Planning and Natural Resources listening to alternatives of broadside billionaire land-clearing. Our work at the Lost Cemetery had shown that even the National Guard headquarters could still be built while an historic graveyard was saved. At this point in time (September 2007) we were *even then* right in the middle of the restoration of Fort Christian, the most visible and significant piece of history on St. Thomas, and everything was running smoothly and in a timely manner (an unusual situation for any public works project in the Virgin Islands, big or small). But politics had now stepped in, and we were given a new woman-boss without much of a valid reason. They say that politics makes strange bedfellows, and we came to learn that the *ad hoc* appointment of political bedfellows was not necessarily so strange after all. She was, after all, a personal friend of the Governor's.

It took Myron two weeks to get all his stuff packed, and even then they were hassling him constantly. Once he was gone Lorraine had his once-tasteful office gutted, even to the carpet, and then the historic whitewashed walls were painted over with a bright sunshine orange, and she ordered all new office furniture, computers, and a personal Blackberry. Then she had the office of her "administrative assistant" revamped as well (the cost of redecorating both of these offices being equivalent to a year of the total office's operating expenses). This girl Friday turned out to be less of an administrative assistant than a personal secretary to Lorraine: she refused to help get out the paperwork, or make travel arrangements, or even get out the timesheets without an argument. However, she was very good at sending out memos on office etiquette and work ethics, despite the fact that neither she nor Lorraine were held to the same strictures. Though we'd always maintained a schedule in the office of 8 to 5, with an hour off for lunch, they came in at 9, or maybe 10, went to lunch at 11, ate and shopped until 2 or 3, and left at 4. I tried engaging Lorraine in some of the serious issues facing us, but she really didn't want to hear it. She also didn't want any decisions to be made unless she made them, which often led to difficulties when she didn't know (or want to know) the background details. Our weekly meeting with the contractor and Public Works on the renovations at Fort Christian immediately took an ugly turn for the worse when she told me I no longer needed to attend, and then she got in a yelling match with the contractor, who ended up shutting down the project, laying off the workers, and going back to St. Croix. We were six months from completion at the time, and on-schedule. It has now been over seven years that the fort's been closed "for repairs." In the absence of any other rational explanation, I lay it at the feet of Ms. Thomson, a very smart woman, but a prima donna and a bit of a bitch. It all became very clear when I learned that she had been chosen the Carnival "Princess" some thirty years earlier, and had obviously not outgrown the title. It also helped that she and the Governor were known to have enjoyed a special relationship. Needless to say, "the Princess" and I did not get along (and oh yeah, she didn't like white people, period, neither the good, the bad, nor the ugly, and made no bones about it).

After two months I knew this was not going to end well, and having just spent the short vacation with Mom, I knew that she was going to need some assistance in the near future. So I wrote a letter to Lorraine's boss, Commissioner Matthews, stating that I was going to have to leave to take care of Ma (which was true—even Mom's doctor was sending us signals that all was not normal). Then I wrote him a separate, private, five-page letter explaining the background problems incurred by his and the Governor's choice for Director and the issues facing the State Historic Preservation Office as a result. I delivered these to his office personally, and he sat down and read them with me sitting there. I was a little nervous because I thought it would piss him off (nobody likes to hear they made bad decisions), but when he was finished, he laid it down on his desk and said, "There's nothing in here that I can disagree with." Except that he wouldn't accept my resignation. "No," he said, "I can't afford for you to leave right now. What'll it take for you to stay one more year, until Lorraine gets settled in the job?" Surprised, I said "Well, I'll have to think about it…" "Call me when you're ready." I called him in two days, said I'd thought it over, and he suggested we have dinner and talk: Hook, Line, and Sinker at 7, Thursday. I show up early and sat at the bar. It was a bad night out, dark storm clouds, lightning, and a heavy downpour starts around 6:45. I figure he's not gonna show, not in this weather, and who'd blame him? But in he comes, wearing a yellow rain slicker, and we get a table and he orders a couple of beers and several expensive finger-food appetizers. After some brief small talk, much of it regarding Lorraine, and some of it more than I wanted to hear, he asks me again, "So, what's it going to take to keep you here for one more year?" I said, "I want another $10,000 on my salary; I want another $10,000 on Sean's salary; and I want another $10,000 on Terry's salary, because we're the ones getting the job done at SHPO and keeping Lorraine afloat. Then I want to move to St. Croix… and I want you to pay the expenses… up front… not one of those deals where I pay, and then get reimbursed. And finally, I want to report to you directly, not to Lorraine. That's what I want." He let out a long whistle, "Geez, you're really negotiating now, aren't you?" "You asked me what I wanted," I told him. He goes, "Well, I'll have to run this by the Governor…" "Okay, lemme know," I told him.

A week goes by and I don't hear from him. Then he calls one day, and says "Okay, the Governor said alright. Except for one thing—you still have to report to Lorraine. She's your supervisor, and that's the law… she's still your boss. But you can call me any time to talk if you're having problems… other than that, the Governor agreed. You'll have to give me a little time though, these things take a little while. I'll get back to you." Need I say it? One year later, nothing had happened. When pressed at various intervals, the Commissioner would counter with, "We're working on it." So, as the anniversary approached, I got my ducks in order and filled out the paperwork for extended sick leave as my Mother's caretaker (this now had become a pressing issue because Ma had obviously become somewhat "Alzheimeric," as I coined it, during the interim). Once I was ready, cleaned up and backed up my files, and bought a plane ticket, I took the five-page letter I'd written the Commissioner the year before and scratched out the date, writing in a new one by hand, not changing a word. Then I sent it to him with a note that I'd be leaving St. Thomas October 1st. He called me up and said, "What can I do to get you to stay?" and I told him "not a thing." I reminded him that he hadn't done what he said he would a year earlier, and the office had gone straight to hell in the meantime while Lorraine strutted and preened, but she still didn't know what we did, why we did it, and, most galling of all, didn't care. I told him that as far as I was concerned it was all his fault; he knew better, and she didn't.

When I told Lorraine that I was leaving on October 1st, she was visibly relieved. I was nothing but a burr in her backside because I wouldn't let her get away with whatever she wanted, and though I never undermined her, or was insubordinate, I was constantly giving her instructive suggestions on what we needed to do, why we needed to do it, and how it needed to be done. As my time for departure to the States approached, and I reminded her that this was a family sick-leave situation, it dawned on her that there was still a lot of work that was going to be needed to be done, like reviewing proposals and archaeological reports, and writing responses to the various divisions for permits: all the things that I did as a matter of routine. Could I do some work from Orlando? Sure, I told her, but I wanted those hours paid for outright, and not counted against my sick leave. "Just send me the reports via FedEx and I'll review them, draft a response, and send them back with an e-mail saying how many hours I'd spent on them." Now she was very happy: the job would still get done and I wouldn't be around to bother her. This worked for approximately six months until she and her cohort started "forgetting" to credit my hours, and paychecks started getting delayed. Having done my part, I wasn't going to stand for working long-distance and then not getting paid. I finally submitted a formal resignation effective May 1st, 2009, and it was just as well; Mom was getting sketchier by the day and by now I seriously needed to concentrate on the situation at home, not the situation a thousand miles away in the islands.

Epilogue: Onward! Through the Fog...

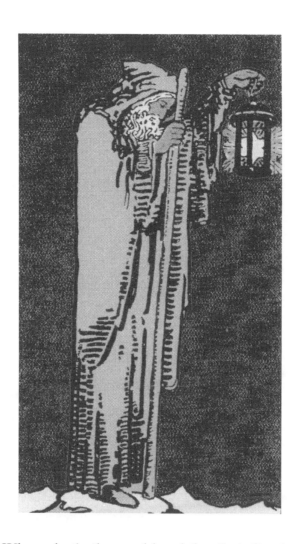

Why, what's the world and time? A fleeting
thought
In the great meditating universe,
A brief parenthesis in chaos.

Insignificance of the World
Thomas Lovell Beddoes,
minor Romantic poet
c. 1825

20.   Mom, the House, and Six Decades Done (2008 -2012)

When I had gotten back to the States on October 1st, Mom was waiting for me at the airport, and when we got to the parking deck, she handed me the keys and asked me to drive. She never drove again. The previous year, her 10-year-old bronze whale of an old-lady Cadillac had begun to sputter, and when she took it in, the bastards at the dealership, as usual, told her it was gonna cost more than a thousand dollars to fix. Paul drove down from Tallahassee, and the two of them traded in the old Cadillac for a newer fire-engine-red model, and although it was not a bad-looking car, Ma never liked it since it had a lot of new-fangled gadgetry that made her nervous. So, once I got to Orlando, she decided that from now on I could drive her wherever she needed to go, which I did, since I didn't have a car of my own yet. In no time flat, I'm one of those fifty-some-odd-year-old guys that one sees all over the country pushing the cart in the grocery store behind the eighty-some-odd-year-old lady. "No, Ma, we don't need any more toilet paper, you've got forty rolls already! I know they're buy-one-get-one-free, but that's not always the great deal it sounds like... Yes, I know we'll use them eventually... Okay, Ma, okay!" She always got me good too. For instance, I might suggest, to speed things up, "While you're looking over the cosmetics, Ma, tell you what... I'll go to the other side of the store and grab the fruit and milk..." I wouldn't be gone four or five minutes tops, maybe looking at a hand of bananas when, over the store loudspeaker: "DAVID BREWER! DAVID BREWER! PLEASE COME TO THE FRONT OF THE STORE! YOUR MOTHER'S LOOKING FOR YOU!" I'd get up to the front of the store and there'd be a coven of middle-aged overweight female cashiers in uniform standing around Mom, consoling her while she's upset and crying; then they'd look at me as if I'd clubbed her with a frozen leg of lamb before having coldly abandoned her in the ice-cream freezer for an hour. I always wondered how she moved so fast when I wasn't around, yet when I was with her she couldn't cover one aisle in fifteen minutes. (I guess I should be thankful my name wasn't Randy Bastid coming over the loudspeaker. As far as the cashiers were concerned, though, it might as well have been Rotten Bastard: "ROTTEN BASTARD! ROTTEN BASTARD! PLEASE COME TO THE FRONT OF THE STORE! YOUR MOTHER'S LOOKING FOR YOU!")

It was both funny and sad. Mom had always been inquisitive, politically astute, and a real newshound. She read voraciously, and loved a good lively conversation, and even more, she loved to play bridge, religiously. I can't count the number of times that she tried to teach me how to play that infuriating game over the decades, and even though I played all the "normal" games fairly well: poker, spades, blackjack, I could never get the grasp of bridge; it was just too complicated. Now, however, I noticed that she had pretty much quit playing, and when her friends would call to ask her to make up a foursome, she'd beg off. What got me mad was that she would use me as the excuse: "Well, I'd love to, but my son is visiting and we have plans..." I'd even offer to drive her and then pick her up at the end, which might have happened once after I got to Orlando in 2008, before she just hung it up for good. It was the personality changes that really started to get me though. Ma was always the sweetest, most giving person in the world; everyone commented on it, and I experienced it myself when she'd pull my butt out of the fire on more than several occasions. Now she's asking me to drive her to the store, to get her hair done, to go out to lunch or a movie, or to just "go for a ride to get out of the house." All of which I was glad to do; but when I started getting cabin-fever and just needed to get away on my own for an hour or so, she flat would not let me take the car! "No, that's *my* car," she'd say, and I couldn't argue, though I tried, "But Ma, I just want to go out for an hour..." "No!" she insisted, "Find another way!" One day I just picked up the keys and headed for the door, but she caught me, and we stood there in the foyer with her tightly grasping a handful of my shirt collar til I handed them back. Well, this was just baffling (I was waiting for my final payoff from the Virgin Islands, and couldn't get a car of my own yet). One Saturday, a month or so later however, they're having a garage sale in the neighborhood, and I'm driving her around, we're looking at stuff, she's buying knick-knacks, and whoa! there's an old-fashioned big-tired, broad-handle-barred, wide-seat cruising street bicycle: $45. The tire is flat, so I talk them down to $35. Deal. I tossed it in the trunk of Ma's car, got it home, filled the tires, which held, and I was back on the streets. Now I was one of the army of chubby old grey-haired guys in t-shirt, shorts, and tennis shoes, wearing the backward ball cap (so it doesn't blow off), that plagues the nation's roads and neighborhood streets nowadays. Thank God Almighty, Free at last!

Dazed In

Every day now I'd be out exploring on my new pedo-mobile, riding all the way up even onto the edge of South Orange Blossom Trail (bad idea!), and cruising the byways, looking for the nearest watering hole where I might grab a quick one while Ma was either taking a nap or watching the news. Yeah, there was the Red Lion, where you could still get a Budweiser for a buck, but again, riding along OBT was ten times riskier than off-track betting, and they didn't call it SOB Trail for nothing: bad dudes, bad girls, and bad cops. As an alternative, I tried going up to the Ramada, which was actually right around the corner from the house, easy walking distance, but the hotel Sports Bar there was often either not open, or when it was it was prohibitively expensive, catering to the captive foreign tourists at the hotel pool. I didn't need that, although I did have time enough there to get friendly with the Oriental bartender that surreptitiously sold hot electronic gizmos off of Craigslist to tattooed guys in leather jackets, who would come in and quickly pay cash, or come back later to loudly complain 'cause the shit didn't work. Otherwise, he was bored and appreciated a little intelligent conversation, so he'd slip me a free drink once in a while, but ultimately his sideline cost him his job. Then one day I'm riding along 33rd Street and I spot a red neon flashing light out the alley window of the Days Inn, four blocks from the house and right next to the county jail. I stop in and it's a nice quiet, dark, and unoccupied bar, with a beautiful, friendly, big-chested blonde bartendress. Beer $2. Perfect. Her name was Sharon. Now pushing just past forty, she had once been a fitness instructor, and the remnants of that profession still showed, although she'd now been tending bar all over Orlando for probably twenty years. Her tits were easily 38Ds but she swore they were genuine, even to the point of "I'll even let you feel one, but just for just a second." Most genuine however, was her attitude. She was bright, wide-smiled, humorous, flirty, and always pleasant; she also poured 'em stiff, and would often lose count (in your favor) when pushing beers. The Days Inn (at 33rd and I-4) was a well-known stopover for truckers, since it was not only cheap, but it also had the requisite large extra-long parking lot and turnaround space that they needed to line up, unhook, and move their tractor-trailers. And if a trucker wanted to sleep, or entertain, in the back of his sleeper cab, instead of getting a room, the management was often generous enough to oblige, especially if the hotel was already more than half-full. They'd give 'em a parking sticker and let them stay, since the boys were still going to spend a pile of money in the bar anyway. To see Sharon.

So I started going to the Days Inn regularly, every day, after 4 (when it opened). I'd tell Ma that I was going out riding my bike, which she thought was a good thing. I'd be gone less than an hour though before she'd be calling me frantically on my cell phone, "Where are you? When are you coming home?" Shit, I was lucky if I got three beers in me before I was pedaling back to the house to calm her down. Then I got an idea. As a routine, after the news, and dinner (another story), she would watch that pompous ass Bill O'Reilly (for an Irishman, a real jerk), and then we'd watch the Daily Show and Stephen Colbert's repeats from the night before, and inevitably she'd be asleep by nine. I'd turn out the lights, give her a kiss on the forehead and cover her up, then go out in the living room to read until maybe 11, before I turned in. What the hell!? She never woke up before morning, though it might be 5 or 6 o'clock when she did. One night around 9-9:30, I tucked her in, and creeping out the front door like I did when I was an errant teenager, I pedaled on down to the Days Inn. (Hey! It wasn't like I was leaving her in the car in a hot parking lot with the windows rolled up!) The place was full of truckers, bail bondsmen, fat chicks with their skinny friends, newly-released inmates from the jail, off-duty cops and whores. It was wonderful! And it was karaoke night too! I threw caution to the wind and ordered a rum and tonic. Ouch! Sharon was taking good care of me; I guess she was happy to see me out at night for once. By 11:30 I'm three sheets to the wind, signing up to sing, and I choose Meat Loaf's *Paradise by the Dashboard Light*, one of my favorites. But it's a duet... damn, I forgot. Does any girl here know the song? "I do," yells Sharon! We belt it out rather badly, but it's memorable nonetheless (I even get the running sexual baseball commentary part down without pausing), and the applause are most gratifying. Everyone else is singing slow and sappy sad country songs. Shit! It's after midnight! And just like that Cinder-fella, I realize I gotta go! Once outside though, I quickly find out that I can't get on the bike, much less pedal and balance at the same time... and then steer too! Silly stupid me, I end up walking the bike back home. Takes me forty-five minutes for a ten-minute walk, and even then I tumble over once or twice, pick it up and keep on going. I get home without incident, and I'm in bed by 1. In the morning, Ma's wondering why I'm sleeping so late... "It's 8:30! I've been up since 5:30! I need a ride to the store!" Oooohhhh, Ma...

Then I fucked up. I don't remember how it happened. Either Sharon had recommended that I bring her in, or I just opened my yap one day and suggested to Ma, "Let's go to the Days Inn." I took her in to meet Sharon, and there they went—they loved each other! At first this was a good thing: between Sharon fawning over her, as well as Sharon's girlfriends, and the random roving trucker making mock passes at her and telling stories of adventures on the road, Ma was happy, mentally engaged, and thoroughly entertained; and I could enjoy a couple (or more) stress-free beers. This went on for months. Then it started getting a little weird. Mom would now start getting her makeup together around noon. She's picking out different dresses, earrings, jewelry, etc. (I'm covertly watching her over the top of whatever book I was reading at the time.) "Aren't you going to take a shower and get dressed?" she'd ask me. "No, Mom," I'd say, "I'm not taking a shower and getting dressed to go to the Days Inn. I just went for a swim in the pool... Okay, okay, I'll put on another shirt," and it didn't matter what I put on, it was always, "Oh, no, not THAT one!" "Dammit, Ma! It's fine!" Finally, she would spend the last half-hour doing her nails. She's done and it's 3:00. She'd sit in the kitchen, staring at the clock. Now it starts approaching 4 o'clock, and she's getting her purse and hands me the car keys. And off we'd go.

Sometimes Sharon would be ten or fifteen minutes late for her own reasons, and when she was, she'd find us sitting in the hotel lobby waiting when she opened the bar's inside doors, me rolling my eyes and apologizing. I'd put some Frank Sinatra or Tony Bennett on the jukebox while Sharon set up the bar and got Ma a coke or coffee and me a beer. Then, Ma started bringing in "presents" for Sharon: earrings, costume jewelry, pendants, scarves... This too, was not a bad thing, as Sharon loved the stuff and treated each, no matter how cheap or trivial, as if it were some holy relic. Sharon had a couple of dogs, a Toto-like terrier, and a tiny teacup Chihuahua, and when she found out how much Mom liked dogs, she started bringing them into the bar, and that kept Ma going for awhile. Then, to reciprocate, Mom started bringing in pictures of our family dogs: portrait photos of pets that had been dead for over twenty years. One day, however, both Sharon and her good friend Jan took me aside and told me that Ma had tried to give each of them some money: not much, maybe 50 bucks each, but they both refused; still, they wanted me to know about it. Luckily, it was right around this time that Ma started giving out on the Days Inn. She was losing patience, hearing, and vitality. By that I mean, that she could only take about an hour, or even less, before she wanted to go home; she didn't always get what people were saying to her (like the toothless, drunk, and mumbling redneck truck drivers, or worse, someone with a Spanish accent, especially when the music was playing), and she was just tired all the time.

High Fine Ants

During the summer of 2009 I finally received my payoff from the Virgin Islands, and after giving Mom a thousand, helping Amy buy a van, and giving the boys a couple hundred each, I noticed a Ford F-150 pickup in a neighbor's carport with a small handwritten "For Sale" sign on it. No one else would have even noticed it, the sign was so small. But the truck was just what I was looking for: relatively new (2003) and with a camper on the back. They wanted $6500 for it, but after some dickering ("I'll pay you cash."), I got them to come down to $5500. Now I was really flying first class, and Ma couldn't tell me when or where I could go. (She got mad though when I brought it home and claimed it blocked her view of the street when I parked it in the driveway, "Can't you park it somewhere else?" It just so happens that you can't see out of the house down the street. So I parked it on the lawn alongside the house in the back yard.) But I also needed a project just to fill my days, and since I couldn't touch anything inside the house without Ma getting upset, I decided to take on the job of painting the outside of the house. She liked this idea, since it needed it anyway, and it gave me something to do, and I also got freedom rides to Home Depot for a half an hour or so. We picked out a nice bright tangerine/peach orange, and I started on the cinder block back patio first, generally working mornings until noon. When I turned the corner however, and got in the bright sunlight, I discovered that there was going to be a lot of scraping and wood repairs to get done first. Ma would come out every half-hour, look up at me standing on the ladder and beg me to come down and stop working "It's too hot!" Sometimes it even worked. But I generally hunkered down and busted nut, sweating gallons (summertime sun be damned), listening to the radio, still glad to have a diversion, and generally ended up in the pool cooling off and rehydrating by twelve. By August it was done.

Ma's 84th birthday was approaching and we made plans to go to Tallahassee to celebrate. I was looking forward to it so I could get a break and let someone else entertain Ma, since it had by now become a constant drain. Earlier that summer, Ma finally broke down and asked me to help her with her finances. Up until now she had guardedly protected any idea of how much she had, how much she spent, or how she spent it. My brother Paul and I had pretty much assumed that she was well-off, between her Social Security, and Dad's pension from Martin Marietta, and the golden parachute of some 100 grand they had given him when he retired, which was safely socked away in a couple of interest-bearing IRAs (although he had sold the thousands of free stock options they had given him over the years for something like $12 a share; today Lockheed Martin sits above $150). Still, there were some disturbing trends. The house was stacked with unopened bags and boxes from designer stores, there were drawers full of old Lotto tickets, and the bastards at the Cadillac dealership never lost an opportunity to hit her for a grand or two no matter how minor the repairs. Then there was that incident with her trying to give Sharon and her friend some money (how far afield had that gone? She always made me roll down the window and give the pitiful sign-carrying nomads on the side of the road a 5-dollar bill!).

I might mention here that Mom had a gun collection, garnered between Dad's guns and some she had bought for sentimental reasons ("Your Daddy carried one of these same M-1 carbines all through the war... did I ever tell you how they charged him $45 for the one he lost when he was wounded?"). Some more were given to her by her bridge-playing buddies when either their husbands died, or some widower's sister-in-law was cleaning out his house before sending him to "The Home." Sweet Holy Moses! She had several handguns, two M-1's, Dad's 1894 Winchester, three shotguns (one of which was an old Mexican silver-plated double-barreled antique that was probably carried by one of Pancho Villa's guerillas), and a couple of what-we-call 'varmint guns.' And a gun collection makes sense… even for a little old lady. But then there was the hoard of Beanie Babies. Not 50… not 100… not 500… but 1500! THAT was worrisome. "They're a good investment!" "No, Mom, they weren't a good investment when they first started selling 'em and they're not worth a plug nickel now!" "They're still in their original packages!" "Goddammit, Ma! Look! Look here on E-bay… Look! 25 cents! And that's for a rare one!" "I've got some rare ones… someday they're going to be worth a lot of money!" "Maybe in a hundred years, Ma… and then only maybe. Jesus Christ! At $6 a pop, you've spent 9,000 dollars on these damn things… You coulda sent the grandkids to college!" "I don't want to talk about it." "Fine!"

Now I don't want to talk about it either. (I'll tell you what I did with them later.) Getting back to her finances… it finally occurred that she couldn't balance her checkbook, couldn't add and subtract, or write the checks to pay her bills, much less understand what was really going on… She asked me to help her. Sure, I said, but there was a problem. What was the problem? "I need to know how much you've got, what your income is, where you keep your money, what accounts…" "Oh," she said, "you need to know all that?" "Yes, Mom, I need to know all that… Let's start with your income." Between her Social Security and Dad's pension from Martin, she couldn't even meet her bills. Why? She had a pile of magazine subscriptions that she never read: Vogue, Cosmopolitan, The New Yorker, Smithsonian, Redbook, Vanity Fair, etc., and the godforsaken bloodsucking middlemen who sold her the non-discounted subscriptions over the phone were asking for payment on magazines she wouldn't receive for another two years! Those were all cancelled, and I wrote a nasty letter to each and every one of them in the most threatening quasi-legal terms I could muster, and what would happen to them if they didn't quit dunning her. Then there were the car payments. The Cadillac dealership had given her squat for the trade-in on her old car (she would have gotten off better by donating it to Goodwill, or better still, having it stolen, or even—god forbid—totaling it), and sure as hell, the new one had been financed through GMAC, General Motors Acceptance Corporation, at the height of their gouge-ability, who charged her an arm and a leg in interest (this was one of the infamous "bailout companies" during, well, here we were, 2007-2008. It now operates under the guise of Ally Financial). Well, she had to make those payments, for now. But most egregious, and frightening, was the fact that she had run up a large debt on 3 credit cards and was just making the interest payments of $600 a month! Barely.

How had she continued to spend money? She had been dipping into her IRAs. I was, to say the least, shocked and dismayed (as I told my brother, "There went the inheritance!" even though neither of us had really been counting on it—but we HAD counted on her being able to live the rest of her life on it). It was an ugly situation. It took me a week but I talked her into taking the rest of the money out of one IRA and paying off two of the credit cards. That at least got her back to where her income would hold up. But that third and final credit card, Bank of America, the worst, was up to something like $23,000, and when it hit $25K, according to the fine print, they would shut her down and demand full payment (and/or put a lien on the house). In the meantime they were hitting her for $345 a month, just in interest! What to do? I went to Ma's bank and picked out a friendly-looking loan officer. I told him the problem and he suggested a home equity loan: "Does she own the house?" Sure she does. "Then take out a loan for say,

25K, pay off the 18% credit card balance, and pay us back at 3-4%. Should drop the payments to $85 or less. She can do it with a signature. Tell me to go ahead and I'll draw up the papers." "Draw up the papers." Then it took another ten days to convince her it was a good deal. Finally I got her to go into the bank, and damn if she didn't balk at the last minute. It took both of us, the loan officer and myself, over an hour of tag-team wrestling to get her to calm down, understand what was happening, why it was a good thing, and sign the papers. Easy as pulling teeth. Out of a horse. A healthy wild horse. With pliers. In the end though, I later discovered there was a catch. (Isn't there always a catch?) Meanwhile, I'm writing the checks for the bills, and she's signing them ("What's this one for?" "That one is your utility bill, Mom." "Well, don't send that one out right away." "Why not?" "I don't like them and I want them to have to wait until the last minute." "Okay, Ma… yeah, that'll teach 'em".)

We go to Tallahassee for her birthday, and there were a lot of histrionics. After we'd been there only a little over an hour, she throws a hissy fit and wanted to go home. "Well, I'm not driving you back, Ma, we just drove five hours getting here." To her grandson: "Dennis, will you please drive me back to Orlando? I'll give you a hundred dollars." "Of course, Grandma, if you really want to go…" Thank God for Amy, who talked her down, and soon she forgot why she wanted to go. Paul took her to a movie the next day, so I got a three-hour break before they got back for the "party." Lots of pictures (I think they all sensed this might be the last one). Sad to say, the very next day, we were on our way… back… to Orlando. In three days, ten hours of which we were side-by-side in the car, me listening to her re-telling old family stories, I got three hours alone.

Losing Wait

As you can see, I was starting to lose it as well. The weather started getting cooler, and I'd finished the outside work for awhile, so we were cooped up together a lot, and if I left the house to go anywhere, I'd be getting a call in fifteen minutes wondering where I was and when I was coming home. Then started the food issue. We'd go shopping and buy all kinds of food; then she'd look in the refrigerator, just staring, and say, "I'm starving!" "Okay, Ma, what would you like, I'll fix anything… how's about some bacon and eggs?" "That would be nice." I'd cook the bacon and eggs, and she'd take one bite (not two… **one!**) of the eggs, eat one strip of bacon, and say, "I'm not hungry, here, you eat this." "No, Ma, I made enough for myself, you eat it… you said you were starving." "I don't want it," and she would throw it out. Well, that made me mad. I tried every trick in the book to get her to eat. She loved bacon, and by now we'd discovered pre-cooked bacon (Aha! Take THAT, you Bare Naked Ladies!), and thank God, 'cause I was getting sick and tired of frying it up. So I would make her most-requested favorite: bacon-lettuce-and-tomato sandwiches, half a sandwich at a time, of which she would take one bite, pull out the two half-slices of bacon, eat them, and throw out the rest (later in the day though, she'd pull out a half a loaf of fresh deli bread to feed the ducks out in the back yard). Sometimes I could get her to eat a cupful of milk and cereal in a bowl (Kellogg's Frosted Flakes), but now, even half of that was going in the garbage (or out to the ducks). It was exasperating. She was still drinking her black coffee (half-cup, steaming hot, no sugar, no cream), and smoking her goddamn cigarettes… which became a contentious issue between us, because, even though I'm very tolerant of smokers (not having really picked up the habit myself), she was buying three packs a day, and smoking two, with the third ending up as a series of long ash-tails, filling ashtrays and/or dropping to the floor (carpet or no). Funny… she never smoked in her car, never smoked at Amy's house in Tallahassee, never smoked in front of her bridge player friends, and never missed it; but when she got in the house, she lit right up and had one going from morning til night. Habit.

When I'd take Ma to the doctor, I'd go in with her, but other than him checking her respiration, pulse, and blood pressure, he'd just ask her a few questions. Luckily, I was there to answer, because, according to her, she was fine, was eating well, wasn't tired, had cut back on her smoking, etc. I'd make it a point to stay back when she went up front to settle the fee, and tell the doctor what was really going on. He'd just shrug and say he couldn't do anything unless she complained. I'm pretty sure that, even with Medicare, it was still $80 a pop, once a month, for a ten-minute visit. Doctors! If I could have gotten her on an apple-a-day regimen, just to keep the leech away, I would have preferred that. As it happened, she decided on her own that she wasn't going back to see him... ever. Nice guy... just a cold fish.

Her health was deteriorating; there was no doubt about it. Besides the mental confusion and repetitiveness, she was getting smaller. I could see it. And she started complaining about back pains. At first it was that she must have slept wrong; then she thought she had lifted something too heavy (she did take a tumble in the driveway one morning trying to bring the large empty rolling trash can back from the curb, but luckily didn't break anything). So I started applying Mentholatum ointment to her lower back when she requested, and this became not just a daily routine, but sometimes hourly. She was now living on black coffee, cigarettes, and maybe three strips of bacon a day. I started buying chocolate milk, always one of her favorites (even dosing it on the sly with some of that old-people nutritive, Ensure), but she quickly lost her taste for it. Then we came upon Thanksgiving, and I started to give thanks. What's the one thing that comes out at Thanksgiving and is available throughout the holiday season (and it ain't turkeys), that you don't see the rest of the year? Egg-nog! And Ma loved egg-nog. So, now, besides the three slices of bacon, she at least had 2 or 3 cups of egg-nog a day, full of nutrients, milk fat, calories, and somewhere in there, I imagine, eggs. She responded immediately. Or so I thought. In retrospect, it probably just postponed the inevitable by several weeks.

Merry Ex-Ma's

We made plans to go out for Thanksgiving dinner. I even made reservations at her favorite restaurant, Mimi's Café. When the day arrived, she decided that she wasn't up to it, could we go tomorrow? Well, tomorrow she didn't feel like it either. We never did go out for dinner. The back pains were getting worse. I'd make a doctor's appointment, and when I was outside doing something, she'd call up and cancel it. I'd make another one, and she'd refuse to go. The doctor's office said they couldn't keep doing this. I told them to make another appointment (now we're in December). Ma says she's not going, and I said, "Fine, I'll go," and I went. Five minutes. I told him about her lack of appetite, the back pains, the personality changes, the memory loss. Sorry, nothing he could do unless she came in. However... he did give me the number for a Medicare home-visit service, where an LPN would come, check on Ma, and then report back to him. Well, that was something anyway. But I still got pissed that they charged *me* $80 for the visit: five minutes. I called the number he gave me and they scheduled an appointment at the house for two days hence. Sure enough, in two days, the LPN arrived, a young handsome Spanish woman, who was very sweet, caring, patient, and thorough. She even got Mom to give some blood samples, which I found surprising, especially since it was kind of tricky with Ma's puny little veins rolling around under her limp and pallid skin. The LPN scheduled another appointment for a week later. Now we're facing Christmas, and it was clear that there was not going to be any travelling to Tallahassee. And Mom didn't want any company coming down either. Okay. I did what I could by stringing some lights and putting a wreath on the door. That was about it. When the LPN showed up a week later, maybe a week before Xmas, she was much more serious in her demeanor. All she did was check Ma's pulse, blood pressure,

463

and respiration, and give her some small pills for "anxiety" and to help her sleep. As I walked her out to her car, she told me that she had gotten the blood samples analyzed and talked to Mom's doctor. They both agreed that it wasn't good: Ma was slowing down considerably. No, no real prognosis, these things just happen. It was time to call hospice. Hospice!? Aww, no… did that mean what I thought it meant? Yes, she said. She'd call them for us, and she assured me that this didn't necessarily mean something was imminent, but they would be able to handle Ma's situation better than she could. I went back in, popped one of Ma's "anxiety" pills for myself, and when she went in her room to watch television, I called my brother, Paul, and told him what the LPN had said. He'd be down right after Christmas.

That Yule day passed like any other day of the week. Paul arrived the next day, Saturday, the 26th, and he understood the situation immediately. Ma was glad to see him and that cheered her a bit, but I think he was a little surprised to see how both ill and ill-tempered she had gotten, and she started off right away by telling him what a mean bastard I'd been to her, which obviously had not been the case. Admittedly, the worst thing that ever happened was a week before he arrived, on a day when she had gotten particularly troublesome, I said to her "Jeez, Ma, y'know, you're getting to be a real pain in the ass" and she made it a point to have me write it down word-for-word on one of her 3x5 index cards so she wouldn't forget—I know, I know, I'll pay for that one in Purgatory for a century or two (later). But we all got along as best we could, and the hospice team came by and made their preliminary assessment. Again, not good, but they were the nicest people one could imagine and they were wonderful about cleaning her up, making her comfortable, and providing Paul and I with lots of "stuff": waterless shampoo, salves, sheet liners, pads, etc., not to mention advice ("Don't worry about the temperament; that's normal." "She'll be sleeping more." "Relax, this is natural." "Couple a weeks."). And they were right about every call. As far as food, Paul and I fell back on the old standby, Campbell's Chicken Noodle Soup, and stocked a half-a-dozen cans, which we heated up a half a can at a time; and still a little eggnog on the side… until New Years, when it disappeared from the store shelves. But by then, she was down for the count.

Last Rites

Ma started sleeping more and more. Where she would normally have been up at 5 or 6, coffee brewing, and already finished reading the paper, now she was sleeping 12 hours until 8 or 9, and barely ever getting up, napping during the day, and asleep again for the night by 8 or 9 in the evening. We'd go in and watch television with her all hours of the day, taking turns talking with her and getting a little soup. Now she was having trouble getting up to go to the bathroom, and would call out if no one was in her room, and Paul and I were lifting her up and setting her down on the toilet, wiping her, etc. Her urine was tea-bag brown, and the hospice said this was a sign of failing kidneys. Thank God Paul was there, or I'd have been unable to cope and then I too would have gone crazy. The hospice folks dropped in every other day now and said to call them if anything happened. "Like what?" we'd ask, still sort of in denial. "You'll know," they said, and left a vial of morphine, "here, this will help her sleep. Just a half a teaspoon." One day out of the blue Sharon and Jan showed up from the Days Inn, and even though Ma was laying down on her side, just breathing heavily, she perked up ever so slightly to see them, promising to get down to the bar when she could. They cried as they left. Then my son Sam showed up; he'd been in town on a work assignment, and came over when we told him it would probably be the last time he saw his Grandma. He came, sat on her bed and, holding her hand, talked to her for a half-hour. It was heartbreaking. Afterwards, I tried to buck up and explain to him that this was all natural, a part of the "circle of life," blah-blah-blah, but he cried as he left too. Then I cried. The crazy religious lady from across the street, a rabid Greek Orthodox, who I usually humored in her fanatic fundamentalism, came over and asked if she could "pray over" Ma; I got pissed off and told her no, that God could hear her prayers just fine over at her own house, thanks anyway. But it did remind Paul and I that we probably had a filial duty to Mom to get a priest in there, pronto. We called St. James and they said they'd have somebody out there the next day. A short wiry young and dark-haired Spanish priest showed up and carried out the last rites, and though Mom was barely conscious when he left, she whispered "You couldn't find an Irish one?" The next day, Sunday, the 17th of January, we'd been up all night with Ma and Paul slept late. I checked on Ma that morning and she was lying on her side, out cold, breathing shallow and rapid. Around 10 or 11 I went into the kitchen to prepare an eyedropper full of the morphine to give Ma if and when she woke up and accidentally knocked it over, spilling some. I slurped it up just for the hell of it. Paul got up and suddenly I felt very sleepy. I laid myself down on the couch to take a nap (which I never do). After a long set of fever dreams, at 3 that afternoon, Paul woke me up, and said, "I think it's over." We went into her bedroom and I checked her pulse, which was silent. She looked peacefully asleep. We said an Our Father and a Hail Mary, then called the hospice and waited, sitting with her for a half-hour or so.

The hospice attendant was, as usual, extremely kind and efficient. She was going to wash and prepare Ma for the funeral home. I asked her if she wanted me to help, but she said only if I wanted to (I didn't), otherwise, she would take care of it, "See if you can find something for her to wear... something comfortable." Paul and I looked around and found one of those snuggle-blanket things they sell on TV that one of the grandkids had sent her for Christmas, pink, her favorite color. "Perfect!" the girl said. When she was done, there was some paperwork, and we thanked her profusely—they really had been exceptionally sensitive and supportive. We called the funeral home and they said they'd send someone right out. One last short vigil, and when they came, they wheeled her out. Alone now, after a few minutes Paul and I drove up to the Days Inn and had a stiff one (or two) with Sharon, toasting "the best Mom there ever was." Remembering something Dad once said when his Mom finally passed, I told Paul, "Well, now we can get free tickets to the Orphan's Ball!"

The next couple of days was nothing but dealing with the funeral home, which meant picking out a casket, putting up a deposit (Paul covered it), bringing clothes, writing the obit, notifying relatives, making arrangements with the church and the cemetery, and digging out what important papers we could find to get a handle on things. Once we settled on a day for the viewing and next-day burial and wake, we let our friends know. This necessitated some cleaning up around the house, which we did as best as we could. Notice came that relatives from Michigan were on their way down, and I made reservations at both the Ramada Inn and the Days Inn for the overflow. Finally, we went downtown and shook hands with the priest at St. James, making sure we got an Irish one this time and not another Spaniard. In anticipation of the poorer kin who'd end up sleeping at the house, Paul and I flipped the mattress over on Ma's bed and I put clean sheets on everything. The friends began to arrive; the relatives rolled into town; and the funeral home called me and Paul to come down and make sure everything was copacetic. I'd also made a tape of Irish tunes for the parlor to play that evening, and I handed them to the director when we came in the door. He led us into the viewing room and as we stepped in, the casket being all the way at the other end of the open hall, we both stopped and looked at each other. Even from this end of the room we could see something wasn't right. We had given them a green dress for Mom. There, out of the open casket, stood a couple of large padded green breasts, that, if there were any truth to the matter, could not have belonged to Mom, who was never more than (what does one say?) a handful, a pair of tomatoes, just short of 'ample,' a childhood concept of cream-filled cupcakes... (I'm doing my best to be circumspect here!). Now, we were looking at a couple of Mamie van Dorens sticking out of the coffin, and pointy ones at that! When we walked on up, slowly, and looked in, there was an expression plastered on Ma's face that (even though her eyes were closed) sort of said "Look at this, will ya!?" The funeral guy saw our slight discomfort and asked, "Is everything alright?" We'd already been through the wringer by now and decided right then and there that Ma probably would have let the obvious humor of it ride. Did it really matter now, anyway? "Yeah, it's fine," we said. "One thing," Paul uttered, and pulled out a pair of her old glasses and put them on her. Ma had had that Lasix surgery a year or two earlier and as a result she saw so well that she had quit wearing her glasses, but we had always seen her wearing them for our entire lifetime, so it seemed the right thing to do. On the way home, we stopped at Goodwill to pick up some decent dead-man's clothes for ourselves to wear to the funeral the next day.

The funeral was nice and subdued, held in the chapel at St. James, rather than the larger cathedral section, and it was better there, being more personal and intimate with friends and family. Surprising to me, there was a sizable contingent of black ladies occupying a couple of pews, young and old, waiting when we got there. I didn't recognize them, but after the service I went up to thank them for coming and found out they were neighbors and friends who had known Mom for years, had seen the announcement in the paper, and felt obligated to come and pay their respects. On leaving the church, Paul had requested the organist play "When the Saints Go Marching In," but she obviously didn't want to do it, not thinking it appropriate, and tried to beg off, offering something more sedate, but he insisted. She compromised by playing the most somber version I'd ever heard; hell, the slow-stepping funeral bands in New Orleans would have been more cheerful. Besides my brother and myself, I quickly conscripted Dennis LeFils, Ed Quinby, Bruce Dacey, Bob Nolin, and my two younger sons, Sam and Dennis, as pallbearers. We drove to the cemetery, where the priest was perfunctorily professional, which we were glad of, and there was a slight small diversion when it was discovered that the coffin was a little too large for the hole, but that was quickly resolved by the gravediggers who sat under a tree nearby. Finally wedged in next to Dad's vault, we tossed in a few handfuls of dirt and a number of roses, and left the men to finish their work. It was a beautiful sunlit and warm January day. Amy went on ahead to meet people at the house, while I went and got the caterings and Paul stopped at the liquor store to load up on refreshments. When we got back to the house, the wake began with toasts to Ma, and I put on a tape of Irish drinking songs that she always liked. There was lots of reminiscing and story-telling and flirting with the single girls from Michigan, and it all ended peaceably, if a bit raucous with my son Dennis going into the pool fully clothed. Mom would have enjoyed it. When they left, a day or two later Paul had to go back to work in Tallahassee, Amy too, and one morning I woke up in the house alone, wondering "What next?"

Beanie Bay-bye

I didn't have to wonder long. Now the real work was facing me. Paul and I figured we'd sell the house; but that meant it had to be cleaned out, first, and cleaned up, second. Well, hell, Mom and Dad had been accumulating crap for over sixty years now ("It's not crap!" Ma would admonish me repeatedly), everything from the aforementioned guns, antiques, furniture, clothes, magazines, knick-knacks, etc., to the dreaded Beanie Babies. Those fuckers were going to be the first thing to go. (I had once threatened Ma that I was going to use them to fill her grave, but this was an empty threat, since it would still have left a mound twenty feet high that the city-maintained cemetery would not have tolerated.) I was thinking over what I could do with them (forget E-bay) and had a flash of brilliance. I called Arnold Palmer's Children's Hospital here in Orlando and asked them if they'd be interested. "Oh yes!" they said, "How many do you have?" When I told them, they got pretty quiet. "Tell you what," I said, "how about I bring over a couple of boxes, there's thirty in a box, and when you run out you call me and I'll bring you some more." "That would be great." Five boxes went into the truck and I was there in twenty minutes. That's 150, or 10%, gone. Needless to say, over the next 6 or 7 months I made another 8 trips or so (slipping in an extra box once in awhile), and they were always glad to see me. Their method of distribution was to hand one out to each kid who got discharged (since, sadly, more than a few kids never made it out the door), and in this manner I dispatched all 1500 of the hideous little pieces of shit. At one point the girl in charge of receiving them asked me if I'd accept a tax write-off for them. Sure I would. We filled out the paperwork, but when it asked for the value of each I was stumped, "I don't know, probably fifty cents" I said. "Well, they're brand new, and still in their bags... the price tag says $6. So you can put that down." Really? Yeah, really. It was only on *the very last boxload* that the young girl came out with her little red hand-truck and while we were unloading them, asked me, "Did anyone in your house ever smoke? One of the nurses said she thought she smelled smoke on the plastic bags... We wouldn't want any of the children, who are already sick..." "What!? Smoke? Smoke? No, no one in our house ever smoked... maybe it's from being in the back of the truck... it'll pick up some of the exhaust back there sometimes if the hatch isn't latched tight... Bye, thanks..."

To get rid of the other stuff, there were garage sales, put on throughout the neighborhood by the Catalina Homeowners Association, and often Paul would come down to help. But these things only yielded $75 or $80 at the end of a long day of dickering, just enough for us to go out for dinner and drinks, and the cleaning of the items, price-marking, and arranging of the stuff was more of a hassle than the $80 profit was worth. Plus, at the end of it, it looked like nothing had left the house! We divvied up the guns, and it was decided that since I was staying in the house and had to both maintain it and fix it up, I could sell the rest of the crap and live off it, while Paul could take anything that he or his family fancied. So, when I was alone, I became somewhat of an E-bay expert by photographing items, writing up descriptions, taking orders and mailing the stuff out. For the most part they were things like figurines, fine Italian ceramic ones known by the artist's name as Lladros. These were embodiments of cute peasant children playing with pigs and sheep and other farm animals when they weren't holding hands and fawning over each other. Someone had once convinced Mom that these, too, were a good investment (since once they were produced, numbered, and sold, the original mold was supposedly destroyed before a new design was made, thus they were limited editions), but it turned out that you'd be lucky to sell them for 50% of what she had paid for them 20 years earlier. There were dozens of them, which I sold one at a time, and they had to be packed with extra care because they were so fragile (the packing and shipping usually ate up half the profit). Unlike the Beanie Babies, at least there was still a minor market for these by some of the other rabid Lladro "collectors" in the world, other little old ladies convinced of their extrinsic investment value.

A Fistful of Dollars

Then there was the matter of the silver dollars. Mom had collected silver dollars since we were kids, adding to a base collection which was all she had inherited from her own Mother back in 1961. Her oldest brother, the psychologically-damaged evil Uncle Donald—the Japanese-interpreting former seminarian of World War II—had not shown up at his mother's funeral in Detroit. Everyone wondered why. When they got back from the large Catholic funeral Mass at St. Theresa's and then the burial at the cemetery, they found the front door to the family house swinging open. Inside, the place had been gutted, generally empty except for a few items laying about. Donald had backed up a moving van and ransacked the place while everybody was at the funeral, depriving both his brother Allen and Mom from getting any of their expected inheritance. He not only took the baby grand piano that had been promised to Mom (who knows, if she had gotten it, maybe I coulda been another Billy Joel "Pianoman"). He took all the costliest antiques, furniture and fixtures, even a gorgeous and expensive old Grandfather clock. Finally, he rolled up the oriental rugs, leaving nothing but the dust bunnies along the walls of the hardwood floors. Ma was so devastated that Paul and I used to plot how to find Uncle Donald and kill him when we were kids. He wasn't located for another ten years (Ma even put a private detective out there looking for him), somewhere out West, by which time he had liquidated everything and was once again broke. The silver dollars were saved because they'd been stashed in a safe deposit box to which only the family lawyer had access, and were subsequently divided between Mom and Allen. The only other items Ma ever got from the estate were two small metal statues of the sword-wielding Don Juan, the Spanish libertine, and Don Diego (aka "Zorro"), the Los Angeles liberator, and a beautiful Nativity set of hand-painted Italian ceramics (which Donald obviously had no interest in). So Ma took the 150 or so silver dollars she got from her Mom and added to them throughout the 1960s and 70s, never turning down an opportunity to increase the growing hoard. She was like Dillinger when she'd accost banks, even loudly berating managers who tried to hold out, and I can't tell you how many times she embarrassed my whole family when she'd break out in tears after spotting one in a cashier's drawer at the grocery store and the recalcitrant clerk refused to hand it over for a paper bill. Well, once Paul left and I'd gotten rid of the Beanie Babies, one day I was cleaning out "the spare bedroom," which had been used as an in-house storage shed for over fifty years, and picked up a buried piece of luggage, or rather *tried* to pick it up, but it wouldn't budge. I'd stumbled on the treasure! Dragging it out into the living room I pulled it all out and counted them, something close to 600 (598-99). Then I put them in stacks by date, knowing that the oldest would be worth the most. Then I got on the Internet. After two days of intensive study in "Walking Liberty" versus "Sitting Liberty" versus Morgans and Eisenhowers, setting them out by mint marks, dates, and condition, I slowly came to realize that their value lay just in the silver content, and that true collectors only paid more for a very, very few oddballs, none of which were in our collection (none!). (I still get an earful from people who have maybe three or four silver dollars, and a couple of silver fifty-cent pieces or dimes, who tell me that *they're really worth a lot more than the weight of the silver*, but they don't listen. Hey, look it up yourself!). The going rate at this time was something like $22-$25 an ounce, which each coin weighed by definition. The best thing to do was mix them back up and divide them in half. I called Paul and told him the news. We had already divided the gold coins, a few Canadians and Krugerrands that we had found mixed in with the important papers. The silver however was a different kettle of fish, so to speak (silverfish!). I boxed up Paul's 300 to carry up to Tallahassee, and put mine in a little plastic ice cooler. He, being the industrious future-planning ant, has decided to continue the hoarding for the coming post-apocalyptic Winter (when he will trade them each for loaves of bread or bullets), whereas I, the wastrel grasshopper, began to sell mine, and did so for over a year, getting up to $35 apiece for them on E-bay from other ant-brained hoarders all over the country. I used the dough to live on, and pay for tools, repairs, and paint for the house, and, oh yeah, drink beer (while I fiddled around).

Go Caddy

Mom had been gone for months now and her little red Cadillac is still in the driveway and GMAC is still asking for $385 a month in payments. Now I won't drive it, and I hate the damn thing too, just like Ma did, and unlike the payments to the bank, where the house is collateral, well here, the car itself is the collateral, and as far as I could tell, this was Ma's personal loan, so I call GMAC, explain the situation, and tell them we don't want the car. They surprise me with the following: No problem, this happens all the time (old people dying and their Caddy's not yet paid for). "We'll come and pick up the car. Not only that, we'll take the car, clean it up, and re-sell it out of the dealership; if the car sells for more than what is owed on it (and that appears to be the case here), we will send you a check for the difference. You and your brother are likely to be reimbursed $2-3,000." Woo! Woo! I tell them to "come and get it." The next day a small ride-on tow truck shows up, I fill out some paperwork, hand them the keys, shake hands and it's gone. Nothing to do now but wait for the check, which, of course, doesn't come. What does come is a nasty letter from GMAC saying they want $2500 for wear-and-tear on the car, immediately, or they're going to sue the estate. I call GMAC Customer Service, and get a crusty old geezer in the Collections department, at first thinking "oh shit, here we go," but I am once again surprised. After listening to my tale of woe: Mom dying, the car payments, them taking the car, and the promise of a check, the guy goes "those bastards!" (Whoa!? Hey, aren't all these phone calls "recorded for some silly purpose or another"?) He doesn't care. He's getting ready to retire and he's sick and tired of these S.O.B.'s making promises and lying and just screwing people around—he's had it, and he's not putting up with it any more. He'll handle it. He took all my information, gave me his personal desk phone number, and said expect a letter within a week. And sure enough, within a week, I got a nice letter from GMAC, even with condolences for the passing of prized customer Flora T. Brewer. The letter also said that no more payments were due to GMAC and they apologized for any misunderstanding. Well, well, well, I figure… *we have met the enemy and he is ours!* Only weeks later, when I was driving by the Cadillac dealership and looked out at all the beautiful used cars for sale did it suddenly occur to me that, when the car was re-sold, probably $1000 of our sale reimbursement check was likely dropped into the old curmudgeon's retirement account for the mere cost of a first-class stamped letter, and that GMAC surely added the other $1500 to their profits that year (not counting the 3-year's interest from the car payments that Ma had already made), and THEY GOT THE CAR, so they could go and do it all over again. DOH!

The Navajocean

One afternoon, I was having a cold one at a new local hangout, Rusty O'Reilly's, a quiet place with a long beautiful dark wood-and-brass bar near where I shopped for groceries. The place was owned by one of those snotty Brits that had already made some money somewhere else and then decided to open a bar pretending to be an old Irish pub (thus, "Rusty O'Reilly's"). The John Bull-shit Englishman was a real jerk, and when he eventually (and predictably) went out of business, it was done with the doors suddenly locked one morning, bright orange tax lien posters pasted on the doors, and the waitresses, barmaids, and kitchen staff standing out front scratching their heads. Well, before this all went down, and it was still a relatively pleasant place to go, on this occasion a guy comes in, and even though there are plenty of open seats, he sits on a stool one down from me. He's short, stocky, dark-skinned, black hair, with glasses and a flat-top haircut, dressed in a short jacket and plain khaki work clothes. Quiet and shy, he nods to me as he sits down and orders a beer. When he orders the second one, the barmaid, a strikingly beautiful strawberry-blonde named Liz, routinely says to him, "You having a good day?" He looks up at her, straight-faced, and softly says, "My father died today." She's a bit shocked, collects herself, and says, "Oh my God, I'm so sorry to hear that" before scurrying away. He goes back to staring at his beer, and after an awkward couple of seconds, I said, "Sorry to hear about your dad…" opening the door for what I'm hoping is a short conversation. "I haven't seen him in ten years," he says, and when he looks up at me with his thick myopic glasses magnifying his sad but dry eyes, I can see he's an Indian, a Native American. "You're a Native American, aren't you?" I asked. "Yes." "What tribe, if you don't mind me asking?" "I'm Navajo." "Well, that's interesting," (I'm intrigued now), "New Mexico?" "No, Arizona… that's where my father was." "So what brought you to Orlando?" He sits up now and turns to me, suddenly glad to have someone to talk to: "Well, growing up in the desert, on the reservation, I always wanted to see the ocean, so I figured I'd come to Florida to see it." (Now that's *really* interesting.) "So, what did you think?" I asked. I'm waiting for some stirring bit of native philosophy, maybe something like "the Great Water moves like a living blue desert," but instead, he says, "I haven't seen it yet." "You haven't seen it yet? How long have you been here?" I pushed. "Eight years." "EIGHT YEARS! You've been here eight years, and you haven't seen the ocean yet!?" I was gasping, "Why not?!" "I've been working six days a week, and I don't have a car. I take the bus everywhere I go. And I haven't been able to take enough time off of work to go and see the ocean and get back in time for work." I started to laugh, and caught myself, "So, what's your name?" "Gene,' he said. "Okay, Gene, I'll tell you what, you tell your boss that you're taking next weekend off, and by God, I'm gonna take you to see the ocean!" "Okay," he says, smiling now. I asked him, "You need a ride home?" "Yes, please." "Okay, let's have one more beer, for your dad…, they're on me, and I'll give you a lift home."

On the way home, I find out he lives near me, on 33rd street, just up the street from the Days Inn, where Sharon worked. But he's living in a warehouse! The warehouse is owned by the guy he works for (ironically, an East Indian), who peddles goo-gaws to the tourists, and who must be a real prick, because he's charging Gene $300 a month to sleep on a pile of cardboard boxes, eat off a hotplate, out of a mini-fridge, on the concrete floor of the warehouse (hotter'n hell in the summer; cold as ice in the winter); all this while paying him some $6 an hour. For entertainment, Gene's got a small black and white TV and a radio (when he's not riding the bus and drinking beer). "Whoa, whoa, whoa!" I tell him, "Gene, this shit is all illegal! This bastard's not treating you right… you need to tell him…" "I don't want to cause any trouble right now," he says, "I need the job, and I'm saving some money to get a car and a place of my own." I give him my phone number and tell him to give me a call after he's talked to his boss. "And you *tell* him," I said, "don't ask him. We're going Friday afternoon and you'll be back Sunday. If there's a problem, you let me know." Well, he calls me the next day and says the boss said okay, then asks if I want to go out and have a beer. We end up going out two days more in a row before Friday arrives; I take him to the Days Inn, introduce him to Sharon, and we go back to Rusty's and by now I know more about hogans, sheep, the desert, and Navajo history than I ever wanted to know, but no matter, we were going to the beach.

Friday comes and I pick up Gene at the warehouse. I'd reserved a room in New Smyrna at the old Sea Vista for two nights and we get into town and cross the Intracoastal, pulling into the weatherworn motel-by-the-sea around 5 o'clock. I checked in and then lead him out to the deck at the tiki bar out back and let him get his first view of the awesome Atlantic. He was mesmerized. After a bit I went and got a couple of beers at the bar, came back and there he was, still silently staring out at the incoming waves. I set the beers down, went back to the room, rifled through my backpack and got my camera. Coming back once again, he hadn't moved, not even to take a sip off his beer. I shot several pictures of him with the beach and ocean in the background. In all the photos he's oblivious of me taking pictures. "Wanna take a walk on the beach?" I ask him, and he just nods. We walk down the tiki bar steps, and even though I'm already in shorts and barefoot, I notice he's still in his work clothes, "well, at least take off your boots," I suggest, "let the sand ease up between your toes…" "No," he says. "Why not?" I ask. "Where I come from, men never take off their shoes." "That's just crazy," I offer, but he plods on toward the surf, getting right up to the shallow wave-water skimming up the sand, then steps back. He stands there, just looking at the waves, smelling it deeply, completely engrossed. People in bathing suits are walking by, glancing over at this guy in a jacket, khakis, and boots, standing at the edge of the outgoing tide, staring out at the waves. "Gene," I suggest, "I'm going back up on the deck, you stay out here as long as you want. If I'm not up there when you get back, we're in Room 23, okay?" He just nodded.

I remember the first time I saw the ocean. It was 1961 and I was 9 years old; we had just moved down from Detroit, and once we were out of school, Mom and Dad decided to take a drive to Daytona. We were in our old brown-and-white Ford Fairlane and Mom drove. Paul and I sat in the backseat. We all had the windows down (no air-conditioning back then) and it took forever to get there. As we came into Daytona, we crested a hill, and there, between a couple of hotel buildings, you could see the ocean. Paul and I were so excited that even Mom and Dad caught the bug. We went straight to the beach before checking into a hotel, and we ran up and down the sand, and into the water up to our knees. It was incredible, just incredible. Yeah, I had seen the Great Lakes (at least Lake Erie), and sure, they went off to the horizon too, but hell, they were dark and dirty, rocky, and both cold and relatively calm. Here was a majestic giant, living, breathing, churning Beast of a Blue-Green God as far as the eye could see, covering half the world! It only took the weekend however, spent at the large tourist hotel (which was another trip altogether), before we soon got used to looking at the water and were later preoccupied with poking Portuguese men-o-war and chasing ghost crabs, building sand castles, and wading in the hotel pool. Sure, the wonder of it passed with its familiarity, but it's been replaced in my old age with a quiet and holy meditative respect instead, like an old, old friend. One of the few times I ever experienced that original awe of seeing the ocean for the first time was when I saw Mammoth Cave as an adult—Sweet Jesus in the Morning! There's another breath-taking marvel!

The next day at New Smyrna, I convinced Gene to put on a pair of shorts, but he still insisted on wearing his boots ("fine, fine, fine, goddamit"). I got him in the truck, "Let's go for a ride on the beach!" and drove south down A1A for a couple of miles before turning onto the sand after paying the toll, then headed north so that his passenger window would be facing the sea. I'm looking at the girls out on their blankets to my left while trying not to run any kids over, and he's staring out at the waves; I took a few more pictures, and they all show him just staring, blank-faced. Once we got back to the ramp near the Sea Vista, I climbed back up off the beach and got back onto A1A, heading south again. I had something I wanted to show him. I drove down to Canaveral National Seashore and convinced the ranger at the gate that I was Park Service and I knew both the Superintendent and the Chief Ranger, so he let us in for free. A quarter-mile down the road and I pulled in to the parking area at the base of Turtle Mound. One of the largest remaining shell mounds in Florida if not the United States (or the world), it was built by the native aboriginal Timucuans over a thousand-year-period before the Europeans arrived, and I thought he'd like to see what the Native Americans of Florida were doing here along the East Coast when the Navajo were still a fiercesome entity in the Northwest, before they moved south and got domesticated in the desert. He loved it! Standing on the top where we could see the ocean to the east and Mosquito Lagoon to the west, he finally opened up and was now animatedly talkative about what it meant to be a real native American. I gave him a quick primer on the Indians of Florida, and what happened when the Spaniards, and then the rest, came. From tens of thousands in the 1500s, the Timucuans were all gone by the mid-1700s. Then I took him to Castle Windy, which is a smaller, but even older shell mound. We talked as we hiked back into the woods of what it must have been like to have lived there. Walking around the mound, I pointed out an old "Indian well," which is a depression in the sand that the natives would dig and re-dig periodically, and then as the brackish water seeped in it would settle, with fresh water rising to the surface, to be skimmed off for drinking. Now it was just a wallow for feral hogs that had overrun the park. We finished off with lunch at JB's Fish Camp on the lagoon waterway, and watched people pulling in reds and trout and flounder. Back at the Sea Vista, we had a few more drinks at the tiki bar, and turned in early. Before leaving the next day, I did my best to talk him into taking off his boots and wading up to his knees in the Atlantic, just to say he did it, but he wouldn't have any part of it. I still don't understand why, and he wouldn't explain. He did ask me to make copies of all the photographs (some of which he had me take of just the waves) so he could send them to his sister in Arizona.

When we got back to Orlando, he thanked me profusely. I made the photocopies for him to send his sister, which he lost, so I made another set, with an extra set for him. He started calling me all the time to go have beers, then it was so he could go shopping, and then it was just that he needed a ride somewhere. I pushed him to get another job, to tell his boss to go fuck himself, but he never made any movement to improve the situation. I put up with it for awhile, until one day at one of my personal hangouts, he got offensively Indian-drunk and started arguing with the patrons, some of who were sweet young ladies who were really very nice, and when he started in on me, I told him that was it. I quit answering the phone, and he eventually quit calling. Every now and then I see him sitting at a bus stop, and if he sees me, he'll wave politely and I'll honk at him.

Rose a' Charon

Back to working on the house, as I got a room cleaned out, I'd scrape the loose drywall, patch it, sand and smooth it, and wash the walls with TSP (trisodium phosphate, the nasty shit they took out of detergents back in the 70s because it was so environmentally unfriendly—but it sure as hell works). The TSP was necessary to take off the first thick layer of tobacco-stain lacquer that Mom and Dad had so carefully built up since 1961. The brown juice would run down my arms as I washed overhead, and after a day I'd be dizzy from the nicotine soaking through my skin via the TSP. But once the walls were patched, sanded and washed, I was ready to put on the first coat of primer, the famous Kilz Stain Blocker. I say first coat because, goddammit, the brown stuff would still ooze through the first one; even after the second I could still detect a hint of tan coloring beneath. Then, two coats of whatever paint, no matter what the "only 1-coat" promises were on the can, or even how dark the color for that matter. That meant four coats, or more precisely, that I painted each room four times before it was done (*after* the scraping, patching, sanding, and washing). It was worth it: it kept me busy, and the rooms looked great in the end. It took the better part of a year to work my way back to the bedrooms before I gave up. There was still a lot of junk to deal with, but bit by bit, I got it out the door, whether by E-bay, Craigslist, or Goodwill. I'd just got the place empty, especially the garage, when I got a phone call from Sharon. She and her boyfriend were (finally) breaking up, and they were getting out of their apartment, him going north and she was moving in with her mom. Could she stash some of her things (furniture, appliances, clothes—in effect, everything) in my garage until they either reconciled or she got back on her feet? The boyfriend and her had been arguing over her drinking, which had put her in the hospital twice (the first time, Mom and I visited her, and seeing her sitting there with two black eyes, a broken nose and chipped teeth convinced everyone that the guy had pummeled her, despite his protestations to the contrary; only later did his story that "she had fallen face-down off the toilet onto the bathroom floor, where he found her in a pool of blood" finally reveal itself to be the truth: the second time it happened, he'd been out of town). I had no idea that she'd been a closet alcoholic. Yeah, she had a glass that she'd sip out of while working at the Days Inn bar, but hell, I'd never seen her intoxicated. Apparently, she'd taken to that last refuge of the alcoholic, straight vodka, and when she went home at night she consumed it by the glassful, didn't eat, and subsequently would pass out, sometimes, yes, on the toilet. "Fine," I told her, "you can store your shit over here." I'd just gotten it cleaned out, so what the hell. How long? "No more than six months, promise." A van, two big college kids, and $300 later, and the garage was full again.

472

When she gets out of rehab a month later, she came by and went through the stuff, but all she grabbed were a couple of bags of clothes. "Where you going?" I asked her. "Oh, Steve and I are getting back together. He's living in Michigan, outside of Detroit now, putting down floors…" "What about the rest of the stuff?" "We'll be back within three months to get it all out, promise." She leaves the house in her little red BMW to drive to Michigan. It's 4 o'clock in the afternoon. Four hours later, she gets across the State line into Georgia before she falls asleep at the wheel and rolls the car over and over, totaling it. Her two little dogs are fine. So's she. Luckily for her, the bottle of vodka was thrown from the car and never spotted by the cops. She calls a friend who picks her up from a nearby hotel, and drives her to Ohio, where Steve meets them and takes her back to Detroit. Two months later, in the middle of the winter, she's found outside a bar in a snowbank, nearly frozen solid. Steve packs her up and sends her back south to Ocala where she rooms up with her mom in the retirement mega-haven known as The Villages. Here she takes her second tumble off the toilet: broken nose (again), two black eyes, broken cheekbone… Back to rehab. When she gets out this time she's happy, healthy, looking good again, gonna get a job bartending at Nancy Lopez's Restaurant at the Village Golf Course (even though she's taken the pledge and is on the wagon). A month later I get a phone call from her good friend Jan: "Sharon's dead. Liver failure." I empty out the garage, giving it all away.

How's For Sale?

Well, now the house really is empty, I've painted all I want to paint for now, and Paul and I decide to put it on the market. Unfortunately, this is the worst market ever for trying to sell a house. We're on the tail end of the greatest mortgage debacle in the history of the country. Houses are boarded up because of the inflated payments finagled by the debt mongers who had sold and re-sold bad-faith mortgages, and thus, there were a number of properties "under water" that banks just held onto for the hell of it and let fall into disrepair. There were also a number of "For Rent" signs everywhere as couples moved out, tried to downsize, and then at least get their payments covered. It was bad. Three years earlier, before the 2008 meltdown, when Ma was still alive, we'd been told the house was approaching a quarter-million (even "as is," with the tobacco stains and all); now the realtors told us we'd be lucky to get $140K, and even then, prices were dropping precipitously. We listed it with one realtor, a family friend, for six months. Not a bite. Then we listed it with a guy who specialized in the neighborhood, so he knew all the tricks; a year goes by and yeah, there's a couple of inquiries, but nothing pans out. We go from $180K to $160 to $140 to $125. "You're following the slide down!" the guy tells us, "you need to get ahead of it!" Even worse, the banks were being stingy and holding on to their money, not doing what banks are supposed to do: loan out the dough at a reasonable return to get the economy stimulated.

A year and a half since Mom passed and Paul's getting antsy. Around this time I get a visit from my oldest son Robin, who is a captain in the Marines, a pilot who flies the V-22 Ospreys, vertical take-off and landing chopper planes. He's in town on leave, and likes the look of the house, now cleaned up and painted. "Dad, I want to buy it," he tells me. I'm hesitant and try to talk him out of it. "I don't think that would be a good idea," I say to him, " it's the worst market ever, and the realtor tells me that without central air and heat, it's probably not going to move anytime soon. I'm just not sure that it would be a good investment for you and I'd really hate for you to end up taking a beating." "Well, I've always liked it, and now it's looking better than ever… lot of memories… I still want it… talk to Paul." Which I did. We decided to let him have it for $116K, and then, even though he had the greatest credit in the world, there was the slightest glitch—he couldn't get a VA loan because it wasn't his primary residence! The military had given him some assistance on his apartment in Okinawa, and therefore, by definition, that was his primary.

Well, whatta bunch of crap! Nonetheless, he was undaunted, "I'll get a conventional loan." I talk to the realtor, and he says no problem (well, small problem)… a conventional loan is going to require a 20% down payment, but I can give that to Robin out of my share of the proceeds from the sale. What!? "How can I do that?" I ask him, "…since the bank can't get the 20% until *after* I get the sale proceeds." "Don't worry," he says, "we do it all the time; the checks are just slid across the table, it all happens at once." "Really? Well, okay then, let's do it." It all went down very smoothly. After the realtor and the title company (of course), Ma's bank got the first check. That is, we paid off the home equity loan first (we still had been making payments, even after Mom died, or else they could have taken the house—THAT was the catch that the friendly loan officer had glossed over [to both me and Mom] when pushing the loan); next, Paul got paid back for the funeral costs; then Paul and I divided the remainder; and only then did I toss $22K to Robin for the down payment. It was all bass-ackwards to me, but the realtor and the bank were happy, and I guess that's all that really mattered (to them). Then, surprised again, Robin said he wanted to put in central heat and air. Well, that was another 12 grand, but there was a company that was willing to do it, and give a long-term loan to cover it. By September it was done. Hallelujah! (Despite all my reservations, Robin was right and I was wrong. He ended up getting the house for 96K, after the 20% down, and the realtor just told me recently that we [he] could turn it over tomorrow for $150K, the market has improved that much. In a couple more years its value should be up around $200-250K again.)

Unbeknownst to just about everybody, in the months before the house had sold I had come to the end of my rope, all my money was gone, and the cupboard was bare. I sold my share of the guns (I really had no use for them and didn't want them in the house anyway), except a long-barreled .38 revolver and Dad's 1894 Winchester (which I pawned to Paul for $500), and that carried me for another couple of months, when, out of the blue, I got a call from an old archaeologist friend of mine, Carlos, who owned an environmental consulting firm out of Ft. Lauderdale. We had always gotten along well when I was the Territorial Archaeologist in the VI and I was reviewing his company's work. I'd always been impressed with the professional quality of their projects, and if I ever needed them to change something or do some extra work to "clear" a property, I never had a problem, whereas other consulting companies would bitch and moan and cry (and worse, argue) about "Why do we have to do this?" Well, he knew that Mom had died, and that I'd been working on the house, but now that things had settled down he asked me, "Hey, how would you like to come work for us… part-time… as a consultant… good pay… per diem… travel… it'd be good for you and good for us… couldn't get better qualifications than the former State Archaeologist… whaddya say?" I didn't say yes; I said "hell, yes!" So here I am, living in the house I grew up in, now owned by my eldest son; still doing some archaeology and keeping a hand in cultural resource management, lots of travel (all this work in the Virgin Islands for the most part, so I get to stay in touch with friends there as well, including both Monica and Betsy). Mom and Dad are resting easy in Greenwood Cemetery, here in downtown Orlando. My brother Paul and his family, as well as my first (and only) wife and best friend Amy, and my two younger sons, Sam and Dennis, both men now, and most of my remaining friends, all live in Tallahassee, a pleasant four-hour drive away. Meanwhile, besides maintaining the house and writing and reading, I hang out at a nice little neighborhood bar called Piper's, owned by a pleasant Scotsman who hires pretty and pleasing young girls in short red-plaid kilts to pour beers. I'm there in the afternoons now listening to the other grey-haired geezers, gomers, and curmudgeons, telling lies and getting in heated battles over the political direction of the country, the fallacy of religion, and the mystery of women.

Life's been good… considering.

Made in the USA
Columbia, SC
30 July 2022

64224929R00263